11th Edition

Business Communication and Character

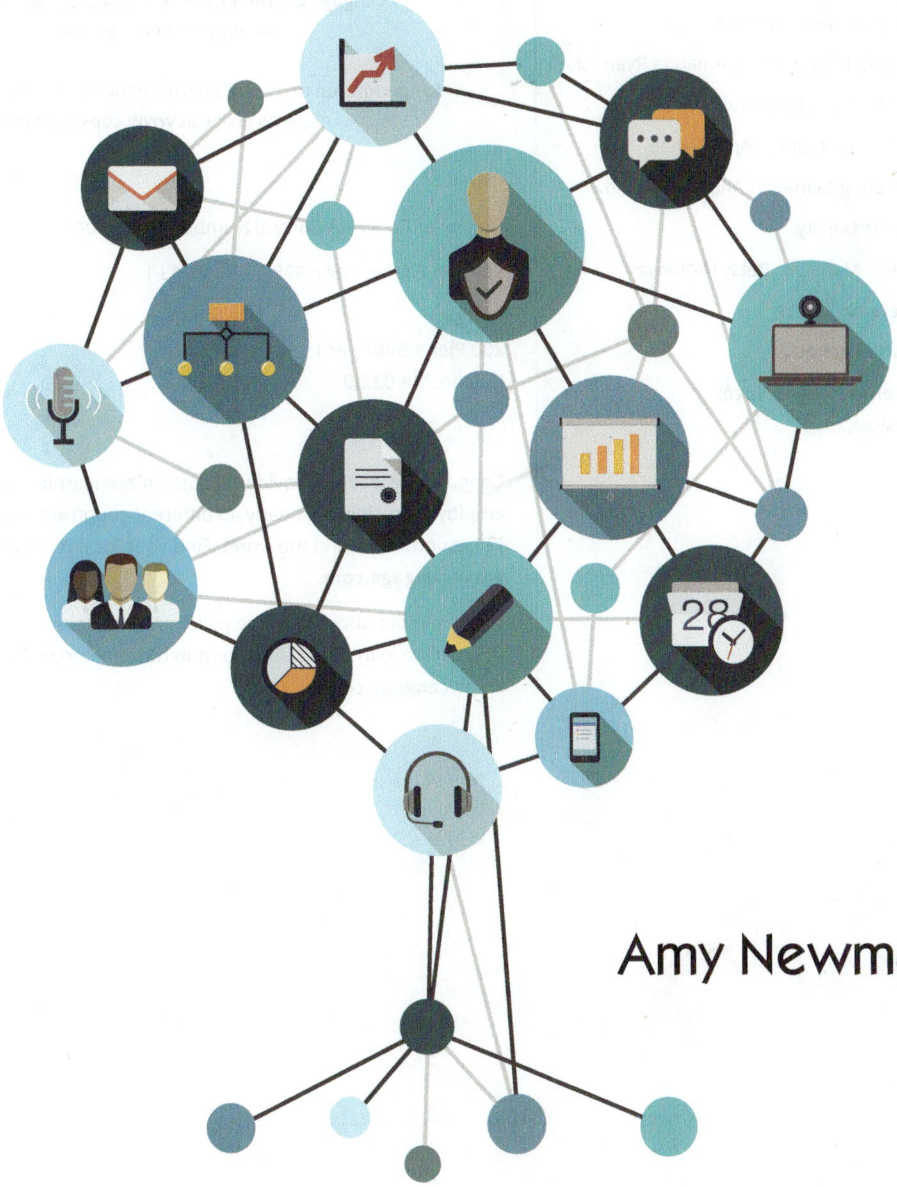

Amy Newman

CENGAGE

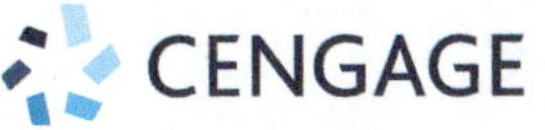

Australia • Brazil • Canada • Mexico • Singapore • United Kingdom • United States

***Business Communication and Character*, 11e**
Amy Newman

SVP, Higher Education Product Management: Erin Joyner

VP, Product Management, Learning Experiences: Thais Alencar

Product Director: Joe Sabatino

Product Manager: Heather Thompson

Product Assistant: Hannah May

Learning Designer: Megan Guiliani

Content Manager: Amanda White

Digital Delivery Quality Partner: Amanda Ryan

VP, Product Marketing: Jason Sakos

Director, Product Marketing: April Danaë

Portfolio Marketing Manager: Anthony Winslow

IP Analyst: Diane Garrity

Senior IP Project Manager: Betsy Hathaway

Production Service: Straive

Designer: Felicia Bennett

Cover and Interior Image Source: Hilch/Shutterstock.com

For product information and technology assistance, contact us at **Cengage Customer & Sales Support, 1-800-354-9706 or support.cengage.com.**

For permission to use material from this text or product, submit all requests online at **www.copyright.com.**

Library of Congress Control Number: 2022930448

Student Edition ISBN: 978-0-357-71813-1

Cengage
200 Pier 4 Boulevard
Boston, MA 02210
USA

Cengage is a leading provider of customized learning solutions with employees residing in nearly 40 different countries and sales in more than 125 countries around the world. Find your local representative at **www.cengage.com.**

To learn more about Cengage platforms and services, register or access your online learning solution, or purchase materials for your course, visit **www.cengage.com.**

Printed at CLDPC, USA, 10-22

Brief Contents

Contents

Part 1 Communicating Character and Building Business Relationships 2

Part 5 Developing and Delivering Presentations and Visuals 360

Part 6 Presenting Yourself for Employment 422

Reference Manual 495

About Amy Newman

Amy Newman is a senior lecturer emerita at Cornell University in the SC Johnson College of Business. She specializes in business communication and served in the Dyson School of Applied Economics and Management and the School of Hotel Administration, where she taught undergraduate and graduate courses in business writing, organizational behavior, persuasive communication, and corporate communication. As the director of Grand Challenges @Dyson, Newman managed a required community-engaged learning curriculum. For eCornell, the university's executive education unit, she developed several online courses in crisis communication and building leadership character.

Before joining Cornell, Newman spent 20 years working for large companies, such as Canon, Reuters, and Scholastic. Internally, she held senior-level management positions in human resources and leadership development. As an external consultant, Newman worked to improve communication and employee performance in hospitality, technology, education, publishing, financial services, and entertainment companies.

A graduate of Cornell University and the Milano School of Policy, Management, and Environment at The New School, Newman is author of *Building Leadership Character* (Sage) and four editions of *Business Communication and Character*. Since 2010, she has maintained a blog, at amynewman.com, of news stories relevant to business communication and character.

Acknowledgments

Business Communication and Character was inspired by my teaching and learning from students at Cornell, and I am grateful for how they have shaped my thinking. When I began my teaching career, I focused on rules and right answers. Students pushed me to be a better educator and a better person. I'm also grateful to my partner, Eric Clay, for challenging my approach to teaching and for deepening my work to include character.

I have thoroughly enjoyed working with the team at Cengage Learning, who, with their staff, nurtured the book every step along the way:

Erin Joyner, Senior Vice President, Higher Education Product Management, who gave me the opportunity to be an author;
Heather Thompson, Product Manager, who gave me a clear vision for the 11th edition;
Megan Guiliani, Learning Designer, who pushed me to write a practical, inclusive book;
Amanda White, Content Manager, whose research and impeccable organization brought the book to life; and
Diane Garrity, Intellectual Property Analyst, whose thoughtful advice allowed for real-life illustrations throughout the book.

Part 1

Communicating Character and Building Business Relationships

CHAPTER 1

Introduction to Business Communication and Character

Learning Objectives

After you have finished this chapter, you should be able to

LO1 Describe the relationship between communication and character.

LO2 Explain components of the character, audience, message (CAM) communication model.

LO3 Identify factors to consider during the character check step of the communication model.

LO4 Describe aspects of the audience to consider in business communication.

LO5 Choose the best medium for your message in a business situation.

The Learning Objectives (LOs) will help you learn the material. You'll see references to the LOs throughout the chapter.

"*I Started Trading Hot Stocks on Robinhood. Then I Couldn't Stop.*"[1]

—Jason Sweig, author of *Your Money and Your Brain*

Chapter Introduction

Robinhood Is Fined $65 Million for Misleading Communications

Investment app Robinhood agreed to pay $65 million in fines for misleading customers. The start-up grew rapidly, attracting younger, inexperienced investors with no-fee accounts, zero minimums, and unlimited trading.[2] Redditors using Robinhood and other apps rocked the market in 2021 when they drove up GameStop, AMC, BlackBerry, and other stocks, causing wild price fluctuations with no connection to company performance.[3]

A lawsuit against Robinhood cited "aggressive tactics" and "gamification"[4] to push users to invest in riskier stocks, resulting in higher trading volume, potentially dramatic losses, and more revenue for the company. A competitor compared using the app to "being in Las Vegas,"[5] and an NBC article describes the persuasive visuals:

> When smartphone owners pull up Robinhood's investment app, they're greeted with a variety of dazzling touches: bursts of confetti to celebrate transactions, the price of bitcoin in neon pink, and a list of popular stocks to trade.
>
> Charles Schwab, meet Candy Crush.[6]

Source: Robinhood, Robinhood.com Homepage, accessed December 18, 2021.

To gamify investing, Robinhood shows playing cards and chances to win.

All is well when stocks go up, but when stocks decline, users must make up the loss. For one 20-year-old man, his bill appeared to be $730,000, and he committed suicide.[7] Robinhood's business model and communication raise questions about the leaders' character.

LO1 Describe the relationship between communication and character.

1-1 Business Communication and Character

Your communication demonstrates who you are as a person—what is considered your character. Your messages and delivery reflect on you personally, communicating not only your ideas but also what you value and how you care to engage with those around you.

You might think of character as a fixed trait, but character is a simple habit that is developed over time. Every day, you make critical choices about whether, how, when, and what to communicate. When you make decisions that have positive outcomes for others and for yourself in the long term, you are choosing to be a person of high character. Over time, you develop "moral muscle memory"[8] and more regularly and more easily make better decisions.

Visit the author's blog at amynewman.com for current communication examples.

Character and communication are inextricable. Communication sends signals to others about your character—strong or weak. Based on your communication, others decide whether they will respect you, listen to you, and choose to work with you. Fortunately, we can choose to develop our character and illustrate strong character in our communication.

1-1a The Value of Proficient Communication Skills

As a result of your work in this course, with this book and your instructor as your guides, you will develop proficient communication skills that employers value. Written, oral, and interpersonal communication as well as leadership and teamwork skills rank highly on lists of skills that employers seek in new hires.[9]

Your communication differentiates you during the job search and on the job. Competence in writing and speaking helps you get hired, perform well, and earn promotions. If you decide to go into business for yourself, communication skills help you find investors, promote your product, and manage your employees. These same skills also help you in your personal life with family, friends, partners, and community members.

In most jobs, people communicate more than they do any other activity. Communication is the process of sending and receiving messages—sometimes verbally through spoken or written words and sometimes nonverbally through facial expressions, gestures, postures, and voice qualities. If you send a message to someone and they receive it, communication will have taken place. At work, you communicate by writing emails, attending meetings, producing reports, posting online, conducting interviews, blogging, delivering presentations, and more. You also communicate with your silence and lack of response.

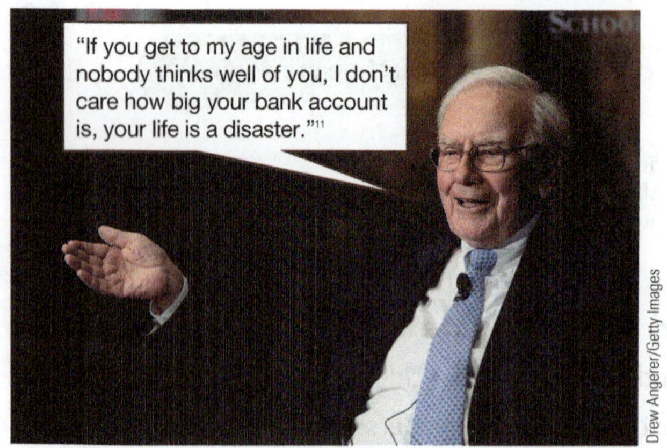

"If you get to my age in life and nobody thinks well of you, I don't care how big your bank account is, your life is a disaster."[11]
Drew Angerer/Getty Images

Chairman and CEO of Berkshire Hathaway Warren Buffett speaks of character in his own life.

1-1b Demonstrating Character Through Communication

Good communication demonstrates that you're a person—and a leader—of good character who makes a positive impact on others over time. In Figure 1, you'll see examples of character dimensions that we'll revisit throughout the book.

Multinational conglomerate holding company Berkshire Hathaway hires for character. Chairman and CEO Warren Buffett, also known for his philanthropy, describes three qualities the company looks for in new employees: intelligence, initiative (or energy), and integrity. He explains, "And if they don't have the latter, the first two will kill you. Because if you're going to get someone without integrity, you want him lazy and dumb."[10]

Character Dimensions and Business Communication | **Figure 1**

CHARACTER DIMENSION	DEFINITION	COMMUNICATION EXAMPLES
Accountability	Taking responsibility	Admitting a mistake and taking steps to solve problems caused
Authenticity	Living as your genuine self	Acting naturally during a job interview
Compassion	Caring for others and for yourself	Listening to an employee who needs your support
Courage	Standing up for principles despite the risks	Initiating a difficult conversation with a coworker
Humility	Recognizing our limits and being willing to learn	Exploring downsides of your proposal
Integrity	Acting consistently with your own and with societal values	Creating a LinkedIn profile that matches your resume
Vulnerability	Being willing to accept emotional exposure	Sharing with your coworkers that you need help meeting a deadline

Vadim Sazhniev/iStock/Getty Images

Michael Burrell/Alamy Stock Photo

Throughout the book, you'll read about the relationship between your personal character and business communication. Next, you'll learn a communication model that begins with you.

1-2 Components of Communication

LO2 Explain components of the character, audience, message (CAM) communication model.

How does communication happen in organizations, and how can you make good decisions about your own communication? In this section, you'll learn the basic process of communication: creating a message and getting a response from the audience. Then you'll see how to use the process at work with the character, audience, message (CAM) model.

1-2a How Communication Happens

Communication consists of several components, shown in Figure 2. The communication need and context drive initial decisions about the message. Next, the communicator creates and sends the message—for example, an email, a presentation, or a tweet—that the audience receives. At this point, the audience becomes the sender of a new message—the response, which includes emotional and other reactions.

Of course, communication is far more complex than this model conveys. Messages themselves are complex compilations of explicit and implicit content as well as obvious and subtle emotion. Also, the audience filters the message according to their own knowledge, biases, experience, background, and so on. Communication barriers get in the way of messages being received as they were intended, and a response could cause the sender to change course.

In addition, when people interact, they create new meaning together. Communication has consequences: outcomes affect understanding and future interactions.[12] We'll explore this phenomenon more in Chapter 3.

Figure 2 | How Communication Happens

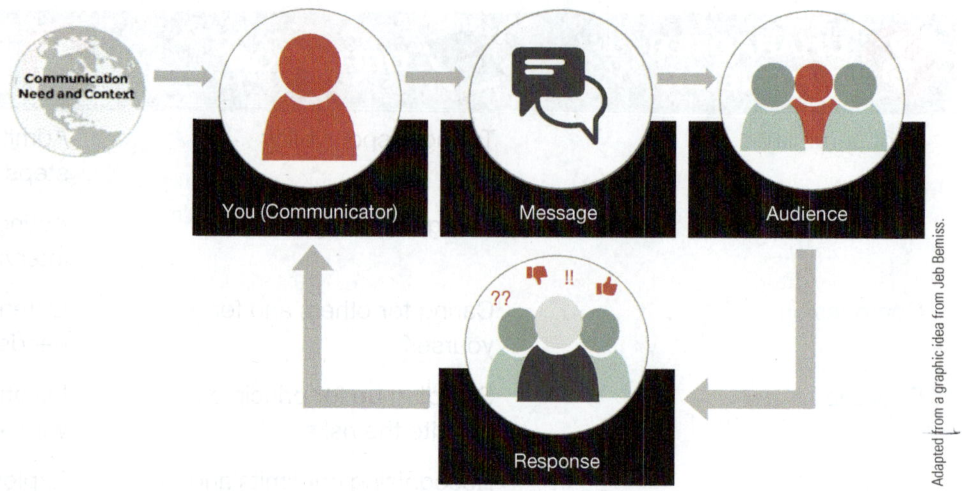

1-2b The CAM Communication Model

With a basic understanding of how communication happens, you can follow three steps to develop your own messages: the CAM model—character check, audience analysis, and message and medium, shown in Figure 3.

Figure 3 | CAM Communication Model

In the CAM model, you'll notice that analyzing your audience comes before you craft your message. The audience receives the message, but first we need to understand ourselves (the character check) and the audience. Then we can send a message that reflects well on ourselves and addresses the needs of those affected.

The rest of this chapter describes what to consider at each stage of the CAM model. Following are a few questions to ask yourself as you make communication decisions:

- **Character Check:** What drives me to communicate? To what am I reacting, and what is my purpose? What impact do I want to have? How do I want others to perceive me? How can I demonstrate good character?
- **Audience Analysis:** How can I tailor my communication to my audience? What context should I consider? How does communication travel within the organization? What barriers might get in the way?
- **Message and Medium:** What is the content of my message, and how will I convey that message?

1-3 Character Check

LO3 Identify factors to consider during the character check step of the communication model.

By checking in with yourself first and developing self-awareness, you more likely will demonstrate good character in your communication. This section gives you tools to improve your self-awareness, stay within the law, and make ethical decisions.

We'll evaluate one example using the CAM model: former United Airlines CEO Oscar Munoz's first communication after a viral video of a passenger being forcibly removed on a plane (Figure 4).[13] The airline needed seats for four United employees, and after passengers didn't accept vouchers for other fights, Dr. David Dao was selected to be bumped. He refused to leave his seat and was dragged down the aisle, first screaming and then unconscious with a bloody face.[14]

United Airlines Communication Example | **Figure 4**

United CEO response to United Express Flight 3411.

This is an upsetting event to all of us here at United. I apologize for having to re-accommodate these customers. Our team is moving with a sense of urgency to work with the authorities and conduct our own detailed review of what happened. We are also reaching out to this passenger to talk directly to him and further address and resolve this situation.

- Oscar Munoz, CEO, United Airlines

How do you feel about your own communication skills? What messages and feedback about your writing and oral presentations have you received from your family and teachers that may affect how you approach this course?

1-3a Self-Awareness and Emotional Intelligence

Self-awareness was identified as "the most important capability for leaders to develop" by the 75 members of the Stanford Graduate School of Business's Advisory Council.[15] Daniel Goleman identifies self-awareness as the first component in his groundbreaking book, *Emotional Intelligence*.[16] He describes self-awareness as an ongoing process of knowing ourselves and our emotions, strengths, and weaknesses—an honest, realistic assessment that isn't too harsh or too optimistic.[17,18]

In each book chapter, look for questions with the "Emotional Intelligence" icon in the margin. Responding honestly will improve how well you understand yourself and how your communication affects your relationships with others.

People with high emotional intelligence (or EQ, for emotional quotient) share the four competencies shown in Figure 5.[19] Which of these competencies did the United Airlines' tweet fail to demonstrate? A few obvious examples are demonstrating empathy, considering customers' needs, and managing conflict.

Author of the book *Insight*, Tasha Eurich extends the definition to include "internal" and "external" self-awareness.[20] You might think that you're self-aware, but Eurich found that only 10 %–15% of us really know ourselves and, just as important, know how others perceive us.[21] Regularly seeking feedback is one way to improve our external awareness.

Figure 5 | Emotional Intelligence Competencies

Self-Awareness: Understanding one's own emotions and how they affect others, recognizing one's strengths and limitations, and demonstrating self-confidence.

Umuarus/iStock/Getty Images

Self-Management: Keeping emotions in check, acting with integrity, being adaptable, striving for excellence, taking initiative, and demonstrating optimism.

bsd555/iStock/Getty Images

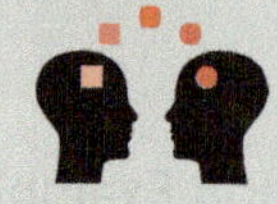

Social Awareness: Demonstrating empathy by recognizing others' perspectives and taking them into consideration, understanding group dynamics, and considering customers' needs.

tomozina/iStock/Getty Images

Relationship Management: Developing others, inspiring people, initiating or managing change, influencing, managing conflict, and working with others toward shared goals.

Passakorn_14/iStock/Getty Images

Assessing our internal and external self-perceptions is particularly critical for character development because character is judged externally as much as it is internally. Ideally, we know ourselves as we are known to others.[22] How did others perceive Munoz's tweet about the passenger? As we'll see next, not very well.

1-3b Communication Need and Purpose

Today's leaders are in a tough spot. They serve many constituencies—employees, shareholders, customers, the media, the board of directors, and other groups.[23] Munoz's primary objective may have been to protect the company and employees, and this intent certainly is understandable.

But his tweet represents a short-term view—likely a response to internal pressure and a desire to protect his job. Munoz begins with a vague reference to the incident and describes how employees are affected: "This is an upsetting event to all of us here at United." He starts the remaining sentences with "I," "Our team," and "We" and doesn't mention the passenger by name. As any CEO would in this situation, he wants to make the problem go away—to "resolve this situation"—but Munoz fails to consider what others need: a real apology and a commitment to do better next time.

Leaders of high character don't try to smooth things over. With external self-awareness, they take a hard look at how others might perceive them. Then they communicate to achieve better outcomes for more people than just themselves. They think strategically and broadly about long-term impacts of their communication.

To determine your own motivation before you communicate, identify the **communication need**—either from your own thinking or from an organizational situation. Be honest about your purpose and what drives you. Are you looking for accolades or revenge? Are you angry and wanting to show who is in charge? Or do you genuinely want to improve the way others work? Getting clear about what a successful outcome of your communication looks like will keep you focused on what matters. At the same time, you do need to consider legal consequences.

1-3c Potential Legal Consequences of Communication

A leaked United Airlines email from Munoz assured employees, "Our employees followed established procedures for dealing with situations like this."[24] Munoz probably wanted to protect United from lawsuits, and he was right to do so. In a business environment, legal considerations are a real threat.

When you work for a company, anything you write and say may become public during a legal investigation. In a discovery process, the company being investigated must produce evidence related to an inquiry, including emails, IMs, texts, recorded phone conversations, voicemail messages, and other communications the attorneys believe are relevant.

When you join a company, you will probably sign several policies about communicating at work. These are designed to protect the company against lawsuits; public relations nightmares; and breaches of confidentiality, privacy, and security.

Your company may provide social media guidelines, such as Intel's, shown in Figure 6.[25] Intel summarizes the advice to employees:

> What do our policies mean? They mean that we trust you. We bring smart people into the Intel family, and we expect you to make smart decisions. This means that you are both the person in the best position to tell the world why Intel is such an amazing place to be and the person best suited to protect Intel from harm.

Intel's Social Media Guidelines | **Figure 6**

3 Rules of Engagement

Disclose
Your presence in social media must be transparent

Protect
Take extra care to protect both Intel and yourself

Use Common Sense
Remember that professional, straightforward and appropriate communication is best

You can protect yourself and your company by paying careful attention to what you put in writing and what you say. A law firm suggests asking yourself, "Would I be comfortable two years from now being cross-examined in federal court in front of a jury about the content of this email I am about to send?"[26] If you wouldn't, then don't send the email. You might ask yourself the same question for all communications related to your company.

1-3d Ethics and Communication

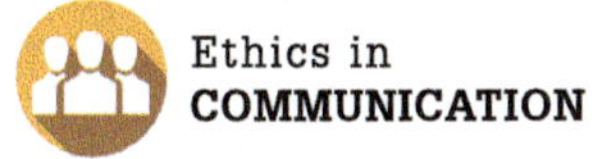

Beyond the legal requirements, companies will expect you to communicate ethically. Each of us has personal ethics, or moral principles, that go beyond legal rules to guide how we act. Our ethics represent our personal belief about whether something is right or wrong. As children, we begin forming our ethics based on how we perceive the behavior of our parents, other adults, and our peer group.

Three types of ethics guide our behavior:

- Professional ethics are defined by an organization. Employees and members are expected to follow these guidelines, which define what is right or wrong in the workplace—often beyond established laws. For example, your university has academic integrity guidelines to discourage cheating.
- Social ethics are defined by society. Cheating also is generally frowned upon by society, as evidenced by public outrage after news reports uncovered incidents of wealthy families inventing athletic profiles, cheating on exams, and offering compensation to get their children admitted into a preferred college.[27]
- Individual ethics are defined by the person and are based on family values, heritage, personal experience, and other factors. You have your own beliefs about cheating that guide your behavior.

Why do ethical people make unethical decisions? Some take the easy route. Others strive to win at any cost. Research shows that circumstance makes people most susceptible to bad behavior[28]—situational ethics. Michael Lewis, who started his career in investment banking and wrote *The Big Short*, warns of "Occupational Hazards of Working on Wall Street":

> The question I've always had about this army of young people with seemingly endless career options who wind up in finance is, What happens next to them? People like to think they have a "character" and that this character of theirs will

endure, no matter the situation. It's not really so. People are vulnerable to the incentives of their environment, and often the best a person can do, if he wants to behave in a certain manner, is to carefully choose the environment that will go to work on his character.[29]

Organizations try to manage ethical behavior, for example, by publishing procedures and codes of ethics, but some of these efforts backfire by removing judgment and good decision making from an employee's job.[30] In the United Airlines example, employees followed strict procedures instead of their conscience.[31,32] In a later email, Munoz admitted, "It happened because our corporate policies were placed ahead of our shared values. Our procedures got in the way of our employees doing what they know is right."[33]

When faced with an ethical decision, consider the questions in the Framework for Ethical Decision Making shown in Figure 7. Using these questions, we can assess the decision of airport employees who dragged Dr. Dao off the plane. Removing a passenger may be legal, but assault is not. The act complied with procedures—to a fault, negatively affecting Dr. Dao, other passengers, and, in the end, company stakeholders and the public. Clearly, the action didn't represent company values, and those involved were most likely embarrassed by the viral video.

Figure 7 | Framework for Ethical Decision Making

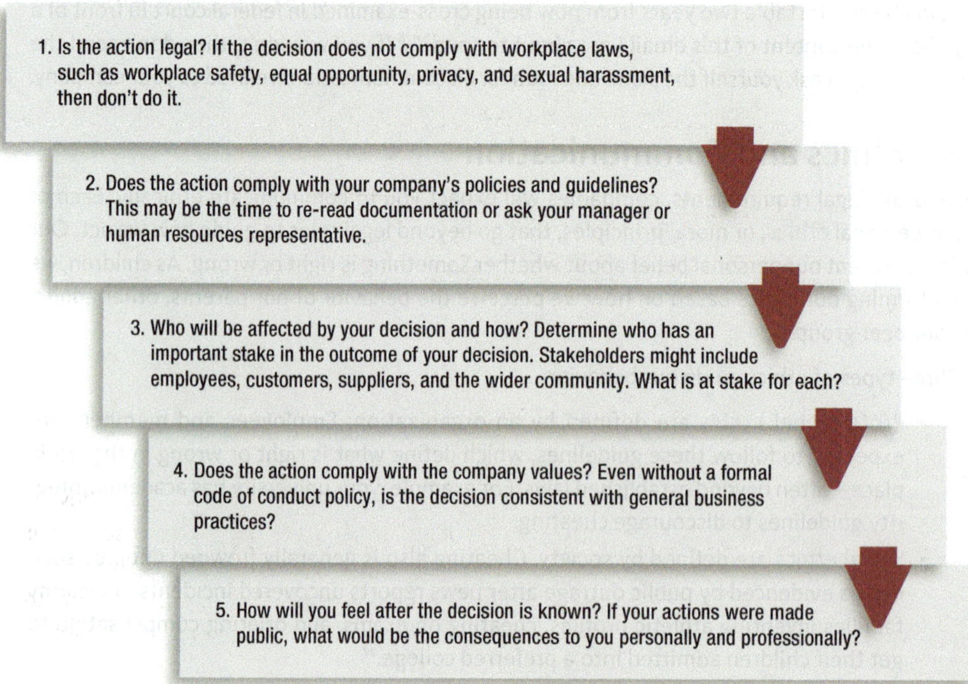

1. Is the action legal? If the decision does not comply with workplace laws, such as workplace safety, equal opportunity, privacy, and sexual harassment, then don't do it.
2. Does the action comply with your company's policies and guidelines? This may be the time to re-read documentation or ask your manager or human resources representative.
3. Who will be affected by your decision and how? Determine who has an important stake in the outcome of your decision. Stakeholders might include employees, customers, suppliers, and the wider community. What is at stake for each?
4. Does the action comply with the company values? Even without a formal code of conduct policy, is the decision consistent with general business practices?
5. How will you feel after the decision is known? If your actions were made public, what would be the consequences to you personally and professionally?

Like character, business ethics are conveyed in our communication. With the name "Robinhood," the investment app is associated with something noble, as the legendary Robin Hood was known for stealing from the rich and giving to the poor. But the company purpose is to generate revenue, and the effect on people's lives can be dire. After checking your own character—with an honest assessment of your purpose, a clear awareness of yourself, knowledge of legal implications, and sound ethical decision making—you will be ready to move to the next step of the CAM model, audience analysis.

1-4 Audience Analysis

LO4 Describe aspects of the audience to consider in business communication.

Communication doesn't happen in a vacuum. Good communicators consider what context drives their message, how communication travels within an organization, and what barriers might interfere. In Chapter 4, you'll learn a more detailed process for analyzing an audience for a particular message. For now, let's review strategic considerations for business communication using the example of applying for a job.

1-4a Communication Context

As an authentic person, you portray yourself similarly in any situation. But realistically, you communicate differently at home with your parents, in class with your professor, at a party with friends, and in a restaurant on a first date. The best communicators are adaptable; they scan the environment and adjust their messages and style to what the situation requires and what is appropriate for the audience.

When you apply for a job, the context drives how you approach your communication. If a friend recommended that you apply for a Starbucks headquarters position in Seattle, you might send an email to her contact to start the conversation. But if you saw a sign up in your local Starbucks in Boulder CO, you would more likely dress well one day, visit the store, and ask to speak with the manager. If your cousin left a position at Starbucks, you might express interest in the opening. But if you learn your cousin was fired, pursuing the job would be hurtful. If you apply for a marketing job, you might send a resume that showcases your creative skills, which wouldn't be appropriate for an application for a financial position.

All these situations require what is called organizational or political savvy. Your ability to navigate and adapt to individual personalities, styles, and situations as well as organizational culture, history, and structure determines your success as a communicator. Next, we'll see how communication travels within an organization.

1-4b Communication Directions

In any organization, communication flows through formal and informal networks. When you know how to navigate these networks, you have a better chance of getting the results you want from your messages. Again, we'll use the example of applying for a job to illustrate how communication moves among people and departments.

The Formal Communication Network

Three types of communication make up an organization's formal communication network—downward, upward, and lateral—shown in Figure 8. Downward communication is the flow of information from managers to their employees (people who report to them). If you send your resume to the head of human resources or chief people officer, that person will probably forward it to a lower-level manager—for example, the director of recruiting, who might pass it along to the college recruiting manager. This process is called cascading communication, which directs information from one level in an organization down to another.

Upward communication is the flow of information from lower-level employees to upper-level employees or managers. Upward communication provides managers with feedback about their communication, suggestions for improving the business, and information needed for decision making. The college recruiter would ask the director of recruiting for approval to bring you to headquarters for an interview.

Lateral communication (also called horizontal communication) is the flow of information among peers within an organization. Through lateral communication, employees coordinate work, share plans, negotiate differences, and support each other. Lateral communication can be challenging in an organization because you're trying to influence coworkers but have no management authority over them.

Figure 8 | The Formal Communication Network

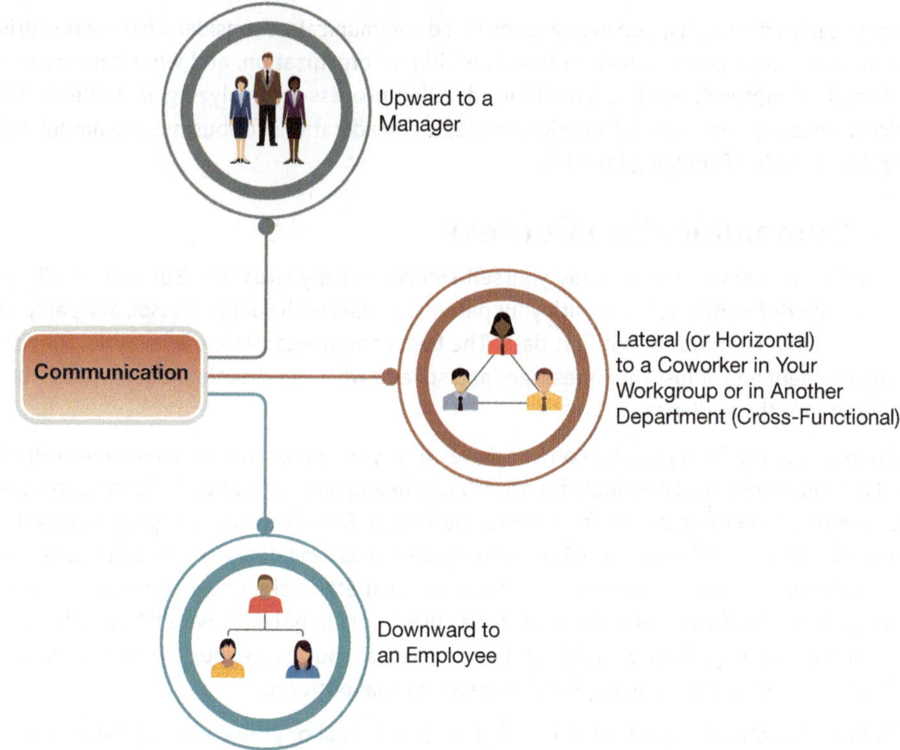

Communication is particularly difficult when the lateral communication is cross-functional—across different departments, divisions, or branches. In these situations, you'll need to rely on your relationship-building and persuasive communication skills to rally support and accomplish your goals. The college recruiter (who typically works in a department called human resources, talent management, people operations, or human capital) supports hiring managers in different lines of business—for example, finance, technology, and sales. During the hiring process, you may be a recruiter's top choice, but the hiring manager, to whom you'll report, typically makes the final decision.

The Informal Communication Network

Employees share information through the informal communication network (or grapevine). If you tell friends who work at Starbucks that you want to work there, they might text each other about which open positions might be the best fit for you. You also might check Glassdoor to see what employees say about the working environment and interview process.

The grapevine has negative consequences too. Without good formal communication, the grapevine will take over. People need information, particularly when they fear changes that may affect them. Although the grapevine is surprisingly accurate,[34] managers who let the grapevine function as employees' main source of information miss out on the chance to convey their own messages. Rather than trying to eliminate the grapevine (a futile effort), competent managers act quickly and use the formal communication network (meetings, email, the intranet, and newsletters) to get ahead of rumors. When managers have a history of sharing timely, accurate information, they are viewed as transparent and develop trust over time.

Savvy managers also identify key influencers in an organization to get accurate messages infused into the grapevine. This process requires organizational savvy as well as relationship management—one component of emotional intelligence, which involves inspiring people, influencing, working with others toward shared goals, and other skills. These skills are important to overcome communication barriers.

Think about a time when you used the informal communication network. How did your relationship skills help or hinder your goals?

1-4c Communication Barriers

Considering the complexity of the communication process, your audience may not receive messages exactly as you intend. Communication barriers may be verbal (what you say) or nonverbal and may be categorized as language, cultural, attitudinal, or emotional.[35,36]

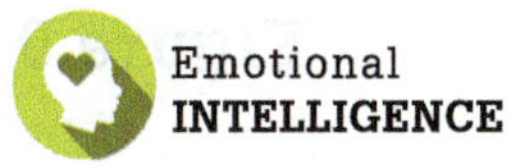

Which of the verbal and nonverbal barriers do you find most challenging? What can you do to overcome these barriers at work and in your personal life?

Language Barriers

The most obvious communication barriers are caused by differences in language. When people speak different languages, they will have trouble understanding each other. An interpreter (for oral communication) or translator (for written communication) may be used, but problems still occur. Important documents should first be translated into the second language and then retranslated into English. You'll learn more ways to communicate across language differences in Chapter 3.

Even when people speak the same language, different accents and terms can get in the way of communication. As the saying goes, "England and America are two nations divided by a common language."[37] Sometimes senders and receivers attribute different meanings to the same word or attribute the same meaning to different words.

Every word has both a denotative and a connotative meaning. Denotation refers to the literal, dictionary meaning of a word. Connotation refers to the subjective, emotional meaning that you attach to a word. For example, the denotative meaning of the word *plastic* is "a synthetic material that can be easily molded into different forms." For some people, the word also has a negative connotation—"cheap or artificial substitute"—or they associate the term with its environmental impact. Are your reactions likely to be the same as everyone else's? Some terms cause an emotional reaction that turns off the receiver and harms your relationship.

John Henshall/Alamy Stock Photo

Poor translations can be funny or confusing.

Similarly, what you intend when you use an expression may differ from its literal interpretation. When the United Airlines CEO wrote that the airline had to "re-accommodate" the passenger, he used company jargon for "find another seat." He certainly didn't mean what we saw on video. Late-night host Jimmy Kimmel criticized the word choice: "That is such sanitized, say-nothing, take-no-responsibility, corporate, B.S. speak."[38]

In Chapter 5, you'll learn more about slang, jargon, clichés, and euphemisms, like those in Figure 9. These terms are useful as business shorthand, particularly for similar groups of people, but they are often misunderstood or perceived negatively by people outside of a group, causing problems in communication.

As a business communicator, your primary goal is to be understood. Dr. Anthony Fauci, director of the National Institute of Allergy and Infectious Diseases, offered this communication advice: "Help people know what you're talking about. The goal isn't to show how smart you are."[39] Ask yourself whether you're trying to impress rather than express; this might convey arrogance or insecurity rather than humility.

Cultural Barriers

Cultural barriers extend beyond mere language differences and affect our communication style and choices. For example, our culture may influence how and when we offer criticism or speak up at meetings. Our culture also affects how we dress and whether and how we might pray at work, which communicates what we value.

Figure 9 | Euphemisms Used to Fire Employees

"We're going to make a few changes around here, and one of them is you."

"I was fired from my second post-high-school job working for a dry cleaning establishment. My boss actually said, 'You're not dry cleaning material.'"

Ragan Communications Forum, "Have you been fired?" www.myragan.com, accessed July 10, 2010.

In addition, culture affects how we perceive others' communication. Organization behavior researcher Nancy J. Adler explains the impact:

> Our interests, values, and culture act as filters and lead us to distort, block, and even create what we choose to see and hear. We perceive what we expect to perceive. We perceive things according to what we have been trained to see, according to our cultural map.[40]

We make judgments—often unfairly—about others' behaviors, and we are prone to stereotyping, assuming that the behavior of one person in a group represents everyone in that group. Instead, you could practice curiosity, being open to learning about others' values and beliefs. We'll explore more cultural differences and approaches to overcome them in Chapter 3.

LEE JIN-MAN/AFP/Getty Images

Microsoft founder Bill Gates was perceived as disrespectful for keeping one hand in his pocket when he met former South Korean President Park Geun-hye, who was later convicted for corruption.

Attitudinal Barriers

Based on our culture and experience, we hold certain attitudes about the world and about work, which affects how we send and receive messages. Our political views, ideas about power and change, personality, motivation, self-esteem, and so on, cause us to interpret communication according to our ways of thinking.

Let's revisit the example of Robinhood from the chapter opening. A young, inexperienced investor who needs to pay tuition reads, "Sign up and get your first stock for free."[41] She gets excited and opens an account. But someone recovering from a gambling addiction reads the same message and wonders what the catch is. She is skeptical and immediately closes the app—not what the Robinhood marketing staff intended.

For another example, let's revisit your application to Starbucks. Your resume includes your work experience at Dunkin' Donuts, which you believe to be an asset to the company. But the recruiter knows the store where you worked and doesn't like how people are managed. He prefers to hire people with no experience and train them "the Starbucks way." Knowing your audience well and adapting your message to them will increase the chance that your message is interpreted as intended, but attitudinal barriers will always exist in communication.

Emotional Barriers

Emotional involvement is essential to communication. As you saw earlier, an audience responds to a message with any number of emotions, and that response affects ongoing communication.

For you, as the communicator, a moderate level of emotional involvement is authentic and appropriate, but too much can hinder communication. If you're excessively angry at a coworker or overly upset about something that happened at home, you might have a difficult time conveying information or fully listening.

These situations provide an opportunity to practice emotional intelligence. Keep your emotions in check, but rather than ignore or push aside how you feel, you might choose to be vulnerable and demonstrate courage—two character dimensions. Try telling your coworkers how you feel and letting people know what's happening outside work. Being open about your life, within reason, gives coworkers the chance to be compassionate with you.

Likewise, you might struggle to communicate when someone else is excessively emotional. In these situations, describe what you observe, ask questions to understand the source of the concern, and demonstrate empathy.[42] Disregarding emotions tends to make communication more challenging, not less.

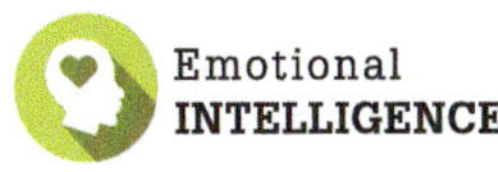

Think about a time when your emotions got in the way of communication. How do you manage your emotions without denying them?

Other Barriers

Additional barriers may cause problems at work. Communication may be impeded by physiological barriers—such as hearing loss, memory loss, and speech difficulties—and by physical barriers—such as dividers between cubicles. Other culprits that interfere with communication are technology problems, such as a slow Internet connection or a misdirected email; environmental noise, such as construction, an uncomfortable chair, or a family member during a Zoom call; and competing and distracting noise, such as too much schoolwork or a messy workspace.

Much can go wrong when we communicate, but knowing how to recognize and overcome barriers increases your chance of success. With a good sense of these factors and others related to your audience, you're ready to focus on your message and the medium.

1-5 Message and Medium

LO5 Choose the best medium for your message in a business situation.

Whether a communication achieves your objectives depends on how well you construct the message (the information to be communicated). Verbal messages (traditionally referred to as "oral") are transmitted through meetings, telephone conversations, voicemails, podcasts, conference calls, or videoconferences. Written messages are transmitted through emails, reports, blogs, web pages, brochures, tweets, posts, or company newsletters. Nonverbal messages are transmitted through facial expressions, gestures, or other body movements. With so many options (channels or media), the real challenge is choosing the best medium—whether traditional or technology based—for your message.

1-5a Traditional Communication Channels

Traditional forms of oral and written communication still exist in all organizations today, although they are declining—particularly since the COVID-19 pandemic, when digital communication flourished.[43] Fortunately, people still do meet in person. One-on-one, team, or large-group face-to-face meetings are the most personal forms of business communication and the best choice for building relationships. At many organizations, flip charts and handouts are used during these meetings and during training programs.

fizkes/Shutterstock.com

Businesspeople meet in person to build relationships.

Organizations still print written communications—slick, colorful brochures; internal newsletters for employees without computer access; financial statements for customers who opt out of the electronic format; sales letters; and periodicals, such as magazines, journals, and newspapers. Complex reports also may be printed because they're difficult to read on a computer screen. In an office, a rare printed memo or postal letter likely will convey important information about pay or benefits.

1-5b Technology-Based Communication Media

In addition to older communication technologies (email and phone), computer-mediated communication (CMC)—for example, instant messaging, videoconferencing, and social media—offers many options for sending and receiving messages.

What is your preference for communicating with others? Do you sometimes avoid talking with someone on the phone and send a text, IM, or email instead? Why do you make this choice?

Email and Phone

Email tends to be the default choice for communication,[44] even when face-to-face communication would work better,[45] and sending an email to someone in the next cubicle is common. More and more, phone calls are viewed as intrusive,[46] and young people are uncomfortable making and receiving calls.[47] Sometimes, we avoid the phone and hide behind email, which could be an issue of courage.

Instant and Text Messaging

Instant messaging (IM) and texting are popular at work. For short messages and quick questions, these channels are ideal, and they may outlive email.[48] Of course, with smartphones, email also may elicit an instant response, but this varies by organization and people. The real value of messaging apps is "presence awareness"—you know when someone is available to respond immediately.

Texting is common in business, and most customers want companies to text them.[49] Because texts are far more likely to be opened than emails, companies use texts for short messages—for example, to confirm deliveries, offer discounts, and send billing and appointment reminders.[50] Internally, busy managers may encourage employees to text rather than email, but companies should have policies in place to describe what is appropriate for this medium.[51]

Videoconferencing

Zoom and Microsoft Teams became go-to applications for online meetings and videoconferencing during the COVID-19 pandemic when people were quarantined. With video, screensharing, whiteboarding, polling, chat, and file-sharing capabilities, these platforms have obvious advantages over in-person meetings—for example, easier scheduling and less travel. In addition, people might feel more at ease at home and more comfortable participating.[52]

Social Media

Social media gives companies tremendous opportunities to connect with people online. Companies engage with customers and the public on the internet, with employees on a proprietary intranet, and with franchisees and others on an extranet.

For many companies, social media focuses on user-generated content (UGC), also called consumer-generated media (CGM). This content is created on social networking sites, a subset of social media. LinkedIn is one example, where people share career and business information. Using a donut analogy, updated from a viral "Social Media Explained" post,[53] Figure 10 describes how a donut shop might use popular social sites.[54]

After introducing a few examples here, we'll discuss communication technologies where relevant throughout the book.

1-5c Choosing Communication Media

Given all these media choices, which is best for your message? For a large-scale change, companies will send multiple messages through a variety of communication channels to reach different audiences. For example, to announce a company acquisition, executives

How a Donut Shop Might Use Popular Social Media Sites | **Figure 10**

Instagram: Look at a photo and read a story about donuts.
Facebook: See how much we like donuts.
Twitter: Read news about the best donut in Cincinnati.
YouTube: Watch our chef make donuts.
TikTok: Watch a short, funny video of people eating donuts.
LinkedIn: Read an article about our history.
Pinterest: Get a recipe to make donuts at home.
Snapchat: See a customer eating donuts.
WhatsApp: Message or call a friend about donuts.
WeChat: Video or call a friend; order and pay for donuts.

Bloomicon/Shutterstock.com; Ingvar Björk/Alamy Stock Photo

might hold a conference call with analysts, meet with the management team in person, send an email to all employees, and write a press release. This coordination is part of a strategic communication plan created at senior levels in an organization.

For simpler communications, consider the questions in Figure 11 about the audience, message, and logistics to guide you. Embedded in the questions is the concept of rich and lean media.[55] The richest media are in person—allowing for real-time, or synchronous, interactivity and cues, such as body language. The leanest media are static, or one-way, and provide no social cues. Although Zoom and other platforms aren't *exactly* like being "live," they are close, and they provide cues that traditional communication channels don't offer, such as voting, tagging, and liking.[56]

Typically, complex and emotional messages are best delivered with rich media, while routine and simple messages may be delivered with lean media. Although perceptions of communication media vary, Figure 12 shows a rough continuum. Do you agree with this sequence? From your own experience and perspective, which would you move, and why? For example, is a Zoom meeting richer than an in-person meeting because it offers more options for interactivity, such as chat and breakouts?

Media choice is complicated further because media are converging, with multiple forms available on one platform or app. For example, are blogs and IMs richer than videos if they include an embedded video?

1-5d Multicommunicating

Imagine that you're meeting with a customer in person and send a text to someone back at the office to ask a quick product question. Or you're on a phone call and respond to an IM. These examples are considered multitasking or, more accurately, multicommunicating, or engaging in overlapping conversations.[57]

Multicommunicating can be effective—up to a point. Can you watch a recorded class lecture, listen to music, and text at the same time? You may think you're good at multitasking,

Figure 11 | Considerations for Choosing Communication Media

Audience

- What is the communicator's relationship with the audience? Is it a strong, existing, or long-term relationship?
- Are interactivity and feedback important?
- At what level of the organization is the audience?
- Is this group, in general, senior, junior, or at the same level as the communicator?

Message

- Is the communication neutral, positive, or potentially bad news? How is the audience likely to react?
- What are the organizational norms for this type of communication?
- Is this message confidential or private in any way?
- Does the message or conversation need to be documented?

Logistics

- What access to technology does the audience have?
- How long is the message? How complex is the information?
- How many people will receive the message?
- How urgent is the message? Does the audience need it immediately?
- Where are the receivers located?
- What is the most practical and efficient delivery method?
- How easily will the receivers understand the message? What's their primary language and reading proficiency?

Figure 12 | Communication Media Continuum

You might find media *roughly* in this order along the continuum.

Rich				Lean
Face-to-Face Meeting	Videoconferencing Online Meeting	Teleconferencing Phone Call Voice Message	Blog Microblog	Brochure Newsletter Flier
In-Person Oral Presentation	Some Social Media Platforms	Video	Email IM Text Message	Report

but Stanford University researchers conclude the opposite: "Heavy multitaskers are lousy at multitasking."[58] More accurately, multitasking means switching, or "rapid toggling," between activities—the interruption of one task to perform another. In a Carnegie Mellon University study, people who were interrupted while reading scored less well on test questions than people who weren't interrupted, making people "20% dumber," according to the study sponsors.[59]

In addition, you can be effective at multicommunicating only if people around you tolerate it. Texting may be acceptable in some meetings but considered rude in others. Pay attention to what your respected peers do and adjust your behavior to match theirs.

1-6 Chapter Closing

After his initial failure, United Airlines CEO Oscar Munoz did a much better job communicating. He demonstrated several character dimensions in subsequent messages.

In an email to customers, Munoz focuses on his audience and tries to rebuild trust. He wrote, "Earlier this month, we broke [customers'] trust when a passenger was forcibly removed from one of our planes. We can never say we are sorry enough for what occurred, but we also know meaningful actions will speak louder than words."[60]

He also appeared on talk shows—a more personal, conversational medium—to convey his apology and commitment to do better in the future. In the next chapter, you learn more about communicating to improve interpersonal and team relationships.

The CAM Model

Every chapter in this book ends with a business communication example to illustrate important concepts covered. These short case studies, which relate to each chapter introduction, include the three components of the CAM model.

The CAM model demonstrates examples of communication so that you can see the *process* of communicating, not just the results. You'll see the model "in action" as an example and then again "in practice," your chance to apply the model using content and tools from each chapter. Over time, using the model will become a habit, and you will consider the steps for all important communications.

Decide Whether Graphics Are Ethical

Consider the chapter introduction: Robinhood uses gaming graphics on its app to make investing seem fun and exciting. Imagine that you are the company's VP of marketing, and the CEO asks you—before the decision was made—whether showing confetti, playing cards, and other graphics is ethical.

>>> CHARACTER CHECK

To help you decide whether the confetti is ethical, you choose a few relevant questions from the chapter, including the Framework for Ethical Decision Making.

1. **Is the confetti consistent with general business practices?**
   Yes, in the gaming industry, but certainly not in financial services.
2. **How would I feel if my decision were publicized? What could be the consequences?**
   I would probably feel embarrassed. Any business has the right to make money, but the confetti might lure people into investing, and I would have a tough time living with myself. I want to be a person of integrity—to be honest about the risks involved and not be associated with a company that misleads customers.

>>> AUDIENCE ANALYSIS

1. **Who will be affected by the decision to use graphics and how?**
   Young, inexperienced users would be affected by this decision because the graphics are designed to attract them. The risks aren't immediately apparent and would be camouflaged, for example, by confetti, which is associated with a party.
2. **What directions of communication are relevant to this decision?**
   Because this is a direct-to-consumer app, people make decisions themselves, without needing approval. Inexperienced investors have no lines of authority to consult, which makes them particularly vulnerable.

>>> MESSAGE AND MEDIUM

1. **What is my assessment?**
   I've made my decision: the confetti and other graphics are unethical, and I'll communicate that message to the CEO.
2. **What main points will I include?**
   I'll focus on our affiliation with the financial services industry and the potential negative impact of showing gaming graphics.
3. **In what medium will I communicate the message?**
   I'll meet with the CEO in person. I want to be sensitive because the news might not be welcomed, and I don't want a document trail in case the company decides to use the graphics despite my recommendation.

CAM

> IN PRACTICE

Write a Company Response

Imagine that you're one of Robinhood's founders and just learned about the suicide of Alex Kearns, who left a note citing a $730,000 debt on the app. Although the negative balance was temporary, sadly, Kearns did not understand this.[61] (You may research the situation further to prepare for this activity.)

You decide to respond to Kearns' death, convey your condolences, and promise changes. Use the CAM model and the following questions to write your post.

>>> CHARACTER CHECK

1. How do I feel about Kearns' suicide? Does this touch on personal experience I have had with suicide?
2. Am I proud of the business model? To what extent is the model responsible for provoking Kearns' suicide?

>>> AUDIENCE ANALYSIS

1. Who is my audience for my message? What impact do I want to have on them?
2. What barriers might get in the way of my message being received as I intend it?

>>> MESSAGE AND MEDIUM

1. What main points will I include in my message?
2. In what medium will I communicate the message? I'll consider the questions in Figure 11 to help me decide, and I might include multiple formats.

When you're finished answering these questions, read the founders' blog post at https://blog.robinhood.com/news/2020/6/19/commitments-to-improving-our-options-offering. How well did the founders' message address your responses to the CAM model questions? What would you have done differently?

REFLECTING ON YOUR COMMUNICATION AND CHARACTER DEVELOPMENT

1. **Complete the VIA Survey of Character Strengths.**

   Research shows that, although we need to acknowledge our weaknesses, focusing more on our strengths—and finding ways to use them—has more positive outcomes for people and for those around them.[62] What are your character strengths? Take a free online survey at www.viacharacter.org.[63] You'll be asked for your email address, but you don't need to purchase a report. You may print the web page with your results. Reflect on your weaknesses and your strengths. How can your strengths compensate for your weaknesses?

2. **Write a speech that someone else might deliver about you in ten years.**

   Imagine that you're winning an award from your company or from a community organization for your leadership. What would someone say about you, particularly about ways you were able to overcome obstacles to accomplish all that you did? Include future examples that illustrate your effect on individuals' work or personal lives; your contribution to your team, your company, and your community; and the values you hold and model for others.[64]

3. **Identify your self-awareness archetype.**

   In her article "What Self-Awareness Really Is (and How to Cultivate It)," Tasha Eurich explains four "archetypes" to categorize current levels of internal and external self-awareness—knowing ourselves and knowing how others perceive us.[65] Ideally, we should seek high external and internal self-awareness.

   From the descriptions in Figure 13, how do you identify? What can you do to move closer to the "aware" category?

Four Self-Awareness Archetypes | **Figure 13**

	LOW EXTERNAL SELF-AWARENESS	HIGH EXTERNAL SELF-AWARENESS
HIGH INTERNAL SELF-AWARENESS	**Introspector** Introspectors have a clear understanding of themselves but do not challenge their own views or search for blind spots by asking for feedback.	**Aware** Awares know themselves and seek to understand how others perceive them. Therefore, they operate at the highest level of self-awareness. At the same time, awares recognize that they must continuously work at introspection and must seek feedback from others to maintain a strong sense of self-awareness.
LOW INTERNAL SELF-AWARENESS	**Seeker** Seekers do not yet have a clear understanding of themselves or an understanding of how others perceive them. Without these insights, seekers often feel stuck or frustrated because they do not know how they can improve their performance or their relationships.	**Pleaser** Pleasers have a strong understanding of how others perceive them, but they do not have a strong sense of themselves. They tend to focus on meeting others' needs or expectations at the expense of their own. In the long run, this may hinder their own success and fulfillment.

4. **Prepare for a job interview question about ethical decision making.**
   Imagine that an employer asks you the question, "Tell me about a time when you took action because a situation conflicted with your values."[66] Write a response that includes context or background about the situation, your action, and the result. Emphasize what you learned from the experience. Also prepare for the interviewer to ask follow-up questions. Write possible questions and your answer to each.

5. **Identify your most common communication barriers.**
   List a few times when you had trouble communicating with someone. Do you see a pattern? Consider language, cultural, attitudinal, emotional, and other barriers described in the chapter. Which barriers do you need to address, and what strategies will you use to prevent these barriers from interfering in future communications?

6. **Choose the phone instead of a text or email.**
   Do you default to using text and email when a phone call might be a better choice? Sometime in the next week, consider a situation that you can address by phone. What makes you uncomfortable about having a voice conversation, and how can you work through these feelings? If it's easier, schedule a time for the call, and give the receiver an idea of what you would like to discuss. If you do make the call, reflect afterward on what went well and what you might do differently in the future.

DEVELOPING YOUR BUSINESS COMMUNICATION SKILLS

LO1 Describe the relationship between communication and character.

BUSINESS COMMUNICATION AND CHARACTER

1. **Analyze a leader's message.**
   Find a recent message that demonstrates or fails to demonstrate strong character. Use your own news sources, or go to amynewman.com and choose Chapter 1 from the right side of the page. What in the leader's message demonstrates character? What do the words convey, and what is not said? If you were an advisor to this leader, what changes would you recommend?

2. **Describe someone you know who has strong character.**
   Do you know someone you would describe as having strong character? What examples from this person's communication demonstrate character?[67]

3. **Find examples of character dimensions.**
   From a movie, series, or TV show, find at least five communication examples that illustrate the character dimensions defined in Figure 1. Briefly describe the scene and what the actor does or says to demonstrate each dimension.

LO2 Explain components of the character, audience, message (CAM) communication model.

COMPONENTS OF COMMUNICATION

4. **Observe communication in action.**
   While watching a movie, series, TV show, or interview, analyze two people talking. Track how communication happens between the initial communicator and the audience. In particular, note how the audience receives the message and creates a new message. How do the two create new messages and meaning together? In other words, how does the initial message evolve to include the response?

5. **Plan an upcoming communication.**
   Think about a message you need to send, and walk through the character, audience, message (CAM) communication model:

Character Check: What drives you to communicate? To what are you reacting, and what is your purpose? What impact do you want to have, and how do you want others to perceive you? How will you demonstrate strong character?

Audience Analysis: How can you tailor your communication to your audience? What context should you consider? How does communication travel within the organization? What barriers might get in the way?

Message and Medium: What is the content of your message, and how will you convey that message?

CHARACTER CHECK

LO3 Identify factors to consider during the character check step of the communication model.

6. **Reflect on your communication.**

   At the end of a day, write down your answers to the following questions:

   a. What communication makes me feel most proud today? What did I do to contribute to the success? What did others do to contribute to the success?

   b. What communication didn't go as well as I hoped? What happened to interfere? What can I do differently in the future to improve the results of similar communications?

   To develop your communication and self-awareness, use this practice at the end of every day.

7. **Describe someone you know who has high emotional intelligence.**

   Do you know someone you would describe as having high emotional intelligence? What examples from this person's communication demonstrate self-awareness, self-management, social awareness, and relationship management?

8. **Rewrite United Airlines' tweet.**

   Given what you know about the United Airlines situation and business communication, rewrite the tweet shown in Figure 4. Try to do a better job of conveying character in this first message about the incident.

9. **Analyze consequences of email in legal action.**

   The U.S. Federal Trade Commission (FTC) sued Facebook for illegal monopolization. Read more about the case at www.ftc.gov/news-events/press-releases/2020/12/ftc-sues-facebook-illegal-monopolization. Research the role email plays in the suit, particularly CEO Mark Zuckerberg's 2012 email about acquiring Instagram. How did the email affect the government's case? What lessons do you take from this situation about your own communication?

10. **Assess how a social media policy is implemented.**

    If you're working now and have access to it, share the organization's policy with the class and describe how the policy is implemented. How do employees both abide by and skirt the policy? In what ways are situations handled that are consistent or inconsistent with the policy? If you were a legal advisor to the organization, what revisions would you suggest?

11. **Apply the Framework for Ethical Decision Making to an employment situation.**

    Imagine that you got a job offer and accepted it. You were happy about your decision until you got another offer—this time from your ideal company and in your ideal location. Write responses to each of the questions in the Framework for Ethical Decision Making (Figure 7). Adapt questions to the situation; for example, in addition to company policies, guidelines, and values, consider those of your college. Given your responses, what would you do? If this has happened to you, explain your decision and the consequences.

12. **Discuss ethical dilemmas.**

Working in small groups, identify at least one ethical dilemma one of you has experienced in each of the following categories. Using the Framework for Ethical Decision Making (Figure 7), analyze how you handled the situation and what, if anything, you could have done differently.

a. Copyright issues or academic integrity—for example, copying someone else's work or discovering that a friend plagiarized a paper.

b. Confidentiality—for example, sharing information although you were asked not to.

c. Employment—for example, fabricating or exaggerating information on your resume.

d. Customer service—for example, giving a customer information you know isn't true.

LO4 Describe aspects of the audience to consider in business communication.

AUDIENCE ANALYSIS

13. **Describe the context of a communication.**

Find a news story on businesswire.com or from your own sources about a CEO leaving a company. These communications are sensitive: leaders need to be respectful to the departing CEO and, at the same time, supportive and enthusiastic about an incoming executive. Research the situation and describe the context. For example, did the CEO resign or get forced out? Was the CEO in place for a long time? How do you see these and other factors considered in the announcement? For example, who is quoted and what do they say?

14. **Describe someone you know who has organizational savvy.**

Do you know someone you would describe as having organizational savvy? Perhaps someone is a good networker or knows just the right things to say in business or group situations. What examples from this person's communication demonstrate organizational savvy?

15. **Create an organization chart to identify a company's formal communication network.**

Think of an organization where you worked recently. Create an organization chart for two or three levels of employees. Identify examples of upward, lateral, and downward messages you remember from your experience.

16. **Identify communication barriers between a manager and an employee.**

In the classic business movie *Office Space*, watch Scene 13, "Flair." This communication does not go very well. Identify the communication barriers in this scene.

An interaction in the movie *Office Space* illustrates communication barriers.

MESSAGE AND MEDIUM

LO5 Choose the best medium for your message in a business situation.

17. Explore how a company uses social media.

What's your favorite company? Which of the platforms shown in Figure 10 does the company use and how? If you're a customer, what other ways does the company communicate with you and for what purposes? Which do you consider most and least effective?

18. Identify clues for ending an email or text chain.

Some emails and texts seem to go on forever. At some point, a phone call might work better to resolve an issue. Talk with a partner about a recent experience and how you knew that the current medium was doing more harm than good. What were the consequences of either sticking with it or changing your approach?

19. Choose communication media for different audiences.

Imagine that you're the owner of a retail store and decide to close three of your 14 locations. Working in groups, identify in the communication plan template in Figure 14 which medium you would use to communicate with each audience. You may have multiple communications for some audiences. Include the rationale for your decisions.

Communication Plan Template | **Figure 14**

AUDIENCE	COMMUNICATION MEDIUM (OR MEDIA)	RATIONALE FOR CHOOSING THE COMMUNICATION MEDIUM (OR MEDIA)
Store managers		
Store employees		
Loyalty customers		
Other customers		
Suppliers		

20. Choose how to reject a job offer.

Image that you were offered a summer internship but decide not to accept it. With a partner, discuss the most appropriate communication medium to use for your message. Would you use a different medium if you received the offer by email or by phone?

CHAPTER SUMMARY

LO1 Describe the relationship between communication and character.

Communication and character are inextricable. Your character—the sum of who you are as a person—is demonstrated in your decisions and in your communications. Fortunately, you can strengthen your character over time. Every day, you make decisions about how you interact and engage with others. You can choose to focus on better outcomes for others and for yourself in the long term.

LO2 Explain components of the character, audience, message (CAM) communication model.

Communication happens when people send messages that audiences receive. To be a communicator of strong character, approach communication as a process. First, check your own character—what drives you to communicate and what outcomes you want for others and for yourself. Second, analyze your audience to tailor your message depending on the context. Third, plan your message and medium—the content and the delivery mechanism.

LO3 Identify factors to consider during the character check step of the communication model.

During the first step, checking your character, consider ways to develop your emotional intelligence, particularly your self-awareness. Take a longer-term view of your communication, including the impact you want to have on others. Stay within the law and use the Framework for Ethical Decision Making to resolve work dilemmas.

LO4 Describe aspects of the audience to consider in business communication.

During the audience analysis phase, adjust your message to different audiences and be mindful of the organizational context. Consider how communication travels within an organization and what communication barriers may be at play.

LO5 Choose the best medium for your message in a business situation.

During the message and medium phase of the CAM model, consider many options of traditional and technology-based communication. Although email is the default medium, richer channels may be better choices for building relationships. Consider the audience, message, and logistics when deciding which medium is best for the situation and context.

Endnotes

1. Jason Sweig, "I Started Trading Hot Stocks on Robinhood. Then I Couldn't Stop," *The Wall Street Journal*, December 4, 2020, www.wsj.com/articles/robinhood-day-trade-i-started-trading-hot-stocks-then-i-couldnt-stop-11607095765, accessed December 24, 2020.
2. Nathaniel Popper and Michael J. de la Merced, "Robinhood Pays $65 Million Fine to Settle Charges of Misleading Customers," *The New York Times*, December 17, 2020, www.nytimes.com/2020/12/17/business/robinhood-sec-charges.html, accessed December 18, 2020.
3. Matt Phillips and Taylor Lorenz, "'Dumb Money' Is on GameStop, and It's Beating Wall Street at Its Own Game," *The New York Times*, January 27, 2021, www.nytimes.com/2021/01/27/business/gamestop-wall-street-bets.html, accessed February 6, 2021.
4. Commonwealth of Massachusetts, Office of the Secretary of the Commonwealth Securities Division, "Administrative Complaint," Robinhood Financial, LLC, Docket No. #-2020-0047, December 16, 2020, https://drive.google.com/file/d/1lwkWVLlFtlCBX-z3N_k-GrZx2ZCQ-g8c/view, accessed December 21, 2020.
5. David Ingram, "Designed to Distract: Stock App Robinhood Nudges Users to Take Risks," NBC News, September 12, 2019, www.nbcnews.com/tech/tech-news/confetti-push-notifications-stock-app-robinhood-nudges-investors-toward-risk-n1053071, accessed December 18, 2020.
6. Ingram.
7. Nathaniel Popper and Michael J. de la Merced, "Robinhood Pays $65 Million Fine to Settle Charges of Misleading Customers," *The New York Times*, December 17, 2020, www.nytimes.com/2020/12/17/business/robinhood-sec-charges.html, accessed December 18, 2020.
8. Mary C. Gentile, "Giving Voice to Values: A Pedagogy for Behavioral Ethics," *Journal of Management Education* 41(2017): 469–479.
9. For example, see "The Attributes Employers Seek on Students' Resumes," National Association of Colleges and Employers, April 19, 2021, www.naceweb.org/talent-acquisition/candidate-selection/the-attributes-employers-seek-on-students-resumes/, accessed May 6, 2021, and "The Impact of COVID-19 on the Hiring of Business School Graduates," Graduate Management Admissions Council, Corporate Recruiters Survey 2020, September 21, 2020, www.gmac.com/-/media/files/gmac/research/employment-outlook/gmac_corporate_recruiters_survey_sept_2020.pdf, accessed May 6, 2021.
10. Warren Buffett, "Integrity," YouTube, March 26, 2017, www.youtube.com/watch?v=tpmY1aK3jP8, accessed January 5, 2021.
11. Tom Popomaronis, "Warren Buffett Says This Is 'The Ultimate Test of How You Have Lived Your Life'—and Bill Gates Agrees," CNBC, September 1, 2019, www.cnbc.com/2019/09/01/billionaires-warren-buffett-bill-gates-agree-this-is-the-ultimate-test-of-how-you-have-lived-your-life.html, accessed May 27, 2021.
12. Ilene C. Wasserman and Beth Fisher-Yoshida, *Communicating Possibilities* (Chagrin Falls, OH: Taos Institute, 2017), p. 3.
13. Oscar Munoz, United Airlines (@united), "United CEO response to United Express Flight 3411," Twitter, April 10, 2017, https://twitter.com/united/status/851471781827420160, accessed December 27, 2020.
14. Michael Goldstein, "Biggest Travel Story of 2017: The Bumping and Beating of Dr. David Dao," *Forbes*, December 20, 2017, www.forbes.com/sites/michaelgoldstein/2017/12/20/biggest-travel-story-of-2017-the-bumping-and-beating-of-doctor-david-dao, December 29, 2020.
15. Bill George, Peter Sims, Andrew N. McLean, and Diana Mayer, "Discovering Your Authentic Leadership," *Harvard Business Review*, February 2007, https://hbr.org/2007/02/discovering-your-authentic-leadership, accessed December 27, 2020.
16. Daniel Goleman, *Emotional Intelligence* (New York: Bantam Books, 1995).
17. Goleman.
18. The subtitle of Goleman's tenth anniversary book is, "Why It Can Matter More than IQ." I want to be careful about overstating the value of emotional intelligence. Although EQ is important for communication and business relationships, researcher Adam Grant and others have proven that cognitive abilities are better predictors of job performance. See, for example, Adam Grant, "Emotional Intelligence Is Overrated," LinkedIn, September 30, 2014, www.linkedin.com/pulse/20140930125543-69244073-emotional-intelligence-is-overrated/, accessed December 21, 2020.
19. Steven B. Wolff, "Emotional Competence Inventory (ECI)," Hay Group, McClelland Center for Research and Innovation, 2005, Technical Manual, www.eiconsortium.org/pdf/ECI_2_0_Technical_Manual_v2.pdf, accessed December 21, 2020.
20. Tasha Eurich, *Insight: The Surprising Truth About How Others See Us, How We See Ourselves, and Why the Answers Matter More than We Think* (New York: Currency, 2018).
21. Tasha Eurich, "What Self-Awareness Really Is (and How to Cultivate It)," *Harvard Business Review*, January 4, 2018, https://hbr.org/2018/01/what-self-awareness-really-is-and-how-to-cultivate-it, accessed December 27, 2020.
22. From Amy Newman, "Four Self-Awareness Archetypes," eCornell Course Materials, "Building Leadership Character," 2019.
23. From Amy Newman, *Building Leadership Character* (Thousand Oaks, CA: Sage, 2019), p. xvii.
24. Email reported by Benjamin Zhang, "United Responds to Crisis by Calling the Passenger 'Disruptive' and 'Belligerent,'" Business Insider, April 10, 2017, www.businessinsider.com/united-airlines-ceo-letter-employee-2017-4, accessed December 27, 2020.

Endnotes

25. "Intel Social Media Guidelines," Intel, www.intel.com/content/www/us/en/legal/intel-social-media-guidelines.html, accessed December 27, 2020.

26. Douglas C. Northup and Ronald J. Stolkin, "Legal Issues Affecting Business E-mails," Fennemore Craig, June 13, 2007, www.fclaw.com/newsletter/materials/Business/EmailsUpdate6-13-07.pdf, accessed April 28, 2015.

27. Jacob Shamsian and Kelly McLaughlin, "Here's the Full List of People Charged in the College Admissions Cheating Scandal, and Who Has Pleaded Guilty So Far," Insider, September 2, 2020, www.insider.com/college-admissions-cheating-scandal-full-list-people-charged-2019-3, accessed December 27, 2020.

28. For an overview, see Dennis Gentilin, *The Origins of Ethical Failures: Lessons for Leaders* (Abingdon, Oxon: Routledge, 2016), chapter 1.

29. Michael Lewis, "Occupational Hazards of Working on Wall Street," *Bloomberg*, September 24, 2014, www.bloomberg.com/view/articles/2014-09-24/occupational-hazards-of-working-on-wall-street, accessed May 9, 2017.

30. Stephen Cohen, "Promoting Ethical Judgment in an Organisational Context," *Journal of Business Ethics* 117 (2013): 513–523.

31. Roomy Khan, "United Airlines Customer Dragging Drama: Are Corporate Mandates Killing the Conscience?" *Forbes*, April 19, 2017, www.forbes.com/sites/roomykhan/2017/04/19/united-airlines-customer-dragging-drama-are-corporate-mandates-killing-the-conscience/, accessed May 9, 2017.

32. Susan Carey, "Behind United's Fateful Move to Call Police," *The Wall Street Journal*, April 16, 2017, www.wsj.com/articles/behind-united-airlines-fateful-decision-to-call-police-1492384610, accessed June 9, 2017.

33. Oscar Munoz, "Actions Speak Louder than Words," United Airlines Email, April 28, 2017, http://bit.ly/2oSYEaA, accessed April 29, 2017.

34. Bruce Fortado, "A Field Exploration of Informal Workplace Communication," *Sociology Mind* 1 (2011): 212–220, file.scirp.org/Html/7877.html, accessed December 30, 2020.

35. "Communication Barriers," Personal Healthcare Inc., http://phicare.com/competencies/communicationbarriers.php, accessed January 1, 2021.

36. K. Usha Rani, "Communication Barriers," *Journal of English Language and Literature* 3 (2016), www.researchgate.net/profile/Usha_Kumbakonam/publication/304038097_COMMUNICATION_BARRIERS/links/57641fd708aedbc345ecb7e2/COMMUNICATION-BARRIERS.pdf, accessed January 1, 2021.

37. Credit to George Bernard Shaw for saying, "England and America. . ." David Marsh, "Lickety Splits: Two Nations Divided by a Common Language," *The Guardian*, November 26, 2010, www.theguardian.com/media/mind-your-language/2010/nov/26/americanisms-english-mind-your-language, accessed January 1, 2021.

38. Derick Hawkins, "'Re-accommodate'? United Ridiculed for Corporate Speak Response to Passenger Dragging," *The Washington Post*, April 11, 2017, www.washingtonpost.com/news/morning-mix/wp/2017/04/11/re-accommodate-united-gets-lampooned-for-its-awkward-response-to-passenger-dragging/, accessed January 2, 2021.

39. Dr. Anthony Fauci, "Cornell Promise: A Commitment to Learning from the COVID-19 Pandemic," Cornell University Interview, October 6, 2020, https://live.alumni.cornell.edu/?v=5f7ca7e4bc6c5900a561225c,accessed January 1, 2021.

40. Nancy Adler, *International Dimensions of Organizational Behavior*, 2nd ed., (Boston, MA: PWS-Kent Publishing Company, 1991), pp. 63–91.

41. Robinhood.com homepage, accessed January 2, 2021.

42. For an interesting article about persuading patients to take medication, see Annemiek J. Linn et al., "Words That Make Pills Easier to Swallow: A Communication Typology to Address Practical and Perceptual Barriers to Medication Intake Behavior," *Patient Preference and Adherence* 5 (2012): 871–885, www.ncbi.nlm.nih.gov/pmc/articles/PMC3526884/, accessed January 2, 2021.

43. Minh Hao Nguyen et al., "Changes in Digital Communication During the COVID-19 Global Pandemic: Implications for Digital Inequality and Future Research," *Social Media + Society* (July 2020), https://doi.org/10.1177/2056305120948255, accessed December 18, 2020.

44. David Lennox, Amy Newman, and Maria Loukianenko Wolfe, "How Business Leaders Communicate in 2012: Classroom Strategies for Teaching Current Practices," Association for Business Communication 11th European Conference, Nijmegen, Netherlands, May 2012.

45. Thomas W. Jackson, Anthony Burgess, and Janet Edwards, "A Simple Approach to Improving Email Communication," *Communications of the ACM* 49 (June 2006): 107–109.

46. Daisy Buchanan, "Wondering Why That Millennial Won't Take Your Phone Call? Here's Why," *The Guardian*, August 26, 2016, www.theguardian.com/commentisfree/2016/aug/26/whatsapp-phone-calls-smartphone-messaging-millennials, accessed December 18, 2020.

47. Anita Hofschneider, "Bosses Say 'Pick Up the Phone,'" *The Wall Street Journal*, August 27, 2013, www.wsj.com/articles/SB10001424127887323407104579036714155366866, accessed December 18, 2020.

48. Judi Brownell and Amy Newman, "Hospitality Managers and Communication Technologies: Challenges and Solutions," *Cornell Hospitality Research* 9 (December 2009).

49. Stephanie Burns, "9 Clever Ways to Use Text Messaging in Your Business," *Forbes*, September 5, 2019, www.forbes.com/

sites/stephanieburns/2019/09/06/9-clever-ways-to-use-text-messaging-in-your-business, accessed December 19, 2020.

50. Burns.

51. Alison E. Curwen, "Texts and E-Mails vs. Oral Communication at Work: Which Is Best?" *SHRM*, April 21, 2017, www.shrm.org/resourcesandtools/hr-topics/employee-relations/pages/written-versus-oral-communication-.aspx, accessed December 18, 2020.

52. Lisa M. Gray et al., "Expanding Qualitative Research Interviewing Strategies: Zoom Video Communications," *The Qualitative Report* 25, pp. 1292–1301, https://search.proquest.com/openview/c264828516f288b941ad22c63c576706/1, accessed December 19, 2020.

53. Doug Ray, Three Ships Media, "Social Media Explained," Instagram, February 3, 2012, www.instagram.com/p/nm695/, accessed December 19, 2020.

54. Adapted from Karine Miron, "Social Media Explained 2019—Infographic," Karinemiron.com, March 20, 2019, www.karinemiron.com/social-media-explained-2019-infographic, accessed December 19, 2020.

55. Kumi Ishii, Mary Madison Lyons, and Sabrina A. Carr, "Revisiting Media Richness Theory for Today and the Future," Wiley, Special Issue Article, *Features of Emerging Technologies*, March 4, 2019, https://onlinelibrary.wiley.com/doi/epdf/10.1002/hbe2.138, accessed March 17, 2021.

56. Zhenyang Luo and Justin Walden, "Fundamental Changes Brought by Computer-Mediated Communication," in Stephanie Kelly (ed.), *Computer-Mediated Communication in Business: Theory and Practice*, (Newcastle upon Tyne, UK: Cambridge Scholars, 2019), p. 2.

57. N. Lamar Reinsch, Jr. et al., "Multicommunicating: A Practice Whose Time Has Come?" *Academy of Management Review* 33 (2008): 391–408.

58. Clare Baldwin, "Media Multitasking Doesn't Work, Say Researchers," Reuters, August 24, 2009, www.reuters.com/article/us-multitasking-stanford/media-multitasking-doesnt-work-say-researchers-idUSTRE57N55D20090824, accessed December 19, 2020.

59. Bob Sullivan, "Students Can't Resist Distraction for Two Minutes . . . and Neither Can You," UCI Donald Bren School of Information & Computer Sciences, May 18, 2013, www.ics.uci.edu/community/news/articles/view_article?id=273, accessed December 19, 2020.

60. Oscar Munoz, "Actions Speak Louder than Words," United Airlines Email, April 27, 2017, accessed May 8, 2021.

61. Keith Griffith, "Nebraska College Student, 20, Commits Suicide After 'Mistakenly' Believing He Owed $730,000 on Online Trading Platform Robinhood," Daily Mail, June 17, 2021, www.dailymail.co.uk/news/article-8433117/College-student-20-commits-suicide-Robinhood-glitch-showed-massive-debt.html, accessed January 2, 2021.

62. Robert Biswas-Diener et al., "Psychological Strengths at Work," Chapter 3, in Eds. Lindsay G. Oades et al., *The Wiley Blackwell Handbook of the Psychology of Positivity and Strengths-Based Approaches at Work* (The Atrium, UK: John Wiley & Sons, 2017).

63. The VIA character survey is based on the book by Christopher Peterson and Martin Seligman, *Character Strengths and Virtues: A Handbook and Classification* (Oxford, UK: Oxford University Press, 2004).

64. Adapted from Amy Newman, "Creating a Personal Leadership Vision," in "Selections from the ABC 2020 Annual Conference, Online: Business Dress and Pajama Bottoms—My Favorite Assignment Goes On," *Business and Professional Communication Quarterly* 84 (June 2021): 169–170.

65. Tasha Eurich, "What Self-Awareness Really Is (and How to Cultivate It)," *Harvard Business Review,* January 4, 2018, https://hbr.org/2018/01/what-self-awareness-really-is-and-how-to-cultivate-it, accessed January 8, 2021.

66. Question adapted from Mary Gentile, *Giving Voice to Values* (New Haven, CT: Yale University Press, 2010), pp. 51–53.

67. Adapted from Amy Newman, *Building Leadership Character* (Thousand Oaks, CA: Sage, 2019), p. 22.

CHAPTER

2 Team and Interpersonal Communication

Learning Objectives

After you have finished this chapter, you should be able to

LO1 Describe ways to improve team communication.

LO2 Explain ways to build relationships when working remotely.

LO3 Apply the steps for team writing in a business situation.

LO4 Identify best practices for in-person and online business meetings.

LO5 Explain examples of nonverbal communication.

LO6 Describe ways to improve listening skills in business situations.

"I have had different jobs, and I've enjoyed just about all of them. But I've never been prouder of the people I work for as I am with these men." [1]

—Michele Roberts, Executive Director, National Basketball Players Association

Chapter Introduction

NBA Players Demonstrate Team Collaboration

Rather than cancel the season during the COVID-19 pandemic, U.S. National Basketball Association (NBA) players agreed to strict quarantine and testing protocols—each doing their part for the good of the team.[2] Writers for *Fortune* magazine called the success of the bubble "a case study in leadership," complimenting the team and Michele Roberts, the executive director of the Players Association.[3]

Mike Ehrmann/Getty Images Sport/Getty Images

U.S. basketball players protest as a team.

As another demonstration of solidarity around that time, players protested police brutality. The LA Lakers joined arms and "took a knee" (kneeled) while wearing "Black Lives Matter" T-shirts during the National Anthem before a game.[4]

On any team, members won't necessarily agree with all team decisions, but when they act as a cohesive unit, they can focus on what they do best—in this case, play basketball.

LO1 Describe ways to improve team communication.

2-1 Work Team Communication

No matter how well you write or speak, your professional and personal success depends on your relationships with others. In Chapter 1, you learned about the importance of character. In this chapter, you learn skills for interacting with people at work—ways to improve your interpersonal communication with team members and people outside your organization.

Your character, and whether you are trustworthy, is on full display when you interact with others one-on-one and in small groups. If you want to be a productive team member, you need strong relational skills. Next, we explore work in teams: team formation, types of team communication, accountability, giving, and team ethics.

2-1a Team Formation

By definition, people who work in organizations communicate with other people. Working in small groups is one of the most enriching—and sometimes one of the most challenging—aspects of a business environment. Because of the difficulties, 86.3% of employers rate "ability to work in a team" as a top attribute they want to see on students' resumes.[5]

A team is a group of individuals who depend on each other to accomplish a common objective. Teams accomplish more work than individuals working alone; a group's total output exceeds the sum of each individual's contribution.

Between two and seven members—with five often as an ideal—seems to work best for effective work teams.[6] Smaller teams often lack the diversity of skills and interests to function well, and larger teams struggle with managing their interactions because two or three people may dominate.

Teams function best when members trust each other and follow established goals and norms.

Developing Trust

In addition to their contributions to work output, teams offer employees a sense of belonging and connection. When team members know each other well, they develop trust over time and rely on each other to achieve work goals and to grow personally and professionally. Trust helps team members accomplish tasks more easily, overcome challenges, avoid personality conflicts, and feel happier at work.[7]

When starting a new or joining an existing team, spend time getting to know each other personally. Share your strengths and weaknesses, work styles, experiences, feelings about the work or project, and so on. What do you have in common outside of work? "Small talk" about light, non-work-related subjects—friends, family, and social activities—before and after meetings is natural and helps establish a supportive and open environment, particularly for virtual teams, which we explore later.

When have you felt that you could trust others on a team? How did you contribute to the relationship?

To develop trust over time, couples researcher John Gottman suggests engaging with each other in small ways. When someone appears upset, our tendency is to turn away and avoid the emotion. But with good emotional intelligence, we seek to understand our team members and offer our support.[8]

Establishing Initial Team Goals and Norms

Early on, teams also need to define their goals. The following questions are a good starting point for your team:

- What is your team's purpose? Why do you exist?
- What will be the impact of your work? Why does it matter?
- What objectives do you need to accomplish? How will you measure success?

Too often, decisions just happen on a team; members go along with what they think everyone else wants. Instead, teams should agree on how they'll operate and make decisions; for example, consider discussing the following early on with your team:

- What if team members miss a deliverable or team meeting? How should they notify the team? What will be the consequences?
- What if two team members are having a conflict? How should it be addressed or resolved?
- Which decisions will be most important for the team? How should the team make those decisions?
- What if team members need help completing a task? How should they handle this situation? How will others respond?

2-1b Types of Team Communication

Three types of communication—conflict, conformity, and consensus—greatly affect a team's performance and how much team members enjoy working together. Let's consider the example of Boeing, the manufacturer of the 737 MAX airplane involved in two crashes that killed 346 people within five months between 2018 and 2019. At the time, Boeing leaders deflected responsibility, but in 2021, the company was charged with fraud and paid more than $2.5 billion to settle criminal charges.[9]

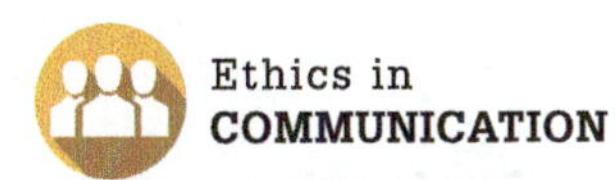

Since the crashes, reports of problematic internal communication have surfaced. Examples illustrate the three types of communication that affect team performance, explained in Figure 1.

2-1c Accountability

Accountability is a critical character dimension for team productivity; all team members are responsible for completing assigned tasks. Developing a culture of accountability means that people are more intrinsically than extrinsically motivated. Rather than blaming and shaming people when mistakes happen, team leaders create an environment where people hold themselves accountable and aren't dependent on external measures.

The continuum in Figure 2 describes four approaches to accountability and the consequences of each.[15] Most of us would want to be and work for a supportive leader.

How do we inspire a culture of accountability? To move team members—or yourself—toward greater independence and self-accountability, identify expected outcomes and a schedule for regular updates. Then, follow the plan and trust that work will be completed unless proven otherwise. When others' work isn't completed, try to practice compassion: ask about obstacles and offer to problem-solve. When your own work isn't completed, take initiative and demonstrate humility by asking for help.

2-1d Giving

To develop more supportive relationships at work, we can take lessons from the natural world to give us new ways of thinking about team communication. Emerging research about forests show that trees communicate with each other through "a complicated web of relationships, alliances and kinship networks."[16] We see a single, standing tree, but the ecosystem beneath the surface is a highly conflicted, collaborative system, with examples of altruism—trees sacrificing themselves for other trees. This research rattles some scientists and challenges more simplistic notions of evolution.[17]

In his book *Give and Take*, Adam Grant describes the value of altruism among humans at work. Although you might believe that focusing on your own needs and goals is the surest way to advance your career, Grant found that "givers," who help others without expecting anything in return,[18] achieve higher levels of individual success in the long run.[19] Givers rely on interdependence[20] and focus on team outcomes. Turns out, generosity pays.

Figure 1 | Types of Team Communication

TYPE	EXPLANATION	EXAMPLE FROM BOEING SITUATION
Conflict: Should teams avoid conflict? 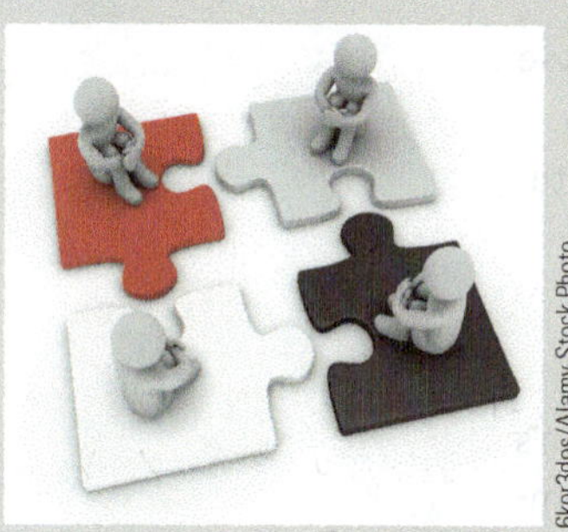 6kor3dos/Alamy Stock Photo	Many leaders and team members work hard to avoid conflict, but conflict is part of what teams are all about. Without conflict, teams miss out on productive discussion and debate. Personal attacks can doom a team, but healthy conflict that focuses on issues rather than personalities takes courage, an important character dimension for team functioning.	Evidence shows that upper management tried to avoid conflict. A Boeing engineer filed a complaint against the company that included these statements: "I was willing to stand up for safety and quality but was unable to actually have an effect in those areas," and "Boeing management was more concerned with cost and schedule than safety or quality."[10]
Conformity: Should team members try to conform?   Panther Media GmbH/Alamy Stock Photo	Conformity is an agreement to ideas, rules, or principles. However, too much conformity can result in **groupthink**, when people think similarly without independent thought. Groupthink stifles opposing ideas and the free flow of information. If pressure to conform is too great, negative information and contrary opinions never surface.	Pressure to conform at Boeing forced employees to mislead regulators so that additional pilot training wouldn't be required to fly the planes. One employee admitted in an email, "Probably true [that the skill isn't intuitive], but it's the box we're painted into. . . . A bad excuse, but what I'm being pressured into complying with."[11] Another employee wrote, "Who will cost Boeing tens of millions of dollars? Burn him at the stake! . . . GET 'ER DONE!"[12]
Consensus: Should teams always strive for consensus?  YAY Media AS/Alamy Stock Photo	**Consensus** means reaching a decision that best reflects the thinking of all team members. With this ongoing process, teams explore divergent and dissenting opinions to pursue a shared, collective view. Consensus is unlike a unanimous vote, which has agreement from everyone, or a majority vote, which could ignore fierce disagreement from the minority.	Boeing decisions ignored employees who held minority views. One employee asked another in a chat, "Would you put your family on a MAX simulator–trained aircraft? I wouldn't." The employee responded, "No."[13] Another employee wrote, "I still haven't been forgiven by God for the covering up I did last year."[14] Clearly, some employees had strong reservations about the company's decisions.

External and Internal Accountability Measures | **Figure 2**

External Measures < ——————————— **> Internal Measures or "Self-Accountability"**

	PUNISHING	MICRO-MANAGING	DIRECTING	SUPPORTING
What Leaders Do	Discipline people for poor performance or work habits	Criticize minor mistakes	Assign and schedule tasks; provide checklists	Specify results, measure progress regularly, and provide coaching
When Leaders Act	After problems surface	Constantly	Before problems surface	Ongoing but not too frequently
Typical Focus	Punishing and blaming	Babysitting and correcting	Teaching and evaluating	Solving problems collaboratively
Likely Outcomes for Employees and Coworkers	Feeling fearful and victimized	Feeling mistrusted and dependent	Feeling devalued; doing the minimum	Feeling valued, self-reliant, and focused on development

2-1e The Ethical Dimension of Team Communication

When you agree to participate on a team, you accept certain standards of ethical behavior, including putting the good of the team ahead of personal gain. In baseball, team ethics are clear. If a runner is on base, the batter may bunt the ball, knowing the batter will probably be thrown out (i.e., the pitcher will get the ball to first base before the batter gets there). The batter makes the sacrifice for the good of the team, so that another teammate can advance a base.

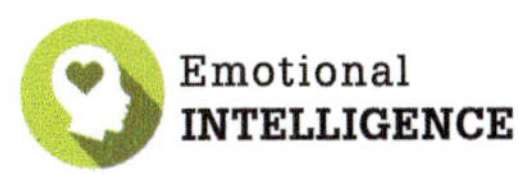

When have you had a difficult time celebrating a team member's success? How did your own feelings get in the way?

Team members also have an ethical responsibility to respect each other's emotional needs. Teams members are encouraged to produce their best work, rather than feel blamed and criticized for not performing up to standard. When a baseball player hits a home run, the entire team celebrates. When a player strikes out, you'll never see team members criticizing the player. Each member also promotes the team's well-being—refraining from destructive gossip, dominating meetings, and sabotaging work.

Team members also act with integrity. They do what they say they will do, which builds trust over time, so team members can count on each other. Team members also uphold the moral standards of the team or larger organization. When the Houston Astros engaged in sign stealing of opposing teams, players disgraced the team and the entire league.[21] However, within one year, two Astros were rehired, one as manager of the Detroit Tigers. Team owner Chris Ilitch said of A.J. Hinch, who had been fired for his role in the cheating scandal, "There was never a doubt in my mind of his character."[22] Would you agree?

2-2 Virtual Team Communication

LO2 Explain ways to build relationships when working remotely.

Teams or team members who work remotely, whether full or part time, have their own communication advantages and challenges. In this section, you learn ways to improve communication when team members aren't physically present by developing social presence, setting goals and norms, choosing a collaboration platform, and using voice and messaging technologies.

2-2a Developing Social Presence

Bringing the team together in person occasionally or, at least, for an initial meeting will build relationships more quickly. When this isn't possible, people do their best from a distance.

Increasing social presence, how close and real we perceive someone who is not physically present, can improve team relationships. Spending time getting to know each other personally is even more important for virtual teams than for in-person teams.[23]

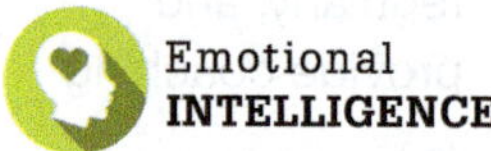

On any team and particularly on virtual teams, be your authentic, genuine self. Personal disclosures help members develop presence and build solidarity among the team.[24] When people reveal more of themselves, they report feeling happier and a greater sense of community.[25,26]

Emotional INTELLIGENCE

When have you been part of a team that knew each other well personally? How did your knowing each other affect team relationships and performance?

Using informal language also helps team members develop presence and increases feelings of connection. Positive, friendly language and emoticons reduce perceived physical distance[27]—within reason. One virtual team member said it well:

> I tend to lighten up with a colleague who uses emoticons and less-than perfect [sic][28] punctuation and sentence structure. On the other hand, too many smiley faces and indecipherable abbreviations make me worry about how productive the person will be. These factors dictate whether I keep the work focused on project-specific communication or create a more open forum of communication that allows for more dialogue outside of or surrounding the project.[29]

2-2b Setting Goals and Norms

For virtual teams, a formal contract with specific agreements about online communication may increase the chance of meeting goals. One study suggests that teams perform best when they first imagine achieving their goals, and then write a charter.[30]

Guidelines for creating a virtual team charter are shown in Figure 3. The examples are minimal: you can expand on these with your team. Although a charter will provide direction and keep team members accountable, try not to be too rigid. Strive for the accountability culture discussed earlier so that all team members are self-driven to contribute to the team's success. As the team develops, revisit the charter and consider updates.

Consider creating shared rhythms and rituals. Some teams find success by scheduling regular meetings and starting with quick check-ins.[31] Others improve productivity by scheduling time for chatter as well as uninterrupted individual work time.[32] Setting additional expectations, such as a 24-hour response time for messages,[33] may keep team members accountable.

The charter also should include preferred technologies. Remote workers are more likely to work late nights and weekends[34] and could be in different time zones, so teams should use both synchronous and asynchronous tools. But try to choose one primary channel, so you and your team members get proficient at relating to each other, at least initially. Also, with fewer technologies, you'll retrieve messages more easily.[35] Next, we explore collaboration platforms and best practices for the more prevalent technologies.

2-2c Choosing a Collaboration Platform

Although working in remote teams can be challenging, online collaborative tools have proven business outcomes. Users report improved productivity, quick solutions to business problems, and higher employee engagement.[36] These tools also increase transparency and make it easier for everyone on a team to contribute.[37] In-person teams reap these same benefits. Of course, these social tools are useful only when people use them consistently and effectively.

As the most popular cloud-based collaboration app,[38] Slack, owned by Salesforce, keeps teams organized. Users set up workspaces and channels, which function as chat rooms. Integrated apps allow users to manage workflow, share screens, make calls, and more. Microsoft Teams competes with Slack and offers similar functionality.

GUIDELINE	EXAMPLE
Purpose: **Why does the team exist? What is the team expected to do?**	*Our purpose is to identify ways to improve workstation ergonomics for headquarters staff.*
Results: **How will we know when the team is successful? What specific outcome or deliverable will we achieve?**	*We'll produce a report with specific recommendations based on employee feedback. The report will include products, a realistic budget, metrics, and an implementation plan. We'll identify specific criteria for evaluating our success.*
Communication: **How will the team communicate and store files?**	*We'll use Slack as our primary communication tool and for storing files. Zoom will be the default for meetings, and we'll meet every Thursday for a half-hour at 3 p.m. EST for check-ins. Otherwise, we'll use our group text. Expected turnaround times are 6 hours for Slack messages and 2 hours for texts. We'll avoid sending messages after 10 p.m. EST.*
Roles and Responsibilities: **What will team members do to ensure success?**	*Ava, Leader: Serves as liaison with senior management, facilitates meetings, and oversees work output.* *Cecilia, Organizer: Schedules meetings and manages the project plan.* *Charlie, Document Manager: Keeps Slack updated, takes meeting minutes, maintains all documentation.* *Manoj, Communicator: Drafts messages to employees and management, including the final report.*
Decision Making: **What decisions will the team make, and how will we make them?**	*We'll decide everything related to the internal work and communication that's within our given budget. If we need to go outside the organization for information, or if we're getting close to the budget, we'll escalate the decision. We'll strive for a consensus, but Ava will make final decisions when we get stuck.*
Conflict Management: **How will the team manage through conflict?**	*After talking through our past team experiences, we decided to address issues directly with each other as they occur —no delaying and no complaining to other people. We'll do our best to not get defensive if someone addresses an issue with us or gives us constructive feedback. If someone needs help or will miss a deadline, we need to know in advance and that person will offer some solutions.*

Despite its ambitions,[39] Slack hasn't killed email. No one can seem to accomplish that mission. But team members can use emotional reactions and feel more connected in a workspace that is more interactive than linear. To manage projects, teams also find Monday.com and Trello useful. Finally, although not a collaborative workspace, Google Drive provides enough functionality for teams to share writing tasks and may be enough for simple projects.

2-2d Calling and Messaging

Chapter 1 provided an overview of communication technologies and how to choose channels for your messages. As you might expect, remote teams that rely on richer forms of communication, such as videoconferencing, are better coordinated. These media help teams build trust, particularly when they are first forming.[40] In this section, you learn best practices for calling and messaging team members.

The phone and voicemail have fallen out of favor—and for good reason with the popularity of texting, as a tech writer explains:

> Why would anyone leave a voice message when shooting off 160 characters can get the job done 99 percent of the time? Worse is the inevitable game of phone tag that comes when neither party can connect in real time.[41]

Still, a phone call is better than email to convey complex information, bad news, or emotional decisions.[42]

Plan outgoing calls to prepare yourself and the receiver. Because some people are uncomfortable talking on the phone and perceive calls as intrusive, consider scheduling time in advance. Plan what you'll say for important calls, particularly the first couple of sentences. Also be prepared to leave a voicemail, which is likely if you don't have an appointment.

Voice tone is critical because, although the phone is a richer medium than email, you don't see body language, which conveys important cues. Avoid reading: use your natural voice and a conversational style. The call is a chance to build a relationship, so be yourself. But avoid saying anything you might regret; conversations can be recorded.

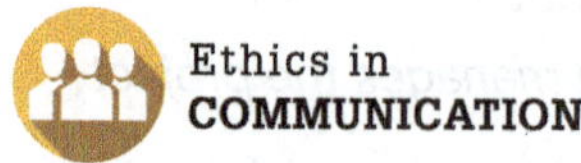

Follow guidelines and norms for texting and instant messaging. Your company probably has a policy that you should follow for security and privacy concerns. In addition, pay attention to norms within your work group. When do people message instead of email? What's the expected response time?

Typically, reserve messaging for short interactions and questions that require an immediate response. Save heavy content and important decisions for email.

Use informal language for messaging, but know that anything you write may become public, as with any communication. Follow grammar, punctuation, and capitalization standards within the organization. Use gifs and emoticons, as discussed earlier, if they are acceptable within your group.

We've talked about the best ways for teams to function and communicate. Now let's look at a specific team activity: collaborating on writing projects.

LO3 Apply the steps for team writing in a business situation.

2-3 Collaborative Writing

The increasing complexity of the workplace makes it difficult for people to have the time or expertise to write long or complex documents on their own. Team writing is common in organizations for sales proposals, recommendation reports, websites, financial analyses, and other projects that require input from people in different functions or departments. These tasks require a strategic approach that includes project planning and commenting on team writing.

2-3a Applying Strategies for Team Writing

Let's take an example of a start-up business. If you and two friends want to open an ice cream store and need funding—from a bank or private investors—you would write a business plan. You would probably all do extensive research to make sure the business is feasible. Then, you might have one person write the financial projections, another write the marketing plan, and so on, until you complete the business plan.

No one person will have expertise in all areas of planning your new business. When you present your idea to investors, each of you will create slides for your part of the presentation. And later, when you create a website, you may divide up the writing for that too.

Consider the steps in Figure 4 when writing as part of a team. During the planning phases, teams typically spend more time collaborating. Then, when the writing starts, they draft sections independently.[43]

Steps for Team Writing | **Figure 4**

Identify Project Requirements	Determine project goals: who is the audience, and what result do you want? Identify project components: what research do you need, what topics will you cover, and what deliverables will you produce? Decide how you'll share information: how will you collaborate online, and when will you meet in person?
Create a Project Plan	Divide work fairly: which tasks suit each team member's strengths and interests? Create a project plan: who will complete which task by when? (See Figure 5 for a sample.)
Draft the Writing	Begin with an outline: what major sections in what order will be included in the final product? Agree on a writing style: if different people write different sections, what style will you use (e.g., how formal)? Share information: if one person will create the entire first draft for consistency, how will each team member provide expertise?
Revise the Writing	Allow enough time for editing the draft: finishing a first draft the day before a project is due does not leave enough time. Provide feedback: see the tips for commenting on team writing (Figure 6). Make sure you have a single "voice" in the project: the final report should be coherent and cohesive. Have each team member review the entire draft: look for errors in content (gaps or repetition) and writing style.
Finalize the Project	Have everyone proofread the final document: you are all responsible for the final version. Be clear about delivery: who will submit the final version, in what format, and by when?

Figure 5 shows the start of a simple project plan. You can create something much more detailed or keep it simple and add to these steps.

2-3b Commenting on Team Writing

Commenting on a peer's writing is useful for both of you. Your peers receive feedback to improve their writing, and you practice techniques to objectively evaluate others'—and eventually your own—writing. When done effectively, giving each other feedback can build a sense of community within the team. Follow the tips in Figure 6.

Figure 5 | Example of a Simple Project Plan

WRITING A BUSINESS PLAN		
WHO	**TASK**	**BY WHEN**
Madeline	Set up a Slack channel.	April 20
Madeline	Draft an outline for the business plan.	April 22
Griffin	Draft company overview section (mission, vision, etc.).	April 24
Beata	Draft management profiles.	April 24
Madeline	Research local ice cream shops and other businesses for competitive analysis section.	April 30
To be continued...		

Figure 6 | Commenting on Team Writing

buffaloboy/Shutterstock.com

Imagine Yourself as the Audience

- Assume the role of reader—not instructor. Your job is to help the writer, not to grade the assignment.
- Read first for context and meaning; comment on the large issues first—the information, organization, relevance, and overall clarity for the audience.

buffaloboy/Shutterstock.com

Encourage Revisions

- Avoid taking over the text. Accept that you are reading someone else's writing—not your own. Make constructive suggestions but avoid making decisions or demands.
- Comment sparingly. Without marking every typo, help the writer apply your feedback throughout the draft.
- Provide specific, useful feedback (not "I liked this part," but "You did a good job explaining this difficult concept").

buffaloboy/Shutterstock.com

Take a Positive Approach

- Emphasize the writer when giving positive feedback and emphasize the text (rather than the writer) when giving negative feedback: "I'm glad you used the most current data from the annual report." "This argument would be more persuasive for me if it contained the most current data."
- Use "I" language (not "You need to make this clearer," but "I was confused by this customer description").

LO4 Identify best practices for in-person and online business meetings.

2-4 Business Meetings

Whether in person or through technology, people meet to share information, provide team progress updates, solicit and provide input, solve problems, make decisions—and start, maintain, and sometimes end relationships. Unfortunately, many meetings are unnecessary and poorly run. In response to one survey, 71% of managers said meetings were "unproductive and inefficient," and more than 60% said meetings kept them from getting their own work done or from doing deep thinking.[44]

Meetings can work well. After choosing an appropriate meeting format, an effective communicator plans, facilitates, participates in, and follows up a meeting.

2-4a Determining the Meeting Format

Choosing an appropriate format for your meeting is an important part of good meeting planning. Because in-person (face-to-face) meetings are the richest type of communication, they are preferable for meeting new people, building relationships, negotiating contracts, delivering bad news, and other important interactions. Video (online) meetings are second best, particularly for time differences and when travel isn't possible, and conference calls (by phone) are useful when video is unavailable. Figure 7 compares the best and worst of face-to-face meetings, conference calls, and video or online meetings.

Comparison of Meeting Formats | **Figure 7**

Description: In-person meetings for any number of people

At their best:
- Build strong, meaningful relationships
- Increase social interaction
- Allow for difficult discussions and complex decision making
- Keep people focused

At their worst:
- Lead to excessive socializing
- Are expensive and show unproven return on investment (when large groups travel)

Face-to-Face Meetings

Rido/Shutterstock.com

Description: Audio conference calls for people in two or more locations (often through speakerphone)

At their best:
- Accommodate one-way and two-way communication
- Connect multiple people in other locations on one medium
- Cost little and are easy to set up

At their worst:
- Cause overlapping conversations because participants lack nonverbal cues
- Fail when connections are lost
- Lead to distractions when people multitask or forget to mute the call

Conference Calls

Tetra Images/Getty Images

Description: Video meetings for any number of people using applications, such as Zoom or Microsoft Teams

At their best:
- Provide the closest alternative to an in-person meeting
- Feel like an in-person meeting
- Cost little
- Include interactive functionality

At their worst:
- Lead to "Zoom fatigue"
- Fail because of technology or user issues

Video or Online Meetings

metamorworks/Shutterstock.com

Companies have more options than those in Figure 7. For example, premier telepresence technology allows participants to feel as if they are in a room together, and webinars, typically for large groups, give the presenter more control over how the audience participates.

2-4b Planning the Meeting

Even without travel expenses, meetings are expensive. Add up the hourly wage of participants and factor in lost time doing other work, and you can calculate just how much a meeting costs. Getting your money's worth from a meeting requires careful planning: identifying the purpose, deciding who will attend, and preparing an agenda.

Identify the Purpose

The first step is always to identify your purpose. The more specific you can be, the better results you will get. A purpose such as "to discuss how to make our marketing staff more effective" is vague and doesn't identify a clear outcome. These purpose statements are clearer and more specific:

- To decide whether to implement a new rewards program for the marketing staff
- To finalize the work schedule for July
- To prioritize candidates for the IT analyst position

Once you identify your purpose, you might realize that you don't need a meeting at all. For one-way communication that doesn't require input or feedback, such as a monthly status update, an email or Slack message might be all you need.

Decide Who Should Attend

Who needs to attend your meeting? Everyone you invite to your meeting should have a specific reason for participating. Ideally, you will include only those who will contribute to the meeting. Who can provide background information? Who will suggest ideas? Who will make the decision?

Meeting invitations—like wedding invitations—can cause friction. You may want to keep your meeting small but feel obligated to include someone. Of course, you want to avoid hurt feelings, but you should balance this with your goal: to run an efficient, productive meeting. Speaking with team members ahead of time about whether they need to attend or involving your manager in the decision may be useful.

Have you delayed or skipped meeting with people to avoid conflict? How did the situation resolve? If you had met, how could the outcome have been better?

On the other hand, avoid excluding people just to prevent conflict. Getting everyone to agree on the same goal during the meeting can be challenging. Instead, speak separately with decision makers and cynics ahead of time to help rally their support before going into the meeting. Or be prepared to address conflicting goals and different points of view during the meeting.

Prepare an Agenda

With your purpose and participants set, you need to decide what topics the meeting will cover and in what order. This **agenda** helps you prepare for the meeting and keeps people focused on the schedule. Knowing the agenda in advance helps participants plan for the meeting and tells them that their contributions are important. You also may assign topics for participants to lead (with their permission, of course). This is one way to engage more people in the meeting and share the responsibility.

Send the agenda with a calendar invitation and room location or online meeting link. Microsoft Outlook and online tools, such as Doodle and When2Meet, help find times when everyone is available. If you schedule the meeting far in advance, you may want to send a reminder a day or two before the date. The more specific the agenda you can provide, the better. Figure 8 is an example of a detailed agenda.

Sample Detailed Agenda | **Figure 8**

IT Analyst Selection Team Meeting

Purpose: To prioritize the candidates and select our first choice for the job offer

March 20

Conference Room C

9:00 – 9:45 a.m.

Topic	Who	Timing
Review requirements of the IT analyst position	Yuri	9:00 – 9:05
Candidate 1		
• Review feedback gathered	Kelly	9:05 – 9:10
• Discuss qualifications	Everyone	9:10 – 9:15
Candidate 2		
• Review feedback gathered	David	9:15 – 9:20
• Discuss qualifications	Everyone	9:20 – 9:25
Candidate 3		
• Review feedback gathered	Eun	9:25 – 9:30
• Discuss qualifications	Everyone	9:30 – 9:35
Agree on the top candidate (and possibly a backup)	Everyone	9:35 – 9:40
Recap and agree on next steps	Yuri	9:40 – 9:45

Notice that this agenda isn't set for one hour. Although one hour is often the default time, some meetings need more or less time and should be scheduled accordingly. Shorter timeframes also give people time between meetings and may keep people on schedule.

Shorter and fewer meetings also avoid **Zoom fatigue**, exhaustion from online meetings caused by excessive focus and cognitive processing. The visual stimulation and the constant emotional effort to appear "on" are overwhelming during online meetings.[45] You might consider hiding your self view during meetings. In addition, watching in speaker view instead of gallery view reduces visual stimulation[46] but may reduce the feel of a face-to-face meeting, so you'll have to choose. Another way to avoid people getting "Zoomed-out" is to plan for interactivity so people stay engaged throughout the meeting.

2-4c Facilitating the Meeting

The best meetings are interactive; otherwise, it's a one-way conversation and why should people join in real time just to listen? Figure 9 offers tips for arriving at, checking in, and checking out of online meetings,[47] and we review a few key points next for setting the stage, facilitating interactivity, managing time, and ending the meeting.

Set the Stage

Even before a meeting starts, you'll set the stage. Arrive a few minutes early and start on time, which communicates that you're serious about the topic, value participants' time, and expect them to be prompt for future meetings. The suggestions under "Arrive" in Figure 9 help build a sense of community online, particularly for larger groups and for people with distractions at home.

Figure 9 | Virtual Meeting Strategies

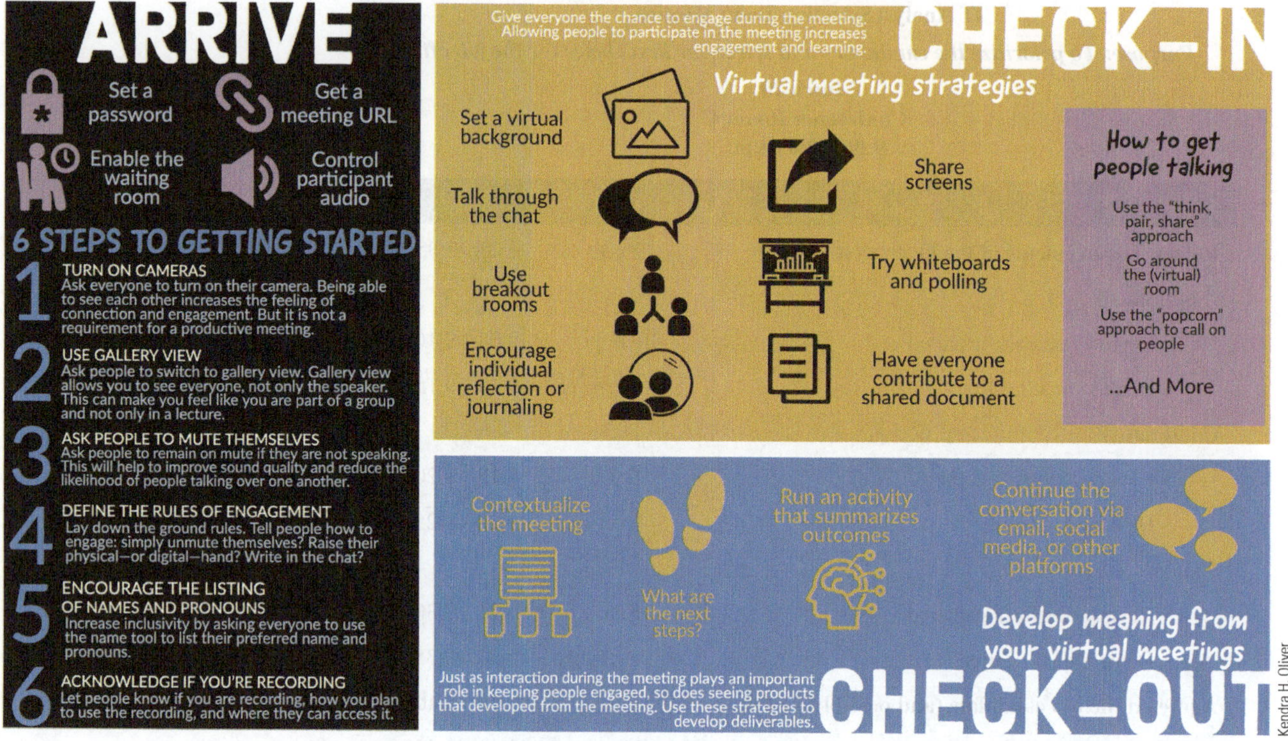

Greet people as they join—whether in person or online—and encourage people to introduce themselves to people they don't know. After socializing for a couple of minutes, get down to business—the first item on your agenda. State the purpose of the meeting, including what you hope to accomplish by the end, and review the agenda briefly.

Facilitate Interactivity

How will you involve people throughout the meeting? Think about parts of the agenda where people can share their ideas, and plan ways to incorporate group activities. For online meetings, follow suggestions in Figure 9 under "Check-In," such as using whiteboard, chat, and breakout features in Zoom and other platforms.

Try to get everyone talking. Before the meeting, prepare people to contribute, for example, "David, I'm really looking forward to hearing whether you think these candidates have the technical skills for the job." During the meeting, draw people out, for example, "Eun, what did you think about Candidate 2's interpersonal skills?"

Manage Time

Use the agenda as your guide throughout the meeting. Keep track of time and refer to the schedule periodically. Steer people back on track, for example, "I'm getting concerned about time. We'll have time to decide on the job title later. Maybe we should move on to Candidate 2 at this point" or "Why don't I check with HR about the title and follow up with you separately, so we can discuss Candidate 2's qualifications?"

At the same time, be flexible and avoid cutting off valuable discussion; sometimes meetings go off track for good reason. You might say something like, "We're running a little behind schedule, but I think the title is important. Do you want to schedule time for tomorrow so we can talk more about this?"

Summarize and End the Meeting

Follow suggestions for "Check-Out" in Figure 9 to summarize the meeting. This reminds people what was decided and reinforces that it was a good use of time. You might say, "So, we all agree to extend an offer to Candidate 2. If she doesn't accept, then we'll start a new search. I'll call her today and will let you know by email what she says. Thanks for a productive meeting, everyone."

End the meeting on time. Participants will appreciate not feeling stressed about getting back to their work or to another meeting on time—and they will be more likely to contribute to meetings in the future.

2-4d Participating in the Meeting

Good facilitation requires good participation. Researchers identified eight "meeting citizenship behaviors," shown in Figure 10.[48] You'll notice that most of these involve contributions, which require attention throughout the meeting.

Meeting Citizenship Behaviors | **Figure 10**

- If given the opportunity beforehand, I provide input regarding the meeting agenda.
- I come prepared to meetings.
- I express my true opinions in meetings.
- I communicate my ideas in meetings.
- I speak up in meetings.
- If I don't agree with the group during a meeting, I say so.
- During meetings, I volunteer information that may help solve someone else's problem.
- I try to make our meetings more productive.

Maintaining focus during meetings can be challenging, particularly when the meeting isn't run well. One study found that students and professionals generally agree on appropriate phone use during meetings. Least-tolerated activities include making or answering calls, writing and sending texts or emails, and checking texts or emails. On the other hand, bringing a phone to the meeting, checking incoming calls and excusing yourself to answer, browsing the web for relevant information, and checking your phone for the time, particularly in informal meetings, were more highly tolerated.[49]

During online meetings, the temptation to do other work is even greater. But checking email or browsing online is more obvious than you might think. You can tell by eye movements and light changes when people are typing or moving between screens. These activities and side conversations—in person or in chat—may be viewed as rude. Also, chats are saved along with video recordings, so be careful about snarky comments that could become public. On audio conference calls, multitasking is less detectable but no less rude.

2-4e Following Up After the Meeting

Regular and informal meetings may require only a short email to confirm what was decided. Formal meetings or meetings where controversial ideas were discussed may require a more formal summary.

Minutes are an official record of the meeting; they summarize what was discussed, what decisions were made, and what actions participants will take. Generally, they should emphasize what was *decided* at the meeting, not what was *said* by the members.

Figure 11 shows an example of meeting minutes for a development committee at a nonprofit organization. To keep this simple, the writer added minutes in blue type to the agenda. Sending

Figure 11 | Meeting Citizenship Behaviors

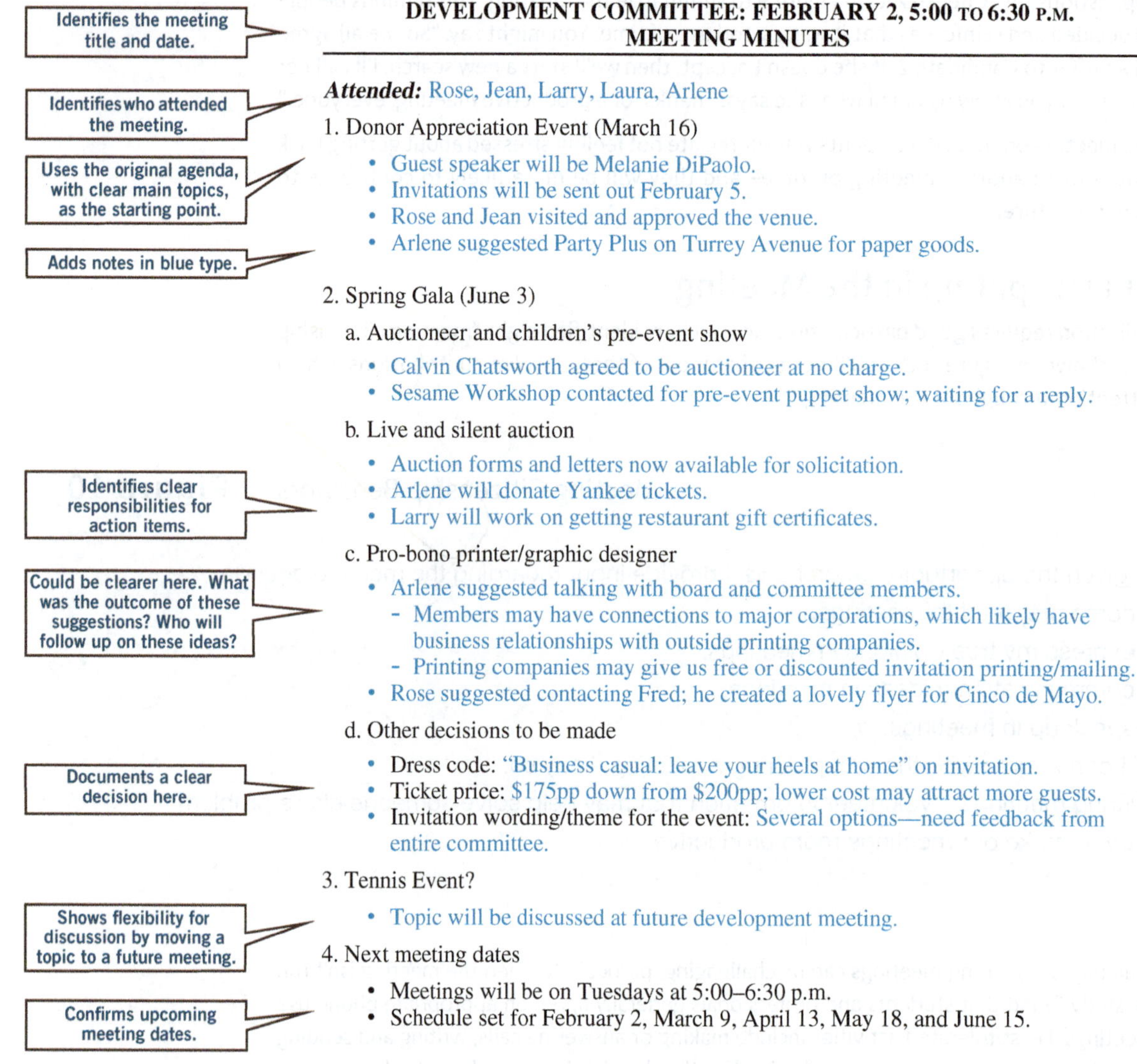

Identifies the meeting title and date.
Identifies who attended the meeting.
Uses the original agenda, with clear main topics, as the starting point.
Adds notes in blue type.
Identifies clear responsibilities for action items.
Could be clearer here. What was the outcome of these suggestions? Who will follow up on these ideas?
Documents a clear decision here.
Shows flexibility for discussion by moving a topic to a future meeting.
Confirms upcoming meeting dates.

DEVELOPMENT COMMITTEE: FEBRUARY 2, 5:00 TO 6:30 P.M.
MEETING MINUTES

Attended: Rose, Jean, Larry, Laura, Arlene

1. Donor Appreciation Event (March 16)
   - Guest speaker will be Melanie DiPaolo.
   - Invitations will be sent out February 5.
   - Rose and Jean visited and approved the venue.
   - Arlene suggested Party Plus on Turrey Avenue for paper goods.

2. Spring Gala (June 3)

   a. Auctioneer and children's pre-event show
   - Calvin Chatsworth agreed to be auctioneer at no charge.
   - Sesame Workshop contacted for pre-event puppet show; waiting for a reply.

   b. Live and silent auction
   - Auction forms and letters now available for solicitation.
   - Arlene will donate Yankee tickets.
   - Larry will work on getting restaurant gift certificates.

   c. Pro-bono printer/graphic designer
   - Arlene suggested talking with board and committee members.
     - Members may have connections to major corporations, which likely have business relationships with outside printing companies.
     - Printing companies may give us free or discounted invitation printing/mailing.
   - Rose suggested contacting Fred; he created a lovely flyer for Cinco de Mayo.

   d. Other decisions to be made
   - Dress code: "Business casual: leave your heels at home" on invitation.
   - Ticket price: $175pp down from $200pp; lower cost may attract more guests.
   - Invitation wording/theme for the event: Several options—need feedback from entire committee.

3. Tennis Event?
   - Topic will be discussed at future development meeting.

4. Next meeting dates
   - Meetings will be on Tuesdays at 5:00–6:30 p.m.
   - Schedule set for February 2, March 9, April 13, May 18, and June 15.

minutes within 24 hours shows meeting participants that their contributions are valued. Minutes may be sent by email or posted to a team's collaboration space.

With good planning, strong facilitation, and timely follow-up, you'll hold meetings that build relationships and that people *want* to attend. Next, you learn how nonverbal communication affects business relationships during meetings and other interactions.

LO5 Explain examples of nonverbal communication.

2-5 Nonverbal Communication

When teams meet in person or online, you use and observe nonverbal communication. Not all messages at work are spoken, heard, written, or read—in other words, verbal. A nonverbal message (e.g., smiling or shaking your head) can convey as much or more than a verbal message, particularly the emotions behind a message.

Common types of nonverbal communication in business are discussed in this section: facial expressions and gestures, body movement, physical appearance, voice qualities, and touch.

2-5a Facial Expressions and Gestures

By far, the most expressive part of your body is your face—particularly your eyes. Using a computational model, researchers mapped how a genuine smile is distributed across a face. Comparing real and posed smiles, they conclude, "A genuine smile is indeed in the eyes."[50]

Can you tell which smile is real in Figure 12? If you guessed the one on the right, you are correct. One clue is how people contract the many muscles in the corners of their eyes, which is hard to fake unless the smile is genuine.[51]

What Smile Is Genuine? **Figure 12**

Prostock-Studio/iStock/Getty Images

How eye contact is perceived varies by culture, and we explore the differences more in the next chapter. Too much eye contact in some Eastern cultures (and in Western cultures when it feels like staring) can be off-putting or offensive. "Elevator eyes"—looking someone up and down in a judging or sexual way—is not appropriate in any business environment.

Eye contact during videoconferencing is tricky. We typically look at people's faces and not directly into the camera. Research shows that looking a bit downward is generally acceptable, but people are sensitive to sideways eye contact.[52] To give the appearance of direct eye contact, place the other person's image as close to the camera as possible and sit back a little, although not so much that your image is too small.[53] To see your own eye contact, take screenshots to compare how you look when you gaze at different parts of your screen and camera.

We need to be cautious about assuming too much based on facial expressions. Previous research concluded that facial expressions are universal rather than cultural,[54] but this traditional view has been challenged.[55] You also might find it harder than you think to identify when someone is lying. Deception research provides few conclusive clues that indicate a lie.[56,57]

Like facial expressions, gestures—for example, hand movements—alone are difficult to decipher.[58] But gestures can illustrate and reinforce your verbal message. Your message will be clearer and seem more consistent when gestures match your speech. You learn more about these movements when we discuss delivering presentations in Chapter 12.

2-5b Body Movement

Body stance (e.g., your posture, where you place your arms and legs, and how you distribute your weight) is another form of nonverbal communication. For example, standing or sitting up straight might convey confidence and connection, while slouching might communicate withdrawal. Although the research was initially challenged,[59] studies show that holding "power poses" before presentations and job interviews increases feelings and perceptions of confidence.[60] Try holding a high-power pose, such as those on the left side of Figure 13, for two minutes to see how it affects you.

Figure 13 | Power Poses

Leaning slightly toward someone would probably convey interest and involvement in the interaction. Try to maintain an open stance with your arms naturally to your sides or in your lap. Leaning back with your arms folded across your chest or putting your hands on your hips or in your pockets might send a negative message, whether or not you intend to.

Your positioning in relation to others also conveys information and may affect how people relate to you. To address the power imbalance, some clinically trained chaplains and health care workers will sit at a level of or below their patients. Patients feel more comfortable speaking across or down to the professional rather than the other way around.[61] Translating these lessons to an office, a business manager might avoid standing over an employee's cubicle, sitting behind a desk, or sitting at the head of a table.

Finally, consider how you walk and what messages you might be sending. Do your pace and gait indicate motivation and excitement or boredom and reluctance? These and other nonverbals might mean nothing at all, but people watching you could be drawing their own conclusions.

2-5c Physical Appearance

Many cultures place great value on physical appearance. In the United States, attractive people are perceived as more intelligent, more likable, and more persuasive than unattractive people.[62] At work, physically attractive people are more likely to be interviewed and hired, get promoted, and earn higher wages.[63]

Although you can't change all your physical features, make choices that enhance your professional image in the business environment, such as using clothing, jewelry, and hairstyle to emphasize your strong points. Observe those around you to identify what is generally acceptable at work—and then consider your own authentic style and what makes you feel comfortable. You might "try on" different looks to test others' reactions and how you feel.

2-5d Voice Qualities

No one speaks in a monotone. To illustrate, read the sentences in the first column of Figure 14 aloud, each time emphasizing the italicized word. Note how the meaning changes with each reading.

Voice qualities, such as volume, speed, pitch, and tone, carry both intentional and unintentional messages. For example, when you are nervous, you may speak faster and at a higher pitch. People who speak too softly risk being interrupted or ignored, and people who speak too loudly are often seen as being pushy or insecure.

You'll also notice obvious gender differences. Men's voices are about an octave lower than women's voices. Vocal coaches will advise women to improve breathing and to amplify their voice to increase resonance. Women who try to increase volume with sheer force risk sounding "shrill"—a disparaging description of a woman's voice.[64]

How Tone Conveys Emotion and Affects Meaning | Figure 14

SENTENCE	POSSIBLE EMOTION AND MEANING
Caleb missed the donor meeting.	You're surprised that Caleb, a reliable team member, rather than Allison, who is unreliable, missed the meeting.
Caleb *missed* the donor meeting.	You're frustrated that Caleb wasn't just late; he didn't attend the meeting at all.
Caleb missed the *donor* meeting.	You're angry that Caleb missed such an important meeting.

2-5e Touch

Touching in the office may be unwelcomed, as the #MeToo Movement—the reckoning of sexual harassment and sexual assault—has shown. Companies typically have policies against "unwelcome, unwanted physical contact,"[65] so be particularly careful about invading others' space. A hug may be well intended but may have a negative impact. At the same time, lightly touching someone's shoulder may be appropriate and expected when someone suffers a tragedy.

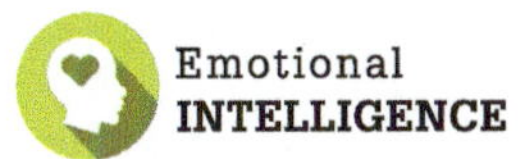

How comfortable are you with touching in a work environment? Do you tend to want physical contact, or do you avoid it?

Shaking hands, traditionally the most common business greeting, is falling out of favor because of concerns about transmissible diseases. If you do shake hands, practice so that you convey confidence, share a real connection, and make a good first impression. Use a firm grip (but not a "death grip"). Avoid placing your hand above the other person's, which may signal dominance.

Consider alternatives to a handshake, such as a genuine smile, a nod, a brief wave, a small bow, a prayer sign ("namaste"),[66] or an elbow bump. When you're more junior in rank, follow the lead of the person you're meeting to avoid potential awkwardness. Without physical contact, we have other ways to build relationships, for example, listening, which we cover next.

2-6 Listening

LO6 Describe ways to improve listening skills in business situations.

We listen to know others and the world around us. Whether you are making a formal presentation to 500 people or speaking with one person over lunch, listening is essential to understanding.

To fully grasp message content as well as emotion, listening is a full-body experience. We use potentially all our senses to appreciate every aspect of communication.

Listening certainly involves much more than just hearing. You can hear and not listen (just as you can listen and not understand). Hearing is a passive process, whereas listening is an active process. When you *perceive* a sound, you're merely aware of it; you don't necessarily comprehend it. When you *listen*, you interpret and assign meaning to the sound.

When your car is operating normally, even though you *hear* the sound of the engine as you're driving, you're barely aware of it; you tune it out. But the minute the engine begins to make a strange sound—not necessarily louder or harsher, but just *different*—you tune back in, listening intently to determine the problem. You *heard* the normal hum of the engine but *listened* to the strange noise. You also may have *experienced* the noise with your body—a rattling or vibration sensation.

Although listening is the communication skill we use the most, it is probably the least developed of the four verbal communication skills (writing, reading, speaking, and listening). Why are we such poor listeners? First, most people have simply not been taught how to listen well; few students receive formal training in listening. Second, we think about four times faster than we speak, so our minds tend to wander and we lose concentration. The good news is that you can improve your listening skills. After a few definitions, you'll learn the value of listening and ways to be a better listener.

2-6a Empathy, Sympathy, and Compassion

Beyond listening is showing **empathy**, understanding and sharing another's feelings. You can listen to your coworkers' stress about workload, but can you really see the situation from their perspective—feel what they feel? Does the interaction bring up your own stress? With this level of communication, you'll more fully help coworkers without judging them.

CHARACTER

Empathy is different from **sympathy**, which is simply understanding and providing comfort. Social work researcher Brené Brown, who has a top-ten Ted Talk,[67] describes empathy as going beyond sympathy. Brown says that empathy is "feeling with people" and "is a vulnerable choice because, in order to connect with you, I have to connect with something in myself that knows that feeling."[68]

Empathy has limitations. It may not be appropriate in all situations and may cause managers to make poor decisions, particularly in crisis situations and when they overidentify with employees' feelings.[69] In addition, empathy alone doesn't solve problems and may cause further unhealthy rumination. In his book *Chatter*, Ethan Kross warns that we also need cognitive assistance "to help us distance, normalize, and change the way we're thinking about experiences."[70]

Still, demonstrating empathy is a good way to begin a conversation and to respond to others. When we take risks to be more vulnerable, we allow others to be more open with us. Later in the book, you learn about **compassion**—noticing, feeling, and demonstrating concern that alleviates suffering.

2-6b The Value of Listening

In friendships and romantic relationships, we generally know the importance of listening and empathy. In a popular video, "It's Not About the Nail" (Figure 15), a couple is arguing. She complains about pain and pressure, and he says, "You do have a nail in your head. . . . I'll bet if we got that out of there . . ." She is frustrated by him: "You always do this. You always try to *fix* things when what I really need is for you to just listen."[71]

Figure 15 "It's Not About the Nail"

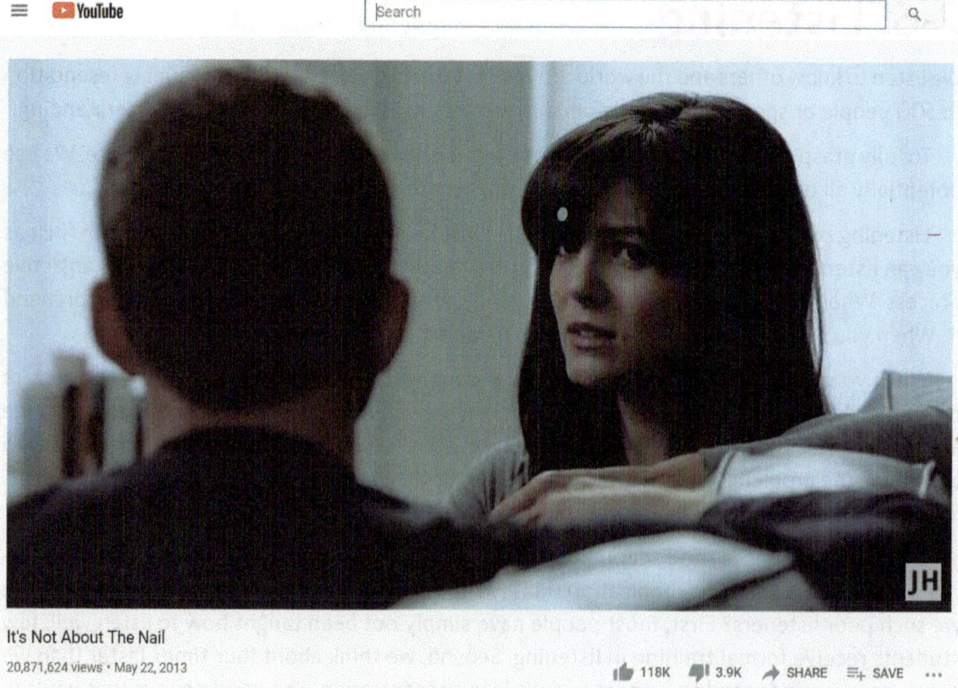

Source: YouTube, LLC

The video is funny because, *stereotypically*, men have trouble listening and instead want to fix problems. But research shows that women are only slightly more empathic than men. This may surprise you, but previous studies relied on self-reports, which lead respondents to answer across gender-role stereotypes, reinforcing our misperceptions. More recent studies were based on experiments and observations.[72]

In business, listening improves tasks and relationships (Figure 16).[73] Imagine trying to tell your manager about a potential new client or an idea to save money—and being ignored. Listening also contributes to feelings of belonging. In one study, 71% of employees surveyed had experienced "social exclusion" at work, for example, ostracism or shunning, in the past six months.[74] Next, you learn strategies to improve your listening skills.

Figure 16 How Listening Improves Business

TASKS	RELATIONSHIPS
Improves problem solving	Increases interpersonal trust
Improves product and service design	Improves customer service and loyalty
Improves accuracy of communication	Increases employee commitment and morale
Reduces misunderstandings about new tasks	Encourages timely feedback
Increases frequency of sharing information	Increases perceptions of integrity

2-6c Keys to Better Listening

To listen more effectively, give the speaker your undivided attention, stay open-minded, avoid interrupting, involve yourself, and respond.

Give the Speaker Your Undivided Attention

In a work environment, some distractions are easier to eliminate than others. You can control whether you multitask, but if you're working from home or in a cubicle, you may not be able to control all the noise and diversions around you. Your coworker may be typing loudly, talking on the phone, or clipping his toenails (true story!). Your best bet is to use your proficient communication skills to explain how the behavior is affecting your work and politely request a change.

Mental distractions can be even more difficult to eliminate. By practicing mindfulness, you can discipline yourself to postpone thinking about an upcoming exam or social event. Temporarily banishing competing thoughts will allow you to give a speaker your undivided attention.

Do you have a daily practice of mindfulness or meditation? How might these mind-training techniques help you?

Try to focus on the content of the message. A speaker's nonverbal communication, such as dress and body language, may seem incongruent with the message or may trigger a reaction in you. You may have your own ideas on how people "should" look or sound, but don't let unimportant factors prevent you from listening openly. Delivery skills can steal our attention—sometimes more than they should. If someone is nervous, speaks too softly, or sounds "boring," challenge yourself to listen beyond these surface issues. Almost always, *what* is said is more important than *how* it is said.

Stay Open-Minded

When approaching a conversation, first check yourself. To demonstrate good character, be honest about your feelings going into an interaction. Try to listen objectively and openly. Demonstrate humility by being willing to accept new information and new points of view, regardless

What prevents you from listening openly to others? How can you listen with a more open mind?

of whether they mesh with your existing beliefs (see Chapter 3). Concentrate on the content of the message rather than the person.

Consider the conversations in Figure 17. In the first conversation, the manager has preconceived notions, and she believes she knows the right answer. She doesn't allow the employee to explain his situation.

In the second conversation, the manager refrains from jumping to conclusions too quickly and solving the problem for the employee. Listening openly gives the manager more information

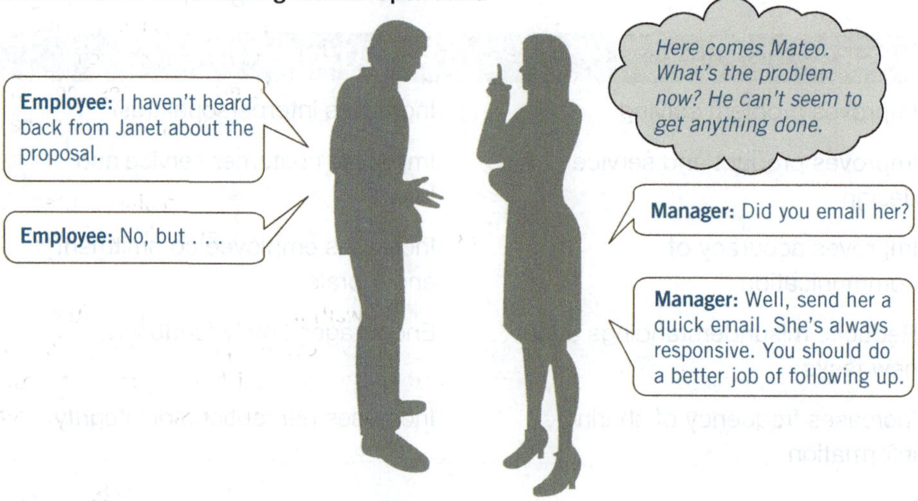

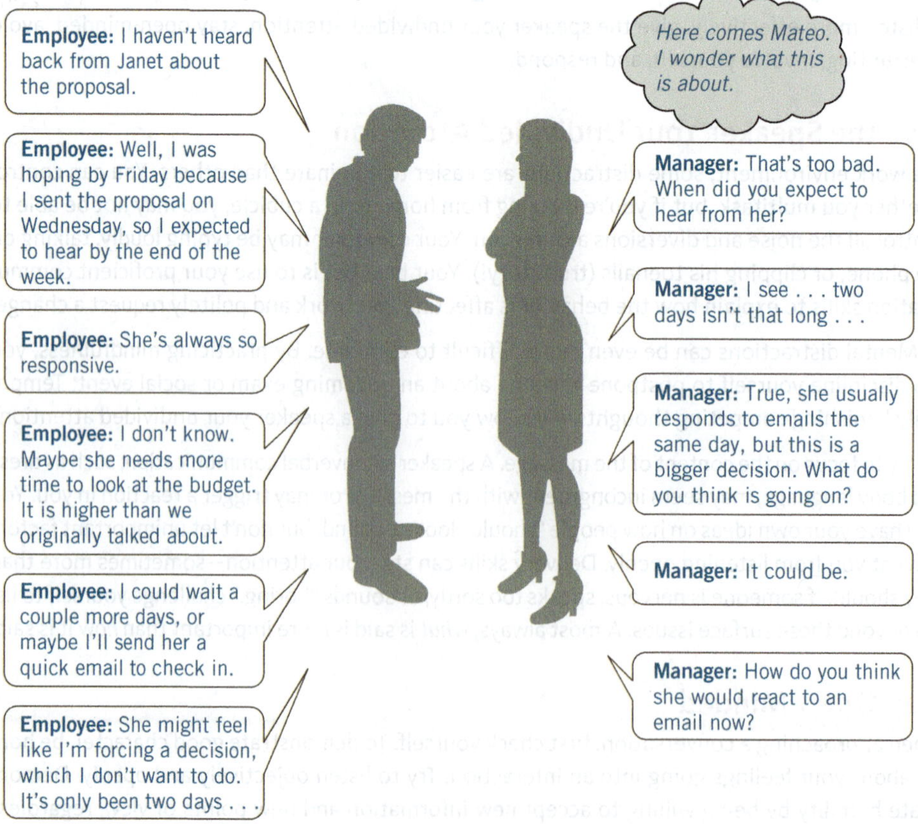

Figure 17 | Two Conversations: Listening with an Open Mind

Conversation 1: Not Listening with an Open Mind
Here comes Mateo. What's the problem now? He can't seem to get anything done.
Employee: I haven't heard back from Janet about the proposal.
Manager: Did you email her?
Employee: No, but . . .
Manager: Well, send her a quick email. She's always responsive. You should do a better job of following up.
Conversation 2: Listening with an Open Mind
Here comes Mateo. I wonder what this is about.
Employee: I haven't heard back from Janet about the proposal.
Manager: That's too bad. When did you expect to hear from her?
Employee: Well, I was hoping by Friday because I sent the proposal on Wednesday, so I expected to hear by the end of the week.
Manager: I see . . . two days isn't that long . . .
Employee: She's always so responsive.
Manager: True, she usually responds to emails the same day, but this is a bigger decision. What do you think is going on?
Employee: I don't know. Maybe she needs more time to look at the budget. It is higher than we originally talked about.
Manager: It could be.
Employee: I could wait a couple more days, or maybe I'll send her a quick email to check in.
Manager: How do you think she would react to an email now?
Employee: She might feel like I'm forcing a decision, which I don't want to do. It's only been two days . . .

from which to evaluate the situation. Sure, it takes a little longer, but in the future, the employee may walk through this type of thinking on his own—and ultimately solve problems more independently.

Don't Interrupt—Usually

In some cultures and when you know someone well, you might have overlapping conversations. You "finish each other's sentences"—a sign of a close friendship.[75]

But in business, interruptions have negative consequences. First, they are considered rude, sending a message that what you have to say is more important. Second, instead of speeding up the exchange, interruptions may drag it out because they interfere with the speaker's train of thought, causing backtracking.

Men are far more likely to interrupt women than the other way around.[76] To reduce interruptions, women should avoid using tentative language, for example, "Can I ask" and "Excuse me."[77] As U.S. Vice President Kamala Harris said during a debate with former Vice President Mike Pence, "Mr. Vice President, I'm speaking.... If you don't mind letting me finish, then we can have a conversation."[78] But responsibility needs to be on the listener.

Don't confuse listening with simply waiting to speak. Even if you're too polite to interrupt, if you're constantly planning what you'll say next, you can hardly listen attentively to what the other person is saying.

Americans tend to have low tolerance for silence. But waiting a moment or two after someone has finished before you respond has several positive effects—especially in an emotional exchange. Silence gives the person speaking a chance to elaborate, which could draw out further insights. Space during a conversation also creates a quieter, calmer, more respectful atmosphere that is more conducive to solving problems.

Yet sometimes we have to take the space we need. You don't have to be subjected to a barrage of complaints or irrelevant talk for too long. In these cases, you may interrupt politely or ask for permission to interrupt. Often, over-talkers will realize they were stuck and dominating the conversation.

Involve Yourself

Because hearing is passive and listening is active, you should be *doing* something while the other person is speaking. Research shows that both verbal and nonverbal actions are important to convey support. Verbal responses signal greater understanding of message content than do nonverbals, probably because verbal responses tend to be more specific, while nonverbals tend to be more generic.[79]

Follow these suggestions to be a more active listener:

- Jot down notes, translating what you hear into writing. Keep your notes brief and focus on the main ideas; don't become so busy writing that you miss the message.
- Listen for what you need. Consider how the information might be useful to you. Personalizing the information will help you concentrate more easily—even if the topic is difficult to follow or if the speaker has annoying mannerisms.
- Maintain eye contact, nod in agreement, lean forward, and use encouraging phrases such as "Uh huh" or "I see."

Respond by Paraphrasing or Reflecting

Also to be a more active listener, consider three levels of responding, each with increasing involvement (Figure 18). To repeat what someone says feels like parroting; it demonstrates that you are hearing but not necessarily listening. Paraphrasing is better: this approach shows that you are interpreting the message and restating it in your own words. Often, reflecting is best: you are telling the person that you hear, understand, and care about the underlying message.

Do you find it difficult to identify others' emotions? How could you improve your ability to empathize?

Figure 18 | Three Levels of Responding

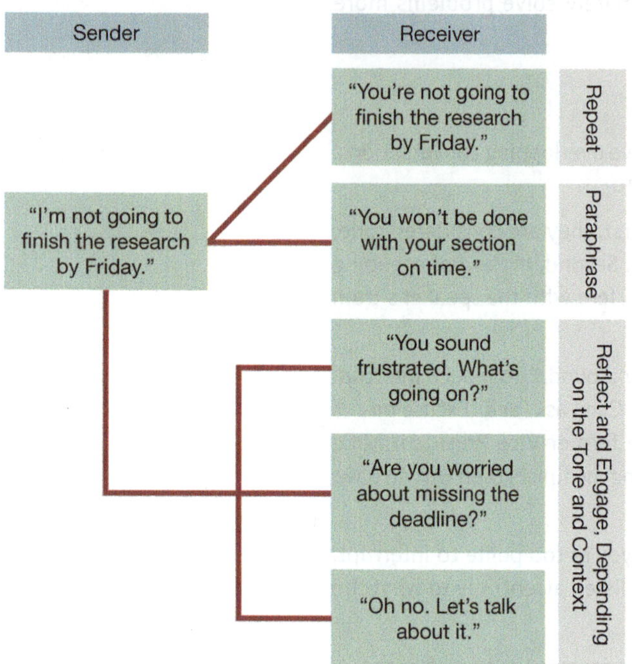

Sender
Receiver
"I'm not going to finish the research by Friday."
"You're not going to finish the research by Friday."
Repeat
"You won't be done with your section on time."
Paraphrase
"You sound frustrated. What's going on?"
"Are you worried about missing the deadline?"
"Oh no. Let's talk about it."
Reflect and Engage, Depending on the Tone and Context

Reflecting is particularly appropriate if you see someone visibly upset (and may be inappropriate for other interactions). Conveying your understanding of the content and the emotions without judgment may open the discussion and encourage the person to talk more about what's happening and how you can help solve the problem. Research shows that people are better at empathizing after they spend time identifying others' emotions throughout a day.[80] As part of emotional intelligence, the ability to demonstrate empathy requires us to be in touch with our own and others' emotions.

Notice how empathy sounds in the conversation between a manager and employee shown in Figure 19. This is a difficult interaction because the manager thinks the work can be done, but she can still see the situation from the employee's point of view. What's important is to reserve judgment and genuinely, physically feel what the employee feels. Telling people to "relax" or "calm down" usually has the opposite effect. At the same time, empathy doesn't always mean agreement. During this interaction, the manager uses empathy to defuse the situation and help the employee solve the problem on his own.

Figure 19 | Listening with Empathy

Manager: What's going on? You look really stressed.
Employee: Chi just asked me for the budget projections by tomorrow.
Manager: Oh, my. I thought he didn't need them until next week.
Employee: Me too. I'm not going to be able to do it all!
Manager: No wonder you're stressed. It's a lot to take on.
Employee: Right. Can I get Robby to help me?
Manager: Robby is working on the North Face proposal and will need the research by Friday to complete it.
Employee: Ugh. I don't know how I'll get it done!
Manager: Let's figure out what's doable. Why don't we meet for a few minutes now to map out what has to be done.
Employee: OK, I guess that will help.
Manager: Good. Let's just take it one step at a time.

2-7 Chapter Closing

When Boeing agreed to the settlement related to the Boeing 737 MAX plane crashes, the new president and CEO, David L. Calhoun, wrote to employees:

> I firmly believe that entering into this resolution is the right thing for us to do—a step that appropriately acknowledges how we fell short of our values and expectations. This resolution is a serious reminder to all of us of how critical

> our obligation of transparency to regulators is, and the consequences that our company can face if any one of us falls short of those expectations.[81]

At the same time, a company statement blamed two former employees:

> The agreement is based on the conduct of two former Boeing employees and their intentional failure to inform the FAA [Federal Aviation Administration] Aircraft Evaluation Group (AEG), the group within the FAA responsible for making pilot training determinations, about changes to the Maneuvering Characteristics Augmentation System (MCAS).[82]

Although the company strives to do better, leaders blamed a couple of individuals and failed to acknowledge much larger issues with team functioning and communication.

In the next chapter, you learn about communicating across differences, which will require your best team and interpersonal skills—and your character.

> IN ACTION

Decide Whether to Remove "Black Lives Matter" Messages

Consider the chapter introduction that describes basketball players protesting police violence. A few months later, NBA Commissioner Adam Silver announced the decision to remove the "Black Lives Matter" lettering from courts and to disallow the message on players' jerseys.[83] Using the CAM model, what questions might he have asked himself before making this decision?

>>> CHARACTER CHECK

1. **What is my role as a leader?**
   Silver has a complicated job with several constituents to consider, including players, fans, and sponsors. Personally, he may agree with the players that "Black Lives Matter" and all that the message means, but he has a responsibility to listen to many perspectives.
2. **Am I willing to disappoint some people?**
   To be effective in his role, Silver cannot please everyone. Whatever decision he makes takes courage—the willingness to assess risk and take a stand.

>>> AUDIENCE ANALYSIS

1. **What context is important to consider?**
   The history of the NBA must factor into the decision. As Silver said in an ESPN interview, "We're completely committed to standing for social justice and racial equality, and that's been the case going back decades. It's part of the DNA of this league."[84]
2. **Who is affected by the decision and how?**
   Players are still committed to the movement and likely want the message to stay visible. Black players, particularly, serve as role models for young people. And yet some fans, as Silver said in the interview, find the message, to put it one way, distracting: "I understand those people who say, 'I'm on your side, but I want to watch a basketball game.'"[85]

>>> MESSAGE AND MEDIUM

1. **How will I communicate the decision to players?**
   Curiously, from the interview and other news sources at the time, it sounded as though Silver hadn't discussed the decision with players. Silver said, "How it [the social justice message] gets manifested is something we're going to have to sit down with the players and discuss for next season."[86]

2. **In what medium will I communicate the message?**
   Silver said they were going to "sit down" to discuss the decision. An in-person meeting is best in this situation because players likely have strong feelings, and some will disagree with the decision. A conversation is also best to listen to ideas on how to continue the players' work.

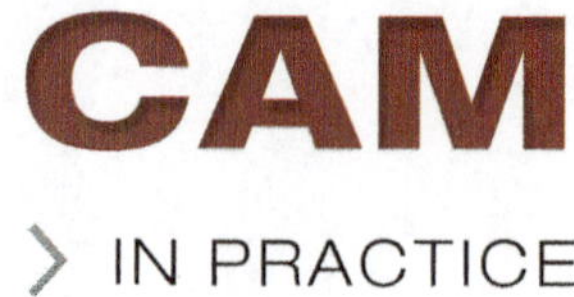

Plan a Meeting with Basketball Players

Imagine that you're NBA Commissioner Adam Silver and will hold a meeting with players about the (almost) final decision to remove "Black Lives Matter" messaging from courts and jerseys.

››› CHARACTER CHECK

1. How do I feel about the decision? How confident am I that this is the right thing to do?
2. What makes me proud about the players' activism, and what concerns do I have about continuing the message?

››› AUDIENCE ANALYSIS

1. How would I describe the players as my audience—those who promote the message and those who haven't supported it?
2. What barriers might get in the way of my message being received as I intend it?
3. What outcomes do I want for players at the end of the meeting? How do I want them to feel, what information do I want them to know, and what do I want them to do?

››› MESSAGE AND MEDIUM

1. What main points will I include in my message?
2. How will I involve players in the meeting? How will I make it interactive?
3. Create an agenda for the meeting.

REFLECTING ON YOUR COMMUNICATION AND CHARACTER DEVELOPMENT

1. **Debrief a negative team experience.**
   Think about a negative experience you had as part of a team. What was your role in the team's failure? Without wallowing in it too much, try to identify what you could have done differently. Get in touch with another member of the team to discuss what happened. Ask for feedback about your contribution to the team and how you might do better in future teams.

2. **Introduce yourself to develop your team relationships.**
   When you're part of a new team, introduce yourself by including some self-disclosure—nothing too personal but a few aspects of your life that will help your team members know you better and feel more comfortable with you. Next, practice communicating informally. Particularly if your communication tends to be more formal, try more conversational language.

3. **Practice giving and receiving peer feedback on writing.**
   Exchange a few pages of writing with a friend or classmate. Following the guidelines in Figure 6, Commenting on Team Writing, provide written feedback, and then discuss your feedback by taking turns. How do you feel giving and receiving feedback on writing? You might try this exercise with one of your favorite papers. This will challenge you to hear constructive feedback even if you don't agree with it.

4. **Observe your nonverbal communication.**
   Next time you're on a video meeting, record yourself speaking and listening. Watch yourself later to observe your nonverbal communication. Are your words aligned with your facial expressions, gestures, and movement? If you notice inconsistencies, what could be the cause? Remember how you felt during these times and try to match your verbal and nonverbal communication more closely.

5. **Assess your listening skills.**
   Reflect on your listening skills by rating the behaviors in Figure 20. For which of the items did you mark "often" or "always"? Next time someone is talking to you, observe these behaviors in yourself and try to listen more carefully.

Figure 20 | Assess Your Listening Skills

	NEVER	SOMETIMES	OFTEN	ALWAYS
I prefer to talk than to listen.				
I have a tough time listening to people whose views are different from mine.				
I have a tough time listening to people complain.				
When someone else is talking, I plan what I'll say next.				
I tend to try to solve problems quickly instead of listening to the whole situation first.				

DEVELOPING YOUR BUSINESS COMMUNICATION SKILLS

LO1 Describe ways to improve team communication.

WORK TEAM COMMUNICATION

1. **Observe a team's communication.**
   Watch a segment of a movie, series, or TV show in which a team is communicating. Search for "team movies" if you need ideas. Write down examples you observe of conflict, conformity, and consensus. Also identify any examples of groupthink. Talk with a classmate about your observations.

2. **Agree on team norms.**
   For a team project in class, agree on team norms. Answer the following questions:
   - What if team members miss a deliverable or team meeting? How should they notify the team? What will be the consequences?
   - What if two team members are having a conflict? How should it be addressed or resolved?
   - Which decisions will be most important for the team? How should the team make those decisions?
   - What if team members need help completing a task? How should they handle this situation? How will others respond?

   In addition to these questions, identify and answer at least three more that are important to the team.

3. **Assess accountability.**
   Think about a past or current job. Looking at Figure 2, External and Internal Accountability Measures, how would you describe leaders in the organization? Did you notice a difference between your immediate manager and others? How did your manager's way of holding you accountable—punishing, micromanaging, directing, or supporting—affect your work? What does this exercise tell you about your preferred way of working?

4. **Address a difficult situation with a team member.**
   Imagine this situation: your manager calls you into her office and asks for product information for a customer. She seems annoyed that you haven't already sent it to her, but this is the first you're hearing about it. She says that one of your team members said you were working on this last week. You remember your team member talking about a customer needing more information, and you offered suggestions for how to find it. You don't remember committing to anything. How will you handle this situation? What will you say to your team member? What will you say to your manager? Will you take responsibility for getting the work done now—or not?[87]

LO2 Explain ways to build relationships when working remotely.

VIRTUAL TEAM COMMUNICATION

5. **Analyze remote informal communication.**
   Review text or instant messages you exchanged with a coworker or classmate. What aspects of the messages are informal, for example, slang, abbreviations, emoticons, and so on? How does your communication compare to your coworker's or classmate's? Which is more effective given the situation?

6. **Create a virtual team charter.**

   If you are part of a remote team, develop a charter to agree on how you'll work together. Refer to Figure 3 for questions about your purpose, results, communication, roles and responsibilities, decision making, and conflict management.

7. **Compare collaboration platforms.**

   In a small group, research a few collaboration platforms. Also share your own experience about the advantages and disadvantages of each. Which platforms might be best for which type of work or team? If you had to choose one for your group, which would it be and why?

8. **Leave a voicemail message.**

   Imagine that you applied for a job and received the following voicemail message from the company's HR manager:

   > Hello. This is Marley Catona from Bank on Me. We received your cover letter and resume, and I'd like to schedule a phone interview with you. Will you please tell me what times you're available this Friday for a half-hour call? You can reach me at 555-1212. Thank you.

   Leave a response on another student's phone. Plan your message in advance but try to sound natural. You'll want to express your enthusiasm for the interview and give specific times when you're available. Use the checklist in Figure 21 to give each other feedback.

COLLABORATIVE WRITING

LO3 Apply the steps for team writing in a business situation.

9. **Create a project plan.**

   Working in groups of four or five, plan an upcoming event. You may choose something real in your lives—a club or social event—or invent something. Complete the first two steps for team writing described in Figure 4: identify project requirements and create a project plan. Include all the tasks you would need to complete in order to plan and hold the event.

10. **Comment on a peer's writing.**

    Working in groups of three, use the tips in Figure 6, Commenting on Team Writing, to provide feedback on other students' writing. If you're working as part of a team, use a writing sample for your project. Otherwise, choose a writing sample for another assignment.

    Spend about 10 minutes reviewing each paper and writing comments. If you have a grading rubric, use it to guide your comments. Identify at least one strength and one suggestion in each of the grading categories.

    When you're finished making comments, compare your notes and describe your feedback and approach. How similar are your comments? Did you agree on which parts were strongest and weakest? What could account for differences? Did you each focus on different aspects of the paper or view some parts more harshly than others? How could this activity help you assess your own writing?

BUSINESS MEETINGS

LO4 Identify best practices for in-person and online business meetings.

11. **Evaluate a meeting.**

    In pairs, think about the best and worst meetings you ever attended. They could have been at work, at school, or with a community organization. List the factors that made each the best and worst. Compare them to the principles in this chapter.

Figure 21 | Checklist for Voicemail Message Feedback

- ❑ Thanks Ms. Catona for the call
- ❑ Includes all relevant information:
  - ❍ First and last name
  - ❍ Reason for calling (responding to Ms. Catona's message)
  - ❍ Times available on Friday
- ❑ Avoids extraneous information and fillers (e.g., overuse of "uh," "um")
- ❑ Uses an appropriate tone:
  - ❍ Professional
  - ❍ Enthusiastic
  - ❍ Natural
  - ❍ Confident, but not overly confident
- ❑ Ends the call clearly and professionally
- ❑ Other: ____________________

12. Observe and practice good meeting citizenship.

Prepare to participate during an upcoming meeting. Review the meeting citizenship behaviors listed in Figure 10. Try to demonstrate as many behaviors as possible and observe other participants to see how many they follow.

After the meeting, reflect on your experience. Which behaviors did you observe others doing? How did their actions affect your view of them and their contribution to the meeting? Which actions were you able to take? How did your participation affect your experience of the meeting? Which of the behaviors will you continue in the future?

How did people use their phones during the meeting? Did you see people making or taking calls or checking or writing text messages? How did you judge those behaviors?

13. Plan a business meeting.

Working in groups of five, choose one of the following scenarios for the next three exercises. For the scenario you and your team members choose, prepare an email and detailed agenda to send to meeting participants. Plan ways to involve people in the meeting. Whether you'll meet in person or online, how can you encourage everyone to participate? If you'll meet online, what platform tools will you use?

Exchange emails and agendas with another group in class. Provide feedback on the purpose, clarity, tone, and level of detail.

Scenario 1

Imagine that you are a dean at your college and you want to expand your student advisory board. Currently, four students are elected to the board every year, but you want to add four to increase diversity and get more perspectives. You also have two new initiatives coming up next year—an alumni weekend event and a student blog—and both require more students to help. Invite the current board members to a meeting to discuss and vote on the proposal.

Scenario 2

Imagine that you work as a sales associate for your local Gap store. The work schedule is always set a month in advance, but you want more flexibility. You ask the four other sales associates in the store to meet with you so you can convince them to plan the schedule only one week in advance. You would need the store manager's approval to do this, but you decide to get your coworkers on board first.

14. Facilitate a meeting.

Use one of the scenarios in the previous exercise to practice facilitating and participating in a meeting. You may do this in person or online.

Have each person assume the role of another participant. The dean or the sales associate will lead the meeting. Conduct a ten-minute meeting. Following the meeting, evaluate its effectiveness. Did you achieve your objective? Explain your answer.

15. Write meeting minutes.

To summarize the meeting for your colleagues in the previous scenario, write up the meeting minutes. Each of you in the group should prepare the minutes separately. Then, as a group, compare your minutes. Which are best and why?

16. Evaluate an online meeting.

Next time you participate in an online meeting, evaluate which of the suggestions in Figure 9 the host follows. How well did the host arrive, check in, and check out of the meeting? Which of the platform features did you use? If you were asked for feedback, what would you suggest the host do differently next time?

NONVERBAL COMMUNICATION

LO5 Explain examples of nonverbal communication.

17. Identify others' emotions.

Throughout the day, keep a list of emotions you see on people's faces. Try to be more precise than happy, sad, or angry. People might feel upset, delighted, anxious, determined, grateful, ambitious, confident, content, bored, disgusted, or a host of other emotions. Practicing identifying others' facial expressions helps you understand their emotions better and improves your own emotional intelligence.

18. Practice direct eye contact online.

With a friend or classmate, schedule time for a video meeting on Zoom or another platform. Practice different gazes to see which appears to be the most direct eye contact. Also take a few screenshots of yourself so you can see how you appear to others.

19. Use your voice tone to convey emotions.

With a partner, practice conveying different emotions. If you go first, read the sentences in the left-side column, changing your tone to reflect each emotion. Also change the order of the sentences to see whether your partner can guess which emotion you're expressing. If you go second, read the right-side column, changing the tone and order of sentences. What helps and hinders the ability to identify the right emotion?

Today is my birthday. (excited)	I didn't get the Bank of America job. (disappointed)
Today is my birthday. (sad)	I didn't get the Bank of America job. (angry)
Today is my birthday. (anxious)	I didn't get the Bank of America job. (indifferent)
Today is my birthday. (emphatic)	I didn't get the Bank of America job. (surprised)

LO6 Describe ways to improve listening skills in business situations.

LISTENING

20. Listen to key ideas and compare notes.

Watch a few minutes of a news report with the class. As you're listening, take notes about the most important points. In small groups, compare a few examples. In what ways are your notes different or similar? Did you miss important points that your classmates wrote down? If so, why do you think this is the case?

21. Identify listening skills from poor listening experiences.

Working in pairs, have one person describe a time when someone didn't listen well. This can be a situation with a family member, friend, doctor, or someone else. Have the listener identify (1) what the person did to demonstrate nonlistening and (2) the effect this had on the speaker. From this experience, write a list of good listening skills.[88]

22. Observe someone listening.

Working in groups of three, have one person talk about a difficult decision. As your classmate describes the situation, have a second person listen, using skills discussed in this chapter. The listener just needs to listen—not give advice or help the speaker solve the problem. The third person in your group should take notes on how the listener uses the skills in Figure 22.

Figure 22 | Checklist for Listening Skills Feedback

SKILLS	RATING				
• Gives the speaker undivided attention	1	2	3	4	5
• Stays open-minded	1	2	3	4	5
• Doesn't interrupt	1	2	3	4	5
• Involves oneself by doing the following:					
— Maintains eye contact	1	2	3	4	5
— Nods in agreement	1	2	3	4	5
— Leans forward	1	2	3	4	5
— Uses encouraging phrases ("Uh huh," "I see")	1	2	3	4	5
— Responds (paraphrases and reflects)	1	2	3	4	5

After about three minutes of conversation, have both the speaker and observer give feedback to the listener. Which skills were used most effectively, and which skills could the listener improve?

If you have time, switch roles so everyone has a chance to practice listening skills. After each person receives feedback, debrief the activity. What did you each learn about yourself and your listening skills?

23. Discuss Brené Brown's TED Talk, "The Power of Vulnerability."

Find Brené Brown's popular TED talk.[89] Watch the video in groups or on your own. In small groups, discuss the video and how her concept of vulnerability relates to empathy. If you're comfortable, take some risks and discuss your personal views of empathy: what do you find easy or difficult about showing empathy toward others?

CHAPTER SUMMARY

LO1 Describe ways to improve team communication.

Teams can accomplish more and better-quality work in less time than individuals can if the teams function properly and develop trust. Otherwise, teams can waste time and experience interpersonal conflicts. Conflict about ideas is a helpful part of the group process, but interpersonal conflicts are detrimental. Consensus and conformity can lead to productivity, but too much focus on either can lead to groupthink. High-functioning team members hold themselves accountable, give more than take, and act ethically.

LO2 Explain ways to build relationships when working remotely.

Remote teams face additional challenges and should spend more time getting to know each other personally, developing social presence, creating a team charter, and choosing a primary collaboration platform. Use the telephone for richer communication that requires more cues for understanding and choose text and instant messaging for simpler and routine communication. How you present yourself on the phone and in short messages demonstrates your professionalism.

LO3 Apply the steps for team writing in a business situation.

For group writing projects, team members should identify project requirements, create a project plan, draft the writing, revise the writing, and finalize the project. When done well, commenting on peers' writing leads to better final products and team relationships.

LO4 Identify best practices for in-person and online business meetings.

To hold a productive meeting, determine the format, identify the purpose, decide who should attend, and prepare an agenda. The best meetings are interactive, so build in ways that everyone can contribute and use available tools for online meetings. Managing time carefully and stating clear outcomes will keep everyone focused—including yourself as a meeting participant.

LO5 Explain examples of nonverbal communication.

Nonverbal communication includes body movement, stance and positioning, physical appearance, voice qualities, and touch. Nonverbals complement verbal messages, convey their own messages, and are difficult to interpret without corresponding language.

LO6 Describe ways to improve listening skills in business situations.

Listening has many positive benefits for business but is the least developed communication skill. Empathy is important to understand another person's feelings, which may differ from your own. Whether listening to a formal presentation or conversing with one or two people, listen more effectively by giving the speaker your undivided attention, staying open-minded about the speaker and the topic, avoiding interrupting the speaker, and involving yourself actively in the communication.

Endnotes

1. Don Riddell, "'I Don't Know What Percentage of Those Men Have Essentially Had Their Lives Saved by Black Women,' Says Head of NBA Players' Union," CNN, March 13, 2021, www.cnn.com/2021/03/13/sport/michele-roberts-nba-players-union-cmd-spt-intl/index.html, accessed May 9, 2021.
2. "NBA Begins New Season Amid COVID Jump, but a Bubble Remains 'a Last Resort,'" PBS NewsHour, December 22, 2020, www.pbs.org/newshour/show/nba-begins-new-season-amid-covid-jump-but-a-bubble-remains-a-last-resort, accessed January 3, 2021.
3. Adam Lashinsky and Brian O'Keefe, "The NBA Bubble Was a One-of-a-Kind COVID-19 Success Story," *Fortune*, October 15, 2020, www.popsci.com/story/health/nba-coronavirus-bubble-success-science/, accessed January 3, 2021.
4. NBA, "Clippers and Lakers Kneel in Solidarity During National Anthem," YouTube, July 30, 2020, www.youtube.com/watch?v=xM7PZpaz1ml, accessed January 3, 2021.
5. NACE Staff, National Association of Colleges and Employers, "Key Attributes Employers Want to See on Students' Resumes, January 13, 2020, www.naceweb.org/talent-acquisition/candidate-selection/key-attributes-employers-want-to-see-on-students-resumes/, accessed December 21, 2020.
6. John R. Pierce, "Communication," *Scientific American* 227 (September 1972): 36.
7. Paul J. Zak, "The Neuroscience of Trust," *Harvard Business Review*, January-February 2017, https://hbr.org/2017/01/the-neuroscience-of-trust, accessed January 20, 2021. Also see Paul J. Zak, *Trust Factor* (New York: AMACOM, 2017).
8. John Gottman, "On Trust and Betrayal," Greater Good, October 29, 2011, http://greatergood.berkeley.edu/article/item/john_gottman_on_trust_and_betrayal, accessed January 20, 2021.
9. "Boeing Charged with 737 Max Fraud Conspiracy and Agrees to Pay over $2.5 Billion," U.S. Department of Justice, January 7, 2021, www.justice.gov/opa/pr/boeing-charged-737-max-fraud-conspiracy-and-agrees-pay-over-25-billion, accessed January 11, 2021.
10. Natalie Kitroeff, David Gelles, and Jack Nicas, "Boeing 737 Max Safety System Was Vetoed, Engineer Says," *The New York Times*, October 2, 2019, https://www.nytimes.com/2019/10/02/business/boeing-737-max-crashes.html, accessed January 11, 2021.
11. Boeing Employee Message, July 21, 2014, https://int.nyt.com/data/documenthelper/6653-internal-boeing-communications/606e3fda752a935bc0df/optimized/full.pdf, page 3, accessed January 11, 2021.
12. Boeing Employee Message, December 18, 2014, https://int.nyt.com/data/documenthelper/6653-internal-boeing-communications/606e3fda752a935bc0df/optimized/full.pdf, page 6, accessed January 11, 2021.
13. Boeing Employee Message, February 8, 2018, https://int.nyt.com/data/documenthelper/6653-internal-boeing-communications/606e3fda752a935bc0df/optimized/full.pdf, page 103, accessed January 11, 2021.
14. Boeing Employee Message, May 15, 2018, https://int.nyt.com/data/documenthelper/6653-internal-boeing-communications/606e3fda752a935bc0df/optimized/full.pdf, page 58, accessed January 11, 2021.
15. Adapted from Craig Redding, "Increasing Accountability," *Organizational Development Journal* 22 (2004): 65, and Amy Newman, "Authenticity, Integrity, and Accountability," eCornell course, "Accountability Continuum."
16. Richard Grant, "Do Trees Talk to Each Other?" *Smithsonian Magazine*, March 2018, www.smithsonianmag.com/science-nature/the-whispering-trees-180968084/, accessed December 12, 2020.
17. Ferris Jabr, "The Social Life of Forests," *The New York Times*, December 2, 2020, www.nytimes.com/interactive/2020/12/02/magazine/tree-communication-mycorrhiza.html, accessed December 12, 2020.
18. Within reason, of course. Grant also found that givers who are "too trusting, too caring, and too willing to sacrifice their own interests for the benefit of others . . . are most likely to land at the bottom of the success ladder." Adam Grant, *Give and Take: Why Helping Others Drives Our Success* (London: Penguin Publishing Group, 2014), p. 7.
19. Adam Grant, *Give and Take: Why Helping Others Drives Our Success* (London: Penguin Publishing Group, 2014).
20. Grant, p. 73.
21. Mike Axisa, "Houston Astros Cheating Scandal: 10 Things We Learned from MLB's Nine-Page Investigative Report," CBS Sports, January 15, 2020, www.cbssports.com/mlb/news/houston-astros-cheating-scandal-10-things-we-learned-from-mlbs-nine-page-investigative-report, accessed December 22, 2020.
22. Jared Diamond, "Three Astros Were Suspended for Cheating. Two Are Already Back," *The Wall Street Journal*, December 24, 2020, www.wsj.com/articles/three-astros-were-suspended-for-cheating-two-are-already-back-11608758747, accessed December 27, 2020.
23. Patti Wojahn, Stephanie K. Taylor, and Kristin Blicharz, "Forming Groups into Teams through Virtual Interactions: Researching Remote Collaborators and 'Getting to Know You'," 2010 IEEE International Professional Communication Conference, July 7–9, 2010, https://ieeexplore.ieee.org/document/5530009, p. 206, accessed January 12, 2021.
24. Ryan Goke and Stephanie Kelly, "Developing Presence," in Stephanie Kelly (ed.), *Computer-Mediated Communication for Business: Theory and Practice* (Newcastle upon Tyne, UK: Cambridge Scholars Publishing, 2019), p. 39.
25. Ralph Van den Bosch and Toon W. Taris, "Authenticity at Work: Development and Validation of an Individual Authenticity Measure at Work," *Journal of Happiness Studies* 15 (2014): 1–18.
26. Vanessa Buote, "Most Employees Feel Authentic at Work, but It Can Take a While," *Harvard Business Review*, May 11, 2016, https://hbr.org/2016/05/most-employees-feel-authentic-at-work-but-it-can-take-a-while, accessed January 15, 2021.

27. Goke and Kelly, p. 39.
28. By coincidence, the author uses less-than-perfect punctuation.
29. Wojahn et al., p. 206.
30. Andrea Freund, "Enabling Success or Cementing Failure: When and why team charters help or hurt team performance," (under review at *Organization Science*), described in Robert I. Sutton, "Remote Work Is Here to Stay. Bosses Better Adjust," *The Wall Street Journal*, August 2, 2020, https://www.wsj.com/articles/remote-work-is-here-to-stay-bosses-better-adjust-11596395367, accessed January 12, 2021.
31. Michael D. Watkins, "Making Virtual Teams Work: Ten Basic Principles," *Harvard Business Review*, June 27, 2013, https://hbr.org/2013/06/making-virtual-teams-work-ten, accessed January 12, 2021.
32. Freund.
33. Goke and Kelly, p. 39.
34. Freund.
35. Goke and Kelly, p. 37.
36. "The Digitization of Collaboration," *Harvard Business Review*, Analytic Services, 2018, https://hbr.org/resources/pdfs/comm/workplace/TheDigitizationOfCollaboration.pdf, accessed December 24, 2020.
37. "The Digitization of Collaboration."
38. Matthew Finnegan, "How to Get the Most Out of Slack," *Computerworld*, July 2, 2020, www.computerworld.com/article/3257934/how-to-get-the-most-out-of-slack.html, accessed December 22, 2020.
39. Finnegan.
40. Jolanta Aritz, Robyn Walker, and Peter W. Cardon, "Media Use in Virtual Teams of Varying Levels of Coordination," *Business and Professional Communication Quarterly* 81 (2018): 222–243.
41. Eric Griffith, "How to Get Rid of Voice Mail," *PC Magazine*, March 15, 2016, www.pcmag.com/news/how-to-get-rid-of-voice-mail, accessed December 23, 2020.
42. David Lennox, Amy Newman, and Maria Loukianenko Wolfe, "How Business Leaders Communicate in 2012: Classroom Strategies for Teaching Current Practices," Association for Business Communication 11th European Conference, Nijmegen, Netherlands, May 2012.
43. Rodney P. Rice and John T. Huguley, Jr., "Describing Collaborative Forms: A Profile of the Team-Writing Process," *IEEE Transactions on Professional Communication* 37 (September 1994): 163–170.
44. Leslie A. Perlow, Constance Noonan Hadley, and Eunice Eun, "Stop the Meeting Madness," *Harvard Business Review*, July-August 2017, https://hbr.org/2017/07/stop-the-meeting-madness, accessed January 13, 2021.
45. Kendra H. Oliver, "Are You Feeling Zoom-Ed Out? You Are Not Alone," Vanderbilt School of Medicine, October 1, 2020, https://medschool.vanderbilt.edu/basic-sciences/2020/10/01/are-you-feeling-zoom-ed-out-you-are-not-alone/, accessed January 14, 2021.
46. Elizabeth Grace Saunders, "I'll Be Right Back. How to Protect Your Energy During Zoom Meetings," *Fast Company*, April 15, 2020, www.fastcompany.com/90490716/ill-be-right-back-how-to-protect-your-energy-during-zoom-meetings, accessed January 16, 2021.
47. Oliver.
48. Benjamin E. Baran, et al., "Leading Group Meetings: Supervisors' Actions, Employee Behaviors, and Upward Perceptions," *Small Group Research* 43 (November 2011): 330–335, https://journals.sagepub.com/doi/pdf/10.1177/1046496411418252, accessed January 14, 2021.
49. Emil B. Towner, Heidi L. Everett, and Bruce R. Klemz, "Not So Different?: Student and Professional Perceptions of Mobile Phone Etiquette in Meetings," *Business and Professional Communication Quarterly* 82 (2019): 317–336.
50. Hassan Ugail and Ahmad Al-dahoud, "A Genuine Smile Is Indeed in the Eyes - The Computer Aided Non-Invasive Analysis of the Exact Weight Distribution of Human Smiles Across the Face," *Advanced Engineering Informatics* 42 (October 2019): 1–10. www.sciencedirect.com/science/article/abs/pii/S1474034619305403, accessed December 12, 2020.
51. Hassan Ugail and Ahmad Al-dahoud.
52. Leanne S. Bohannon et al., "Eye Contact and Video-Mediated Communication: A Review," *ScienceDirect* 34 (2013): 177–185, www.sciencedirect.com/science/article/pii/S0141938212001084, accessed January 16, 2021.
53. Bohannon
54. Paul Ekman, E. Richard Sorenson, and Wallace V Friesen, "Pan-cultural Elements in Facial Displays of Emotion," *Science* 164 (April 1969): 469–479, https://pubmed.ncbi.nlm.nih.gov/5773719/, accessed December 12, 2020.
55. See discussion in Malcolm Gladwell, *Talking to Strangers* (London, UK: Allen Lane, 2019), pp. 259–261.
56. Timothy J. Luke, "Lessons from Pinocchio: Cues to Deception May Be Highly Exaggerated," *Association for Psychological Science* 14 (2019): 646–671, https://journals.sagepub.com/doi/pdf/10.1177/1745691619838258, accessed December 12, 2020.
57. Timothy R. Levine, "Five Reasons Why I Am Skeptical That Indirect or Unconscious Lie Detection Is Superior to Direct Deception Detection," "*Frontiers in Psychology* 10 (2019), www.ncbi.nlm.nih.gov/pmc/articles/PMC6706798/, accessed December 12, 2020.
58. Robert M. Krauss, Palmer Morrel-Samuels, and Christina Colasante, "Do Conversational Hand Gestures Communicate?" *Journal of Personality and Social Psychology* 61 (1991): 743–754.

59. Kim Elsesser, "Power Posing Is Back: Amy Cuddy Successfully Refutes Criticism," *Forbes*, April 3, 2018, www.forbes.com/sites/kimelsesser/2018/04/03/power-posing-is-back-amy-cuddy-successfully-refutes-criticism, accessed May 12, 2021.
60. Amy J. C. Cuddy, S. Jack Schultz, and Nathan E. Fosse, "P-Curving a More Comprehensive Body of Research on Postural Feedback Reveals Clear Evidential Value for Power-Posing Effects: Reply to Simmons and Simonsohn (2017)," *Psychological Science* 29 (2018): 656–666. https://doi.org/10.1177%2F0956797617746749.
61. Eric Clay, email, July 8, 2017.
62. Timothy A. Judge, Charlice Hurst, and Lauren S. Simon, "Does It Pay to Be Smart, Attractive, or Confident (or All Three)?" *Journal of Applied Psychology* 94 (2009): 742–755.
63. Dario Maestripieri, Andrea Henry, and Nora Nickels, "Explaining Financial and Prosocial Biases in Favor of Attractive People: Interdisciplinary Perspectives from Economics, Social Psychology, and Evolutionary Psychology," *Behavioral and Brian Sciences* 40 (2017), https://doi.org/10.1017/S0140525X16000340.
64. Stephanie Watson, "The Unheard Female Voice," The ASHA Leaders, ASHAWire, February 1, 2019, https://leader.pubs.asha.org/doi/10.1044/leader.FTR1.24022019.44, accessed May 11, 2021, https://doi.org/10.1044/leader.FTR1.24022019.44.
65. "Anti-harassment Policy and Complaint Procedure (includes Dating/Consensual Relationship Policy Provision)," Society for Human Resources Management, www.shrm.org/resourcesandtools/tools-and-samples/policies/pages/cms_000534.aspx, December 22, 2020.
66. John Egan, "Waving Goodbye to the Handshake: 7 Alternatives to a Workplace Custom," SHRM, April 27, 2020, www.shrm.org/resourcesandtools/hr-topics/employee-relations/pages/coronavirus-handshake-alternatives.aspx, accessed January 20, 2021.
67. TED.com, "The Ten Most Popular TEDx Talks," 2. The Power of Vulnerability, Brené Brown, www.ted.com/playlists/180/the_10_most_popular_tedx_talks, accessed December 22, 2020.
68. Brené Brown, "Brené Brown on Empathy," YouTube, December 10, 2013, www.youtube.com/watch?v=1Evwgu369Jwhttps://www.youtube.com/watch?v=1Evwgu369Jw, accessed June 1, 2021.
69. Sam Walker, "Joe Biden Promises Empathy, but That's a Difficult Way to Lead," *The Wall Street Journal*, November 14, www.wsj.com/amp/articles/joe-biden-promises-empathy-but-thats-a-difficult-way-to-lead-11605330019, accessed December 22, 2020.
70. Ethan Kross, *Chatter: The Voice in Our Head, Why It Matters, and How to Harness It* (New York: Crown, 2021), p. 94.
71. Jason Headley, "It's Not About the Nail," YouTube, www.youtube.com/watch?v=-4EDhdAHrOg, accessed January 15, 2021.
72. Sandra Baez et al., "Men, Women...Who Cares? A Population-Based Study on Sex Differences and Gender Roles in Empathy and Moral Cognition," *PLOS ONE*, https://doi.org/10.1371/journal.pone.0179336, accessed January 15, 2021.
73. Judi Brownell, "Fostering Service Excellence through Listening: What Hospitality Managers Need to Know," *Cornell Hospitality Report* 9 (April 2009).
74. Jane O'Reilly and Sara Banki, "Research in Work and Organizational Psychology: Social Exclusion in the Workplace," in Paolo Riva and Jennifer Eck (eds.), *Social Exclusion* (New York: Springer, 2016), https://doi.org/10.1007/978-3-319-33033-4_7, pp. 133–155.
75. Jack Sidnell, "Comparative Studies in Conversational Analysis," *Annual Review of Anthropology* 36 (2007): 229–224, https://doi.org/10.1146/annurev.anthro.36.081406.094313.
76. Stephanie Watson, "The Unheard Female Voice," The ASHA Leaders, ASHAWire, February 1, 2019, https://leader.pubs.asha.org/doi/10.1044/leader.FTR1.24022019.44, accessed May 11, 2021, https://doi.org/10.1044/leader.FTR1.24022019.44.
77. Watson.
78. Helier Cheung, "VP Debate: Did Gender Play a Role in the Interruptions?" BBC, October 8, 2020, www.bbc.com/news/election-us-2020-54467093, accessed May 17, 2021.
79. Graham D. Bodie, et al., "The Role of 'Active Listening' in Informal Helping Conversations: Impact on Perceptions of Listener Helpfulness, Sensitivity, and Supportiveness and Discloser Emotional Improvement," *Western Journal of Communication* 79 (2015): 151–173.
80. Alan Alda, *If I Understood You, Would I Have This Look on my Face?: My Adventures in the Art and Science of Relating and Communicating* (New York: Random House, 2018).
81. "Boeing Reaches Agreement with Department of Justice," Boeing Communications, January 7, 2021, https://boeing.mediaroom.com/news-releases-statements?item=130799, accessed January 15, 2021.
82. "Boeing Reaches Agreement."
83. Adam Silver, "Adam Silver Talks NBA Bubble, When Next Season Could Start | NBA Countdown," ESPN, October 4, 2021, https://youtu.be/R4PbOVFw4l8, accessed January 15, 2021.
84. Silver.
85. Silver.
86. Silver.
87. Adapted from Amy Newman, *Building Leadership Character* (Thousand Oaks, CA: Sage, 2019), p. 132.
88. Becky Norman, adapted from Derek, "Trainers' Tips: Active Listening Exercises," TrainingZone, August 7, 2018, www.trainingzone.co.uk/develop/cpd/trainers-tips-active-listening-exercises, accessed January 16, 2021.
89. Brené Brown, "The Power of Vulnerability," YouTube, January 3, 2011, https://www.youtube.com/watch?v=iCvmsMzlF7o, accessed June 1, 2021.

CHAPTER

3 Communicating Across Differences

Learning Objectives

After you have finished this chapter, you should be able to

LO1 Describe two approaches for shifting your mindset.

LO2 Define three types of conflict common in business environments and how to approach each.

LO3 Apply steps to engage in a difficult conversation in a business situation.

LO4 Identify ways to adapt language to audiences to honor differences.

LO5 Compare how people in high- and low-context countries communicate.

"[Carlos Ghosn] nurtured hero worship and took too much credit for positive developments" in a "culture that values discretion and humility."[1]

—Jeff Kingston, Director of Asian Studies at Temple University Japan

Chapter Introduction

Carlos Ghosn Succeeds, and Then Fails, in Intercultural Communication

Carlos Ghosn had a dramatic career pioneering the Renault-Nissan-Mitsubishi Alliance in Japan and ending with his arrest for financial misconduct.[2] Before his trial, Ghosn escaped from Japan to Lebanon in a "big black box" on a private plane.[3]

A popular business figure in Japan, Ghosn was touted as "an inspirational advocate of cross-cultural understanding and diversity within the business world."[4] Holding French, Brazilian, and Lebanese citizenships, he attributed part of his success to working across cultural differences: "The Alliance is making progress because it respects individual and cultural identities."[5]

Joseph Eid/AFP/Getty Images

Carlos Ghosn gives a one-hour news conference that a *Guardian* writer calls "lengthy and often rambling."[9]

Although his tough business decisions made Nissan profitable,[6] in the end, Ghosn's lack of cultural sensitivity may have caused his downfall. He defied Japanese cultural norms by closing plants and eliminating jobs. In addition, his lavish lifestyle and boastful nature were not appreciated and may have hastened charges of underreporting pay and misusing funds for personal gain.[7]

A professor of intercultural communication and management highlights Ghosn's lack of "the key intercultural competence needed by all those working across cultures: self-awareness, the ability to perceive and reflect upon himself."[8] Leaders who work across differences also must practice curiosity and humility.

LO1 Describe two approaches for shifting your mindset.

3-1 Shifting Your Mindset

Working across differences tests our character, particularly our willingness and ability to put ourselves aside at times in favor of others' ideas, values, and cultures. Chapter 2 compared listening with a closed and open mind. Similar principles apply when you communicate across differences, but the interactions may be more difficult and the stakes higher.

We start this chapter with a look at yourself—your own cultural identities. How we view ourselves often shapes how we view others. We sometimes judge ourselves and others harshly without knowing why. Instead, we can expand our thinking by allowing ourselves to feel uncomfortable, which happens when we meet people who are unlike us and when we are in unfamiliar situations. After exploring these topics, you learn strategies to shift your mindset and approach yourself and others with more humility and curiosity than judgment.

3-1a Acknowledging Your Own Cultural Identities and Views

Wouldn't it be great if everyone were just like you? Probably not. In a business environment, how would you allocate work when everyone has the same skills? How would you generate new ideas when everyone thinks the same way?

When people think of diversity, they often jump to differences in race and gender, but diversity is far more complex. At work, people differ by skill set, education, experience, thought, workstyles, sexual orientation, socioeconomic status, generation, physical abilities, family status, religious beliefs, political beliefs, core values—and by race, ethnicity, and gender.

Diversity doesn't mean a particular group of people; we are all diverse. An obvious example is in workstyles. When you start working with a team, you notice how differently people approach a project. Stephanie sees only problems, Kai jumps right to a solution, and Tamika wants to put together a schedule.

Consider your own affiliations and identities. Communicating across differences doesn't only mean adapting to *others*. Through our interactions, we come to understand and accept *ourselves* in new ways.

Self-awareness is key to intercultural communication[10] (or cross-cultural communication), which takes place between people from different cultures. When we talk about culture, we mean the customary traits, attitudes, and behaviors of a group of people. A message is created by someone from one culture to be understood by someone from another culture. More broadly, multiculturalism refers to appreciating diversity among people, typically beyond differences in countries of origin.

You might take the first step in shifting your mindset about working across differences by asking yourself the questions in Figure 1.

How comfortable are you answering these questions? What could contribute to your level of comfort or discomfort?

Why do we misjudge people? We are all prejudiced in some way, which means only that we *pre-judge* others—a useful survival skill for early humans to avoid threats. Similarly, we stereotype people, which means we attribute to an individual an assumption we have about the group to which they belong that may or may not be true.

Of course, trouble ensues when we take action based on wrongly held beliefs. When you're assigned to work with a team of students on a project, how do you judge the student-athlete, the student whose native language isn't English, or the student who wears a hijab or a yarmulke? Research on implicit (or unconscious) bias indicates that we have certain preferences or aversions and we are completely unaware or mistaken about them.

Companies recognize the dangers of implicit bias and have taken steps to make team members more aware. For example, HSBC, Deloitte, BBC, and Google have implemented blind hiring to reduce bias in the selection process.[11] By redacting applicants' name, address, dates, hobbies, interests, volunteer work, and/or college,[12] companies hope to increase diversity and hire the best talent.

Figure 1 Questions About Your Identity and Views

- With what groups do I affiliate or feel as though I belong?
- What is most important about my own cultural identity?
- What has shaped my cultural identity throughout my life?
- What do others need to know about me to understand and respect me?
- What is the hardest part of living up to my own cultural expectations?
- When have I felt ashamed of who I am?
- When have others misunderstood or misjudged me because of my affiliation or identity?
- When have I misunderstood or misjudged others because of their affiliation or identity?
- How open am I to people who are different from me?
- Do I interact regularly with people who are different from me?
- Do I avoid interacting with certain people? Why?

3-1b Learning When We're Uncomfortable

The lessons and examples in this chapter will challenge you and may make you feel uncomfortable. But we learn the most when we are uncomfortable, as shown in Figure 2.[13] When we're comfortable, we may be complacent, with our minds on autopilot. When we're struck by fear or panic, we may be reactive, unable or unwilling to learn.

Figure 2 We Learn When We're Uncomfortable

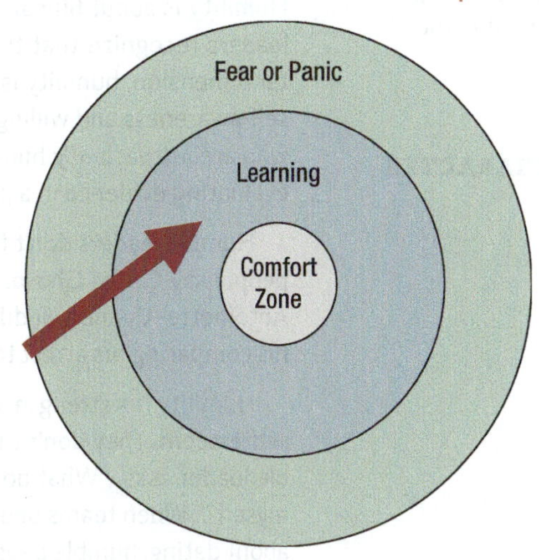

When we are uncomfortable enough, we can learn. We recognize that what we believe to be true is questioned. We learn to reconcile our ideas with different ways of thinking, and we might learn that multiple truths exist.[14]

Changing your mindset takes courage, which American poet Maya Angelou called the greatest virtue:

> [W]ithout courage, you cannot practice any other virtue consistently. You can be kind for a while; you can be generous for a while; you can be just for a while, or merciful for a while, even loving for a while. But it is only with courage that you can be persistently and insistently kind and generous and fair.[15]

Next, you learn strategies you can use to understand yourself and others better.

3-1c Reducing Blanket Judgments of Others

In this section, you learn ways to reduce judgment of others, particularly negative judgments. You'll increase understanding of yourself by asking why you're judging, choosing humility, observing without judging, getting perspective, being curious, and getting up close.

Ask Why You're Judging

How we judge others might tell us more about ourselves than about the other person. Swiss psychiatrist Carl Jung said, "Everything that irritates us about others can lead us to an understanding of ourselves."[16] A coworker seems too pushy with customers. Is this true, or is the real issue that you hesitate to close a sale? Does another coworker really talk too much, or is the issue that you don't get the airtime you want? When you're judging someone, ask yourself the questions in Figure 3.[17]

Figure 3 | Why Am I Judging?

- Is it because of a preconceived notion?
- Is it because of my knowledge or experiences?
- Is it because of my strong values?
- Is it because of my limited view of the world?
- Am I biased?
- Am I jealous?
- Does the judgment hold true for me instead?

Think about a time when you judged someone else and learned something about yourself in the process.

Being honest about your judgment may reduce its hold on you, allow you to view the other person more objectively—and help you learn about yourself. As a bonus, when we stop judging others, we tend to care less about what they think of us.

Choose Humility

Humility is about human limits: seeing and handling our own and others' limitations. Humble leaders recognize that their view or way of being is not the only way of being. As a character dimension, humility is essential to communicating across differences because it drives our self-awareness and willingness to learn. Because they accept that they could be wrong, people who are *intellectually* humble do a better job distinguishing between real and "fake" news and evaluating evidence in a persuasive argument.[18]

Humble leaders don't flaunt success; they don't see themselves as better than others. When people say Carlos Ghosn, the former leader of Nissan, lacked humility, they point to his Marie Antoinette–themed wedding in Versailles (with costumes), his brazen escape from the law, and his comparing his arrest to the attack on Pearl Harbor.[19]

Humility is a strength at work and at home. Perhaps paradoxically, humble leaders have high self-esteem. They don't think less of themselves, but they think about themselves less. A humble leader asks, "What do others see that I need to see?" and "What can they teach me about myself?" When teams openly admit and learn from mistakes, they perform better.[20,21] In a study about dating, humble people got more dates and were rated as more attractive than people who are arrogant.[22]

Observe Details Without Judging

When we're humble and realize that our judgments may be wrong, we can view situations more objectively. Do you interpret the person in the next image as serious, sad, angry, deep in thought, worried, or something else? How might the wheelchair, the setting, or physical characteristics affect your perception? What do you observe about yourself as you observe the image? In other words, what does your interpretation say about you?

Training our minds to observe without interpreting or judging is challenging, and a regular practice of mindfulness and meditation can help. Research shows that mindfulness reduces stress and work conflicts and increases satisfaction and resilience.[23] In one study, students reduced their anxiety about taking tests by participating in a mindfulness program.[24] Because of the positive results, Deutsche Bank, BASF, Monsanto,[25] Target, Google, General Mills,[26] and other companies encourage employees to practice mindfulness at work.

When we practice mindfulness, we train ourselves to stay present or "in the moment." A beginner might experience greater clarity, comfort, and calm. Over time, mindfulness helps us observe thoughts and feelings without letting them overtake us—it gives us perspective.

AnnaStills/Shutterstock.com

How do you interpret this image?

Practice Getting Perspective

To expand our own point of view, we need the capacity to take different perspectives. Perspective taking means taking others' points of view; we seek to understand others' thoughts, feelings, and motivations.[27] When people develop this capacity, they develop and repair trust,[28] communicate more clearly, help others more, and reduce stereotyping and prejudices.[29,30]

Try different strategies to understand other perspectives. "Zoom in, zoom out" is useful when we're either too close to a situation to see the big picture or too far to see the detail.[31] Amazon CEO Jeff Bezos is known for keeping one chair empty at meetings to represent the customer perspective.[32] One study found that writing about challenges from others' perspectives helped to shift thinking about certain groups.[33]

However, some researchers warn that, although perspective taking has many relational benefits, it may entrench people in their own views.[34] The better approach is often to just ask.[35] Find out why people believe what they believe. As researchers conclude, *getting* perspective is even better than *taking* perspective.[36,37] We don't simply imagine another point of view: we come to understand it by asking questions and by listening. That requires genuine curiosity.

Be Curious

Asking others about themselves and their perspectives demonstrates curiosity. We approach situations saying, "I wonder . . ." instead of "I know . . ." In her TED Talk "Why You Think You're Right—Even if You're Wrong," Julia Galef explains the difference between soldier and scout mindsets. Soldiers want to overpower the enemy, so they are motivated by proving they are right and the enemy is wrong. Scouts map what exists even if it contradicts their own thinking. Galef says the scout mindset is open, curious, and grounded.[38]

In his book *Think Again*, Adam Grant encourages us to act like scientists. He explains, "instead of drawing conclusions about people based on minimal clues, [scientists] test their hypotheses by striking up conversations."[39]

Get Up Close

Finally, we judge others less when we come to know them better. Commentator and author David Brooks writes, "Real change seems to involve putting bodies from different groups in the same room, on the same team, and in the same neighborhood."[40] Part of the value of a more diverse workforce is that people get to test their judgments—and recognize how often they are wrong.

Social work researcher Brené Brown writes, "People are hard to hate close up."[41] That applies to us as well. The more self-awareness we develop, the better we'll know and appreciate ourselves, which in turn makes us more open to others. Next, you'll see how a more open mindset will help you manage through conflict.

LO2 Define three types of conflict common in business environments and how to approach each.

3-2 Managing Through Conflict

Like shifting your perspective, managing through conflict takes courage. In Chapter 2, you learned that conflict is one type of team communication. Although people often want to avoid conflict, doing so stunts personal growth, team development, and work outcomes. Without conflict, teams don't experience harmony; they experience apathy.[42] No one cares enough to challenge others' ideas and, therefore, the best ideas don't emerge.

Courageous people don't shy away from confrontation that will bring about positive change. Particularly when that change may result in benefits for others, engaging in conflict demonstrates your good character. In this section, you learn about types of conflict, how to decide whether to engage, and ways to engage productively.

3-2a Assessing Types of Conflict

Three types of conflict are common in organizations. Task conflict involves the work: assignments, resource allocation, goals and expectations, and policies and procedures. Relationship conflict occurs when personalities or styles differ. These conflicts can stymie a group by eclipsing task conflicts. In other words, when people don't like each other, they see only the personality issues and can't hear useful differences about tasks.[43] Values conflict can be caused by differences in politics, religion, morals, identities, and other factors.[44] Differences in such values as security, achievement, and status can affect group process quickly and are often overlooked.[45]

Two situations at Amazon illustrate values conflict well. Amazon employees have taken several actions to persuade the company to reduce its carbon emissions, stop using fossil fuels, and cut ties with oil companies. Company leaders believe they are doing enough, but many employees have protested.[46] Amazon employees also tried to unionize for better pay and working conditions, but company leaders believe their wages and benefits are competitive.[47]

When managed well, these types of conflicts may improve team cohesion, effectiveness, and satisfaction.[48] Unhealthy conflict damages work output and relationships.

More problematic conflict arises when people are uncivil. Workplace civility means showing respect and concern for others—a baseline way of interacting at work. Workplace bullying negatively affects work and relationships and leads to people feeling unsafe. Like bullies in schools, bullies at work intimidate, offend, or humiliate someone, often in front of others. At work, people who are bullied can experience negative job outcomes, anxiety, depression, and, in extreme situations, suicide.[49] Between 10 and 15% of European and American employees report being bullied at work.[50]

Cyberbullying is increasingly common online, and the effects are particularly harmful and difficult to control. Anonymity, a large audience, and direct access to the victim offer cover and fuel to a bully, and the permanent nature of content causes lasting problems.[51]

Leadership is key to changing toxic environments. Pervasive incivility should be reported through designated channels, such as employee hotlines or human resources. Laws in most countries protect people from harassment, and strong, consistent leadership can resolve these damaging conflicts.

For other types of conflict, employees decide what, if any, action to take. An Amazon employee described her activism: "It's exactly what Amazon has taught me to be: bold, audacious, and tackle big problems."[52] She is describing her courageous decision to engage in conflict.

3-2b Deciding Whether to Engage in Conflict

Before taking action to address a conflict, check yourself, as you would when applying the CAM model. What is your motivation? Be sure that your goals reflect good character—wanting better outcomes for others—rather than self-righteousness, a steadfast belief that your way is the right way.

Also check your mental and physical state. It sounds basic, but are you hungry or tired? Would you view the situation and react in the same way tomorrow or next week?[53] Everyone has bad moods, including your teammates. Let fleeting issues pass. Not every eye-roll or negative comment needs to be addressed.

After checking yourself, consider the risks. What's at stake for you personally and professionally if you do or do not take action? Consider the risks and questions in Figure 4.[54] With answers to these questions, you'll decide whether the potential positive outcomes outweigh the risks.

Risks of Taking Action to Address a Conflict | **Figure 4**

Ambiguity
Can I accept unclear and conflicting perspectives, including my own? Am I willing to accept that my assessment may not be correct?

Anttoholo/iStock/Getty Images

Vulnerability
Am I willing to be exposed emotionally? Can I withstand public judgment and feeling ashamed, even if I'm wrong?

Anttoholo/iStock/Getty Images

Loss
What do I risk personally and professionally by taking action? Could I be ostracized, and will I damage relationships? Could I get fired?

Anttoholo/iStock/Getty Images

You may be tempted to leave a team or a job to avoid conflict. Sometimes that is the best option, particularly if you're in an abusive situation. But most times, addressing conflict is the better, more courageous choice.

In his classic book *Exit, Voice, and Loyalty*, Albert O. Hirschman discusses the tradeoffs between voicing complaints and leaving an organization.[55] Amazon employees could quit instead of complaining about the company's impact on the environment or lack of work breaks. They risk quite a lot in speaking up.

But leaving does nothing to solve the problem they care about deeply and may harm the company in the long run. Also, when individuals quit, they leave others to carry more weight. The more constructive choice is to use their voices and demonstrate loyalty to their cause, to each other, and ultimately, to the company.

3-2c Engaging Productively

Once you decide to engage in a conflict, first identify the type. Task, relationship, and values conflicts should be approached differently.[56]

Task Conflicts

Think of task conflicts as group problems. It's tempting to defuse conflicts by making one member a scapegoat: "We'd be finished with this report by now if Sam had done his part; you can never depend on him." Rarely is one person solely responsible for the success or failure of a group effort. Were expectations clear to Sam? Was he waiting for data from someone else? Did he need help but couldn't get it from the rest of the team? What is the team's role in encouraging or allowing behavior, and what can each of you do differently to encourage more productive behavior?

In *Think Again*, Adam Grant explains that Steve Jobs resisted creating a phone, believing it was for the "pocket-protector crowd" and wasn't cool enough. Team members encouraged him—not by arguing their point, but by "planting seeds" and "activating his curiosity" with questions: "We've already put 20,000 songs in your pocket [with the iPod]. What if we put everything in your pocket?"[57]

Task conflicts may seem easy to resolve, but underlying issues related to relationships and values may be at play. Try to get underneath the surface disagreement. For example, differences about scheduling may reflect deeper value differences around work quality or work–life balance.

Relationship Conflicts

Relationship differences may be addressed best by getting to know people personally and coming to appreciate what is different about each of you. Also find commonalities so you can focus more on your similarities than on your differences. If your personality differences seem insurmountable, try to separate the person from the idea.

On a team, it takes a brave leader—an official leader or any team member—to address relationship conflicts directly: "I'd like to talk about how we interact with each other at these meetings. It seems like we often end up fighting—it's not productive, and someone usually gets hurt. Does anyone else feel that way? What can we do differently?"

Values Conflicts

Values conflicts may be resolved by affirming others' positive qualities.[58] Do you respect your teammates' integrity? Can you acknowledge that they stand up for what they believe?

Some values conflicts may never be resolved but could bring about greater understanding and deeper relationships. In these situations, your humility will be tested as you pursue a dialogue rather than inflict your views on others.

If teams did their work in getting to know each other, as discussed in Chapter 2, conflicts will be minimized and easier to resolve, but they will never be eliminated. In the next section, you learn more specific skills for communicating during conflicts.

LO3 Apply steps to engage in a difficult conversation in a business situation.

3-3 Engaging in Difficult Conversations

In the end, work conflicts often come down to communication—a difficult conversation. According to authors of the book *Crucial Conversations*, people tend to handle these situations either with silence (sarcasm, sugarcoating, avoiding, or withdrawing) or with violence (controlling, labeling, or attacking).[59] In this section, you learn better approaches to prepare for and encourage dialogue during a difficult conversation, including when to give and receive critical feedback.

3-3a Preparing for a Difficult Conversation

Managing through tough conversations requires everything discussed so far in this chapter: humility, perspective getting, curiosity, and of course, a willingness to engage in conflict. Before you prepare for the physical (or virtual) interaction, prepare yourself emotionally and mentally.

This is a good time for another character check. Can you be humble and make space for the other person? Can you focus on affirming, appreciating, encouraging, and validating?[60] Understanding others' goals and perspectives is just as important as conveying your own, and addressing their concerns when you don't share them demonstrates your respect for their well-being.

You might be tempted to fire off a text message, but richer communication channels are best for these challenging interpersonal situations. In-person conversations are ideal, and video or the phone can work, particularly if that's how you typically communicate. To get started, ask yourself the questions in Figure 5.

Figure 5 Prepare for a Difficult Conversation

Prepare Yourself

What is the situation or problem that you need to address?

What do you hope to accomplish? Be specific about the ideal outcome.

What assumptions do you have about this situation or about the person? Which of these assumptions do you need to confirm or clarify?

What could be the reasons for the behavior from the other person's perspective? In other words, could you be wrong about some of your interpretations? Does the person have good intentions even if the behavior is a problem?

How might you, intentionally or unintentionally, be contributing to the situation? Be careful about blaming others without examining your own responsibility.

How do you think the person might respond? Prepare for a few possible reactions.

Choose a Time and Setting

When could be a good time for you and for the other person to discuss the situation? When will you have enough time and space, so you are not rushed or distracted by other meetings or issues? Allow for extra time in case the conversation runs long.

Are you ready to listen openly to another point of view? If you are not ready, postpone the conversation until you are.

Ask for permission to start the conversation. You might say something like, "I'd like to talk with you about something sensitive (or difficult). Is now an okay time?" or "I like to talk about ____________. When is a good time for us to meet in the next couple of days?"

If you meet in person, find a private setting where you won't get interrupted. Depending on the issue, emotions may run high, or the information may be confidential.

3-3b Encouraging a Dialogue

Dialogue is different from discussion or debate, which you might think of as "winning" an argument, as shown in Figure 6.[61] With a dialogue, no one is right or wrong; you are both trying to understand the other and come to a new way of looking at a difficult situation. Compare aspects of dialogue to emotional involvement with loved ones and in community situations. Although not always appropriate for business, you might find characteristics of these interactions, described in the last column, useful for deepening relationships at work and increasing a sense of belonging.

Figure 6 | Differences Among Debate, Discussion, and Dialogue

IN DEBATE, WE ...	IN DISCUSSION, WE ...	IN DIALOGUE, WE TRY TO ...	WHEN WE'RE EMOTIONALLY INVOLVED, WE MIGHT ...
Succeed or win	Present ideas	Broaden our own perspectives	See each other as whole people instead of focusing on ideas or perspectives
Look for weakness and logical flaws	Look for answers and solutions	Look for shared meaning	Discover new, shared meaning
Stress disagreement	Persuade others	Find places of agreement	Adopt the other's point of view
Focus on "right" and "wrong"	Share information	Bring out areas of ambiguity and ambivalence	Allow for discomfort
Listen with a view of countering	Listen for places of disagreement	Listen without judgment and with a view to understand	Just listen, without needing an explanation
Discount the validity of feelings	Avoid feelings	Validate and explore feelings	Share without restraint
Disregard relationships	Maintain relationships	Build relationships	Commit to the other's well-being

To move closer to a dialog, encourage the other person to participate in the conversation with you. This requires a good start, active listening, sharing your perspective, problem solving, and ending well. Follow the suggestions below.

Start the Conversation

Begin the conversation positively and focus on shared goals—what you have in common.

- Approach your manager: "I'd like to talk about the project lead position. I know that Alibaba is an important client, and I'm disappointed that I wasn't selected."
- Approach a coworker: "I have concerns about our interaction during the meeting yesterday. I'd like to tell you what I observed [or how I feel], and then I'd like to hear your view. I think we have different perceptions about this, but I know that we both want the department to be represented well."

Listen Actively and Openly

Try to just listen while the person shares other perspectives.

- Encourage the person to keep talking until nothing else needs to be said.
- Say, "Tell me more...," "I see...," and nod your head to let the person know you are listening attentively and not judging.
- Keep listening until you *really* see where the person is coming from. You may not agree with the person's choices or behavior, but you can almost always understand a situation from another point of view.
- Try the active listening techniques discussed in Chapter 2, such as paraphrasing what the person says into your own words. Keep perfecting it until the other person agrees that you fully understand.

Share Your Perspective

Describe your observations and reactions.

- Focus on behaviors instead of making global statements. "I was upset when you asked Margot to lead the project instead of me," rather than, "You always ask Margot," "You don't trust me," or "You never give me a chance."
- Explain as much as you can about why you hold your perspective. "I hear that Margot has more experience with the client. At the same time, I have more experience with the system, and I wrote most of the proposal."
- Be honest about your own vulnerabilities, defenses, or baggage. "Something similar happened at my previous job, and I'm wondering what I can do differently to give you more confidence in my abilities."
- Take responsibility for your part. "Maybe I wasn't clear about how important it was for me to work with this client" or "Maybe I needed to step up more during the planning phase."
- Consider sharing your perspective before asking the other person's perspective, depending on the situation.

Problem-Solve

Discuss how you can work together to prevent a similar situation in the future.

- Ask the other person for ideas and try to acknowledge and build on them.
- Offer your own suggestions—what you can do differently and what you would like from the other person.
- Try to find a shared purpose or outcome for the larger organization. What will be improved in addition to your relationship?

End the Conversation

Try not to rush the closing.

- Summarize the results and check that the other person agrees with the conclusions or planned steps.
- Thank the person for speaking with you, and end on a positive note.

The steps are only guidelines to follow. Conversations may veer off course, and sometimes that is best. At some point in the conversation, try to "reflect in action" to zoom out and get perspective. By quickly answering the questions in Figure 7, you'll know whether you need to make adjustments to improve the outcome.

When conversations get heated, you can only control yourself. Regardless of what the other person says or does, what *you* say and do matters. You could modify your language, tone, or

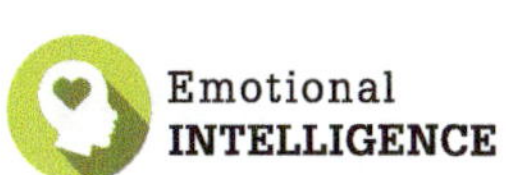

How easily can you step back or zoom out during a difficult conversation? Practice slowing down a charged interaction to improve the outcome.

approach, or slow the conversation down to give each of you more time to talk. Consider moving to another location, taking a walk, or continuing the conversation at a later time if you are stuck and doing more damage than good.

Figure 7 | Reflection in Action

	Intellectual Reflection Are you getting the results you want? Why or why not? How is the person (or people) reacting to you? What do you observe about the others' tone of voice or body language?
	Emotional Reflection How do you feel right now? Are you frustrated, angry, annoyed, satisfied, excited, hopeful, or something else? How are your emotions affecting the interaction? Are they encouraging cooperation and support, or are they getting in the way?
	Physical Reflection What is your body language right now, and what is it communicating to the other person? How do you feel physically? Does your physical feeling denote an underlying reaction that is inconsistent with the character you want to demonstrate?

GoodStudio/Shutterstock.com

GoodStudio/Shutterstock.com

GoodStudio/Shutterstock.com

3-3c Giving and Receiving Constructive Feedback

One example of a difficult conversation is when you give or receive constructive (or negative) feedback. Imagine a work environment—or a class—in which you never receive feedback on your performance. How would you know what you do well and what skills you need to develop? Feedback is the only way to know what needs to be improved.

Giving and receiving feedback needs to be part of a team's culture—how you'll work together. In Chapter 8, you learn about giving and receiving performance feedback in a manager–employee relationship. Here we focus on team members or other coworkers.

In her book *Radical Candor*, Kim Scott supports an honest, open approach to giving feedback. Practicing radical candor means that you know and care about people personally and, at the same time, challenge them directly.[62] An example of responding to someone who sends an email and forgets the attachment is shown in Figure 8.

Figure 8 Radical Candor for Giving Feedback

Care Personally

Challenge Directly

Ruinous Empathy	**Radical Candor**
Do nothing because you're worried about ***the sender's*** feelings.	Reply to sender: "I didn't receive the attachment."
Do nothing because you're worried about ***your*** feelings.	Reply to all: "You forgot the attachment!"
Manipulative Insincerity	**Obnoxious Aggression**

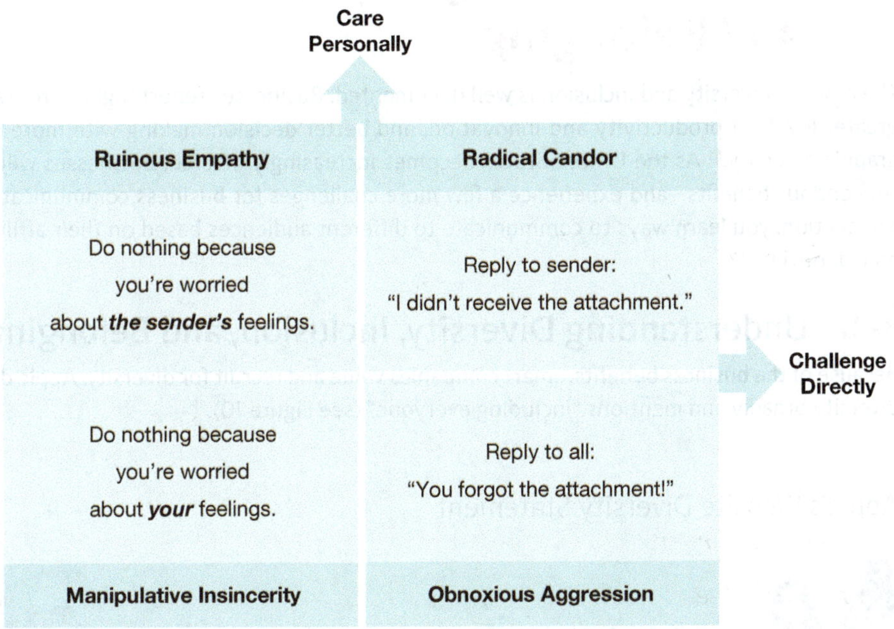

When you give feedback, follow the suggestions in Figure 9, which apply to both positive and negative feedback. Focusing on the specific behavior instead of the person and taking responsibility for the feedback will improve the chance that the discussion will go well. Here's one example, and you can practice using language that feels natural for you:

> "**When you** interrupted Keisha during the meeting, **I felt** frustrated **because** I wanted to hear what she had to say—she's the client and will decide whether she works with us or with a competitor." [Pause for discussion or say something like, "How do you see it?"]

Figure 9 How to Give Positive and Negative Feedback

DESCRIBE BEHAVIORS	GIVE SPECIFIC EXAMPLES	SPEAK FOR YOURSELF	USE ENCOURAGING LANGUAGE
State objectively what you saw or heard. Words like *unprofessional*, *irresponsible*, and *lazy* are labels that we attach to behaviors. Instead, describe the behaviors and drop the labels.	To say, "You never finish work on time" is probably untrue and unfair. Give specific, recent examples from your own observations, if possible.	Don't refer to absent, anonymous people ("A lot of people here don't like it when you . . ."). Use "I" statements instead: "I felt disregarded when you didn't include my suggestions in the report."	Try saying, "What I appreciate about you . . ." "I think you could be even more effective if you . . ." and "I wonder whether . . ."[63]

Typically praise in public but criticize in private. Your goal is to change behaviors—not embarrass people. Next, you learn ways to communicate across differences to improve inclusivity and belonging at work.

LO4 Identify ways to adapt language to audiences to honor differences.

3-4 Communicating to Improve Inclusivity and Belonging

The case for diversity and inclusion is well documented. Businesses report higher profitability, greater levels of productivity and innovation, and better decision making with more demographic diversity.[64] As the United States becomes increasingly diverse, businesses will enjoy tremendous benefits—and experience a few more challenges for business communicators. In this section, you learn ways to communicate to different audiences based on their affiliations and identities.

3-4a Understanding Diversity, Inclusion, and Belonging

Because of the business benefits, smart companies value and recruit for diversity. Apple defines diversity broadly and mentions "including everyone" (see Figure 10).[65]

Figure 10 | Apple's Website Diversity Statement

Different together.
At Apple, we're not all the same. And that's our greatest strength. We draw on the differences in who we are, what we've experienced, and how we think. Because to create products that serve everyone, we believe in including everyone.

Source: Apple Inc.

Many companies today go beyond demographic diversity and strive for **inclusion** and **belonging**. Diversity is a baseline objective: companies simply count the numbers of people. Beyond the numbers, inclusion is about behaviors, such as inviting people to meetings and implementing their ideas. Belonging is the highest level of achievement—how people feel. Do people feel valued? Do they feel as though they are part of a community?[66]

Belonging is the newest concept and aims to address employees' feelings of isolation. When asked to distinguish between belonging and fitting in, an eighth grader said, "I get to be me if I belong. I have to be like you to fit in."[67] This wise student is also describing authenticity.

3-4b Bringing Your Whole Self to Work

At the beginning of the chapter, you reflected on your affiliations and identities. How comfortable are you "bringing your whole self to work," as former Pepsi Chairman and CEO Indra K. Nooyi explains?

> The only way we will hold on to the best and brightest is to grasp them emotionally. No one may feel excluded. It's our job to draw the best out of everyone. That means employees must be able to immerse their whole selves in a work environment in which they can develop their careers, families and philanthropy, and truly believe they are cared for.[68]

We judge a person's character partly by how genuine they seem. Are they authentic and real, or do they put on an act for different people in different settings? One study found that 75% of employees want their colleagues to share more of themselves.[69]

Being authentic at work has personal benefits. When people share more of who they are, they report greater job satisfaction, a stronger sense of community, lower job stress, and higher levels of engagement.[70,71] People who carry secrets experience more stress and negative health effects. A study of people who concealed their sexual orientation showed that the secret quite literally "weighed them down," as the expression goes. They found physical tasks more difficult and were less likely to offer others help with physical tasks.[72]

At this point, you might be wondering how much of yourself to reveal in business situations. Of course, this is a personal decision, and self-disclosure carries risk. Management researchers suggest that you consider the timing and relevance and how much you share. Also pay attention to what and how others share—and their reactions to your disclosures.[73] Put safety first; you may choose not to disclose information that could cause intolerable harm.

How accurately can you assess others' reactions to your disclosures? Improving the accuracy will improve your external self-awareness.

In addition, being authentic doesn't mean being a narcissist—it's not all about you.[74] Oversharing personal aspects of yourself, feeling inferior or superior because of your identity, or lacking empathy for others are not healthy features of authenticity.[75]

Don't expect immediate intimacy from others. By being trustworthy and with measured vulnerability, you'll develop relationships over time.

3-4c Using Inclusive Language

Communication, particularly language, is an important part of fostering belonging in an organization. How we interact with people affects how they feel about themselves and ultimately how they contribute.

Terminology used to refer to groups is constantly evolving because of preference and because terms become dated and carry negative connotations. English actor Benedict Cumberbatch referred to Black actors as "colored."[76] An Ohio State Senator and medical doctor made the same mistake and threw in a racist generalization. He was fired from his job at a health care company.[77] People have little tolerance for outdated terms.

Most of the following advice is from the American Psychological Association (APA) Style guide, a good source for current language.[78]

Race and Ethnicity

APA style explains the difference between race and ethnicity:

> *Race* refers to physical differences that groups and cultures consider socially significant. For example, people might identify their race as Aboriginal, African American or Black, Asian, European American or White, Native American, Native Hawaiian or Pacific Islander, Māori, or some other race. *Ethnicity* refers to shared cultural characteristics such as language, ancestry, practices, and beliefs. For example, people might identify as Latin or another ethnicity.
>
> Be clear about whether you are referring to a racial group or to an ethnic group. Race is a social construct that is not universal, so one must be careful not to impose racial labels on ethnic groups. Whenever possible, use the racial and/or ethnic terms that your participants themselves use.
>
> Be sure that the racial and ethnic categories you use are as clear and specific as possible. For example, instead of categorizing participants as Asian American or Hispanic American, you could use more specific labels that identify their nation or region of origin, such as Japanese American or Cuban American. Use commonly accepted designations (e.g., census categories) [see Figure 11[79,80]] while being sensitive to participants' preferred designation.[81]

Whenever possible, use terms that people prefer. For example, "Latin" and "Hispanic" mean different things to different people, and some people prefer gender-neutral terms, such as "Latin@" or "Latinx."[82] "People of color" may be falling out of favor, with more precise language preferred.[83] As a *New Yorker* writer recommends, "Say Black if you mean Black." The BIPOC Project explains that Black, Indigenous and People of Color (BIPOC) is used to "dismantle white

Figure 11 | U.S. Census Categories for Race and Gender

Is Person 1 of Hispanic, Latino, or Spanish origin?

☐ **No**, not of Hispanic, Latino, or Spanish origin

☐ Yes, Mexican, Mexican Am., Chicano

☐ Yes, Puerto Rican

☐ Yes, Cuban

☐ Yes, another Hispanic, Latino, or Spanish origin – *Print, for example, Salvadoran, Dominican, Colombian, Guatemalan, Spaniard, Ecuadorian, etc.*

What is Person 1's race?
Mark ☒ *one or more boxes* ***AND*** *print origins.*

☐ White – *Print, for example, German, Irish, English, Italian, Lebanese, Egyptian, etc.*

☐ Black or African Am. – *Print, for example, African American, Jamaican, Haitian, Nigerian, Ethiopian, Somali, etc.*

☐ American Indian or Alaska Native – *Print name of enrolled or principal tribe(s), for example, Navajo Nation, Blackfeet Tribe, Mayan, Aztec, Native Village of Barrow Inupiat Traditional Government, Nome Eskimo Community, etc.*

☐ Chinese

☐ Filipino

☐ Asian Indian

☐ Other Asian – *Print, for example, Pakistani, Cambodian, Hmong, etc.*

☐ Vietnamese

☐ Korean

☐ Japanese

☐ Native Hawaiian

☐ Samoan

☐ Chamorro

☐ Other Pacific Islander – *Print, for example, Tongan, Fijian, Marshallese, etc.*

☐ Some other race – *Print race or origin.*

supremacy and advance racial justice.[84] "Minority" is outdated because it's often inaccurate and because it implies a deficiency related to a "majority."[85]

What we call ourselves is not a trivial matter. The terms used to refer to other groups are not ours to establish, and it's easy enough to use terms that others prefer.

Gender

Avoid confusing *gender* and *sex* in your writing and speech. **Gender** is a social construct and reflects how people feel and behave. **Sex** refers to someone's biology. In most business situations, use "gender," which also avoids associations with sexual behavior.

Differences in male and female communication styles may be exaggerated. As with most behaviors, more differences exist within a gender group than between groups. Newer and more useful research[86] focuses more on the negative impacts of stereotypes and **stereotype threat**, which could cause people to behave in ways expected of them.

The Human Rights Campaign defines **gender identity** as "one's innermost concept of self as male, female, a blend of both or neither—how individuals perceive themselves and what they call themselves." For **transgender** people, how they identify or express their gender "is different from cultural expectations based on the sex they were assigned at birth."[87] Some people prefer such terms as "gender-nonconforming," "genderqueer," and "gender-nonbinary."[88] Recognizing the many ways people identify, Facebook offers more than 50 gender options for user profiles.[89]

Because some people don't identify as strictly male or female, such pronouns as *he*, *she*, *him*, or *her* don't fit. You might ask people what pronouns they use and consider using *they* until you know. For strict grammarians, *they* is a plural pronoun, but its use as a singular pronoun is increasingly acceptable,[90] particularly because other variations—for example, *ze*, *xe*, *hir*, and *ey*—aren't yet consistently used in business settings. Whenever possible, use gender-neutral language described in Figure 12.

Generations

Because people are living and working longer, up to five generations of employees could be working together.[91] Faulty stereotypes do exist, and research shows that younger employees' negative views of "older" workers extends to those in their 50s.[92] But organizational psychology scholars conclude that "sweeping group differences depending on age or generation alone don't seem to be supported."[93]

Therefore, problems at work are primarily from our own stereotypes. Be careful about your assumptions of any workers based on their age, and always avoid age-biased language.

Sexual Orientation

Although same-sex marriage is now legal and more accepted in the United States, can people who identify as LGBTQ+ (lesbian, gay, bisexual, transgender, queer/questioning, plus) bring their whole selves to work? Can they speak about their social and family lives just as straight people talk about theirs?

To pave the way for others, Apple CEO Tim Cook wrote "I'm proud to be gay," an open letter in a major business magazine.[94] Homophobic and heterosexist language is still far too common and should never be used in the workplace.

Ability

People sometimes feel uncomfortable interacting with people with disabilities. Avoid making assumptions based on your observations. Physical disabilities say nothing about someone's intelligence, and people may live with many disabilities, such as mental illness, that aren't visible. Depending on the situation, just use your natural way of speaking and eye contact, or you might ask if someone needs assistance.[95] Try to be yourself and be patient.

Figure 12 | Strategies for Inclusive and Gender-Neutral Language

Use neutral job titles to avoid implying that a job is held by only men or only women.

Instead of	Use
salesman	sales representative, sales associate
male nurse	nurse
waitress	server
stewardess	flight attendant

Avoid words and phrases that unnecessarily imply gender.

Instead of	Use
you guys	everyone
manmade	artificial, manufactured
manpower	human resources, employees
mankind	people, humans

Use appropriate personal titles and salutations.

- If a woman has a professional title, use it (Dr. Martha Ralston, the Rev. Deborah Connell).
- In emails and letters, avoid Ms., Miss, Mrs., or Mr. by including the person's full name (Dear Cara Simpson) or by using the receiver's title (Dear Investor, Dear Neighbor, Dear Hiring Manager).

Find alternatives to gendered pronouns (e.g., "Each manager must evaluate his employees annually") and "one," which is considered formal.

- Use plural nouns and pronouns. "All managers must evaluate their employees annually."
- Use second-person pronouns (*you*, *your*). "You must evaluate your employees annually."
- Omit the pronoun. "Each manager must evaluate employees annually."
- Use *they* as a singular pronoun unless you need to abide by strict grammar rules.

Instead of using potentially disparaging language, choose "people-first language" unless someone prefers otherwise.[96] With people-first language, you identify the person before the disability; for example, say, "people with disabilities" and "Alejandro is a sophomore who has epilepsy."

We still have "handicapped" parking spaces, but this is an outdated term. When referring to people, the term implies a limitation and a disadvantage. Also avoid condescending euphemisms, for example, "special needs," "physically challenged," and made-up words like "handicapable."[97] For advice for writing about specific disabilities, see the National Center on Disability and Journalism guide.[98]

Religion

Whether we were raised in a certain tradition or adopted it later in life, religion helps people create meaning in their lives. At many companies, discussing religious beliefs, like political beliefs, is discouraged. But some companies allow people to practice what is most important to them during the day. Texas Instruments, Gogo, and other companies have dedicated prayer rooms for their employees.[99]

At the same time, people who don't practice religion should not be forced to do so. Unless the organization is identified with a particular religion, and new hires know this before accepting a job, managers should not, for example, ask employees to pray before business meals.

Be mindful about religious differences. Not everyone wants to hear "Merry Christmas" when they don't celebrate the holiday. Try to avoid assumptions based on appearance, names, or the majority.

Other Characteristics

In the office, family background and income level might give people an advantage. Someone raised in a family of business executives might understand important work behaviors, for example, what to wear and how to interact with senior-level managers. What if someone can't afford to wear designer clothes or go out to lunch with the team? Try to be sensitive to financial pressures and how they affect relationships and perception.

What else do we bring to work? Veteran status, political views, whether we have children, and many other qualities make each of us unique and full contributors to an organization. We are all members of groups with different customs, values, and attitudes.

3-4d Offending and Taking Offense

"Walking on eggshells"—carefully measuring every word we say—is no way to work. We can't build trusting relationships if we avoid topics or people for fear of offending them. We will offend sometimes and will be offended other times. We all make assumptions that aren't accurate or use terms that unintentionally offend.

In her book *35 Dumb Things Well-Intended People Say*, Maura Cullen tells about using the word *blackmail* during a meeting, which someone found to have racial connotations.[100] Was the woman being overly sensitive? Who's to judge? Cullen didn't; she simply replaced the word with *coerced* and then spoke with her colleague after the meeting so they could understand each other better.

Apologies may repair a relationship but only if they are genuine. Taking the time to understand the offense and how it affected the other person are key and may bring you closer in the long run. Ibram X. Kendi, historian and author of the bestselling book *How to Be an Antiracist*, writes, "The heartbeat of racism is denial, and the heartbeat of antiracism is confession."[101]

When something offends you at work, you have every right to say so. Try to focus on your reaction instead of on the other person. Calling someone a racist likely won't improve your working relationship or change the person's behavior. Use the tips for engaging in conflict and managing difficult conversations. With a constructive approach, you'll contribute to the type of place where everyone feels valued and wants to work.

3-5 Adapting to International Cultural Differences

LO5 Compare how people in high- and low-context countries communicate.

To be successful in today's global business environment, leaders need to appreciate international differences among people. Although English may be the standard language for business, by no means do we have one standard for all business communication. In this section, you learn ways to improve your adaptability and communication across international differences.

We discuss communicating with people from different cultures, but keep in mind that each member of a culture is an individual. We generalize here to teach broad principles for communication, but we adapt to people who may think, feel, and act quite differently from a cultural norm or stereotype.

When have you misjudged others based on their country of origin?

3-5a Understanding Cultural Differences

Cultures differ widely in what they value. For example, Figure 13 shows that international cultures vary in how much they emphasize individualism, time orientation, power distance, uncertainty avoidance, formality, materialism, and context sensitivity. Of course, differences exist within a

To help you understand differences, compare your own culture with another via the Hofstede Centre (https://www.hofstede-insights.com/product/compare-countries).

country and can be dramatic even within the United States, given our diverse population, large immigrant communities, and differences between people who live in rural and urban places.

We can look at communication differences even more deeply through a lens of "high-context" and "low-context" cultures, the last value listed in Figure 13. A continuum of a few countries is shown in Figure 14. Next, you learn ways that cultures throughout the world differ in verbal communication and relationships, group-oriented behavior, body language and gestures, time, and space.

Figure 13 | Cultural Values

LOW	VALUE	HIGH
Japan China Mexico Greece	***Individualism***: Cultures in which people see themselves first as individuals and believe that their own interests take priority.	United States Canada Great Britain Australia Netherlands
Pacific Rim and Middle Eastern countries	***Time Orientation***: Cultures that perceive time as a scarce resource and that tend to be impatient.	United States Switzerland
United States Israel Germany Ireland Sweden	***Power Distance***: Cultures in which management decisions are made by managers simply because they are managers.	France Spain Japan Mexico Brazil
United States Canada Australia Singapore	***Uncertainly Avoidance:*** Cultures in which people want predictable and certain futures.	Israel Japan Italy Argentina
United States Canada Scandinavian countries	***Formality***: Cultures that attach considerable importance to tradition, ceremony, social rules, and rank.	China India Latin American countries
Scandinavian countries	***Materialism***: Cultures that emphasize assertiveness and the acquisition of money and material objects.	Japan Austria Italy
Northern European countries	***Context Sensitivity***: Cultures that emphasize the surrounding circumstances (or context), make extensive use of body language, and take the time to build relationships and establish trust.	Asian and African countries

To learn more about cultural differences, read Geert Hofstede, *Culture's Consequences: Comparing Values, Behaviors, Institutions and Organizations Across Nations,* 2nd ed. (Thousand Oaks, CA: Sage Publications).

Verbal Communication and Relationships

According to anthropologist Edward T. Hall, high-context cultures—for example, China and Japan—rely less on words and more on subtle actions and reactions of communicators. Communication for these cultures is more implicit and emphasizes relationships among people.[102]

On the other hand, low-context cultures, for example, the United States, rely on more explicit communication—the words people use. In these cultures, tasks tend to be more important than relationships, so people use a direct style of communication.[103]

The American expression, "The squeaky wheel gets the grease," describes a direct approach to getting your way. Compare this to the Chinese proverb, "A harsh word dropped from the tongue cannot be brought back by a coach and six horses," which warns against direct, emotional language and emphasizes the weight of one's words.[104]

Figure 14 High- and Low-Context Cultures

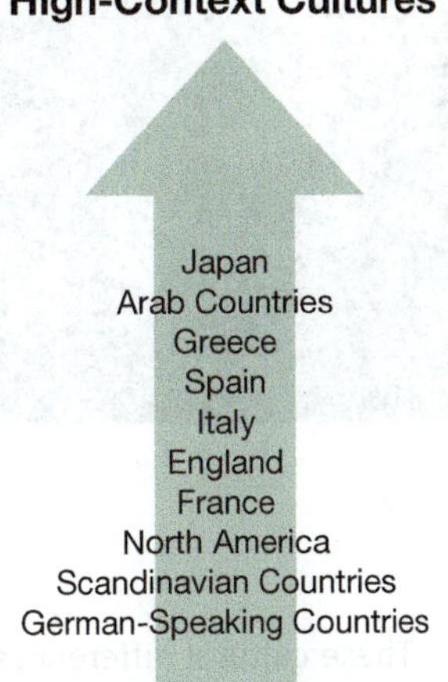

Silence is valued and can have great meaning in high-context cultures. Many non-Western cultures use silence during meetings to contemplate a decision, whereas businesspeople from the United States and Canada tend to have little tolerance for silence in business negotiations.[105] As a result, Americans and Canadians may rush in and offer compromises and counterproposals that would have been unnecessary if they were more comfortable with the silence—and more patient. For successful intercultural communications, we read between the lines because what is left unsaid or unwritten may be just as important as what is said or written.

Again, you'll notice differences within the United States. For example, people in some regions speak more quickly, whereas others speak more slowly and allow more space between speakers.

Apple "Behind the Mac" ads in Japan and the United States illustrate the differences in context sensitivity. Research on intercultural advertising shows that Asian ads tend to be more symbolic and emphasize harmony, while American ads are more likely to mix rational, emotional, and entertaining messaging.[106]

The 30-second Japanese commercial, shown at left in Figure 15, highlights Apple products in popular Japanese anime films and series. As the video description on YouTube states, the commercial is "meta" and uses Japan's "beloved storytelling format."[107] The video uses symbolism in adaptations of the Apple logo: a pear, a heart, and an apple with a second bite.

By contrast, the one-minute U.S. ad, shown at right in Figure 15, is subtitled "Greatness." The video is a photo series of famous Americans with the voiceover, "There's a certain type of person, who doesn't take 'no' for an answer. They don't walk in quietly. They parade in, trailblazing…. They don't wait for greatness. They make it." The video message is literal, emphasizes bold communication—and spotlights individual celebrities and their achievements,[108] which you'll read more about next.

Group-Oriented Behavior

In capitalistic societies, such as the United States and Canada, individual effort is often stressed more than group effort, and a competitive atmosphere prevails. But in other cultures, teamwork is more highly valued than originality and independence of judgment. The Japanese say, "A nail standing out will be hammered down," and go to great lengths to reach decisions through group consensus.

Figure 15 | Comparing Japanese and American Apple Commercials

Source: YouTube, LLC

These cultural differences are evident when you apply for a job. If you're from an individualistic culture, you're likely to submit a resume touting your skills, experience, and personal achievements. Recruiters from these cultures appreciate this approach and hire the best qualified person. Although recruiters from more group-oriented cultures also hire the best person for the job, they give preference to applicants who are trustworthy and loyal. They tend to hire people they or others in the company know well.[109]

The Toyoda family changed the company name to Toyota in 1937 for its clearer sound and more favorable number of strokes for writing the name.[111]

Closely related to the concept of group-oriented behavior is the notion of "saving face." People save face when they avoid embarrassment. When Akio Toyoda, the Japanese president of Toyota Motor Corporation, apologized for many vehicle recalls, he demonstrated emotion and great humility—far more than might have been expected of an American business leader.[110] Certainly far more than we heard from American leaders, for example, Boeing's Dennis A. Muilenburg.

AP Images/Koji Sasahara

Akio Toyoda apologizes at a recall press conference for Toyota Motor Company.

In cultures that place high value on human relationships, people are reluctant to offend others. Latin Americans tend to avoid an outright "no" in their business dealings, preferring instead a milder, less explicit response. "Yes" to a Japanese person might mean "Yes, I understand you" rather than "Yes, I agree." To an American, the Japanese style of communication may seem too indirect and verbose.

At one point during Toyoda's testimony before Congress, the committee chair said, "What I'm trying to find out . . . is that a yes or a no?" To Japanese viewers, this sounded rude and disrespectful.[112]

Body Language and Gestures

Body language, especially gestures, also varies among cultures. For example, hand gestures differ greatly in meaning, as shown in Figure 16.[113] Even within the United States, the "okay" sign is now considered a hate symbol in certain contexts, associated with white supremacy.

How eye contact is valued and perceived varies greatly by culture. One study found that people from an East Asian culture perceived people who made direct eye contact as "angrier and more unapproachable and unpleasant" than did those from a Western European culture.[114] Eye-tracking technology reveals that Westerners focus more on eyes and mouths, while people from East Asian countries focus more holistically on faces.[115] These studies support the idea that East Asians may find direct or excessive eye contact rude. By contrast, in some Western cultures, eye contact increases feelings of connection and trust. A Netherlands study of Airbnb host photos showed that direct eye contact increased intentions to book.[116]

What Hand Gestures Mean in Different Countries | **Figure 16**

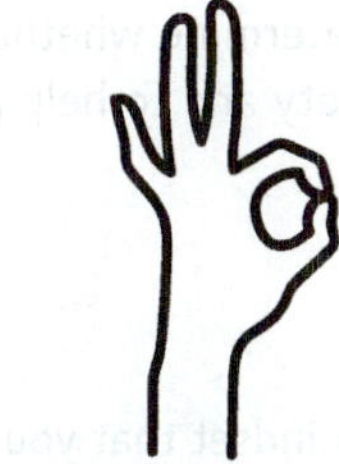

OK Sign

France: Something or someone is worthless

United States: "OK" or symbol for white supremacists

Turkey: Insult toward gay people

Pelin Kahraman/Shutterstock.com

Thumbs-up

United States: Approval

Iran: Obscene gesture

Malaysia: Used to point

Pelin Kahraman/Shutterstock.com

Curling Index Finger

United States: Used to summon someone over

Many Asian countries: Used to summon dogs

Philippines: Offensive gesture

Pelin Kahraman/Shutterstock.com

Pointing

Universally perceived as rude when directed at someone

Pelin Kahraman/Shutterstock.com

Time

The meaning given to time also varies greatly by culture. Americans and Canadians are much more time-conscious than members of South American or Middle Eastern cultures. Punctuality is key in Switzerland, Germany, Britain, the Netherlands, Austria, Scandinavia, and other countries.[117] As the American saying goes, "Time is money."

Others see time as more flexible. Latin American and Middle Eastern cultures tend to be more casual about time. For example, if your Mexican host asks to meet at 3:00, it's most likely *más o menos* (Spanish for "more or less") 3:00. How a Spaniard's day might be planned and lived is illustrated in Figure 17.[118] Businesspeople in Asian and Latin American countries also tend to favor long negotiations and slow deliberations.

Spanish Schedules in Theory and in Reality | **Figure 17**

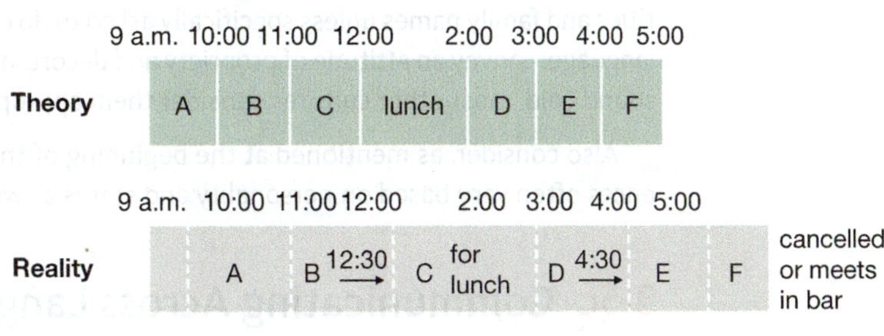

Time is related not only to culture but to status, situations, and individual preferences. You would likely be on time for a job interview, but you might not worry about being five minutes late for your lunch date, particularly if you send a text. On the other hand, your lateness might communicate that you don't care enough to be on time. Not everyone will be forgiving, and you may be perceived as arrogant—as if your time is more important than theirs.

Space

When Americans are on a crowded elevator, they tend to look down, up, or straight ahead—anything to avoid too much contact with other people. Most people in the U.S. culture are uncomfortable in such close proximity to strangers. Yet Middle Easterners and Latin Americans tend to prefer closer interpersonal space.

Our feelings about space are partly an outgrowth of our culture and partly a result of geography and economics. One study found that how much interpersonal space people prefer also depends on age, gender, and temperature.[119] Differences also vary by context and situation. You'll sit closer to a friend than you will an interviewer.

Our preferences for distance have changed dramatically with concerns about transmissible disease. Consider your own personal space needs and the needs of others. Look for social cues, such as facial expressions or people backing away, to determine whether they prefer more or less space.[120] Try to accommodate differences for safety and to help people feel comfortable.

3-5b Adapting to Different Cultures

Adapting to different international cultures requires the same open mindset that you would adopt in working through conflict, engaging in difficult conversations, and communicating to improve belonging. But international differences may be more pronounced, so more flexibility may be required. We fight against our tendency toward ethnocentrism, the belief that an individual's own cultural group is superior. With good character, we ask ourselves, why do I need to feel special or better?

Instead, we work toward cultural competence, agility, and humility. Cultural competence means you can "understand people from different cultures and engage with them effectively."[121] Beyond competence, cultural agility means that you are adept at navigating cross-cultural situations.[122] You might work with people in several different countries and need to adjust with grace and ease.

Cultural humility is deeper still, involving self-reflection and the recognition that you are never done learning. When you communicate with people from other cultures, take time to plan your interactions. When traveling to other countries, learn about the geography, form of government, largest cities, culture, and current events. Become familiar with the customs, for example, giving (and accepting) gifts, exchanging business cards, and entertaining guests.

You might err on the side of formality. Compared to U.S. and Canadian cultures, most other cultures value and respect a more formal approach to business dealings. Call others by their titles and family names unless specifically asked to do otherwise. With your verbal and nonverbal language, convey an attitude of propriety and decorum. Although you may think these strategies sound cold, most other cultures consider them appropriate.

Also consider, as mentioned at the beginning of this chapter, individual differences. Preferences often vary based on personality and status as well.

3-5c Communicating Across Languages

Following are tips when communicating with someone who speaks a language different from yours:[123]

- **Verbals.** Avoid slang, jargon, and other figures of speech. American expressions, such as "They'll eat that up" or "out in left field," may be confusing. Use humor sparingly; humor is risky—it may be lost on your counterpart, or worse, it may offend someone. Choose simpler words, enunciate a bit more, rephrase sentences, and slow down your rate of speech,[124] but don't be condescending. Also be careful about your assumptions: don't equate others' poor grammar or mispronunciation with a lack of intelligence.
- **Visuals and nonverbals.** Use a variety of media: handouts (distributed before a meeting to allow time for reading), visuals, models, and so on. Provide written summaries and access to materials after the meeting. Use appropriate facial and hand gestures to reinforce meaning.
- **Pace.** Pause to allow more time for understanding and for questions. Listeners in other languages may need time to translate or may have a different rhythm from yours. Avoid jumping in to fill silences.

- **Comprehension.** Check for understanding after speaking. Ask open-ended questions ("What can I clarify?" or "What other information do you need?") instead of close-ended questions ("Do you have any questions?" or "Do you understand?"). Observe reactions, particularly facial expressions, to see where people may be getting stuck. When listening, check your own understanding by rephrasing and getting verification.
- **Support.** Encourage non-native speakers verbally and nonverbally, for example, by smiling and nodding your head. Be patient and don't interrupt or finish people's sentences for them unless they ask for help. Draw people out with questions without singling them out, which could be embarrassing.

When you're communicating as a non-native speaker, much of the same advice applies. Speak more slowly, enunciate words carefully, pause. and provide visuals to increase comprehension.[125] You might tell others about your level of understanding and speaking. Try to be accurate and not underestimate your ability.

Some level of confidence is essential to increasing fluency. Practice means sometimes getting words wrong. In most business situations, people will be patient and forgiving. Try not to be embarrassed about your "accent." Everyone has an accent. Even native speakers—within a country and sometimes within a town—speak differently, and it is nearly impossible to eliminate an accent in a non-native language.[126]

3-6 Chapter Closing

Photos of Carlos Ghosn's opulent French wedding later emerged in stark contrast to workers protesting across France for higher wages.[127] Ghosn did offer to reimburse the company $57,000, a rental fee he charged to the company and used for the wedding.[128] But this figure pales in comparison to the $12 million Ghosn is suspected of using for personal expenses.[129]

As of this writing, Ghosn is still trying to "clear his name," according to an Associated Press report more than two years after his arrest. Ghosn still "denies any wrongdoing" and blames "people who organized the plot" against him.[130]

Working and communicating across differences requires some skill but mostly humility and an open mindset. No matter how much you prepare to work with people who are different from you, you will always be surprised. Someone will do or say something unexpected. The more you can approach these situations with humility and wonder, the more you will enjoy communicating across differences rather than view it as a burden.

In the next chapter, you learn about business writing, which also requires understanding others—in this case, your audience or reader.

Decide Whether to Engage in Conflict About Extravagant Wedding Plans

Consider the chapter introduction, which described Carlos Ghosn's extravagant spending. Imagine that you are a member of the company board of directors at the time and are deciding whether to engage in conflict about Ghosn's wedding plans in Versailles. Using the CAM model, what questions might you ask yourself before making the decision?

CHARACTER CHECK

1. **What is my role as a board member?**
   Although Mr. Ghosn is the board chair, members of the board of directors have a fiduciary responsibility to the company. A wedding is a personal event, yet a company leader is a public figure. As a board member, I should be cautious about overstepping, but even without the (future) knowledge that Mr. Ghosn may have spent company funds on the wedding, the perception is poor.
2. **What are the potential consequences of my engaging in this conflict?**
   Looking at the factors in Figure 4, the situation certainly is ambiguous, with conflicting perspectives, including my own. I may face harsh backlash from Mr. Ghosn because this is a private, celebratory occasion. Other board members may disagree, and I could be ostracized, although I won't likely lose my position over it.

AUDIENCE ANALYSIS

1. **What context is important to consider?**
   Mr. Ghosn is an outsider but has been extraordinarily successful in the company's turnaround. He may feel entitled to do as he pleases.
2. **Who is affected by the decision and how?**
   Company image may suffer if the wedding continues as planned. Even if Mr. Ghosn is using his own funds, the wedding is quite showy for a leader of a Japanese company. With a Marie Antoinette theme, the party includes people wearing period dresses and powdered wigs. He appears to be flaunting fame and wealth.

>>> MESSAGE AND MEDIUM

1. **What is my decision?**
   I will address the situation directly with Mr. Ghosn.
2. **What are the main points of my message?**
   I will describe how this situation reflects on company image and ask Mr. Ghosn to reconsider his plans.
3. **In what medium will I communicate the message?**
   An in-person conversation is best because this is a sensitive, potentially emotional issue.

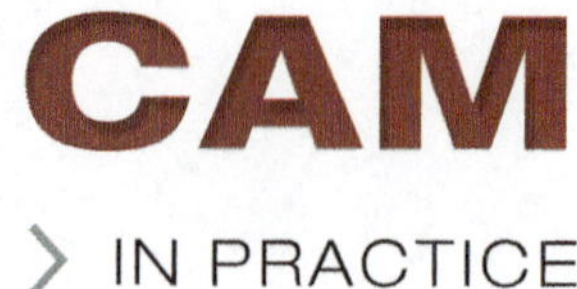

> IN PRACTICE

Prepare for a Difficult Conversation About the Extravagant Plans

Imagine that you are the board member who has decided to express concerns about Ghosn's wedding plans and ask him to reconsider the extravagance. Prepare to have a difficult conversation.

>>> CHARACTER CHECK

1. How do I feel about the decision to address this situation with Mr. Ghosn? How confident am I that this is the right thing to do?
2. How can I separate the personal celebration, the business impact, and my own feelings about such an event? In other words, how might my judgment of Mr. Ghosn get in the way of a productive conversation?

>>> AUDIENCE ANALYSIS

1. Knowing what I do about Mr. Ghosn, how do I expect him to react? How can I prepare myself for his reaction?
2. What other barriers might get in the way of my message being received as I intend it?
3. What outcomes do I want to achieve in this conversation?

>>> MESSAGE AND MEDIUM

1. What main points will I include in my message? What cultural values describe the possible negative public perception?
2. What would be a good setting for the meeting? Will I involve other board members? Why or why not?

REFLECTING ON YOUR COMMUNICATION AND CHARACTER DEVELOPMENT

1. Complete a Social Identity Wheel.

To develop self-awareness, complete the Social Identity Wheel in Figure 18.[131] Write your identities in the open sections, and then respond to the statements in the middle.

With a friend you trust and know well, share the Identity Wheel you created as a reflection activity. What do you feel most and least comfortable sharing? How does talking about your responses change how you think about yourself? How does your friend respond, and how might that change how you think about yourself?

Identity Wheel | **Figure 18**

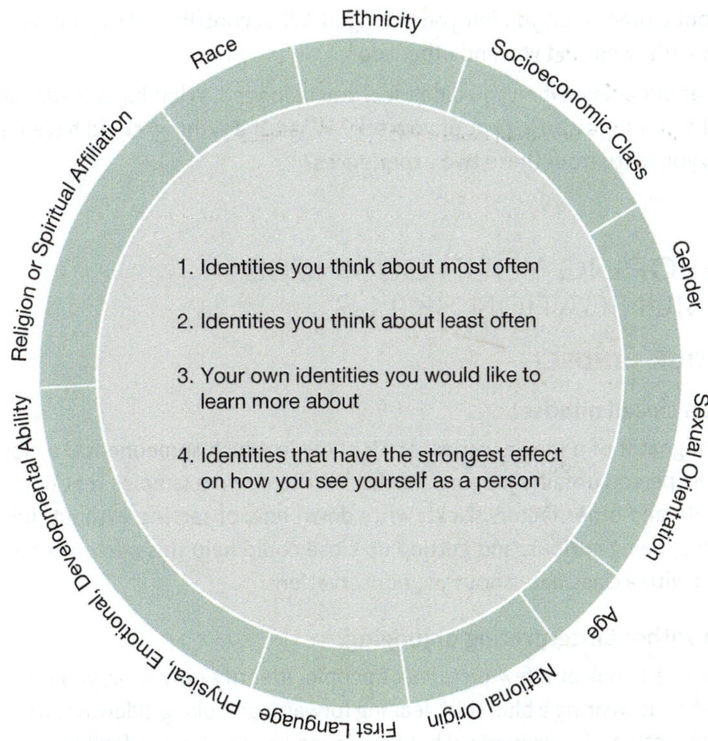

2. Take an Implicit Bias test.

At Harvard's Implicit Bias site (https://implicit.harvard.edu/implicit/takeatest.html), you'll find tests about your perceptions on race, age, gender, sexual orientation, religion, weight, skin tone, and more. Take at least one of these tests. How did you do? Did the results surprise you? Why or why not?

3. Practice mindfulness to gain perspective.

If mindfulness isn't part of your daily practice, try it for at least five minutes a day for a week. Consider one of Thich Nhat Hanh's guided breathing meditations,[132] or follow instructions from the Greater Good Science Center at the University of California, Berkeley.[133] Thich Nhat Hanh and the website follow similar steps to walk you through the process: finding a comfortable position, relaxing your body, observing your breathing, and focusing your attention.

After one week, reflect on and consider sharing your experience with a friend, family member, or classmate. How do you feel? Do you experience greater clarity, comfort, or calm? Will you continue the practice?

4. **Reflect on a difficult conversation.**

   Think about a difficult conversation you initiated recently. What was the situation, and what led to your decision to address rather than ignore it? What did you risk? Which skills and steps discussed in this chapter did you use? What went well, and what would you do differently next time you encounter a similar situation?

5. **Reflect in action.**

   The next time you're involved in a difficult conversation, check in with yourself by asking the questions in Figure 7. Try to reflect intellectually, emotionally, and physically. What does your assessment tell you about your experience? What adjustments can you make to improve the situation?

6. **Reflect on belonging.**

   Think about a time when you felt you belonged. What contributed to your feeling this way? In other words, what did you and others do?

   Think about a time when you didn't feel you belonged. What happened? Did you try too hard to "fit in" or hide an aspect of yourself? What, if anything, could have been avoided? What can you learn from these two experiences?[134]

DEVELOPING YOUR BUSINESS COMMUNICATION SKILLS

LO1 Describe two approaches for shifting your mindset.

SHIFTING YOUR MINDSET

1. **Observe a closed mindset.**

   Watch a segment of a movie, series, or TV show in which someone has a closed mindset. How is this person unfairly judging another? Write down examples that demonstrate failing humility and other factors. Next, write down how observing without judging, getting perspective, being curious, and getting up close could help this person keep a more open mind. Talk with a classmate about your observations.

2. **Observe without interpreting or judging.**

   In small groups, look at a few pictures of people. Identify only what you see, for example, that someone is wearing a blue shirt, leaning forward, or looking sideways. Try not to include any interpretations, for example, what people may be thinking or feeling.

3. **Review your resume for potential bias.**

   Identify parts of your resume that might lead to bias in the hiring process. Assume the worst: that someone is biased against your name, address, dates, hobbies, interests, volunteer work, and/or college. What are you willing to change—or not? Of course, you can present yourself just as you are.

4. **Consider an employment decision.**

   You're a candidate for a new job and ask to meet your prospective team. You're glad you did because no one on the team is like you; you are the only __________. (Fill in the blank.) What is this characteristic, and how important is it that you are different? Will you take the job?[135]

LO2 Define three types of conflict common in business environments and how to approach each.

MANAGING THROUGH CONFLICT

5. **Identify types of conflicts.**

   As you watch movies or other shows this week, notice examples of conflicts. For each, identify the type of conflict—task, relationship, or values. How do people work through them? How do they tackle different types of conflicts differently? What do they do that is successful, and what could they do differently to improve the outcomes?

6. **Analyze a past team conflict.**
   Think about a team conflict you had in the past. Or, if you're working as part of a team now, discuss a conflict you had. Identify whether it was a task, relationship, or values conflict. How did you handle it? What was the outcome? How could you handle conflicts in the future?

7. **Decide whether to address a conflict.**
   Talk with a partner in class about a conflict you're currently experiencing. Walk through the questions in Figure 4 about ambiguity, vulnerability, and loss to decide whether to engage in the conflict. What do you decide and why?

ENGAGING IN DIFFICULT CONVERSATIONS

LO3 Apply steps to engage in a difficult conversation in a business situation.

8. **Plan a difficult conversation about plagiarism.**
   Imagine that one of your team members submitted her section of a report for a class project, but you suspect it's not the student's own work. In a footnote on the last page are someone else's name, the same course number, and last year's date. The student submitted the work online, and your three team members also have access to the file.

   With a small group, follow the steps in Figure 5 to prepare for one of you to lead a conversation with this student. Prepare another student to play the role of the second student. As you prepare, invent whatever details you would like.

9. **Role-play a difficult conversation about plagiarism.**
   Using the scenario described in Exercise 8, have the student leading the discussion follow the steps for encouraging a dialogue. Start the conversation, listen actively and openly, share your perspective, problem-solve, and end the conversation. Review suggestions in the chapter for each step of the process without being too rigid: these are only guidelines.

   Have other students in your group observe and take notes. After the conversation, first ask the student who played the role of the one who submitted the work how the conversation went—what went well, and how could the discussion have gone better? Next, have the observers give their feedback. Finally, have the student who led the conversation summarize the feedback and describe possible changes for the future.

10. **Plan, role-play, and reflect on a difficult conversation about customer service.**
    Use the process described in Exercises 8 and 9 to plan and role-play another situation. Imagine that a coworker's behavior falls into the "obnoxious aggression" category of radical candor. Earlier in the day, you overheard your coworker tell a customer, "You need to be more careful with the product. It's not a toy, and you'll be responsible if it breaks again."

    This time, in the middle of the role play, stop and have both students reflect in action. Use the questions in Figure 7. Based on your responses, what changes in your approach will you make for the rest of the conversation?

    After taking this break, finish the conversation. What changes did you make, and how, if at all, did they affect the outcome?

11. **Plan an upcoming difficult conversation.**
    Think about a situation you may have been avoiding. Use the steps in Figure 5 to prepare yourself to have a difficult conversation. Before choosing a time and place, talk with a partner about your responses to the first set of questions. How do you feel about scheduling the conversation? What, if anything, is holding you back? What other work can you do to be fully prepared?

LO4 Identify ways to adapt language to audiences to honor differences.

COMMUNICATING TO IMPROVE INCLUSIVITY AND BELONGING

12. Compare diversity statements.

Find and compare diversity, inclusion, and/or belonging statements from two or three of your favorite companies. Answer the following questions, and then share your responses with another student:

- How easy was it to find the statement on the company website?
- Which parts of the statement fit the definitions of diversity, inclusion, and belonging? Does the statement focus on one more than the others?
- In what ways does the statement reflect the company, brand, products, or services? In other words, could any company use the same statement, or is it unique to that company?
- Comparing the statements, which is best and why?

13. Discuss your views of using inclusive language.

In small groups, discuss how you feel about using inclusive language, for example, the advice in Figure 12. Allow space for everyone to be honest and respectful of different points of view. For example, not everyone likes the idea of using *they* as a singular pronoun or being asked what pronouns they use, while others may feel that using gender-neutral pronouns is important. Still others may feel that pronouns they use are essential to their identity.

14. Discuss misjudgments.

With a classmate, describe a time each of you were misjudged because of your affiliation or identity. Next, describe a time when you misjudged someone else. What are the similarities and differences among these four situations? What can you learn from talking them through?

LO5 Compare how people in high- and low-context countries communicate.

ADAPTING TO INTERNATIONAL CULTURAL DIFFERENCES

15. Advise someone who is traveling to another country.

Imagine that a colleague is traveling abroad and wants your advice. With a classmate, choose one country that neither of you knows well. Prepare a short email with suggestions about greetings, dining, meetings, and other relevant information.

16. Analyze how well a company adapts to international audiences.

Choose a large, global company and explore its website. Do you find multiple versions of the company's site for different countries? In what ways does the company adapt its writing style, use of graphics, and other features to different cultures? Write a brief report on your findings and include screenshots of the company's website(s) to illustrate your points.

17. Compare cultural values of two countries.

Choose two countries and compare their cultures at https://www.hofstede-insights.com/product/compare-countries. What similarities and differences do you notice? What, if anything, surprises you?

18. Describe a culture to the class.

If your country of origin is different from where you're studying, you may volunteer to describe the culture to the class. Or you may volunteer if you have traveled to another country. Answer the following questions:

- How would you describe the culture based on the values in Figure 13?
- What similarities and differences do you notice between your country and where you're studying?
- What did you expect when you either came to this country or visited the other? What surprised you?
- Do you prefer one country to the other? If yes, which and how so?

CHAPTER SUMMARY

LO1 Describe two approaches for shifting your mindset.

Communicating successfully across differences starts with self-awareness—our own identity and views. To reduce critical judgment of others, ask yourself why you're judging, choose humility, observe without judgment, practice getting perspective, be curious, and get up close. The better we know ourselves and others, the more we value differences.

LO2 Define three types of conflict common in business environments and how to approach each.

Managing through task, relationship, and values conflicts takes courage and skill. Abusive behaviors may require leadership interventions, but other conflicts are natural and improve team functioning and relationships when engaged in and handled well. To decide whether to engage in conflict, consider whether you can withstand the ambiguity, exposure, and potential loss.

LO3 Apply steps to engage in a difficult conversation in a business situation.

Engage in difficult conversations by preparing yourself, choosing a time and setting, and encouraging a dialogue, rather than a debate or discussion. Work toward increasing understanding and building a relationship rather than "winning." Give and receive feedback in ways that demonstrate caring personally and challenging directly.

LO4 Identify ways to adapt language to audiences to honor differences.

Improving inclusivity and belonging at work starts with your bringing your whole, authentic self to work, as much as is appropriate and possible for you. Choose inclusive language for different groups by adapting to others' preferences, which change over time and vary by people. Differences within groups are greater than between groups, so avoid unfairly stereotyping. Offense is inevitable and presents an opportunity to increase understanding, change behavior, and inevitably, build a deeper, more trusting relationship.

LO5 Compare how people in high- and low-context countries communicate.

Cultures vary in how much they emphasize individualism, time orientation, power distance, uncertainty avoidance, formality, materialism, and context sensitivity. Individual differences affect people's behavior, yet understanding cultural differences helps us prepare to communicate internationally. Adapting requires cultural competence, humility, and agility. When communicating with or as a non-native speaker, verbal, visual, nonverbal, and other approaches will help increase understanding.

Endnotes

1. Daniel Shane, "After Carlos Ghosn, Japan May Never Hire Another Foreign CEO," *Forbes*, November 30, 2018, www.cnn.com/2018/11/30/business/japan-foreign-ceos-carlos-ghosn, accessed May 24, 2021.
2. Nissan Motor Co., Ltd., "Announcement Regarding Changes of Representative Directors," *The Wall Street Journal*, November 22, 2018, www.wsj.com/edition/resources/documents/print/NissanPDF.pdf, accessed January 17, 2021.
3. Nick Kostov, "Inside Carlos Ghosn's Great Escape: A Train, Planes and a Big Black Box," *The Wall Street Journal*, January 7, 2020, www.wsj.com/articles/inside-carlos-ghosns-great-escape-a-train-planes-and-a-big-black-box-11578445084, accessed January 17, 2021.
4. Carlos Ghosn, "Our Differences Are Many, Our Potential Is Great," Speech delivered at the Arab Bankers Association of North America Award Dinner, New York City, NY, October 15, 2014, https://www.linkedin.com/pulse/our-differences-many-potential-carlos-ghosn, accessed January 17, 2021.
5. Bill Snyder, "Carlos Ghosn: Five Percent of the Challenge Is the Strategy. Ninety-five Percent Is the Execution," Insights by Stanford Business, July 9, 2014, www.gsb.stanford.edu/insights/carlos-ghosn-five-percent-challenge-strategy-ninety-five-percent-execution, accessed January 17, 2021.
6. Snyder.
7. Peter Franklin, "Unethical, Criminal or Victim?" Business Spotlight, April 2019, p. 45, https://www.business-spotlight.de/business-englisch-lesen/unethical-criminal-or-victim, accessed January 17, 2021.
8. Franklin.
9. Graeme Wearden, "'A Kind of Nightmare': Carlos Ghosn's Press Conference - Key Points," *The Guardian*, January 8, 2020, www.theguardian.com/business/2020/jan/08/carlos-ghosn-press-conference-key-points-nissan-renault, accessed January 17, 2021.
10. Adapted from Michael Vande Berg, "From the Inside Out: Transformative Teaching and Learning." Presented at the Workshop on Intercultural Skills Enhancement (WISE) Conference at Wake Forest University, February 3, 2016, http://global.wfu.edu/files/2016/03/Training-WISE-workshop-second-version-2-3-16.pdf., accessed January 22, 2021.
11. Justin Parkinson and Maisie Smith-Walters, "Who, What, Why: What Is Name-Blind Recruitment?" BBC, October 26, 2015, www.bbc.com/news/magazine-34636464, accessed January 23, 2021.
12. Daniel Brtz, "Can Blind Hiring Improve Workplace Diversity?" Society for Human Resources Management, March 20, 2018, www.shrm.org/hr-today/news/hr-magazine/0418/pages/can-blind-hiring-improve-workplace-diversity.aspx, accessed January 22, 2021.
13. Andy Molinsky, "If You're Not Outside Your Comfort Zone, You Won't Learn Anything," *Harvard Business Review*, July 29, 2016, https://hbr.org/2016/07/if-youre-not-outside-your-comfort-zone-you-wont-learn-anything, 2016, accessed January 21, 2021.
14. Tommy J. Van Cleave and Chris Cartwright, "Intercultural Competence as a Cornerstone for Transformation in Service Learning," in Corey Dolgon, Tania D. Mitchell, and Timothy K. Eatman (eds.), *The Cambridge Handbook of Service Learning and Community Engagement* (New York: Cambridge University Press, 2017), p. 209.
15. Jena McGregor, "Maya Angelou on Leadership, Courage and the Creative Process," *The Washington Post*, May 28, 2014, www.washingtonpost.com/news/on-leadership/wp/2014/05/28/maya-angelou-on-leadership-courage-and-the-creative-process/, accessed January 21, 2021.
16. Carl Gustav Jung, "Quotable Quote," Goodreads, www.goodreads.com/quotes/5846-everything-that-irritates-us-about-others-can-lead-us-to, accessed January 23, 2021.
17. Prakhar Verma, "How to Develop a Non-Judgemental Attitude to Live More Peacefully," Medium, September 27, 2018, https://medium.com/swlh/how-to-stop-judging-and-start-living-91bef2834c9a, accessed January 23, 2021.
18. Mark R. Leary et al., "Cognitive and Interpersonal Features of Intellectual Humility," *Personality and Social Psychology Bulletin* 43 (2017): 793–813.
19. David Hellier, Corinne Gretler, and Jeff Green, "The Ghosn Brand Is Broken. These Spin Doctors Say How to Fix It," *Bloomberg*, January 12, 2020, www.bloomberg.com/news/articles/2020-01-12/the-ghosn-brand-is-broken-these-spin-doctors-say-how-to-fix-it, accessed January 23, 2021.
20. Bradley P. Owens, Michael D. Johnson, and Terence R. Mitchell, "Expressed Humility in Organizations: Implications for Performance, Teams, and Leadership," *Organization Science* 24, (2013): 1517–1538.
21. Arménio Rego et al., "Leader Humility and Team Performance: Exploring the Mediating Mechanisms of Team PsyCap and Task Allocation Effectiveness," *Journal of Management* 45 (January 2017): 1009–1033.
22. Daryl R. Van Tongeren, Don E. Davis, and Joshua N. Hook, "Social Benefits of Humility: Initiating and Maintaining Romantic Relationships," *Journal of Positive Psychology* 9 (2014): 313–321.
23. Fung Kei Cheng, "What Does Meditation Contribute to Workplace?: An Integrative Review," *Journal of Psychological Issues in Organizational Culture* 6 (2016): 18–34.
24. Aslak Hjeltnes et al., "Facing the Fear of Failure: An Explorative Qualitative Study Of Client Experiences in a Mindfulness-Based Stress Reduction Program for University Students with Academic Evaluation Anxiety," *International Journal of Qualitative Studies on Health and Well-being* 10 (2015).

25. Fung Kei Cheng, "What Does Meditation Contribute to Workplace?: An Integrative Review," *Journal of Psychological Issues in Organizational Culture* 6 (2016): 18–34.
26. Kimberly Schaufenbuel, "Why Google, Target, and General Mills Are Investing in Mindfulness," *Harvard Business Review*, December 2015, https://hbr.org/2015/12/why-google-target-and-general-mills-are-investing-in-mindfulness, accessed January 30, 2021.
27. Salvatore Zappalà, "Perspective Taking in Workplaces," *Journal for Perspectives of Economic, Political, and Social Integration* 19 (2014): 55–70.
28. Michelle Williams, "Building and Rebuilding Trust: Why Perspective Taking Matters," in Roderick M. Kramer and Todd L. Pittinsky (eds.), *Restoring Trust in Organizations and Leaders: Enduring Challenges and Emerging Answers* (New York: Oxford University Press, 2012), https://doi.org/10.1093/acprof:oso/9780199756087.003.0009 accessed June 29, 2017.
29. Summarized in Salvatore Zappalà, "Perspective Taking in Workplaces," *Journal for Perspectives of Economic, Political, and Social Integration* 19 (2014): 55–70.
30. To read more on how neuroscience research distinguishes between empathy and perspective taking, see Julia Stietz, "Dissociating Empathy From Perspective-Taking: Evidence From Intra- and Inter-Individual Differences Research," *Psychiatry*, March 14, 2019, www.frontiersin.org/articles/10.3389/fpsyt.2019.00126/full, accessed January 24, 2021.
31. Rosabeth Moss Kanter, "Managing Yourself," *Harvard Business Review*, March 2011, https://hbr.org/2011/03/managing-yourself-zoom-in-zoom-out, accessed January 23, 2021.
32. John Koetsier, "Why Every Amazon Meeting Has at Least 1 Empty Chair," *Inc.*, April 5, 2018, www.inc.com/john-koetsier/why-every-amazon-meeting-has-at-least-one-empty-chair.html, accessed January 23, 2021.
33. Alex Lindsey et al., "The Impact of Method, Motivation, and Empathy on Diversity Training Effectiveness," *Journal of Business and Psychology* 3 (2015): 605–617.
34. Adam Grant, *Think Again* (New York: Viking, 2021), p. 178.
35. Tal Eyal, Mary Steffel, and Nicholas Epley, "Research: Perspective-Taking Doesn't Help You Understand What Others Want," *Harvard Business Review*, October 9, 2018, https://store.hbr.org/product/research-perspective-taking-doesn-t-help-you-understand-what-others-want/H04KXF, accessed January 23, 2021.
36. Tal Eyal, Mary Steffel, and Nicholas Epley, "Perspective Mistaking: Accurately Understanding the Mind of Another Requires Getting Perspective, Not Taking Perspective. *Journal of Personality and Social Psychology* 114 (2018): 547–571, https://doi.org/10.1037/pspa0000115.
37. Nicholas Epley, "Be Mindwise: Perspective Taking vs. Perspective Getting," *Behavioral Scientist* (2014), https://behavioralscientist.org/be-mindwise-perspective-taking-vs-perspective-getting/, accessed April 14, 021.
38. Julia Galef, "Why You Think You're Right—Even if You're Wrong," TED Talk, February 2016, www.ted.com/talks/julia_galef_why_you_think_you_re_right_even_if_you_re_wrong, accessed July 1, 2017.
39. Grant, p. 178.
40. David Brooks, "2020 Taught Us How to Fix This," *The New York Times*, December 31, 2020, www.nytimes.com/2020/12/31/opinion/social-change-bias-training.html, accessed January 23, 2021.
41. Brené Brown, "Braving the Wilderness Excerpt," September 7, 2017, Brené Brown Blog, https://brenebrown.com/blog/2017/09/07/braving-the-wilderness-excerpt/, accessed January 23, 2021.
42. Kathleen M. Eisenhardt, Jean L. Kahwajy, and L.J. Bourgeois III, "How Management Teams Can Have a Good Fight," *Harvard Business Review*, July-August 1997, https://hbr.org/1997/07/how-management-teams-can-have-a-good-fight, accessed February 3, 2021.
43. Shankar Vedantam and Adam Grant, "The Easiest Person to Fool," Hidden Brain Episode, NPR, https://hiddenbrain.org/podcast/the-easiest-person-to-fool/, accessed February 3, 2021.
44. Katie Shonk, "3 Types of Conflict and How to Address Them," Harvard Law School Program on Negotiation, October 1, 2020, www.pon.harvard.edu/daily/conflict-resolution/types-conflict/, accessed January 24, 2021.
45. David J. Woehr, Luis M. Arciniega, and Taylor L. Poling, "Exploring the Effects of Value Diversity on Team Effectiveness," *Journal of Business and Psychology* (2013): 107–121.
46. Barbara Ortutay, "Hundreds of Amazon Workers Challenge Company on Climate Practices Despite Risk to Jobs," *Fortune*, January 27, 2020, https://fortune.com/2020/01/27/amazon-employees-climate-change-challenge-job-threats/, accessed January 25, 2021.
47. Steven Greenhouse, "'We Deserve More': An Amazon Warehouse's High-Stakes Union Drive," *The Guardian*, February 23, 2021, www.theguardian.com/technology/2021/feb/23/amazon-bessemer-alabama-union, accessed May 24, 2021.
48. Amanuel G. Tekleab, Narda R. Quigley, and Paul E. Tesluk, "A Longitudinal Study of Team Conflict, Conflict Management, Cohesion, and Team Effectiveness," *Group and Organization Management* 34 (February 4, 2009): 170–205.
49. Dwayne Devonish, "Workplace Bullying, Employee Performance and Behaviors," *Employee Relations* 35 (May 29, 2013): 630–647.
50. Sarah Branch, Sheryl Ramsay, and Michelle Barker, "Workplace Bullying, Mobbing and General Harassment: A Review," *International Journal of Management Reviews* 15 (July 2013): 280–299.

51. Beth Tootell, Stephen Croucher, and Jo Cullinane, "Cyberbulling in the Workplace," in Stephanie Kelly (ed.), *Computer-Mediated Communication in Business: Theory and Practice* (Newcastle upon Tyne, UK: Cambridge Scholars, 2019), p. 163.
52. Karen Weise, "Over 4,200 Amazon Workers Push for Climate Change Action, Including Cutting Some Ties to Big Oil," *The New York Times*, April 10, 2019, www.nytimes.com/2019/04/10/technology/amazon-climate-change-letter.html, accessed January 25, 2021.
53. Ethan Kross describes "distancing" and other ways to manage negative thoughts in *Chatter: The Voice in Our Head, Why It Matters, and How to Harness It* (New York: Crown, 2021).
54. Rushworth M. Kidder, *Moral Courage* (New York: HarperCollins, 2005).
55. Albert O. Hirschman, *Exit, Voice, and Loyalty: Responses to Decline in Firms, Organizations, and States* (Cambridge, MA: Harvard University Press, 1970).
56. Katie Shonk, "3 Types of Conflict and How to Address Them," Harvard Law School Program on Negotiation, October 1, 2020, www.pon.harvard.edu/daily/conflict-resolution/types-conflict/, accessed January 24, 2021.
57. Shankar Vedantam and Adam Grant, "The Easiest Person to Fool," Hidden Brain Podcast, NPR, https://hiddenbrain.org/podcast/the-easiest-person-to-fool/, accessed February 3, 2021.
58. Katie Shonk, "Strategies to Resolve Conflict over Deeply Held Values," Harvard Program on Negotiation, Daily Blog, November 30, 2020, www.pon.harvard.edu/daily/conflict-resolution/strategies-to-resolve-conflict-over-deeply-held-values, accessed May 25, 2021.
59. Kerry Patterson, Joseph Grenny, Ron McMillan, and Al Switzler, *Crucial Conversations* (New York: McGraw-Hill, 2002).
60. Karl Albrecht, "The Paradoxical Power of Humility," *Psychology Today*, January 8, 2015, www.psychologytoday.com/blog/brainsnacks/201501/the-paradoxical-power-humility, accessed January 26, 2021.
61. Adapted from "Creating Community Across Difference," Intergroup Dialogue Project, Cornell University, 2018, which is adapted from University of Michigan Program on Intergroup Relations, 2008. Original source: Daniel Yankelovich, *The Magic of Dialogue: Transforming Conflict into Cooperation* (New York: Simon & Schuster, 1999).
62. Kim Scott, *Radical Candor: Be a Kick-Ass Boss Without Losing Your Humanity* (New York: St. Martin's Press, 2017), p. 40.
63. Bill Burnett and Dave Evans, *Designing Your Life: How to Build a Well-Lived Life* (New York: Alfred A. Knopf, 2016).
64. "Good for the Bottom Line: A Review of the Business Case for Diversity and Inclusion," Hearing Before the Subcommittee on Diversity and Inclusion of the Committee on Financial Services, U.S. House of Representatives, May 1, 2019, Serial No 116-22, https://www.govinfo.gov/content/pkg/CHRG-116hhrg37521/pdf/CHRG-116hhrg37521.pdf, accessed January 27, 2021.
65. "Different Together," Apple, www.apple.com/diversity/, accessed January 27, 2021.
66. Jena McGregor, "First There Was 'Diversity.' Then 'Inclusion.' Now HR Wants Everyone to Feel Like They 'Belong,'" December 30, 2019, *The Washington Post*, www.washingtonpost.com/business/2019/12/30/first-there-was-diversity-then-inclusion-now-hr-wants-everyone-feel-like-they-belong, accessed January 27, 2021.
67. Brené Brown, *Daring Greatly: How the Courage to Be Vulnerable Transforms the Way We Live, Love, Parent and Lead* (New York: Avery, 2015), p. 232.
68. "Indra Nooyi's Leadership Lessons: Head, Heart & Hands," Enactus Career Connections in "Eleven pearls of wisdom from outgoing PepsiCo chief Indra Nooyi," January 2, 2014, accessed January 27, 2021.
69. Vanessa Buote, "Most Employees Feel Authentic at Work, but It Can Take a While," *Harvard Business Review*, May 11, 2016, https://hbr.org/2016/05/most-employees-feel-authentic-at-work-but-it-can-take-a-while, accessed January 27, 2021.
70. Ralph Van den Bosch and Toon W. Taris, "Authenticity at Work: Development and Validation of an Individual Authenticity Measure at Work," *Journal of Happiness Studies* 15 (2014): 1–18.
71. Vanessa Buote, "Most Employees Feel Authentic at Work, but It Can Take a While," *Harvard Business Review*, May 11, 2016, https://hbr.org/2016/05/most-employees-feel-authentic-at-work-but-it-can-take-a-while, accessed June 21, 2021.
72. Michael L. Slepian, et al., "The Physical Burdens of Secrecy," *Journal of Experimental Psychology* 141 (2012): 619–624, https://web.stanford.edu/group/ipc/pubs/Slepian-Masicampo-Toosi-Ambady_Physical-Burdens-of-Secrecy_in-press_JEPG.pdf, accessed January 18, 2021.
73. Lisa Rosh and Lynn Offerman, "Be Yourself, but Carefully," *Harvard Business Review*, October 2013, https://hbr.org/2013/10/be-yourself-but-carefully, accessed January 27, 2021.
74. Laura Guillen, Natalia Karelaia, and Hannes Luc Leroy, "The Authenticity Gap: When Authentic Individuals are Not Regarded as Such and Why it Matters," INSEAD Working Paper No. 2016/08/DSC, March 6, 2016, https://papers.ssrn.com/sol3/papers.cfm?abstract_id=2734779, accessed April 14, 2021.
75. Brené Brown, "My Response to Adam Grant's New York Times Op/ED: Unless You're Oprah, 'Be Yourself' Is Terrible Advice," LinkedIn, June 5, 2016, www.linkedin.com/pulse/my-response-adam-grants-new-york-times-oped-unless-youre-bren%C3%A9-brown/, accessed April 14, 2021. Adam Grant, "The Dangers of Being Authentic," LinkedIn, June 5, 2016, https://www.linkedin.com/pulse/dangers-being-authentic-adam-grant/, accessed April 14, 2021.

76. Nick Thompson, "Benedict Cumberbatch Apologizes for 'Colored Actors' Remark in U.S. Interview," CNN, January 28, 2015 http:www.//cnn.com/2015/01/27/entertainment/benedict-cumberbatch-colored-apology/index.html, accessed January 28, 2021.
77. Darrel Rowland, "Ohio Sen. Steve Huffman Who Cited 'Colored' People Not Washing Their Hands Fired from Job," *The Columbus Dispatch*, June 10, 2020, www.dispatch.com/story/news/2020/06/10/gop-ohio-senator-questions-whether-minorities-get-covid-19-unwashed-hands/5339187002/, accessed January 28, 2021.
78. "Bias-Free Language," APA Style, https://apastyle.apa.org/style-grammar-guidelines/bias-free-language, accessed January 28, 2021.
79. Nicholas Jones, "Update on the U.S. Census Bureau's Race and Ethnic Research for the 2020 Census," United States 2020 Census, www.census.gov/content/dam/Census/newsroom/press-kits/2014/article_race_ethnic_research_2020census_jones.pdf, accessed January 28, 2021.
80. "Your Guide to the 2020 Census," United States 2020 Census, https://2020census.gov/content/dam/2020census/materials/languages/guides/Large_Print-Guide.pdf, accessed January 28, 2021.
81. "Racial and Ethnic Identity," APA Style, https://apastyle.apa.org/style-grammar-guidelines/bias-free-language/racial-ethnic-minorities, accessed January 28, 2021.
82. "Racial and Ethnic Identity."
83. E. Tammy Kim, "The Perils of 'People of Color,'" *The New Yorker*, July 29, 2020, www.newyorker.com/news/annals-of-activism/the-perils-of-people-of-color, accessed January 28, 2021.
84. "Our Mission," The BIPOC Project, www.thebipocproject.org/, accessed January 28, 2021.
85. Rashaad Lambert, "'There Is Nothing Minor About Us': Why *Forbes* Won't Use The Term Minority To Classify Black And Brown People," *Forbes*, October 8, 2020, www.forbes.com/sites/rashaadlambert/2020/10/08/there-is-nothing-minor-about-us-why-forbes-wont-use-the-term-minority-to-classify-black-and-brown-people/?sh=55228d9d7e21, accessed June 2, 2021.
86. See, for example, Marianne Schmid Mast and Keou KambiwaKadji, "How Female and Male Physicians' Communication Is Perceived Differently," *Patient Education and Counseling* 101 (2018): 1697–1701, and Courtney von Hippel, et al., "Stereotype Threat and Female Communication Styles," *Personality and Social Psychology Bulletin* 37 (2011): 1312–1342.
87. "Sexual Orientation and Gender Identity Definitions," Human Rights Campaign, www.hrc.org/resources/sexual-orientation-and-gender-identity-terminology-and-definitions, accessed January 28, 2021.
88. "Gender," APA Style, https://apastyle.apa.org/style-grammar-guidelines/bias-free-language/gender, accessed January 28, 2021.
89. Will Oremus, "Here Are All the Different Genders You Can Be on Facebook," *Slate*, February 13, 2014, https://slate.com/technology/2014/02/facebook-custom-gender-options-here-are-all-56-custom-options.html, accessed January 28, 2021.
90. "Singular 'They,'" AP Style, https://apastyle.apa.org/style-grammar-guidelines/grammar/singular-they, accessed January 28, 2021.
91. Lori A. Trawinski, "Leveraging the Value of an Age-Diverse Workforce," Society for Human Resources Management Foundation, www.shrm.org/foundation/ourwork/initiatives/the-aging-workforce/Documents/Age-Diverse%20Workforce%20Executive%20Briefing.pdf, accessed January 28, 2021.
92. Robert M. McCann, Howard Giles, and Hiroshi Ota, "Aging and Communication Across Cultures," in Ling Chen (ed.), *Intercultural Communication* (Berlin: De Gruyter Mouton, 2017).
93. Eden King, et al., "Generational Differences at Work Are Small. Thinking They're Big Affects Our Behavior," *Harvard Business Review*, August 1, 2019, https://hbr.org/2019/08/generational-differences-at-work-are-small-thinking-theyre-big-affects-our-behavior, accessed January 28, 2021.
94. Tim Cook, "Tim Cook Speaks Up," *Bloomberg*, October 30, 2013, www.businessweek.com/articles/2014-10-30/tim-cook-im-proud-to-be-gay, accessed January 28, 2021.
95. "Enhancing Your Interactions with People with Disabilities," American Psychological Association, www.apa.org/pi/disability/resources/publications/enhancing, accessed January 28, 2021.
96. National Center on Disability and Journalism, "Disability Language Style Guide," https://ncdj.org/style-guide, accessed January 28, 2021.
97. "Disability," AP Style, https://apastyle.apa.org/style-grammar-guidelines/bias-free-language/disability, accessed January 28, 2021.
98. National Center on Disability and Journalism, "Disability Language Style Guide," https://ncdj.org/style-guide, accessed January 28, 2021.
99. Kathy Gurchiek, "Prayer and Meditation Rooms Can Increase Inclusion," March 23, 2018, Society for Human Resources Management, www.shrm.org/resourcesandtools/hr-topics/behavioral-competencies/global-and-cultural-effectiveness/pages/prayer-meditation-rooms-can-increase-inclusion.aspx, accessed January 28, 2021.
100. Maura Cullen, *35 Dumb Things Well-Intended People Say* (Garden City, NJ: Morgan James Publishing, 2008).
101. Ibram X. Kendi, Facebook post, www.facebook.com/ibramxkendi/posts/1018094395255469, accessed January 28, 2021.

102. Elizabeth A. Tuleja, "Intercultural Communication for Business," in James S. O'Rourke IV (ed.), *Managerial Communication Series* (Canada: Thomson South-Western, 2005).

103. Geert Hofstede, *Culture's Consequences: Comparing Values, Behaviors, Institutions and Organizations Across Nations*, 2nd ed. (Thousand Oaks, CA: Sage, 2001).

104. He Bai, "A Cross-Cultural Analysis of Advertisements from High-Context Cultures and Low-Context Cultures," *English Language Teaching* 9 (2016): 21–27.

105. Quan Yuan, "Analysis of Silence in Intercultural Communication," International Conference on Economy, Management and Education Technology (2015), www.atlantis-press.com/proceedings/icemet-15/25837457, accessed January 29, 2021.

106. Chang-Hyun Jin, "An Empirical Comparison of Online Advertising in Four Countries: Cultural Characteristics and Creative Strategies," *Journal of Targeting, Measurement and Analysis for Marketing* 18 (2010): 253–261.

107. "Apple Japan - Behind the Mac," YouTube, March 11, 2020, https://youtu.be/SWlgADuY8xQ, accessed January 29, 2021.

108. "Behind the Mac - Greatness," Apple, November 10, 2020, https://youtu.be/b3VcGKv9Cfw, accessed January 29, 2021.

109. Nancy J. Adler, *International Dimensions of Organizational Behavior*, 5th ed. (Mason, OH: South-Western, Cengage Learning, 2008), p. 29.

110. Jim Lehrer et al., "Toyota Chief's Emotional Apology Resonates in Japan," PBS NewsHour, February 25, 2010, www.pbs.org/newshour/show/toyota-chiefs-emotional-apology-resonates-in-japan, accessed January 29, 2021.

111. "Toyota Motor Company," The Yamasa Institute, http://yamasa.org/japan/english/destinations/aichi/toyota.html, accessed January 29, 2021.

112. Roland Kelts, "Toyota and Trust: Was the Akio Toyoda Apology Lost in Translation?" *CS Monitor*, February 25, 2011, www.csmonitor.com/Commentary/Opinion/2010/0225/Toyota-and-trust-Was-the-Akio-Toyoda-apology-lost-in-translation, accessed January 29, 2021.

113. David Anderson, Matthew Stuart, Mark Abadi, and Shayanne Gal, "5 Everyday Hand Gestures That Can Get You in Serious Trouble Outside the US," *Business Insider*, January 5, 2019, www.businessinsider.com/hand-gestures-offensive-different-countries-2018-6, accessed February 6, 2021. Kathleen Crislip, "Hand Gestures in the World with More Than One Meaning," TripSavvy, June 26, 2019, www.tripsavvy.com/hand-gestures-with-more-than-one-meaning-3149620, accessed February 6, 2021. Sophie Forbes, "17 Gestures That Can Cause Offense Around the World," ShermansTravel, February 4, 2020, www.shermanstravel.com/advice/18-gestures-that-can-cause-offense-around-the-world, accessed February 6, 2021. Courtney Subramanian, "12 Gestures That Will Accidentally Piss People Off Around the World," Thrillist, March 15, 2015, www.thrillist.com/travel/nation/ok-symbol-thumbs-up-and-other-hand-gestures-that-mean-different-things-abroad, accessed February 6, 2021. Maria Inês Teixeira, "15 Insulting Gestures in Different Cultures," Lingoda, June 8, 2020, https://blog.lingoda.com/en/15-insulting-gestures-in-different-cultures/, accessed February 6, 2021. Chris Miller, "The Meaning of Hand Gestures Around the World," English Live, https://englishlive.ef.com/blog/english-in-the-real-world/hand-gestures/, accessed February 6, 2021. Vanessa Swales, "When the O.K. Sign Is No Longer O.K.," *The New York Times*, December 15, 2019, www.nytimes.com/2019/12/15/us/ok-sign-white-power.html, accessed February 6, 2021. Sophie Thompson, "Cultural Differences in Body Language to be Aware of," VirtualSpeech, August 25, 2017, https://virtualspeech.com/blog/cultural-differences-in-body-language, accessed February 6, 2021.

114. Hironori Akechi et al., "Attention to Eye Contact in the West and East: Autonomic Responses and Evaluative Ratings," *PLOS ONE* (2013), www.ncbi.nlm.nih.gov/pmc/articles/PMC3596353/, accessed January 29, 2021.

115. Caroline Blais, "Culture Shapes How We Look at Faces," *PLOS ONE* (August 20, 2008), https://journals.plos.org/plosone/article?id=10.1371/journal.pone.0003022, accessed January 29, 2021.

116. Peter Broeder and Elena Remers, "Eye Contact and Trust Online," The IEEE 12th International Conference on Application of Information and Communication Technologies / AICT 2018, https://pure.uvt.nl/ws/portalfiles/portal/30017845/Broeder_Remers2018.pdf, accessed January 16, 2021.

117. Richard Lewis, "How Different Cultures Understand Time," *Business Insider*, June 1, 2014, https://www.businessinsider.com/how-different-cultures-understand-time-2014-5, accessed January 30, 2021.

118. Lewis.

119. Agnieszka Sorokowska, "Preferred Interpersonal Distances: A Global Comparison," Journal of Cross-Cultural Psychology 48 (2017): 577–592, https://doi.org/10.1177/0022022117698039.

120. Robin Welsch, "Interpersonal Distance in the SARS-CoV-2 Crisis," *Human Factors: The Journal of the Human Factors and Ergonomics Society* 62 (September 9, 2020), https://doi.org/10.1177%2F0018720820956858.

121. Louise J. Rasmussen, "Cross-Cultural Competence: Engage People from any Culture," Global Cognition, July 14, 2020, www.globalcognition.org/cross-cultural-competence/, accessed January 29, 2020. Also see Louise J. Rasmussen and Winston R. Sieck, "Culture-General Competence: Evidence from a Cognitive Field Study of Professionals Who Work in Many Cultures," *International Journal of Intercultural Relations* 48 (September 2015): 75–90.

122. Marcelle I. Wilson Davis, "Global Leadership," *Journal of Business Diversity* 18 (November 2018). See also Paula Caligiuri,

Cultural Agility: Building a Pipeline of Successful Global Professionals (San Francisco: Jossey-Bass, 2012).

123. Most of this advice is from Nancy J. Adler, *International Dimensions of Organizational Behavior*, 5th ed. (Mason, OH: South-Western, Cengage Learning, 2008), p. 90.

124. Adam Evans and Harika Suklun, "Workplace Diversity and intercultural Communication: A Phenomenological Study," *Cogent Business and Management* 4 (2017), www-tandfonline-com.proxy.library.cornell.edu/doi/full/10.1080/23311975.2017.1408943, accessed January 1, 2021.

125. Deborah Grayson Riegel, "3 Tips for Presenting in English When You're Not a Native Speaker," *Harvard Business Review*, April 6, 2018, https://hbr.org/2018/04/3-tips-for-presenting-in-english-when-youre-not-a-native-speaker, accessed January 30, 2021.

126. Nick Stockton, "What's Up with That: Why It's So Hard to Lose an Accent," *Wired*, September 30, 2014, www.wired.com/2014/09/whats-up-with-losing-accents/, accessed January 30, 2021.

127. Liz Alderman, "Carlos Ghosn May Have Spent Company Funds on Wedding Party, Renault Says," *The New York Times*, February 7, 2019, www.nytimes.com/2019/02/07/business/carlos-ghosn-versailles-renault.html, accessed February 1, 2021.

128. Leo Lewis, "Ghosn Offers to Reimburse Versailles for Birthday and Wedding Cost," *Financial Times*, February 8, 2019, www.ft.com/content/b74d1f92-2b56-11e9-a5ab-ff8ef2b976c7, accessed February 1, 2021.

129. Nick Kostov, "Carlos Ghosn Rang Up $12 Million in Suspect Expenses, Audit Finds," *The Wall Street Journal*, April 30, 2019, www.wsj.com/articles/carlos-ghosn-rang-up-12-million-in-suspect-expenses-audit-finds-11556628319, accessed February 1, 2021.

130. Jeffrey Schaeffer and Zeina Karam, "Defiant Ghosn Pins Hopes on French Probes to Clear His Name," AP News, May 26, 2021, https://apnews.com/article/beirut-middle-east-lebanon-business-a63fd5544e82a47022e128ab16c314c9, accessed May 26, 2021.

131. Adapted from "Personal Identity Wheel," University of Michigan, Inclusive Teaching, https://sites.lsa.umich.edu/inclusive-teaching/social-identity-wheel/, accessed January 31, 2021.

132. See, for example, "Breathing Meditation with Thich Nhat Hanh," YouTube, January 9, 2008, https://youtu.be/E7XJdkL4j3Y, accessed January 31, 2021.

133. The Greater Good Science Center at the University of California, Berkeley, "Mindful Breathing," http://ggia.berkeley.edu/practice/mindful_breathing, accessed June 4, 2017.

134. Adapted from Amy Newman, *Building Leadership Character* (Thousand Oaks, CA: Sage, 2019), p. 86.

135. Newman, p. 87.

Part 2 Developing Your Business Writing Skills

CHAPTER 4

Writing and Designing

Learning Objectives

After you have finished this chapter, you should be able to

LO1 Describe steps in the business writing process.

LO2 Answer five questions to analyze a business audience.

LO3 Describe one approach to organizing your ideas for a message.

LO4 Identify differences between writing emails and writing for the web.

LO5 Explain four principles for designing documents and websites.

LO6 Apply steps to revise and proofread a business message.

"The most important qualification is surprisingly missing from most of State Farm's online information about the Steer Clear program. To be eligible, all vehicles in a driver's household must be insured with State Farm." [1]

—Grace Kim, Bankrate reviewer

Chapter Introduction

State Farm Designs an Attractive but Imperfect Web Page

State Farm advertises a program for young drivers with clear, concise writing and engaging graphics on one web page.[2] With little text, the page conveys the main points of the program.

The image is bold and relevant, with overlay text to name and describe the program. Both phrases use rhetorical devices. "Steer Clear" is an example of assonance, or rhyming, and "Driver Discount" is an example of alliteration, or repeated consonant sounds.

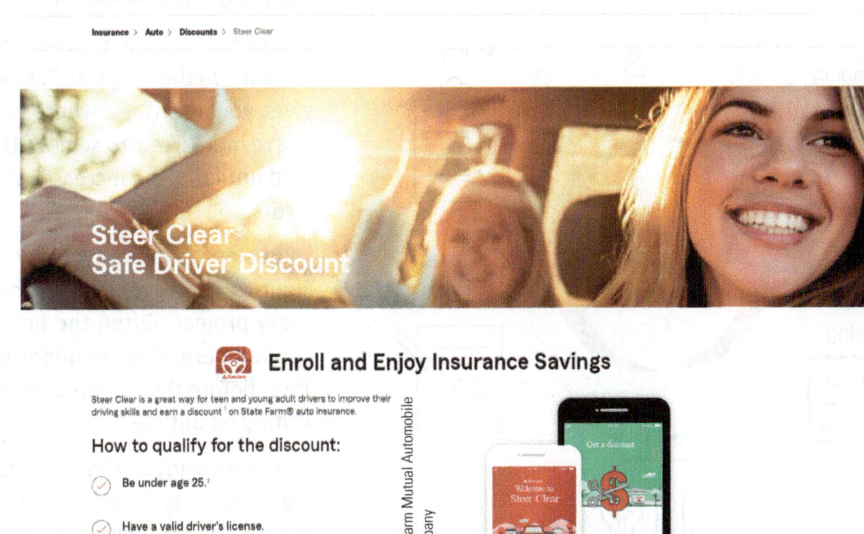

Source: State Farm Mutual Automobile Insurance Company

https://www.statefarm.com/insurance/auto/discounts/steer-clear.

State Farm uses a mix of text and graphics for a web page.

Splashes of red give the page a cohesive look. The State Farm logo, wheel icon, check marks, and app graphics are well placed and reflect a modern style. The app screenshots feature a hallmark of the program designed to attract young people.

The page isn't perfect. A financial product reviewer noted that the bullets listing driver requirements aren't parallel. She also identified an obvious, intentional omission: drivers must carry State Farm insurance.[3]

LO1 Describe steps in the business writing process.

4-1 Business Writing Process Overview

Our writing, like our character, is a work in progress. As you develop your writing, you lay the foundation for your future career—documenting your achievements, hopes, and plans. You are judged, as you judge others, on what and how you write. Committing to improving your writing is a commitment to improving your character and how you are perceived.

Figure 1 | The Writing Process

Peacefully7 and limeart/iStock/Getty Images

How do you start? When faced with a writing task, some people just start writing. They try to do everything at once: choose the best words, organize paragraphs, format, proofread—all at the same time. This may seem like the most efficient writing process, but it's not. With this approach, writers often get bogged down with details that prevent them from making progress and producing the best result.

Instead, writing in steps is the better strategy and will save you time in the long run. For example, spending time planning gives you a sense of where you want to go. With clear goals, you're more likely to achieve them. Similarly, waiting to proofread until the end increases the chance that you'll catch more errors.

Business writers typically perform the steps described in Figure 1. However, this process will vary for everyone and every project. Often the process is far more recursive than implied here. Writers might begin researching and drafting ideas before they complete some aspects of planning, such as writing an outline.[4]

The amount of time you devote to each step depends on the complexity, length, and importance of the writing project. You may go through all the steps when writing a business plan but not when answering an email inviting you to a meeting.

Next, you learn how to analyze your audience—the first step in the writing process.

LO2 Answer five questions to analyze a business audience.

4-2 Audience Analysis

Your first step is to consider your audience for the message—the reader or readers of your writing. An audience analysis helps you understand your message from the reader's perspective. This process gives you a sense of the audience's potential mental filters—how they might interpret the message—and how to adjust your approach accordingly.

In this section, you learn detailed questions for analyzing your audience, which is also the second step in the CAM communication model. Analyzing your audience takes character, particularly a willingness to understand their point of view.

4-2a Understanding Audience Analysis

Your audience may be just one person or a group of diverse people all over the world. We can't always understand our audiences perfectly, but we do our best to anticipate what they need and how they might react to our message. For a strategic-level communication—for example, announcing a big change in a company, such as a merger or acquisition—multiple messages would be sent to different audiences. Here, we consider just one message at a time.

Audience Analysis Example (Moving the Office to the Suburbs) | **Figure 2**

	Response	Effect on My Communication
Who is the audience?	**Primary audience:** Employees in the Chicago office, who will be moving **Secondary audience:** Employees in the Boston office, who may be concerned that they will move next.	I'll focus on the Chicago employees, but Boston employees will find out about the move, so I should plan communication for that group too. The Boston office may move within the next two years.
What is your relationship with the audience?	As the Chicago office manager, I know these employees well and have credibility with them, but I don't know the Boston employees well.	The Chicago employees trust me, and I won't take advantage of that trust. I'll be transparent and tell them what I know in a conversational, respectful tone. The Boston office manager will communicate with the Boston group.
How will the audience likely react?	Employees who live near the new location will be happy, but most will not and may resent the company's plan to reduce costs while increasing travel expenses for them.	I'll acknowledge the controversy and the negative impact on people's lives. I'll also be honest about the rationale for the decision and what we can and can't do to support employees.
What does the audience already know?	Employees know this was a possibility because we have been looking to reduce costs, but they may be surprised about the timing.	I'll reiterate the rationale for the move and provide evidence for the decision compared to other options. I won't be a jerk about it, but employees can infer that the alternative was to reduce staff.
What is unique about the audience?	Many employees don't own cars and make minimum wage. They may not be able to afford to move because of fewer rental properties.	I need to understand the hardship this move creates and will offer whatever I can, including relocation assistance and transportation credits.

Let's take an example of moving an office from downtown Chicago to a suburb. In Figure 2, you can see how analyzing an audience helps the writer tailor a message.

4-2b Applying the Five Questions

Following are considerations for each of the five questions for analyzing your audience.

Who Is the Primary Audience?

When you have more than one audience, identify your primary audience (e.g., the decision maker) and your secondary audience (others who will also read and be affected by your message). Focus on the primary audience but try to satisfy the needs of the secondary audience as well. If this is too much to accomplish in one message, write separate messages to different audiences.

When Peloton's CEO and Founder John Foley sent an email to customers about shipment delays for bikes and treadmills (Figure 3), he may not have considered his audiences. The email distribution included Peloton app subscribers who don't own their products—and might be reluctant to purchase one in the future because of the delays.

When have you found it difficult to consider your audience's perspective? What barriers have prevented you from accepting another's point of view? Recognizing your own judgment may help you appreciate your audience and tailor a message.

Figure 3 | Peloton Email to Customers

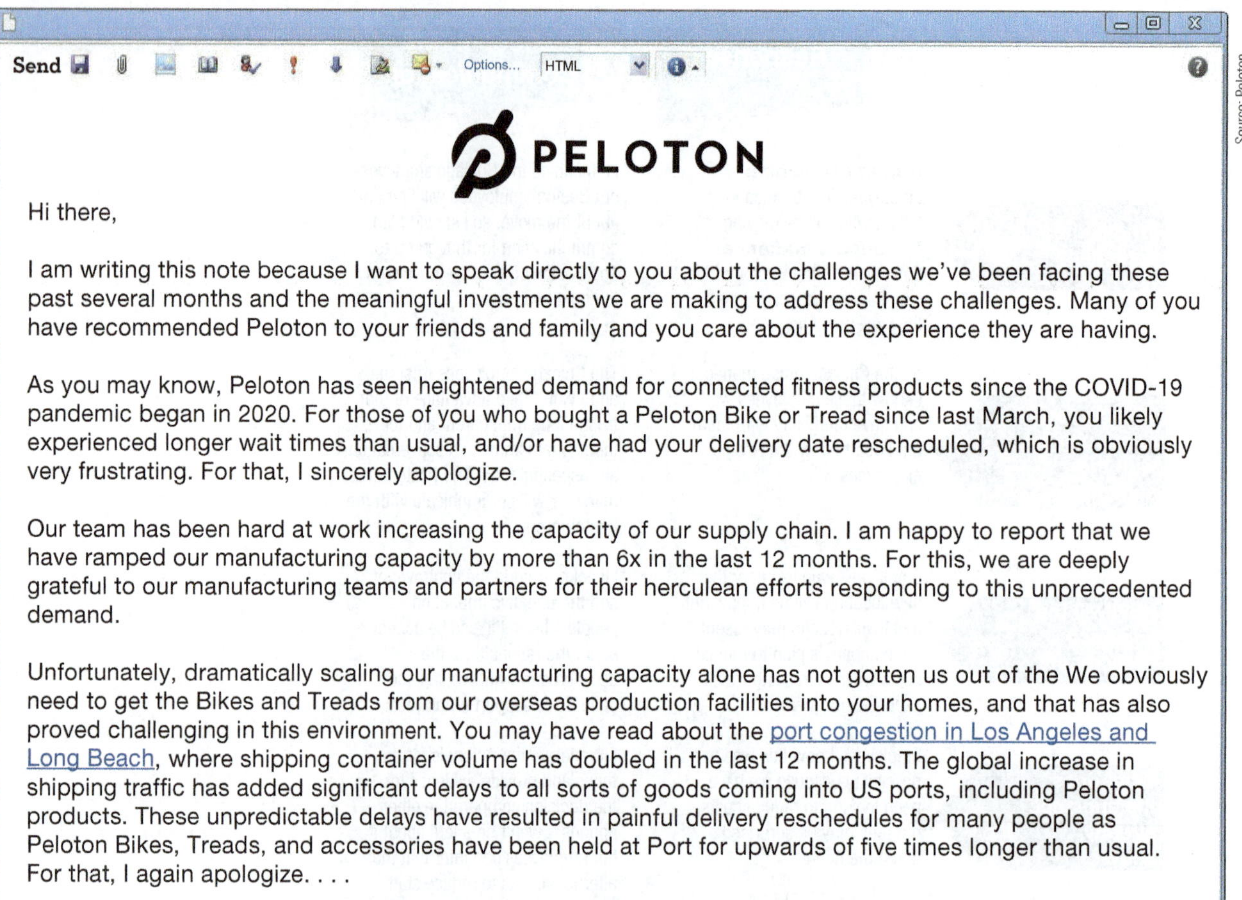
Send Options... HTML

PELOTON

Hi there,

I am writing this note because I want to speak directly to you about the challenges we've been facing these past several months and the meaningful investments we are making to address these challenges. Many of you have recommended Peloton to your friends and family and you care about the experience they are having.

As you may know, Peloton has seen heightened demand for connected fitness products since the COVID-19 pandemic began in 2020. For those of you who bought a Peloton Bike or Tread since last March, you likely experienced longer wait times than usual, and/or have had your delivery date rescheduled, which is obviously very frustrating. For that, I sincerely apologize.

Our team has been hard at work increasing the capacity of our supply chain. I am happy to report that we have ramped our manufacturing capacity by more than 6x in the last 12 months. For this, we are deeply grateful to our manufacturing teams and partners for their herculean efforts responding to this unprecedented demand.

Unfortunately, dramatically scaling our manufacturing capacity alone has not gotten us out of the We obviously need to get the Bikes and Treads from our overseas production facilities into your homes, and that has also proved challenging in this environment. You may have read about the port congestion in Los Angeles and Long Beach, where shipping container volume has doubled in the last 12 months. The global increase in shipping traffic has added significant delays to all sorts of goods coming into US ports, including Peloton products. These unpredictable delays have resulted in painful delivery reschedules for many people as Peloton Bikes, Treads, and accessories have been held at Port for upwards of five times longer than usual. For that, I again apologize. . . .

Source: Peloton

In addition, Foley's email doesn't distinguish current delays from previous sales. If you were waiting for a bike—Peloton's primary audience—you're probably frustrated and want a more targeted email. The bottom line for you is, when will you get your bike? Foley fails to address this critical question. Separate emails would have worked better in this situation.

What Is Your Relationship with the Audience?

Does your audience know you? If your audience doesn't know you, establish your credibility by assuming a professional tone and give enough evidence to support your claims. Are you writing to someone outside or inside the organization? If outside, your message may be more formal and contain more background information than if you're writing to someone inside the organization.

What is your status in relation to your audience? Messages to your manager might be a little more formal, less authoritarian in tone, and more informative than communications to peers or people who report to you. Study your manager's own messages to understand the preferred style and adapt your messages accordingly.

When you communicate with people who report to you, be respectful rather than patronizing. Try to instill a sense of collaboration and include employees in your message rather than talking down to them. For example, use "we" when you refer to the company or department. But be sincere and avoid platitudes, for example, "Employees are our greatest assets."

How Will the Audience Likely React?

If the reader's initial reaction to both you and your topic is likely to be positive, your job is relatively easy. Typically, your message can be short and straightforward, and you can provide little, if any, justification.

But if you expect your reader's reaction—either to your topic or to you personally—to be negative, now you have a real sales job. Your best strategy is to call on external evidence and expert opinion to bolster your position. Begin with areas of agreement, stress how the audience will benefit, and try to anticipate and answer any objections the reader might have. Through logic, evidence, and tone, build a case for your position. You learn more strategies for persuasive communication and conveying bad news in Chapters 7 and 8.

What Does the Audience Already Know?

Understanding what the audience already knows helps you decide how much content to include and what writing style is most appropriate. When writing to multiple audiences, adapt to the key decision maker (the primary audience). In general, it is better to provide too much rather than too little information.

Beware the "curse of knowledge."[5] When you're close to a situation, the message is clear to you, but others need more explanations. Concrete language and stories help reduce this gap so that people get the information they need easily.

What Is Unique About the Audience?

The success or failure of a message often depends on little things—the extra touches that say to the reader, "You're important, and I've taken the time to learn about you." What can you learn about the interests or demographics of your audience that you can build into your message? What particular questions and concerns can you anticipate and address?

4-2c Adjusting a Message for a Manager

Let's look at another example to illustrate the crucial role that audience analysis plays in communication. Assume that you are a marketing manager at Seaside Resorts, a chain of small hotels along the California, Oregon, and Washington coasts. You know that many of the larger hotel chains have loyalty (or frequent-stay) programs, which reward repeat customers with free nights and other perks.

You want to write a message recommending a loyalty plan for Seaside. Assume that Haney, your immediate manager and the vice president of marketing, will be the only reader of your email and has the authority to approve or reject your proposal. Compare three versions of Haney's background and perspective and how you might adjust your approach for each (Figure 4).

Figure 4 | Adjusting Your Communication Approach to Your Audience

Haney's Background and Perspective	Notes for Your Communication Approach
Haney has 20 years of management experience in the hospitality industry, and she respects your judgment.	Haney knows about loyalty programs and has confidence in you, so you can present what you know clearly, concisely, and directly.
Haney started in her position at Seaside Resorts just three months ago and is still learning about the hotel industry. Up to this point, your relationship with her has been cordial, but she isn't familiar with your work.	You'll need to build credibility with Haney without sounding cloying. In addition to your research, you might want to include information about your experience with loyalty programs. But be careful about bragging that you know more than she does.
Haney has implied that she doesn't completely trust your judgment. In the past, she has been hesitant about accepting your ideas without extensive research on her own.	Present research specific to your resort and include an external review for more credibility. Include all costs and potential downsides to build trust and to demonstrate that you took time to develop a comprehensive proposal.

LO3 Describe one approach to organizing your ideas for a message.

4-3 Planning

After thoroughly analyzing your audience, you can begin planning your message. Planning involves making conscious decisions about the message purpose, content, and organization.

4-3a Purpose

If you don't know why you're writing the message (i.e., what you hope to accomplish), then you won't know whether you have achieved your goal. In the end, how well you wrote your message doesn't matter if you don't meet your objectives.

You might find it easier to start with a general purpose and then refine it into a specific objective. A communication objective describes what you expect the reader to do as a result of your message. For the hotel loyalty program example, your general purpose might be this:

General Purpose: To describe the benefits of a loyalty program at Seaside Resorts.

This goal is a good starting point, but it isn't specific enough. It doesn't identify the intended audience or the outcome you expect. If the audience is the marketing vice president, do you want her to simply understand what you have written? Commit resources for more research? Agree to implement the plan immediately? How will you know if your message achieves its objective? This is one example of a more specific communication objective:

Specific Objective: To persuade Haney to approve developing and implementing a loyalty program for a 12-month pilot in Seaside's three Oregon resorts.

This purpose is now specific enough to guide you in writing the message and evaluating its success. Additional examples of general-purpose statements converted to more useful objectives are shown in Figure 5. These communication objectives state what you expect the audience to do and how you hope people will feel after reading your message.

Identifying a Communication Objective | **Figure 5**

General-Purpose Statement	Specific Communication Objective
To communicate the office move.	To explain the rationale and process for the move to employees, while maintaining morale and minimizing employee turnover.
To apply for the sales associate position.	To convince the HR manager to call me for an interview based on my qualifications for the job.
To deny a customer's request for a replacement phone.	To maintain the customer's goodwill by explaining the rationale for the denial.

4-3b Content

After you analyze your audience and identify the objective of your message, the next step is to decide what information to include. For simple messages, such as a quick text or routine email, this step is easy. However, most communication projects require many decisions about what to include. How much background information is needed? What research or data best supports the conclusions? Are expert opinions needed? Would examples, anecdotes, or graphics help comprehension? The trick is to include enough information so that you don't lose or confuse the reader yet avoid including irrelevant material that wastes the reader's time and obscures important data.

One useful strategy to get started is **brainstorming**—jotting down ideas, facts, examples, and anything else you think might be helpful in constructing your message. Aim for quantity, not quality. Don't evaluate your output until you run out of ideas. Then begin to refine, delete, combine, and revise your ideas to form your message.

Another approach is **mind mapping** (also called *clustering*), a process that avoids the step-by-step limitations of lists. Instead, write your main idea in the middle of the page. Then, write down possible points and link them with a line either to the main idea or to another point. As you think of other details, add them where they might fit.

The mind map visual offers flexibility and encourages free thinking. Figure 6 shows an example of mind mapping for the loyalty program idea, developed in the program coggle.it. You may find writing by hand more freeing. Either way, by putting your ideas down and showing how they relate, you're beginning to organize your message, which is the next step in the planning process.

4-3c Organization

After you have brainstormed around a main idea, you may choose to organize your points into an outline. Particularly for longer writing projects, students who spend time outlining find it useful to organize their writing and their thinking, to make the writing process easier, to keep them focused, and to save their ideas.[6] Think of your outline as a living representation of your writing—not a rigid plan.

In this step, you identify the hierarchy and sequencing of topics. First, classify or group related ideas. Next, differentiate between the major and minor points so that you can line up minor ideas and evidence to support the major ideas.

The diagram in Figure 7 shows the loyalty program idea shaping up into a well-organized message. You'll notice that some items changed from the mind map. This is typical: you'll rethink some ideas and hone others. For example, maybe you changed your mind about needing physical loyalty cards.

Figure 6 | Mind Map of Loyalty Program Ideas

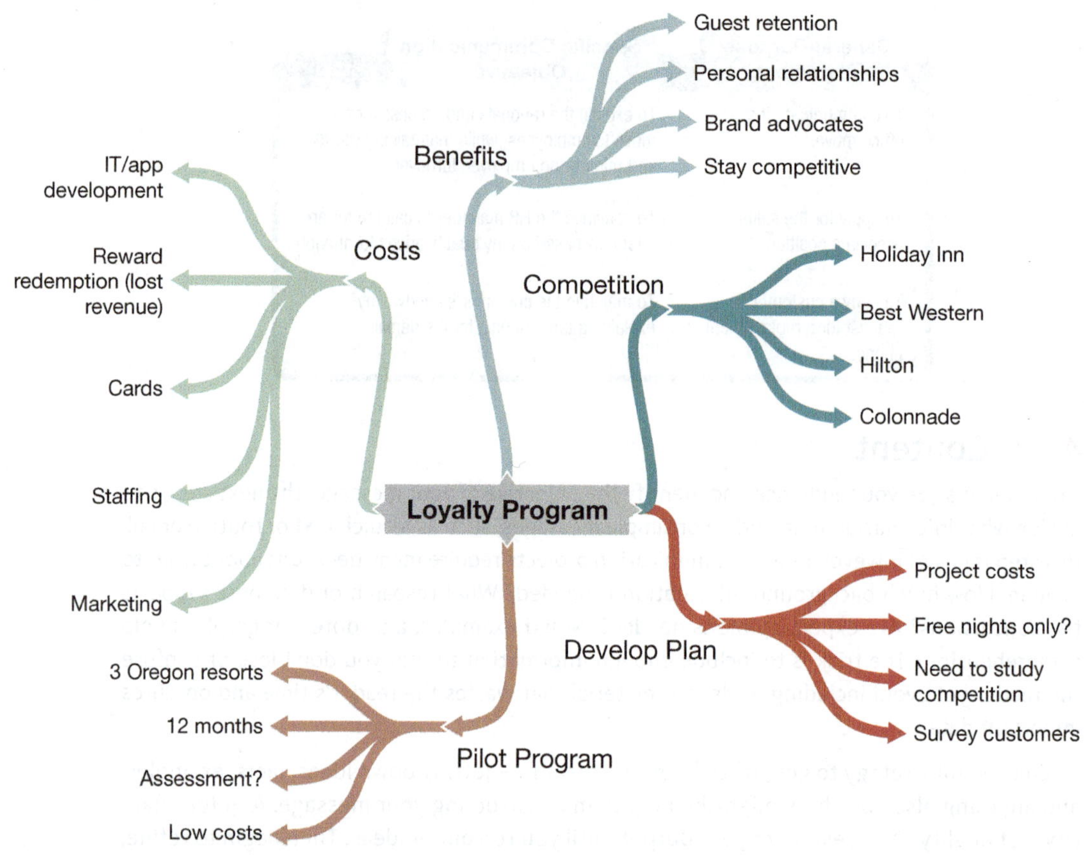

Figure 7 | Organization for Loyalty Program Message

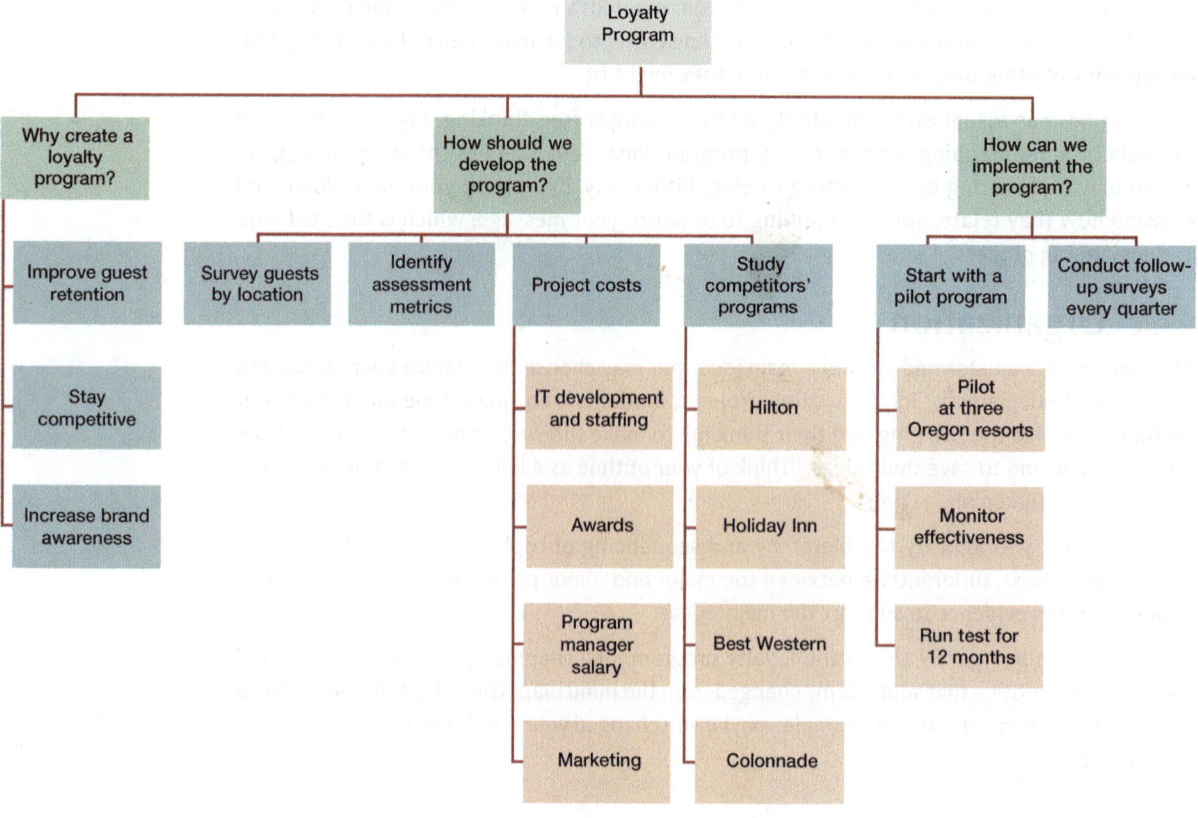

Rather than create a hierarchical diagram, you may present your ideas in outline form, shown in Figure 8. You'll notice an introduction before the first section. For most business communication, audiences expect to see the main point up front. This is the direct organizational plan: your conclusion or recommendation is first, with explanations following. Of course, you may skip the chart or outline for shorter and less important business writing.

Message Organization in Outline Format | **Figure 8**

Loyalty Program Message Outline

Introduction: Include purpose, summary of main points, and preview of topics to be covered.

Section 1: Why should we create a loyalty program?

(1) Improve guest retention
(2) Stay competitive
(3) Increase brand awareness

Section 2: How should we develop the program?

(1) Survey guests by location
(2) Identify assessment metrics
(3) Project costs
  (a) IT development and staffing
  (b) Awards
  (c) Program manager and salary
  (d) Marketing
(4) Study competitors' programs
  (a) Hilton
  (b) Holiday Inn
  (c) Best Western
  (d) Colonnade

Section 3: How can we implement the program?

(1) Start with a pilot program
  (a) Pilot at three Oregon resorts
  (b) Monitor effectiveness
  (c) Run test for 12 months
(2) Implement at other hotels gradually
(3) Conduct follow-up surveys every quarter

Conclusion: Summarize points, describe next steps, and request action.

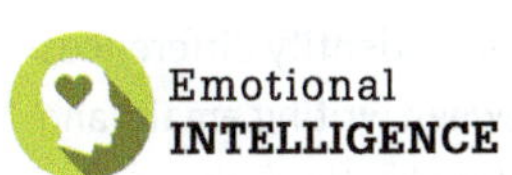

Do you prefer a more direct or indirect style of communication? Do you tend to get to the main point right away or give explanations and examples before conveying the main point? Does your own style sometimes get in the way of what's best for the audience and situation?

For longer written communications (e.g., long memos, proposals, or reports), consider writing your introductory paragraph first. For the direct approach, the introduction explains why you're writing (the purpose), what your conclusions are (your main points), and what topics the reader can expect (the preview). For the indirect organizational plan, you also will cover these points, but you would provide more background information—and discuss your purpose and main points later in the introduction. Compare three approaches, shown in Figure 9, for an introductory paragraph for the loyalty proposal. These build on our earlier examples of analyzing the audience (Figure 4).

In the less direct introduction examples, notice how much softer the tone is for the reader. The main point is more of an invitation than a recommendation.

After you have organized your ideas, you're ready to begin drafting your message.

Figure 9 | Adjusting an Introductory Paragraph to Your Audience

Version of Haney	Approach for the Introductory Paragraph
Haney is experienced and respects you.	***Most Direct:*** The purpose of this proposal is to recommend implementing a loyalty program in our three Oregon resorts. A loyalty program will improve guest retention and increase brand awareness. I'll discuss why we should establish a loyalty program, how we should develop the program, and how we can implement a pilot for our guests.
Haney is new to the hotel industry and doesn't know you well.	***Less Direct:*** The attached *Wall Street Journal* article discusses the success of loyalty programs at four small hotels, including my former employer. Each found that the program improved guest retention and increased brand loyalty. The purpose of this proposal is to recommend that Seaside implement a similar program. I'll describe how loyalty programs work, analyze the costs and benefits for Seaside, and recommend a pilot program.
Haney has not supported your ideas in the past.	***Least Direct:*** The attached *Wall Street Journal* article discusses the success of loyalty programs at four small hotels. I became interested in this idea for Seaside and would like to share my research with you. I found that 75% of our competitors have a loyalty program, and a recent Hotel and Lodging survey shows that nearly half of the 5,000 respondents choose specific hotels (even if they are more expensive) in order to accrue points. Small hotels have found that loyalty programs have increased guest retention and improved brand awareness. In this proposal, I'll describe loyalty programs at our competitors and the potential costs and benefits for Seaside. Dr. Kenneth Lowe, professor of hospitality services at Southern Cal, read and commented on my first draft. I would be glad to talk about how we might start with a small pilot program.

LO4 Identify differences between writing emails and writing for the web.

4-4 Drafting

After planning your message, you're ready to begin **drafting**—composing a preliminary version of a message. The more work you did to plan and organize your message, the easier this step will be. In this section, you learn how to start the process and how to write for different media: emails, memos, letters, and the web.

4-4a Letting Go

Probably the most important thing to remember about drafting is to just let go. Let your ideas flow as quickly as possible, without worrying about style, correctness, or format. If this is difficult for you, you might experience **writer's block**—the inability to focus on the writing process and to draft a message. If you do, consider the following typical causes:

- *Procrastination*: Putting off what we dislike or don't feel confident doing.

- *Impatience*: Getting bored with the naturally slow pace of the writing process.
- *Perfectionism*: Believing that our draft must be perfect the first time.

Try to tame your inner critic. Telling yourself that you're not a good writer or that you write too slowly can reinforce old beliefs about yourself. Business writing is different from academic writing: you might find it easier and more fun.

Also separate the drafting stage from the revising stage, so you're not trying to find the perfect word or correct spelling in the first draft. You'll have time to edit later. It's much easier to polish a page full of writing than a page full of nothing. Striving for perfection will interfere with your creativity, and you might start to question your ability, which makes it even harder to tackle writing. Try each of the strategies in Figure 10 for avoiding writer's block at least once. Then, choose what works best for you.

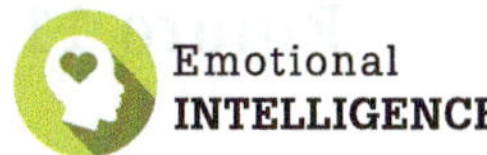

How do you feel about your own writing? Have you been told that you're a good writer or a poor writer? Do you tell yourself that you hate writing? Consider how these messages may cause writer's block. Instead, try to think positively: you can learn to write well.

Figure 10 Strategies for Overcoming Writer's Block

1 Choose the right environment.
- Go to a quiet library—or a busy coffee shop.
- Experiment until you find a place where you write best.

2 Minimize distractions.
- Close web browsers and your email to avoid notifications.
- Leave your phone in another room so you're not tempted to pick it up.

3 Schedule a reasonable block of time.
- For short writing projects, block out enough time to plan, draft, and revise the entire message in one sitting.
- For long or complex projects, schedule blocks of about two hours, or set milestones, such as writing one section and then taking a break.

4 State your purpose in writing.
- Define the objective of your message clearly and concisely.
- Write the objective someplace prominently so you always keep it in mind.

5 Write freely.
- Start by freewriting; write without stopping for 5 to 10 minutes.
- Write anything, without judgment; if you get stuck, write, "I'll think of something soon."

6 Think out loud.
- Picture yourself telling a colleague what you're writing about, and explain aloud the ideas you're trying to get across.
- Sharpen and focus your ideas by speaking rather than writing them.

7 Avoid perfectionism.
- Think of your writing as a draft—not a final document.
- Don't worry about style, spelling, or punctuation at this point. The artist in you must create something before the editor can refine it.

8 Write the easiest parts first.
- Skip the opening paragraph if you're struggling with it.
- Start with a section that's easiest for you to write.

4-4b Writing Emails, Memos, and Letters

In Chapter 1, we discussed several options for conveying your message. How you draft your message depends on which medium you choose. In this section, we look at writing guidelines for email, memos, and letters. Email is so pervasive in organizations that many people don't consider it writing—but of course it is. In business, emails can be one-word confirmations or longer messages with attachments. Email is the default communication choice in many organizations, with people sending and receiving 126 messages a day on average.[7] With so many messages to manage, how you write emails will determine whether yours are read and understood. See guidelines for drafting email messages in Figure 11 and an email example that meets these criteria in Figure 12.

Figure 11 | Writing Effective Email Messages

Openings and Closings

Follow your company's standards for salutations.

Write "Dear," "Hi," "Hello," or "Good morning" as salutations, depending on what people in your organization typically use. If you're writing an email to a prospective employer, err on the side of formality with "Dear Carly Thomas," followed by a comma. Although a comma after "Hi" as in, "Hi, Jasmine," is technically correct, you may find that few people in your company use this as a convention. Also, most people will skip the salutation (and signature) after one round of emails. It's silly to continue using someone's name in quick response emails.

Consider an opening statement.

You might start an email to build a genuine connection, for example, "I hope you're managing through this heat" or "It was good to see you last week." Starting with "I hope you're doing well" is getting dated and may sound trite.

Follow conventions for closings and signatures.

Like salutations, use standard closings that reflect your organization's culture. See what other people write, for example, "Thank you" or "Best regards." Pay attention to differences in emails sent internally and externally.

Use a signature line.

You may set up a personalized signature line for emails you send. Typically, this includes your name, title, company, and possibly your phone number. If your company has guidelines, follow what's required. If not, keep your signature line simple and professional: avoid fancy fonts, colors, and quotes for business email.

Audience

Complete the "To" field last.

Draft your email before you add the receiver's name. This way, you won't send the email accidentally before you proofread.

Use an appropriate tone.

Tone is difficult to assess in an email, so be careful with humor. Emails can be formal or informal but err on the side of formality with people you don't know well and those more senior to you in the organization. Readers may view you as less professional if you overuse exclamation points.[8] Also avoid sending business emails with romantic content or when you are emotional.[9] You may regret them later.

Think through who needs to be on copy.

Include only people who need to receive a copy and ask for your manager's preference. In some organizations, using BCC (blind carbon copy—sending someone a copy of your email without others knowing) is considered sneaky. This can become an ethical issue—and can come back to bite you if the person on BCC replies to all. A better alternative is to be open about who else is seeing the message or, if you must, forward an email after it has been sent.

Content

Be concise.

For all business writing, but particularly for emails, keep them as short as possible. Because people read emails on their phone, more than a couple of paragraphs is often considered too long. Crop and embed images rather than attach them for easier reading.[10] If you need to write more, consider including a summary in the email and attaching a formatted document instead.

Provide context.

Initiating an email and responding to one require different approaches. When you initiate an email, provide enough context for the reader—your purpose for writing and background information. Emails should be concise, but don't sacrifice clarity.

Organization

Use a specific, descriptive subject line.

Use subject lines that convey what you need or how the email will benefit the reader. Consider "New logo for your feedback," "Please change the Kraft meeting to Thursday," or "Need shipping info to close the Alaska deal." Inspire your reader to open the email by making it easy to respond. Use "urgent" and "important" labels sparingly. What is important to you might not be important to the reader, and overuse will be a turnoff.

Make emails easy to skim.

Particularly for email, which people read quickly, make sure your main points are clear and up front. Include a "call to action"—what you are asking the reader to do. Use bullets where it makes logical sense.

Keep paragraphs short.

You may lose your audience with dense paragraphs. Even single-sentence paragraphs are acceptable in email to improve readability.

Figure 12 Sample Email

To: Mauren Withers
From: Keith Stapleton
Subject: Need More Detailed Bio by Friday

Maureen,

I just saw the compiled biographies of all speakers for the ALP conference next week. Yours is considerably shorter than the others, so I thought you might want to add more detail about your background:

- Previous work at Seagram
- Previous positions with Mott
- Education and certificates

I'm attaching a more typical example in case you want to compare yours.

If you would like to provide a new version, please email it to me by Friday, June 9. This way, we can make sure your bio is included with the others in the printed brochure.

Thank you,

Keith

Keith Stapleton, Event Planning Assistant
Center for Leadership Development
1161 West Palm Street
Columbus, OH 43230
(614) 555-8700

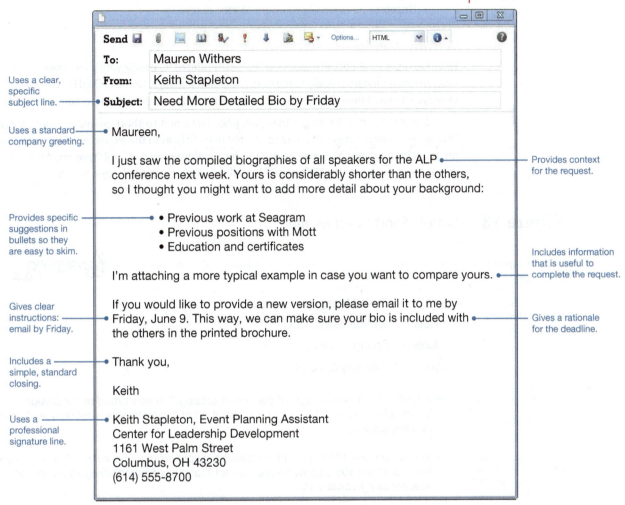

Uses a clear, specific subject line.

Uses a standard company greeting.

Provides context for the request.

Provides specific suggestions in bullets so they are easy to skim.

Includes information that is useful to complete the request.

Gives clear instructions: email by Friday.

Gives a rationale for the deadline.

Includes a simple, standard closing.

Uses a professional signature line.

International **COMMUNICATION**

In addition to conforming to organizational norms for email, pay attention to variations by country and region. Cultural differences discussed in Chapter 3 are as apparent in email messages as in any business communication. For example, in cultures that emphasize relationships rather than tasks, you may see longer emails with more personal information. Although an email from a U.S. manager may jump right into the main point, an email from a Latin American manager may start with a longer introduction about the weather or an update about the family.

Managing Email

One survey found that people spend, on average, five hours each day checking email—three hours on work email and two hours on personal email.[11] Here are a few ways to manage your email consumption:[12]

- Send fewer emails; you'll receive fewer in return.
- Turn off notifications on your computer and phone to stop interruptions and the time spent getting back to your other work (about 64 seconds);[13] instead, check email hourly or less often.
- Move emails out of your inbox after you read them; respond to all emails that require less than a minute.
- Use search functionality to find emails instead of wasting time filing them into folders and trying to retrieve them; if you must, use very few folders.[14]
- Use programs like Slack to manage messages by project.

- Set up filters for content you want to read later.
- Unsubscribe to emails you want to stop receiving.

Writing Memos

Email has replaced almost all memos—traditionally printed for people within an organization. Sometimes *memo* is used generically to mean an important message. Delta CEO Ed Bastian wrote, "CEO employee memo: Protecting our future," but the message was posted on the company's website.[15]

Today, memos may be longer than one page (attached to short emails) or short messages that serve as cover notes (attached to printed material), as in the example in Figure 13. In some organizations, memos also may be printed for employees who do not have regular access to a computer at work. See the Reference Manual for an example of a longer memo.

Figure 13 | Sample Short Cover Memo

Is printed on paper with a company logo. — Aggresshop

Includes standard memo heading with the writer's initials. —

To: Store Managers

From: Andrea Jewel, CEO A.J.

Subject: Spring Catalog

Date: February 8, 20XX

Refers to attached printed materials (a good reason to send a printed memo). — Attached is a preview copy of our spring catalog. I'm very proud of our Design Team, who created a beautiful representation of Aggresshop's most unique clothing and accessories.

Asks for feedback by email, which is the more typical communication medium for the company. — You will receive 100 copies of the catalog in your store by February 20. If you would like more than 100 copies, please contact Maryanne (msunger@aggresshop.com) by Wednesday, February 15.

Includes information related to the printed catalogs; this also may be sent by email. — Catalogs will be shipped to customers on February 22—one week earlier this year in response to your requests.

Closes on a positive note. — Best of luck for a successful spring season.

Writing Letters

Letters are written to people outside your organization and are reserved for formal communication. In your business career, you may write cover letters for jobs, sales letters to customers, proposal letters for new business, or thank-you letters to donors. See the Reference Manual for an example.

Because letters are for external audiences, a more formal approach is appropriate:

- Include your return address and the date.
- Use a formal salutation, typically, "Dear Sara Patel," followed by a colon (although commas are often used).
- Print your letter on company stationery or with an image of the company's logo. Many organizations will provide image files for you to paste into a document.
- Write longer paragraphs (typically three to seven sentences) and few bulleted lists.
- Use a professional closing, such as "Sincerely" or "Regards," and then leave a few lines to sign your name above your full typed name. Your title and department may follow your name.

4-4c Writing for the Web

When writing for the web, think like a user—your audience. Why would people visit your site? What do they want to see? Follow these guidelines to provide a good user experience, drive traffic to your site, and make your site accessible.

Developing Content for Scanning

We may want to believe that users will read every word on our website, but they will not. People generally scan sites looking for what interests them.[16] Consider the following tips when writing web text:[17]

- Use simple, commonly used words that people understand.
- Use minimal text and more graphics.
- Put relevant information up front—in headings, subheadings, and paragraphs.
- "Chunk" content into manageable sections.
- Use parallel bullets wherever possible.
- Write concisely and keep sentences and paragraphs short.
- Vary font sizes and font enhancements for headings, body text, and links.
- Use pronouns and active voice.

The Choice Hotels website follows these principles (Figure 14).[18] The most important information is prominent, and minimal text encourages users to select their language, follow simple tabs at the top, or most important, book a room. When users scroll down the page, they read plain language, chunked information, "you" or implied "you" as the subject, active voice, (mostly) parallel bullets or a short paragraph, and clear button text.

Consider using web analytics to collect and analyze data about your users. After you understand users' experience on your site, you can develop new content that will keep them engaged and coming back.

Optimizing for Search

Your website's ranking in search engine results determines how much traffic will be driven to your site. Consider these tips to improve search engine optimization (SEO):[19]

- **Research, select, and place keywords.** Use Google Analytics to determine how keywords rank in search engines. Some bloggers find words that rank highly and write about those topics. However, resist repeating a keyword too frequently, which can impact SEO negatively. Instead, find synonyms and develop related content. Place a keyword in a header and add text that explains it.
- **Develop quality content.** Write useful, relevant content and demonstrate credibility to improve search engine results. A clear, conversational, persuasive writing style affects readability, which can improve SEO. Write as you would speak, with natural language and contractions. Clear organization and accurate grammar also may affect search results.
- **Design for easy use.** Optimizing a website for mobile use improves SEO, as does using effective anchor text (descriptive links) and keeping permalinks (the page URL) short. Accessibility also affects ranking, which we discuss next.

Developing an Accessible Website

Not everyone has the same access or experience when navigating the web. Web accessibility guidelines ensure that sites are useable by people with visual, motor, auditory, cognitive, and other disabilities.[20] Developing an accessible website or webpage also means that people with a slow internet connection or a mobile device have a similar experience to those using fast desktops and laptops.[21]

The U.S. government has identified guidelines for web accessibility.[22] Following are a few tips to ensure that your web content and design are inclusive:[23]

- **Write clearly.** Simple language makes your site easier to navigate and easier to read.
- **Create logical structure.** Headings for lists and data tables make the organization explicit and facilitate navigation by keyboard, typically by tabbing.
- **Provide alternative text.** For people who are blind and/or use a screen reader, add meaningful labels to describe web content they can't see, for example, images and color.
- **Write descriptive text for links.** Links should be explicit instead of, for example, "click here."
- **Include captions and transcripts.** Add text captions and/or transcriptions for videos and audio.
- **Check PDF and other non-HTML content.** HTML is preferrable, but you can improve Microsoft Office documents using the Accessibility Checker in the Review tab.

Figure 14 | Choice Hotels Website

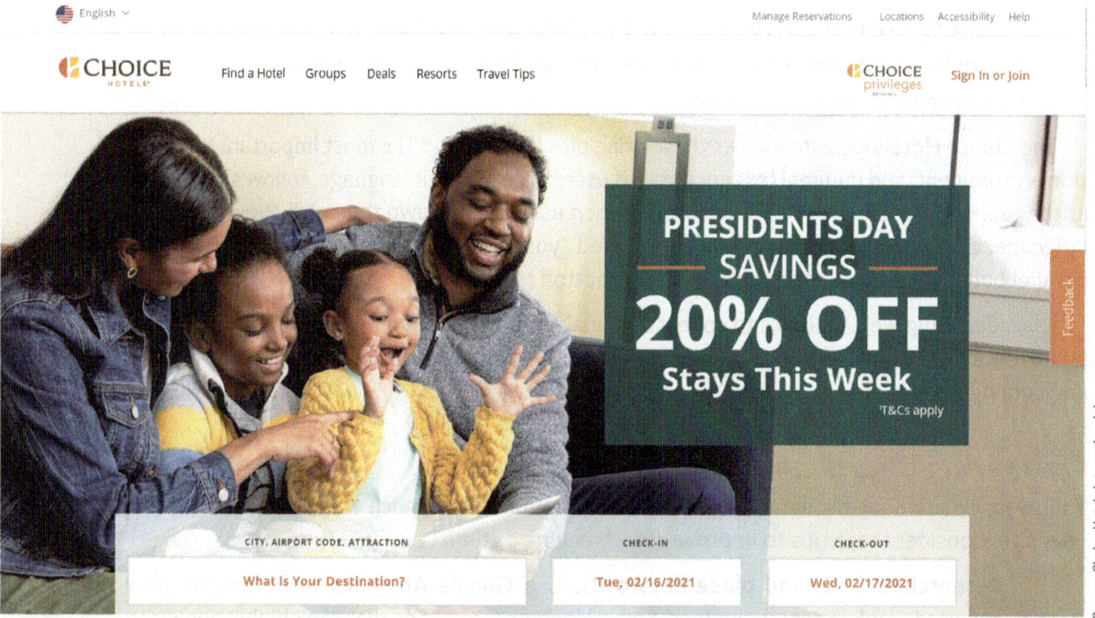

Source: Choice Hotels International, Inc.

Source: Choice Hotels International, Inc.

4-5 Designing

LO5 Explain four principles for designing documents and websites.

How your document, blog post, or website looks affects readability and interest. Good design invites your audience to read your work and helps them understand and find information easily.

In this section, you learn design principles to meet your audience's needs and your communication objectives. In later chapters, you learn about creating visuals from data and designing presentation slides.

4-5a Design Principles

Four principles—contrast, repetition, alignment, and proximity (or C.R.A.P.)[24]—describe key elements of a well-designed document or web page (Figure 15).

Figure 15 C.R.A.P. Design Principles

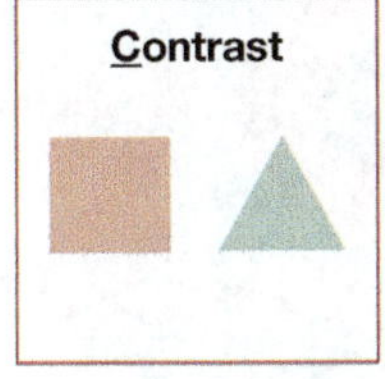

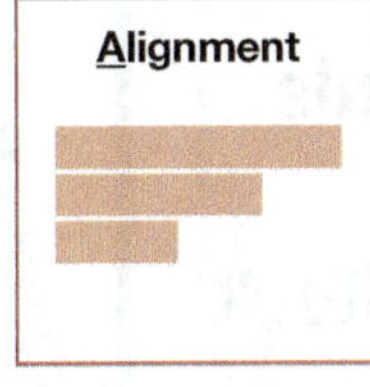

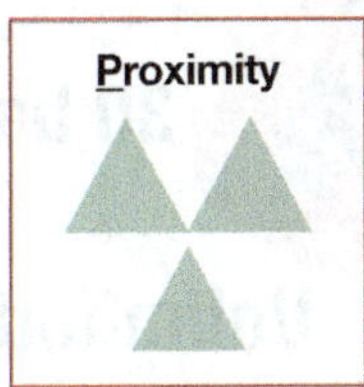

Contrast

Good contrast means that elements stand out and are easily distinguished. Compare the two designs in Figure 16. In the bad example, the colors blend together, making the text and images difficult to distinguish. When you convert images to grayscale, good contrast is more apparent.

You'll notice other issues with these graphics. Lines run through text, which, like graphics behind text, interferes with reading. Also, the font sizes are too similar, so the reader doesn't know what is most important.

Repetition

Repetition creates unity in your design. Consistent sizes and colors of text and graphical elements allow readers to scan and find information easily. Look at a few pages in this book. You see similar fonts, a consistent color palette, and the same style for figures. Overall, these features create a cohesive look and feel.

You also see repetition in how content is presented. Each chapter starts with an introduction, includes headings and subheadings to provide visual contrast and a hierarchy of ideas, and ends with the CAM communication model, exercises, and a summary. You know what to expect.

Alignment

Alignment creates unity by connecting elements. With clear, consistent alignment, text and graphics match up: you either see physical lines, or you can imagine them. Lining up components conveys order and a clean look.

Left or center alignment work best. For graphical interest, you might see text or images lined up on the right side of a document or web page, but for English speakers, who read from left to right, this alignment can be jarring.

Proximity

Proximity shows how elements are related. Instead of spacing elements evenly, group them to convey relationships. A caption clearly describes an image when it's placed closely. When you look at a web page, squint. Do you see groups of elements, or does everything blur together?

More specific design principles for documents and the web are next.

Figure 16 | Good and Bad Contrast

Good Contrast

Olga Miltsova/Shutterstock.com; Natutik/Shutterstock.com

Bad Contrast

Olga Miltsova/Shutterstock.com; Natutik/Shutterstock.com

Olga Miltsova/Shutterstock.com; Natutik/Shutterstock.com

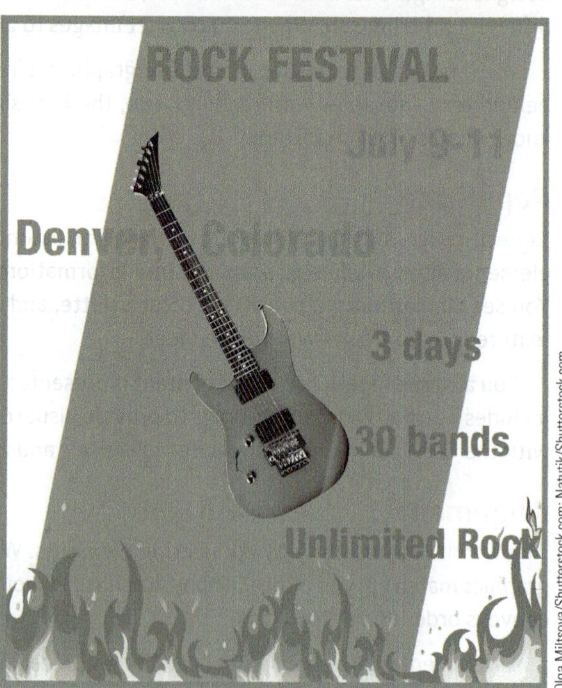

Olga Miltsova/Shutterstock.com; Natutik/Shutterstock.com

4-5b Document Design

Fonts, spacing, graphics, and other elements create the physical appearance of your writing—the **document design**. Readers understand and navigate a well-designed document easily.

You might be tempted to use all the space on a page, but **white space**—the unused parts of a page—shows the reader where to look. Use one-inch margins, line spacing between paragraphs, and space around graphics and within tables to make text easier to read and to provide a clean look with more visual appeal. Otherwise, documents look cluttered and may turn off your reader.

Notice how much white space is used in the second Choice Hotels website image in Figure 14. You also see good alignment and symmetry on the page; it looks balanced.

Bullets are another good way to increase white space and draw a reader's attention to important text, as you see in the earlier sample email in Figure 12. Use bullets when you have more than two points with parallel information.

Choose standard fonts that are easy to read. Serif fonts, with small lines connecting to the letters, have a more classic look. Sans serif fonts (without lines) present a more modern look. Figure 17 shows common fonts and sizes for business documents. On the job, choose the one most often used at the company.

Figure 17 Common Fonts and Sizes for Business Documents

Serif Fonts
Cambria 12
Georgia 12
Times New Roman 12

Sans Serif Fonts
Arial 10
Calibri 11
Verdana 10

Distinguish headings and subheadings with larger fonts, bold text, and different colors. Use all capital letters for some titles, but avoid overuse, which could appear as shouting.[25] You also may use italics for emphasis and underlining, although the lines may be perceived as hyperlinks.

Break up text with graphics when you need to illustrate points. Text can flow around images, but place graphics against margins instead of in the middle of the page to avoid interrupting a sentence. For business, typically avoid adding photos and other elements just for visual appeal; they could detract from your message. Instead, create or find meaningful graphics that help your reader understand your main points.

4-5c Web Design

For web design, many of these same suggestions apply. Because web pages have less text and more graphics, C.R.A.P. principles—contrast, repetition, alignment, and proximity—are more evident and may be even more important than in a written document. Two jobs are popular for ensuring proper web design. User interface (UI) designers create the look-and-feel for web pages and apps, while user experience (UX) designers evaluate users' interactions, for example, how easy a site is to navigate.[26]

Eye-tracking software tells us how users read a web page and, therefore, where to place important information. Common patterns, depending on page content, are shown in Figure 18. Users' eyes typically follow the F-Pattern when reading text-heavy pages and the Z-Pattern when more elements are introduced. When users follow the Z-Pattern, they see all four quadrants on a page and probably won't miss anything. Of course, these patterns are drawn for languages that are read from left to right and may be reversed for other languages.[27]

When content is presented in distinct cells on a web page, eyes often follow a lawn-mower pattern. Users begin in the top left cell, travel to the right, and then drop down to the next row, as you would when mowing a lawn.[28]

The Gutenberg Diagram shows another way users might read a content-heavy website. In this scanning pattern, you see that users might miss important elements at the top-right and the bottom-left of the screen—the fallow areas. However, you can disrupt this pattern with visual cues, as Amazon does.[29]

Figure 18 | Reading Patterns

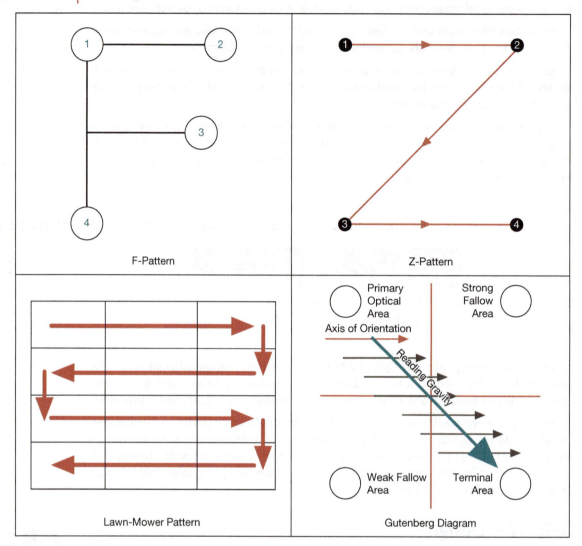

F-Pattern

Z-Pattern

Lawn-Mower Pattern

Primary Optical Area

Strong Fallow Area

Axis of Orientation

Reading Gravity

Weak Fallow Area

Terminal Area

Gutenberg Diagram

Go to any Amazon product page and you'll see that it follows the Gutenberg Diagram. An image of the product is shown top-left, and the "Buy Now" and "Add to Cart" buttons are in the strong fallow area, drawing the user's eye (and mouse click) to this quadrant, so that nothing is missed. Users fixate and click on "buy" buttons more quickly when they are placed in this quadrant or in the terminal area.[30] Squint your eyes on any Amazon product page, and you'll see what is most visible.

Website and app design raises ethical questions. The Robinhood investment app has been criticized for leading users too aggressively through the process of buying stock. A computer scientist describes an example:

> For instance, once you start a trade on Robinhood, it is easier to move forward than to back out of it.
>
> [Although] confirming the purchase requires a swipe up, there is no clear cancel button. To back out of a trade, the user has to press a link labeled 'edit' on the top-left corner and then press an X button.[31]

Website builders make it easy to create well-designed pages. Wix, Squarespace, Duda, and GoDaddy are just a few options, and many are free for basic features.[32]

4-6 Revising and Proofreading

LO6 Apply steps to revise and proofread a business message.

Much of your writing will happen during the **revising** stage, when you modify your draft to make improvements. Revising involves checking content, style, and correctness. After you spend time revising, you can proofread your message and then send it off to your readers.

4-6a Revising

How much time you spend revising depends on the importance of the message and your time constraints. For important writing projects and when possible, put your draft away for some time—the longer, the better. This break helps you distance yourself from your writing. If you revise immediately, you'll remember what you meant to say rather than what you actually wrote, which may prevent you from spotting errors.

Also consider asking coworkers for feedback, so you get a more objective point of view. This demonstrates humility—your perspective-taking ability and your willingness to admit that you can do better. This step may prevent embarrassment for you and your company.

Revising for Content

To revise for content, first reread your purpose statement and then the entire draft to get an overview of your message. Imagine yourself as the reader and answer these questions:

- Is the purpose of the message clear?
- Is the content appropriate for the purpose?
- Is the content sensitive to how the reader might react?
- Are main points up front and sequenced logically?
- Is all the information necessary?
- Is important information missing?
- Is the message cohesive?

Although you may be proud of your first draft, don't be afraid of making changes to improve your writing, even if it means striking out whole sections and starting over. The goal is to produce the best possible message.

Revising for Style

Read each paragraph again (out loud, if possible). Reading out loud gives you a feel for the rhythm and flow of your writing. Long sentences that made sense as you wrote them may leave you out of breath when you read them out loud. Also check for clarity and tone. Could parts of the message be misinterpreted—or be considered offensive or off-putting?

Revising for Correctness

Editing, ensuring that the writing conforms to standard English, requires your detailed attention. Editing involves checking for correctness—identifying problems with grammar, spelling, punctuation, and word usage.

Unfortunately, you can't rely solely on your computer's grammar and spellchecker or other programs. These tools aren't 100% accurate, and they miss the context of your writing. Take responsibility to catch your own errors that may reflect negatively on your credibility or cause misunderstandings.

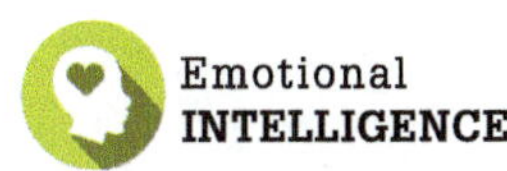

Do you take time to proofread? If not, what gets in the way? Try to be honest about the obstacles: lack of planning, procrastination, not feeling good about your writing, or something else.

4-6b Proofreading

Proofreading is the final quality-control check for your message. Business readers may judge errors harshly, believing that the writer doesn't know what is correct or didn't take the time to find out. Errors may reflect poorly on your character. A sign outside the Portage Community Education Center in Michigan read, "Our teachers make a differance."[33] That was embarrassing.

Proofread for content, typographical, and formatting errors:

- **Content errors.** Was any material omitted unintentionally? As you revise, you may move, delete, or duplicate text. Check to be sure that your message makes sense.
- **Typographical errors.** Next, read through your message slowly, checking for typographical errors. Look carefully for hard-to-spot errors (see Figure 19).
- **Formatting errors.** Visually inspect the message for format. Are all the parts included and in the correct position? Does the message look attractive on the page or online?

Figure 19 | Proofreading Tips

Look for Hard-to-Spot Errors

- Misused words that spellcheckers won't flag—for example, *form* instead of *from*.
- Repeated or omitted words—for example, articles (*the*, *a*, *an*).
- Proper names and numbers.
- Titles and headings, particularly if you use "all caps," which some spellcheckers skip (although you can change this option).

Catch More Errors

- Proofread important writing in print, not on your monitor, laptop, or phone.
- Print on yellow or pink paper to see your work differently.
- Wait a few hours or overnight after your last revision before you start proofreading.
- Use a ruler to guide and slow down your eyes as you proofread.
- Read backward, one sentence at a time.

After you make changes, be sure to proofread again. By correcting one mistake, you might inadvertently introduce another. You're finished proofreading only when you read through the entire message without making any changes. For important messages, consider asking someone else to proofread your writing as well.

4-7 Chapter Closing

Over time, you'll develop your own process of writing and designing business messages. With more experience and confidence, you'll learn to write efficiently yet avoid taking shortcuts that could damage your credibility and relationship with your reader. Your reader will view you as someone who cares about their needs and presents information in a way that values their time.

On its website, State Farm leads the user through the enrollment process—"3 Easy Steps"—for the Steer Clear safe driver discount. As you will learn in the next chapter, the writing style works well for the purpose and audience—and doesn't detract from the company's objective, which is to sell more car insurance.

Encourage State Farm Web Writers to Change the Text

Consider the chapter introduction, which described State Farm's "Steer Clear" program for young drivers. Imagine that you're the head of the sales department and have heard several callers complain that drivers must carry State Farm insurance to be eligible for the program.

You plan to talk with the web writers about the situation and ask them to consider being more explicit about this requirement. Using the CAM model, what questions might you ask yourself before speaking with the group?

››› CHARACTER CHECK

1. **What is my role as sales department leader?**
   I want to support the company's sales process and encourage people to carry our insurance, but I also don't want people to feel misled. When some people find out that they must be State Farm customers—and cancel their current policy—they get angry.
2. **Can I be humble and admit I may be wrong?**
   Yes, because I don't have data to support my view: I can't say what percentage of people are turned off compared to the percentage that buy insurance. Also, if text on the website states that State Farm insurance is required, I don't know how many fewer people, if any, would call about the program. But I know we make some people angry, and it puts my sales associates in an awkward position. It takes courage for me to address this situation with another department.

››› AUDIENCE ANALYSIS

1. **What is my relationship with the audience?**
   Sales and marketing departments often have a healthy tension. More typically, the sales department is pushing the marketing department to exaggerate benefits or downplay costs. In this case, it's the opposite.
2. **What do I know about the audience, and how might they react?**
   The web writers are expert marketers, and I should be careful about questioning their knowledge and intention. They might believe that the requirement is obvious: of course, people have to have State Farm insurance in order to get the discount. They might feel frustrated or disrespected. The group is also busy with web updates, and this would be another project for them.

>>> MESSAGE AND MEDIUM

1. **What are the main points of my message?**
   I'll explain what the reps have experienced with callers and identify the web text that is causing problems.
2. **In what medium will I communicate the message?**
   A video meeting is probably best because the web writers work remotely, and I can share my screen to show the current text and proposed new text.

Revise State Farm Website

〈 IN PRACTICE

Imagine that you're one of the State Farm web writers, and you'll rewrite text shown in the chapter opening to be more explicit: to take advantage of the "Steer Clear" program, drivers need State Farm insurance.

››› CHARACTER CHECK

1. How do you feel about the original wording? What do you see as the impact of revising the text?
2. How do you feel about the change? It's fine to be opposed to or ambivalent about the change.

››› AUDIENCE ANALYSIS

1. Who are your primary and secondary audiences for the web page?
2. What do you know about each?
3. What information does your audience need in order to make an informed decision about the program?

››› MESSAGE AND MEDIUM

1. Draft new text for the home page. How can you be clearer about the requirements and still make a sale?
2. In addition to text on the website, how, if at all, would the change affect the graphics?

REFLECTING ON YOUR COMMUNICATION AND CHARACTER DEVELOPMENT

1. **Reflect on your writing history and confidence level.**
   What has been your experience with writing? Think about a few pivotal projects or assignments throughout your life. What feedback have you received about your writing from family, friends, coworkers, classmates, and instructors?

   How have these experiences shaped your confidence level? What are some older messages about your writing that may no longer be true?

   How does your business writing differ from your academic writing experience? About which do you feel more confident? How can you transfer skills from one to the other?

2. **Assess how you feel about writing.**
   In Figure 20, rate how you feel about your writing.[34]

Figure 20 | How Do You Feel About Your Writing?

Statement	Rating Disagree Strongly … Agree Strongly
1. I avoid writing.	1 2 3 4 5 6 7
2. I fear my writing being evaluated.	1 2 3 4 5 6 7
3. I am apprehensive when I have to write something professional or for evaluation.	1 2 3 4 5 6 7
4. I dislike having my friends read what I write.	1 2 3 4 5 6 7
5. Writing is not fun.	1 2 3 4 5 6 7
6. I dislike seeing my thoughts written out.	1 2 3 4 5 6 7

   When you finish, consider how your responses affect your writing. How can you dispel negative messages and shift your thinking about yourself and your writing? What would a compassionate friend say to you? For example, "You have improved over time and will continue to improve during this class."

3. **Document your writing process.**
   As you're working through your next writing assignment, document how you spend time and how confident you feel at each step of the writing process. Use the chart in Figure 21.

Figure 21 | Document Your Writing Process

WRITING PROCESS STEP	HOW MUCH TIME I'M SPENDING	HOW CONFIDENT I FEEL Not at all … Very
Audience Analysis		1 2 3 4 5
Planning		1 2 3 4 5
Drafting		1 2 3 4 5
Designing		1 2 3 4 5
Revising		1 2 3 4 5
Proofreading		1 2 3 4 5

You might have guessed that there are no right or wrong answers for how much time is appropriate at each step; this will vary for everyone and every writing project. You also may complete this matrix for another project or two—shorter and longer ones.

When you look at your time spent, what does it tell you? If you spent most of your time planning, maybe that is just what you needed to do. If you feel that writing is a slow, difficult process for you, can you reframe your thinking to accept that writing *is* a slow process—for everyone who wants to write well?

When you assess confidence level, try to hone in on areas that you want to improve so you banish negative thinking about *all* aspects of your writing. Do you have trouble organizing your ideas but feel proficient at revising or proofreading your work? Or maybe you have an easy time drafting—letting your ideas flow—but struggle with design?

On the other hand, if you're a fast writer, what does that say about you and your writing process? Perhaps you're not spending enough time revising your writing to improve the finished product. Do you need to slow down some steps of the process to create a better product?

4. **Analyze writer's block.**

   After you complete the first three exercises, consider why you experience writer's block, if you do. What could be getting in your way of enjoying the writing process more?

5. **Identify obstacles to audience analysis.**

   Do you tend to rush through the process of analyzing your audience? Do you sometimes feel as though you know best what information to include and how to present it? If so, what could prevent you from getting an outside view? Consider suggestions from Chapter 3 about shifting your mindset. Try to practice curiosity, humility, and perspective taking.

6. **Free-write about your writing.**

   Spend 10 minutes freewriting—continuously, without judgment—about a current assignment. How do you feel about the assignment and your work so far? What issues are you facing? What are your plans for the next step in the process?[35] Save a minute or so to write about how the freewriting affects your work and your feelings about your work.

DEVELOPING YOUR BUSINESS COMMUNICATION SKILLS

BUSINESS WRITING PROCESS OVERVIEW

LO1 Describe steps in the business writing process.

1. **Describe steps in the writing process.**

   Review the Peloton situation and email in Figure 3. Imagine that you're an executive coach for the CEO of Peloton. Describe the steps in the writing process that he should take to ensure that future messages are tailored to specific audiences. Explain how the writing process would avoid future communication issues.

2. **Identify missing steps.**

   Find a company message you consider to be a failure. What steps in the writing process may have been missed? For example, is the purpose not specific; the audience not well defined; the organization unclear; or the message cluttered, unclear, or riddled with errors? On which step should the writer have spent more time and attention?

AUDIENCE ANALYSIS

LO2 Answer five questions to analyze a business audience.

3. **Analyze a new wealth management client.**

   Imagine that you work for a wealth management firm, which manages financial assets for individuals. You have a prospective new client, whose previous financial manager was her brother-in-law, who recently retired. Looking at her portfolio, you realize that she's heavily invested in just one stock, which you believe is too risky. This is a tricky situation because you want her to choose you as her manager, and her history is with a close family member.

In small groups, discuss the five questions for analyzing your audience. How does the information you gathered affect your approach in telling this client that her asset mix should change in order to reduce her risk exposure?

4. **Decide how to communicate with multiple audiences.**

   Your college is merging with another local college. Identify the many audiences affected by this decision—both internal and external to the college. Who needs to know about the change?

   Once you have identified these groups, decide which audiences need to receive different messages. One way to decide is to analyze each audience, the information they need, and how they might react.

5. **Analyze an instructor as the audience.**

   If you were a business communication instructor and received this email from a student, how would you react? Analyze your instructor as an audience for this student's message and consider changes the student might make to achieve the purpose.

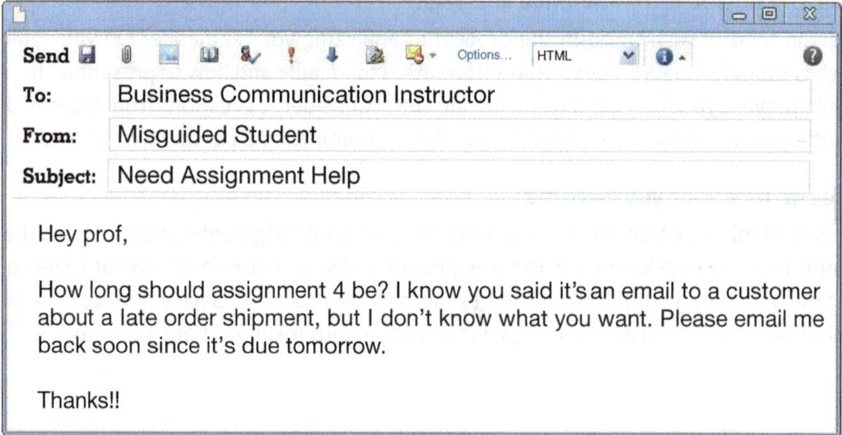

Send Options... HTML

To: Business Communication Instructor

From: Misguided Student

Subject: Need Assignment Help

Hey prof,

How long should assignment 4 be? I know you said it's an email to a customer about a late order shipment, but I don't know what you want. Please email me back soon since it's due tomorrow.

Thanks!!

6. **Analyze audiences for a football team.**

   When a football team changed its name from the Washington Redskins, the leaders had many audiences to consider. Find articles to read more about the story, and then list the audiences who would have an opinion on the situation. Describe how each might have felt about the change.

LO3 Describe one approach to organizing your ideas for a message.

PLANNING

7. **Use coggle.it.**

   Prepare for your next writing assignment by putting your ideas on coggle.it. Use one of their designs without paying. Practice writing freely, organizing your thoughts, and moving main and subpoints around. Share your experience with a classmate.

8. **Identify a message objective and analyze the organization.**

   Find a company message or use one you found for a previous exercise. Write down the specific objective—what did the writer hope to accomplish? Do you believe the message achieved that objective? Why or why not?

   Next, analyze how the message is organized. Is the main point up front? Is the organization logical and easy to follow? How might you reorganize the message for easier reading and a more logical flow?

9. **Identify general-purpose statements and communication objectives for several situations.**

   Read the following situations and write a general-purpose statement and a specific communication objective—the results you want—for each.

   - As the manager of a small retail clothing store, you write an email to let employees know they're getting a $3 per hour wage increase.
   - As the assistant manager of a movie theater, you write an email to tell a customer you found the earring she lost the night before.
   - As a newly hired advertising director, you write an email to the president of the company requesting a 10% increase in your advertising budget.
   - As a CEO, you write a blog post on your investor website about your company's falling stock price.
   - As a marketing manager, you write a letter to customers announcing a new product that will be available in your store starting next month.
   - As a student, you write a letter to your college newspaper editor about the increase in tuition costs.
   - As a warehouse manager, you write an email to an employee who left the facility unlocked last night.

10. **Plan the organization of messages.**

    For the situations in Exercise 9, imagine what the audience reaction might be and write a sequential outline of your points. Explain why you chose the order you did.

11. **Brainstorm new ice cream flavors.**

    Working in groups of three or four—without censoring your ideas—come up with as many new ice cream flavors as you can. Make a list of all the suggestions, and then share your list with the other groups in the class. How does your list compare to other groups' lists? How big is the combined list? Which group generated the most ideas? What do they believe contributed to their success?

12. **Organize a product review.**

    Prepare to write a review of a product you used or purchased recently. Use the process outlined in this chapter:

    - Brainstorm ideas. What do you think is important to include in your review? Draw a mind map.
    - Create a hierarchy of ideas. How will you organize your main and supporting points?
    - Develop an outline. Write a more detailed, sequential plan for the product review.

DRAFTING

LO4 Identify differences between writing emails and writing for the web.

13. **Write a draft product review.**

    Now that you have your outline for Exercise 12, draft your product review. Practice freewriting for this activity to avoid moving to the revision stage too quickly. Don't worry about formatting for this exercise; just practice moving from an outline to a written document.

14. **Write a draft email to your organization members.**

    Using the principles discussed for effective email communication, write a draft email to members of an organization to which you belong. This can be real or imagined—a sports team, fraternity or sorority, hobby club, religious group, or nonprofit organization.

    Your purpose is to move some of your meetings online. You may choose the schedule—every other meeting, once a month, or whatever makes sense for the organization.

Provide enough reasons to convince the other members that this is a good decision. You believe this will save travel and meeting time because you'll work more efficiently. Invent whatever details you need to make your email realistic.

When you're finished, compare your email to a classmate's. How do they differ, and how are they similar? What are the best aspects of each?

15. Write a company memo to announce a new organizational structure.

Imagine that you just acquired a company and plan to bring in an entirely new management team—five of your classmates. In a separate message to employees, you have communicated the rationale for the changes. Now, you would like to introduce your new team to the rest of the organization.

Write a two-page memo. After a brief introduction, in which you refer to previous communications about the change, include one short paragraph (about 50 words) for each of the five new executive team members. In each paragraph, include the following information: executive's name, new title, and previous experience. Invent whatever details you would like.

16. Format a letter.

You have just finished collecting donations for the American Cancer Society. To thank people for donating, you will send individual letters. Using guidelines in this chapter and in the Reference Manual, format your letter. You do not need to write the letter; just create the template with the date, addresses, salutation, and closing. You may create your own letterhead or use a standard return address.

17. Write blog posts.

Imagine that you work for your favorite company and have been asked to write a few entries on their blog. Write three short posts (about 50 words each). Write one post about an upcoming national holiday, one post to promote a product or service, and one post to link to a recent news story about the company. Use the principles for writing for the web and try to optimize the search results.

18. Improve SEO of a blog.

With a small group, select a keyword that interests you. Search for the word in any search engine and analyze the results. When you follow pages that rank highly, note how they use the word, for example, in headings and content. What other features of the site mentioned in this chapter could influence the ranking?[36]

19. Evaluate a website for accessibility.

Look at one of your favorite websites. Evaluate whether the site meets accessibility guidelines outlined in this chapter. What criteria are met, and what, if anything, should the designers do to make the page more inclusive?

LO5 Explain four principles for designing documents and websites.

DESIGNING

20. Evaluate a website for design.

Look at the same website you evaluated in Exercise 19. Now consider the design. Which reading pattern seems to drive the design? Where are the most important elements, and how does the design draw your eye to them? Finally, consider the overall look and feel. Do you find it attractive and inviting? Why or why not?

21. Find examples of contrast, alignment, repetition, and proximity.

Browse a few websites to find good examples of contrast, alignment, repetition, and proximity. With a small group, discuss how these principles improve the site design and your user experience.

22. Redesign a document.

Find a dense document that has little white space and few headings or graphics. You might look at a legal court filing, a company's privacy statement, or an apartment lease. How could you redesign the document to include principles from this chapter? If you can, import the document into an editable form, so you can redesign it on your computer. Otherwise, make notes about what you would suggest the writer do to improve the readability.

REVISING AND PROOFREADING

LO6 Apply steps to revise and proofread a business message.

23. Revise your email to organization members.

Revise your draft email to the student organization (from Exercise 14). What changes will you make to improve the message? Follow these steps for the revision process:

a. Read the email once, revising for content. Make sure that all needed information—and no unnecessary information—is included for the audience. Check the sequencing.

b. Read the email a second time, revising for style. Make sure that the words, sentences, paragraphs, and overall tone are appropriate. How might the readers react?

c. Read the email a third time, revising for correctness. Make sure that grammar, punctuation, and word choice are error free.

24. Revise another student's email.

Exchange draft emails (from Exercise 23) with other students in class (so that you're not revising the paper of the person who is revising yours). Using the process described in Exercise 23, revise the other student's message, and then return the draft to the writer with your suggestions.

25. Revise a previous message.

Bring in a one-page message (email, memo, or letter) you have written in the past. Exchange papers with other students (so that you're not revising the paper of the person who is revising yours). Spend a few minutes asking the writer to give you background information about the message: purpose, audience, and so on. Then, follow the three-step revision process described in Exercise 23.

Return the paper to the writer. Then, using the suggestions, prepare a final version of the message. You don't have to take every suggestion; just those you believe will improve your message. Submit both the marked-up version and the final version of your paper to your instructor. For each suggestion that you didn't accept, write a short note about why you decided to ignore it.

26. Proofread a letter.

Proofread the following lines of a letter using the line numbers to indicate the position of each error. Proofread for content, typographical errors, and format. For each error, indicate by a "yes" or "no" whether the error would have been identified by a computer's spelling checker. How many errors can you find?

1. April 31 2022
2. Mr. Thomas Johnson, Manger
3. JoAnn @ Friends, Inc.
4. 1323 Charleston Avenue
5. Minneapolis, MI 55402
6. Dear Mr. Thomas:
7. As a writing consultant, I have often asked auld-
8. iences to locate all the errors in this letter.

9. I am always surprised if the find all the errors.
10. The result being that we all need more practical
11. Advise in how to proof read.
12. To avoid these types of error, you must ensure that
13. That you review your documents carefully. I have
14. Prepared the enclosed exercises for each of you
15. To in your efforts at JoAnne & Friend's, Inc.
16. Would you be willing to try this out on you own
17. Workers and let me know the results.
18. Sincerely Yours
19. Mr. Michael Land,
20. Writing Consultant

27. Proofread a job posting.

Review the following passage and see how many errors you can find. Look for spelling, formatting, and punctuation errors.

Finance Management Trainee

Program Overview
Bank on Me; a financial services company based in NYC; is now recruit a select number of candidates for its finance management training program. This is a comprehensive two year financial training program to provide you with experience in the magor financial areas of the bank.

In addition to ongoing classroom training, the trainees complete projects in one or more of the following area:

- Analyzing and reporting on internal operations
- Forecasting financial trends
- Developing models and performing financial analyze of investments
- Supporting the corporations internal planning and management accounting functions
- Prepare external reports for shareholders and regulatory authorities
- Providing guidance on accounting policy issues and/or taxation issues

Position Qualification

- Associates or bachelors degre
- Financial course work
- At least on summer of finance related experience
- Minimum 3.5 GPA
- Demonstrated leadership experience
- Spanish language, a plus
- Microsoft Excel proficiency
- Strong communication skills
- Excellent attention detail

About Bank on Me
Founded in 1964, Bank on Me offer consumer and commercial banking services at 630 branches throughout the North east U.S. We offer personal and busines checking accounts, loans, credit cards, and other financial products. We also provide home loans and assistance to commercial property owners and investors. At Bank on Me we prid ourselves on superior customer service and have won several service awards that demonstrate this commitment.

Contact Information
Please send your cover letter and resume to the following:
Marley Catona
Recruting Officer
Bank on Me
555 New York Ave.
New York, NY 10022

CHAPTER SUMMARY

LO1 Describe steps in the business writing process.

The writing process varies for everyone, depending on their preferences and the project, but most writers find it helpful to follow separate steps. Spend time analyzing your audience, planning, drafting, designing, revising, and proofreading.

LO2 Answer five questions to analyze a business audience.

Before writing, carefully analyze your audience. Identify who the audience is (both primary and secondary), determine what the audience already knows, consider your relationship with the audience, anticipate the audience's likely reaction, and identify any unique characteristics of the audience.

LO3 Describe one approach to organizing your ideas for a message.

Identify the general purpose and then the specific objective of your message. Based on your audience analysis, determine what information to include and in what order. Consider brainstorming, creating a mind map, or writing an outline to develop and organize your ideas.

LO4 Identify differences between writing emails and writing for the web.

Select an appropriate environment for drafting and schedule enough time. Concentrate on getting the information down without worrying about style, correctness, or format. Adjust your writing for different media. Follow conventions for email, memos, and letters. When writing for the web, follow guidelines for developing content, optimizing search results, and improving accessibility.

LO5 Explain four principles for designing documents and websites.

When designing documents and writing for the web, follow guidelines for contrast, alignment, repetition, and proximity. Include white space and professional fonts for a clean look and easy reading. Design web pages that help people navigate easily.

LO6 Apply steps to revise and proofread a business message.

Revise for content, style, and correctness. Leave a time gap between writing and revising the draft. When you proofread, read through your message carefully to catch content, typographical, and formatting errors. Consider asking someone else for feedback as you revise and proofread.

Endnotes

1. Grace Kim, "State Farm Steer Clear Review," *MSN*, February 8, 2021, www.msn.com/en-us/money/personalfinance/state-farm-steer-clear-review/ar-BB136VWb, accessed February 4, 2021.
2. "Steer Clear," State Farm Website, www.statefarm.com/insurance/auto/discounts/steer-clear, accessed February 4, 2021.
3. Kim.
4. Matthew J. Baker, "Pain or Gain?: How Business Communication Students Perceive the Outlining Process," *Business and Professional Communication Quarterly* 82 (2019): 273–296.
5. Chip Heath and Dan Heath, "The Curse of Knowledge," *Harvard Business Review*, December 2006, https://hbr.org/2006/12/the-curse-of-knowledge, accessed February 7, 2021.
6. Baker.
7. "Email Statistics Report," The Radicati Group, Inc., www.radicati.com/wp/wp-content/uploads/2015/02/Email-Statistics-Report-2015-2019-Executive-Summary.pdf, accessed February 12, 2021.
8. Shannon L. Marlow, Christina N. Lacerenza, and Chelsea Iwig, "The Influence of Textual Cues on First Impressions of an Email Sender," *Business and Professional Communication Quarterly* 81 (2018): 149–166.
9. Stephanie Kelly, "Writing Effective Emails," in Stephanie Kelly (ed.), *Computer-Mediated Communication in Business: Theory and Practice* (Newcastle upon Tyne, UK: Cambridge Scholars, 2019), p. 121.
10. Kelly, p. 126.
11. Giselle Abramovich, "If You Think Email Is Dead, Think Again," Adobe Blog, September 8, 2019, https://blog.adobe.com/en/publish/2019/09/08/if-you-think-email-is-dead--think-again.html, accessed February 12, 2021.
12. Andrew Quagliata, "Get Out of Your Inbox," Blog Post, October 3, 2019, andrewquagliata.com, accessed February 12, 2021, and Matt Plummer, "How to Spend Less Time on Email Every Day," *Harvard Business Review*, January 22, 2019, https://hbr.org/2019/01/how-to-spend-way-less-time-on-email-every-day, accessed February 12, 2021.
13. Thomas Jackson, Ray Dawson, and Darren Wilson, "The Cost of Email Interruption," *Journal of Systems and Information Technology* 5 (2001): 85–92, https://repository.lboro.ac.uk/articles/journal_contribution/The_cost_of_email_interruption_/9402233, accessed June 28, 2021.
14. Ofer Bergman, "The Effect of Folder Structure on Personal File Navigation," *Journal of the American Society for Information Science and Technology* 61 (2010): 2426–2441.
15. Ed Bastian, "CEO Employee Memo: Protecting Our Future," *Delta*, May 14, 2020, https://news.delta.com/ceo-employee-memo-protecting-our-future, accessed February 12, 2021.
16. "How People Read Online: New and Old Findings," Nielsen Norman Group, April 5, 2020, https://www.nngroup.com/articles/how-people-read-online, accessed February 16, 2021.
17. Adapted from "Writing for the Web," usability.gov, accessed February 16, 2021.
18. Choice Hotels Homepage, choicehotels.com, accessed February 16, 2021.
19. Jenna Pack Sheffield, "Search Engine Optimization and Business Communication Instruction: Interviews with Experts," *Business and Professional Communication Quarterly* 83 (2020): 153–183.
20. "People with Disabilities on the Web," WebAIM, https://webaim.org/intro/, accessed February 13, 2021.
21. "Developing Accessible Websites," University of Washington, www.washington.edu/accessibility/web/, accessed February 13, 2021.
22. "How to Meet WCAG (Quick Reference)," W3C Web Accessibility Initiative, www.w3.org/WAI/WCAG21/quickref/, accessed February 13, 2021.
23. "Principles of Accessible Design," WebAIM, https://webaim.org/intro/, accessed February 13, 2021.
24. Robin Williams, *The Non-Designer's Design Book* (Berkeley, CA: Peachpit Press, 2014).
25. "All caps" are not necessarily harder to read, as previously believed. See, for example, Kevin Larson, "The Science of Word Recognition," Microsoft Typography Blog, https://docs.microsoft.com/en-us/typography/develop/word-recognition, February 5, 2018, accessed February 13, 2021, and Susan Weinschenk, "100 Things You Should Know About People: #19 - It's a Myth That All Capital Letters Are Inherently Harder to Read," The Team W Blog, December 23, 2009, accessed February 13, 2021.
26. "What Is UI Design? What Is UX Design? UI vs UX: What's the Difference," UX Planet, February 24, 2019, https://uxplanet.org/what-is-ui-vs-ux-design-and-the-difference-d9113f6612de, accessed February 14, 2021.
27. Doaa Farouk Badawy Eldesouky, "Visual Hierarchy and Mind Motion in Advertising Design," *Journal of Arts and Humanities* 2 (2013): 148–162.
28. "How People Read Online: New and Old Findings," Nielsen Norman Group, April 5, 2020, https://www.nngroup.com/articles/how-people-read-online, accessed February 16, 2021.
29. Eldesouky.
30. Ania Hernandez and Marc L. Resnick, "Placement of Call to Action Buttons for Higher Website Conversion and Acquisition: An Eye Tracking Study," Proceedings of the Human Factors and Ergonomics Society 57th Annual Meeting (2013), https://jourals.sagepub.com/doi/pdf/10.1177/1541931213571232, accessed February 13, 2021.
31. Michael Wursthorn and Euirim Choi, "Does Robinhood Make It Too Easy to Trade?: From Free Stocks to Confetti," *The Wall Street Journal*, August 20, 2020, www.wsj.com/articles/confetti-free-stocks-does-robinhoods-design-make-trading-too-easy-11597915801, accessed February 13, 2021.
32. Jeffrey L. Wilson, "The Best Website Builders for 2021," *PC Magazine*, December 16, 2020, www.pcmag.com/picks/the-best-website-builders, accessed February 13, 2021.

33. "Spelling Can Make a Huge 'Difference,'" Pinterest Image, www.pinterest.com/pin/714735403357013518/, accessed February 12, 2021.
34. Measure from Hamlet Autman and Stephanie Kelly, "Reexamining the Writing Apprehension Measure," *Business and Professional Communication Quarterly* 80 (2017): 516–529.
35. Thanks to Holly Lawrence for this idea in "Personal, Reflective Writing: A Pedagogical Strategy for Teaching Business Students to Write," *Business Communication Quarterly* 76 (2013): 192–206.
36. From Jenna Pack Sheffield, "Search Engine Optimization and Business Communication Instruction: Interviews with Experts," *Business and Professional Communication Quarterly* 83 (2020): 153–183.

CHAPTER

5

Improving Your Writing Style

Learning Objectives

After you have finished this chapter, you should be able to

LO1 Identify four principles of writing style.

LO2 Explain ways to choose the best words for a business message.

LO3 Write three types of sentences.

LO4 Describe components of a logical paragraph.

LO5 Compare examples of appropriate and inappropriate tone.

"*We love our fans more than anything, but you should know that the demogorgon is not always as forgiving. So please don't make us call your mom.*"[1]

—Netflix attorney

Chapter Introduction

Netflix Attorney Writes a Fun Cease-and-Desist Letter

We typically don't think of lawyer letters as fun, but Netflix gives us a good example of a natural, light-hearted tone despite the serious subject.

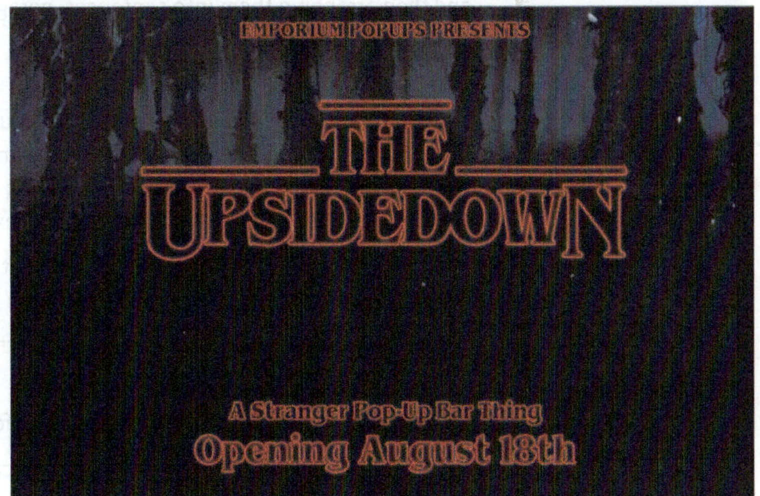

A bar uses the *Stranger Things* theme.

The Upside Down, a pop-up bar in Chicago, used the Netflix series *Stranger Things* as its theme. Featuring Christmas lights, waffles on a table bolted to the ceiling, the family sofa, and themed drinks,[2] the bar is more than a nod to the hit show.

Companies write "cease-and-desist" letters to demand that people or businesses stop using their brand or imagery. Most letters are threatening and, as one lawyer notes, "pretty boring."[3] But here's an excerpt from the Netflix letter:

> Look, I don't want you to think I'm a total wastoid, and I love how much you guys love the show. . . . But unless I'm living in the Upside Down, I don't think we did a deal with you for this pop-up.[4]

Business communicators often get the best results, and build better relationships, by writing naturally.

LO1 Identify four principles of writing style.

5-1 Developing Writing Style

When you think of "style," what comes to mind? Designer clothes? A Tesla? A good haircut? At W Hotels, housekeepers are called "room stylists."[5] They clean and arrange items to make a guestroom functional and appealing. When you style your business writing, you're working toward a clear, professional message for your audience. You also reveal your character by paying attention to your writing and to your reader.

When we talk about writing **style**, we mean how an idea is expressed. Style is everything but the content (or the message substance) and mechanics. **Mechanics** are elements in communication that show up only in writing, for example, spelling, punctuation, abbreviations, and capitalization. In this chapter, you'll learn to create an effective style by choosing the best words and then arranging them into sentences, paragraphs, and complete messages.

5-1a Style and Character

CHARACTER

In discovering your own style, you convey your character. Readers come to know you through your writing. Throughout this chapter, you learn about a natural, conversational style—as if you were talking with your audience directly. This approach builds a relationship with your reader and conveys your credibility. Compare these examples.

☒ NOT As the company founder, I do not want to change the business plan to incorporate your suggestions at this point in time.

☑ BUT I'm concerned that changing the business plan now will delay our chances for funding.

☒ NOT The applicant did not include references, so we will not accept the application.

☑ BUT We'll accept the application when we get references.

Style is also a matter of character because we focus on our audience instead of on ourselves, as you see in the second examples above. We choose good style to appeal to our audience rather to inflate or obscure our own position. At work, we follow conventions to make our writing easier to read and understand, but we don't talk down to our readers.

Emotional INTELLIGENCE

Do you have a particular writing style? If so, how would you describe it, and what does it say about you?

5-1b Principles of Style

In what ways does the thank-you email in Figure 1, based on a real email, lack style? The email is grammatically correct and easy to read, but what's the problem? What might it say about the writer's character?

Figure 1 Thank-You Email Lacking Style

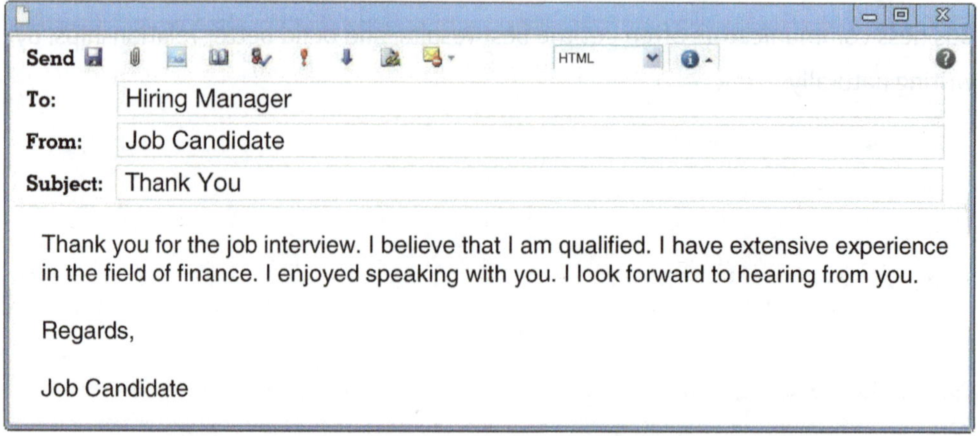

Compare Figure 1 to Figure 2, which oozes style. From her book *Year of Yes*, Shonda Rhimes, who created *Grey's Anatomy* and *Scandal* and produced *Bridgerton*, writes about her own writing process.[6,7] Although not a business writing example, we see Rhimes's attention to word choice, sentence structure, paragraph organization, and tone. Her choices are deliberate and engage the reader. These same principles apply to creating style in business writing, as shown in Figure 3.

Figure 2 Writing Excerpt with Style

> "Without ever committing to a plan, without ever actively trying, without ever realizing it is going to happen, the storyteller inside me steps forward and solves the problem. My inner liar leaps in to take over my brain and begins to spin the yarns. Begins to just . . . fill in the blank space. To paint over the nothingness. To close the gaps and connect the dots."
>
> —Shonda Rhimes

Figure 3 Principles of Style

Words	Sentences	Paragraphs	Tone
• Write clearly. • Write concisely.	• Use a variety of sentence types. • Use active and passive voice appropriately. • Use parallel structure.	• Keep paragraphs unified and coherent. • Control paragraph length.	• Find your own professional, conversational voice. • Convey a confident, courteous, sincere tone. • Stress positive language and the "you" attitude.

5-2 Choosing the Best Words

LO2 Explain ways to choose the best words for a business message.

As the building blocks for writing, words can make or break your message. Clear, concise writing is essential for business communication.

5-2a Write Clearly

The most basic guideline for writing is to write clearly—to write messages the reader can understand and act on. You can achieve clarity by following these guidelines:

- Be accurate and complete.
- Use simple words.
- Use specific, concrete language.
- Avoid dangling expressions.
- Avoid clichés, slang, and unnecessary jargon.

Be Accurate and Complete

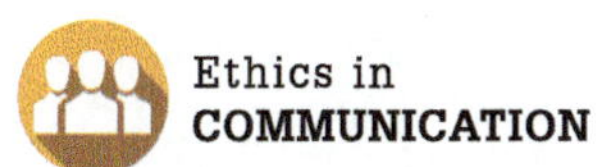

Your credibility as a writer depends on the accuracy of your message. If a writer is careless, doesn't prepare, or intentionally misleads the reader, the damage is immediate and long lasting. The headlines in Figure 4 use correct grammar, but are they accurate?[8]

Figure 4 | Unintentionally Funny Headlines

Students Cook and Serve Grandparents
Red Tape Holds Up New Bridge
Homicide Victims Rarely Talk to Police
Journalists Say Voters Hold Key to November Election
Hospitals Resort to Hiring Doctors
"We Hate Math," Say 4 in 10—A Majority of Americans
City Unsure Why the Sewer Smells
Federal Agents Raid Gun Shop, Find Weapons
Marijuana Issue Sent to a Joint Committee

The accuracy of a message depends on what is said, how it is said, and what is left unsaid. To demonstrate good character, use judgment to make sure your communication is ethical. The headline "Dow Falls the Most in History"[9] may be technically correct, but if the stock market is at an all-time high before the drop, this could be misleading. As a percentage, the decline might not be that significant.

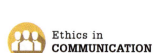

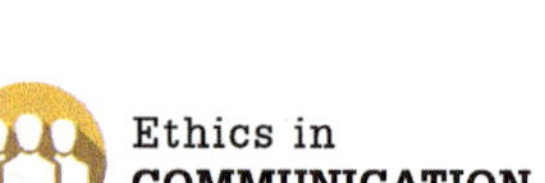

In addition to exaggerating information, inaccurate word choices can downplay events. When Volkswagen was charged with lying to regulators about car emissions, former CEO Martin Winterhorn referred to "irregularities"[10] and said, "We are working very hard on the necessary technical solutions"[11] as if the trouble were caused by a glitch rather than deceit. The company later admitted to installing software to mask emissions.

Closely related to accuracy is completeness. A message that lacks important information may create inaccurate impressions. A message is complete when it contains all the information the reader needs—no more and no less—to react appropriately.

Use Simple Words

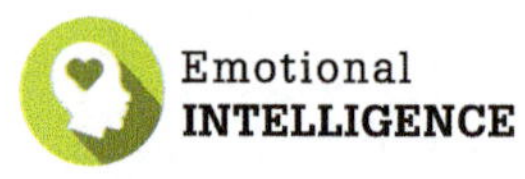

Do you sometimes write to impress? Think about a time when you inflated your word choice, and the audience misunderstood or otherwise had a negative reaction.

To make your message easy to understand, choose simple words that your audience understands. A Princeton University study, "Consequences of Erudite Vernacular Utilized Irrespective of Necessity: Problems with Using Long Words Needlessly," found that undergraduates use more complex words in papers to sound more intelligent. However, according to the researcher, this strategy backfires: "Such writing is reliably judged to come from less intelligent authors."[12]

Short and simple words are more likely to be understood, less likely to be misused, and less likely to distract the reader. Literary authors often write to *impress*; they select words to amuse, excite, or anger. Business writers, on the other hand, write to *express*—to help the reader understand. If you're aware of the writing in a business message, then it's probably distracting you from the main points.

Write approximately as you would speak. The "before" example in Figure 5 uses unnecessarily long words, and the "after" shows simpler choices. The markings, shown using the Track Changes feature in Microsoft Word, are useful when editing your own or a team member's writing. You may use long words, but use them in moderation. And when a shorter word works just as well, choose that one for business writing.

Use Specific, Concrete Language

An abstract word identifies an idea instead of a concrete object. For example, *communication* is an abstract word, but *newspaper* is a concrete word, a word that identifies something you can see or touch. Abstract words are necessary at times, but more specific, concrete language helps the reader visualize what we mean.

Figure 5 Before and After Track Changes

Before Track Changes	After Track Changes
After ascertaining that the modification of the plan was too onerous, we enumerated the substantial number of reasons to terminate the accord. On Tuesday, we'll initiate deliberations to utilize a more undemanding course of action in the future.	After ~~ascertaining~~ learning that ~~the modification of~~ changing the plan was too ~~onerous~~ difficult, we ~~enumerated~~ listed the ~~substantial number of~~ many reasons to ~~terminate~~ end the ~~accord~~ contract. On Tuesday, we'll ~~initiate~~ start ~~deliberations~~ talking about ~~to utilize a more undemanding course of action~~ an easier process ~~in~~ for the future.

Ambiguous words, such as, *a few*, *some*, *several*, and *far away*, may be too broad for business communication. What does ASAP (as soon as possible) mean to you? Does it mean within the hour, by the end of the day, or something else? A more specific deadline—for example, January 14 at 3:00 p.m.—will improve your chances of getting what you need when you need it.

When possible, choose specific words (words that have a definite, unambiguous meaning) and concrete words (words that bring a picture to your reader's mind).

☒ NOT The vehicle broke down several times recently.

☑ BUT The delivery van broke down three times last week.

☒ NOT He became emotional when he didn't get his way.

☑ BUT The user sent a long email in all capital letters when he found out that his data plan changed.

☒ NOT Airbnb will save the planet!

☑ BUT "By staying in Airbnb listings rather than hotels [in one year], Airbnb guests in Europe achieved energy savings equal to that of 826,000 homes and reduced water usage equal to 13,000 Olympic-sized swimming pools."[13]

☒ NOT The vice president was bored by the presentation.

☑ BUT The vice president yawned and looked at her watch during the presentation.

Specific terms tell readers how to react. In the last example, another interpretation of the behavior is that the vice president was tired. Concrete descriptions are more accurate. The Airbnb example, above, translates large numbers by comparing energy savings to something the reader can picture.

Investopedia calculates Apple's market capitalization as more than the gross domestic products of Canada, Brazil, and Italy—and more than three times the U.S. budget deficit. These comparisons are more concrete and understandable than $2.08 trillion.[14]

Other vague words are **euphemisms**, or expressions used to replace words that may be offensive or inappropriate. Sensitive communicators use euphemisms when appropriate; for example, some consider "passed away" more pleasant than "died."

But euphemisms may signal a failing of character—the courage to say what we mean, particularly when it's bad news. Disneyland announced that it was "sunsetting" its Annual Passport program.[15] This is a legal term and a vague description of ending a popular program for park guests.

Euphemisms for firing people have become a corporate joke. Now companies downsize, rightsize, smartsize, rationalize, amortize, reduce, redeploy, reorganize, restructure, offshore, outsource, and outplace. We evade the truth when we overuse euphemisms instead of being more direct.

Avoid Dangling Expressions

A dangling expression is any part of a sentence that doesn't logically fit in with the rest of the sentence. Its relationship with the other parts of the sentence is unclear.

☒ NOT After reading the proposal, a few problems occurred to me. *(As written, the sentence implies that "a few problems" read the proposal.)*

☑ BUT After reading the proposal, I noted a few problems. *(Now, the subject of the sentence is clear: "I" is doing the action stated in the introductory clause.)*

☒ NOT Dr. López gave a presentation on the use of drugs in our auditorium. *(Are drugs being used in the auditorium?)*

☑ BUT Dr. López gave a presentation in our auditorium on the use of drugs. *(By moving "auditorium" closer to "presentation," the writer clarifies what the word is modifying.)*

☒ NOT Yulin explained the proposal to Serena, but she was not happy with it. *(Who is "she"? Who was not happy—Yulin or Serena?)*

☑ BUT Yulin explained the proposal to Serena, but Serena was not happy with it. *(By repeating "Serena," the writer clarifies who was not happy.)*

Avoid Clichés, Slang, and Unnecessary Jargon

People get tired of hearing the same expressions again and again. A cliché is an expression that has become trite through overuse. Because audiences have heard them many times, using clichés may send the message that the writer is unoriginal and couldn't be bothered to tailor the message to the audience.

Avoid these overused expressions in your writing:

According to our records	Our company policy
Thank you for your attention	For your information
If you have any other questions	Please be advised that
Do not hesitate to	Feel free to

Slang is an informal expression, often short-lived, that is identified with a specific group of people. *FOMO* (fear of missing out) and *hangry* (hungry + angry) are two examples that may be outdated by the time you read this.

Business has its own slang. Imagine hearing the expression *throw the baby out with the bathwater* for the first time. In business, we find *low-hanging fruit* for a *quick win*, or we do a *deep dive* or *drill down* into the *customer journey* to *move the needle*—if we have the *bandwidth*. The expressions are dizzying and get tiresome.

Jargon is technical vocabulary used within a special group—sometimes called the "pros' prose." Do you know what these technology terms and acronyms mean?

CRM	FAQ	JPEG	phishing
POS	trojan horse	VoIP	API
thumbnail	VPN	patch	CAD

Closely related to jargon are **buzzwords**, which are important-sounding expressions used mainly to impress other people. Be careful of turning nouns and other types of words into verbs by adding *-ize*: *incentivize*, *operationalize*, *globalize*, *commoditize*, and *maximize*.

Every field has its own specialized words, and jargon offers an efficient way of communicating with people in the same field. But problems arise when jargon is used to exclude someone who doesn't understand it. Consider this advice from Elon Musk, CEO of SpaceX and Tesla:

> Don't use acronyms or nonsense words for objects, software, or processes at Tesla. In general, anything that requires an explanation inhibits communication. We don't want people to have to memorize a glossary just to function at Tesla.[16]

Unclear writing costs money. A study found that company stock trades at lower prices when their annual reports are difficult to read. The lack of clarity causes investors to distrust company leaders and view the stock more negatively.[17]

Research also indicates that writers who avoid jargon and use standard grammar are viewed as more confident.[18] This also was true for writers who avoided unnecessary words, which you learn about next.

5-2b Write Concisely

If you want the attention of businesspeople, who are inundated with email and other content, develop a concise writing style. Demonstrating principles in this chapter, Warren Buffett, CEO of Berkshire Hathaway, revised a passage from a mutual fund prospectus—a document that describes a financial security, or investment (Figure 6).[19] The original version is unclear—and not concise. You'll find redundancies, wordy expressions, hidden verbs and nouns, and other issues you can avoid when you revise.

Revised Mutual Fund Prospectus Excerpt | **Figure 6**

Before

"Maturity and duration management decisions are made in the context of an intermediate maturity orientation. The maturity structure of the portfolio is adjusted in the anticipation of cyclical interest rate changes. Such adjustments are not made in an effort to capture short-term, day to day [sic][20] movements in the market, but instead are implemented in anticipation of longer term [sic], secular shifts in the levels of interest rates (i.e., shifts transcending and/or not inherent to the business cycle). Adjustments made to shorten portfolio maturity and duration are made to limit capital losses during periods when interest rates are expected to rise. Conversely, adjustments made to lengthen maturation for the portfolio's maturity and duration strategy lies in analysis of the U.S. and global economies, focusing on levels of real interest rates, monetary and fiscal policy actions and cyclical indicators."

Words: 136

Sentences: 5 (all passive voice)

Average sentence length: 27.2

After

"We will try to profit by correctly predicting future interest rates. When we have no strong opinion, we will generally hold intermediate-term bonds. But when we expect a major and sustained increase in rates, we will concentrate on shorter-term issues. And, conversely, if we expect a major shift to lower rates, we will buy long-term bonds. We will focus on the big picture and won't make moves based on short-term considerations."

Words: 74

Sentences: 5 (none passive voice)

Average sentence length: 14.8

Do you sometimes add "fluff" to your writing? If so, how can you challenge yourself to develop a more concise style?

Avoid Redundancy and Wordy Expressions

A **redundancy** is the repetition of an idea that has already been expressed or implied. Don't confuse redundancy and repetition. Repetition—using the same word more than once—is occasionally effective for emphasis (as we discuss later). Redundancies, however, serve no purpose and should be avoided.

☒ NOT Signing both copies of the lease is a necessary requirement.

☑ BUT Signing both copies of the lease is necessary.

☒ NOT Combine the ingredients together.

☑ BUT Combine the ingredients.

Not	But
ATM machine	ATM
PIN number	PIN
new innovation	innovation
divide up	divide
any and all	any *or* all
11:00 a.m. in the morning	11:00 a.m.
free gift	gift

Although wordy expressions aren't necessarily writing errors (like redundancies), they do slow the pace of communication. Substitute one word for a phrase whenever possible.

☒ NOT In view of the fact that the model failed twice during the time that we tested it, we are at this point in time searching for other options.

☑ BUT Because the model failed twice when tested, we are searching for other options.

The original sentence contains 28 words; the revised sentence contains 13. You've "saved" 15 words, or 54% of the original sentence. Warren Buffet did almost as well, saving 46% in the prospectus. Here are more overused, wordy expressions:

Not	But
are of the opinion that	believe
in the event of	if
due to the fact that	because
pertaining to	about
for the purpose of	for *or* to
with regard to	about
in order to	to

Overusing prepositions also can cause wordiness. Consider these examples and their shorter equivalents:

Not	But
The cover of the book	The book cover
Department of Human Resources	Human Resources Department
The tiles on the floor	The floor tiles
Our benefits for employees	Employee benefits
The battery in my phone	My phone battery

In the previous revised examples, nouns (e.g., book) are used as adjectives. Following are other ways to use adjectives to condense your writing.

Not	But
This brochure, which is available free of charge	This free brochure
The report with sales numbers for July	The July sales report

Also search for the word *that* in your writing to see whether you could tighten the sentence without it.

Not	But
These are experiences **that** shape our thinking.	These experiences shape our thinking.
Bank of America is a company **that** has branches all over the world.	Bank of America has branches all over the world.
Sign up for a workshop **that** will teach you how to cook.	Sign up for a cooking workshop.

Avoid Hidden Verbs and Hidden Subjects

A hidden verb is a verb changed into a noun, which weakens the action. Verbs are *action* words and should convey what happens in the sentence. They provide interest and forward movement.

☒ NOT Carl made an announcement that he will give consideration to our request.

☑ BUT Carl announced that he will consider our request.

What is the real action? It is not that Carl *made* something or that he will *give* something. The real action is hiding in the nouns: Carl *announced* and will *consider*. Notice that the revised sentence is much more direct—and four words, or 33%, shorter.

Here are more actions that should be conveyed by verbs instead of hidden in nouns:

Not	But
arrived at the conclusion	concluded
has a requirement for	requires
came to an agreement	agreed
held a meeting	met
gave a demonstration of	demonstrated
made a payment	paid

Like verbs, subjects play a prominent role in a sentence and should stand out, rather than be obscured by an expletive. An **expletive** (not to be confused with profanity) is an expression, such as *there is* or *it is*, that begins a clause or sentence and for which the pronoun has no antecedent, or reference. Avoid expletives for clearer subjects and conciseness.

☒ NOT It was suggested that you be removed from the project team.

☑ BUT I spoke with the team about removing you from the project.

Business writers sometimes use expletives to avoid a clear subject—and possibly to avoid taking responsibility. The revision, above, may sound a bit harsh, but the leader is owning the decision instead of evading the issue.

Consider the variations in Figure 7, with particular attention to the changes in subjects and verbs.

Figure 7 | Changing a Sentence to Avoid an Expletive

Clunky expletive	To increase the number of candidates, it is recommended that Alta use an online recruiting system.
"I/we" as subject	To increase the number of candidates, I/we recommend that Alta use an online recruiting system.
Noun phrase as subject	Using an online recruiting system will increase Alta's number of candidates.
"Alta" as subject	To increase the number of candidates, Alta should/can use an online recruiting system.
"Candidates" as subject	More candidates will apply if Alta uses an online recruiting system.

These variations are all grammatically correct—but they emphasize different subjects. For example, the first variation, with no clear subject, might be used to distance the source from the advice, which may be appropriate in some situations. In the second variation, the source takes ownership for the advice. The third, fourth, and fifth variations all avoid the expletive in the first sentence, but notice how each emphasizes a different subject: using the online recruiting system, Alta, and candidates, respectively. You would choose the version that achieves your communication objective.

LO3 Write three types of sentences.

5-3 Writing Effective Sentences

A sentence has a subject and predicate and expresses at least one complete thought. Beyond these criteria, sentences vary widely in style, length, and effect.

Sentences are also very flexible. You can move sentence parts around, add and delete information, and substitute words to express different ideas and emphasize different points. To build effective sentences, use a variety of sentence types, active and passive voice appropriately, and parallel structure.

5-3a Use a Variety of Sentence Types

The three sentence types—simple, compound, and complex—are all appropriate for business writing. Only simple sentences were used in the thank-you email in Figure 1 at the beginning of this chapter. In the example in Figure 8, we see a variety of sentence types. These paragraphs are part of an email the global managing partner at McKinsey, a management consulting firm, sent to staff after the company reached a settlement agreement for its role in driving opioid sales.[21,22]

Simple Sentences

A simple sentence contains one independent, or main, clause (i.e., a clause that can stand alone as a complete thought). Because it presents a single idea and is often short, a simple sentence is effective for emphasis. But simple sentences can be longer and include compound subjects and verbs, as you see in the last example:

- "We fell short of that bar." (See Figure 8.)
- I quit.
- Employees can enroll in the company's 401(k) plan.
- Both part- and full-time employees can enroll in the company's 401(k) plan and in an individual retirement account.

Sentence Variety in McKinsey Email Excerpt | **Figure 8**

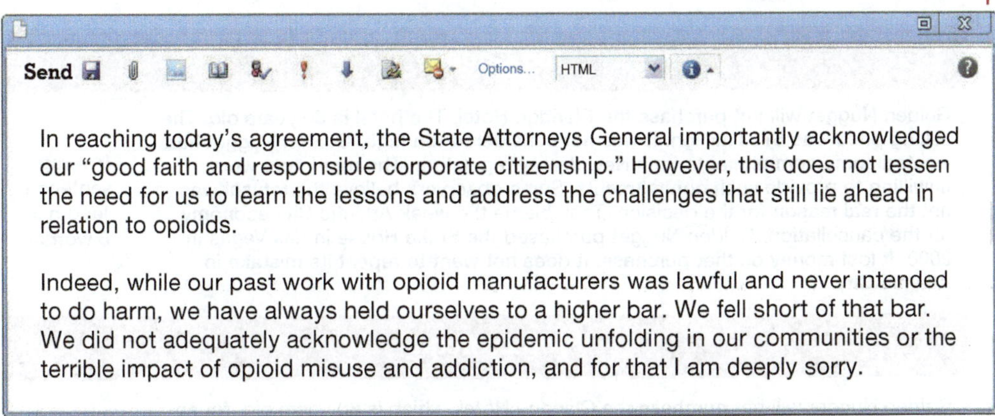

Send
Options...
HTML
In reaching today's agreement, the State Attorneys General importantly acknowledged our "good faith and responsible corporate citizenship." However, this does not lessen the need for us to learn the lessons and address the challenges that still lie ahead in relation to opioids.
Indeed, while our past work with opioid manufacturers was lawful and never intended to do harm, we have always held ourselves to a higher bar. We fell short of that bar. We did not adequately acknowledge the epidemic unfolding in our communities or the terrible impact of opioid misuse and addiction, and for that I am deeply sorry.

Compound Sentences

A compound sentence contains two or more independent clauses. Parts of the following sentence are related, and each idea receives equal emphasis.

- "We did not adequately acknowledge the epidemic unfolding in our communities or the terrible impact of opioid misuse and addiction, and for that I am deeply sorry." (See Figure 8.)
- Stacey listened, and I nodded.
- Morris Technologies made a major acquisition last year, but it turned out to be a mistake.
- East Hill Mines moved its headquarters to St. Louis in 2009; however, it stayed there only five years and then moved back to King City.

Complex Sentences

A complex sentence contains one independent clause and at least one dependent clause. In these sentences, one part of the sentence is dependent, or subordinate, to the main clause:

- "In reaching today's agreement, the State Attorneys General importantly acknowledged our 'good faith and responsible corporate citizenship.'" (See Figure 8.)
- Although it cost $235, the scanner will save valuable input time.
- George Bosley, who is the new CEO at Hubbell, made the decision.
- I will move to Austin when I start my new job.

Sentence Variety

Using a variety of sentence patterns and sentence lengths keeps your writing interesting. As we saw in Figure 1, and you'll see in Figure 9, too many short sentences sound simplistic and choppy. But too many long sentences can be boring and difficult to read.

In the last paragraph, you notice varied sentence types and lengths. The first two sentences are complex, the third is simple, and the last is compound. Lengths vary from 12 to 27 words, which are appropriate for business writing. With this variety, the writing is interesting and easy to read.

5-3b Use Active and Passive Voice Appropriately

Voice is the aspect of a verb that shows whether the subject of the sentence acts or is acted on. In the active voice, the subject *performs* the action expressed by the verb. In the passive voice, the subject *receives* the action expressed by the verb. Passive sentences add some form of the verb *to be* to the main verb, so passive sentences are always somewhat longer than active sentences.

Sometimes people use passive voice to avoid taking responsibility. In what situations might this be appropriate—and inappropriate?

Figure 9 | Sentence Variety for Greater Interest and Easier Reading

Too Choppy	
Golden Nugget will not purchase the Claridge Hotel. The hotel is 60 years old. The asking price was $110 million. It was not considered too high. Golden Nugget had wanted some commitments from New Jersey regulators. The regulators were unwilling to provide such commitments. Some observers believe the refusal was not the real reason for the decision. They blame the weak Atlantic City economy for the cancellation. Golden Nugget purchased the Stake House in Las Vegas in 2000. It lost money on that purchase. It does not want to repeat its mistake in Atlantic City.	(Average sentence length = 8 words)
Too Difficult	
Golden Nugget will not purchase the Claridge Hotel, which is 60 years old, for an asking price of $110 million, which was not considered too high, because the company had wanted some commitments from New Jersey regulators, and the regulators were unwilling to provide such commitments. Some observers believe the refusal was not the real reason for the decision but rather that the weak Atlantic City economy was responsible for the cancellation; and since Golden Nugget purchased the Stake House in Las Vegas in 2000 and lost money on that purchase, it does not want to repeat its mistake in Atlantic City.	(Average sentence length = 50 words)
More Variety	
Golden Nugget will not purchase the 60-year-old Claridge Hotel, even though the $110 million asking price was not considered too high. The company had wanted some commitments from New Jersey regulators, which the regulators were unwilling to provide. However, some observers blame the cancellation on the weak Atlantic City economy. Golden Nugget lost money on its 2000 purchase of the Stake House in Las Vegas, and it does not want to repeat its mistake in Atlantic City.	(Average sentence length = 20 words)

Active Old Navy offers a full refund on all orders.

Passive A full refund on all orders is offered by Old Navy.

Active PwC audited the books last quarter.

Passive The books were audited last quarter by PwC.

Use active sentences most of the time in business writing, just as you naturally use active sentences in most of your conversations. Note that verb *voice* (active or passive) has nothing to do with verb *tense*, which shows the time of the action. As the following sentences show, the action in both active and passive sentences can occur in the past, present, or future.

☒ NOT A very logical argument was presented by Hal. (*Passive voice, past tense*)

☑ BUT Hal presented a very logical argument. (*Active voice, past tense*)

☒ NOT An 18% increase will be reported by the eastern region. (*Passive voice, future tense*)

☑ BUT The eastern region will report an 18% increase. (*Active voice, future tense*)

Passive sentences are most appropriate when you want to emphasize the *receiver* of the action, when the person doing the action is either unknown or unimportant, or when you want to be tactful in conveying negative information. As with expletives, beware of using passive voice to intentionally obscure who is responsible for the action.

All the following sentences are appropriately stated in the passive voice:

- Protective legislation was blamed for the drop in imports. *(Emphasizes the receiver of the action)*
- Transportation to the construction site will be provided. *(Downplays the unimportant doer of the action)*
- Several complaints have been received regarding the new policy. *(Conveys negative news tactfully)*

Revisit Figure 6 to see how Warren Buffet changed the passive sentences to active sentences with *we* as the subject. Understandably, financial firms are concerned about promising outcomes, for example, high returns on funds. But the original passage fails to tell us who is taking the action. Buffet solves this problem by adding cautious words: *try*, *generally*, and *expect*.

5-3c Use Parallel Structure

The term **parallelism** means using similar grammatical structure for similar ideas. For coherence, match adjectives with adjectives, nouns with nouns, infinitives with infinitives, and so on. Julius Caesar's "I came, I saw, I conquered" and Abraham Lincoln's "government of the people, by the people, and for the people" illustrate parallel structure. Compare these sentences and notice how parallelism conveys a rhythm—a flow or movement.

☒ NOT The new dispatcher is competent and a fast worker.

☑ BUT The new dispatcher is competent and fast.

☒ NOT The new grade of paper is lightweight, nonporous, and it is inexpensive.

☑ BUT The new grade of paper is lightweight, nonporous, and inexpensive.

☒ NOT The training program will cover time-off policies, how to resolve grievances, and managing your workstation.

☑ BUT The training program will cover how to manage time off, grievances, and workstations.

☒ NOT One management consultant recommended either selling the children's furniture division or its conversion into a children's toy division.

☑ BUT One management consultant recommended either selling the children's furniture division or converting it into a children's toy division.

☒ NOT Gwen is not only proficient in Microsoft Word but also in Excel.

☑ BUT Gwen is proficient not only in Microsoft Word but also in Excel.

In the last two sets of sentences, note that correlative conjunctions (such as *either/or*, and *not only/but also)* must be followed by words in parallel form.

Also use parallel structure in numbered and bulleted lists and in report headings and presentation slide titles that have equal weight (Figure 10).

Revising for Parallel Phrasing | **Figure 10**

Before	After
Agenda: Planning for Independent Research • What is independent research? • Reasons we should use independent research for this project • Starting the process	**Agenda: Planning for Independent Research** • What is independent research? • Why is independent research appropriate for this project? • How should we begin the research process?
What is the process for conducting independent research? • Pick a topic • Faculty sponsor • Setting up a timeline • Resources • Figure out a method • Data study • You should deliver results	**What is the process for conducting independent research?** **D.I.S.C.U.S.S.** • Discover topic • Identify faculty sponsor • Set up timeline • Consult resources • Use methods • Study data • Shape deliverables

LO4 Describe components of a logical paragraph.

5-4 Developing Logical Paragraphs

A paragraph is a group of related sentences that focus on one main idea, often identified in the first sentence of the paragraph—the topic sentence. The body of the paragraph supports this main idea by giving more information, analysis, or examples. Effective paragraphs are unified, coherent, and an appropriate length.

5-4a Keep Paragraphs Unified and Coherent

Although closely related, unity and coherence are not the same. A paragraph has unity when all its parts work together to develop a single idea consistently and logically. A paragraph has coherence when each sentence links smoothly to the sentences before and after it.

Unity

A unified paragraph gives information that is directly related to the topic, presents this information in a logical order, and omits irrelevant details. The following excerpt is a middle paragraph in a memo arguing against the proposal that Collins, a baby-food manufacturer, should expand into producing food for adults:

☒ NOT [1] We cannot focus our attention on both ends of the age spectrum. [2] In a recent survey, two-thirds of the under-35 age group named Collins as the first company that came to mind for the category "baby-food products." [3] For more than 50 years, we have spent millions of dollars annually to identify our company as the baby-food company, and market research shows that we have been successful. [4] Last year, we introduced Peas 'n' Pears, our most successful baby-food introduction ever. [5] To now seek to position ourselves as a producer of food for adults would simply be incongruous. [6] Our well-defined image in the marketplace would make producing food for adults risky.

Before reading further, rearrange these sentences to make the sequence of ideas more logical.

As written, the paragraph lacks unity. You may decide that the overall topic of the paragraph is Collins's well-defined image as a baby-food producer. So Sentence 6 would be the best topic sentence. You might also decide that Sentence 4 brings in extra information that weakens paragraph unity and should be left out.

☑ BUT Our well-defined image in the marketplace would make producing food for adults risky. For more than 50 years, we have spent millions of dollars annually to identify our company as the baby-food company, and market research shows that we have been successful. In a recent survey, two-thirds of the under-35 age group named Collins as the first company that came to mind for the category "baby-food products." To now seek to position ourselves as a producer of food for adults would simply be incongruous. We cannot focus our attention on both ends of the age spectrum.

Coherence

A coherent paragraph weaves sentences together so that the writing is integrated. To achieve coherence, use transitional words, use pronouns, and repeat key words:

- **Transitional words.** Transitional words help the reader see relationships between sentences. Figure 11 shows commonly used transitional expressions for the relationships they express.

Common Transitional Expressions | **Figure 11**

Relationship	Transitional Expressions
Addition	Also, besides, furthermore, in addition, too
Cause and effect	As a result, because, consequently, therefore
Comparison	In the same way, likewise, similarly
Contrast	Although, but, however, nevertheless, on the other hand, still
Illustration	For example, for instance, in other words, to illustrate
Sequence	First, second, third, then, next, finally
Summary/conclusion	At last, finally, in conclusion, therefore, to summarize
Time	Meanwhile, next, since, soon, then

- **Pronouns.** Because pronouns stand for words already named, using pronouns binds sentences and ideas together. Pronouns are italicized here:

    If Collins branches out with additional food products, one possibility would be a fruit snack for youngsters. Funny Fruits were tested in Columbus last summer, and *they* were a big hit. Roger Johnson, national marketing manager, says *he* hopes to build new food categories into a $200 million business. *He* is also exploring the possibility of acquiring other established name brands. *These* acquired brands would let Collins expand faster than if *it* had to develop a new product of *its* own.

- **Repeated key words.** Use purposeful repetition to link ideas and thus promote paragraph coherence. Here is a good example:

    Collins has taken several *steps* recently to enhance profits and project a stronger leadership position. One of these *steps* is streamlining operations. Collins' line of children's clothes was *unprofitable*, so it discontinued the line. Its four produce farms were also *unprofitable*, so it hired an outside professional *team* to manage them. This *team* eventually recommended selling the farms.

5-4b Control Paragraph Length

How long should a paragraph of business writing be? Long blocks of unbroken text look boring and may unintentionally obscure an important idea buried in the middle. On the other hand, a series of extremely short paragraphs can weaken coherence. Compare the messages in Figure 12. Which is more inviting to read? Information is easier to digest when broken into small chunks with paragraph breaks, headings, bullets, and in this example, sub-bullets.

Paragraphs can be any length, and occasionally one- or two-sentence paragraphs might be effective, particularly in emails. However, most paragraphs of good business writers fall into the 60- to 80-word range—long enough for a topic sentence and three or four supporting sentences.

A paragraph is both a logical unit and a visual unit: logical because it discusses only one topic and visual because the end signals readers to pause and digest the information. Although a single paragraph should never discuss more than one major topic, complex topics may be divided into several paragraphs.

Figure 12 | Comparing Paragraph Length: Which Is More Inviting to Read?

Our goal is to transition the organization as smoothly as possible. Over the next 90 days, we will implement the transition plan. By October 15, we will transfer sales representatives to new divisions. Each sales representative will be moved from our current regional teams to a new team: consumer, small business, or corporate. Managers will work closely with representatives to determine strengths, experience, and preferences. By October 31, we will identify account type. All sales representatives will categorize current accounts for the new divisions: consumer, small business, and corporate. By November 30, we will transition accounts to new teams. For business accounts with new sales representatives, we will follow this process. For small business accounts, the former and new sales representative will send an email to the account contact, followed by a phone call and visit (if possible) by the new sales representative. For corporate accounts, the former sales representative will send an email and schedule a conference call or visit by both the former and new sales representatives.

Our goal is to transition the organization as smoothly as possible. Over the next 90 days, we will implement the transition plan:

- **Transfer sales representatives to new divisions (by October 15)**
  Each sales representative will be moved from our current regional teams to a new team: consumer, small business, or corporate. Managers will work closely with representatives to determine strengths, experience, and preferences.
- **Identify account type (by October 31)**
  All sales representatives will categorize current accounts for the new divisions: consumer, small business, and corporate.
- **Transition accounts to new teams (by November 30)**
  For business accounts with new sales representatives, we will follow this process:
  — For small business accounts, the former and new sales representative will send an email to the account contact, followed by a phone call and visit (if possible) by the new sales representative.
  — For corporate accounts, the former sales representative will send an email and schedule a conference call or visit by both the former and new sales representatives.

LO5 Compare examples of appropriate and inappropriate tone.

5-5 Creating an Appropriate Tone

Tone in writing refers to your attitude toward the reader and the subject of the message. Adopting an appropriate tone requires character. Consider how your message affects your reader, just as your tone of voice affects your listener during a conversation. An inappropriate tone may reflect negatively on you, signaling either a lack of confidence or a lack of humility to get your point across without degrading the reader.

Read the Netflix "cease-and-desist" letter described in the chapter introduction (Figure 13).[23] Compare the letter to language used in a U.S. Olympic Committee missive sent to a group of knitters who staged a "Ravelympics":

> We believe using the name "Ravelympics" for a competition that involves an afghan marathon, scarf hockey, and sweater triathlon, among others, tends to denigrate the true nature of the Olympic Games. In a sense, it is disrespectful to our country's finest athletes and fails to recognize or appreciate their hard work.[24]

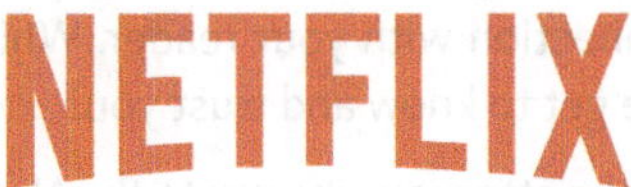

August 23, 2017

Emporium Arcade Bar
% Danny and Doug Marks
2363 N. Milwaukee Ave
Chicago, IL 60647

Via email (dkmarks@gmail.com, info@emporiumchicago.com)

Danny and Doug,

My walkie talkie is busted so I had to write this note instead. I heard you launched a *Stranger Things* pop-up bar at your Logan Square location. Look, I don't want you to think I'm a total wastoid, and I love how much you guys love the show. (Just wait until you see Season 2!) But unless I'm living in the Upside Down, I don't think we did a deal with you for this pop-up. You're obviously creative types, so I'm sure you can appreciate that it's important to us to have a say in how our fans encounter the worlds we build.

We're not going to go full Dr. Brenner on you, but we ask that you please (1) not extend the pop-up beyond its 6 week run ending in September, and (2) reach out to us for permission if you plan to do something like this again. Let me know as soon as possible that you agree to these requests.

We love our fans more than anything, but you should know that the demogorgon is not always as forgiving. So please don't make us call your mom.

Thanks,

Director/Senior Counsel - Content & Brand IP

Knitters were outraged, and a spokesperson for the Olympic Committee admitted that the letter "was definitely too strident in its tone."[25]

The Netflix letter illustrates guidelines to achieve an appropriate tone in business writing:

- Find your own professional, conversational voice.
- Write confidently.
- Use a courteous and sincere tone.
- Use appropriate emphasis and subordination.
- Use positive language.
- Stress the "you" attitude.

5-5a Find Your Own Professional, Conversational Voice

Business writing is less formal than you might think. A natural, conversational tone shows your personality and builds a connection with your reader. While maintaining professionalism, be your authentic self so people get to know and trust you.

In addition to the humor, the attorney who wrote the Netflix letter chose informal language. *Look* and *love* give you the sense that the writer is talking directly to the reader.

The writer also used contractions: *don't*, *I'm*, *you're*, *it's*, and *we're*. Except for the most formal reports, contractions are acceptable in business writing. To write as you speak, choose these combined words.

Tone should be appropriate for the audience and situation. Imagine that you're sending a LinkedIn message to someone who graduated from your school recently. Compare the examples in Figure 14.

Figure 14 | The Conversational Writing Style

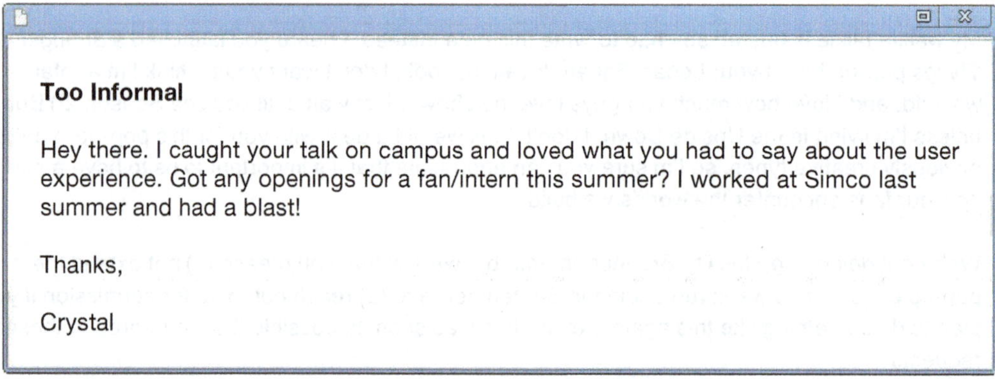

Too Informal

Hey there. I caught your talk on campus and loved what you had to say about the user experience. Got any openings for a fan/intern this summer? I worked at Simco last summer and had a blast!

Thanks,

Crystal

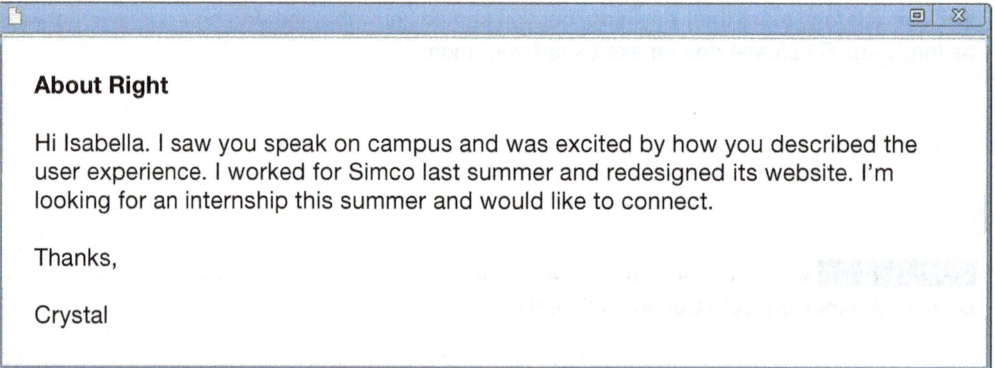

About Right

Hi Isabella. I saw you speak on campus and was excited by how you described the user experience. I worked for Simco last summer and redesigned its website. I'm looking for an internship this summer and would like to connect.

Thanks,

Crystal

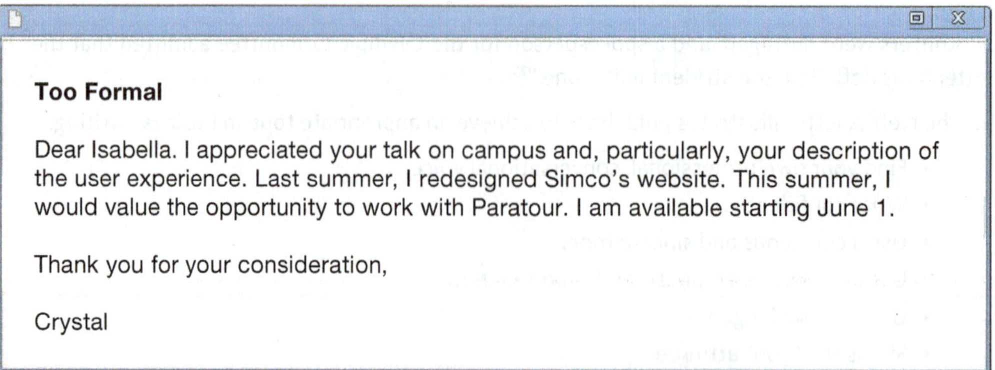

Too Formal

Dear Isabella. I appreciated your talk on campus and, particularly, your description of the user experience. Last summer, I redesigned Simco's website. This summer, I would value the opportunity to work with Paratour. I am available starting June 1.

Thank you for your consideration,

Crystal

The formal version is longer, which is typical, and sounds stilted. You might not say *appreciate*, *particularly*, *value*, or *opportunity* if you talked with Isabella directly.

Although the middle version is labeled "about right," no tone is perfect. Over time, you'll develop your own, unique writing style for different contexts. You'll find a natural tone that sounds like you, conveys your enthusiasm, and demonstrates confidence, which we discuss next.

5-5b Write Confidently

Do you tend to sound overconfident or unsure of yourself? What challenges do you face in striking the right tone?

To achieve your communication objective, your message should convey a confident attitude. The more confident you are about your writing, the more likely your audience will understand your explanation, accept your decision, or complete your request.

Be especially wary of beginning sentences with "I hope," "If you agree," "I think," and other self-conscious terms.

☒ NOT If you'd like to take advantage of this offer, you can call us.

☑ BUT To take advantage of this offer, call us today.

☒ NOT I hope that you will agree that my qualifications match your job needs.

☑ BUT My qualifications match your job needs in the following respects.

In some situations, the best strategy is simply to omit information. Why focus on your lack of work experience in a cover letter or imply that your product may need to be returned?

☒ NOT Let us know if you experience any other problems.

☑ BUT Your headphones should work perfectly now.

A word of caution: Do not appear *overconfident*; avoid sounding presumptuous or arrogant. Be especially wary of using strong phrases, such as "I know that" and "I am sure you will agree that."

☒ NOT I'm sure that you'll agree our offer is reasonable.

☑ BUT This solution gives you the data you need while protecting the client's privacy.

Context matters. The lawyer who wrote the Netflix letter sounds confident and unyielding: "Let us know as soon as possible that you agree to these requests." For a cease-and-desist letter, this tone is appropriate. For other types of business writing, this may sound too pushy or presumptuous.

5-5c Use a Courteous and Sincere Tone

A courteous, sincere tone builds goodwill for you and your organization and increases the likelihood that your message will achieve its objective. For example, lecturing the reader or filling a letter with **platitudes** (trite, obvious statements) sounds condescending. Also, readers are likely to find offensive such expressions as "you failed to," "we find it difficult to believe that," "as you know," or "your complaint."

☒ NOT Companies like ours cannot survive unless our customers pay their bills on time.

☑ BUT By paying your bill before May 30, you will maintain your excellent credit history with our firm.

☒ NOT You sent your complaint to the wrong department. We don't handle shipping problems.

☑ BUT We have forwarded your letter to the shipping department. You should be hearing from them within the week.

Your reader is sophisticated enough to know when you're being sincere. To achieve a sincere tone, avoid exaggeration (especially using too many modifiers or too strong modifiers), obvious flattery, and expressions of surprise or disbelief.

☒ NOT Your satisfaction means more to us than making a profit, and we will work night and day to see that we earn it.

☑ BUT We have taken these specific steps to resolve the issue.

☒ NOT I'm surprised you would question your raise, considering your overall performance last year.

☑ BUT Your raise was based on an objective evaluation of your performance last year.

The best way to achieve an appropriate tone is to genuinely think well of your reader. With conversational language, the Netflix writer sincerely compliments the bar owners: "I love how much you guys love the show." When you communicate across a difference of status or power, adopt an attitude of respect and equality to avoid sounding too pompous or too deferential.

Also be mindful of tone in short messages. In text messages, punctuation, abbreviations, and capitalizations can make all the difference in how a message is received. How do you interpret the messages in Figure 15?

Figure 15 | What Tone Does Each Text Message Convey?

Researchers found what you likely already know: a period sounds fierce. Some people perceive periods in texts to signal passive-aggressiveness or anger; others use periods to simply end a sentence.[26] Knowing the writer/reader and context may help you determine whether the period carries more weight than the small dot implies. Reading too much into a cue can be as damaging as missing one, so be cautious either way.

In any form of writing, tone is difficult to determine. To avoid misunderstandings, as discussed earlier, you might pick up the phone instead.

5-5d Use Appropriate Emphasis and Subordination

Imagine that you're asked to compare Zoom and Google Meet as online meeting platforms for 75 employees. Through your research, you find that Google Meet is free for up to 100 people, but that version doesn't include the functionality of Zoom, and group meetings are restricted to one hour. The paid version of Google Meet is too expensive—$8 per employee per month—and includes programs you don't use. Zoom costs $149.90 per year for up to 100 employees. You conclude that Zoom is worth the expense.

As you plan an email to your manager, consider ways to show the relative importance of each feature. To emphasize an idea, use the strategies in Figure 16. To subordinate an idea, simply use the opposite strategy. The Netflix letter maintains a positive tone by subordinating the threat in an introductory (dependent) clause ("We're not going to go full Dr. Brenner on you") and emphasizing the request in the independent clause ("but we ask that you please. . .").

CHARACTER

Your goal is not to mislead the reader. Demonstrate good character by making your conclusions clear. If you believe that Zoom is the *slightly* better choice, you can say so without exaggerating differences.

5-5e Use Positive Language

You are more likely to achieve your objectives with positive instead of negative words, such as *cannot* and *will not*. Negative language also often has the opposite effect of what is intended. Don't think of elephants. What are you thinking of now?

Ways to Emphasize Ideas | Figure 16

Put the idea in a short, simple sentence. Or put the idea in the main clause of a sentence.

- **Simple:** *Zoom is the best platform for our use.*
- **Complex:** *Although Google Meet is free, Zoom has more functionality.*

Place the major idea first or last. Within a paragraph or a sentence, the order of emphasis is first, last, middle.

Zoom is worth the expense. For $149.90 per year, Zoom includes polling, breakout groups, hand raise, and attendance reports. Google Meet includes none of those features for free. To access them (and programs we don't use) would cost $8 per user per month, or $7,200 per year.

Devote more space to the idea.

The functionality is important. We'll use an online platform for training and meetings, and we want to encourage interactivity. In addition, Google Meet limits group meetings to one hour, which is not long enough for our workshops.

Choose language that indicates importance.

The most important factor for us is interactivity during meetings. Cost is a minor consideration.

Include repetition (within reason).

Zoom has more functionality—functionality that allows people to participate during our meetings.

Use design elements to emphasize key ideas (again, within reason)**.** Use bullets, bold, italics, color, indenting, etc.

*The same functionality in Google Meet would cost **more per month** than Zoom will cost **in a year**.*

Positive language builds goodwill and usually provides more information to your reader. Note the differences in tone and detail in the following sentences:

☒ NOT The briefcase is not made of cheap imitation leather.

☑ BUT The briefcase is made of 100% belt leather for years of durable service.

☒ NOT I do not yet have any work experience.

☑ BUT My two terms as secretary of the Management Club taught me the importance of accurate recordkeeping and gave me experience in working as part of a team.

Stress what *is* true and what *can* be done rather than what is not true and cannot be done. Avoid *mistake*, *damage*, *failure*, *refuse*, and *deny*, which carry negative connotations. In one short paragraph about "Ravelympics," we see *denigrate*, *disrespectful*, and *fails*.

☒ NOT We can't replace the blender because the warranty has expired.

☑ BUT Although the warranty expired, we can offer you a replacement blender.

☒ NOT Failure to follow the directions may cause the blender to malfunction.

☑ BUT Following the directions will ensure that your blender lasts for many years.

5-5f Stress the "You" Attitude

If you're like most people reading or hearing a message, your reaction probably is, "What's in it for me?" or "How does this affect me?" To focus on the reader, adopt the "you" attitude to emphasize what the *receiver* (the listener or the reader) wants to know. These revised examples focus on receiver benefits—how the reader will benefit.

☒ NOT Our Jabra Speak 710 model comes with a travel pouch.

☑ BUT Take the Jabra Speak 710 with you in its protective travel pouch.

☒ NOT We will be open on Sundays from 1:00 p.m. to 5:00 p.m., beginning May 15.

☑ BUT You can shop on Sundays from 1:00 p.m. to 5:00 p.m., beginning May 15.

If the benefits aren't apparent, then show how someone *other than you* benefits. The Stranger Things bar owners have nothing to gain from doing what the Netflix lawyer asks except avoiding legal action. But the lawyer appeals to them personally instead of threatening them: "You're obviously creative types, so I'm sure you can appreciate that it's important to us to have a say in how our fans encounter the worlds we build." The only threat is presented as a joke and another allusion to the show: "So please don't make us call your mom."

Stressing the "you" attitude focuses the attention on the reader, which is where the attention should be—most of the time. However, when you refuse someone's request, disagree with someone, or talk about someone's mistakes or shortcomings, avoid connecting the reader too closely with the negative information. In these situations, avoid second-person pronouns (*you* and *your*), and use passive sentences or other subordinating techniques to stress the receiver of the action rather than the doer.

☒ NOT You should have included more supporting evidence in your presentation.

☑ BUT Including more supporting evidence would have made the presentation more convincing.

☒ NOT You failed to return the speaker within the 10-day period.

☑ BUT We give full refunds on speakers returned within 10 days.

5-6 Chapter Closing

Another Netflix-themed bar, Strange Patio!, popped up in Chicago a few years later. The company attorney might have more work to do—or the owners may have asked permission this time. Legal claims filed by and against Netflix, as for any company, continuously challenge lawyers to work on their writing style.

The same is true for business writers like you. Over time, you'll apply the principles of style, summarized in the Checklist for Revising Your Writing, and will see big improvements in your work. You'll also see your personality come through as you develop your own business writing style.

Checklist for Revising Your Writing

WORDS

- ☑ **Write clearly.** Be accurate and complete; use simple words; use specific, concrete language; avoid dangling expressions; and avoid clichés, slang, and unnecessary jargon.
- ☑ **Write concisely.** Avoid redundancy and wordy expressions; avoid hidden subjects and verbs.

SENTENCES

- ☑ **Use a variety of sentence types.** Use simple sentences for emphasis, compound sentences for equal relationships, and complex sentences for subordinate relationships.
- ☑ **Use active and passive voice appropriately.** Choose active voice most often to emphasize the doer of the action; use passive voice to emphasize the receiver.
- ☑ **Use parallel structure.** Match adjectives with adjectives, nouns with nouns, infinitives with infinitives, and so on.

PARAGRAPHS

- ☑ **Keep paragraphs unified and coherent.** Develop a single idea consistently and logically; use transitional words, pronouns, and repetition when appropriate.
- ☑ **Control paragraph length.** Use a variety of paragraph lengths.

TONE

- ☑ **Find your own professional, conversational voice.** Write mostly as you would speak in business to build connections and show your personality and strong character.
- ☑ **Write confidently.** Use a confident tone without sounding arrogant or presumptuous.
- ☑ **Use a courteous and sincere tone.** Build goodwill by being genuine and avoiding platitudes, exaggeration, obvious flattery, and expressions of surprise or disbelief.
- ☑ **Use appropriate emphasis and subordination.** Emphasize and subordinate through sentence structure, position, amount of space, language, repetition, and design.
- ☑ **Use positive language.** Stress what you *can* do or what *is* true rather than what you cannot do or what is not true
- ☑ **Stress the "you" attitude.** Emphasize what the receiver wants to know and how the receiver will be affected by the message; stress receiver benefits.

Write a Friendly "Cease-and-Desist" Letter

Consider the chapter introduction, which described The Upside Down, the *Stranger Things*–themed bar. Imagine that you're the Netflix lawyer who is charged with sending a "cease-and-desist" letter (Figure 13) to the bar owners.

Using the CAM model, what questions might the lawyer have considered before writing the letter?

CHARACTER CHECK

1. **What is my role as the Netflix attorney?**
   I'm in an important function at Netflix, and I have legal expertise that is critical to protecting the company's assets. However, I don't need to be arrogant or threatening. I'd like to find a way to convey my legal points without being intimidating.
2. **What if my letter became public?**
   Most "cease-and-desist" letters are formal and follow a template. If I write a letter that's fun, I risk embarrassment. Other attorneys may think it's silly or question my authority. I might face ridicule or be ostracized, but I'm willing to be courageous and take what I think is a better approach.

AUDIENCE ANALYSIS

1. **What do I know about the audience?**
   The bar owners love the show! I want to acknowledge that and not spoil the relationship or cause negative publicity. They probably didn't mean harm and may have intended flattery—in addition to wanting to generate revenue.
2. **How might they react?**
   They may be disappointed but not surprised. Most business professionals know that you can't use commercial branding without permission.

MESSAGE AND MEDIUM

1. **What are the main points of my message?**
   I'll balance appreciation with a solution. I want to be clear about what is not acceptable and what needs to happen: the bar can stay open for only the planned six weeks. If they want to use the show as a theme for other ventures, they need to ask permission.
2. **In what medium will I communicate the message?**
   A "cease-and-desist" is the best approach because it's a standard written legal document.

Responding to a "Cease-and Desist" Letter

〈 IN PRACTICE

Imagine that you're one of The Upside Down bar owners. You receive the Netflix attorney's letter. How will you respond?

>>> CHARACTER CHECK

1. What was my intent when I created the pop-up bar? I want to be honest about my purpose.
2. What are my options, including doing nothing? What are the ethical and potential legal considerations of each option?

>>> AUDIENCE ANALYSIS

1. What do I know about corporate attorneys? How do I feel about them?
2. Considering my options, what is the potential impact on others? Who would be affected and how?

>>> MESSAGE AND MEDIUM

1. What do I decide to do and why?
2. If I decide to respond, what will be my main points? What medium will I choose and why?

REFLECTING ON YOUR COMMUNICATION AND CHARACTER DEVELOPMENT

1. **Consider jargon for your area of expertise.**

   Think about a topic you know well, for example, a stock or investment, a business, a video game, a sport or hobby, a political issue, or an academic area. Write an email to someone who is also an expert on the subject. Include at least six jargon terms you would typically use.

   Now assume that you're sending the same email to someone who is not at all familiar with the topic. Revise your original message to make it appropriate for this reader.

   How do you feel while writing the revision? Is it frustrating? Have you used jargon to show off your expertise in the past? Describe how using jargon might exclude people who aren't familiar with your topic.

2. **Describe your writing style.**

   How would you describe your typical writing style? Now that you learned guidelines for business writing, how willing are you to flex your style to meet the needs of your audience? In what ways is it easy and difficult for you to adapt to business writing?

   Another way to think of this question is to consider adapting your writing for different occasions and audiences. How might your business writing style vary for different situations—sending an email to network with a family friend, thank a coworker, or update your manager on a project?

3. **Reframe creativity.**

   Some students find learning business writing frustrating because they believe they can't be creative. Do you feel this way? Business messages do follow some standard formats. Try to identify ways you can show your creativity and personality within these guidelines, even in formal documents like reports and cover letters.

4. **Reevaluate your tone.**

   Think about a time when someone felt hurt or offended by something you wrote. This could be a business, school, or personal situation. What did the person say about your writing?

   How would you describe your role in the situation? What, specifically, in your writing led to the bad feelings or misunderstanding? In your writing since then, how have you been mindful about the potential impact of your choices?

DEVELOPING YOUR BUSINESS COMMUNICATION SKILLS

LO1 Identify four principles of writing style.

DEVELOPING WRITING STYLE

1. **Analyze writing style.**

   Find an email that you received recently from a company or organization. Analyze the writing style by looking carefully at the words, sentences, paragraphs, and tone. How do you describe the style? Do you find it appropriate for you as the audience? What would improve the style? Compare emails and your analysis in small groups.

2. **Identify style issues.**

   Read these paragraphs, which are from the retailer BJ's website during the COVID-19 pandemic.[27] What are the major style issues?

   > We are here to serve you in these challenging times. BJ's provides essential services in our communities, giving you access to food and other products

> you and your families need during this time. We are considered an essential business and will continue to operate under state of emergency and shelter-in-place orders recently issued in the United States.
>
> We continue to closely monitor the coronavirus situation and our priority remains the health and safety of our team members, members and communities. We continue to follow recommendations and guidelines from the Centers for Disease Control and Prevention (CDC) and other health organizations to help ensure our clubs exceed our already high standards for general hygiene and health practices.
>
> We'll continue to take precautions to keep our clubs and other facilities clean and help ensure the well-being of our team members, members and community, following protocols from health experts and relevant federal and state agencies.

CHOOSING THE BEST WORDS

LO2 Explain ways to choose the best words for a business message.

3. Announce a new initiative using clear, simple language.

As the CEO of a growing business, you want to help employees save for retirement. Many of your employees receive minimum wage and have little experience with investing money. Write an email to employees explaining what a 401(k) plan is, why employees should participate, and how it will work at your company. You may need to research 401(k) plans first; you will find information on U.S. government websites, such as www.irs.gov.

For this new initiative, you will probably have in-person meetings, too, to explain the new plan. Imagine this email as a starting point.

4. Use simple language.

Revise the paragraph below to make it more understandable.

> The privileged juvenile was filled with abundant glee when her fashion mogul employer designated her as the contemporary representative of an ostentatious couture line. Although she was temporarily employed for the summer for an internship in the design department, her adolescent ambition was to enrich her life as a model. Subsequent to altering her hair, administering makeup, and adorning herself with the fashion designer's creations, she advanced in front of the photographer's lenses, beginning the succession of fulfilling her dreams.

5. Use concrete language to explain food waste.

Imagine that you're trying to convince world leaders to develop initiatives to reduce food waste. You found this information:

> Roughly one third of the food produced in the world for human consumption every year—approximately 1.3 billion tons—gets lost or wasted.[28]

Those sound like big, impressive numbers, but can you present this information in a more meaningful, actionable way? What could be a relevant, concrete comparison?

6. Revise to fix modifier and other issues.

Rewrite to clarify these sentences:

a. The actor was accosted after the play by a young man.

b. To become a policy, the management team must agree unanimously.

c. After attending the meeting, the minutes were prepared by the board secretary.

d. The manager fired an employee because he was insane.

e. Although the owners have changed, they continue to expand.

f. Sam only wants to work on weekends.

g. As a company, I want to be fair to all employees.

7. Write clearly and avoid slang.

These two sentences are filled with business slang and clichés. Revise them using simple, clear language.

> Using the synergies amongst our competitors, we can formulate a program that not only capitalizes on the strengths of each of our respective constituencies but that raises the bar to a new level for each and every one of us.
>
> At the end of the day, we need to think outside the box to look for low-hanging fruit, or we'll never reach our end goal.

8. Eliminate wordy expressions.

Revise the following sentences to eliminate wordy phrases by substituting a single word wherever possible. You may find other opportunities to tighten for conciseness.

a. Push the red button in the event that you see smoke rising from the cooking surface.

b. More than 40% of the people polled are of the opinion that government spending should be reduced.

c. Please send me more information pertaining to your new line of pesticides.

d. Due to the fact that two of the three highway lanes were closed for repairs, I was nearly 20 minutes late for my appointment.

e. Chef Ramsay, who was formerly my instructor at culinary school, is in today's society the owner of several restaurants, which are all over the world.

f. The newest sports automobile trend is to install seats made out of leather.

g. Google is now taking applications for job positions at this point in time, in spite of the fact that they just laid off employees.

h. We have the ability to vote for the best performer on TV by text messaging the on-screen telephone number.

9. Tighten a paragraph for conciseness.

By how many words can you reduce this paragraph without changing the meaning?

> New York City is the most natural choice of a location for an innovative restaurant like Fellerton. It is no secret that New York City is a world capital in restaurant innovation. In fact, New York City residents and locals alike consider themselves the most experimental eaters in the country as well as the top foodies. It is also home to Restaurant Week, which has since spread to cities all over the world. The fact that people living in New York City are adventurous eaters means they are more likely to accept and praise an unheard of restaurant concept like Fellerton.

10. Eliminate hidden verbs and hidden subjects.

Revise the following sentences to eliminate hidden verbs and hidden subjects.

a. The jury needs to carry out a review of the case to make a decision about whether the actress has a violation of her alcohol probation.

b. For our road trip during spring break, we must undertake the calculations of our driving travel time from California to New York.

c. If you cannot make the payment for the $135 tickets, you will not be able to make backstage visitations for the Lollapalooza concerts.

d. After much deliberation, the group came to a decision about how to make a response to the lawsuit.

e. Although Hugh wanted to offer an explanation of his actions, his boss refused to listen.

f. If confused about the assignment, there are some diagrams that you should review.

g. It is our intent to complete the project by Friday at 3:00 p.m.

h. There are four principles of marketing that we need to consider.

11. Rewrite a legal document.

Find any legal document, for example, one of the many privacy or user agreements you click through to use apps. Copy the original text, and then revise it for clarity and conciseness. By how many words (and what percentage of the text) can you reduce the document without changing the meaning?

WRITING EFFECTIVE SENTENCES

LO3 Write three types of sentences.

12. Identify types of sentences.

Copy a few paragraphs from an article in a major online newspaper. In a new document, identify whether each sentence is simple, complex, or compound. Find the percentage of simple, complex, and compound sentences by dividing the total number of sentences by each type. Notice how the author varies types of sentences for a sophisticated writing style.

13. Practice writing different types of sentences.

Write a simple, a compound, and a complex sentence that incorporates both items of information in each bullet. For the complex sentences, emphasize the first idea in each item.

a. The new phone will be available on Wednesday / The phone will have more features than the older model.

b. The captain got promoted to a major today / He will lead the army.

c. Tim was promoted / Tim was assigned additional responsibilities.

d. Eileen is our corporate counsel / Eileen will draft the letter for us.

14. Practice sentence variety.

Rewrite the following paragraph by varying sentence types and sentence lengths to keep the writing interesting.

> Smartfood was founded by Ann Withey, Andrew Martin, and Ken Meyers in 1984. The product was the first snack food to combine white cheddar cheese and popcorn. Ann Withey perfected the Smartfood recipe in her home kitchen after much trial and error. Smartfood sales were reportedly only $35,000 in 1985. During that time, the product was available only in New England. By 1988, sales had soared to $10 million. This attracted the attention of Frito-Lay. The snack-food giant bought Smartfood in 1989 for $15 million. Since the purchase, Frito-Lay has not tampered with the popular Smartfood formula. It has used its marketing expertise to keep sales growing, despite the growing number of challengers crowding the cheesy popcorn market.

15. **Vary sentence length.**
Write a long sentence (40 to 50 words) about a company or person you admire. Then revise the sentence so that it contains 10 or fewer words. Finally, rewrite the sentence so that it contains 16 to 22 words. Which sentence is the most effective? Why?

16. **Use active and passive voice.**
Working in groups of three, identify whether each of the following sentences is active or passive. Then, discuss whether the sentence uses active or passive voice appropriately and why. Next, change the sentences that use an inappropriate voice.

Sentence Example	Active or Passive Voice?	Appropriate Use? (If not, then rewrite the sentence.)
a. A very effective sales letter was written by Paul Mendelson.		
b. Our old office will be sold to a real estate developer.		
c. You failed to verify the figures on the quarterly report.		
d. The website designed by Catalina Graphics did not reflect our company's image.		

17. **Check and revise sentences for parallel structure.**
Determine whether the following sentences use parallel structure. Revise sentences to make the structure parallel.
    a. The executive at Ernst & Young writes reports quickly, accurately, and in detail.
    b. The bride hates wearing heels, and on her wedding day, she just wanted to wear flats, be able to dance around, and be comfortable.
    c. The store is planning to install a new point-of-sale system that is easier to operate, easier to repair, and cheaper to maintain than the current system.
    d. Angelina's children like to go swimming, biking, and play tennis.
    e. According to the survey, most employees prefer either holding the employee cafeteria open later or its hours to be kept the same.
    f. The quarterback is expert not only in calling plays but also in throwing passes.
    g. Our career guide will cover writing resumes, cover letters, and techniques for interviewing.

DEVELOPING LOGICAL PARAGRAPHS

LO4 Describe components of a logical paragraph.

18. **Order sentences into a logical paragraph (Honda Accord).**
Place a number (from 1 to 7) next to each sentence to represent its position within the paragraph. *Hint:* The broadest statement will be the first sentence—the topic sentence.

The Accord has 17-inch alloy wheels.	
The car's wide-opening doors provide easy access to the interior.	
With an automatic reverse feature, the moonroof is safe.	
The Accord is a good choice for today's active driver.	
The Honda Accord is a well-designed, functional car that will attract attention.	
In a variety of colors, the Accord will stand out in the crowd.	
The one-touch power moonroof with tilt is easy to operate.	

19. Order sentences into a logical paragraph (Nick's Pizza).

Place a number (from 1 to 8) next to each sentence to represent its position within the paragraph.[29] *Hint:* The broadest statement will be the first sentence—the topic sentence.

But, as Nick says, "I decided I needed to do what felt like the right thing to do: communicate openly, clearly, and honestly."	
Going against the advice of his publicist and his banker, Nick decided to send an email explaining the situation to his customers and asking for their patronage.	
Analysts credit Nick's transparency and authenticity for saving the business.	
Some started a Facebook page, while others frequented Nick's Pizza and spread the word.	
This strategy also defies conventional wisdom, which warns of suppliers cutting off a potentially failing business and customers avoiding a place in trouble.	
When Nick's Pizza & Pub was going out of business, Nick turned to his customers for support—and he got it.	
Nick saw an immediate increase in sales, and today it's still a viable restaurant.	
Customers responded.	

20. Use transitions for paragraph coherence.

Revisit the Honda Accord paragraph in Exercise 18. Now that you have sentences in a logical order, add transitions to improve coherence.

21. Adjust paragraph length.

Read the following paragraph and determine how it might be divided into two or more shorter paragraphs to help the reader follow the complex topic being discussed.

> Transforming a manuscript into a published book requires several steps. After the author submits the manuscript, the copy editor makes any needed grammatical or spelling changes. The author reviews these changes to be sure that they haven't altered the meaning of any sentences or sections. Next, the publisher begins the design process. At this point, designers select photographs and other artwork and create page layouts, which show how the pages will look when printed. The author and publisher review these page proofs for any errors. Only after all corrections have been made does the book get published. From start to finish, this process can take as long as a year.

LO5 Compare examples of appropriate and inappropriate tone.

CREATING AN APPROPRIATE TONE

22. Revise a sales email to convey a confident tone.

> Hi Raj,
>
> I'm wondering whether you enjoyed our first shipment of organic vegetables that we dropped off last week. Did you receive them? How did they look and taste to you?
>
> If you would like to order more, let me know.
>
> Otherwise, I hope you have a great day!
>
> Jordine

23. Revise sentences to convey a confident tone.

Revise the following sentences to convey an appropriately confident attitude.

a. Can you think of any reason not to buy the latest Android?

b. I hope you agree that my offer provides good value for the money.

c. Of course, I am confident that my offer provides good value for the money.

d. You might try to find a few minutes to visit our gallery on your next visit to galleries in this area.

24. Discuss tone in text messages.

In small groups, discuss text messages you received recently that caused misunderstandings. What was the situation and what went wrong? If you can, share the messages to gauge how your classmates might have reacted. What could cause these differences? What ideas does your group have for reducing misunderstandings in texts?

25. Revise the tone in a paragraph.

Rewrite this passage to avoid platitudes, obvious flattery, and exaggeration.

> You, our loyal and dedicated employees, have always been the most qualified and the hardest working in the industry. Because of your faithful and dependable service, I was quite surprised to learn yesterday that an organizational meeting for union representation was recently held here. You must realize that a company like ours cannot survive unless we hold labor costs down. I cannot believe that you don't appreciate the many benefits of working at Allied. We will immediately have to declare bankruptcy if a union is voted in. Please don't be fooled by empty rhetoric.

26. Revise an email to a neighbor.

Revise this note to convey a better tone. This can be casual and fun but try to build a better relationship.

> To Apartment 4,
>
> You guys are so inconsiderate. You're way too noisy and keep me up all night. Why do you have to stay up so late and blast music? At least you can invite me to your parties.
>
> From Sleepless in Apartment 3.

27. Vary emphasis in a memo.

Assume that you have evaluated two candidates for the position of sales assistant. This is what you have learned:

- Carl Barteolli has more sales experience.
- Elizabeth Larson has more appropriate formal training (earned a college degree in marketing and attended several three-week sales seminars).

Write a memo to Robert Underwood, the vice president, recommending one of these candidates. First, assume that formal training is the most important criterion, and write a memo recommending Elizabeth Larson. Second, assume that experience is the most important criterion, and write a memo recommending Carl Barteolli. Use appropriate emphasis and subordination in each message. You may make up any reasonable information needed to complete the assignment.

28. Use positive language.

Revise the following paragraph to eliminate negative language.

> We cannot issue a full refund at this time because you did not enclose a receipt or an authorized estimate. I'm sorry that we will have to delay your reimbursement. We are not like those insurance companies that promise you anything but then disappear when you have a claim. When we receive your receipt or estimate, we will not hold up your check. Our refusal to issue reimbursement without proper supporting evidence means that we do not have to charge you outlandish premiums for your automobile insurance.

29. Make a positive impression.

Revise the following signs often seen in stores:

a. "No shirt, no shoes, no service."

b. "American Express cards not accepted."

c. "No returns without receipts."

d. "No smoking."

e. "No dogs allowed."

30. Stress the "you" attitude.

Revisit BJ's website in Exercise 2. You probably noticed that every sentence starts with "we." Revise the text using "you" to focus on the customer instead.

31. Use a "you" attitude and positive language.

Rewrite this email from a facilities manager to country club members. How can you stress the "you" attitude and focus on good news without misleading members?

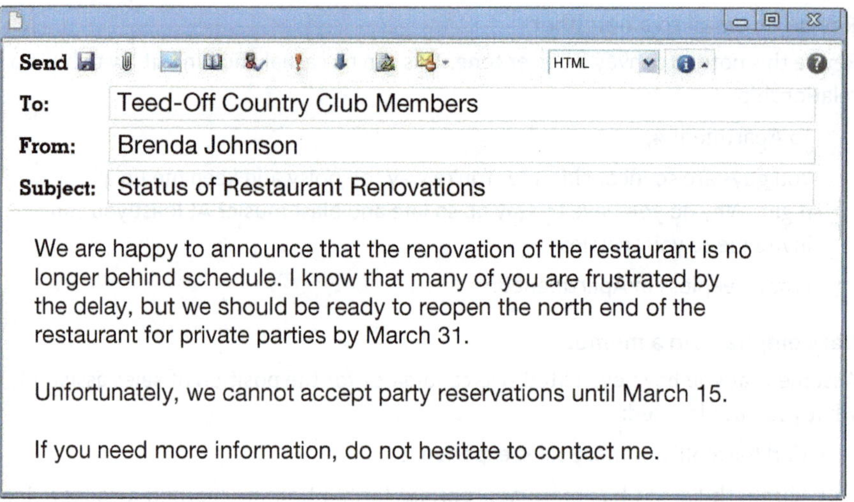
To: Teed-Off Country Club Members
From: Brenda Johnson
Subject: Status of Restaurant Renovations

We are happy to announce that the renovation of the restaurant is no longer behind schedule. I know that many of you are frustrated by the delay, but we should be ready to reopen the north end of the restaurant for private parties by March 31.

Unfortunately, we cannot accept party reservations until March 15.

If you need more information, do not hesitate to contact me.

CHAPTER SUMMARY

LO1 Identify four principles of writing style.

When describing writing, style means how an idea is expressed. Four principles of style are words, sentences, paragraphs, and tone.

LO2 Explain ways to choose the best words for a business message.

Achieve clarity by making your message accurate, by using simple words, and by avoiding dangling expressions and unnecessary jargon. Write to express—not to impress. Use longer words only if they express your idea more clearly. Use specific, concrete language and avoid clichés, slang, jargon, and buzzwords. To achieve conciseness, make every word count. Avoid redundancy, wordy expressions, and hidden verbs and subjects.

LO3 Write three types of sentences.

Choose simple sentences for emphasis, compound sentences for two or more ideas of equal importance, and complex sentences for two or more ideas of unequal importance. Use active voice to emphasize the doer of the action and passive voice to emphasize the receiver of the action. Express similar ideas using a similar grammatical structure.

LO4 Describe components of a logical paragraph.

Your paragraphs should be unified and coherent. Develop only one topic per paragraph, and use transitional words, pronouns, and repetition to move smoothly from one idea to the next. Although you should vary paragraph lengths, most range from 60 to 80 words in business documents.

LO5 Compare examples of appropriate and inappropriate tone.

Demonstrate confidence that you will achieve your objectives. However, avoid sounding presumptuous or arrogant. To achieve an appropriate tone, use emphasis and subordination, prefer positive rather than negative words, and keep the emphasis on the reader.

Endnotes

1. Netflix Director/Senior Counsel, Content & Brand IP, posted by LMA Community Member, "Netflix Sent the Most Epic Letter Asking This 'Stranger Things' Themed Pop-Up Bar To Shut Down," Boredpanda, www.boredpanda.com/LETTER-STRANGER-THINGS-BAR-NETFLIX/, accessed February 14, 2021.
2. Netflix.
3. Reg P. Wydeven, "Sometimes Lawyers Are Cool," McCarty Law, October 10, 2017, https://mccartylaw.com/2017/10/sometimes-lawyers-are-cool/, accessed February 15, 2021.
4. Netflix.
5. "Stylist / Housekeeping Attendant," Marriott Careers, https://jobs.marriott.com/marriott/jobs/20203797, accessed February 15, 2021.
6. Shonda Rhimes, *The Year of Yes* (New York: Simon & Schuster, 2015), p. xxii.
7. Rhimes also teaches a master class in script writing for television: Master Class, www.masterclass.com/classes/shonda-rhimes-teaches-writing-for-television, accessed February 15, 2021.
8. From the former Newseum, archived at The Why Not 100, April 1, 2015, http://thewhynot100.blogspot.com/2015/04/73-best-headline-fails.html, accessed February 15, 2021.
9. One example is a CNN news story: Anneken Tappe, "Dow Falls 1,191 Points—the Most in History," CNN Business, February 27, 2020, www.cnn.com/2020/02/27/investing/dow-stock-market-selloff/index.html, accessed February 15, 2021.
10. Curtis Hutchinson, "Volkswagen Group Boss Winterkorn Resigns," MotorTrader.com, September 23, 2015, www.motortrader.com/motor-trader-news/automotive-news/volkswagen-group-boss-winterhorn-resigns-23-09-2015, accessed February 15, 2021.
11. Volkswagen Group, "Video Statement Prof. Dr. Martin Winterkorn," YouTube video, September 22, 2015, www.youtube.com/watch?v=wMPX98_H0ak, accessed April 21, 2017.
12. Daniel M. Oppenheimer, "Consequences of Erudite Vernacular Utilized Irrespective of Necessity: Problems with Using Long Words Needlessly," *Applied Cognitive Psychology* 20 (2006): 139–156. Quoted in Richard Morin, "Nerds Gone Wild," The 2006 Ig Nobel Awards, Pew Center Research Publications, October 6, 2006, http://pewresearch.org/pubs/72/nerds-gone-wild, accessed March 15, 2015.
13. "How the Airbnb Community Supports Environmentally Friendly Travel Worldwide," Airbnb News, April 19, 2018, https://news.airbnb.com/how-the-airbnb-community-supports-environmentally-friendly-travel-worldwide/, accessed July 1, 2021.
14. Mark Kolakowski, "At $2.08 Trillion, Apple Is Bigger Than These Things," Investopedia, March 17, 2021, www.investopedia.com/news/apple-now-bigger-these-5-things/, accessed July 4, 2021.
15. "Update on Disneyland Resort Operations," Disneyland Website, https://disneyland.disney.go.com/travel-information/#annual-passports, accessed February 17, 2021.
16. Catherine Clifford, "Elon Musk's 6 Productivity Rules, Including Walk Out of Meetings That Waste Your Time," CNBC, April 18, 2018, www.cnbc.com/2018/04/18/elon-musks-productivity-rules-according-to-tesla-email.html, accessed February 17, 2021.
17. Byoung-Hyoun Hwang and Hugh Hoikwang Kim, "It Pays to Write Well," *Journal of Financial Economics* 124 (2017): 373–394.
18. Kim Sydow Campbell, Jefrey S. Naidoo, and Jordan Smith, "When Your Boss Says, 'You Need to Sound More Professional': Writing Style and Writer Attributions," *International Journal of Business Communication* (2021): 1–24, https://doi.org/10.1177/23294884211025735.
19. Remarks by Arthur Levitt, U.S. Securities and Exchange Commission, "Taking the Mystery out of the Marketplace: The SEC's Consumer Education Campaign," National Press Club, Washington, D.C., October 13, 1994, www.sec.gov/news/speech/speecharchive/1994/spch012.txt, accessed February 17, 2021.
20. "Sic" identifies an error in the original writing: missing hyphens in "day-to-day."
21. Kevin Sneader, "Today's Settlement on Opioids and Setting a Higher Standard," McKinsey email, February 4, 2021, www.mckinseyopioidfacts.com/wp-content/uploads/2021/02/todays-settlement-on-opioids-and-setting-a-higher-standard.pdf, accessed February 17, 2021.
22. Michael Forsythe and Walt Bogdanich, "McKinsey Settles for Nearly $600 Million Over Role in Opioid Crisis," *The New York Times*, February 3, 2021, www.nytimes.com/2021/02/03/business/mckinsey-opioids-settlement.html, accessed February 17, 2021.
23. Netflix.
24. Adrian Chen, "Knitters Outraged After U.S. Olympic Committee Squashes Knitting Olympics—and Disses Knitters," Gawker, June 20, 2012, http://gawker.com/5920036/us-olympics-committee-is-mad-at-knitting-olympics-for-denigrating-real-athletes, accessed February 19, 2021.
25. Kevin Allen, "U.S. Olympics PR Chief Shares Lessons from Knitting Controversy," PR Daily Europe, June 26, 2012, www.prdaily.com/u-s-olympics-pr-chief-shares-lessons-from-knitting-controversy/, accessed February 19, 2021.
26. Danielle N. Gunraj, et al., "Texting Insincerely: The Role of the Period in Text Messaging," *Computers in Human Behavior* 55 (2016), https://doi.org/10.1016/j.chb.2015.11.003.

27. “BJ’s Response to Coronavirus,” BJ’s Website, https://newsroom.bjs.com/BJs-Response-to-Coronavirus/default.aspx, accessed February 21, 2021.

28. “Worldwide Food Waste,” UN Environment Program, www.unep.org/thinkeatsave/get-informed/worldwide-food-waste, accessed March 5, 2021.

29. Carol Roth, “Humble Email Saves Suburban Chicago Pizza Pub,” *Crain’s Chicago Business*, March 15, 2012, www.chicagobusiness.com/article/20120315/BLOGS06/120319853/suburban-chicago-restaurateur-s-unusual-plea-to-customers-pays-dividends, accessed July 7, 2021.

Part 3

Crafting Written Messages

CHAPTER 6

Neutral and Positive Messages

Learning Objectives

After you have finished this chapter, you should be able to

LO1 Describe the value of positive messages in business.

LO2 Explain how to organize a neutral message.

LO3 Apply guidelines for writing a goodwill message in a business situation.

LO4 Apply guidelines for responding to online feedback in a business situation.

LO5 Explain ways to engage customers and employees on social media.

> *"Wow, it's hard for us to come up with the right words to say. THIS is what we stand for. THIS is Dairy Queen."* [1]
>
> —Dairy Queen Facebook post

Chapter Introduction

More than 900 Cars "Pay It Forward" at Drive-Through

A Minnesota Dairy Queen shared good news on Facebook: a driver paid for the next car's order, and this continued for more than two days and 900 cars.[2] With an exuberant use of exclamation points, a writer for the store tracked how many customers contributed.[3] Sales totaled more than $10,000, some of which the company donated.

Actor John Krasinski picked up the story for his web sensation, "Some Good News."[4] The series reported only positive stories and was so successful that CBS purchased it after just a few episodes.[5]

When celebrated, small acts of gratitude and generosity can bring about big results.

Dairy Queen Grill & Chill (522 C St NE, Brainerd, MN)
December 3, 2020 ·

UPDATE 8:44pm: We are still going strong!!!! OVER 275 cars have paid it forward!!! If we can keep it going like this for the rest of the night we will be opening tomorrow with money forward!!! Way to go DQ Fans!!! and THANK YOU!!!

Update: We are still going strong now over 150 cars paying it forward here at DQ...
Not sure if its the sun shining, or the Christmas Spirit is already here... But it started with one and we are now at about 48 cars that have paid it forward! Lets keep this caring train going!
#DQ #payitforward #wereallinthistogether #spreadthejoy

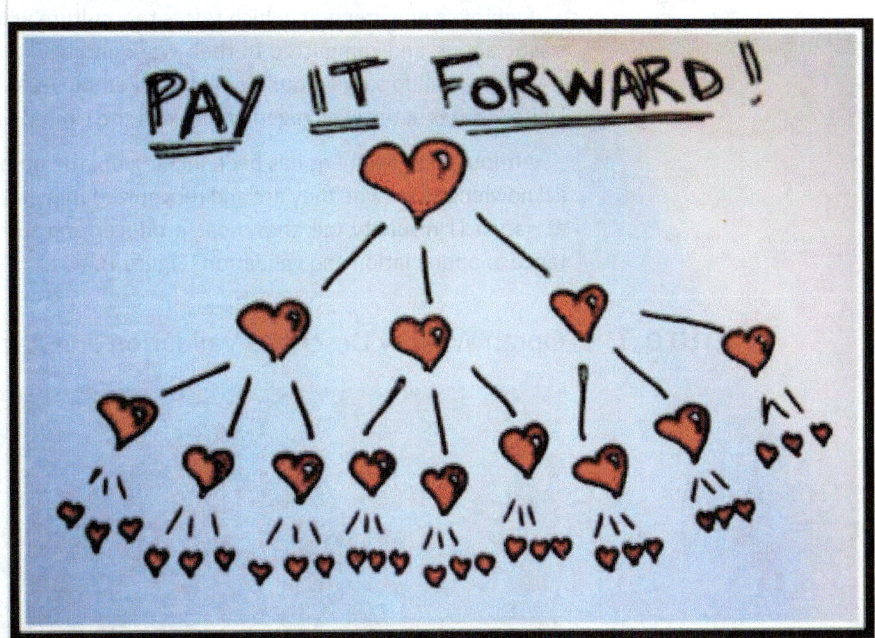

Source: Facebook

Dairy Queen updates Facebook users with a positive message.

LO1 Describe the value of positive messages in business.

6-1 Creating a Positive Work Environment

In Chapters 2 and 3, we discussed the value of developing positive working relationships and creating a culture where people feel as though they belong. Writing positive messages contributes to both.

Most people love getting compliments and thank-you notes. Research shows that people underestimate how surprised and happy someone will be to receive a genuine note of appreciation. Instead, they worry that their message will be awkward.[6]

Managing our self-doubt to write a note simply out of a sense of gratitude is an important aspect of character. Can you be grateful without expecting something in return? The good news is that you likely will feel better. When people practice gratitude, they experience benefits to their own well-being.[7]

In this chapter, you learn how to write positive and neutral messages, which are probably the most common type of business writing.

6-1a Appreciation at Work

We need more positivity at work. A LinkedIn poll found that 80% of professionals experience the "Sunday Scaries,"[8] that post-weekend, pre-work anxiety that one employee calls "low-grade, existential dread."[9]

Negative stereotypes about business, some of which are true, have launched memes and media, for example, *Corporate*, a dark comedy series about the world of work. The lead characters, two "junior executives-in-training," have tyrannical bosses who pressured them to fire other employees, do personal chores, and develop a marketing campaign to promote a war.[10]

Employee engagement, which refers to a culture where employees feel "involved in, enthusiastic about, and committed to their work and workplace,"[11] has been dismal for many years. An annual Gallup survey found only 15% of employees worldwide and 35% of employees in the United States actively engaged and 14% in the United States feeling disengaged.[12]

Although engagement has been inching up, the numbers show that employees need to feel acknowledged for who they are and recognized for what they do. In her commencement speech at Harvard University, talk show host, producer, and author Oprah Winfrey described the importance of appreciation and validation (Figure 1).[13]

Figure 1 | Oprah Winfrey Describes Validation and Appreciation

UPI/Alamy Stock Photo

I have to say that the single most important lesson I learned in 25 years talking every single day to people was that there's a common denominator in our human experience.... The common denominator that I found in every single interview is we want to be validated. We want to be understood. I've done over 35,000 interviews in my career. And as soon as that camera shuts off, everyone always turns to me and inevitably, in their own way, asks this question: "Was that OK?" I heard it from President Bush. I heard it from President Obama. I've heard it from heroes and from housewives. I've heard it from victims and perpetrators of crimes. I even heard it from Beyoncé in all of her Beyoncé-ness. She finishes performing, hands me the microphone, and says [Oprah whispers], "Was that OK?"... [We] all want to know one thing: "Was that OK?" "Did you hear me?" "Do you see me?" "Did what I say mean anything to you?"

Employee recognition increases job satisfaction, motivation, and feelings of competency.[14] At work, we tend to take good work for granted and give feedback only when we notice problems. In one study, more than 25% of employees said they considered changing jobs because of "lack of recognition for their efforts."[15] Hearing only complaints can be demoralizing and might discourage people from making any changes at all.

6-1b Types of Positive and Neutral Messages

Positive messages may travel within or outside an organization. Internally, a manager recognizes an employee's contribution to a project, a coworker congratulates another on the birth of a child, or an employee thanks a manager for constructive feedback. Externally, a customer thanks a sales associate in a store or writes a positive review online.

In addition to these positive messages, business communication is often about routine topics. Externally, a small business owner asks about a service discount or a customer asks about product availability. Internally, a manager sends an email about a minor policy change or an employee asks a coworker for information to include in a report. Although routine, these messages are important to run a business.

To distinguish these examples from more difficult communication—persuasive and bad-news messages covered in the following chapters—we refer to these as neutral messages. Positive and neutral communications may be presented in any communication medium. In this chapter, you see examples of email, letters, handwritten notes, and social media posts.

6-2 Writing Neutral Messages

LO2 Explain how to organize a neutral message.

Typically, neutral messages are shorter and more direct than persuasive and bad-news messages. Your audience will likely be interested in what you have to say, so a quick audience analysis may be all you need. Then you can begin drafting your message, starting with the main idea, followed by explanations and details, and then a friendly closing.

6-2a Start with the Main Point

When writing a positive or neutral message, put your main point up front. Notice how news is announced in the first sentence of the three company messages shown in Figure 2.

When requesting information—a neutral, routine message—ask for what you need clearly and directly in the first sentence or two. You may use a question, a statement, or a polite request, which asks the reader to act rather than actually giving a yes-or-no answer.[19] At times, you might find it awkward to ask for information or help. The examples in Figure 3 might make it easier for you to start your message.

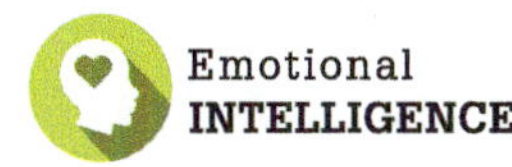

How comfortable are you asking for information or help? What holds you back, and how can you overcome your hesitations?

Figure 2 | Main Points Start Company Announcements

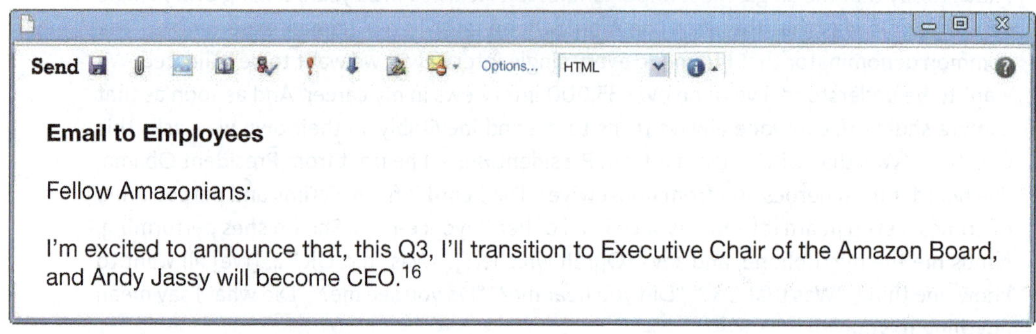
Send Options... HTML

Email to Employees

Fellow Amazonians:

I'm excited to announce that, this Q3, I'll transition to Executive Chair of the Amazon Board, and Andy Jassy will become CEO.[16]

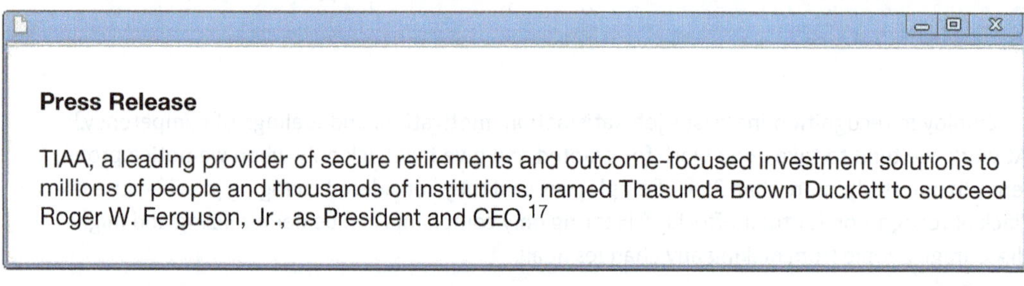
Press Release

TIAA, a leading provider of secure retirements and outcome-focused investment solutions to millions of people and thousands of institutions, named Thasunda Brown Duckett to succeed Roger W. Ferguson, Jr., as President and CEO.[17]

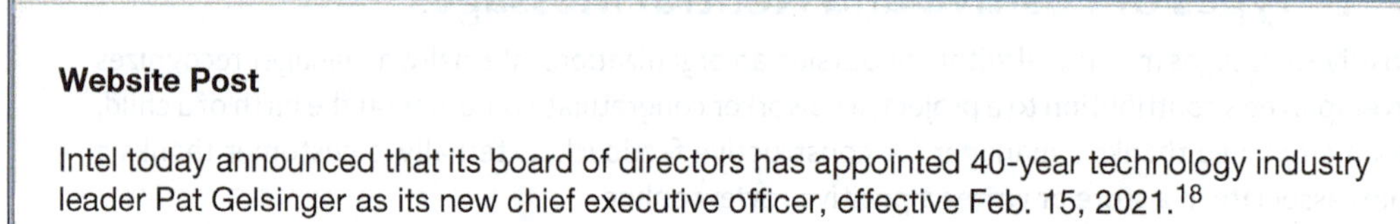
Website Post

Intel today announced that its board of directors has appointed 40-year technology industry leader Pat Gelsinger as its new chief executive officer, effective Feb. 15, 2021.[18]

Figure 3 | Examples of Requests

Direct Question
When do you expect the Ray-Ban Sunmasters to be back in stock?

Statement
Please let me know when you're available to meet about the donation.

Polite Request
Would you mind telling me how you arranged for summer housing in Dallas?

Remember that you are imposing on the goodwill of the reader. Ask as few questions as possible—and never ask for information that you can easily get on your own. If many questions *are* necessary, number them in a logical sequence; most readers will answer questions in order and will be less likely to skip one unintentionally. Yes-or-no questions or short-answer questions are easy for the reader to answer, but when you need more information, use open-ended questions.

6-2b Provide an Explanation and Details

Most of the time, you'll need to explain your initial request. Include background information (the reason for asking) either immediately before or after making the request. For example, suppose you received a request for information about someone's job performance. Unless you were also told that the request came from a prospective employer and that the applicant gave your name as a reference, you might be reluctant to provide any information.

As another example, imagine that you're writing to a former employer or professor asking for a letter of recommendation. You might need to give some background about yourself to jog the reader's memory. Put yourself in the reader's position. What information would you need to answer the request accurately and completely?

A reader is more likely to cooperate if you can show how responding to the request will benefit the reader. But you can skip the benefits if they feel contrived, or when they're obvious. An email asking employees to recycle their paper would probably not need to discuss the value of recycling, which most people already know.

From the audience's perspective, what are the issues with the request in Figure 4? Consider the timing, tone, and Johara's potential concerns. For an improved version, see Figure 5.

Ineffective Email Request | **Figure 4**

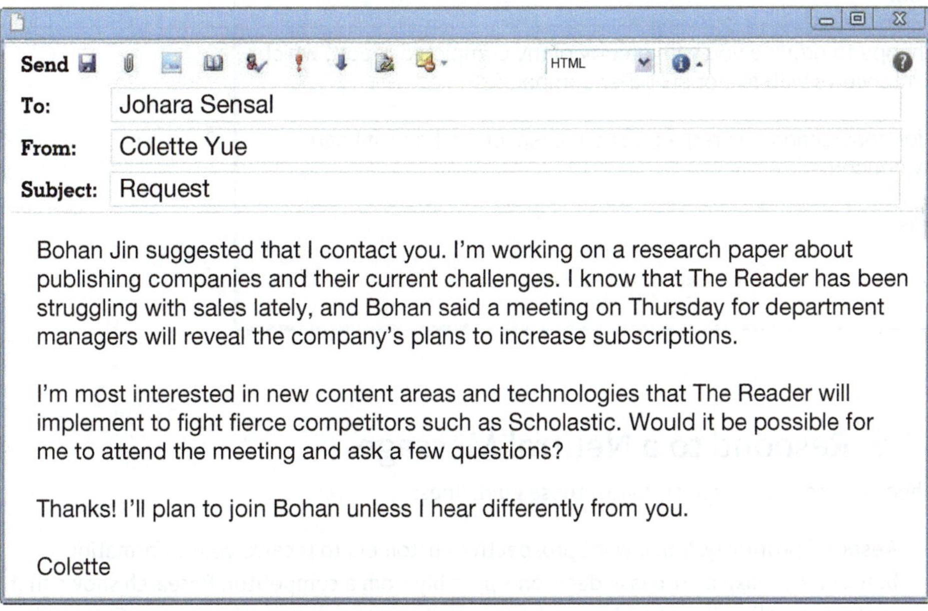

Send

HTML

To: Johara Sensal

From: Colette Yue

Subject: Request

Bohan Jin suggested that I contact you. I'm working on a research paper about publishing companies and their current challenges. I know that The Reader has been struggling with sales lately, and Bohan said a meeting on Thursday for department managers will reveal the company's plans to increase subscriptions.

I'm most interested in new content areas and technologies that The Reader will implement to fight fierce competitors such as Scholastic. Would it be possible for me to attend the meeting and ask a few questions?

Thanks! I'll plan to join Bohan unless I hear differently from you.

Colette

6-2c End on a Positive Note

Use a friendly, positive tone in your last paragraph, as in the example in Figure 5. In your closing, express appreciation for the assistance, state and justify any deadlines, or offer to reciprocate. Make your closing specific to the purpose and original.

☒ NOT I need the information by October 1.

☑ BUT May I please have the information by October 1, so I can include upcoming performances on our new website?

☒ NOT Thank you in advance for your assistance in this matter.

☑ BUT Thank you for providing this information, which will help us make a fairer evaluation of Janice Henry's qualifications for this position.

☒ NOT Let me know how I can help you in the future.

☑ BUT Please let me know if I can return the favor by attending the meeting with Gupta Associates next week.

Figure 5 | Effective Email Request

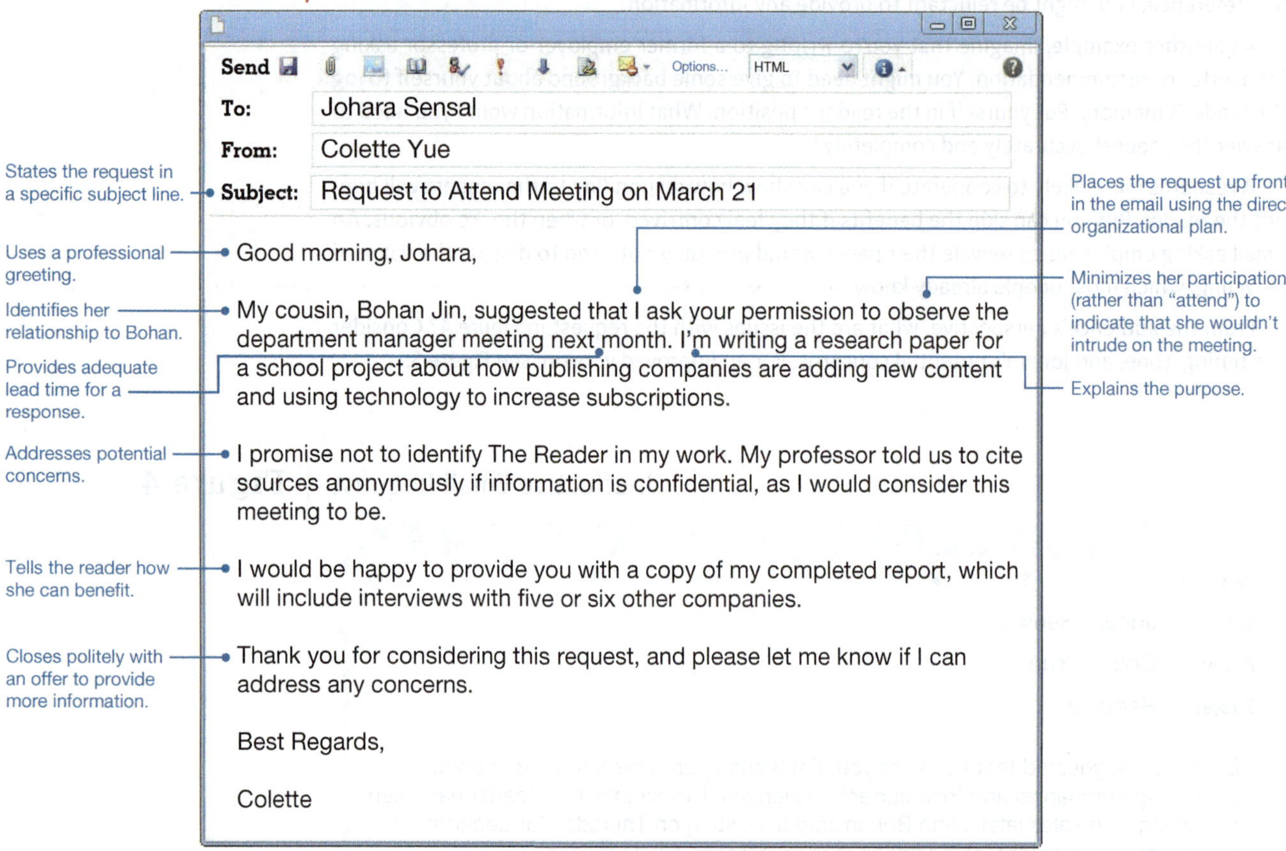

Send
Options...
HTML
To: Johara Sensal
From: Colette Yue
Subject: Request to Attend Meeting on March 21
Good morning, Johara,
My cousin, Bohan Jin, suggested that I ask your permission to observe the department manager meeting next month. I'm writing a research paper for a school project about how publishing companies are adding new content and using technology to increase subscriptions.
I promise not to identify The Reader in my work. My professor told us to cite sources anonymously if information is confidential, as I would consider this meeting to be.
I would be happy to provide you with a copy of my completed report, which will include interviews with five or six other companies.
Thank you for considering this request, and please let me know if I can address any concerns.
Best Regards,
Colette
States the request in a specific subject line.
Uses a professional greeting.
Identifies her relationship to Bohan.
Provides adequate lead time for a response.
Addresses potential concerns.
Tells the reader how she can benefit.
Closes politely with an offer to provide more information.
Places the request up front in the email using the direct organizational plan.
Minimizes her participation (rather than "attend") to indicate that she wouldn't intrude on the meeting.
Explains the purpose.

6-2d Respond to a Neutral Message

When you receive a request, follow these guidelines:

Respond promptly. You'll want prospective customers to receive your information before they make a purchase decision—possibly from a competitor. Research shows that customers will wait up to 24 hours for an email response but want it sooner. One study found that one-third of customers want a response within an hour.[20]

Similarly, on Twitter, customers expect a response to a complaint between 1 and 3 hours; on Facebook, customers want responses between 3 and 6 hours.[21] Customers may tolerate more time for neutral requests, but quicker responses are best.

CHARACTER

For internal email, response time varies by organization, culture, and age. Younger people tend to reply more quickly and, in some settings, you can expect a response within two minutes.[22] Ask about expectations, so you become known as someone who is reliable. As people trust your responsiveness, they will trust your character. Apologize if you take too long to reply, but too many apologies will damage your credibility.

Respond courteously. Your response represents the organization or department. A reply that sounds terse or burdened misses an opportunity to build goodwill.

☒ NOT Although Aetna usually provides that type of information, I can give it to you this one time.

☑ BUT Here is the information. In the future, you may contact Aetna directly at . . .

Put your main point up front. Make it easy for the reader to understand your response by putting the "good news"—the fact that you're responding favorably—up front. This pattern is the same as for a neutral request.

☒ NOT I saw your email last week about speaking at the meeting.

☑ BUT I would be glad to speak at your Engineering Society meeting on August 8. Thank you for thinking of me.

Personalize your response. Even if you start with a template, include your reader's name and tailor the message to specific requests.

Promote your company, products, or services—within reason. You may choose a subtle sales approach when responding to simple requests.

Close your response on a positive, friendly note. Avoid such clichés as, "If you have additional questions, please don't hesitate to let me know." Use original wording, personalized for the reader.

In the next example, Southside Brewery responds to a customer inquiry with personalized, thorough information (Figure 6).

Figure 6 Personalized Response to a Customer's Inquiry

Send Options... HTML

Dear Derek,

Southside Brewery would be happy to host Moniker's office party. Thank you for thinking of us for your event. Yes, we have a private room that will accommodate up to 25 people, and we do have availability on December 9.

We offer two options for private parties: a full menu or a fixed-price limited menu. For the full menu, your guests would simply order from our regular lunch menu, and we would charge you accordingly. If you prefer a limited menu, we could offer a fixed price depending on the items you choose. For example, for $15 per person (not including beverages and dessert), your guests could choose from these items:

- Southwest Chicken Salad
- Salmon Teriyaki
- Ground Beef Burger

If you prefer different menu items, we can work up pricing based on your preferences.

You also asked about a special occasion cake, and we certainly can arrange this for you. We work closely with a bakery that would create something according to your specifications.

I would be happy to meet with you to talk about your requirements and to finalize plans.

Thanks again for your inquiry, and I hope to speak with you soon. You can call me at (215) 555-6760 or email me at ron@southsidebrewery.com.

Answers the customer's inquiry about a specific date in the first paragraph.

Explains two options to meet the customer's needs.

Offers sample menu items in easy-to-read bullets.

Encourages more customization.

Addresses another specific request.

Closes on a positive note.

LO3 Apply guidelines for writing a goodwill message in a business situation.

6-3 Writing Goodwill Messages

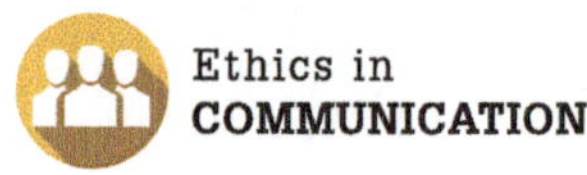

People send positive or goodwill messages out of a sense of kindness and to maintain or build relationships. With no true business objective, these messages convey congratulations, appreciation, or sympathy. Goodwill messages achieve their objective precisely because they have no ulterior motive. Even subtle sales promotion would make receivers suspect the sincerity of your message.

Of course, businesses may reap advantages from goodwill messages. Customers like to deal with people who take the time to acknowledge what's important to them and, as you read earlier, employees are more likely to stay with a company when they feel recognized. But this is not the goal of a sincere goodwill message.

In this section, you learn guidelines for writing goodwill messages and then considerations for different purposes: recognition, congratulations, appreciation, and sympathy.

6-3a Guidelines for Goodwill Messages

You may send a goodwill message by texting or calling instead of writing—especially for minor occasions. People appreciate these timely acknowledgments. But an email or a handwritten note can feel more thoughtful and permanent, particularly because they require extra effort and people receive fewer of them. To write effective goodwill messages, follow the guidelines in Figure 7.

Figure 7 | Guidelines for Goodwill Messages

Be prompt.

Send a goodwill message while the reason is still fresh in the reader's mind. A welcome note to a new employee, for example, should be sent within the first few days on the job.

Be direct.

State the major idea in the first sentence or two, even for sympathy notes; because readers already know the bad news, you don't need to shelter them from it.

Be specific.

If you're thanking or complimenting someone, mention a specific incident or anecdote. Show the significance or impact on others.

Be sincere.

Avoid language that is too flowery or too strong (e.g., "awesome" or "the best I've ever seen"). Use a conversational tone, as if you were speaking to the person directly, and focus on the reader—not on yourself. Take special care to spell names correctly and to make sure your facts are accurate. You may use exclamation marks, but don't overdo it.

Be brief.

You may not need an entire page to get your point across. A personal note card or a one-paragraph email may be plenty.

Goodwill messages vary by culture. What may be appropriate, even expected, in one country may be improper in another. Also, what is emphasized in a goodwill message may differ by culture. In a study comparing Chinese and American graduation cards, Chinese messages reflected far more "process-focused themes" of hard work and continuous self-improvement, whereas American cards emphasized "person-focused themes," such as individual traits.[23] Do your research before writing goodwill messages to people from cultures you don't know well.

6-3b Recognition Notes

Messages should be sent to recognize when someone does a particularly good job. A short note can be directed to the person and, when appropriate, an immediate supervisor. Be clear about how the work was exceptional and how it benefitted others. An internal example, from a manager to an employee, is shown in Figure 8. An external example, from a resident in Hampton, Virginia, to a police officer, is shown in Figure 9.[24]

6-3c Congratulatory Notes

Congratulatory notes are sent for major business achievements—receiving a promotion, winning new business, receiving an award, opening a new branch, or announcing a retirement. These notes are also appropriate for personal milestones—engagements, weddings, births, graduations, and other occasions. The example in Figure 10 is from a manager to an employee in another department.

Emotional INTELLIGENCE

How often do you send notes to recognize, congratulate, or thank people? Why don't you send them more often? How do you feel when you get notes from others?

Figure 8 Internal Recognition Note to an Employee

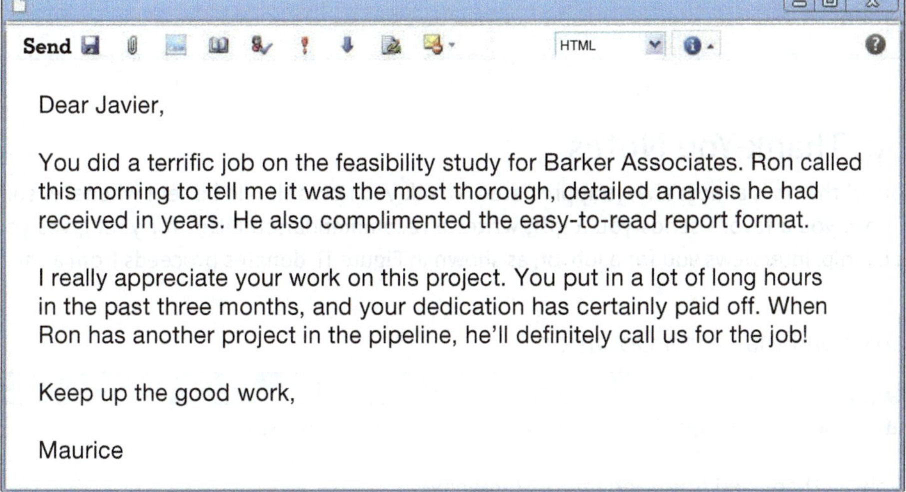

Send HTML

Dear Javier,

You did a terrific job on the feasibility study for Barker Associates. Ron called this morning to tell me it was the most thorough, detailed analysis he had received in years. He also complimented the easy-to-read report format.

I really appreciate your work on this project. You put in a lot of long hours in the past three months, and your dedication has certainly paid off. When Ron has another project in the pipeline, he'll definitely call us for the job!

Keep up the good work,

Maurice

Figure 9 External Recognition Note About a Police Officer

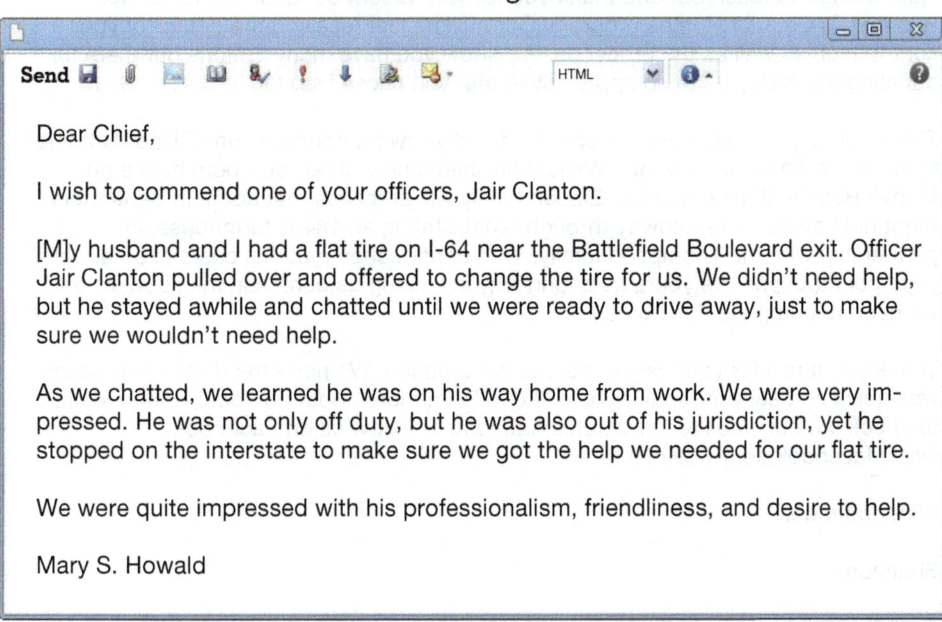

Send HTML

Dear Chief,

I wish to commend one of your officers, Jair Clanton.

[M]y husband and I had a flat tire on I-64 near the Battlefield Boulevard exit. Officer Jair Clanton pulled over and offered to change the tire for us. We didn't need help, but he stayed awhile and chatted until we were ready to drive away, just to make sure we wouldn't need help.

As we chatted, we learned he was on his way home from work. We were very impressed. He was not only off duty, but he was also out of his jurisdiction, yet he stopped on the interstate to make sure we got the help we needed for our flat tire.

We were quite impressed with his professionalism, friendliness, and desire to help.

Mary S. Howald

Figure 10 | Internal Congratulatory Note

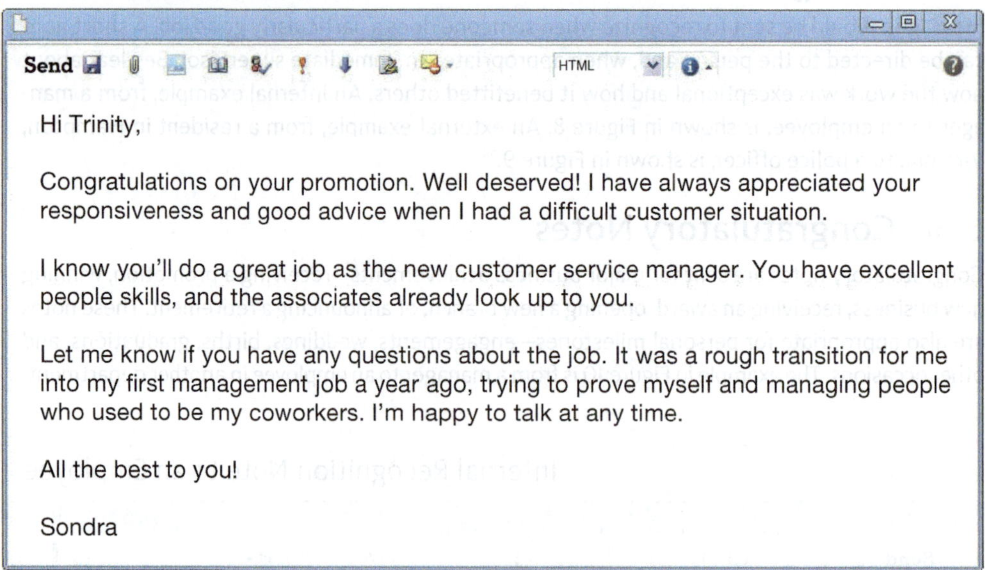

Hi Trinity,

Congratulations on your promotion. Well deserved! I have always appreciated your responsiveness and good advice when I had a difficult customer situation.

I know you'll do a great job as the new customer service manager. You have excellent people skills, and the associates already look up to you.

Let me know if you have any questions about the job. It was a rough transition for me into my first management job a year ago, trying to prove myself and managing people who used to be my coworkers. I'm happy to talk at any time.

All the best to you!

Sondra

6-3d Thank-You Notes

A note of thanks is almost always appreciated. Thank-you notes should be sent whenever someone does you a favor—sends you a gift, writes a recommendation letter for you, gives you a scholarship, interviews you for a job, or, as shown in Figure 11, donates proceeds from a car.

Figure 11 | Thank-You Email for a Donation

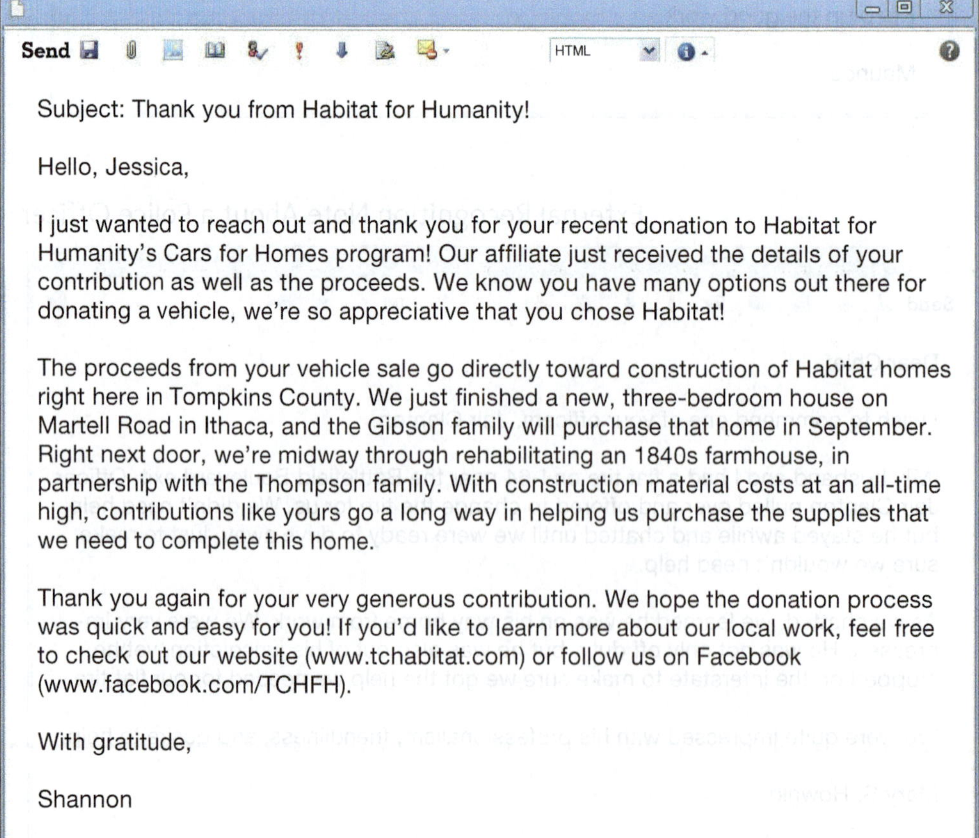

Subject: Thank you from Habitat for Humanity!

Hello, Jessica,

I just wanted to reach out and thank you for your recent donation to Habitat for Humanity's Cars for Homes program! Our affiliate just received the details of your contribution as well as the proceeds. We know you have many options out there for donating a vehicle, we're so appreciative that you chose Habitat!

The proceeds from your vehicle sale go directly toward construction of Habitat homes right here in Tompkins County. We just finished a new, three-bedroom house on Martell Road in Ithaca, and the Gibson family will purchase that home in September. Right next door, we're midway through rehabilitating an 1840s farmhouse, in partnership with the Thompson family. With construction material costs at an all-time high, contributions like yours go a long way in helping us purchase the supplies that we need to complete this home.

Thank you again for your very generous contribution. We hope the donation process was quick and easy for you! If you'd like to learn more about our local work, feel free to check out our website (www.tchabitat.com) or follow us on Facebook (www.facebook.com/TCHFH).

With gratitude,

Shannon

The Habitat for Humanity email[25] is personalized to the donor, noting specifically how the funds were used. The executive director reinforces the organization's mission by describing how they work in partnership with local families.

6-3e Sympathy Notes

Expressions of sympathy or condolence to a person who is having a difficult time personally are especially tough to write but are especially appreciated. People who have health problems, had a car accident, or didn't get a promotion they wanted need to know that others are thinking of them and that they are not alone.

How do you feel about sending sympathy notes? What holds you back, and how can you overcome your hesitations?

Compassion is an important dimension of character and can relieve others' suffering. Sometimes, we resist offering compassion because we don't notice others' pain, know what to say, blame the person for their problems, or simply don't take the time.[26] Handwritten notes convey extra care in these situations, for example, the one shown in Figure 12, which expresses sympathy to a coworker.

Figure 12 Sympathy Note to a Coworker

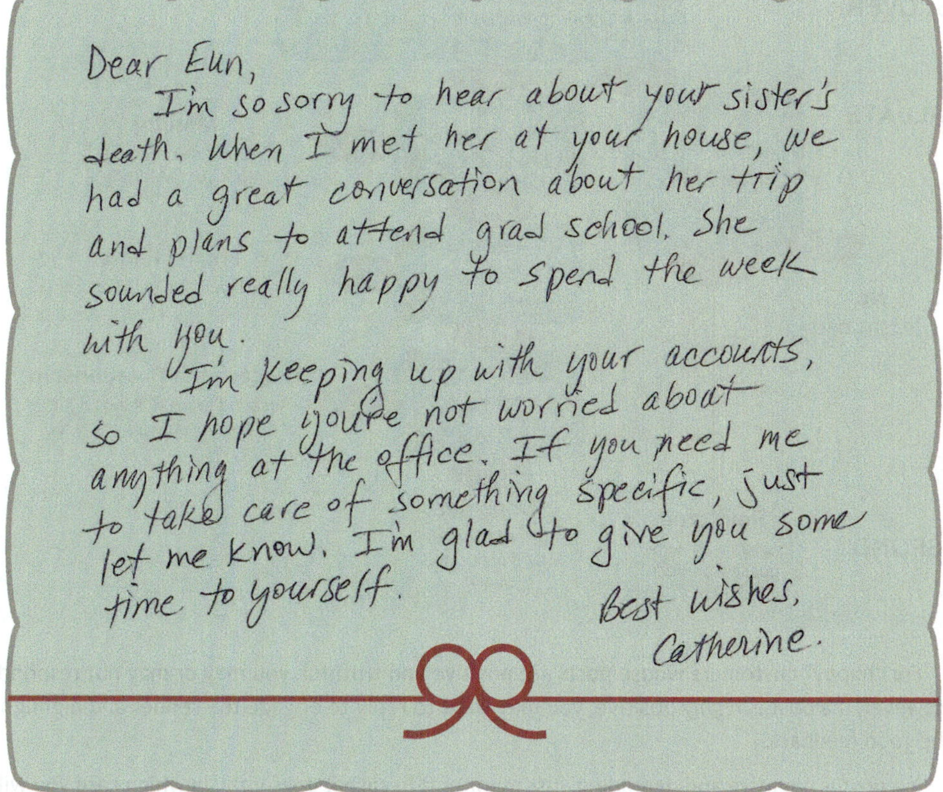
Dear Eun,

I'm so sorry to hear about your sister's death. When I met her at your house, we had a great conversation about her trip and plans to attend grad school. She sounded really happy to spend the week with you.

I'm keeping up with your accounts, so I hope you're not worried about anything at the office. If you need me to take care of something specific, just let me know. I'm glad to give you some time to yourself.

Best wishes,
Catherine

6-4 Addressing Social Media Comments

LO4 Apply guidelines for responding to online feedback in a business situation.

So far, we discussed one-to-one requests and responses. For customers on social media platforms—review sites, blogs, and social networks—the communication opportunities are greater and the stakes higher. Companies can win customers and build a positive reputation online, but slow and poorly written responses can lose customers and damage a company's image—with potentially millions of people watching. In this section, we explore whether and how to respond to customers online.

6-4a Deciding Whether to Respond

Smart companies practice social listening. They monitor the constant stream of social media posts to learn what people are saying about their brand, products, and services.

After they find these mentions of their company, social media managers decide whether and how to respond to online content. For large companies that can afford them, aggregators scan the web for comments about the company. These programs automatically collect and analyze the online messages. Smaller companies have staff members who use tools such as Google Alerts to search the web for mentions.

The flowchart shown in Figure 13, typical for organizations that pay attention to online customer feedback, helps guide a company's response. Companies won't necessarily respond to every online post. One study warns of overcommenting to customer reviews. When large hotels responded to about 40% of reviews, they got the maximum positive impact on ratings and revenue. Otherwise, posting too many management responses could turn off customers.[27]

Figure 13 | Social Media Response Guidelines

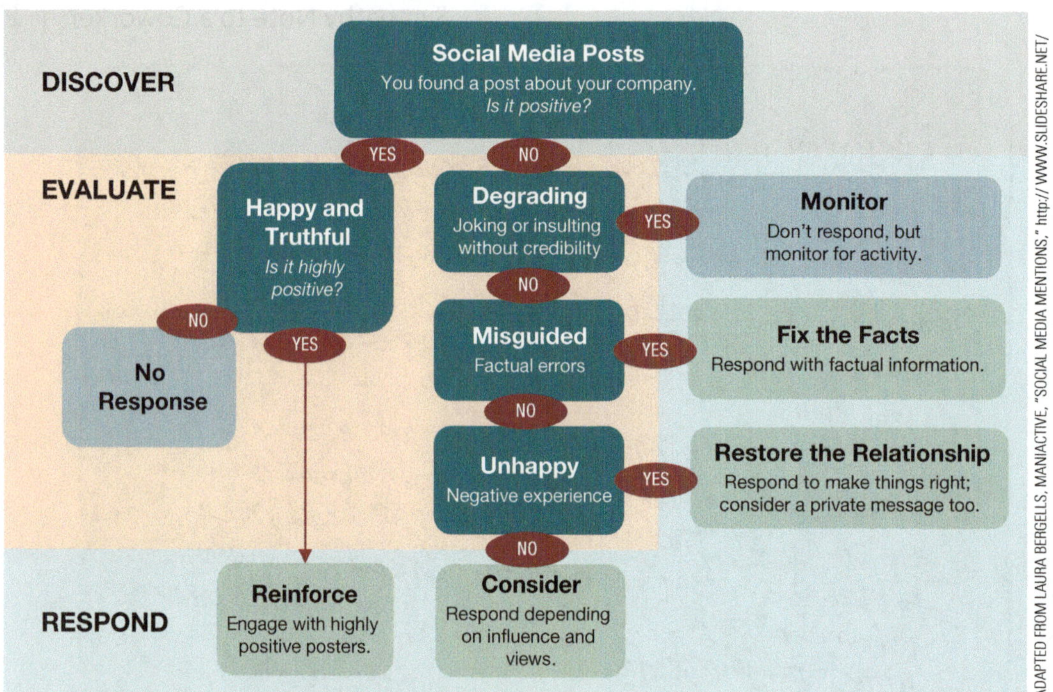

ADAPTED FROM LAURA BERGELLS, MANIACTIVE, "SOCIAL MEDIA MENTIONS," http://WWW.SLIDESHARE.NET/MANIACTIVE/SOCIAL-MEDIA-RESPONSE-FLOW-CHART, ACCESED March 20, 2015, AND FROM THE U.S. AIR FORCE BLOG ASESMENT FLOW CHART, http://WWW.AF.MIL/SHARED/MEDIA/DOCUMENT/AFD-091210-037.PDF, ACCESED March 20, 2015.

For "happy" customers whose posts are positive and truthful, you may or may not respond. However, if a post is *highly* positive, you may want to reply to engage the sender and highlight the good feedback.

If a post is negative and degrading, just monitor it in case it goes viral, in which case you will have to respond. Otherwise, responding to an insulting troll might just inflame the situation. If posts are misguided or unhappy, you will want to respond. Let viewers read the company voice and get the facts or see how you're fixing a negative experience.

Unhappy customers may need additional communication. You might try to reach out with a private message—and let public viewers see that you're doing so—to get more information about a negative experience and offer solutions, such as replacing a damaged item. This detail is best handled privately.

For neutral comments, for example, the Yelp post in Figure 14, management *could* respond but does not. The review is neither so positive that the company should draw attention to it nor so negative that the company should apologize and take action. It can stand alone.

Neutral Customer Review | **Figure 14**

Tiffany P.
Stockton, CA

We tend to forget this place exists, but then a special occasion comes up, and we are reminded again. We've attended a wedding rehearsal dinner here, had an anniversary dinner here, and even had our engagement dinner here. It's a cozy little place with exceptionally good service. The food is delicious although sometimes lacks in quantity. But they offer a full bar and a great variety of food as well as lovely desserts. This is a great place all around.

Source: Yelp, Inc.

6-4b Responding to Positive Reviews

Yelp offers the following advice for responding to customer reviews:

- Start by thanking the reviewer for providing feedback about their experience.
- Highlight something positive they said in the review.
- Conclude by inviting them back.[28]

Except for the last point, this advice also applies to employee reviews. The post from Glassdoor, shown in Figure 15,[29] is highly positive and does warrant a management response to acknowledge the feedback. Particularly for a start-up like Maidbot, the leader's voice is important for prospective employees to hear. In this example, the CEO responds personally, shows his appreciation, and highlights the work culture and team. Negative reviews require special attention. We discuss these in Chapter 7.

Highly Positive Employee Review and Management's Response | **Figure 15**

Source: Glassdoor, Inc.

5.0 ★★★★★ ✓

Current Employee, more than 3 years

Upward trajectory; gaining momentum

Aug 19, 2020 - Technical Leadership in Austin, TX

✓ Recommend ✓ CEO Approval ✓ Business Outlook

Pros

- Outstanding engineering team (high talent, low ego)
- Competent management (planning, strategy, product)
- Individual influence on product and direction
- Growth and learning actively encouraged
- Projects are consistently fun and interesting
- Flexible hours and good benefits

Cons

- Long hours sometimes necessary; but frequently known in advance
- Small team means bigger impact from illness or leave

Maidbot Response

I appreciate you providing your honest perspective on Maidbot and leaving your review. Your feedback on our strong team, competent leadership dynamic, encouragement of learning and growth, and work on exciting projects is refreshing to hear. Building a strong culture with a world-class team is one of our top priorities so we can build an incredible company. Thank you for being part of our A player team and for all of the contributions you have brought to the company.

Sincerely,
Micah Green
Founder, President, and CEO

LO5 Explain ways to engage customers and employees on social media.

6-5 Engaging Customers and Employees on Social Media

Simply responding to customers and prospective and current employees online isn't enough. Ask social media managers in any company, and they will likely say the same thing: it's all about the "conversation."

Social media provides company leaders with the opportunity to engage with stakeholders directly. To build meaningful relationships online, companies are proactive, seeking out customers and finding creative ways to interact.

You know this from your own experience as a customer: your favorite brands tend to find you. Young people flocking to new social networks will soon see new content from companies vying for their attention. Next, you learn how companies engage customers and employees online.

6-5a Engaging Customers Online

A Gallup study found that few people are influenced by companies' social media presence alone. Instead of chasing fans and followers, companies focus on building relationships with existing customers to convert them to brand advocates. To do this, Gallup suggests that companies be authentic, responsive, and compelling.[30]

American Airlines prides itself on responding to tweets in a conversational way. When the company's social media teams brainstormed words for their Twitter responses, they came up with "genuine," "authentic," "transparent," "savvy," "clear," "professional," and "warm"—never "scripted."[31]

DiGiorno Pizza used these principles in its social media campaign, #DeliverDiGiorno.[32] During October, National Pizza Month, the company delivered a free pizza to people within a designated city who tweeted the hashtag (Figure 16). Happy customers tweeted with the hashtag a second time when they received their package, but there was one catch: the pizza was frozen. Still, the campaign was a good way to engage people and promote its frozen product.[33]

Figure 16 | DiGiorno's Engaging Social Media Campaign

@DiGiorno

We're getting in the delivery game during National Pizza Month!

Tweet #DeliverDiGiorno + your city and you could have DiGiorno delivered!

Source: Twitter, Inc.

6-5b Engaging Employees Online

Companies engage employees, in addition to customers, using social technologies. With a robust intranet site, senior-level managers can communicate with employees directly to convey one consistent brand message. Leaders who excel at internal communication are genuine, authentic, and transparent—the same qualities companies demonstrate on social media.

An intranet site also is a good way to encourage employees to participate in conversations about the company—and to keep their comments internal. One popular social networking tool for employees is Yammer (owned by Microsoft). Rather than posting embarrassing information about a company on public websites, employees can give feedback about products, organizational changes, and management on an employee-only intranet site.

6-6 Chapter Closing

Every employee can be a leader in creating a more positive environment at work. Dairy Queen amplified a customer's generosity and promoted a positive image of the company. By responding to and engaging stakeholders inside and outside the organization, you can contribute to a culture where people feel valued and connected to the company and to each other.

Writing positive messages is a foundational skill to prepare you for more challenging situations, such as when you need to persuade others, which we discuss next.

› IN ACTION

Decide How to Convey the "Pay It Forward" News

Consider the chapter introduction, which described the caravan of cars paying for Dairy Queen orders.

Imagine that you're Tina Jensen, the store manager, and have to decide what else, if anything, to communicate about the event on Facebook. Using the CAM model, what questions might Tina consider before posting more on social media?

››› CHARACTER CHECK

1. **How do I feel about the success and my role?**
   I'm incredibly grateful that more than 900 cars participated in what became a community event. My staff and I encouraged people to keep it going, but I don't take credit for our customers' generosity.
2. **Should I use the event to promote Dairy Queen?**
   I posted updates with car counts, but I don't feel comfortable promoting our products. This is such a positive story that I don't want to ruin it and draw negative attention.

   On the other hand, the publicity could inspire people at other companies or in other communities to do the same.

››› AUDIENCE ANALYSIS

1. **Who is my audience on Facebook?**
   Customers may read what I write, and I could see attracting a more public audience from shared posts.
2. **How might they react if I promote the store?**
   They might be turned off and feel as though this whole event was self-promotional and self-serving, but that's not at all the case. I could donate a percentage of the profits that accrued during this time.

››› MESSAGE AND MEDIUM

1. **What are the main points of my message?**
   I'll post one more message and then will stop, so I'm not "milking" the story for our own purposes. The message will provide a link to a local news story and mention our donations.
2. **In what medium will I communicate the message?**
   I'll keep the medium the same—on the Facebook page.

Write an Opinion Letter

〈 IN PRACTICE

Imagine that you started the Dairy Queen caravan by paying for the next car. You want to write an open letter for your local newsletter about the event.

››› CHARACTER CHECK

1. What drives me to write the letter? Consider a purpose that celebrates the event.
2. Now consider a possible selfish purpose.

››› AUDIENCE ANALYSIS

1. Who would likely read my letter and what might interest them?
2. How might they react to my letter?

››› MESSAGE AND MEDIUM

1. What will be my main points?
2. Is a letter in the local newspaper the best medium? What, if any, alternatives might work better?

REFLECTING ON YOUR COMMUNICATION AND CHARACTER DEVELOPMENT

1. **Consider your own views about business.**
   If you have business experience, either as an intern or a full-time employee for a company, do you relate to negative stereotypes about work? How did you contribute to the culture—either positively or negatively? In retrospect, could you have contributed more positively? What could you have done differently?

2. **Reflect on the "Sunday Scaries."**
   Have you experienced anxiety on Sundays or another day of the week in anticipation of the next work or school day? What were the circumstances? What patterns did you observe when this happened, and what conclusions can you draw about the work, the people, the classes, or yourself?

   How can you use the extra energy from your anxiety to gain clarity about your work or school situation? How can you reframe the situation or address issues that cause the anxiety?

3. **Reflect on your response time.**
   Within how many minutes or hours, on average, do you respond to email? Does your answer vary for different contexts, for example, work, school, volunteer, or club/organization email? How would others describe your response time? Are you satisfied with your answers to these questions, or do you want to respond to others more quickly? If you do want to improve, what would it take?

4. **Write a thank-you note.**
   Think about someone who had a positive influence on your life—a former teacher, coach, pastor, friend, relative, etc. Write a thank-you note following the guidelines in this chapter. Reflect on the process. What drives you to write, and what makes you hesitate?

5. **Analyze your response to a tragedy.**
   Think about a recent time when someone close to you suffered a tragedy. Did you write a sympathy note or offer compassion in a different way?

   Reflect on the experience. Did offering compassion come easy to you, or was it difficult? What factors affected your response?

DEVELOPING YOUR BUSINESS COMMUNICATION SKILLS

CREATING A POSITIVE WORK ENVIRONMENT

LO1 Describe the value of positive messages in business.

1. **Describe your ideal work environment.**
   In small groups, describe your ideal work environment. Try to be specific. Identify the people, the office or home space, and the work itself. If you had to prioritize, what would be most important?

2. **Describe your best and worst manager.**
   With a partner, describe the best and worst manager you have had. If you haven't had work experience, think about a coach, teacher, or someone else who inspired you to be your best—and another who didn't support you or actively discouraged you.

Another approach to this question is to think about a time when you felt most and least recognized. How did these people affect your thinking about recognition at work? What can you learn as you develop your own leadership style?

3. **Identify types of emails or text messages.**

   Review the past 50 or so emails or texts you received. Place them in categories: neutral, positive, sales/persuasive, bad news, and others. What conclusions can you draw based on the types of messages that you receive?

   Now review the messages you sent to others. How do those categories compare? What conclusions can you draw about your own messages?

WRITING NEUTRAL MESSAGES

LO2 Explain how to organize a neutral message.

4. **Identify the main point in neutral messages.**

   Read the neutral messages you received recently, identified in Exercise 3. Where is the main point in each? What percentage of the messages include the main point up front?

   Analyze the messages that don't have the main point up front. What conclusions can you draw about these messages and the author's approach? How does the organization affect the readability and, perhaps, your interest or inclination to respond?

5. **Request alumni organization membership information.**

   Whether you're graduating this year or a few years from now, you may want to join a local alumni organization. Write an email to the head of the alumni association in the area you might live. Include two questions that you can't find answered on a website. You might ask about specific club activities, benefits of joining, or steps to enroll.

   When you receive a response, compare emails with your classmates. Is the alumni association communicating consistently across regions (if your association has multiple locations), and are representatives of the organization customizing emails to each of you? If you were advising the organization's leaders, what suggestions would you make for them to improve their communications?

6. **Complete a form request.**

   Find a company's website that provides a form for submitting questions or requests online. Complete the form and analyze the process with a classmate. How easily could you find and complete the form? Also compare responses when you receive them. Did the company representatives follow the guidelines discussed in this chapter? What do you wish they had done differently?

7. **Identify issues with a neutral request.**

   In small groups, discuss a request you received that you didn't fulfill. Provide context, including relevant background about the person making the request, your situation at the time, and what the person was asking.

   Explain why you didn't fulfill the request. Could the sender have done something differently?

   Next, describe a situation in which *you* requested information that wasn't fulfilled. Could you have done something differently?

8. **Respond to a speaking request.**

Imagine that your favorite high school teacher asks you to speak to the junior class. You receive the following email:

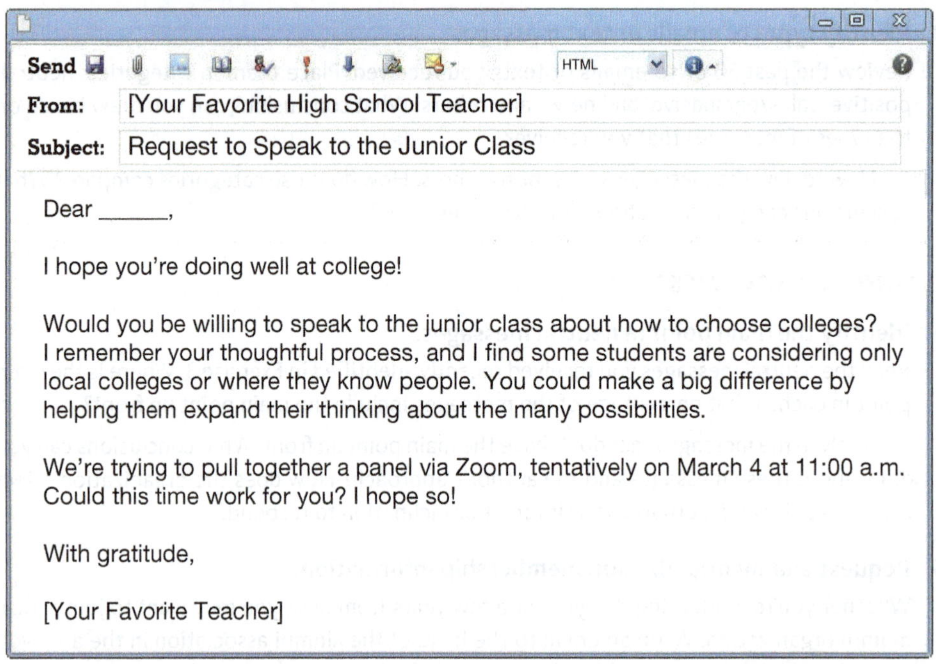
Send
From: [Your Favorite High School Teacher]
Subject: Request to Speak to the Junior Class

Dear ______,

I hope you're doing well at college!

Would you be willing to speak to the junior class about how to choose colleges? I remember your thoughtful process, and I find some students are considering only local colleges or where they know people. You could make a big difference by helping them expand their thinking about the many possibilities.

We're trying to pull together a panel via Zoom, tentatively on March 4 at 11:00 a.m. Could this time work for you? I hope so!

With gratitude,

[Your Favorite Teacher]

Write a response to your high school teacher to accept the invitation. Next, exchange responses with another student for feedback. How well did your classmate follow the guidelines for responding to neutral requests? What differences do you observe in how each of you chose to respond? What could account for those differences (e.g., connections to the school or other factors)?

WRITING GOODWILL MESSAGES

LO3 Apply guidelines for writing a goodwill message in a business situation.

9. **Write a recognition email.**

Imagine that you're a store manager for a local Costco. Brian, one of the sales associates who reports to you, has a reputation of going above and beyond to help customers. You just received a copy of this email, which a customer sent to Brian.

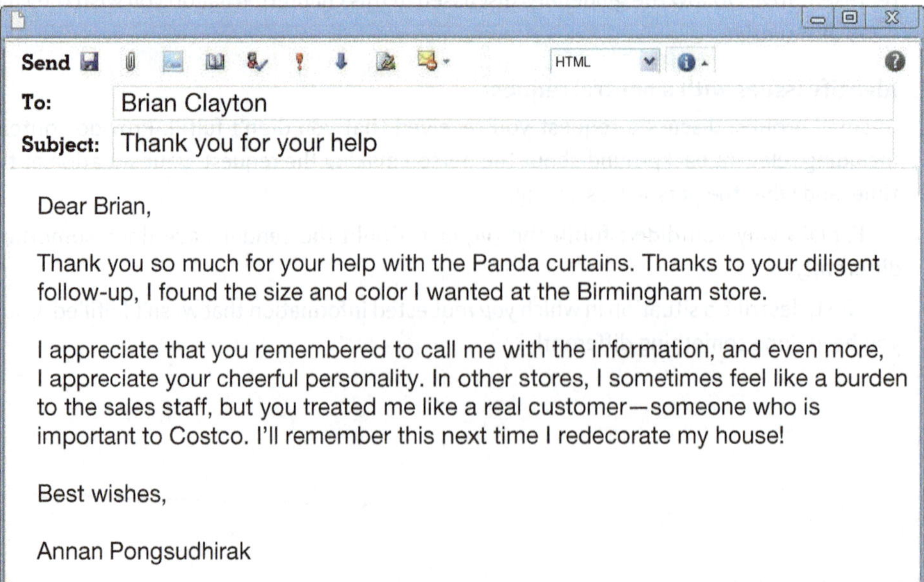
Send
To: Brian Clayton
Subject: Thank you for your help

Dear Brian,

Thank you so much for your help with the Panda curtains. Thanks to your diligent follow-up, I found the size and color I wanted at the Birmingham store.

I appreciate that you remembered to call me with the information, and even more, I appreciate your cheerful personality. In other stores, I sometimes feel like a burden to the sales staff, but you treated me like a real customer—someone who is important to Costco. I'll remember this next time I redecorate my house!

Best wishes,

Annan Pongsudhirak

As a good manager who takes the time to recognize employees' work, you write your own email to Brian. In addition to acknowledging this customer's feedback, include other examples of Brian's performance (which you can invent).

10. Write a congratulatory email.

Imagine that your former boss just won a "Manager of the Year" award. Handwrite a note congratulating the manager and make it meaningful by referring to your own experience as an employee. Include whatever details and examples you believe are relevant when congratulating your boss for the award.

11. Write a thank-you email.

Imagine that you just received an offer for a summer internship. You got the job through someone you know, who connected you to the hiring manager to discuss possibilities at the company.

Write an email to thank your contact for making the connection. Invent whatever details you would like, for example, what the job entails, where it's located, and so on.

Next, compare your note to those of two other students. What differences do you notice? How well did each of you follow the guidelines for writing goodwill messages?

12. Write a sympathy note.

Think about someone you know who recently suffered a significant loss—e.g., a job, a health issue, a divorce, or a death. Write a message that you can send as a handwritten note or in an email. Will you send the message? Why or why not? Consider your own feelings about offering compassion and what might prevent you from following through. What might be good reasons to follow through?

13. Write a goodwill note a day.

During the next week, write one quick goodwill note—email, text, or handwritten—every day. At the beginning of each day, think about someone to recognize, congratulate, thank, or offer compassion. At the end of the week, discuss the experience in class. Did you find it difficult or easy? How did you feel? Will you keep up the practice, perhaps once or twice a week? Why or why not?

ADDRESSING SOCIAL MEDIA COMMENTS

LO4 Apply guidelines for responding to online feedback in a business situation.

14. Decide whether to respond to online reviews.

Find about ten mentions of your favorite brand on Twitter. Using the Social Media Response Guidelines in Figure 13, to which of the posts do you think the company should respond?

Next, analyze which posts received a response and how the feedback was addressed. From these examples, how well is your favorite brand responding on social media? What would improve the response?

15. Analyze a company's response to employee reviews.

On Glassdoor, search for a company for which you might like to work. How well is management responding to reviews? Discuss your analysis in small groups.

16. Provide recommendations for responding to employee reviews.

Imagine that the company you searched for in Exercise 15 hires you as a social media consultant. They want your recommendations for ways they can improve management responses on Glassdoor.

Write a short report to provide the value of responding to employee reviews on Glassdoor, a strategy for responding to social media comments, and guidelines for management responses.

17. **Provide a sample management response.**

To provide further guidance to the company you focused on in Exercises 15 and 16, write a sample management response. Choose a highly positive employee review on Glassdoor and follow Yelp's advice: thank the employee for providing feedback and highlight something positive in the review.

Switch responses with a classmate. Does the other student's review inspire you to work for the company? Specifically, what about the response leaves you with a positive or negative impression?

18. **Write a response to a highly positive customer comment.**

Imagine that you just found this comment about your new dog-training company online. Using the Yelp guidelines, write a response that shows appreciation for the comment.

> Doggie Do is the best! My Doberman, Oscar, wasn't house trained, but now he's a new dog. Amelia at Doggie Do immediately took control, and now Oscar is a well-behaved little pooch—and the rest of the family is much happier. I'd recommend Amelia to anyone having trouble with a new pet.

LO5 Explain ways to engage customers and employees on social media.

ENGAGING CUSTOMERS AND EMPLOYEES ON SOCIAL MEDIA

19. **Analyze a brand's "voice" on social media.**

Choose a company that interests you and visit at least three social networks where it has a presence. Screen-capture a few posts from each site to compare. Does the company convey a similar voice across all platforms? Does the writing reflect the brand and sound appropriate for the brand? In other words, do you associate the writing with the brand? Explain your analysis to a classmate.

20. **Compare companies' tweets.**

You read about American Airlines' principles for writing tweets. Read a few recent tweets at https://twitter.com/AmericanAir and compare them to another airline's writing style. Which sounds more genuine and authentic? Which do you prefer and why?

Now compare these tweets to organizations in different industries. Read tweets from a bank, a clothing retailer, a technology company, and a nonprofit organization. Describe differences you observe in writing style.

21. **Compare social media engagement.**

Now choose one of the organizations from Exercise 20 and visit it on different social platforms. What does the company do to engage customers?

Write a short report to the VP of marketing to identify what the company does well and how it could improve. You might recommend changes in writing style or platforms, or you might suggest ideas for engaging more people or for engaging people in more creative ways. Include principles learned from this chapter and from your own experience interacting with organizations on social networks.

22. Consider a social network for an organization's intranet.

In small groups, have students describe their intranet experience, if any, from an employer or other organization. For the rest of the group, discuss how a company where you worked could have used an intranet. What social networking functionality might have been useful? What could have been the benefits?

Next, consider potential obstacles to implementing an intranet. In other words, why do some companies have an intranet and others don't?

CHAPTER SUMMARY

LO1 Describe the value of positive messages in business.

People want to be appreciated and enjoy receiving positive messages. To counteract negative stereotypes and work stress, managers should recognize people for their work. Positive and neutral messages may be internal or external.

LO2 Explain how to organize a neutral message.

When writing a neutral message, for example, to request action or ask a question, start with the main point, provide explanations or details, and end on a positive note. When responding to a neutral message, respond promptly and personalize your message.

LO3 Apply guidelines for writing a goodwill message in a business situation.

Write goodwill messages to maintain or build relationships. Goodwill messages express recognition, congratulations, appreciation, or sympathy. Write promptly after an event and be direct, specific, sincere, and brief.

LO4 Apply guidelines for responding to online feedback in a business situation.

Follow a strategy for social listening and deciding whether and how to respond to social media comments. Highly positive comments may deserve a response, while neutral comments can be left alone. Typically respond to misguided and unhappy customers but avoid overresponding and inflaming trolls.

LO5 Explain ways to engage customers and employees on social media.

Companies that truly engage customers and employees through social media develop stronger connections with these audiences. Externally, with an authentic brand voice, companies inspire re-posts and extend their reach. Internally, companies encourage feedback and build relationships among employees.

Endnotes

1. Dairy Queen Grill & Chill (522 C St NE, Brainerd, MN), December 10, 2020, Facebook Post, www.facebook.com/DQ45423/posts/233405651466565, accessed February 22, 2021.
2. Jamie Yuccas, "'It Is a Selfless Act': 900 Customers Pay for Each Other's Meals at Dairy Queen in Minnesota," CBS Evening News, December 21, 2020, www.cbsnews.com/news/dairy-queen-minnesota-900-customers-pay-it-forward, accessed February 22, 2021.
3. Dairy Queen Grill & Chill.
4. "Holiday Special with Dwayne Johnson: Some Good News with John Krasinski," *SomeGoodNews*, YouTube, December 20, 2020, https://youtu.be/3GwU4GKzLXY, accessed February 22, 2021.
5. Nicole Lyn Pesce, "John Krasinski Tries Explaining to Furious Fans Why He Sold 'Some Good News' to CBS," MarketWatch, May 20, 2020, www.marketwatch.com/story/john-krasinski-tries-explaining-to-furious-fans-why-he-sold-some-good-news-to-cbs-2020-05-28, accessed February 22, 2021.
6. Amit Kumar and Nicholas Epley, "Undervaluing Gratitude: Expressers Misunderstand the Consequences of Showing Appreciation," *Psychological Science* 20 (2018): 1423–1435.
7. For example, see David DeSteno's work at www.davedesteno.com/publications/tag/gratitude and his book, *Emotional Success: The Power of Gratitude, Compassion, and Pride* (New York: Houghton Mifflin Harcourt, 2018).
8. Blair Heitmann, "Your Guide to Winning @Work: Decoding the Sunday Scaries," LinkedIn, September 28, 2018, https://blog.linkedin.com/2018/september/28/your-guide-to-winning-work-decoding-the-sunday-scaries, accessed February 24, 2021.
9. Joe Pinsker, "Why People Get the 'Sunday Scaries,'" *The Atlantic*, February 9, 2020, www.theatlantic.com/family/archive/2020/02/sunday-scaries-anxiety-workweek/606289/, accessed February 24, 2021.
10. "Corporate," IMDB, www.imdb.com/title/tt5648202, accessed February 24, 2021.
11. Jim Harter and Kristi Rubenstein, "The 38 Most Engaged Workplaces in the World Put People First," Gallup, March 18, 2020, www.gallup.com/workplace/290573/engaged-workplaces-world-put-people-first.aspx, accessed December 19, 2020.
12. Harter and Rubenstein.
13. Oprah Winfrey, "Oprah Winfrey Harvard Commencement Speech," YouTube, May 30, 2013, www.youtube.com/watch?v=GMWFieBGR7c, accessed February 26, 2021.
14. Mussie T. Tessema, Kathryn J. Ready, and Abel B. Embaye, "The Effects of Employee Recognition, Pay, and Benefits on Job Satisfaction: Cross Country Evidence," *Journal of Business and Economics* 4 (2013): 1–12.
15. "Achievers Survey Finds Without Recognition, Expect Employee Attrition in 2018," Achievers, January 18, 2018, www.achievers.com/press/achievers-survey-finds-without-recognition-expect-employee-attrition-2018, accessed February 26, 2021.
16. Jeff Bezos, "Email from Jeff Bezos to employees," Amazon Website, February 2, 2021, www.aboutamazon.com/news/company-news/email-from-jeff-bezos-to-employees, accessed February 25, 2021.
17. "TIAA Appoints Thasunda Brown Duckett President and CEO," TIAA Website, February 25, 2021, www.tiaa.org/public/about-tiaa/news-press/press-releases/pressrelease812.html, accessed February, 25, 2021.
18. "Intel Appoints Tech Industry Leader Pat Gelsinger as New CEO," Intel Website, January 13, 2021, https://newsroom.intel.com/news-releases/intel-appoints-tech-industry-leader-pat-gelsinger-as-new-ceo/#gs.u049t0, accessed February 25, 2021.
19. A polite request can take a period instead of a question mark, such as, "May I please have your answer by March 3," but by convention, most people use a question mark.
20. Jeff Toister, "How Quickly Should You Respond to Email?" Toister Solutions, April 7, 2020, www.toistersolutions.com/blog/how-quickly-should-you-respond-to-email, accessed July 26, 2021.
21. Doga Istanbulluoglu, "Complaint Handling on Social Media: The Impact of Multiple Response Times on Consumer Satisfaction," *Computers in Human Behavior* 74 (2017): 72–82, https://doi.org/10.1016/j.chb.2017.04.016.
22. Farshad Kooti et al., "Evolution of Conversations in the Age of Email Overload," 24th International World Wide Web Conference, April 2, 2015, https://arxiv.org/abs/1504.00704, accessed July 26, 2021.
23. Karen Choi and Michael Ross, "Cultural Differences in Process and Person Focus: Congratulations on Your Hard Work Versus Celebrating Your Exceptional Brain," *Journal of Experimental Social Psychology* (2010), www.sciencedirect.com/science/article/pii/S0022103110002581.
24. Mary S. Howald, "Praise and Thank You's," Hampton, Virginia Website, https://hampton.gov/2290/Praise-Thank-Yous, accessed February 26, 2021.
25. Names and addresses have been changed.
26. Jennifer L. Goetz, "Compassion: An Evolutionary Analysis and Empirical Review," *Psychological Bulletin* 136 (2010): 351–374.
27. Chris K. Anderson and Saram Han, "Hotel Performance Impact of Socially Engaging with Consumers," Cornell University, School of Hotel Administration, April 5, 2016, https://ecommons.cornell.edu/handle/1813/71227, accessed February 27, 2021.
28. "Dos and Dont's of Responding to Reviews on Yelp," Yelp Official Blog, September 1, 2020, https://blog.yelp.com/2020/09/dos-donts-responding-to-reviews-yelp, accessed March 1, 2021.
29. Current employee, "Upward Trajectory; Gaining Momentum," Maidbot Review on Glassdoor, August 19, 2020,

www.glassdoor.com/Reviews/Maidbot-Reviews-E1565237.htm, accessed February 27, 2021.

30. "The Myth of Social Media," Gallup, June 11, 2014, online.wsj.com/public/resources/documents/sac_report_11_socialmedia_061114.pdf, accessed March 1, 2021.

31. Matt Wilson, "American Airlines Responds to Every Tweet with Original, Non-Scripted Answers," PR Daily, August 1, 2012, www.prdaily.com/Main/Articles/12296.aspx, accessed March 3, 2021.

32. @DiGiorno, Twitter, "We're Getting in the Delivery Game During National Pizza Month!" September 23, 2019, https://twitter.com/DiGiorno/status/1176206789056061440, accessed March 19, 2021.

33. Michelle Cyca, "7 of the Best Social Media Campaigns (and What You Can Learn from Them)," Hootsuite, https://blog.hootsuite.com/social-media-campaign-strategy/, August 12, 2020, accessed March 19, 2021.

CHAPTER

7 Persuasive Messages

Learning Objectives

After you have finished this chapter, you should be able to

LO1 Identify ways to tailor persuasive messages to different audiences.

LO2 Compare strategies to persuade an audience in a given situation.

LO3 Describe parts of an effective internal or external persuasive message.

LO4 Describe parts of an effective response to negative feedback.

"As several decades of awareness-raising and initiatives to engage the public have shown, climate change doesn't communicate itself." [1]

—Roz Pidcock, head of communication at a climate change working group

Chapter Introduction

Climate Researchers Identify Ways to Persuade

More than 90% of climate scientists agree that humans are causing global warming, yet Americans' understanding lags the rest of the world.[2] Only 59% of people in the United States, compared to 80% or more in Greece, South Korea, France, Spain, and Mexico, believe that climate change is a major threat.[3]

farzand01/Shutterstock.com

People evacuate after a hurricane in Bekasi, Indonesia.

Researchers have identified six principles to persuade the public that climate change is happening and is human made:

1. Be a confident communicator
2. Talk about the real world, not abstract ideas
3. Connect with what matters to your audience
4. Tell a human story
5. Lead with what you know
6. Use the most effective visual communication.[4]

Eliciting compassion for victims of environmental disasters can be particularly effective for changing beliefs and inspiring climate policy.[5] These strategies are effective for many types of persuasion.

LO1 Identify ways to tailor persuasive messages to different audiences.

7-1 Planning Persuasive Messages

Every day, people try to persuade you: companies advertise their products, friends convince you to go to the movies, and instructors encourage you to learn new concepts. In business, managers guide employees, consultants promote their ideas, and entrepreneurs raise funding. We use persuasion to motivate people to do something or believe something that they would not otherwise have done or believed.

Persuasion becomes an issue of character when we cross ethical lines and when we're manipulated ourselves. Convincing someone to take harmful action or to buy an unneeded product raises questions of integrity and trust. Similarly, getting duped into harming others or going into debt raises questions of compassion and judgment. The principles in this chapter are tools for you to persuade others—and to protect yourself.

One way to reconcile the ethical tension inherent in persuasion is to think about *inspiring* people rather than *persuading* them. Inspiration implies a more audience-focused mindset by which people make their own choices. We explore these concepts in this section, and you learn ways to understand resistance, analyze your audience, and tailor persuasive messages.

7-1a Persuading Ethically

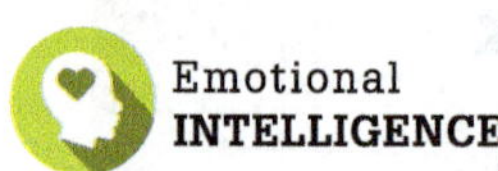

Have you crossed an ethical line when trying to persuade others? What was the situation, and how do you feel about it in retrospect? Would you do anything differently next time?

Persuasion is not coercion. In some cases, people may be forced to do something, but they can't be forced to believe something. They must be persuaded in ways that are acceptable to them.

As business communicators, we have a responsibility to act ethically in building relationships with our audience. We "pitch" our ideas—sometimes quite aggressively, as you may have seen on shows like *Shark Tank*—but investors and others seeking a long-term relationship want to do business with someone who is trustworthy.

For transactional, one-time sales, ethics come into play more often. Imagine trying to rent an apartment when you're in a desperate situation: you have only one day to find a new place. Knowing this, the landlord tells you that three other people are coming to see it later in the day, even though that's not true. People who prey on others' limitations just to make a sale are not acting ethically.

Have you been in situations in which you felt gullible? Have you fallen for a scam and realized too late? What influenced you, and how can you avoid this in the future?

Thousands of regulators and litigators sued Juul for the e-cigarette company's aggressive marketing toward youth.[6] Although the company claimed that the products were intended to help people quit smoking, alluring images, sophisticated packaging, and sweet flavors got teens hooked on vaping.[7]

Notice how the ad in Figure 1 might appeal to teens.[8] Only later did Juul's ads include the warning, "This product contains nicotine. Nicotine is an addictive chemical."[9]

Juul is not going down without a fight. As it settles lawsuits, the company is spending millions of dollars on federal lobbying, and the *American Journal of Health Behavior* has published studies—funded by Juul—showing how the product helps people quit smoking.[10]

To persuade, we need to overcome resistance. But we must do so ethically. We explore types of resistance next.

Technically, *compliance-gaining* refers to changing behavior, and *persuasion* refers to changing attitudes or beliefs. We use *persuasion* here for both.

Juul's Persuasive Messaging Attracted Teens | **Figure 1**

Source: JUUL.

7-1b Understanding Resistance

Persuasion is required when people resist what we ask of them. Following are a few examples of resistance you may encounter when you try to change behavior, attitudes, or beliefs.

Persuasive Message	Possible Resistance
You want your manager to give you a promotion.	Your manager may have budget restrictions or may believe your performance doesn't warrant a promotion.
You want your coworkers to join a union.	Your coworkers may be afraid of losing their job or paying union dues but not getting a higher salary.
You want to sell a new product to an existing customer.	The customer may be happy with the current product or may not want to spend more money.
You want an employee to work overtime.	The employee may have other plans or may believe your request is unfair or unnecessary.
You want a supplier to give you a discount on products.	The supplier may not have authority to grant your request or may be concerned about fairness to other customers.

Emotional **INTELLIGENCE**

How comfortable are you overcoming resistance? Do you tend to shy away from persuasion, or do you embrace the opportunity to convince others of your point of view?

In each of these situations, you must overcome the resistance. You'll have the best chance if you know your audience and adapt your message to them.

7-1c Analyzing Your Audience

In Chapter 4, you learned an approach for analyzing your audience. These five questions, shown again in Figure 2, are particularly useful for persuasive messages.

Typically, people react to persuasion in one of four ways. We try to avoid it, challenge the message, selectively process information, or assert our own views.[11] When faced with a persuasive message, we might fear change or loss of freedom. We also might sense that we're being deceived.[12] These concerns explain why people might be skeptical of or hostile to our attempts to persuade.

Not everyone will be resistant. For example, if you announce a change in an organization, people may be indifferent or even supportive. Too often, these groups are ignored as we put all our time and energy trying to persuade the active resisters. But indifferent people can be inspired to move, and supportive people can be inspired to persuade others.

Figure 2 | Audience Analysis

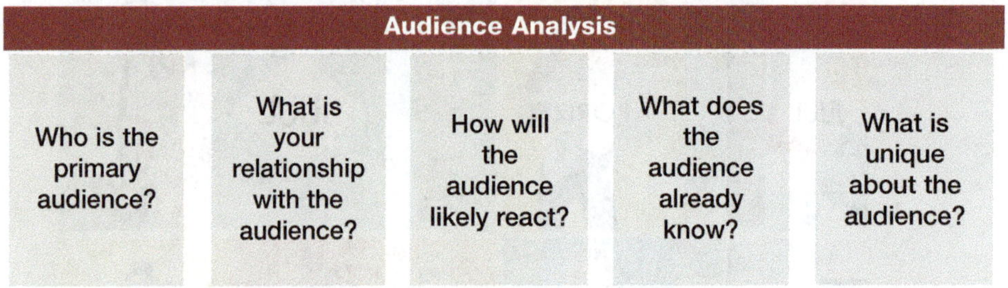

Audience Analysis				
Who is the primary audience?	What is your relationship with the audience?	How will the audience likely react?	What does the audience already know?	What is unique about the audience?

Spend time analyzing your audience to pinpoint areas of resistance. Ask questions to understand their concerns, so you can either change course to accommodate them or address each when you tailor your messages.

7-1d Tailoring to Your Audience

Targeted and tailored messages achieve better results than generic messages that aren't modified for different audiences.[13] Targeted messages are adapted to different audience segments based on group similarities, such as cultural identifications. Research also shows that deeper cultural messaging may have better results than surface messaging. For example, when communication encouraging healthier behavior referred to Asian American, Pacific Islander, or Hispanic values, traditions, religious beliefs, or norms instead of references to music, clothing, or food, the messages were more persuasive, and people were more likely to follow the health advice.[14]

Although advertisers can target a consumer based on, for example, other online purchases and websites visited, managers who know their audience personally can tailor a persuasive message to their specific needs. Tailored messages are adapted to individuals. When people perceive messages as personally relevant, they are more likely to be persuaded.[15]

Even more persuasive than targeted or tailored messages is the process of interpersonal communication.[16] Chapter 3 discussed the value of shifting your mindset to be more open and curious. To change someone's else's mind, particularly about a core belief, apply these same principles. Generally, listen more than you speak.

LO2 Compare strategies to persuade an audience in a given situation.

7-2 Applying Persuasive Strategies

With your audience in mind, develop a toolkit of strategies to change behavior or attitudes. Start with "why," demonstrate credibility, appeal to emotion, develop logical arguments, and apply principles of influence.

7-2a Start with "Why"

In his book and popular TED Talk, Simon Sinek encourages leaders to start with "why."[17] Too often, Sinek says, we focus on what or how—what our idea is or how our product works. Instead, as we discussed earlier, the audience comes first. This requires empathy, our ability to see the situation from the other's perspective.

Tailoring your message to why your audience should care increases the likelihood that they will be persuaded. Let's say you manage a team of eight employees and, because of cutbacks, need to persuade them to take on additional responsibilities. They each have different motivations for complying.

Focusing on "Why" for Different Employees	
For employees who . . .	*You might focus on how taking on additional responsibilities will . . .*
Are ambitious and want to be promoted.	Make them eligible for higher-level positions in the future.
Are social and care about the team.	Help the overall team performance.
Have a strong work ethic.	Increase their contribution to the organization.

Stress the "you" attitude to achieve the results you want. Audiences need to know, "What's in it for me?" and you can address this if you know your audience well. Your job is to let the reader know the benefits of doing as you ask. Emphasize the reader, not yourself or your product.

☒ NOT Our firm would like to do an energy audit of your business.

☑ BUT An energy audit will tell you which investments will save the most money over time.

7-2b Demonstrate Credibility

In his work *Rhetoric*, Aristotle identified three methods by which people can be persuaded:

- Ethos, demonstrating credibility
- Pathos, appealing to emotion
- Logos, developing logical arguments.

These methods remain as relevant today as they were when Aristotle wrote about them more than two thousand years ago. As part of your process of analyzing your audience, consider which of these methods—or what combination—will work best to persuade each person or group. First, we explore credibility.

You might hear clues about your audience's resistance to your credibility. You might hear questions about your experience, such as "What's your background?" or "How long have you been working with Wells Fargo?" Or you might face an audience who is skeptical about your character or ethics. In these situations, your audience may question your motives: "Why are you recommending this proposal to us now?" or "What is our financial agreement with you?"

To address these concerns, demonstrate your credibility. Consider discussing your background up front, sending your bio ahead of time, bringing a more experienced person with you to a meeting, showing examples of your work, or providing references. The more your audience connects with you as a person, the more they may accept you and your opinions.

The graphic in Figure 3 illustrates credibility. The high percentages represent overwhelming scientific consensus about climate change.[18,19]

Integrity is an important component of your character and credibility. When you demonstrate integrity—following through on your commitments and abiding by high moral values—you'll be perceived as trustworthy. Integrity also involves transparency. Communication should be complete and convey the whole truth.

Consider acknowledging opposing viewpoints. Most business audiences are smart enough to know potential downsides of your idea. If you ignore obvious obstacles, you miss an opportunity to address them—and your omission could damage your credibility. By presenting an entire, integral argument, you let the audience decide how to respond.

Figure 3 | Credibility in Climate Change Communication

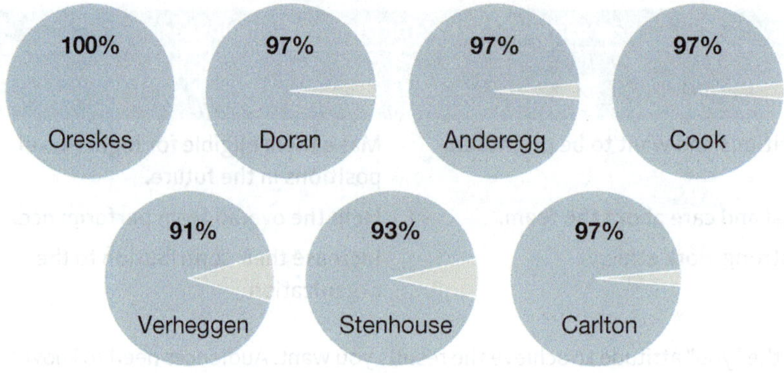

7-2c Appeal to Prosocial Emotions

Some audiences are more persuaded by emotional appeals—and some topics lend themselves more to emotional appeals. Growing evidence shows that prosocial messaging, which promotes the welfare of others, is more persuasive than self-interest appeals.[20]

In the chapter opening, you read about the effect of compassion on climate change beliefs and interests. Images, video, and human anecdotes elicit emotions better than facts and figures do. When we hear or watch stories, our brains release chemicals that make us feel more connected to others and make the storytellers appear more trustworthy, compassionate, and generous.[21] In writing, we also can demonstrate our genuine emotion.

Write stories using the ABT—*and, but, therefore*—format to create and build tension.[22] *And* or another agreement word begins your story and provides context. *But* or another contradiction word signals a shift in the story, which is the problem you identify. *Therefore* or another consequence word describes the result or solution to the problem. The story in Figure 4 illustrates this structure.[23]

This story illustrates another prosocial behavior—gratitude.[24] The author describes feeling grateful for spending time outdoors, which also inspired his action.

7-2d Develop Logical Arguments

To persuade some audiences, logical appeals work best. When an audience challenges your argument ("How can you be sure we'll get the results you promise?") or asks for data ("What's the return on investment for your proposal?"), focus on logic.

Develop a coherent, well-organized argument. Preview your claims and provide convincing evidence to support each. A cohesive argument is complete and focused—neither missing important information nor straying into irrelevant topics.

With sound reasoning, logical arguments conclude that benefits outweigh costs. The benefits and costs may be tangible or intangible, for example, monetary or social.

Aristotle defined the three aspects of logic this way:

- Fact: indisputably verifiable
- Inference: probably verifiable
- Opinion: possibly verifiable.

Typically, factual data is most persuasive; however, inferences drawn on available data and expert opinion also may convince your audience. The example in Figure 5 is a logical argument. We might consider the population growth—from 114 million to 190 million

Emotional Appeal in Climate Change Communication | **Figure 4**

As a parent of two boys, I have always enjoyed being able to share with them the experiences and activities that I enjoyed as a child and seeing the joy on their faces running into the sea on a warm summer's day or throwing snowballs in the winter.

And I got great solace knowing that we were part of an unbroken chain connecting past and future generations.

But as I have brought them up, I have seen the changing seasons become disrupted, and I experienced that as a very deep and profound challenge to my own sense of well-being and my sense of what it meant to be a good father.

Therefore, I made the decision quite late in life to learn what I could about what was happening and what I could do about it, so I returned to university, studied the social science of climate change, and now here I am standing in front of you.

Logical Argument in Climate Change Communication | **Figure 5**

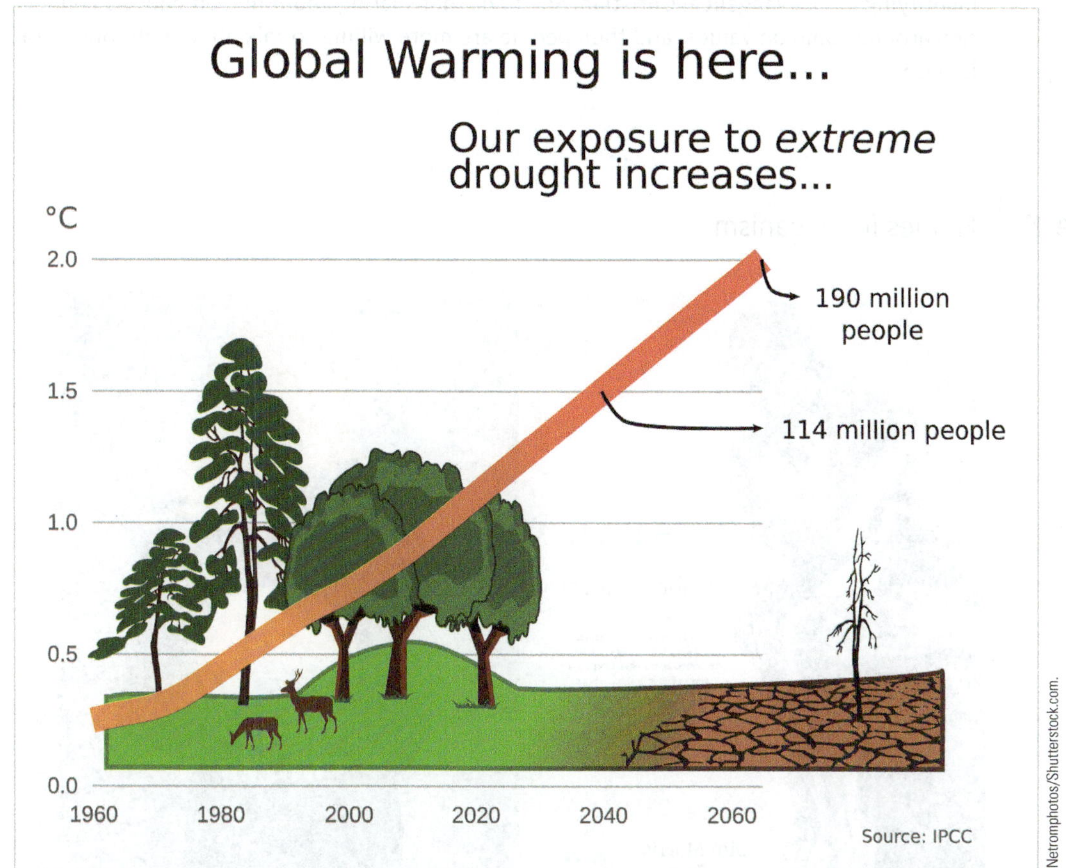

DNetromphotos/Shutterstock.com.

people—a fact. But concluding that this growth will increase exposure to extreme drought might be considered an inference based on assumptions about the effects of more people on the planet.

You'll notice overlap in ethos, pathos, and logos examples. Figure 3 primarily conveys credibility but includes data. Figure 5 primarily conveys data but shows animals and trees and uses emotional language ("extreme").

What we choose to emphasize also contributes to a logical argument. **Framing** is how we present an idea to an audience. For example, Figure 6 illustrates different frames to promote veganism. The "Think" poster, published by People for the Ethical Treatment of Animals (PETA), stresses health benefits. Although the organization's major concern is animal welfare, the marketers chose a different frame for this message. In contrast, the sweatshirt imprint stresses the negative effect of eating meat on the environment. Which of these frames would more likely convince you to become a vegan?

7-2e Apply Principles of Influence

Seven principles of influence from marketing psychology also should be part of your toolkit. Psychologist Robert Cialdini identified the following from his business research.[25]

Liking: People Like Those Who Like Them

"Uncover real similarities and offer genuine praise."

Note that Cialdini emphasizes honesty and authenticity—"real" and "genuine"—rather than forced connection or false praise. Climate scientist Katharine Hayhoe talks about openly identifying as an evangelical Christian. She finds that sharing about herself builds a connection around common values, and then people are more willing to talk about environmental issues.[26]

Figure 6 | Frames for Veganism

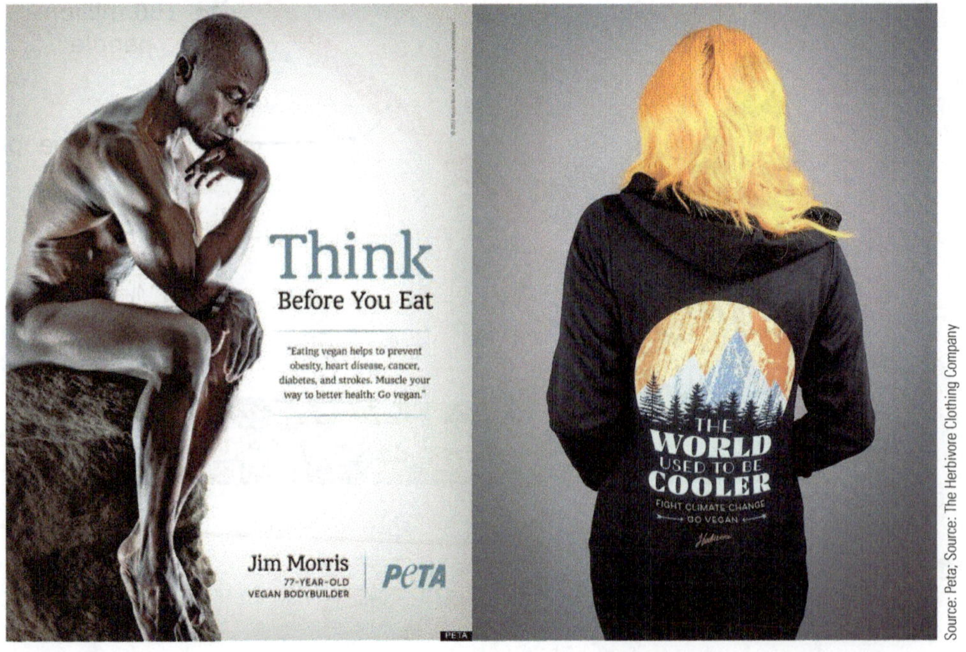

Source: Peta; Source: The Herbivore Clothing Company

Reciprocity: People Repay in Kind

"Give what you want to receive."

In fundraising letters, organizations may include a small gift, banking on the principle of reciprocity—that you will be more likely to donate in return. At work, if you help a coworker with a project, you are far more likely to get help when you need it.

Social Proof: People Follow the Lead of Similar Others

"Use peer power when it's available."

Peer *pressure* could be unethical, but showing people that others have already signed onto an idea will persuade them to agree. Employees who advocate for change within their company have an easier time enlisting support as more join on. As another example, the World Wide Fund for Nature (WWF) in the United Kingdom has a rolling count of people who sign up on its website (Figure 7).

Figure 7 WWF Uses Social Proof and Commitment and Consistency

WWF LEARN WHERE WE WORK WHAT WE DO WHO WE ARE SUCCESS STORIES

JOIN THE FIGHT AGAINST CLIMATE CHANGE

Enter your details to join **156,512** people in demanding the UK tackles the climate crisis.

Source: WORLD WILDLIFE FUND (WWF)

Commitment and Consistency: People Align with Their Clear Commitments

"Make their commitments active, public, and voluntary."

If you sign a petition, you are more likely to donate to an organization. That's why the WWF wants you to sign up to receive email. Minutes taken during a meeting serve a similar purpose: once people commit to a task, they are more likely to follow through.

Authority: People Defer to Experts

"Expose your expertise; don't assume it's self-evident."

Authority relates most closely to credibility. With both humility and confidence, tell people that you know what you're talking about. For example, if you're trying to persuade people to adopt your solution, you might offer evidence of how you have solved similar problems in the past. Companies hire celebrities to endorse their products because the public perceives them to be credible. However, to comply with U.S. laws, people must disclose when they receive compensation—to acknowledge that they are paid to act as experts.

Scarcity: People Want More of What They Can Have Less Of

"Highlight unique benefits and exclusive information."

When you shop online and see "Only 2 left at this price!" or "Order before May 14," the company is using the principle of scarcity. We place a higher value on what we can't have, for example, first-class seats on airplanes and access to limited-occupancy nightclubs.

Unity: People Are Influenced by Shared Identities

"Identify in terms of a group . . . to form a sense of self-esteem and pride."[27]

Cialdini added this seventh principle after noticing shared identities as an undercurrent of the others, helping us make quick decisions about, for example, whether we like the person or view someone as an authority.[28] We are more likely to be persuaded by people with whom we identify, for example, if we're part of the same family, religious group, college, or hometown. When people hear "we," are asked for advice, or are treated as an insider, they are more likely to comply with our requests.[29]

Be careful with these seven principles and all persuasive strategies. They are powerful tools but should never be abused to take advantage of people. Damaged relationships may never heal. Next, we see how persuasion is used in written messages.

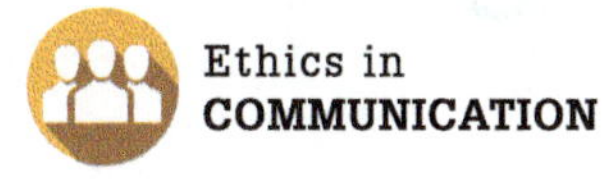

LO3 Describe parts of an effective internal or external persuasive message.

7-3 Writing Persuasive Messages

In business, you'll create many types of persuasive messages. In this section, you learn how to use persuasive strategies in short internal and external written communication.

7-3a Internal Persuasive Messages

When you have an idea at work but don't have the authority to implement it, you'll need to persuade your manager that the idea is worthwhile. In the example shown in Figure 8, a restaurant employee presents an idea to improve the owner's business.

Figure 8 | Short Persuasive Proposal Example

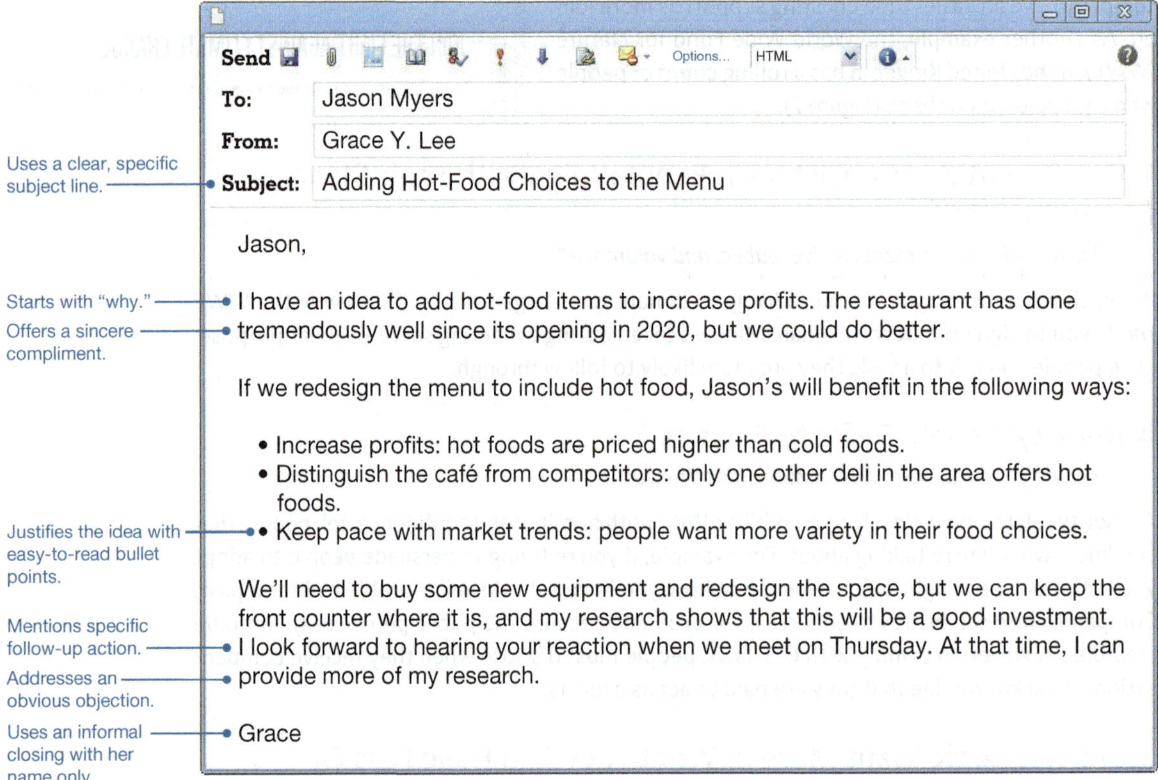

Send
Options...
HTML
To: Jason Myers
From: Grace Y. Lee
Subject: Adding Hot-Food Choices to the Menu
Jason,
I have an idea to add hot-food items to increase profits. The restaurant has done tremendously well since its opening in 2020, but we could do better.
If we redesign the menu to include hot food, Jason's will benefit in the following ways:
• Increase profits: hot foods are priced higher than cold foods.
• Distinguish the café from competitors: only one other deli in the area offers hot foods.
• Keep pace with market trends: people want more variety in their food choices.
We'll need to buy some new equipment and redesign the space, but we can keep the front counter where it is, and my research shows that this will be a good investment. I look forward to hearing your reaction when we meet on Thursday. At that time, I can provide more of my research.
Grace
Uses a clear, specific subject line.
Starts with "why."
Offers a sincere compliment.
Justifies the idea with easy-to-read bullet points.
Mentions specific follow-up action.
Addresses an obvious objection.
Uses an informal closing with her name only.

In Chapter 10, about writing reports, we see the Jason's Deli example as a longer, more formal proposal. In this example, Grace provides just enough information to get the owner interested in her idea. Next, we explore decisions for organizing and justifying these types of messages.

Organizing a Short, Internal Persuasive Message

Grace adapts the message to her audience. She starts with the "why" by focusing on what Jason cares about most—profits. She offers a sincere compliment—an example of liking and emotional appeal—and uses "we" language.

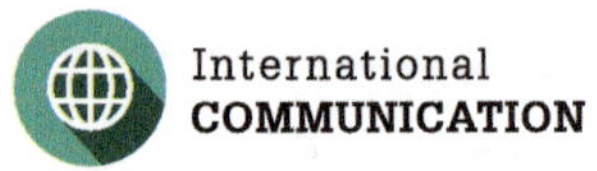

In this example, Grace uses the direct approach. The main point is in the email subject line and in the first paragraph. As you learned in Chapter 4, include your main point up front for most busy, U.S. audiences. But consider a less direct structure, with more context in the introduction, when writing to someone who resists your message or prefers a less direct style (e.g., someone from a high-context culture).

Compare the title slides in Figure 9, which might be used in a presentation to propose closing a company division and laying off employees. The first may be too specific for an idea that will probably meet resistance. The second title, "Roper Division," is too general and tells the audience nothing about your idea. The third is probably best for the topic: the title provides context for the presentation but does not reveal the conclusion up front.

Direct and Indirect Title Slides | **Figure 9**

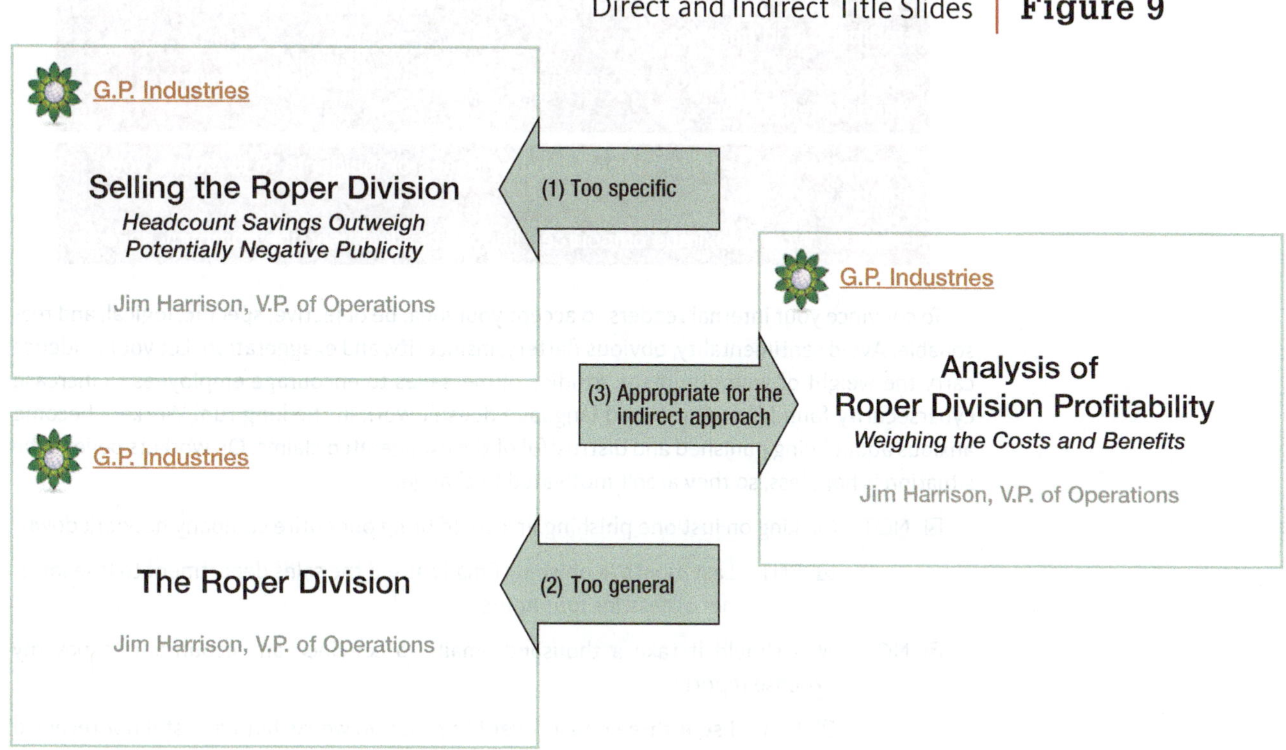

In the last paragraph of her email shown in Figure 8, Grace addresses the obstacle of cost. If Grace doesn't mention the investment, which will be significant, Jason might automatically reject the idea, believing that Grace didn't think it through.

At times, an objection may be so obvious that you might include it at the beginning of a persuasive message. Acknowledging a major concern is audience focused, for example, "In the staff meeting, you said that we don't have a budget for renovations. I have an idea for redesigning the space that will pay for itself within about 16 months."

In her email, Grace also mentions something that won't change: the front counter. Including some continuity in her vision may reduce Jason's resistance.[30]

Grace ends with an invitation to talk more. She demonstrates humility by seeking Jason's feedback and demonstrating her credibility by referring to her research. With this approach, her manager will be ready to listen to her justification.

Justifying Your Idea or Request

How you support your idea depends on what would persuade your audience, what is relevant to the situation, and what information you have available. For internal communications, you have an advantage because you know your audience well and can tailor a message to what's most important to them. You also have access to relevant data.

Generally, the more evidence you can include, the better. However, for simple ideas presented in short messages, focus on your strongest supporting points to avoid overwhelming your audience. Use a variety of evidence—facts and statistics, expert opinion, and examples, as shown in Figure 10.

Figure 10 | Types of Evidence

Facts and Statistics: Use objective statements and statistics that can be verified. Choose a few relevant data points to avoid overwhelming the reader.

Example: The Roper Division represents 34% of our overhead expenses.

Expert Opinion: Include experts to support your points, particularly if your credibility is in question.

Example: According to a recent study by Accenture's Supply Chain Management group...

Examples: Use relevant, representative cases or incidents to illustrate your points.

Example: When Maximus outsourced its logistics last year, the company saved...

To convince your internal readers to accept your idea, be objective, specific, logical, and reasonable. Avoid sentimentality, obvious flattery, insincerity, and exaggeration. Let your evidence carry the weight of your argument. Studies of messages to encourage employees to increase cybersecurity found that fear-based language doesn't work in the long run. Workers become anxious about being punished and distrustful of the exaggerated claims. Or, workers believe the situation is hopeless, so they aren't motivated to change.[31]

☒ NOT Clicking on just one phishing link could bring our entire company network down.

☑ BUT Last month, a phishing email caused the sales department to lose internet access for four hours.

☒ NOT Why should it take a thousand emails to convince an accountant to pay my expense report?

☑ BUT I sent three emails over the past two weeks but have still not received reimbursement for my Chicago trip.

7-3b External Persuasive Messages

The heart of most business is sales—selling a product or service. You read promotional messages in postal mail, on websites, in email, and on signage. In your career, you may write these messages as a sales manager for a large company, as the owner of a start-up company, or as a development officer for a nonprofit organization.

Neighbors Link, a nonprofit organization, offers services to immigrants and their families. The example in Figure 11 shows text in a mailed, folded card used for a fundraising campaign.[32]

Each year, the average American receives 41 pounds of direct, or marketing, mail. Most is viewed as junk mail and ends up in the landfill, but it can be effective. More than 5% of people respond to these solicitations, whereas less than 1% respond to email promotions.[33]

For both, writers face stiff competition. A marketing tool called the AIDA plan is used in social media marketing as well as other types of sales communication.[34] AIDA refers to first gaining the reader's *attention*, then creating *interest* in and *desire* for the benefits of your product, and finally motivating *action*. Next, we explore ways to write external persuasive messages.

Attract Attention

The Neighbors Link message attracts attention because it stands apart from other types of direct mail. The card format is unusual and looks like a personal message, so recipients are more likely to open it. Then, images of adorable children and others engaged in activities draw readers in to learn more.

Nonprofit Fundraising Message | **Figure 11**

"At Neighbors Link, I was finally able to smile naturally. Here I felt that my journey was worth it, even though I lost many things. Here I gained hope, motivation, and strength. Here I obtained the energy to keep fighting every day and that helps me to keep on being a little happier. Here I found extraordinary people whom I will never forget. I will always carry them in my heart."

– Rocio, Parenting Journey Participant

We know that supporting Neighbors Link takes courage and commitment to the vision of a fully integrated society. We are making progress because there are so many people like you who are willing to step forward and take a stand—people like you who value diversity and the richness that new cultures bring to our community.

Neighbors Link collaborates with over a hundred community partners throughout Westchester County—businesses, health care providers, houses of worship, schools, law enforcement, and government officials—who work with us to provide education, employment, and empowerment for immigrant families. Through these efforts, we have created a positive environment for immigrants and the whole community.

You can be part of this movement. You can help those in our community who are making tremendous sacrifices to build a better life for themselves and their families. By keeping Neighbors Link strong, we can secure the vision of healthy integration. Please make your most generous gift today.

You may consider a relevant, catchy opening in promotional materials. A rhetorical question ("What's the difference between extravagance and luxury?"), an unusual fact ("The average family washes one ton of laundry every year"), or a challenge ("Which tastes like instant coffee?") can attract attention. But avoid blatant sales tactics and gimmicky tricks. With all the phishing scams and "clickbait" today, people might react negatively and question your character.

Tell Stories

The Neighbors Link card tells a short story. In quotes, a participant in one of the programs describes her own journey, recognizing the pain of her past and painting a picture that we can imagine—her smile. This story doesn't exactly follow the ABT method discussed earlier, but we experience the movement in her life and hear her gratitude for the organization's work.

Sell Benefits, Not Features

Similar to starting with "why," focus on the **benefits** to the audience or the impact, not on product or service **features**. Neighbors Link talks about the community served—not about its history or programs. The "why" for donors isn't the tax benefit, but the good feeling they get from making a difference in immigrants' lives and being part of important work.

Use action verbs when talking about benefits. Within reason, use colorful adjectives and adverbs and positive language, stressing what your product *is* rather than what it is *not*.

☒ NOT The ski lodge isn't in one of those crowded resort areas.

☑ BUT Enjoy a private escape on the snow-capped peaks of the Canadian Rocky Mountains.

Focus on claims that you can support with evidence. Avoid generalities, superlatives, and too many or too strong adjectives and adverbs. In one study, website reviewers described inflated language as "loathsome."[35]

☒ NOT The Sherwood scooter is the best buy on the market.

☑ BUT The May issue of *Independent Consumer* rated the Sherwood scooter the year's best buy.

☒ NOT Everyone enjoys the convenience of our Bread Baker.

☑ BUT Our Bread Baker comes with one feature we don't think you'll ever use: a 30-day, no-questions-asked return policy.

Choose Clear, Vivid Language

As always, adapt your language to your audience and write concisely. People rarely want to read long blocks of text and dense paragraphs. Where possible, choose bullets instead. Many of the principles you learned in Chapter 4 for web writing apply to sales messages.

The collaboration software Basecamp uses engaging "you" language on its website homepage, as shown in Figure 12.[36] Notice how the text also describes a story: before and after Basecamp. Strong action verbs appear to be handwritten: *create* and *involve*.

Figure 12 | Website Sales Message

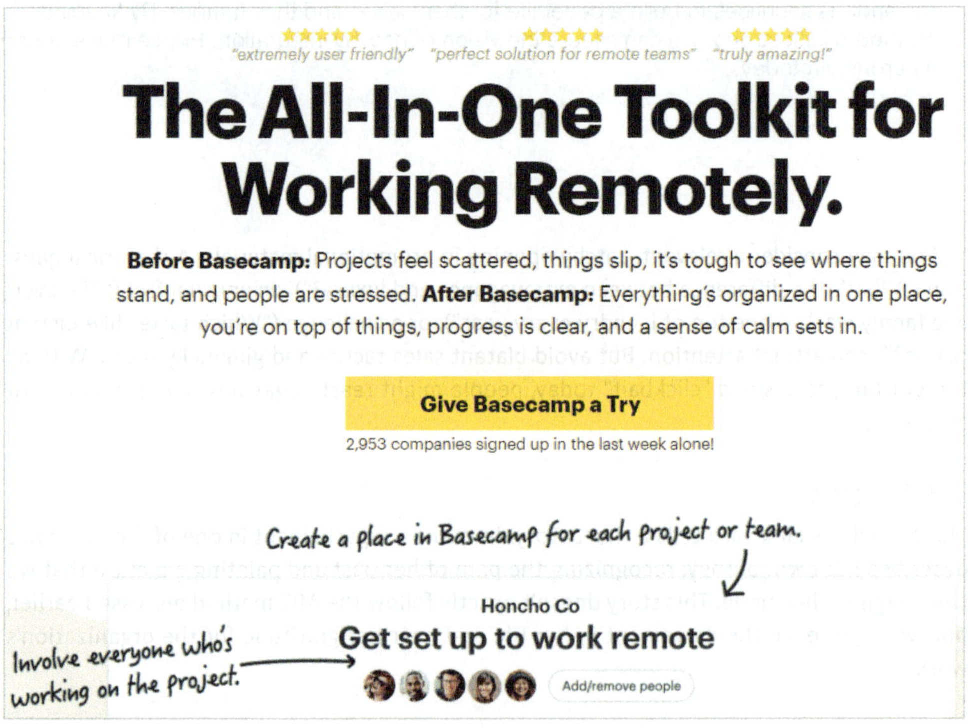

This example illustrates additional persuasive strategies. The stars and reviews at the top of the page are visual and provide credibility. We read a story with emotional language: *stressed*, *scattered*, *slipping*, and then *organized* and *calm*. Below the yellow button, we see a large number of companies—social proof.

Both Neighbors Link and Basecamp use rhetorical devices—a stylistic approach to persuade and evoke emotion. In the nonprofit example, we read repetition in sounds ("courage and commitment") and in phrases ("people like you"). In the Basecamp example, we see subtle rhyming ("create a place" and "get set"). Such devices can be effective in persuasive messages, but try not to overuse them, which can sound forced.

Include a Call to Action

In all persuasive messages, state the specific action you want. The Neighbors Link message ends, "Please make your most generous gift today." The Basecamp website has a prominent yellow box: "Give Basecamp a Try."

The Basecamp box illustrates Cialdini's "commitment and consistency" principle. If users sign up for a trial, they are likely to find value and keep using the program. For expensive items or complex services that people will not buy immediately after reading your message, encourage them to call a representative, request more information, or visit a store.

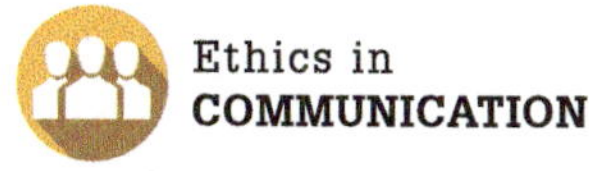

To apply the scarcity principle, you can provide an incentive for prompt action. Offer a gift to the first 100 people who respond or encourage purchases before the holiday rush or during a three-day sale. But make your push for action *gently*. Any tactic that smacks of high-pressure selling is likely to increase reader resistance and, again, may lead the reader to question your ethics.

☒ NOT Hurry! Hurry! These sale prices won't be in effect long.

☑ BUT Order before September 30 to take advantage of our lowest prices of the year.

Use confident language when asking for action, avoiding hesitant phrases, such as "If you want to save money" or "I hope you agree that this product will save you time." When asking the reader to part with money, mention a reader benefit in the same sentence.

☒ NOT If you agree that this ice cream maker will make your summers more enjoyable, you can place your order.

☑ BUT Order by June 25 to have homemade ice cream during the July 4 weekend.

If price is a selling point, introduce it early and emphasize it often. In most cases, however, price is not the reason people will buy your product and should be subordinated. Introduce the price late in the message, after most of the benefits, and consider presenting it in smaller units, for example, monthly instead of annual subscriptions.

If your goal is not an immediate sale, consider other strategies. For example, using the social proof principle, make it easy for people to share or like web content. Juul used this approach, unethically but effectively, by sponsoring parties and creating hashtags that inspired teens to share pictures of themselves using the product.[37]

Use the Checklist for Persuasive Messages to increase your chances of achieving your goals. Next, we discuss writing and responding to negative feedback.

Checklist for Persuasive Messages

ATTRACT THE READER'S ATTENTION

- ☑ Start with "why"—why the reader should care—in most persuasive messages. Avoid misleading statements and sales gimmicks.
- ☑ Consider a less direct style if you expect a lot of resistance to internal messages.

CREATE INTEREST AND BUILD DESIRE

- ☑ Provide evidence for each of your claims—facts, expert opinions, and examples.
- ☑ Explain benefits to your readers, not features—what they will achieve from implementing your idea or buying your product or service.
- ☑ Tell stories to help your readers imagine accepting your ideas.
- ☑ Use action-packed, positive language and engaging graphics for sales messages.

MOTIVATE ACTION

- ☑ Address obvious objections to reduce resistance.
- ☑ Make the desired action clear and easy to take.
- ☑ Ask confidently, avoiding hesitant language.

LO4 Describe parts of an effective response to negative feedback.

7-4 Writing and Responding to Negative Feedback

Wouldn't it be great if all customers were happy all the time? Of course, this isn't the case. Throughout your career—both as a customer and as a provider of a product or service—you will have to address situations when expectations are not met. To convince a business that its product is faulty or to convince a customer that your product is *not* faulty requires persuasion. In this section, we look at principles for repairing company image, writing complaints and online reviews, and responding to negative feedback.

7-4a Repairing Company Image

Context and relationships matter.[38] Sometimes, negative feedback is best handled in person or with a phone call. If you work for Deloitte and have a two-year consulting relationship with a company, you would hope that the client would call with a complaint rather than post a rant on YouTube. In return, you would offer to meet the client in person rather than try to address concerns by email.

For more transactional, high-volume businesses, in which you don't necessarily know your customer, you will likely see comments posted on social media sites. As we discussed in Chapter 6, responding to highly positive comments online is important, but when responding to negative online feedback, the stakes are even higher.

How well you handle negative customer feedback affects your company's image. When a customer has a negative service experience, the situation may be exacerbated in two ways: the customer writes about the experience on a public website, and the company mishandles the online comment. Responding well is critical to service recovery—ideally, turning an upset customer into a loyal one. Often, you can improve your chances of rebuilding a relationship with personal communication.

Failing to respond well to criticism, companies often create their own crisis situation—a significant threat to the organization. One example is Boeing, which you read about in Chapter 2. Failing to take responsibility and apologize for the plane crashes, the former CEO faced challenging questions, particularly during one news conference (Figure 13).[39,40] Ignoring negative feedback rarely helps a bad situation.

What punctuation errors can you find in this tweet?

Figure 13 Boeing Fails to Respond to Difficult Questions

The Seattle Times @seattletimes

Boeing CEO in a news conference after a shareholders meeting, would not concede that there was anything wrong with the original 737 MAX's MCAS flight-control system. As he left the room, a reporter shouted: "346 people died. Can you answer some questions?" st.news/2GTcV3B

Source: Twitter, Inc.

CHARACTER

7-4b Writing Complaints and Online Reviews

Think about times when a company disappointed you. Did you complain? Deciding whether and how to give negative feedback can be a matter of character. You might consider whether you genuinely want to suggest improvements, whether you were wronged—or whether you contributed to the situation, for example, by feeling self-righteous or by simply having a bad day.

If you decide to take action, present yourself as a credible customer with an issue worth the company's attention. Follow these principles for writing a complaint letter or negative online review:

- **Consider an indirect style.** Although you'll want to get to the issue quickly, asking for compensation in your first paragraph may turn off the reader. Instead, build your case gradually to convince the reader to fulfill your request.

☒ NOT I'd like my $55 bus ticket refunded.

☑ BUT Recently, I planned to take the bus to Houston, but I missed it because it left early.

- **Give specific evidence about what went wrong.** For the bus example, giving the specific location, date, time, and witnesses, if possible, makes your argument more credible and persuasive. Avoid generalizations and vague descriptions.

☒ NOT The bus always leaves early.

☑ BUT On Thursday, September 14, I was scheduled to take the bus at 3:15 from Minor Hall. When I arrived at 3:05 with my luggage, two people told me they saw the bus leave at 3:00.

- **Maintain a calm, objective tone.** Your anger may be understandable, but it could hinder your ability to get a positive response from the company. Consider asking a friend for feedback before you send email or post feedback online.

☒ NOT What's the deal with this? Even Amanda, at your central office, said the bus left early, and she was upset about it too!

☑ BUT I called the central office and spoke with Amanda, who contacted the driver and confirmed that the bus had left at 3:00. She said she was surprised the bus left before 3:15, which was its scheduled departure.

- **Close with a confident, respectful tone.** After you provide details, ask for reasonable compensation and a response.

☒ NOT I hope you'll send me the $55 I paid for the ticket and $200 for my waiting time until I could catch a ride with a friend.

☑ BUT I request reimbursement for the $55 ticket. My confirmation email is below.

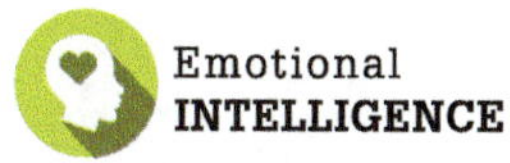

What could get in the way of your using a calm, objective tone when writing a complaint? How can you avoid writing something that could reduce your chance of getting a positive response?

With such clear explanations and an appropriate tone, this is a persuasive message to which any reasonable company would respond.

If you weren't requesting compensation for a dissatisfying bus experience, you could have posted a review online instead. Whether you post on the company's Facebook page or a public review site, such as Yelp, the audience is slightly different: a company representative may read your post, but your primary audience is the public—including people considering taking the bus.

The same principles of organization, evidence, and tone apply for online reviews, but respect may be even more important for public comments. If your post is unreasonable or angry, you may embarrass yourself and regret it later. Also, before you post, you might want to give the company the opportunity to address concerns privately through a phone call, email, direct message on Twitter, or feedback form on the company's website.

The review about a television, as shown in Figure 14, is honest, measured, and reasonable. The customer isn't happy, but the feedback is clear and useful for other consumers—and the manufacturer.

Negative Online Review for a TV | 

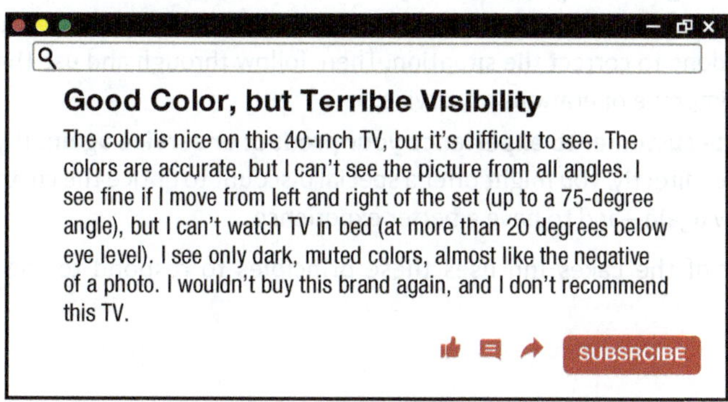

Good Color, but Terrible Visibility

The color is nice on this 40-inch TV, but it's difficult to see. The colors are accurate, but I can't see the picture from all angles. I see fine if I move from left and right of the set (up to a 75-degree angle), but I can't watch TV in bed (at more than 20 degrees below eye level). I see only dark, muted colors, almost like the negative of a photo. I wouldn't buy this brand again, and I don't recommend this TV.

SUBSCRIBE

7-4c Responding to Negative Feedback

Hearing negative feedback can be difficult but is a good opportunity to improve the business and rebuild relationships. As we know by now, ignoring the feedback or responding rudely will surely lose one already angry customer and may lose even more if the feedback is posted online. We want to avoid situations from escalating—and to handle them well when they do turn into crises.

Addressing Negative Reviews and Other Feedback

Worse than not responding to negative feedback is actively discouraging social media posts. A guest house in Hudson, New York, tried to fine people $500 for each negative review posted by one of their wedding guests.[41] Clearly, the management wasn't "engaging" customers, as we discussed in Chapter 6, but pushed them away. The business has since closed.[42]

Let's look at a better example of responding to negative reviews. If you owned the Lakes Inn and saw the online travel review in Figure 15, how would you respond?

Figure 15 Lakes Inn Review

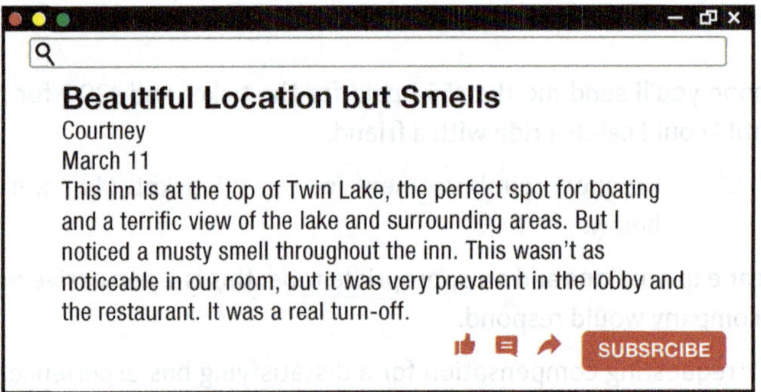

Beautiful Location but Smells
Courtney
March 11
This inn is at the top of Twin Lake, the perfect spot for boating and a terrific view of the lake and surrounding areas. But I noticed a musty smell throughout the inn. This wasn't as noticeable in our room, but it was very prevalent in the lobby and the restaurant. It was a real turn-off.
SUBSCRIBE

Overall, the review is positive, but the guest makes one negative comment that should be addressed. According to the Social Media Response Guidelines described in Chapter 6, this guest could be considered "Unhappy." Responding is appropriate for this guest and because a negative review may influence other travelers.

Follow these guidelines—similar to those for positive reviews—when responding to negative feedback:[43]

- **Show appreciation for the feedback.** Thank the writer for the feedback—even negative comments give you the opportunity to respond and restore your company's reputation.
- **Reinforce positive aspects of the feedback.** Many comments will include some positive points; highlight those for other readers.
- **Address negative aspects directly.** Paraphrase negative comments and include a statement of empathy—the impact on the customer.[44] Explain what you will do or have already done to correct the situation. Then, follow through and use the negative feedback to improve operations or service.
- **Invite the customer to experience your product or service again.** If you can contact the writer directly, you might offer a special discount to entice the customer to try your company again—and to have a better experience.

The manager of the Lakes Inn uses these principles to respond to the guest's review (Figure 16).

Management Response to a Negative Review | **Figure 16**

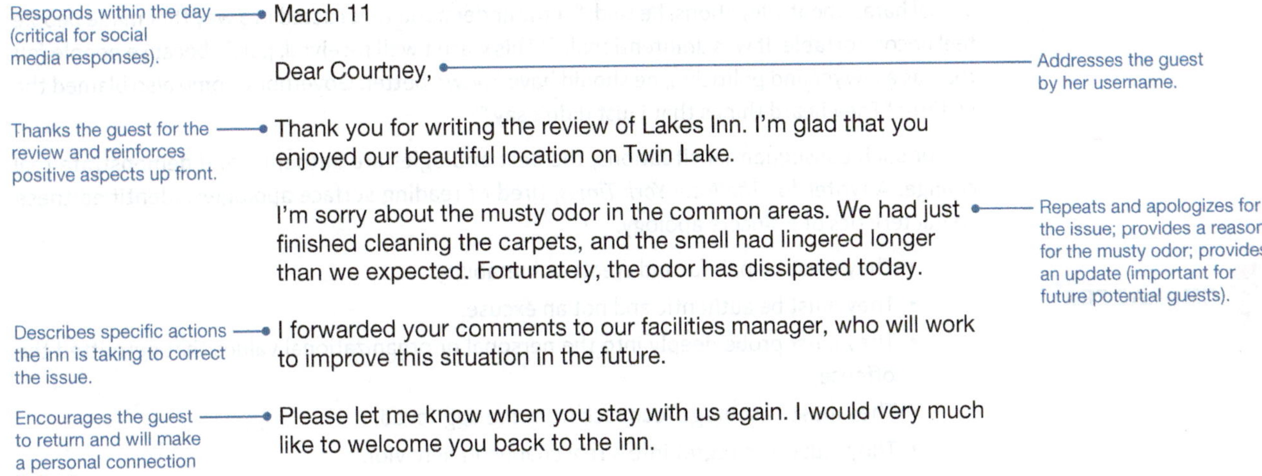
Responds within the day (critical for social media responses). — March 11

Dear Courtney, — Addresses the guest by her username.

Thanks the guest for the review and reinforces positive aspects up front. — Thank you for writing the review of Lakes Inn. I'm glad that you enjoyed our beautiful location on Twin Lake.

I'm sorry about the musty odor in the common areas. We had just finished cleaning the carpets, and the smell had lingered longer than we expected. Fortunately, the odor has dissipated today. — Repeats and apologizes for the issue; provides a reason for the musty odor; provides an update (important for future potential guests).

Describes specific actions the inn is taking to correct the issue. — I forwarded your comments to our facilities manager, who will work to improve this situation in the future.

Encourages the guest to return and will make a personal connection if she does. — Please let me know when you stay with us again. I would very much like to welcome you back to the inn.

Handling Crisis Situations

Sometimes, despite management's best efforts, situations spiral out of control. People aren't always fair on social media sites: the anonymity and mob mentality overtake good sense. When a company's or an individual's reputation is at risk, the best strategy is to apply crisis communication principles to protect and defend the brand. Often, this starts with an apology.

Apologies can increase the company's credibility, move the business forward, and improve the outcome of litigation.[45,46,47] Researchers found that the most effective apologies express regret, explain what went wrong, acknowledge responsibility, declare repentance, offer reparation, and request forgiveness.[48,49] Responsibility and repair are most important. Wrongdoers must accept accountability and not blame others, particularly those they have harmed.[50] Apologies include the phrases "I apologize" or "I am sorry," rather than "I regret."[51]

For minor offenses, informal apologies work well. When OurBus emailed a link that wasn't yet available, the company sent a brief email with the subject, "Our bad. That code doesn't quite work yet . . . " (Figure 17).[52]

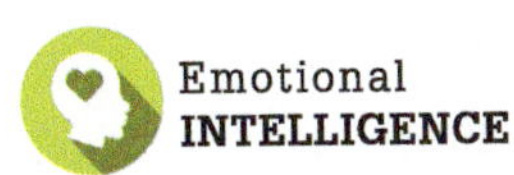

Do you perceive apologies as signs of strength or weakness? Consider your own experience making and receiving apologies at work and in your personal life.

Informal Apology | **Figure 17**

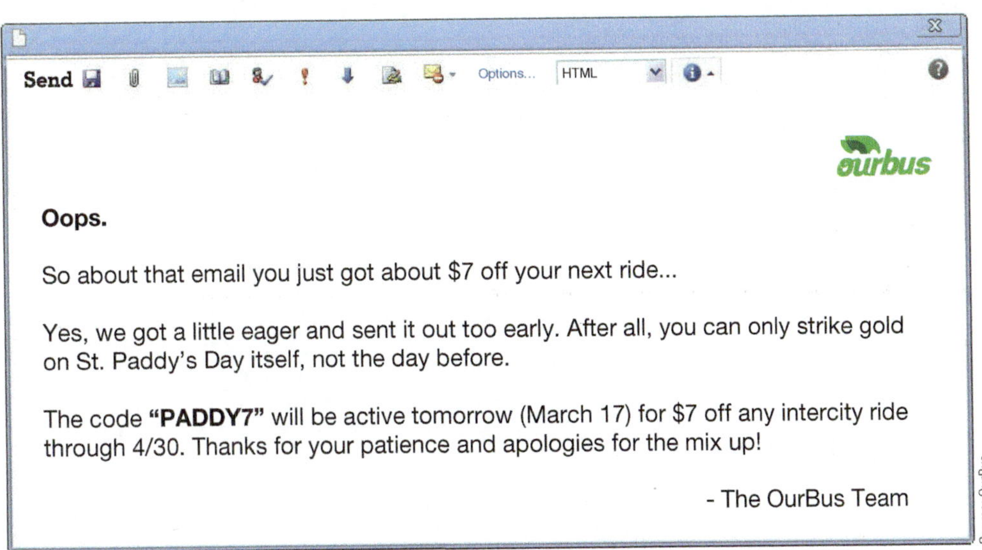

Oops.

So about that email you just got about $7 off your next ride...

Yes, we got a little eager and sent it out too early. After all, you can only strike gold on St. Paddy's Day itself, not the day before.

The code **"PADDY7"** will be active tomorrow (March 17) for $7 off any intercity ride through 4/30. Thanks for your patience and apologies for the mix up!

- The OurBus Team

Source: OurBus

As you might imagine, people are more likely to forgive when something is done out of ignorance than out of malintent. When former New York Governor Andrew Cuomo responded to sexual harassment allegations, he said, "I now understand that I acted in a way that made people feel uncomfortable. It was unintentional."[53] This wasn't well received, partly because people felt that, as a lawyer and politician, he should have known better. Governor Cuomo also blamed the victims: "They heard things that I just didn't say."[54]

For such consequential situations, the best apologies are authentic and demonstrate real change. A writer for *The New York Times*, tired of reading surface apologies, identified these characteristics of a sincere apology:

- They must be painful and create vulnerability.
- They must be authentic and not an excuse.
- They must probe deeply into the personal or organizational values that permitted the offense.
- They must encourage feedback from the aggrieved.
- They must turn regret into a real change in behavior.[55]

Responding to negative feedback is a make-or-break situation for business professionals. If handled well, you can win over a customer for life. If handled poorly, you risk losing much more than one dissatisfied customer.

7-5 Chapter Closing

Throughout your career, you'll persuade and be persuaded. Whether you're inspiring management to reduce emissions or seeking funding for your start-up, you now have a toolkit of proven strategies. The more you tailor these to your audience, while maintaining high ethical standards, the more likely you'll get the result you want.

Persuasive messages are challenging because, by definition, they meet resistance. But you'll be challenged even more when you deliver bad news, which we explore next. In these situations, your message may affect people in deep, personal ways.

Persuade the Company President to Start an Employee Assistance Fund

Consider the chapter introduction, which described persuasive messaging about climate change. Imagine that you're an employee at a company located in a high-risk flood zone.

To prepare for environmental disasters and other emergencies that affect employees' lives, you want to convince your company president to start an employee assistance fund. The company would start the fund with $10,000 and encourage employees to contribute. When employees are faced with emergencies, including personal tragedies, for example, a death in the immediate family, an illness, or a fire, the fund provides tax-free relief. Using the CAM model, what questions might you consider before writing an email to the president?

>>> CHARACTER CHECK

1. **What is my motivation for inspiring this initiative?**
   Last year, my house flooded after a hurricane. We didn't have enough insurance to cover the damage. I'd like to get funding for people in similar situations. Yes, I could benefit in the future, too, but mostly I want to help others avoid going through what my family and I did.
2. **Do I want to get credit for the idea?**
   Well, it won't look bad for me to propose this! The president asked for our ideas for new programs, and this seems like a good one to propose. Still, that's not my primary motivation.

>>> AUDIENCE ANALYSIS

1. **What's the "why" for the president?**
   The president invited our ideas, so she must want to hear them. She has spoken about our vulnerability to hurricanes, and we have a disaster plan for the company, so the issue is important to her.
2. **What are the possible downsides or areas of resistance?**
   She might object to the initial $10,000, and we can start with less, but I will argue that this shows the company's commitment before asking employees to donate. She might not like the idea of asking employees to contribute, but I will share my research, which says that employee assistance funds increase employees' connection to the company. We do have a high turnover rate, so this might increase loyalty. She also might think the fund is overly complicated or might be abused by employees, but I'll share a few success stories from other companies.

>>> MESSAGE AND MEDIUM

1. **What are the main points of my message?**
   I'll focus on the benefits of starting a fund and make it easy for her to agree by describing how these funds work. I'll also volunteer to take the lead. I can draft program guidelines and a message to employees.

2. **In what medium will I communicate the message?**
   I'll send a one-page proposal and attach it to an email. In the email, I'll write just a short paragraph with a few bullet points. At the end, I'll offer to meet to discuss the idea further.

Persuade Employees to Donate

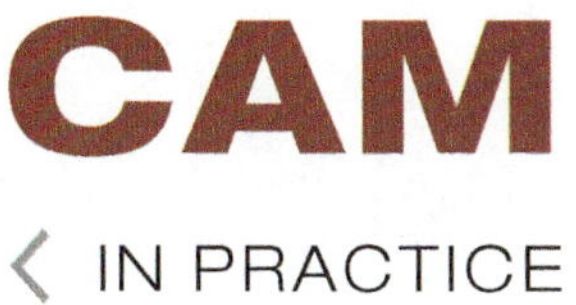

‹ IN PRACTICE

Imagine that your president gave you approval to start the employee assistance fund previously described. Plan a persuasive message to encourage employees to donate.

››› CHARACTER CHECK

1. I have personal reasons for starting the fund. How much will I disclose in my message?
2. At the same time, how will I convey my sincere desire to support employees during times of need without seeming self-interested, particularly in the company recognition that may come with my initiative?

››› AUDIENCE ANALYSIS

1. What is the "why"—the benefits—to employees of contributing to the fund?
2. How might employees react to my message?

››› MESSAGE AND MEDIUM

1. What will be my main points?
2. In what medium will I convey my message to employees?

REFLECTING ON YOUR COMMUNICATION AND CHARACTER DEVELOPMENT

1. **Reflect on a time when you persuaded someone.**

   Have you ever persuaded someone to do something that was in your self-interest but not in their best interest? Most of us have at some point. Describe the situation. What was your motivation? What was the other person's resistance? What strategies did you use? How did the action affect the other person negatively? How do you feel about the situation now?

2. **Consider a time when you were persuaded.**

   Now reflect on a time when you were the victim of someone else's persuasion. Apply the same questions above.

   Taking the two examples together, what do you learn about yourself, and what changes might you consider for the future?

3. **Assess your response to persuasion.**

   Do you often find yourself duped? Do you tend to fall for marketing ploys and buy products you don't need? Do you follow clickbait online and end up on irrelevant ads or websites? Which persuasive strategies were used, and how could you ward against them in the future?

4. **Describe your decision process for complaints.**

   How do you decide whether to complain about a company's product or service? To another student, describe two situations: one in which you complained and one in which you didn't. What were the circumstances and your thinking process in these situations? Discuss how each turned out and what you might do differently in the future.

5. **Analyze your apologies.**

   How comfortable are you in offering apologies? Do you tend to avoid them, or do you offer them easily when you are wrong or make a mistake?

   What prevents you from offering apologies more freely? Or, do you offer them *too* freely, for example, when you are not wrong? Spend some time considering the potential consequences of your approach to apologies.

DEVELOPING YOUR BUSINESS COMMUNICATION SKILLS

LO1 Identify ways to tailor persuasive messages to different audiences.

PLANNING PERSUASIVE MESSAGES

1. **Assess the ethics of a marketing campaign.**

   Identify a company's ad campaign—something you have seen in print or online—and analyze the ethics. Who is the audience? Does the product or service benefit them in some way? Could the purchase affect people negatively? How comfortable would you feel promoting the product or service in a similar way?

2. **Consider the ethics of product endorsements.**

   Some companies hire college students to promote their products. What's your view of this strategy? Consider how the company, the hired students, and the customers are affected. Who benefits most and least in these arrangements?

3. **Assess what is important to team members.**

   Think about a team you know well, e.g., a volunteer organization, a school club, a small group at work, or a sports team. Now think about an idea you might introduce to the team—an idea that team members might resist.

What would be important to know about each team member that might influence how you tailor your message? Consider questions such as the following:

- How long has this person been a part of the team?
- How important is the team to the person?
- What level of commitment to the team have you observed?
- How might the person react to your idea?
- How will this person, specifically, be affected by the change?
- What questions or objections would this person have?

4. **Analyze resistance.**

   Think about something you want for which you need to persuade someone. Describe the person's possible resistance. What makes the situation difficult? How can you, ethically, overcome each point of resistance?

APPLYING PERSUASIVE STRATEGIES

LO2 Compare strategies to persuade an audience in a given situation.

5. **Identify the "why" and framing.**

   Find an email you received from a nonprofit organization trying to persuade you. How well does it focus on you and convince you that you should care? How are issues framed? Explain other ways the issues could be presented to inspire the reader.

6. **Rewrite to emphasize benefits.**

   Rewrite the following excerpt to stress benefits instead of features. In addition, instead of the paragraph format, write a list of bullet points that focus on the reader. Consider starting each bullet with an action verb, and you may invent whatever details you would like.

   > Our headphones are soft, padded, and foldable. They connect with Bluetooth and can be switched easily to different devices. It takes 5 minutes to recharge them, and the charge will last for another hour.

7. **Analyze use of credibility, emotional appeals, and logic in a sales call.**

   In the movie *Boiler Room*, Giovanni Ribisi's character (Seth) is a trainee working at a shady brokerage firm that sells stock in fake companies. During a sales call to a prospective customer (Harry), Seth uses persuasion—but not in a professional, ethical way. You'll find the clip on YouTube at https://youtu.be/eY4UVrXzyhE.

   As you watch the scene, note how Seth uses credibility (ethos), emotional appeals (pathos), and logical arguments (logos) to convince Harry to buy stock. Write down specific text that illustrates each strategy.

8. **Analyze use of credibility, emotional appeals, and logic in a speech.**

   Find a speech online. You might watch a commencement speaker or a company executive. Identify examples of credibility (ethos), emotional appeals (pathos), and logical arguments (logos). Which of the three are used more than the others? Do you find the balance appropriate given the situation and audience?

WRITING PERSUASIVE MESSAGES

LO3 Describe parts of an effective internal or external persuasive message.

9. **Write an article to warn people about quick-cash businesses.**

   To discourage people from signing up at the Promise/Cash Center site shown in Figure 18, write an article for a blog that warns consumers about questionable business practices. Your objective is to convince people that, even though fast cash sounds good, it's not in their best interest in the long term.

Figure 18 | Website Using Questionable Ethics

Yuri Arcurs/Shutterstock.com; Tatiana Popova/shutterstock.com

Consider these questions as you draft your article:

a. What evidence will you use? Research outside sources to support your view. Include data, expert opinion, and examples where relevant.

b. What will you write up front to capture and keep the reader's attention?

c. How will you address potential obstacles or objections from readers?

d. What is a catchy title for your article?

10. Write an email to suggest an idea.

Similar to Grace Lee's suggestion in Figure 8, write an email to a current or previous employer. Think of an idea that would improve the business: a new procedure, an upgraded system, an innovative product, or some other way to increase sales, improve service, or increase operational efficiencies. Choose something simple enough to convey in a short message. Put your main point up front and use a clear, specific subject line to capture attention.

11. Design a homepage for a website to sell headphones.

Using the bullets you created for Exercise 6 as a starting point, design a web page to sell the headphones. In addition to the bullets, what other text and graphics will you include? You can use web design software—or just draw a mock version in PowerPoint or another program. Consider ways to capture attention, create interest, and motivate action.

Now look at a website for any company that sells headphones. How does yours compare? What can you learn from their text and design, and what could the company learn from yours?

12. Write fundraising messages for your school.

a. **Write a message for your school website.** Imagine that you're working for your college's alumni office. You're asked to write text for the website about donating to the school. What will you emphasize, and how will you encourage alumni to donate? Compare your final text to your school's website.

b. **Write a direct mail message to alumni who have donated $500–1,000.** Now write an email to people who have donated in the past. Think of ways you can tailor your message to this group.

c. **Write a message to recent graduates.** Now consider a different audience: students who graduated within the past three years. Write a message to this group. How will you tailor to this audience? What medium will you use for your message?

Compare messages in small groups and focus on the decisions you made for the different audiences.

WRITING AND RESPONDING TO NEGATIVE FEEDBACK

LO4 Describe parts of an effective response to negative feedback.

13. Write a complaint to a business.

Think about a negative customer service experience you had recently. Draft a message you can send to the business manager by email to explain what happened. Be sure to use a credible tone and specific examples to persuade the company that your experience is valid. Also find a way to encourage a response from the company. You may ask for reasonable compensation, if appropriate.

14. Give feedback on someone else's draft complaint.

After you complete Exercise 13, switch emails with another student. Imagine that you're the business manager receiving this complaint. Use the form in Figure 19 to give feedback to your partner. Circle a rating for each question and prepare comments to justify your feedback.

Figure 19 Feedback About a Complaint Email

	NOT AT ALL	SOMEWHAT	YES	DEFINITELY
1. The organization works well for the purpose.	1	2	3	4
2. The tone is appropriate for the audience.	1	2	3	4
3. Enough details and examples explain the situation.	1	2	3	4
4. Requests for compensation are reasonable.	1	2	3	4
5. Correct grammar and punctuation make the letter credible.	1	2	3	4

15. Write a negative review online.

Rewrite your customer complaint email from Exercise 13 for an online review. For your post to an online review site, you have a different reader: the public. Consider making changes for a broader audience, who, like the business manager, cares about your credibility, tone, and details. But, unlike the business manager, this audience may make a purchase decision based on your review.

16. Respond to another student's review.

Give the review you completed in the previous exercise to another student in class. Imagine that you're the business manager responsible for responding to online reviews. First, decide how you would respond to this post. Would you ignore it, write an online response, or try to call or email the customer directly? Then, talk with your partner about your decision. Is this what the writer would prefer? Why or why not?

Next, assume that you'll write a response online. Draft your response and again ask your partner for feedback. Would the writer be satisfied with the response?

Finally, rewrite the response to perfect it with feedback from your partner.

17. Rewrite a company response to negative feedback.

Find an example of a company that doesn't respond well to online feedback. Look on Glassdoor, Yelp, TripAdvisor, or another review site. Rewrite the management response according to principles in this chapter.

18. Write an email reply to a customer demanding a refund.

Imagine that you're the customer service manager at a small company, and one of your employees has escalated a customer complaint to your attention. The customer reported that a custom luxury product does not function as advertised, and the customer is demanding a refund.

Write an email to this customer to explain why you can't grant the refund. Invent whatever details you would like and describe action you can take to fix the problem. Try to restore the customer's confidence in your company.

19. Write an email to a customer who posted negative feedback.

Imagine that you work for the Colonnade Hotel and Resort, and a customer posted a video of his negative experience checking into the hotel (Figure 20). The customer also posted a negative review of the hotel on a travel website (Figure 21). You'll find the video at https://www.amynewman.com/communication-tools.

Prepare an email to the customer, addressing his concerns. How can you win over this very angry customer?

Figure 20 | Dissatisfied Customers at the Hotel

Courtesy of Amy Newman

Figure 21 | Negative Review of the Colonnade Hotel and Resort

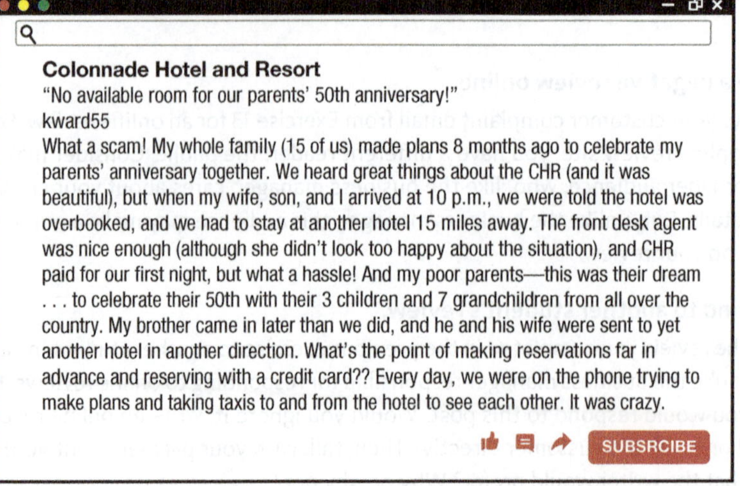

Colonnade Hotel and Resort

"No available room for our parents' 50th anniversary!"

kward55

What a scam! My whole family (15 of us) made plans 8 months ago to celebrate my parents' anniversary together. We heard great things about the CHR (and it was beautiful), but when my wife, son, and I arrived at 10 p.m., we were told the hotel was overbooked, and we had to stay at another hotel 15 miles away. The front desk agent was nice enough (although she didn't look too happy about the situation), and CHR paid for our first night, but what a hassle! And my poor parents—this was their dream . . . to celebrate their 50th with their 3 children and 7 grandchildren from all over the country. My brother came in later than we did, and he and his wife were sent to yet another hotel in another direction. What's the point of making reservations far in advance and reserving with a credit card?? Every day, we were on the phone trying to make plans and taking taxis to and from the hotel to see each other. It was crazy.

SUBSRCIBE

20. **Write an apology.**

Find an example in the news of a company that has made a mistake or suffered some backlash. Write a blog post that meets the criteria for effective apologies. As always, consider the context—the situation and audience—as you write your message.

Compare your message to one that the organization publishes—or not. How do you assess the way the organization handled the crisis?

CHAPTER SUMMARY

LO1 Identify ways to tailor persuasive messages to different audiences.

The more you know your audience, the more likely you can persuade them. Consider possible resistance and tailor your message accordingly. However, be mindful about ethical lines. Never misuse people's trust to persuade them to do something that is ultimately not in their best interest.

LO2 Compare strategies to persuade an audience in a given situation.

Develop a toolkit of strategies to change behavior or attitudes. Focus on why your reader should care about your message, demonstrate your credibility, appeal to prosocial emotions, and develop logical arguments. Apply seven additional principles—liking, scarcity, social proof, commitment and consistency, authority, reciprocity, and unity—to persuade your audience.

LO3 Describe parts of an effective internal or external persuasive message.

Capture the reader's attention by starting with benefits to the reader rather than features of your idea, product, or service. Provide a variety of evidence—facts, expert opinion, and examples—to support your claims. Tell stories and use vivid language and graphics for sales messages. Finally, make action easy to take.

LO4 Describe parts of an effective response to negative feedback.

To write a complaint or negative review as a customer, use an appropriate tone and provide enough evidence to support your points. When responding to negative feedback, consider a personal approach if you know the customer; otherwise, respond online promptly, thank the customer, acknowledge the feedback, apologize when appropriate, explain how the problem will be fixed, and ask for repeat business. When faced with a crisis situation, protect and defend the company's reputation and, if appropriate, make an authentic apology that reflects real change.

Endnotes

1. Adam Corner and Chris Shaw, "Principles for Effective Communication and Public Engagement on Climate Change: A Handbook for IPCC authors," The Intergovernmental Panel on Climate Change (IPCC), January 2018, www.ipcc.ch/site/assets/uploads/2017/08/Climate-Outreach-IPCC-communications-handbook.pdf, p. 3, accessed March 8, 2021.
2. Anthony Leiserowitz, et al., "Climate Change in the American Mind," Yale University and George Mason University Report, December 2020, https://climatecommunication.yale.edu/wp-content/uploads/2021/02/climate-change-american-mind-december-2020.pdf, accessed March 8, 2021.
3. Moira Fagan and Christine Huang, "A Look at How People Around the World View Climate Change," Pew Research Center, April 18, 2019, www.pewresearch.org/fact-tank/2019/04/18/a-look-at-how-people-around-the-world-view-climate-change, accessed March 8, 2021.
4. Corner and Shaw.
5. Hang Lu and Jonathan P. Schuldt, "Compassion for Climate Change Victims and Support for Mitigation Policy," *Journal of Environmental Psychology* 25 (2016): 192–200.
6. Sheila Kaplan, "Juul Is Fighting to Keep Its E-Cigarettes on the U.S. Market," *The New York Times*, July 5, 2021, www.nytimes.com/2021/07/05/health/juul-vaping-fda.html, accessed August 5, 2021.
7. Kathleen Chaykowski, "The Disturbing Focus of Juul's Early Marketing Campaigns," *Forbes*, November 16, 2018, www.forbes.com/sites/kathleenchaykowski/2018/11/16/the-disturbing-focus-of-juuls-early-marketing-campaigns, accessed March 8, 2021.
8. "Pods," Juul, Research into the Impact of Tobacco Advertising, Stanford University, Website, http://tobacco.stanford.edu/tobacco_main/main_pods.php, accessed March 7, 2021.
9. "Pods."
10. Kaplan.
11. Marieke L. Fransen, Edith G. Smit, and Peeter W. J. Verlegh, "Strategies and Motives for Resistance to Persuasion: An Integrative Framework," *Frontiers in Psychology* (2015), https://doi.org/10.3389/fpsyg.2015.01201.
12. Fransen et al.
13. For an example from health communication, see Seth M. Noar and Rosalie Shemanski Aldrich, "The Role of Message Tailoring in the Development of Persuasive Health Communication Messages," *Annals of the International Communication Association* 33 (2009), https://doi.org/10.1080/23808985.2009.11679085.
14. Yan Huang and Fuyuan Shen, "Effects of Cultural Tailoring on Persuasion in Cancer Communication: A Meta-Analysis," *Journal of Communication* 66 (2016), https://doi.org/10.1111/jcom.12243.
15. For example, see Arie Dijkstra, Karien Ballast, "Personalization and Perceived Personal Relevance in Computer-Tailored Persuasion in Smoking Cessation," *British Journal of Health Psychology* 17 (2011): 60–73, https://doi:10.1111/j.2044-8287.2011.02029.
16. Seth M. Noar and Rosalie Shemanski Aldrich, "The Role of Message Tailoring in the Development of Persuasive Health Communication Messages," *Annals of the International Communication Association* 33 (2009), https://doi.org/10.1080/23808985.2009.11679085.
17. Simon Sinek, "How Great Leaders Inspire Action," TED Talk, May 4, 2010, https://youtu.be/qp0HIF3SfI4, accessed March 8, 2021.
18. John Cook, "The Research Agrees: Humans Are Causing Climate Change (Consensus on Consensus)," Global Change Institute, YouTube, April 12, 2016, https://youtu.be/pEb49cZYnsE, accessed March 8, 2021.
19. John Cook et al., "Consensus on Consensus: A Synthesis of Consensus Estimates on Human-Caused Global Warming," *Environment Research Letters* 11 (2016): 1–7.
20. Jillian Jordan, et al., "Don't Get It or Don't Spread It? Comparing Self-interested Versus Prosocial Motivations for COVID-19 Prevention Behaviors." *PsyArXiv*, April 3, 2020, https://psyarxiv.com/yuq7x, accessed December 19, 2020.
21. Paul J. Zak, "How Stories Change the Brain," Greater Good Science Center, University of California, Berkeley, December 17, 2013, https://greatergood.berkeley.edu/article/item/how_stories_change_brain, accessed June 7, 2021.
22. Randy Olson, *Houston, We Have a Narrative* (Chicago: The University of Chicago Press, 2015).
23. Adam Corner, "The Power of Narrative Approaches to Communications," The Climate Communication Project, https://theclimatecommsproject.org/the-power-of-narrative-approaches-to-communications, accessed August 6, 2021.
24. David DeSteno, *Emotional Success: The Power of Gratitude, Compassion, and Pride* (New York: First Mariner Books, 2019).
25. Robert Cialdini, "Harnessing the Science of Persuasion," *Harvard Business Review*, October 2001, https://hbr.org/2001/10/harnessing-the-science-of-persuasion, accessed March 9, 2021.
26. "Katharine Hayhoe on How to Talk About Climate Change (Highlights Video)," Climate Outreach, YouTube, December 1, 2017, https://youtu.be/NbLQ9vhHkyM, accessed March 8, 2021.
27. Alex Birkett, "Cialdini's 7th Persuasion Principle: Using Unity in Online Marketing," CXL, September 7, 2016, https://cxl.com/blog/cialdini-unity/, accessed August 6, 2021.

28. Stephen J. Dubner, "How to Get Anyone to Do Anything," Freakonomics Podcast, Episode 463, May 26, 2021, https://freakonomics.com/podcast/frbc-robert-cialdini, accessed August 6, 2021.

29. Birkett.

30. Adam Grant, *Think Again* (New York: Viking, 2021), p. 178.

31. Sean T. Lawson et al., "The Impact of Fear Appeals in the US Cyber Security Debate," in N. Pissanidis, H. Roigas, and M. Veenendaal (eds.), 8th International Conference on Cyber Conflict, 2016.

32. Neighbors Link, Mt. Kisco, NY.

33. Elisabeth Leamy, "How to Stop Junk Mail and Save Trees—and Your Sanity," *The Washington Post*, February 13, 2018, www.washingtonpost.com/lifestyle/home/how-to-stop-junk-mail-and-save-trees-and-your-sanity/2018/02/12/6000e4c4-05d9-11e8-b48c-b07fea957bd5_story.html, accessed March 9, 2021.

34. Shahizan Hassana, Siti Zaleha Ahmad Nadzimb, and Norshuhada Shiratuddin, "Strategic Use of Social Media for Small Business Based on the AIDA Model," *Procedia—Social and Behavioral Sciences* 172 (2015): 262–269.

35. Hsi-Liang Chu, Yi-Shin Deng, and Ming-Chuen Chuang, "Persuasive Web Design in e-Commerce," in Fiona Fui-Hoon Nah (ed.), *HCI in Business, HCIB* 2014, Lecture Notes in Computer Science, Vol. 8527, Springer, https://doi.org/10.1007/978-3-319-07293-7_47.

36. Basecamp Homepage, Basecamp.com, accessed December 17, 2021.

37. Kathleen Chaykowski, "The Disturbing Focus of Juul's Early Marketing Campaigns," *Forbes*, November 16, 2018, www.forbes.com/sites/kathleenchaykowski/2018/11/16/the-disturbing-focus-of-juuls-early-marketing-campaigns, accessed March 8, 2021.

38. For a discussion of German e-complaints, see Sofie Decock, Bernard De Clerck, and Rebecca Van Herck, "Interpersonal Strategies in E-Complaint Refusals: Textbook Advice Versus Actual Situated Practice," *Business and Professional Communication Quarterly* 83 (2020): 285–308.

39. "Boeing Shareholders Meeting News Conference," April 29, 2019, www.c-span.org/video/?460231-1/boeing-ceo-dennis-muilenburg-holds-news-conference, accessed March 12, 2021.

40. The Seattle Times (@seattletimes), "Boeing CEO in a news conference after a shareholders meeting, would not concede that there was anything wrong with the original 737 MAX's MCAS flight-control system. As he left the room, a reporter shouted: "346 people died. Can you answer some questions," Twitter, April 30, 2019, https://twitter.com/seattletimes/status/1123099160893378561, accessed March 12, 2021.

41. Mara Siegler, "Hotel Fines $500 for Every Bad Review Posted Online," NYPost.com, Page Six, August 4, 2014, http://pagesix.com/2014/08/04/hotel-charges-500-for-every-bad-review-posted-online/, accessed March 13, 2021.

42. "Union Street Guest House," Yelp, www.yelp.com/biz/union-street-guest-house-hudson, accessed August 10, 2021.

43. "Dos and Don'ts of Responding to Reviews on Yelp," Yelp Official Blog, September 1, 2020, https://blog.yelp.com/2020/09/dos-donts-responding-to-reviews-yelp, accessed March 1, 2021.

44. Hyounae Min, Yumi Lim, and Vincent P. Magnini, "Factors Affecting Customer Satisfaction in Responses to Negative Online Hotel Reviews: The Impact of Empathy, Paraphrasing, and Speed," *Cornell Hospitality Quarterly* 26 (2015): 223–231.

45. David B. Wooten, "Say the Right Thing: Apologies, Reputability, and Punishment," *Journal of Consumer Psychology* 19 (2009): 225–235.

46. Steven Fink, *Crisis Communications: The Definitive Guide to Managing the Message* (New York: McGraw-Hill, 2013), p. 179

47. Megan A. Adams, Joseph B. Elmunzer, and James M. Scheiman, "Effect of a Health System's Medical Error Disclosure Program on Gastroenterology-Related Claims Rates and Costs," *The American Journal of Gastroenterology* 109 (2014): 460–464.

48. W. Timothy Coombs, "Crisis Management and Communications," Institute for Public Relations, September 23, 2014, https://instituteforpr.org/crisis-management-communications, accessed March 13, 2021.

49. Roy J. Lewicki, Beth Polin, and Robert B. Lount Jr., "An Exploration of the Structure of Effective Apologies," *Negotiation and Conflict Management Research* 9 (2016): 177–196.

50. Lewicki et al.

51. Sorry Watch, "The Six Steps to a Good Apology," sorrywatch.com, accessed March 17, 2021.

52. OurBus, Email, March 16, 2019.

53. Andrew Cuomo, "N.Y. Gov. Andrew Cuomo on Sexual Harassment Allegations: I'm Going to Learn from This," March 3, 2021, YouTube, https://youtu.be/bW3iJt9WR6c, accessed March 13, 2021.

54. Andrew Cuomo, "Governor Cuomo Responds to Independent Reviewer Report," YouTube, August 3, 2021, https://youtu.be/IGGIN99FVho, accessed August 7, 2021.

55. Dov Seidman, "Calling for an Apology Cease-Fire," *The New York Times*, February 3, 2014, http://dealbook.nytimes.com/2014/02/03/calling-for-an-apology-cease-fire, accessed March 13, 2021.

CHAPTER

8 Bad-News Messages

Learning Objectives

After you have finished this chapter, you should be able to

LO1 Identify goals in communicating a bad-news message.

LO2 Describe factors to consider when writing a bad-news message.

LO3 Write a bad-news reply to a given business request.

LO4 Compare bad-news announcements about operations, the organization, and jobs.

LO5 Describe principles for giving and receiving constructive performance feedback.

> *"COVID-19 is having a more severe and sudden financial impact on our business than 9/11 and the 2009 financial crisis combined."*[1]
>
> —Arne Sorenson, former CEO, Marriott International

Chapter Introduction

Marriott International Suffers Impact of COVID-19 and Lays Off Employees

When the COVID-19 pandemic reached the United States, hotels were hit hard. As the country was shutting down, former Marriott CEO Arne Sorenson spoke of the record low occupancy rates and the impact on staff. In a video, he looks visibly upset when he says, "There is simply nothing worse than telling highly valued associates—people who are the very heart of this company—that their roles are being impacted by events completely outside of their control."[2]

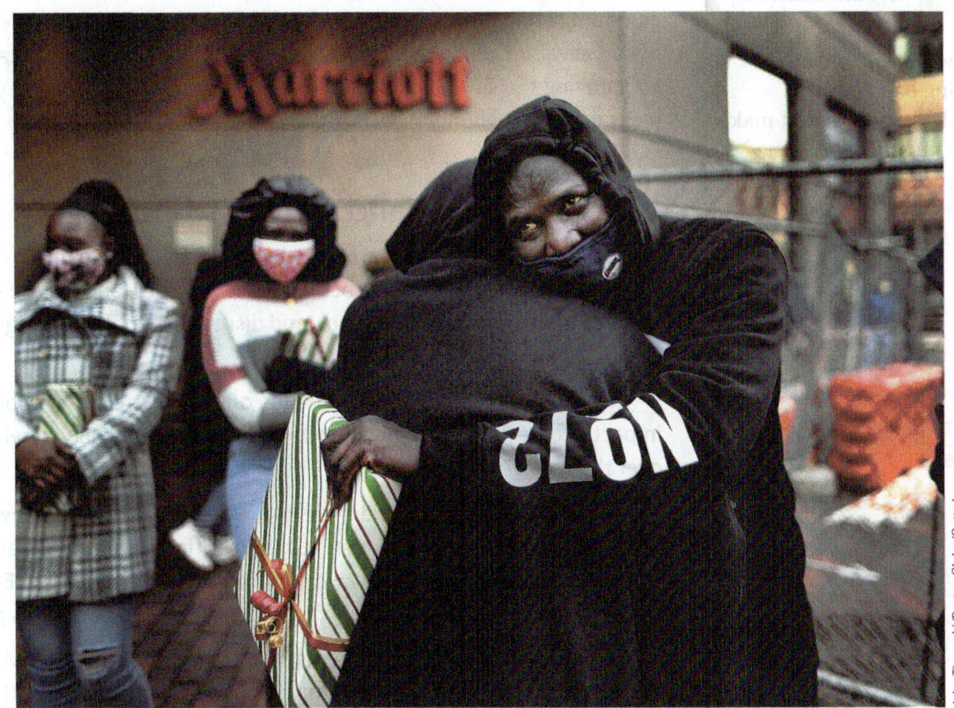

John Tlumacki/Boston Globe/Getty Images

An 18-year Marriott employee hugs a coworker after getting laid off from a Boston hotel.

Throughout that year, Marriott laid off staff in several locations, including Boston, where hotels saw the worst declines in the country. At the Marriott Copley Place, more than half the employees were out of jobs.[3]

Three months after the Boston layoffs, Marriott announced more bad news: Arne Sorenson had died from pancreatic cancer. Bad news will always happen and is often unexpected. How company leaders communicate with stakeholders affects how people respond.

LO1 Identify goals in communicating a bad-news message.

8-1 Planning Bad-News Messages

At some point, we'll all send or receive bad news. Closing an office, discontinuing a product, denying credit—bad news is part of being a leader and running a business.

How you write your messages won't change the news, but it may determine how your reader responds. The potential negative consequences are serious: people who don't like the news or the way you present it are more likely to tell others. We discussed how mishandling negative feedback can turn into crisis situations. The same applies to bad news delivered in ways that confuse the message or disrespect the audience.

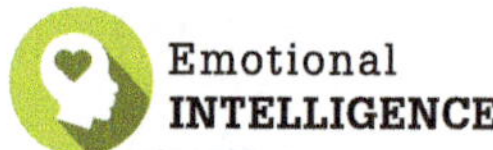

How do you feel about giving bad news? Understanding what makes you uncomfortable may help you improve how you communicate these messages.

Like persuasive messages, bad-news messages require careful planning. According to Andrew Grove, a founder of Intel Corporation, "The worse the news, the more effort should go into communicating it."[4] Grove should know: Intel, like most companies, has communicated its share of bad news, including thousands of layoffs. In this section, you learn to plan bad-news messages by applying the CAM model: checking your character, analyzing your audience, and choosing a message and medium.

8-1a Character and Context Check

Just as people don't like hearing bad news, few enjoy giving it—and most people don't do it well. We feel inadequate, hide behind text messages, and use weak, weaselly words. Or, we feel self-righteous, become belligerent, and disregard people's feelings entirely. Delivering bad news takes courage.

Communicating bad news demands our highest character because, by definition, we will impact people negatively. Bad news also highlights an unequal relationship: the giver has power over the receiver.

We use several character dimensions when delivering bad news. Integrity and transparency show that leaders care about how people are affected. Demonstrating humility may mean admitting our own mistakes and how we contributed to the situation. Being vulnerable means we are willing to be sad ourselves, even if the decision doesn't affect us personally.

Arne Sorenson certainly demonstrated vulnerability in the Marriott video described in the chapter opening. In addition to conveying the bad news about the organization, he addressed his "new bald look," the result of cancer treatments. He admits, "This is the most difficult video message we have ever pulled together. . . . Our team was a bit concerned about using a video today" because of his appearance.[5]

A leader's responsibility is to be both caring and competent. You have several goals in communicating bad news, shown in Figure 1, some of which may sound harsh but are essential to protecting the business.

Figure 1 Goals in Communicating Bad News

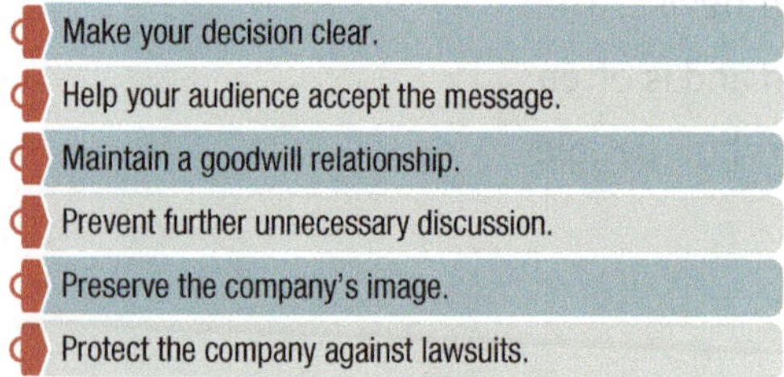

Make your decision clear.
Help your audience accept the message.
Maintain a goodwill relationship.
Prevent further unnecessary discussion.
Preserve the company's image.
Protect the company against lawsuits.

When faced with communicating bad news, first consider the context for the message.[6] Is the message minor (e.g., an unimportant delayed shipment) or major (e.g., a significant company reorganization)? How formal is the company culture? A more formal culture may require longer messages, a more formal tone, and more in-person meetings. What are the legal and ethical considerations? Should corporate attorneys review the message? If so, can you maintain a personal tone and empathy toward the reader, while meeting legal requirements? What is the urgency of the message? Does your audience need to know the information and take action quickly?

Rarely is bad news given in a vacuum. At the end of the chapter, we look at examples of layoff emails, arguably the worst news employees can hear. But long before these decisions are communicated, managers can keep employees informed about organizational problems, such as declining revenue, so they aren't blindsided by the news. Explaining decisions before they're finalized connects employees to the company and positions bad news within a larger organizational context.[7]

In addition to assessing the context for your communication, you'll want to analyze your audience.

8-1b Audience Analysis

Understanding your audience's perspective is a critical step, particularly when communicating bad news. The audience analysis questions in Chapter 4, Figure 2, help us determine how to convey the message so it's as well received as possible. Throughout this chapter, we consider audiences for different types of bad-news messages.

As a general assessment, you can assume that your audience does not like to hear or read bad news. They may feel disappointed, sad, indignant, angry, frustrated, guilty, or a whole host of emotions. Of course, in the end, you have no control over people's reactions, but you can consider their needs.

For organizational changes that affect multiple audiences, consider planning communications for each. Groups will be affected differently, and each should receive a tailored message.

When Marriott announced the acquisition of Starwood Hotels, the company sent different messages to Marriott and Starwood employees, emphasizing different aspects of the decision. Such a large change brings mixed effects. For Marriott, the news was mostly good, but any change makes people uncertain and anxious. For Starwood, people expected layoffs, which came eventually. The template shown in Figure 2 walks you through the process of communication planning when you have multiple audiences.

Communication Planning Template | **Figure 2**

Audience	Create one row for each audience group or person. You may refine the audience groups as you proceed through the Audience Analysis.
Audience Analysis	Identify information needs and potential emotional reactions of each audience group. You may need to refine your initial audience list into smaller or bigger groups if you realize they have different needs.
Communication Objectives	Review the information needs and potential emotional reactions and define specific objectives your message(s) must meet. What do you want each audience to do, think, or feel differently after receiving your communication?
Message and Medium	Consider the identified communication objectives and determine the number of messages and the best medium so that audiences get what they need and feel supported.
Messenger	If you have multiple messages, you will likely have multiple messengers. Consider who is best equipped to deliver each message and who will be best received by each audience group.
Timing or Sequence	People need time to understand, accept, and adapt to change. More complex changes require more messages, and the delivery, timing, and sequence will affect how well people accept and implement the change.

Do you avoid giving bad news in person? Have you hidden behind technology rather than confront someone face-to-face? What were the consequences?

8-1c Message and Media Choice

Even in bad times, messaging can still inspire hope, resiliency, and optimism,[8] as you see in Marriott's announcement, shown in Figure 3, about Arne Sorenson's illness.[9] A positive organizational culture, which we discussed earlier, makes news easier for people to understand and accept. When leaders convey a negative message, they can still inspire people to seek solutions, take action, and carry on with their lives.[10] Later, we discuss specific messaging depending on the type of bad news.

Figure 3 | Marriott Announces Bad News with a Positive Message

Marriott International Statement on Health of President and CEO Arne Sorenson

Marriott International, Inc. (NASDAQ: MAR) today announced that President and CEO Arne Sorenson was diagnosed on Wednesday with stage 2 pancreatic cancer. Sorenson, 60, received the diagnosis from a medical team at Johns Hopkins Hospital in Baltimore after a series of tests. Sorenson will remain in his role while undergoing treatment.

In a message to Marriott International associates, Sorenson noted, "The cancer was discovered early. It does not appear to have spread, and the medical team—and I—are confident that we can realistically aim for a complete cure. In the meantime, I intend to continue working at the company I love. Let me make one request: look ahead with me. We have great work underway at Marriott. I am as excited by what we can accomplish together as I have ever been."

Sorenson's treatment plan will begin next week with chemotherapy. His doctors anticipate surgery near year-end 2019.

As with any business communication, your medium choice depends on the context and audience. If bad news has serious negative consequences—for example, a layoff—then a face-to-face meeting is most appropriate. Researchers describe good reasons for delivering bad news in rich media. Meeting in person or, second best, by video allows people to use and detect body language and to convey respect and sensitivity.[11] Human resources professionals generally agree that the personal touch in these situations is most caring and humane.[12]

Other choices for eliminating jobs, such as text messages, may cause negative press. An article criticized a restaurant layoff with the headline, "This Company Is Laying off Employees via Text Message: Fast casual chain Dig offers a real-time case study in how not to handle tough economic times."[13] Each affected employee received a phone call 15 minutes later, but that doesn't make headlines. Texts may be most efficient, but the perception is never good.

However, if you're responding to a simple request, you might consider how the original message was sent. A request by phone probably warrants a response by phone. A quick IM request ("Can you please join the meeting at 2?") needs only a quick IM reply ("Sorry, I'm meeting with Theo at 2").

When news needs to be delivered quickly to many people, email may be the best option. Compared to face-to-face meetings, email has the following advantages for delivering bad news:

- Allows the sender to determine precise wording.
- Gives the reader time to absorb and understand the message before reacting.
- Ensures a consistent message when sent to many people.
- Controls the message timing when sent to many people.
- Provides a permanent record of what was communicated.
- Ensures a more accurate and complete message.

This last point makes sense when you consider how people feel about giving bad news. Because they struggle with the communication, senders often delay, distort, or incompletely communicate the message. Email may provide just enough distance to help senders communicate more clearly.[14]

8-2 Writing Components of Bad-News Messages

LO2 Describe factors to consider when writing a bad-news message.

Bad-news messages are so varied and potentially sensitive that no one structure or approach applies. To achieve your objectives and meet audience needs, consider how to organize the message, explain the decision, give the bad news, and close the message.

8-2a Organizing the Message

Delivering bad news is complex and requires us to consider options along a continuum of direct and indirect organizational plans—not one or the other.[15] The decision also involves far more than where to place the news and in what order to provide more information. The organization is part of your overall approach and tone.

How you open your bad-news message depends on the content of the message, your relationship with the reader, the reader's expectations, and other factors.[16,17] Will you present the news right up front or wait until the very end? The decision is even more complicated with email: is your message in the subject line or within the body of the email?

You might choose a subject that hints at bad news but isn't too specific. The title of Marriott's press release was, "Marriott International Statement on Health of President and CEO Arne Sorenson."[18] If the title had included "pancreatic cancer," which has a low survival rate, readers would have gotten an immediate impression that was more negative than the company wanted to convey.

Do you prefer to hear bad news directly or more indirectly, perhaps after an explanation of the decision? Does your own style get in the way of how you deliver bad news to others? In other words, do you use your preferred style rather than what might be best for your audience?

Most people prefer to *receive* bad news up front, with explanations following, and most U.S. messages about bad news use this direct organizational plan.[19] At the same time, people prefer to *give* bad news later—to ease into it. This approach makes the giver feel better but doesn't help the receiver understand or accept the news.[20,21] Not much, if any, research supports the "sandwich approach": starting with something positive, giving the bad news, and then ending on a positive note.[22] On the contrary, ending on a highly positive note may sound insincere and may demotivate the person from making behavioral changes based on the news.[23,24,25]

When deciding how and when to present the bad news, consider these questions:

- **What is the content of your message?** If the bad news is a small, insignificant issue, then consider presenting the news up front and following with a brief rationale. If the news affects people personally and may elicit an emotional reaction, you may want to provide a brief rationale before delivering the bad news. And if the situation is highly complex, you may need to provide more explanations before you state the news. Still, don't wait too long, or your reader might feel manipulated, as though you're hiding information.

- **How important is the news?** In a crisis situation or when the information may prevent harm, the news should be right up front. When responding to repeated, unreasonable requests or in other situations when a forceful "no" is in order, also present the news clearly and early on.
- **What are the reader's expectations?** Even in worst-case scenarios, if employees know the news is coming, a more direct approach may work best. Again, delaying the inevitable will frustrate the reader. But if an employee is expecting a positive response about a proposal, a softer approach for your negative feedback, with your rationale first, may be more appropriate. Cultural expectations, as discussed in Chapter 2, also affect structure; people in high-context cultures may prefer a less direct style than people in low-context cultures.

- **What is your relationship with the reader?** When writing to people who report to you, you might choose a less direct style: employees likely will read your entire message, and you can explain the rationale to help them understand a decision that affects them negatively. On the other hand, senior-level managers may prefer news up front to avoid too much reading. Also consider how well you know your audience. For people you communicate with regularly, a more direct style may be acceptable, while people you don't know well may need more relationship building, which happens in indirect messages.

To ease into a bad-news message, some writers start with a one- or two-sentence, neutral buffer before stating the bad news. Again, this buffer won't necessarily soften the blow, but it may be appropriate, particularly when writing to customers and job applicants.

But keep buffers short. Imagine a situation where an employee is called into a manager's office and doesn't know what to expect. In the exchange shown in Figure 4, does the manager use buffers well, or is the employee simply rebuffed? A long, false buffer is not ethical communication and reflects poorly on your character, as though you don't have the courage to present bad news.

Figure 4 | Buffered or Rebuffed?

1 Manager: "Hi, Melissa, how are you doing today?"
2 Employee: "Great. I finished the Gap proposal yesterday, and I'm waiting for their response."
3 Manager: "How do you think the proposal turned out? You're so good at pricing and figuring out exactly what the client needs."
4 Employee: "Thank you. I enjoy writing proposals, and I'm confident about Gap."
5 Manager: "That's great. I'm glad to hear it. But . . ."
6 Employee: "Yes? Is something wrong?"
7 Manager: "Well, no, nothing is wrong, but Paul called, and we didn't get the Gap project."
8 Employee: "We didn't? Why didn't you just say so?"

We use a buffer in a sincere effort to help the reader accept the disappointing news, not to manipulate or confuse the audience. Consider the more effective buffer examples in Figure 5. In these written messages, the bad news comes immediately after this opening.

8-2b Explaining the Decision

Presumably, you have good reasons for reaching your negative decision. Explaining your reasons may help your audience accept the decision and will demonstrate your empathy—understanding that the news may disappoint or upset the receiver. Most of your message should focus on the reasons rather than on you or the bad news itself.

Emotional INTELLIGENCE

When you communicate bad news, how much time do you spend considering the situation from the other person's perspective?

For bad-news messages about unimportant issues and in crisis situations, provide the reasons concisely and matter-of-factly. In emergency situations, no one has time for long explanations—these can come later.

Effective Buffer Examples | **Figure 5**

Audience and Situation	Opening Sentences
Consultant submits a proposal.	Thank you for your thorough proposal and reference list. Clearly, you have done a lot of work in this space. We had a tremendous response to our request and chose a local firm for the project.
Customer asks for a refund.	We have reviewed the situation and understand that the charger hasn't met your expectations. At the same time, the charger was on sale, and the receipt notes, "No returns or refunds." Would you like to exchange the charger for a different model?
Supplier requests more space in the store to display a product.	I appreciate that you chose our store to increase marketing for your product. Our research shows that displays aren't worth the impact on space and traffic flow.
Employee asks for time off.	I understand that you want to take time off before the New Year, and you have certainly earned it. Sebastian asked for that same week off two months ago, and we'll need you to cover the office then.

Present reasons honestly and convincingly. If possible, explain how the reasons benefit the reader or, at least, benefit someone other than your organization, as illustrated in these examples:

- **Why don't you provide copies of company records?** To protect the confidentiality of customer transactions.
- **Why did you raise prices?** To create a more sustainable manufacturing process.
- **Why don't you exchange worn clothes?** To offer higher-quality products to our customers.

To help readers accept your decision when using the direct plan, present a brief rationale along with the bad news in the first paragraph. When Marriott laid off 68 employees at a Hawaiian property, the company sent a letter as an email attachment to local government officials (Figure 6).[26] As required by law, this notice explains the reasons for the bad news, which are summarized in the first paragraph and elaborated on in the third paragraph.

Show the reader that your decision was a *business* decision, not a personal one. Also show that the request was taken seriously, and don't hide behind company policy. People are turned off by hearing "That's just our policy" if it doesn't make sense to them. If the policy is a sound one, established for good reasons, then explain the rationale.

☒ NOT Company policy prohibits our providing an in-store demonstration product.

☑ BUT We surveyed our dealers three years ago and found that the space taken up by in-store demos and the resulting traffic problems were not worth the effort. Dealers also had trouble selling demo products, even with large discounts.

As in the Marriott example, most of your message will be the reasons justifying your decision, but be concise, or your readers may become impatient. Don't belabor a point or provide more background than is necessary. If you have several reasons for refusing a request, present the strongest ones first for the most emphasis and omit weak reasons. Why invite a rebuttal? Stick with your most convincing arguments.

Figure 6 | Marriott Explains the Layoff Decision

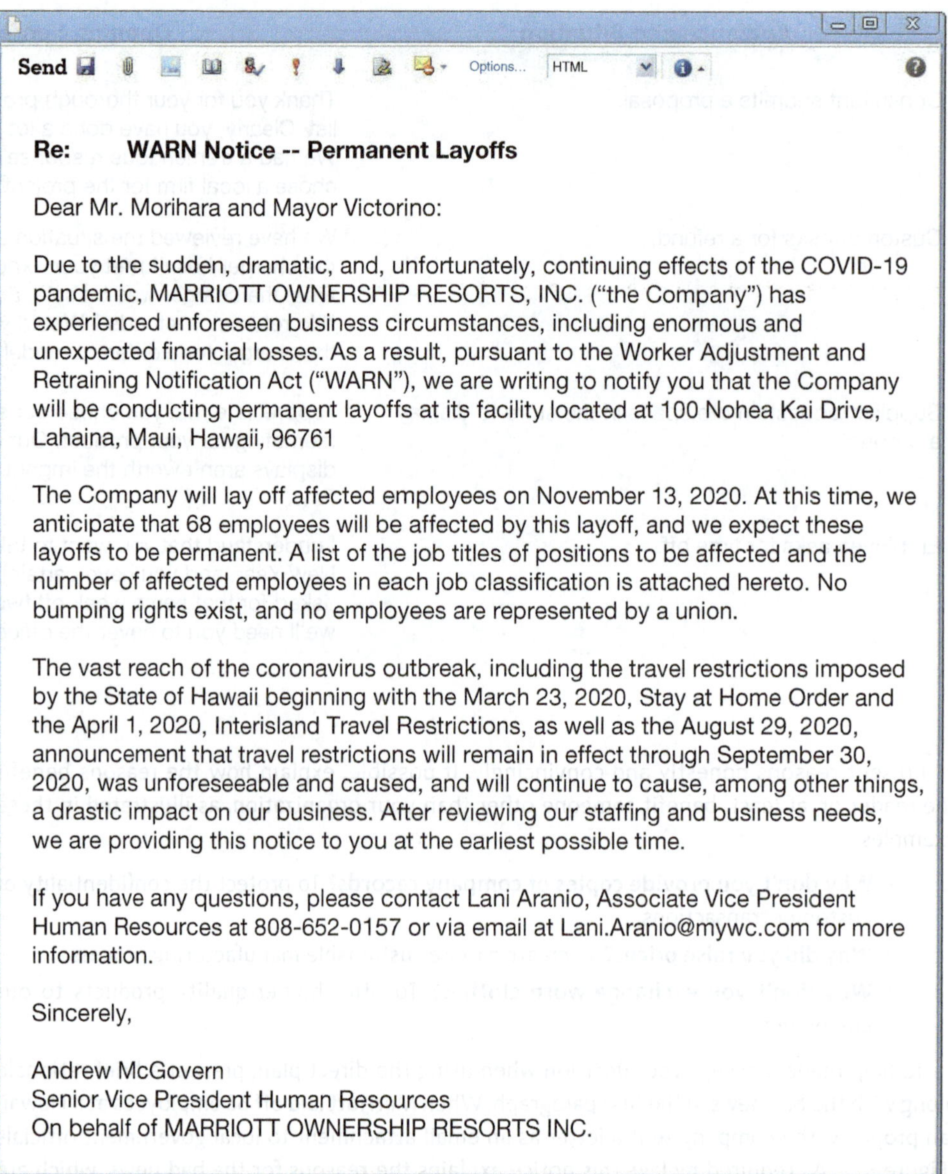

Send | Options... | HTML

Re: WARN Notice -- Permanent Layoffs

Dear Mr. Morihara and Mayor Victorino:

Due to the sudden, dramatic, and, unfortunately, continuing effects of the COVID-19 pandemic, MARRIOTT OWNERSHIP RESORTS, INC. ("the Company") has experienced unforeseen business circumstances, including enormous and unexpected financial losses. As a result, pursuant to the Worker Adjustment and Retraining Notification Act ("WARN"), we are writing to notify you that the Company will be conducting permanent layoffs at its facility located at 100 Nohea Kai Drive, Lahaina, Maui, Hawaii, 96761

The Company will lay off affected employees on November 13, 2020. At this time, we anticipate that 68 employees will be affected by this layoff, and we expect these layoffs to be permanent. A list of the job titles of positions to be affected and the number of affected employees in each job classification is attached hereto. No bumping rights exist, and no employees are represented by a union.

The vast reach of the coronavirus outbreak, including the travel restrictions imposed by the State of Hawaii beginning with the March 23, 2020, Stay at Home Order and the April 1, 2020, Interisland Travel Restrictions, as well as the August 29, 2020, announcement that travel restrictions will remain in effect through September 30, 2020, was unforeseeable and caused, and will continue to cause, among other things, a drastic impact on our business. After reviewing our staffing and business needs, we are providing this notice to you at the earliest possible time.

If you have any questions, please contact Lani Aranio, Associate Vice President Human Resources at 808-652-0157 or via email at Lani.Aranio@mywc.com for more information.

Sincerely,

Andrew McGovern
Senior Vice President Human Resources
On behalf of MARRIOTT OWNERSHIP RESORTS INC.

8-2c Giving the Bad News

If you explained the reasons well, the decision will appear logical and reasonable—the *only* logical and reasonable decision that could have been made under the circumstances.

To retain the reader's goodwill, state the bad news in positive or neutral language, stressing what you *can* do rather than what you *cannot* do. Review Figure 5 for examples that avoid *cannot*, *are not able to*, *impossible*, *unfortunately*, *sorry*, and *must refuse*.

☒ NOT Your financial consulting firm is not appropriate for our type of business.

☑ BUT To maintain confidentiality for our clients, we prefer to manage our finances internally.

Phrase the bad news in impersonal language. Avoid *you* and *your* to distance the reader from the bad news; otherwise, the news may feel like a personal rejection. Also avoid *but* and *however* to introduce the bad news; readers may not remember what was written before the *but*—only what was written after it.

☒ NOT Your proposal is detailed, but your cost estimates are too high.

☑ BUT We appreciate the time you spent developing a detailed cost estimate. In the end, we chose a firm more in line with our budget.

Avoid giving the receiver opportunities to debate the decision. Present the news as final.

☒ NOT The contract is scheduled to end on April 2, but if you need more time, let us know.

☑ BUT The contract will end on April 2.

8-2d Closing the Message

End a bad-news message gently but avoid sales promotions or other tactics that benefit you. When a chef posted an apology for sexual misconduct, he ended on a bad note (Figure 7).[27] The recipe is an obvious attempt at distraction, which came across as self-serving. Although we discussed apologies as persuasive messages, you can see how they also may be considered bad news.[28]

Obvious Promotion in a Closing | **Figure 7**

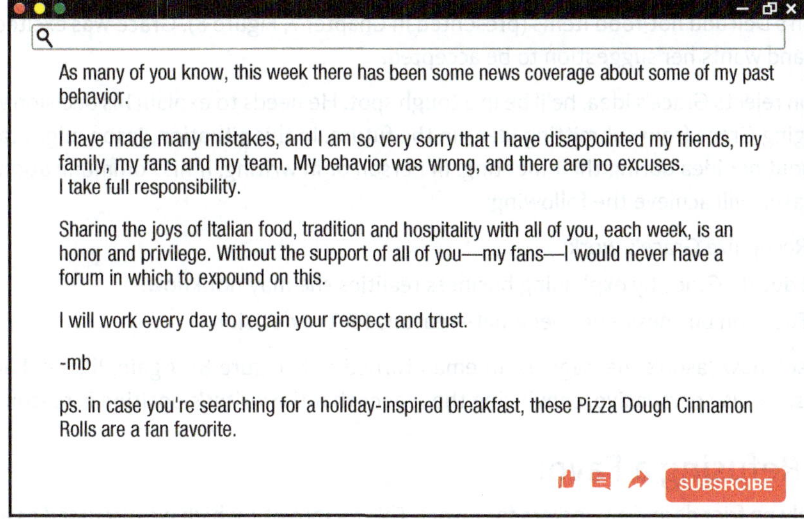

As many of you know, this week there has been some news coverage about some of my past behavior.
I have made many mistakes, and I am so very sorry that I have disappointed my friends, my family, my fans and my team. My behavior was wrong, and there are no excuses. I take full responsibility.
Sharing the joys of Italian food, tradition and hospitality with all of you, each week, is an honor and privilege. Without the support of all of you—my fans—I would never have a forum in which to expound on this.
I will work every day to regain your respect and trust.
-mb
ps. in case you're searching for a holiday-inspired breakfast, these Pizza Dough Cinnamon Rolls are a fan favorite.
SUBSRCIBE

You may write something positive at the end, but you don't have to if it doesn't fit the situation.[29] Instead, think of the ending as a forward-looking statement.

☒ NOT Despite the negative customer feedback, I know you can turn the situation around!

☑ BUT I look forward to working with you to improve your relationships with our long-term customers.

Instead of meaningless clichés that invite more communication, you might offer an alternative, suggestion, or genuine good wishes, depending on the situation. Try to focus on benefits to the reader.

☒ NOT You're welcome to check back to see whether the speakers have come in.

☑ BUT The Torino 920 is similar and on sale. Here's a link for more information.

☒ NOT Let me know if I can do anything else to help.

☑ BUT Even though we don't take large dogs overnight, try Lunabell's in Saratoga.

☒ NOT Your background isn't a fit for us, but I wish you all the best in your future endeavors.

☑ BUT I'm glad I got to know you more, and I'm sure you'll find a better fit for your background and experience.

The rest of this chapter discusses strategies for writing bad-news replies, writing bad-news announcements, and giving and receiving constructive feedback.

LO3 Write a bad-news reply to a given business request.

8-3 Writing Bad-News Replies

Even the best bad-news message can test a reader's goodwill, particularly when the reader has made a request that you reject. What seems like a simple answer may cause the same negative reactions discussed earlier—disappointment, anger, sadness, and so on.

In this section, you learn principles for writing three types of negative replies while maintaining a positive relationship: rejecting an idea, refusing a favor, and refusing a customer's request.

8-3a Rejecting an Idea

Bad-news messages that reject someone's idea or proposal can be challenging to write. Put yourself in the role of the person making the suggestion, for example, Grace Lee, who recommended that Jason's Deli add hot-food items (presented in Chapter 7, Figure 8). Grace was excited about her idea and wants her suggestion to be accepted.

If Jason rejects Grace's idea, he'll be in a tough spot. He needs to explain his decision without discouraging Grace from submitting ideas in the future. In this situation, Jason might talk with Grace about her idea during their meeting. In person or in writing, if his communication is successful, Jason will achieve the following:

- Recognize Grace's work.
- Educate Grace by explaining business realities she may not know.
- Focus on business—not personal—reasons for the decision.

Let's see how Jason's message as an email turned out (Figure 8). Again, like all bad-news messages, it's also persuasive, convincing the reader that the writer's position is reasonable.

8-3b Refusing a Favor

People rely on friends and coworkers for favors. This reciprocity, which we discussed as a principle of influence, strengthens connections among people over time. But, for business or personal reasons, we cannot always accommodate requests.

How you write a message refusing a favor depends on the circumstances. If someone wrote a thoughtful message trying to persuade you to make a large time commitment, a longer, more thoughtful response is appropriate.

But most requests for favors are routine, and you may write a brief, direct response. A coworker asking you to attend a meeting in her place, an employee asking for a deadline extension, or a supplier wanting to change a service agreement may not be deeply disappointed if you decline. The writer probably has not spent a great deal of energy composing the request and simply wants a "yes" or "no" response.

Imagine a situation where an employee requests free conference admission for a planning committee. In Figure 9, Swati Mellone gives her refusal in the first paragraph. After denying the request, she gives clear reasons for the decision and offers a possible alternative without making promises.

8-3c Refusing a Customer Request

For a customer already upset by the failure of the product or service, denying a request can make the situation even worse. You risk losing goodwill and watching the situation go viral through social media sites.

Email Rejecting an Idea | **Figure 8**

Send | Options... | HTML

To: Grace Lee

From: Jason Myers

Subject: Re: Adding Hot-Food Choices to the Menu

Dear Grace,

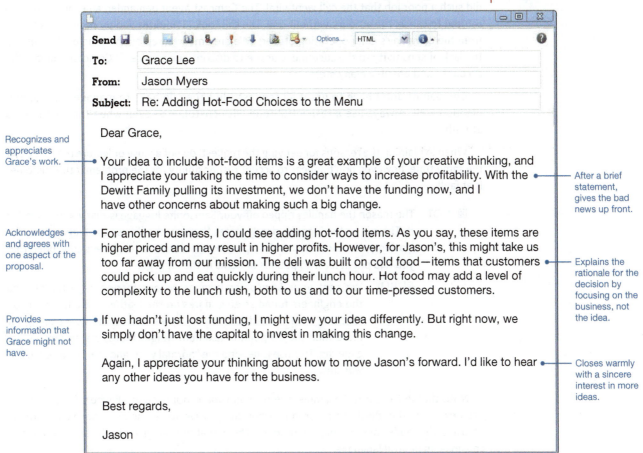

Recognizes and appreciates Grace's work.

Your idea to include hot-food items is a great example of your creative thinking, and I appreciate your taking the time to consider ways to increase profitability. With the Dewitt Family pulling its investment, we don't have the funding now, and I have other concerns about making such a big change.

After a brief statement, gives the bad news up front.

Acknowledges and agrees with one aspect of the proposal.

For another business, I could see adding hot-food items. As you say, these items are higher priced and may result in higher profits. However, for Jason's, this might take us too far away from our mission. The deli was built on cold food—items that customers could pick up and eat quickly during their lunch hour. Hot food may add a level of complexity to the lunch rush, both to us and to our time-pressed customers.

Explains the rationale for the decision by focusing on the business, not the idea.

Provides information that Grace might not have.

If we hadn't just lost funding, I might view your idea differently. But right now, we simply don't have the capital to invest in making this change.

Again, I appreciate your thinking about how to move Jason's forward. I'd like to hear any other ideas you have for the business.

Closes warmly with a sincere interest in more ideas.

Best regards,

Jason

Email Refusing a Favor | **Figure 9**

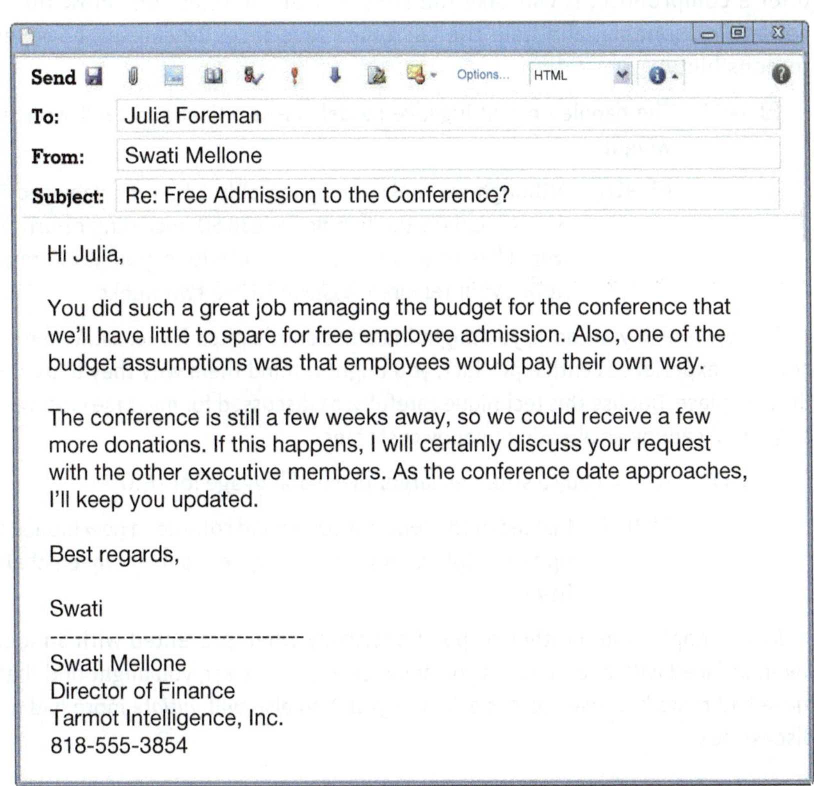

Send | Options... | HTML

To: Julia Foreman

From: Swati Mellone

Subject: Re: Free Admission to the Conference?

Hi Julia,

You did such a great job managing the budget for the conference that we'll have little to spare for free employee admission. Also, one of the budget assumptions was that employees would pay their own way.

The conference is still a few weeks away, so we could receive a few more donations. If this happens, I will certainly discuss your request with the other executive members. As the conference date approaches, I'll keep you updated.

Best regards,

Swati

Swati Mellone
Director of Finance
Tarmot Intelligence, Inc.
818-555-3854

When a customer tried to cancel his Comcast cable subscription, the service representative did such a poor job that the call went viral. The Comcast agent demanded an explanation and refused to cancel the account without one. The call took 18 minutes and prompted an apology from the company's chief operating officer: "We are embarrassed by the tone of the call and the lack of sensitivity to the customer's desire to discontinue service."[30] Comcast still lost the account—and possibly many more.

Companies don't have to grant all requests, but they do have to manage the communication well. Always use a respectful tone with customers—even when the customer is at fault.

When explaining the reasons for denying the request, do not accuse or lecture the reader. At the same time, however, don't appear to accept responsibility for the problem if the customer is at fault.

☒ NOT The reason the handles ripped off your Samsonite luggage is that you overloaded it. The tag on the luggage clearly states that you should use the luggage only for clothing, with a maximum of 40 pounds. However, our engineers concluded that you had put at least 65 pounds of items in the luggage.

☑ BUT We sent your Samsonite luggage to our testing department, and the engineers found stretch marks on the leather and a frayed nylon stitching cord. This kind of wear comes from contents weighing far more than the 40-pound maximum weight that is stated on the luggage tag. This use is beyond the "normal wear and tear" covered in our warranty.

Note that in the second example, the pronoun *you* is not used at all when discussing the bad news. By using third-person pronouns and the passive voice, the example avoids directly accusing the reader of misusing the product. The actual refusal, given in the last sentence, is conveyed in neutral language.

As with other bad-news messages, close on a friendly, forward-looking note. If you can offer a compromise, it will take the sting out of the rejection, show the customer that you are reasonable, and help the customer save face. Be careful, however, not to take responsibility.

☒ NOT The handle on that luggage model is less reliant and can't withstand that much weight.

☑ BUT Although we replace luggage only when it's damaged in normal use, we can replace the handle for $38.50, including return shipping. If you would like us to do so, please call with payment information, and we'll return your repaired luggage within two weeks.

Somewhere in your note, you might include a subtle pitch for resale. When customers have negative experiences with a product, you might remind them why they bought the product in the first place. But use this technique carefully; as discussed for message closings, a strong pitch may simply annoy an already-unhappy customer.

☒ NOT You can buy a stronger, larger piece of luggage for $610.

☑ BUT Instead of the repair, if you would consider a new model, the Fortify has updated styling and the same quiet spinner wheels that you currently have.

Most people would rather respond positively when presented with an idea, asked for a favor, or faced with a request. As you advance in your career, you might find that you're giving more bad news because more is asked of you. You also will *initiate* more bad news, which we discuss next.

8-4 Announcing Bad News

LO4 Compare bad-news announcements about operations, the organization, and jobs.

We just discussed strategies for writing negative replies. Often, however, we're initiating bad news about a current situation or planned event. Quite often, these messages go to a large internal or external audience. These are just some of the many examples of bad news that companies need to communicate:

- The company suffered a bad fiscal quarter.
- An executive is leaving.
- Employees will be laid off.
- Prices are increasing.
- Stores will close.
- Bonuses were cut.
- Departments will be consolidated.
- The company has been acquired.
- The company is accused of wrongdoing.
- A product is being recalled.
- Service cannot be fulfilled.
- A fire caused damage.

Not every organizational change is negative for all audiences, as we saw with the Marriott acquisition of Starwood. The news of a departing executive may be good for a successor but bad for employees who liked working with that person. For this reason, messages about corporate change must be tailored to each audience affected, with particular attention paid to those affected negatively. We explore bad news announcements about normal operations, the organization, and jobs.

8-4a Bad News About Normal Operations

Let's look at how Netflix recently announced a subscription price increase to different audiences (Figure 10). The increase is bad news for customers but good news for investors (as long as the company doesn't lose too many subscribers). With the subject line, "We're updating our prices—here's why," an email to customers presents the news concisely and sells the benefits: more programming.[31] In other words, if you pay more, we can offer more value.

On an earnings call with investors, the chief operating officer says the opposite—in effect, when customers perceive more value, we can charge more. Greg Peters responds to a question about potentially losing customers, or "churn," by describing an "iterative" process.[32] Analysts reported that Netflix would likely gain $500 million in revenue despite some cancellations.[33] This explains the short email to customers with a simple request at the bottom: "We hope you'll stay with us for years to come." The company knows that customers are unlikely to leave—and the impact will be minimal if they do.

For one article, a company spokesperson said something else: "As always, we offer a range of plans so that people can pick a price that works best for their budget."[34] Of course, this point—the option of moving to a lower-rate subscription plan—isn't mentioned in the email to customers. After all, Netflix wants to maximize profits.

When announcing any bad news—no matter how small it seems—take care to adjust your message to different audiences. Any operational change and how you convey the message has potential consequences.

8-4b Bad News About the Organization

If your organization is experiencing serious problems, your employees, customers, and investors should hear the news from you—not from a newspaper, a blog, or the grapevine. For serious problems that receive widespread attention, a large company's public relations department will issue a news release. In a crisis situation, the management team will have a crisis communication plan to ensure clear, consistent messages to all internal and external audiences.

Figure 10 | Netflix Announces a Price Change to Different Audiences

Email to Customers

Send · Options... · HTML

NETFLIX

We're bringing you new TV shows & movies

Hi Amy,

We're updating our prices to bring you more great entertainment. Your monthly price will increase by $1 to $13.99 on December 17, 2020.

This update will allow us to deliver even more value for your membership—with stories that lift you up, move you, or simply make your day a little better.

Questions? Visit the Help Center to learn more or contact us. Or manage your membership anytime by visiting your Account.

Thank you for choosing Netflix—we hope you stay with us for years to come. We look forward to showing you what we have in store.

The Netflix team

Earnings Call with Investors

Greg Peters, Chief Operating Officer and Chief Product Officer

[I]t's almost reversing it, which is that we are looking for signals and signs from our members that are telling us essentially that we have added more value. So you think about engagement with the service and retention and churn characteristics, acquisition.

Those are the things that we're really looking for that are key to basically saying, OK, we've added more value in the service. Now it's the right time to go back to those members and ask them to pay a little bit more so that we can reinvest it and keep adding it. So it's really that sort of iterative, feel-our-way-forward kind of orientation that we have.

As soon as you have enough information, announce the bad news. Be transparent about what you know and honest about what happened. With the email subject, "Notice of Data Breach," the example shown in Figure 11 uses conversational language to address a breach directly. After these paragraphs, the email includes the headings What Happened, What Information Was Involved, What We Are Doing, What You Can Do, and For More Information.[35]

Although you should be transparent, recognize that anything you write may be made public and could be taken out of context. When writing bad news about the company, choose your words carefully: you can't always control how your message is interpreted, as in the example in Figure 12. In this situation, the president has every right—and the responsibility—to defend the company. However, when reported, the facts are presented unfairly.

The last sentence of the president's statement would have been more effective had it been worded differently, for example, "Fences are unnecessary in such isolated sites and, in fact, can cause safety hazards of their own." We can't control every interpretation of our message, but we do need to be particularly careful when announcing bad news.

8-4c Bad News About Jobs

One of the toughest parts of a manager's job is communicating bad news about employees' jobs. When decisions affect people personally—particularly their livelihood and their self-esteem—no one wants to be the messenger.

Companies regularly make decisions that have negative results for employees: they reduce benefits, relocate, change policies, and eliminate jobs. Maintaining employees' goodwill in these

Bad News About the Organization | **Figure 11**

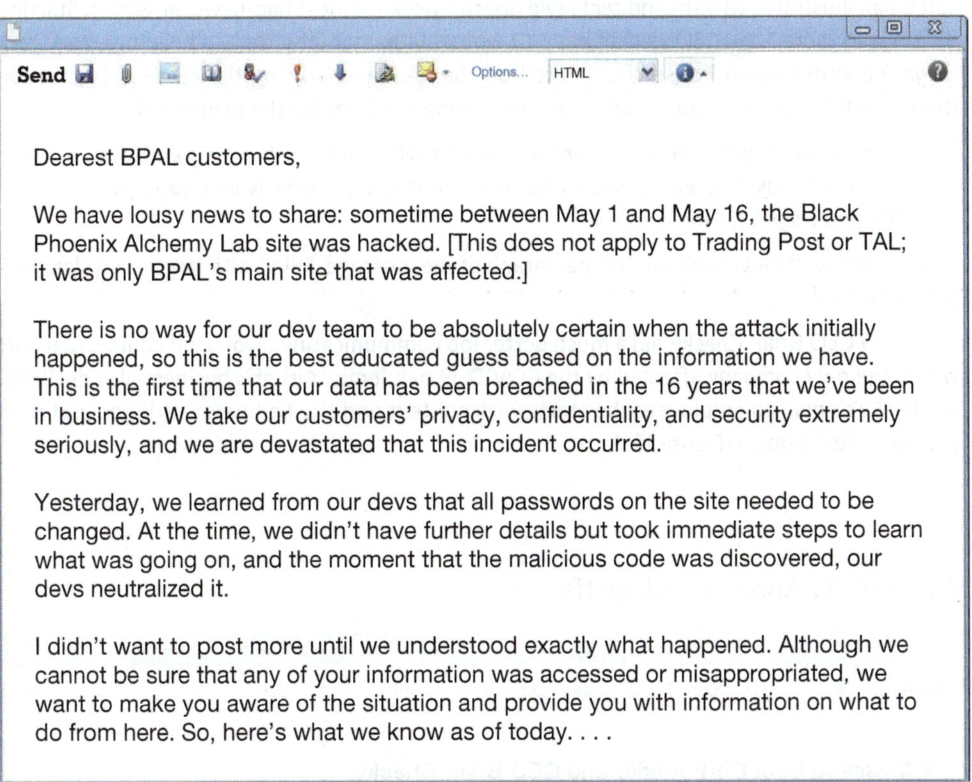

Dearest BPAL customers,

We have lousy news to share: sometime between May 1 and May 16, the Black Phoenix Alchemy Lab site was hacked. [This does not apply to Trading Post or TAL; it was only BPAL's main site that was affected.]

There is no way for our dev team to be absolutely certain when the attack initially happened, so this is the best educated guess based on the information we have. This is the first time that our data has been breached in the 16 years that we've been in business. We take our customers' privacy, confidentiality, and security extremely seriously, and we are devastated that this incident occurred.

Yesterday, we learned from our devs that all passwords on the site needed to be changed. At the time, we didn't have further details but took immediate steps to learn what was going on, and the moment that the malicious code was discovered, our devs neutralized it.

I didn't want to post more until we understood exactly what happened. Although we cannot be sure that any of your information was accessed or misappropriated, we want to make you aware of the situation and provide you with information on what to do from here. So, here's what we know as of today. . . .

Misinterpreting a President's Message | **Figure 12**

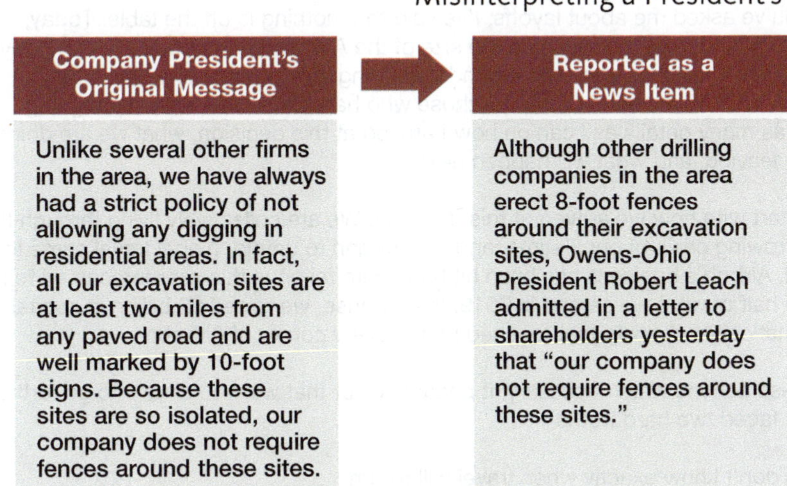

Company President's Original Message	Reported as a News Item
Unlike several other firms in the area, we have always had a strict policy of not allowing any digging in residential areas. In fact, all our excavation sites are at least two miles from any paved road and are well marked by 10-foot signs. Because these sites are so isolated, our company does not require fences around these sites.	Although other drilling companies in the area erect 8-foot fences around their excavation sites, Owens-Ohio President Robert Leach admitted in a letter to shareholders yesterday that "our company does not require fences around these sites."

situations is just as important as maintaining customers' goodwill. Employees have the same ability to use traditional news channels and social media to gossip about the company, and with or without cause, they can sue you.

In addition, of course, treating employees with respect and compassion is the right thing to do. At some point, your company hired these employees, hoping for a promising future with them. The company breaks that trust when it announces layoffs.

In layoff emails, we see a range of approaches, some more effective than others. A Microsoft email illustrates why the indirect style doesn't work for most bad-news messages. Starting with "Hello there," the CEO's email has 1,111 words, 14 paragraphs, and no headings. *New York Magazine* writer Kevin Roose commented on the message, voicing the reader's frustration throughout. In this segment, he criticizes the writing and begs for the main point:

> *"Financial envelope"? You don't literally keep all of Microsoft's cash in a big envelope, do you? Anyway, "changes." I know what that's supposed to mean. Now, please, give it to me straight: tell me I'm fired.*[36]

The news isn't clear until the 11th paragraph of the message. Filled with jargon and slang, it's painful to read.

Airbnb CEO Brian Chesky did a much better job communicating layoffs. Of course, Marriott wasn't the only company affected by the COVID-19 pandemic. Airbnb's business also declined. In Chesky's email to employees, he starts with context and the bad news early on, and then provides the rationale (Figure 13).[37]

Figure 13 | Airbnb CEO Announces Layoffs

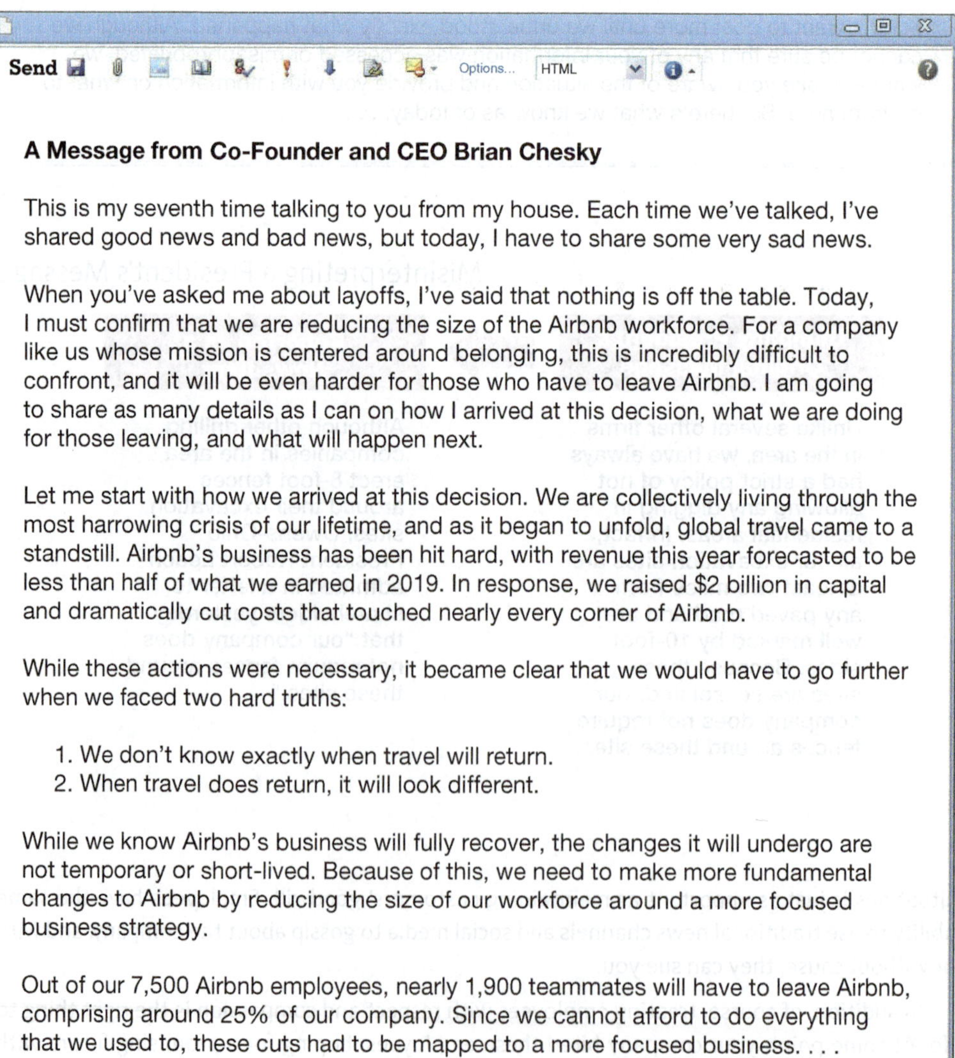

A Message from Co-Founder and CEO Brian Chesky

This is my seventh time talking to you from my house. Each time we've talked, I've shared good news and bad news, but today, I have to share some very sad news.

When you've asked me about layoffs, I've said that nothing is off the table. Today, I must confirm that we are reducing the size of the Airbnb workforce. For a company like us whose mission is centered around belonging, this is incredibly difficult to confront, and it will be even harder for those who have to leave Airbnb. I am going to share as many details as I can on how I arrived at this decision, what we are doing for those leaving, and what will happen next.

Let me start with how we arrived at this decision. We are collectively living through the most harrowing crisis of our lifetime, and as it began to unfold, global travel came to a standstill. Airbnb's business has been hit hard, with revenue this year forecasted to be less than half of what we earned in 2019. In response, we raised $2 billion in capital and dramatically cut costs that touched nearly every corner of Airbnb.

While these actions were necessary, it became clear that we would have to go further when we faced two hard truths:

1. We don't know exactly when travel will return.
2. When travel does return, it will look different.

While we know Airbnb's business will fully recover, the changes it will undergo are not temporary or short-lived. Because of this, we need to make more fundamental changes to Airbnb by reducing the size of our workforce around a more focused business strategy.

Out of our 7,500 Airbnb employees, nearly 1,900 teammates will have to leave Airbnb, comprising around 25% of our company. Since we cannot afford to do everything that we used to, these cuts had to be mapped to a more focused business. . . .

After these opening paragraphs, Chesky describes changes to the business; the decisions and process for reducing staff; the severance, stock, health care, and job support people will receive; and next steps, which include the timeframe for individual meetings. He closes with warm thoughts, particularly for those leaving the organization (Figure 14).[38]

Figure 14 Chesky Ends the Layoff Message

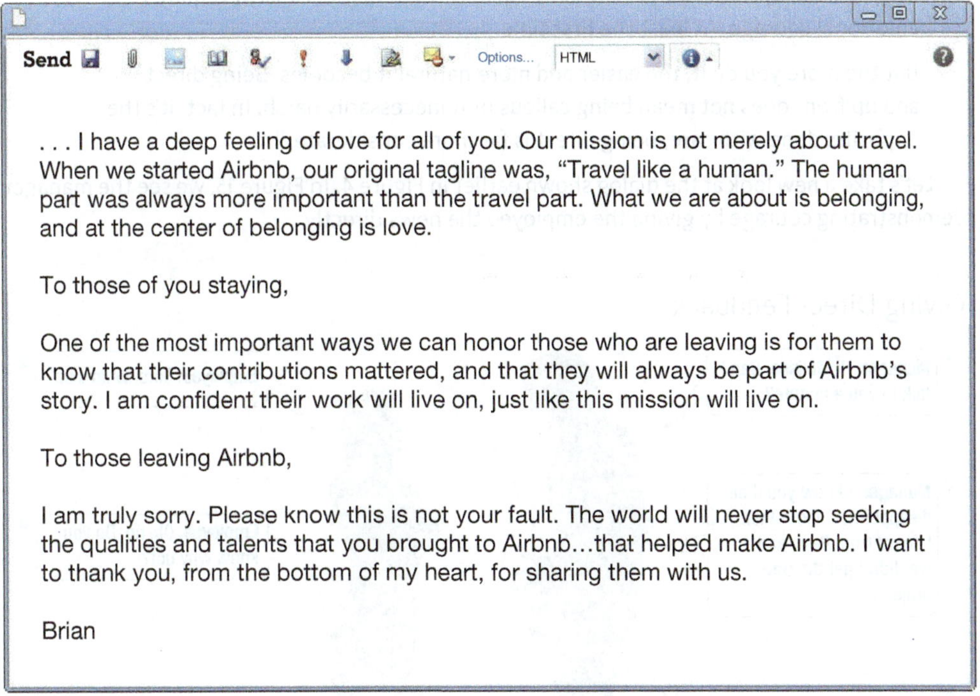

. . . I have a deep feeling of love for all of you. Our mission is not merely about travel. When we started Airbnb, our original tagline was, "Travel like a human." The human part was always more important than the travel part. What we are about is belonging, and at the center of belonging is love.

To those of you staying,

One of the most important ways we can honor those who are leaving is for them to know that their contributions mattered, and that they will always be part of Airbnb's story. I am confident their work will live on, just like this mission will live on.

To those leaving Airbnb,

I am truly sorry. Please know this is not your fault. The world will never stop seeking the qualities and talents that you brought to Airbnb…that helped make Airbnb. I want to thank you, from the bottom of my heart, for sharing them with us.

Brian

After a company-wide announcement of layoffs, managers and human resources representatives typically meet with affected employees individually. The meetings allow the employee to hear the news in person and receive important information about benefits and resources available to them.

As a manager, you also might terminate an employee's job for performance. Unless an employee does something egregious—for example, steals or assaults someone—the decision is a culmination of constructive feedback, which we discuss next.

8-5 Giving and Receiving Constructive Performance Feedback

LO5 Describe principles for giving and receiving constructive performance feedback.

Another challenging situation for managers and employees is giving and receiving negative (or constructive) feedback about job performance. Managers may avoid giving feedback or "sugar-coat" the message.[39] But these managers do employees a disservice, denying them the chance to improve. Often, people want constructive feedback even more than they want positive feedback.[40]

On the other hand, managers may avoid giving constructive feedback because employees don't receive it well. How you react may improve how much feedback you receive—and in turn, how well it's delivered.

Many of the principles about team feedback in Chapter 2 apply to performance feedback. The difference in these situations is the power dynamic.

8-5a Giving Constructive Feedback

As a manager, when you give an employee feedback in person or in writing, get to the main point early, just as you would in other bad-news messages. A *Harvard Business Review* writer supports this direct approach:

> Next time you have a conversation you're dreading, lead with the part you're dreading. Get to the conclusion in the first sentence. Cringe fast and cringe early. It's a simple move that few of us make consistently because it requires emotional courage. At least the first time.

> But the more you do it, the easier and more natural it becomes. Being direct and up front does not mean being callous or unnecessarily harsh. In fact, it's the opposite; done with care, being direct is far more considerate.[41]

Let's take a new look at the dialog shown earlier in Figure 4. In Figure 15, we see the manager demonstrating courage by giving the employee the news directly.

Figure 15 | Giving Direct Feedback

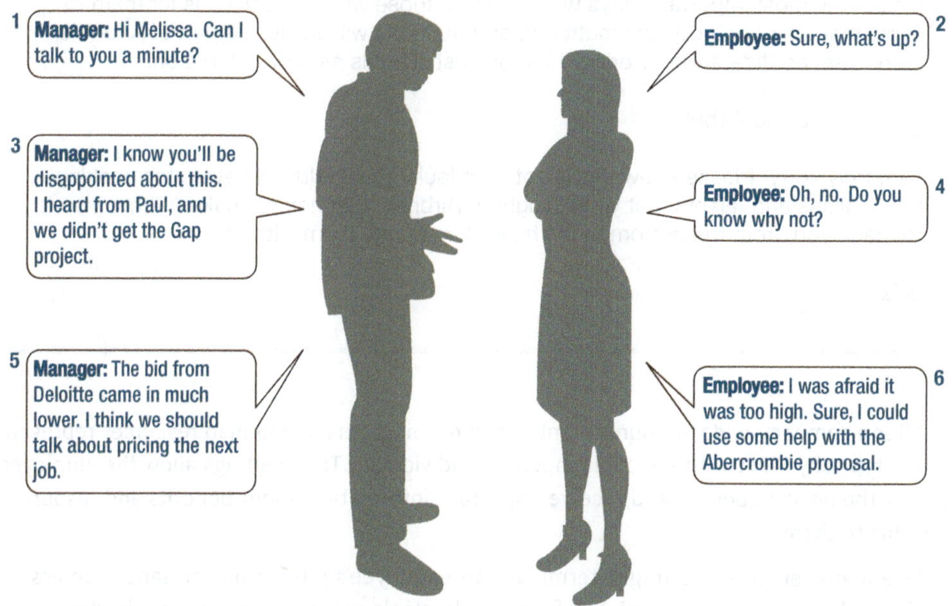

The best feedback is specific and actionable, meaning the employee can do something about it. Use principles discussed in Chapter 2 for giving constructive feedback to team members.

☒ NOT You need to be more professional.

☑ BUT Let's talk about how the Zoom meeting started yesterday. I have some suggestions for how you might adjust your lighting and background.

☒ NOT Your spreadsheet is impossible to read.

☑ BUT I'm having trouble understanding what's most important for me to learn from the data.

Let's use the second example, about data. In this situation, ideally, your performance feedback is a series of questions to the employee:

- Who is your audience for this information?
- What do you think is most important for the audience to see?
- How did you decide which data to include in the spreadsheet?
- How did you choose to organize the data chronologically?

Turn your feedback into a coaching session. A conversation, rather than one-way delivery of negative feedback, encourages employees to find their own solutions and could reduce their defensiveness.

When you look at your responses to the questions in Figure 16, which, if any, would you consider working on for yourself personally and professionally?

8-5b Receiving Constructive Feedback

You know that constructive feedback is necessary for your development, but how do you react when you hear it? Knowing that we all have some negative reactions to constructive feedback, answer the questions in Figure 16. Of course, how you receive it depends on how the feedback is delivered, how well you respect your manager, how confident you are about your work, and so on. Try to think about your typical response.

Figure 16 How Do You React to Constructive Feedback?

1. Feel personally attacked. ("She doesn't like me." "We never got along.")	Never	Sometimes	Always
2. Think the worst. ("I'm going to get fired." "They're going to give this project to someone else.")	Never	Sometimes	Always
3. Blame yourself too harshly. ("I'm terrible at this." "This job is too hard for me.")	Never	Sometimes	Always
4. Blame others. ("Why is this *my* fault?" "Why isn't he talking to _____ about this?")	Never	Sometimes	Always
5. Accept all the feedback no matter what. ("I don't agree, but she must be right." "This doesn't align with my values, but I'll change anyway.")			
6. Argue with the feedback. ("That's not what happened." "She doesn't know the situation.")	Never	Sometimes	Always
7. Shut down. ("If he doesn't like my work, I won't continue on the project." "This is hopeless.")	Never	Sometimes	Always
8. Ignore the feedback. (Too bad if they don't appreciate my work." "I'm not changing.")	Never	Sometimes	Always

What did you learn about yourself that can help you improve how you receive feedback? Next time you hear constructive feedback, try these strategies:

- **Resist your first reaction.** Naturally, your instinct may be fear, anger, or panic. Take a breath and don't interrupt.
- **Adopt an open, curious mindset.** Try to listen without judging. Practice perspective taking—think beyond the impact on you personally. Consider what could happen in the future, despite the immediate bad news.
- **Demonstrate good listening skills.** Use the skills you developed for communicating across differences: pay attention, stay open-minded, don't interrupt, and involve yourself by taking notes, asking questions, nodding, and paraphrasing.
- **View the feedback as an opportunity.** Understanding and acting on constructive feedback may improve your job performance, your feelings about yourself and your work, and your relationship with your manager and your coworkers.
- **Know that your reaction has consequences.** If you respond well to feedback, your manager will likely tell you more ways to improve and will view you as someone who can be coached and promoted within the organization.
- **Thank your manager.** We know that constructive feedback isn't easy to give. Consider saying something like, "I appreciate your telling me this. It was tough to hear, but it's important for me to know, and I'll definitely work on it."

Make it easy for your manager to give you the feedback you need to improve. Ask for feedback about a specific project or task rather than general feedback—and react positively when you hear it.

8-6 Chapter Closing

Even the best leaders of the highest character struggle with delivering bad news. Our good character is what makes the news difficult: we don't want to disappoint or hurt others. But bad news is a part of doing business. Often, negative short-term effects uphold larger organizational commitments and values—and lead to long-term success.

Everyone who receives bad news deserves respect and an explanation. To be credible, that explanation should be rooted in a business decision, which may be driven by data—our next topic.

Cancel a Planned Wedding

Consider the chapter introduction, which described Marriott's temporary closures because of the COVID-19 pandemic. Imagine that you're the conference director at a property that has several weddings booked in the coming months.

Before you have a chance to notify everyone that dates must be postponed because of city regulations, a couple emails you. They want to keep the planned wedding and ask guests to wear masks. Using the CAM model, what questions might you consider before responding to the couple?

››› CHARACTER CHECK

1. **How do I feel about the decision to postpone and the couple's request?**
   I have mixed feelings about everything. The city has banned any event with more than 10 people, and I think that's just too conservative, particularly if everyone wears a mask. We have a big room and can space people adequately. However, it's not my decision, and I've been instructed by the general manager that we will follow the city's guidelines.

   I also feel that it's unfair for the couple to make this request. They know the rules, and we are required to follow them.

2. **What character dimensions should I focus on for myself?**
   I'm tempted to write a curt note in response—I'm not happy about the decision either—but they are guests, and this is disappointing news for them, so I will be professional and respond with compassion. I also will demonstrate integrity by abiding by the law and will be transparent about our lack of ability to rebook a date until we know more about the number of COVID-19 cases.

››› AUDIENCE ANALYSIS

1. **How will the couple likely react?**
   They won't be happy regardless of what I say. They had guests from around the country scheduled to attend, and we planned this wedding together for almost a year. Still, they probably will accept the decision because many guests won't be able to travel anyway.

2. **What is my relationship with them?**
   We have worked well together, overall, but I have found them demanding at times, for example, negotiating many aspects of menu and room décor. I have done my best to accommodate them, but they have not always been happy with my responses to their requests. In this case, they might perceive me, again, as an obstacle to something they want. I'm particularly concerned about their wanting to rebook, and it's impossible to predict when the ban will be lifted.

>>> MESSAGE AND MEDIUM

1. **What are the main points of my message?**
   I will be clear that the wedding needs to be postponed. I will present the news as a decision outside of my control and include a link to the local government website explaining the ban. Of course, I will apologize for the situation and recognize the significant impact on them and their friends and families. But I don't want to open the door for negotiation because the decision is final.

2. **In what medium will I communicate the message?**
   I'll respond by email, which is how I received their message and how most of our communication has transpired. Scheduling a phone or video call would only delay the news and invite questions that I simply can't answer.

Announce a Property Closing

‹ IN PRACTICE

Imagine that you are the general manager for a Marriott property that has suffered because of the COVID-19 pandemic. Plan and write an email telling employees that 30% of the staff—mostly housekeeping and front desk employees—will be furloughed (temporarily laid off without pay). You do not know when you'll be able to reinstate them, but while on furlough, employees can collect unemployment insurance, and the company will cover their health benefits. Invent whatever details you would like.

››› CHARACTER CHECK

1. How do I feel about the decision to furlough staff? Particularly consider that the lowest-paid employees are most affected and that my own job and salary aren't affected.
2. How do I feel about my ability to deliver the news? What character dimensions—for example, courage, humility, vulnerability, integrity, and compassion—do I believe I can demonstrate well, and where might I fall short?

››› AUDIENCE ANALYSIS

1. Who are my primary and secondary audiences? Consider that the email might be distributed beyond my intended audiences.
2. How might they react to my email?

››› MESSAGE AND MEDIUM

1. What will be my main points?
2. How will I organize the email? Consider the opening, headings, and closing.
3. The email will announce the news. What additional communications will be required for affected employees?

REFLECTING ON YOUR COMMUNICATION AND CHARACTER DEVELOPMENT

1. **Reflect on your experience giving bad news.**
   Think about a time when you had to deliver bad news. What was the context, who was the audience, and how did you approach the situation? What were your main points, and what medium did you choose? How did you feel, and how was the message received?

   Consider the principles described in this chapter. Which did you use successfully, and what could you have improved? In what ways might a different approach have affected the outcome?

2. **Reflect on your experience receiving bad news.**
   Now answer the questions from the first reflection question about bad news you received. If it's not too painful, think about a time when you received news that was disappointing or upsetting. Could the sender have done anything to make it less difficult to hear?

3. **Reflect on bad news delivered via text message.**
   Now think about a time when you either delivered bad news or received bad news via a text message. Why did you choose—or why do you think the sender chose—a text message instead of a richer, more personal medium? What was the outcome, both on how the news was accepted and on the long-term relationship?

   In retrospect, was a text the best choice for the medium? If the message had been delivered by a phone call or in person, how, if at all, might the outcome have changed?

4. **Identify your preference for receiving bad news.**
   How do you typically prefer to receive bad news? Do you want news directly, with the main point up front, or do you prefer being eased into it? Do you prefer straightforward language, or do you prefer a softer tone? How do your preferences differ based on the situation or the person delivering the news?

   How does this preference affect your own approach to delivering bad news? Does your own preference for receiving—or for delivering—news focus too much on you instead of on the audience?

5. **Analyze your typical reaction to receiving constructive feedback.**
   Review your responses to the reaction statements in Figure 16. Why do you think you react the way you do? Can you identify something in your history or personality that might drive your response?

   What did you identify as possible ways to change your typical reaction? How realistic are these changes for you? What might prevent you from making them?

DEVELOPING YOUR BUSINESS COMMUNICATION SKILLS

LO1 Identify goals in communicating a bad-news message.

PLANNING BAD-NEWS MESSAGES

1. **Analyze the Marriott CEO message.**
   Watch Arne Sorenson's video discussed in this chapter. (Go to https://youtu.be/SprF-goU6aO0, or search YouTube to find "COVID-19: A message to Marriott International associates from President and CEO Arne Sorenson," March 20, 2020.) Discuss the following questions in small groups:

   a. Identify ways in which Sorenson demonstrates character—his humility, vulnerability, courage, compassion, and so on. In addition, does he convey hope, resiliency, and optimism?

   b. Who are his primary and secondary audiences? Note the title of the video, and yet the video is published on YouTube.

c. What are his key messages? What main points do you take away from the video?

d. What are your thoughts about the medium? Was a video the best choice? Why or why not?

2. Analyze a company recall announcement.

When products are recalled for safety reasons, the U.S. Food and Drug Administration posts company messages on its website. In groups of three or four, discuss the Whole Foods announcement shown in Figure 17.[42] Although these messages tend to be rather formulaic, analyze the context, audience, and medium. What are the objectives, and does the company achieve them?

Product Recall Announcement | **Figure 17**

Company Announcement

Whole Foods Market is voluntarily recalling Cranberry Biscotti purchased from six stores in Maryland, Pennsylvania, and Virginia. The product is being recalled because it may contain undeclared Tree Nuts (Pistachio) that were not listed on the product label due to mislabeling. People who have an allergy or severe sensitivity to Tree Nuts (Pistachio) run the risk of a serious or life-threatening allergic reaction if they consume this product.

The affected products were sold in the Bakery department with sell-by dates through April 3, 2021, and can be identified by the PLU code **41712**. The product was sold by weight in clear plastic containers. All affected product has been removed from store shelves. The issue was identified as a result of a customer complaint, and one illness has been reported to date.

The affected product was sold at the following Whole Foods Market stores: [list omitted].

Customers who purchased this product at Whole Foods Market can bring a valid receipt into the store for a full refund. Consumers with additional questions can call 1-844-936-8255 between the hours of 7:00 a.m. and 10:00 p.m. CST, Monday through Friday, or 8:00 a.m. and 6:00 p.m. Saturday through Sunday.

3. Create a communication plan.

Imagine that you're closing a restaurant that is part of a large chain. Use the communication plan template in Figure 2 as your guide for how to deliver the bad news to different audiences. Identify at least five internal and five external audiences for your messages, and work across the columns to analyze each.

4. Consider media choices for bad-news messages.

Discuss these situations in small groups and decide what medium—for example, email, text, video meeting, or in-person meeting—to use for each message. Try to come to consensus, although you may not find a perfect answer. You also may consider multiple messages.

- If you managed a restaurant and had to tell 18 employees that the restaurant will be closed tonight because of allegations of food poisoning, how would you deliver the news?
- If you laid off a manager and the entire department of eight people who work in four different countries, how would you deliver the news to the group?
- If an employee works in California, and you (the manager) work in New York, how would you tell the employee, whom you have known for two years, that you're leaving the company?
- If you just learned from Human Resources that one of your direct reports has been hospitalized, how would you communicate with the employee? How would you communicate with the employee's coworkers to let them know that the employee will be out for at least two weeks?

LO2 Describe factors to consider when writing a bad-news message.

WRITING COMPONENTS OF BAD-NEWS MESSAGES

5. Compare message organization.

In small groups, find as many bad-news messages as you can—rejections from colleges or jobs, emails you received, or public messages. In each message, how quickly does the writer get to the bad news? Do you notice an introductory sentence or a longer buffer? How does the message end? What do the writers say in closing? Which messages are most and least effective?

6. Revise a template layoff email.

Find a sample layoff email online. (You may use one posted by the Society for Human Resources. Search for "SHRM layoff letter.") Revise the template, which sounds cold and stilted. Use your own, professional, natural style to provide employers with one approach to delivering the bad news.

7. Analyze bad news in a company annual report.

Think about a public company that had a difficult year. Find the annual report and read the CEO's letter, which is typically at the beginning of the report. Consider the context, audience, message, and medium, and describe how the CEO explains the bad news. What is effective about the message, and what could be improved?

8. Decide how to explain bad news.

Imagine that you built a successful company with 40 employees and decided to sell to a major corporation. You will leave, and the acquiring company has indicated that most employees will be laid off. A few employees in specialized technology roles will stay on—at least until the new company fully integrates your app into its existing platform.

The truth is that you sold because they offered a great buyout, and you want to move on to a new business idea. You see yourself as a serial entrepreneur and would rather start a new business than run a mature company. About 10 employees have equity in the business, and they will also get a windfall, but most employees don't have any equity.

In small groups, discuss how you will deliver the news to your employees. What will you give as your reasons for selling, and how will you describe the potential impact on them? Write a few sentences to explain the news.

LO3 Write a bad-news reply to a given business request.

WRITING BAD-NEWS REPLIES

9. Send an email rejecting an idea for online ordering.

Imagine that you run a local used bookstore, where you receive the email shown in Figure 18 from a new employee.

Figure 18 | Email Idea from an Employee

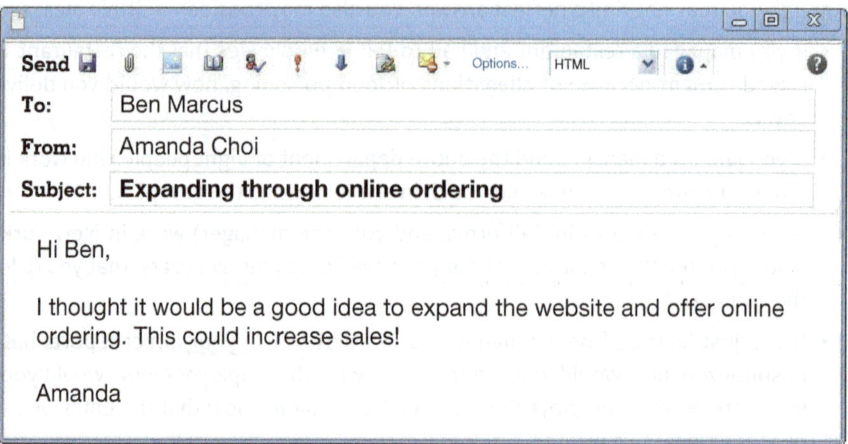

Write an email response to this employee rejecting the suggestion. You can invent whatever rationale you'd like, and keep in mind that this employee did not put a lot of thought into the suggestion.

10. Write an email refusing an employee's request.[43]

You manage the conventions department for a hotel, where you supervise an employee named Robert. Robert is responsible for meeting with companies that hold events at the hotel. This morning, you received the email shown in Figure 19 from Robert.

Email Request from an Employee | **Figure 19**

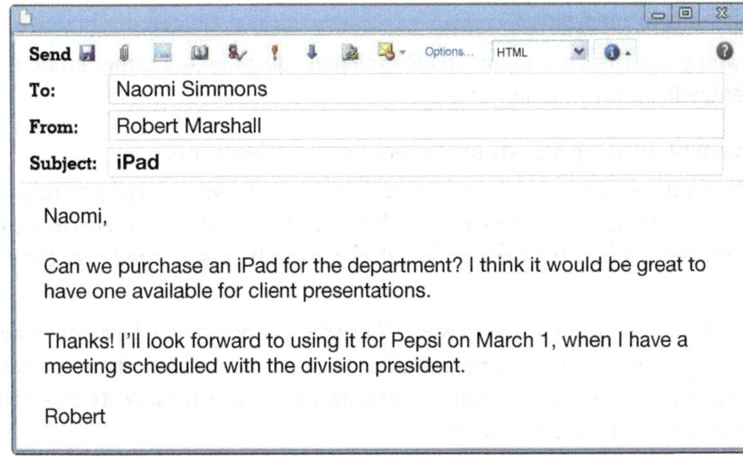
To: Naomi Simmons
From: Robert Marshall
Subject: iPad

Naomi,

Can we purchase an iPad for the department? I think it would be great to have one available for client presentations.

Thanks! I'll look forward to using it for Pepsi on March 1, when I have a meeting scheduled with the division president.

Robert

You won't be able to approve this request for the following reasons:

- You have no budget for this capital expense. It's possible to budget for this next year, but you're not sure an iPad just for client presentations would be worth the expense. You really don't see the point because you recently spent a lot on printing beautiful materials, which Robert takes to clients with him.
- Robert started working at your company only one month ago. Although you encourage ideas, you do not like Robert's presumptuous tone.
- Also, you'd like to encourage Robert to put more time and thought into his ideas. Although not a huge expense, an iPad for your department would need to be justified—and Robert would benefit from supporting his suggestions more convincingly.
- His preliminary marketing plan was due two days ago, but he hasn't submitted it yet. You'd like him to focus on his current responsibilities as a priority.
- On the other hand, you hired Robert because of his strong work background and excellent skills, and you hope he will have a long career with your company. Also, the hiring process was lengthy and expensive, and you have no desire to go through it again. You don't want to discourage him.

Write an email to Robert that rejects his request. Next, exchange emails with another student. At this point, your instructor may give you more information about Robert's perspective. If you were Robert, how would you react to the email? Provide feedback to the original writer.

11. Write an email denying a request for a salary advance.

Imagine that you own a website design firm, and an employee asks you for a favor: a one-month salary advance. This is one of your best employees, someone who has worked with you for more than five years, and you know she's buying a house. But you cannot advance her the money for these reasons:

- It's against your company policy (according to your employee handbook).
- You want to be fair to everyone and cannot accommodate others' requests.

- You don't want to set a precedent.
- You don't believe it's your responsibility.

Decide how you'll organize the email and which of these reasons you will present to the employee. You don't need to include everything unless you believe it will explain your rationale and maintain the employee's goodwill.

12. Write an email rejecting an exception.

You're the president of a campus business club that is offering students mock interviews with a school alumnus. An interested student emailed you to sign up after the deadline, asking to be added to the schedule. All time slots are already taken, and you decide not to ask the alumnus to add a slot.

What will you write back in an email? Exchange drafts with another student and give each other feedback on your approach.

13. Write an email refusing a customer's request to waive a fee.

Imagine that you work for a bank's credit card division, and you're trying to resolve a complaint from a customer. Through an online form on the website, you receive a customer's message, requesting that the bank waive $75 of overdraft fees accrued over the past three months.

Your policy doesn't require you to waive these fees, although you have for some customers. However, you deny this customer's request because the customer had similar overdraft fees in the previous quarter, so the customer is aware of these fees. Write an email to communicate your decision to the customer.

LO4 Compare bad-news announcements about operations, the organization, and jobs.

ANNOUNCING BAD NEWS

14. Announce a price increase.

Write a statement that would appear on a website about an increase in the price of a service, product, or subscription. Choose the company and invent whatever details you would like. If the company has announced an increase, write your message first, and then compare it to the company's. Which do you prefer and why?

15. Write an email to tell employees about a product recall.

Based on the Whole Foods recall, shown in Figure 17, write an email to employees. This is a different audience, so consider how the tone and information provided might differ. Exchange drafts with another student to compare your approaches.

16. Announce a discontinued product.

Prepare a statement for a company's website about one of your favorite products. Sadly, the product will no longer be available. How will you explain the decision and still keep good customers like yourself? Invent whatever details you would like.

17. Write an email announcing employee layoffs.

You are the SVP of human resources for a financial software company that has 7,500 employees. The company has decided to sell AccountSoft, one of its major products. The software has suffered declining sales for the past two years, and it no longer fits with the new mission of the company, which is to sell to small businesses and individuals, rather than larger accounting firms.

You will have individual conversations with employees who are affected by the layoffs, but first you advise the CEO to send an email to all employees to announce the decision to sell AccountSoft and to prepare employees for the downsizing and what will happen next.

As you write this email for the CEO, consider that not all employees from the Account-Soft division will be laid off. The sales and marketing staff (about 150 people) will be leaving the firm, but the software developers will go to the acquiring firm, Accounting Support Services, Inc. This was your agreement with Accounting Support Services as part of the acquisition deal.

Write the email to communicate the decision clearly and help employees understand and accept the message.

18. Write a memo announcing no bonus.

You are the manager of a fitness equipment manufacturing plant called Muscles Galore. The plant has been in operation for seven years. Over the years, your employees have been very productive, and sales have been high. Therefore, Muscles Galore has been able to give generous holiday bonuses (usually more than $1,000) to all its employees for the last five years.

This year, however, because of a slow economy, you will not be able to offer the holiday bonus. Fitness equipment sales are down about 15% from last year. Your projections indicate that the economy is recovering, and sales should be up about 20% next year. If the projections are accurate, you should be able to offer the bonus again next year—but you won't make any promises. Write an email to your employees letting them know the bad news.

GIVING AND RECEIVING CONSTRUCTIVE PERFORMANCE FEEDBACK

LO5 Describe principles for giving and receiving constructive performance feedback.

19. Role-play giving and receiving feedback.

Think about a time at a former job or internship when a coworker's performance didn't meet your expectations. Imagine that you are that person's manager and plan to give feedback. Follow these steps:

a. Identify the issue. What are a few specific examples that illustrate that the performance isn't up to standard? What is the impact of the performance?

b. Think about ways you can approach a meeting with the employee as a coaching conversation. What questions can you ask to get the employee's point of view first?

c. Plan your first couple of sentences to open the meeting. You can let the employee know that you want to talk about something serious but try to leave it open so you have a good interaction. For example, "I'd like to talk with you about your interaction with the customer just now" or "Can we spend some time debriefing last night's meeting?" Use your own, natural language.

When you're ready, role-play this situation with another student playing the role of the employee, who is open to and appreciates the manager's feedback. Have a third student observe the interaction, take notes, and give feedback using principles for giving and receiving feedback discussed in the chapter.

20. Document your feedback.

After your meeting with the employee, described in Exercise 19, write an email confirming what you talked about. Try to be supportive but avoid "sugar-coating" the feedback.

21. Document your feedback for a different type of interaction.

As you did in Exercise 20, document your feedback to the employee. But this time, imagine that the employee was defensive and got angry during the conversation. If the employee had argued about the feedback, how would that change what you write in your follow-up email? Share your draft with other students to get their reactions and suggestions to improve your message. Unlike the employee, try to listen with an open mind!

CHAPTER SUMMARY

LO1 Identify goals in communicating a bad-news message.

Delivering bad news tests your character and requires courage, vulnerability, and integrity. When writing a bad-news message, your goals are to convey the bad news clearly, help the audience accept the decision, maintain the reader's goodwill—and protect the company from further discussion, reputation damage, and lawsuits. Consider the communication context, audience, and media choice before writing your message. Large-scale announcements require a communication plan.

LO2 Describe factors to consider when writing a bad-news message.

As you begin drafting, decide how to organize the message based on the content, importance, reader's expectations, and your relationship with the reader. Explain the decision by focusing on the reasons and reader benefits. Typically, deliver the news using positive or neutral language and close on a friendly, helpful note.

LO3 Write a bad-news reply to a given business request.

When rejecting someone's idea, tact is especially important. Devote most of your message to presenting reasons based on business, not personal, decisions. Most requests for favors are routine and should receive a brief, direct response. For customer requests, the tone of your refusal must convey respect, even when the customer is at fault.

LO4 Compare bad-news announcements about operations, the organization, and jobs.

Announcements of bad news may be either internal or external and may be about normal operations, the organization, or jobs. When people are affected personally, put more time and care into crafting a message that treats the reader with respect and dignity.

LO5 Describe principles for giving and receiving constructive performance feedback.

Telling employees what they could do differently gives them the chance to improve their job performance. Use a direct approach and allow for a conversation in which the employee has time and space to react. When receiving feedback, try to stay open-minded and view the feedback as a good learning opportunity, even if it's painful or you don't, at first, agree with what you hear.

Endnotes

1. Arne Sorenson, "COVID-19: A Message to Marriott International Associates from President and CEO Arne Sorenson," Marriott International, YouTube, March 20, 2020, https://youtu.be/SprFgoU6aO0, accessed March 16, 2021.
2. Sorenson.
3. The Boston Globe Staff, "Marriott Copley Terminates Half Its Staff; Thousands of Hotel Workers Unemployed Around Boston," *The Boston Globe*, November 16, 2020, www.boston.com/travel/local-news/2020/11/16/marriott-copley-terminates-half-its-staff, accessed March 16, 2021.
4. Bill Quirke, "Don't Shoot the Messenger: Conveying Bad News and Change," *Strategic Communication Management* 12 (Apr/May 2008): 24.
5. Sorenson.
6. Sofie Decock, Bernard De Clerck, and Rebecca Van Herck, "Interpersonal Strategies in E-Complaint Refusals: Textbook Advice Versus Actual Situated Practice," *Business and Professional Communication Quarterly* 83 (2020): 285–308.
7. Sandra L. French and Tracey Quigley Holden, "Positive Organizational Behavior: A Buffer for Bad News," *Business Communication Quarterly* 75 (June 2012): 208–220.
8. French and Holden.
9. Marriott News Center, "Marriott International Statement on Health of President and CEO Arne Sorenson," Marriott.com, May 3, 2019, https://news.marriott.com/news/2019/05/03/marriott-international-statement-on-health-of-president-and-ceo-arne-sorenson, accessed March 19, 2021.
10. French and Holden.
11. Robert Bies, "The Delivery of Bad News in Organizations: A Framework for Analysis," *Journal of Management* 39 (2013): 136–162.
12. Chris Russell, "Laid Off via Text Message: HR Execs Respond," HR Lancers, https://hrlancers.com/blog/laid-off-via-text-message-hr-execs-respond, April 27, 2020, accessed March 19, 2021.
13. Maya Kosoff, "This Company Is Laying off employees via Text Message," Marker, March 20, 2020, https://marker.medium.com/millennial-farm-to-table-chain-digs-crisis-response-layoffs-via-text-message-e30145418f54, accessed March 19, 2021.
14. Stephanie Watts Sussman and Lee Sproull, "Straight Talk: Delivering Bad News Through Electronic Communication," *Information Systems Research* 10 (June 1999): 150–166.
15. Valerie Creelman, "The Case for 'Living' Models," *Business Communication Quarterly* 75 (June 2012): 176–191.
16. Creelman.
17. Decock, De Clerck, and Van Herck.
18. Marriott News Center, "Marriott International Statement on Health of President and CEO Arne Sorenson," Marriott.com, May 3, 2019, https://news.marriott.com/news/2019/05/03/marriott-international-statement-on-health-of-president-and-ceo-arne-sorenson, accessed March 19, 2021.
19. French and Holden.
20. Kitty O. Locker, "Factors in Reader Responses to Negative Letters," *Journal of Business and Technical Communication* 13 (1999): 5–48.
21. Angela M. Legg and Kate Sweeny, "Do You Want the Good News or the Bad News First?: The Nature and Consequences of News Order Preferences," *Personality and Social Psychology Bulletin* 40 (2014): 279–288.
22. Locker.
23. Ann Nguyen, "Do You Want the Good News or the Bad News First?: News Order Influences Recipients' Mood, Perceptions, and Behaviors," University of California, Riverside, *Undergraduate Research Journal* (2011): 31–36.
24. French and Holden.
25. Locker.
26. Marriott Ownership Resorts, Inc., Maui Ocean Club, "WARN Notice—Permanent Layoffs," *Via Email*, September 2, 2020, https://labor.hawaii.gov/wdc/files/2020/09/WARN-2020.09.03-HI-MAUIOC-MORI-STATE-MAYOR-Notice2.pdf, accessed March 20, 202
27. Emily Stewart, "Mario Batali's Sexual Misconduct Apology Came with a Cinnamon Roll Recipe," *Vox*, December 16, 2017, www.vox.com/2017/12/16/16784544/mario-batali-cinnamon-roll-apology, accessed August 11, 2021.
28. Locker.
29. Locker.
30. Chris Morran, "Comcast Memo: Rep from 'Painful' Retention Call Was Doing 'What We Trained Him to Do,'" *Consumerist*, July 21, 2014, http://consumerist.com/2014/07/21/comcast-memo-rep-from-painful-retention-call-was-doing-what-we-trained-him-to-do/, accessed March 21, 2021.
31. Netflix, "We're Updating Our Prices—Here's Why," Email, November 17, 2020.
32. Greg Peters, "Netflix (NFLX) Q4 2020 Earnings Call Transcript," January 19, 2021, Netflix, posted by The Motley Fool, www.fool.com/earnings/call-transcripts/2021/01/20/netflix-nflx-q4-2020-earnings-call-transcript/, accessed March 21, 2021.
33. Todd Spangler, "Netflix U.S. Price Hikes Could Boost 2021 Revenue by $500M Even with Subscriber Cancellations, Analysts Say," *Variety*, October 30, 2020, https://variety.com/2020/digital/news/netflix-us-price-hikes-cancel-2021-revenue-increase-1234819628/, accessed March 21, 2021.
34. Julia Alexander, "Netflix Is Raising the Price of Its Most Popular Plan to $14 Today, Premium Tier Increasing to $18," The Verge, October 29, 2020, www.theverge.com/2020/10/29/21540346/netflix-price-increase-united-states-standard-premium-content-product-features, accessed March 21, 2021.

35. Elizabeth Barrial, "Notice of Data Breach," Black Phoenix Alchemy Lab, posted by Snarly, "This Is How You Do a Corporate Apology," May 18, 2018, https://sorrywatch.com/this-is-how-you-do-a-corporate-apology/, accessed March 21, 2021.
36. Kevin Roose, "Microsoft Just Laid Off Thousands of Employees with a Hilariously Bad Memo," *New York*, July 17, 2014, https://nymag.com/intelligencer/2014/07/microsoft-lays-off-thousands-with-bad-memo.html, accessed March 21, 2021.
37. Brian Chesky, "A Message from Co-Founder and CEO Brian Chesky," Airbnb Website, May 5, 2020, https://news.airbnb.com/a-message-from-co-founder-and-ceo-brian-chesky, March 22, 2021.
38. Brian Chesky.
39. Susie S. Cox, "Giving Feedback: Development of Scales for the Mum Effect, Discomfort Giving Feedback, and Feedback Medium Preference," *Performance Improvement Quarterly* 23 (2011): 49–69.
40. Jack Zenger and Joseph Folkman, "Your Employees Want the Negative Feedback You Hate to Give," *Harvard Business Review Blog*, January 15, 2014, http://blogs.hbr.org/2014/01/your-employees-want-the-negative-feedback-you-hate-to-give/, accessed March 21, 2021.
41. Peter Bregman, "How to Start a Conversation You're Dreading," *Harvard Business Review Blog Network*, July 7, 2014, http://blogs.hbr.org/2014/07/how-to-start-a-conversation-youre-dreading, accessed August 17, 2021.
42. Whole Foods Company Announcement, "Allergy Alert Issued for Undeclared Tree Nuts in Mislabeled Cranberry Biscotti at Six Whole Foods Market Stores," U.S. Food & Drug Administration, March 11, 2021, www.fda.gov/safety/recalls-market-withdrawals-safety-alerts/allergy-alert-issued-undeclared-tree-nuts-mislabeled-cranberry-biscotti-six-whole-foods-market#recall-announcement, accessed March 23, 2021.
43. Adapted and used with permission from David Lennox, Cornell University.

Part 4 Preparing Data and Writing Reports

CHAPTER 9

Managing and Visualizing Data

Learning Objectives

After you have finished this chapter, you should be able to

LO1 Identify types of data.

LO2 Explain criteria for evaluating information.

LO3 Write an effective survey question for a given research question.

LO4 Choose a data visualization for a given business situation.

LO5 Describe three ways to avoid presenting misleading information.

"I can't remember the last time a deck on earnings made me laugh out loud on the subway."[1]

—Polina Marinova, *Fortune* magazine writer

Chapter Introduction

SoftBank Invents Data for Charts

WeWork, which provides shared office space to startups, grew and fell spectacularly. With his charismatic sales presence, Founder and CEO Adam Neumann described WeWork as a technology company—a more attractive investment than a real estate company. One analyst found 110 mentions of "technology" in its prospectus but no data to support the claim.[2] Still, Neumann garnered significant investment in the faltering company, including billions of dollars from Softbank.

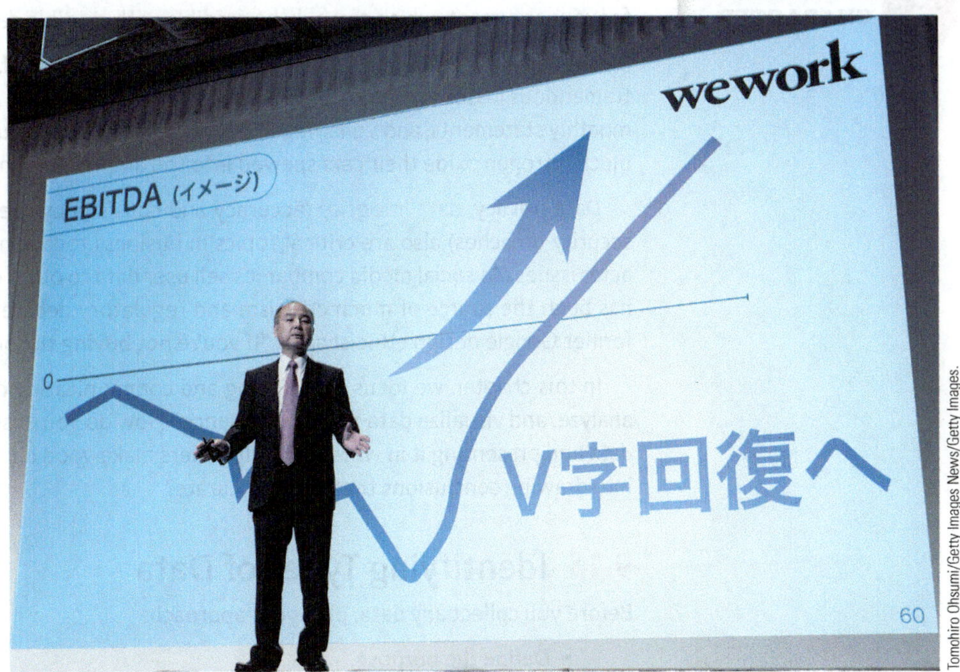

Softbank CEO presents an optimistic view of WeWork.

Tomohiro Ohsumi/Getty Images News/Getty Images.

Softbank also was overly enthusiastic about WeWork. At a press conference in Tokyo, CEO Masayoshi Son explained a staggering $8.2 billion loss with imaginative charts. On one slide, shown here, a curved line shows "hypothetical" earnings—with no data. Another slide showed three boxes: profits with an arrow going up, operating expenses with an arrow going down, and earnings with an arrow going up—with no data.[3] Long notes at the bottom of the slides admit that the illustrations are based on nothing:

> This hypothetical illustration is provided solely for illustrative purposes, reflects the current beliefs of SBG [Softbank Group] as of the date hereof, and is based on a variety of assumptions and estimates. . . .

Softbank's charts became an internet joke and only hurt WeWork's already damaged reputation.

LO1 Identify types of data.

9-1 Identifying Types and Sources of Data

Company leaders need data—facts and statistics—to make good business decisions. A venture capitalist analyzes market data to decide whether to invest in a company. A product development manager uses customer survey data to determine why some products are selling better than others. A human resources manager surveys staff to pinpoint causes of low morale. Based on the information—the meaning of the data in context—the venture capitalist may pass on the investment, the product manager may reduce a price, and the HR manager may offer employees more job flexibility.

The data you choose and how you present it reveal your character. Data lays the foundation for your argument, which can only be credible with credible data and credible communication.

In addition to egregious failings in how data is presented, data falsifications have caused tremendous losses in reputation, wealth, and goodwill. Bernie Madoff sent investors fabricated monthly statements, and Volkswagen developed software to dupe emissions tests, masking how much nitrogen oxide their cars spewed into the air—4,000% more than the legal U.S. limit.[4]

Data privacy, data integrity (accuracy and consistency over time), and data theft (through security breaches) also are critical topics in business today and illustrations of potential character issues. As social media companies sell user data to other companies, their business model has been the source of much criticism and regulatory debate. In the movie *Social Dilemma*, a former Google design ethicist says, "If you're not buying the product, you are the product."[5,6]

In this chapter, we focus on sourcing and communicating data. How do you find, evaluate, analyze, and visualize data for your audience? How do you ensure that you are getting the best data and presenting it in ways that help others make good decisions, rather than mislead them into drawing conclusions that aren't accurate?

9-1a Identifying Types of Data

Before you collect any data, plan your approach:

- Define the purpose.
- Analyze the intended audience.
- Determine what data is needed to solve the problem or make a decision.

Your data will come from several sources. You may include data that you already have (either in your mind or from previous work), you may need to find data from other sources, or you may have to generate new data.

Start the data-collection phase by factoring your problem—breaking it down to determine what data you need to collect. Before Chipotle created a children's menu with healthy options, a product development manager likely searched for answers to the following questions:

- What are the industry trends? How prevalent is the move toward healthier menus for kids?
- How might Chipotle customers respond to the change? Will they choose healthier meals? If so, what kinds of meals would they prefer?
- What is the nutritional content of our current menu options for kids?
- How much would healthier food cost?

Although the word *data* is technically the plural form of *datum*, this book uses the term as a collective noun and with a singular verb. This approach is more common and sounds more natural and conversational.[7]

The manager may want both quantitative and qualitative data. Quantitative data is numerical, for example, the percentage of competitors who have menus for kids or the grams of proteins in a menu item. Qualitative data is descriptive and can't be measured, for example, interview responses of kids talking about food or parents explaining what is important to them when dining out with their kids. A comprehensive, yet manageable approach to research will keep you focused on your goal: to provide enough information so that you can feel confident in your decision.

To answer the research questions, the Chipotle manager will need secondary and primary data. **Secondary data** is collected by someone else for some other purpose; it may be published or unpublished (Figure 1). **Primary data** is collected by you, as a researcher, to solve a specific problem. Because you are collecting the data yourself, you have more control over its accuracy, completeness, objectivity, and relevance. The three main methods of primary data collection are surveys, observation, and experimentation.

Examples of Secondary Data | **Figure 1**

Published (Public and Readily Available)	Unpublished (Private and Available Only to Insiders)
Journal, magazine, and newspaper articles	Some company reports and documentation (e.g., employee performance reviews)
Company, organization, and government websites	Company records (e.g., sales data)
Some public company reports (e.g., annual report)	Company communications (e.g., email)
Blogs and social media posts	Personal files (e.g., expense reports)
Books	Medical records
Government and court records	
Technical documentation	

Although secondary and primary data are both important sources for business reports, we usually start our data collection by reviewing data that is already available—it costs less and saves time. Not all situations require collecting new (primary) data, but most do require some type of secondary data.

Let's look back to our example of a restaurant offering healthier menu items for children. As the owner, you would certainly rely on secondary sources to learn about industry trends. Why commission your own research when the National Restaurant Association and industry publications probably have published studies and articles about the topic? Also, studying secondary data can provide sources for additional published information and provide guidance for possible primary research.

For these reasons, our discussion of data collection first focuses on secondary sources. Secondary data is neither better than nor worse than primary data; it is simply *different*. One of the challenges is finding secondary data appropriate for your purpose.

9-1b Searching for Relevant Sources

You may be tempted to start all searches by googling keywords, but you have better options available. Particularly as a student, you can access subscription-based information through your school's library. Databases such as ABI/Inform, Business Source Complete, Factiva, and Mergent are good choices for business-related newspapers, magazines, and journals for your research. Figure 2 compares search results for Google, Google Scholar, and Business Source Complete.

Accessing Google may be easier than a library database, but you never know what you'll get. Library databases include information already evaluated by scholars and publishers. In the long run, a database will save you time and give you the best results for your report.

Wikipedia can be a good starting point for research but not as a citation. Although librarians may advise against using Wikipedia, several studies demonstrate its reliability.[8] However, relying *only* on Wikipedia is sloppy for two reasons. First, anyone can post to this free, collaborative

Figure 2 | Comparing Search Results

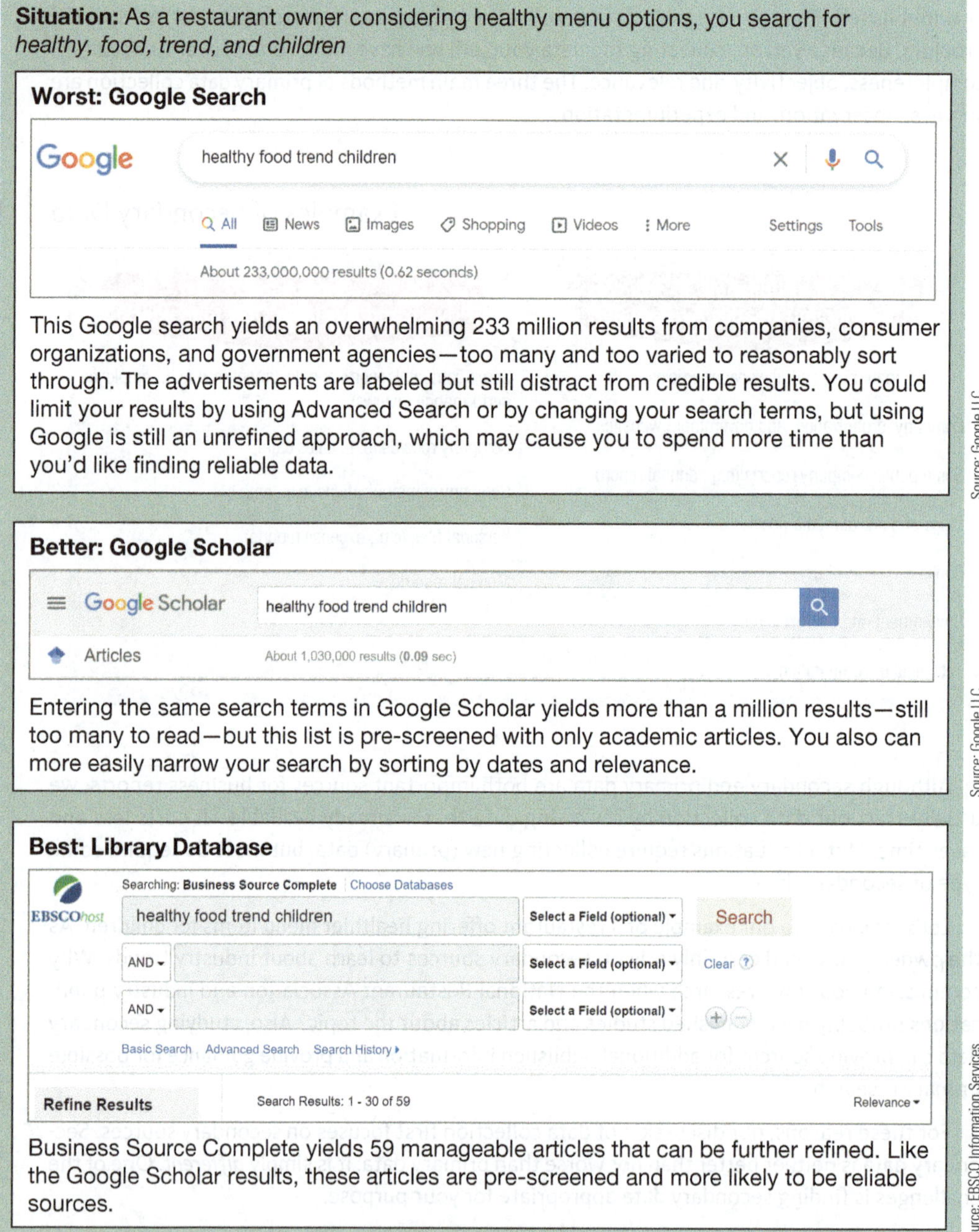

encyclopedia, so you should check all sources in the footnotes yourself. Second, you'll want a variety of sources; citing Wikipedia directly for anything other than definitions may tell your reader you didn't do your homework. Instead, follow links and footnotes to read and cite those sources instead.

Situation: As a restaurant owner considering healthy menu options, you search for *healthy, food, trend, and children*
Worst: Google Search
Google
healthy food trend children
All News Images Shopping Videos More Settings Tools
About 233,000,000 results (0.62 seconds)
This Google search yields an overwhelming 233 million results from companies, consumer organizations, and government agencies—too many and too varied to reasonably sort through. The advertisements are labeled but still distract from credible results. You could limit your results by using Advanced Search or by changing your search terms, but using Google is still an unrefined approach, which may cause you to spend more time than you'd like finding reliable data.
Source: Google LLC
Better: Google Scholar
Google Scholar
healthy food trend children
Articles
About 1,030,000 results (0.09 sec)
Entering the same search terms in Google Scholar yields more than a million results—still too many to read—but this list is pre-screened with only academic articles. You also can more easily narrow your search by sorting by dates and relevance.
Source: Google LLC
Best: Library Database
EBSCOhost
Searching: Business Source Complete Choose Databases
healthy food trend children
Select a Field (optional)
Search
AND
Select a Field (optional)
Clear
AND
Select a Field (optional)
Basic Search Advanced Search Search History
Refine Results
Search Results: 1 - 30 of 59
Relevance
Business Source Complete yields 59 manageable articles that can be further refined. Like the Google Scholar results, these articles are pre-screened and more likely to be reliable sources.
Source: EBSCO Information Services

9-1c Avoiding Bias

Algorithms determine what we see on the web, which could lead to bias.[9] Our social media feeds send us posts that we are prone to "like"—favor and share. Some platforms allow users to control their feed by changing views to the latest or most recent posts. But we still tend to follow people and organizations that align with our interests and beliefs. This skewed content further skews our thinking.

Our limited view makes it more difficult for us to challenge our own biases. One author analyzed 175 cognitive biases and grouped them into four major problems, shown in Figure 3.[10]

Cognitive Bias Problems and Examples | **Figure 3**

1 Too Much Information

Because of information overload, we filter what we read, and we pay more attention to what is funny or bizarre. A common trap is **confirmation bias:** focusing on information that reinforces our existing beliefs.

2 Not Enough Meaning

When information is too confusing, we make sense by drawing conclusions that might not be valid, placing higher value on the familiar, oversimplifying complex information, and assuming we know what others think.

3 Need to Act Fast

Our sense of competition compels us to make quick decisions, which leads us to feel overconfident and self-important, favor immediacy over delayed action, and continue investing in something we started.

4 Limited Memory

We can't remember everything, so we omit or insert details, draw generalizations based on associations and stereotypes, and choose too few examples as representations of larger events and lists.

We have no easy way to ward against all these cognitive biases. Being aware of them may encourage us to resist temptations despite limits on our time and resources. Research indicates that people who have higher IQs are *more* likely to succumb to stereotypes, and people who are better at managing quantitative information are *worse* at evaluating evidence that conflicts with their views.[11] Their quick minds could lead to hasty conclusions. If this describes you, you might have to fight particularly hard to ensure that you're using a variety of sources for data and, as we discuss next, properly evaluating the information you find.

To which of the issues described in Figure 3 do you most relate?

9-2 Evaluating Sources of Information

LO2 Explain criteria for evaluating information.

False information is a serious issue. Misinformation is rampant on the web, and people fall easily for fake news stories with unsupported claims and manipulated video. In a study of middle school, high school, and college students, Stanford University researchers describe students' ability to evaluate information on the web as "bleak."[12]

Once you find information that seems relevant to your research questions, you'll need to evaluate the quality of the sources. With higher quality sources, you'll write more credible reports and make better business decisions.

Whether you're reading an article on a blog or a research study, look at the source critically—and be careful about what you repost or forward to others. Your character is at stake when you promote stories or information that isn't true.

Do you tend to believe what you read on the internet? How can you be more careful about accepting information that isn't substantiated?

9-2a Evaluating Internet Resources

We know that anyone can post anything on the internet. Fake websites, "native advertising" (e.g., embedded articles that are hard to distinguish from the rest of the site), sponsored ads, "deepfake" videos,[13] product endorsements, and conspiracy theories all make it difficult to know what is factual (verifiable) and what is an opinion or promotional.

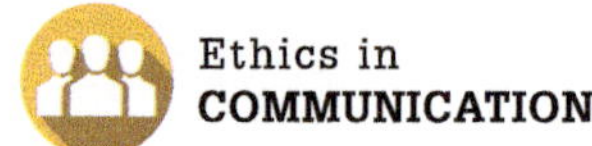

One of the most spectacular conspiracy theories of our time is "PizzaGate." When Hilary Clinton was running for U.S. president, a story of her operating a human-trafficking ring out of a pizza shop in Washington, D.C., went viral. Many credible organizations debunked the news, and Alex Jones, a popular radio host, apologized for his role in spreading the bogus story.[14] Still, the theory resurfaced years later on TikTok.[15]

When you find content on the internet, ask the questions in Figure 4 to evaluate the source. The advice, adapted from an international association of librarians, is useful for identifying fake news and other misinformation.[16]

Figure 4 | Evaluating Web Sources

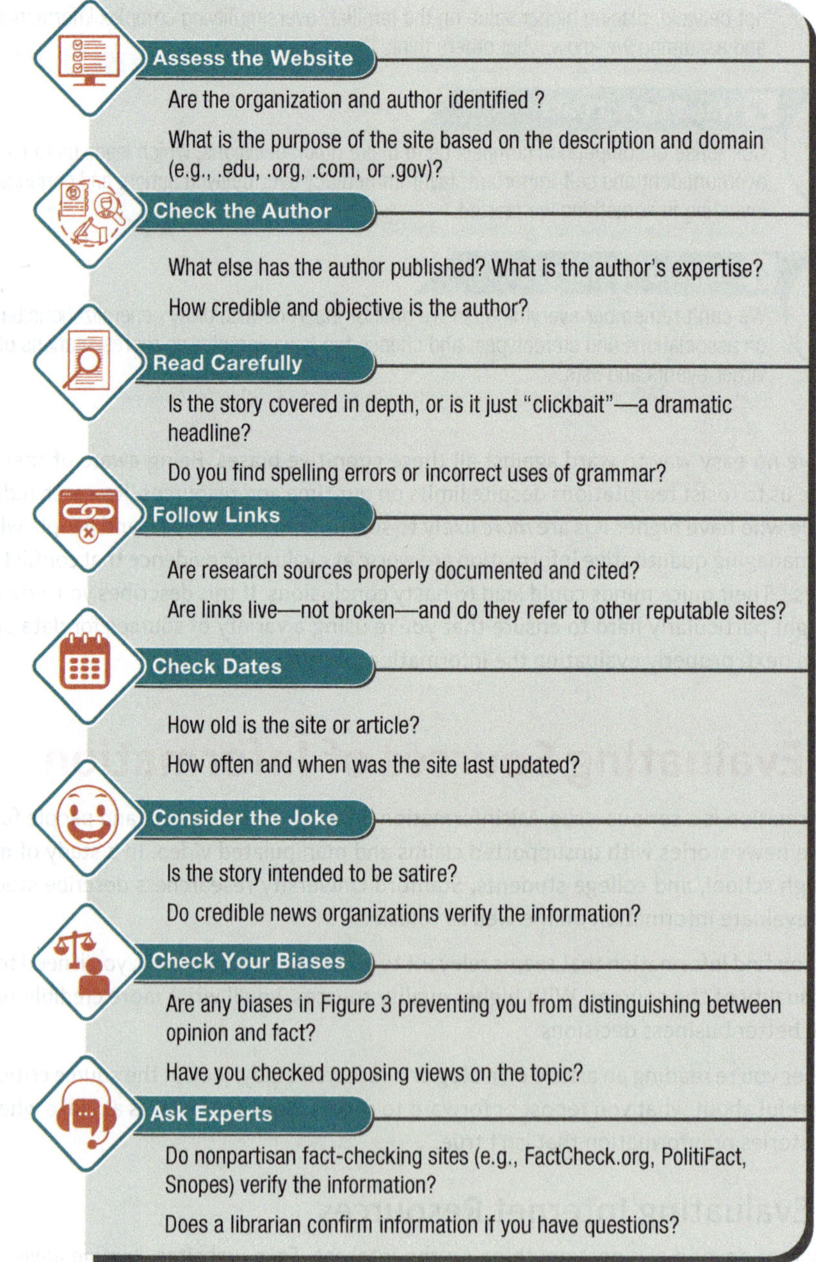

Assess the Website
Are the organization and author identified ?
What is the purpose of the site based on the description and domain (e.g., .edu, .org, .com, or .gov)?
Check the Author
What else has the author published? What is the author's expertise?
How credible and objective is the author?
Read Carefully
Is the story covered in depth, or is it just "clickbait"—a dramatic headline?
Do you find spelling errors or incorrect uses of grammar?
Follow Links
Are research sources properly documented and cited?
Are links live—not broken—and do they refer to other reputable sites?
Check Dates
How old is the site or article?
How often and when was the site last updated?
Consider the Joke
Is the story intended to be satire?
Do credible news organizations verify the information?
Check Your Biases
Are any biases in Figure 3 preventing you from distinguishing between opinion and fact?
Have you checked opposing views on the topic?
Ask Experts
Do nonpartisan fact-checking sites (e.g., FactCheck.org, PolitiFact, Snopes) verify the information?
Does a librarian confirm information if you have questions?

9-2b Evaluating Research Studies

Research studies in academic journals offer more credible sources of information that could be more appropriate for your purpose. Ask yourself the questions in Figure 5 about research you consider incorporating into your report. Data that fails even one of these five tests should probably not be used as a credible source.

Evaluating Research Studies | **Figure 5**

What was the purpose of the study?

People who have a vested interest in the outcome of a study may take shortcuts to get the answer they want. But people who approach research with a genuine interest in answering a question are more likely to select their samples carefully, ask clear and unbiased questions, and analyze data objectively.

Example: Which study about children's food preferences is more trustworthy—one conducted by the U.S. National Institute of Health or one conducted by Sabrett Hot Dogs?

How was the data collected?

Were appropriate procedures used? Even if you're not an experienced researcher, you can make sure data was collected properly and from a large enough representative sample.

Example: If you want to learn your customers' reactions to healthier menu items, you wouldn't ask only two guests who visited the restaurant on Saturday. You would ask a large percentage of your customers and include individuals and families, early and late diners, and so on.

How was the data analyzed?

As we'll see later in this chapter, how we analyze data depends on the type of data we collect. In some situations, even though the analysis is appropriate for the original study, it may not be appropriate for your particular purpose.

Example: Let's say you find a study about eating preferences by age. If the researchers used the broad category "younger than 21," the study won't help you understand how your target group (children 6–9 years old) responded.

How consistent is the data with that from other studies?

When you find the same general conclusions in several independent sources, you can have greater confidence in the data.

Example: If four studies conclude that children don't like fish unless it is fried, and a fifth study reached an opposite conclusion, you might be skeptical of the fifth study.

How old is the data?

Data that was true at the time it was collected may not be true today.

Example: A 1980 study of children's food preferences may not be relevant to your decision today, when more food choices are available, people are dining out more frequently, and people are more health conscious.

Even the most respected academic journals make mistakes. Published, peer-reviewed studies have been retracted for all kinds of reporting errors—some purposeful, some sloppy, and some unintentional. A 1998 study claimed that the measles, mumps, and rubella vaccine caused autism. Despite many studies since that time showing no link, some people still believe the misinformation and refuse vaccines for their children. This distrust has resulted in measles outbreaks.[17]

LO3 Write an effective survey question for a given research question.

9-3 Collecting Data Through Surveys

If your research fails to find enough high-quality secondary data to help you make a decision, you will probably need to collect primary data. For example, in addition to publicly available data, the Chipotle product manager might want information about the company's own customers. In this type of situation, people design and distribute their own surveys with questions they write themselves.

9-3a Using Surveys for Data Collection

A **survey** is a data-collection method that gathers information through online or telephone questionnaires or interviews. Technically, a **questionnaire** is a written instrument with questions to obtain information from recipients. These terms are often used interchangeably, and we'll use *survey* here to mean an online questionnaire, which is the most common method for business research.

Online surveys offer advantages over interviews and other data-collection methods. First, they preserve the anonymity of respondents, which increases the validity of your results because they may give more complete and honest information. Second, no interviewer is present to potentially bias the results. Finally, respondents can answer at a time convenient for them, which is not always the case with telephone or interview studies. Online tools also make it easy to create surveys. Qualtrics, SurveyMonkey, and other programs provide templates for you to generate a form, distribute the questionnaire, and analyze results.

The big disadvantage of surveys is the low response rate, and those who do respond may not be representative (typical) of the population. Social media platforms and sites, such as Mechanical Turk, connect participants with researchers. With a short message about the purpose of your research and how much time is required to complete a questionnaire, you can find respondents for little pay. If you're gathering information from your own customers, you can email the questionnaire or provide a website for customers to visit. You might offer a free item or 10% off in return. Customers who complete a Chipotle satisfaction survey, shown in Figure 6, get a chance to win free burritos for a year.[18,19]

Surveys are best used when you have short, simple questions. With an online survey, you can't adapt questions to different groups easily, but you can and should make your survey accessible, as you see in the Chipotle example.

9-3b Choosing Types of Survey Questions

With a survey tool like SurveyMonkey, you have many options for types of questions. Consider two broad categories: open and closed. An **open-ended question** allows respondents to write their own answers, while a **closed-ended question** includes a list of predefined answers.

Plan to have a balance of both. Closed-ended questions allow you to quantify and categorize results and are easier for your respondents to answer. Open-ended questions require more time and expertise for your respondent but provide richer, more in-depth responses. When you're gathering information from a small number of people and want qualitative responses, choose more open-ended questions. If you wanted to understand why turnover is high in your company, you would certainly want exiting employees to explain their reasons for leaving, which could be complicated.

Common types of closed-ended questions and examples are shown in Figure 7. These are considered multiple-choice questions, the most common type of question on SurveyMonkey's platform.[20] For the following examples, we'll imagine a start-up seeking feedback about its app, Maror.

Chipotle Customer Satisfaction Survey: Multiple-Choice Questions | Figure 6

VOICE OF THE GUEST

We'd love to hear your thoughts, feelings, and impressions from your experience at Chipotle. So much so, that we'll give you a chance to win burritos for a year just for participating.

Turn Off Accessibility Friendly Version

To complete this survey, you must be 13 years of age or older (sorry kids).

Please select the type of survey invite you received:

- ◯ Receipt with a survey code
- ◯ Label on my digital order
- ◯ Email with a survey link
- ◯ I do not have a survey invite

Next

Español

© 2021 SMG. All rights reserved.

ADA Accessibility SMG Terms of Service SMG Privacy Policy USA Sweepstakes Rules Canada Sweepstakes Rules Privacy Policy

Source: Chipotle.com

Additional Types of Closed-Ended Questions | Figure 7

Question Type	Example
Rating scale ***Respondents choose a number within a range.*** Can be used to determine "Net Promoter Score" to determine the health of a business and how likely customers are to recommend the business.	How likely are you to recommend Maror to a friend or family member? 1 ... 10 Not at all likely ... Extremely likely
Likert Scale (a type of rating scale) ***Respondents choose within a range of five to seven options.*** Used to gauge attitudes, beliefs, and opinions.	To what extent do you agree with the following statement? The Maror app is easy to use. ☐ Strongly agree ☐ Agree ☐ Neither agree nor disagree ☐ Disagree ☐ Strongly disagree
Ranking Questions ***Respondents order items according to preference or importance.*** Used to force prioritization to show relativity.	Please rank the following new features in order of importance to you, where 1 is most important and 5 is least important. Customizable account page Bar chart visualizations of account balances Two-factor authentication News feed on the home page Chat with other users

You have more choices than ranking and rating questions. For example, image-choice questions provide respondents with pictures, which can be used to compare preferences for logos, product labels, or web designs. Click-map questions provide points on an image, which can be used to compare preferences for parts of a package, store, or app.

You also have several options for how people respond. The Chipotle example in Figure 6 uses radio buttons (circles), while the examples in Figure 7 use a slider, checkboxes, and dropdowns. Choose a variety to keep the user engaged.

9-3c Writing Survey Questions

Because the target audience has limited time, make every question count. Each question should be essential to your research and yield information you can't get from public or company sources. Why waste respondents' time with questions you can't act on or answers you can find on your own? Follow the guidelines in Figure 8 for constructing a survey.

Figure 8 | Constructing a Survey

Content

- Ask only for information that is not easily available elsewhere.
- Have a purpose for each question. Make sure that all questions directly help you solve a problem or make a decision. Avoid asking for unimportant or merely "interesting" information.
- Use precise wording so that no question can possibly be misunderstood. Use clear, simple language, and define unfamiliar or confusing terms.
- Use neutrally worded questions and deal with only one topic per question. Avoid loaded, leading, or multifaceted questions.
- Ensure that the response choices are both **exhaustive** (one appropriate response for each question) and **mutually exclusive** (no overlapping categories).
- Be careful about asking sensitive questions, such as information about age, salary, or morals. Consider using broad categories for such questions (instead of narrow, more specific categories).
- Pilot-test your survey on a few people to check that all questions function as intended. Revise as needed.

Organization

- Arrange the questions in some logical order. Group questions that deal with a particular topic. If your survey is long, divide it into sections.
- Arrange the alternatives for each question in some logical order—such as numerical, chronological, or alphabetical.
- Give the survey a descriptive title, provide whatever directions are necessary, and include instructions for returning the survey.

To get valid and reliable data from your target audience, your language must be clear, precise, and understandable. Imagine spending time and money on a survey and then making a decision based on invalid data. At best, you would have to disregard the data; at worst, you might decide, for example, to offer a product that few people buy. The quality of the information you include in your reports and presentations reflects on your character, and the collection process starts with neutral (unbiased) questions.

☒ NOT Do you think our company should open an on-site childcare center as a means of ensuring the welfare of our employees' small children?

❒ Yes

❒ No

This wording of the question favors the "pro" side, which biases the responses. A more neutral question will result in more valid responses.

☑ BUT Which one of the following possible additional benefits would you most prefer?

- ❐ A dental insurance plan
- ❐ An on-site childcare center
- ❐ Three personal-leave days annually
- ❐ Other (Please specify:__________)

Also be certain that each question contains a single idea.

☒ NOT Our company should spend less money on advertising and more money on research and development.

- ❐ Agree
- ❐ Disagree

Suppose respondents believe that the company should spend more (or less) money on advertising *and* on research and development? How would they answer? The solution is to put each of the two ideas in a separate question.

Finally, ensure that your categories are mutually exclusive, with no overlap.

☒ NOT In your opinion, what is the major cause of high employee turnover?

- ❐ Lack of air conditioning
- ❐ Noncompetitive financial package
- ❐ Poor health benefits
- ❐ Poor working conditions
- ❐ Weak management

The problem with this item is that the "lack of air conditioning" category overlaps with the "poor working conditions" category, and "noncompetitive financial package" overlaps with "poor health benefits." Also, all four of these might overlap with "weak management." Intermingling categories will confuse the respondent and yield unreliable survey results.

Respondents may be hesitant to answer sensitive questions, for example, about their age or salary. Even worse, they may deliberately provide *inaccurate* responses. To improve your chances of getting sensitive information, try the following:

- Assure the respondent (in your cover letter or email) that the survey is anonymous.
- Use broad categories (accurate estimates are better than incorrect data).
- Include a list of options rather than a fill-in response.

Emotional
INTELLIGENCE

Do you find some survey questions too sensitive to answer? How has this affected your response to questionnaires?

☒ NOT What is your gross annual salary?

$____________________

☑ BUT Please check the category that best describes your annual salary:

- ❐ Less than $25,000
- ❐ $25,000–50,000
- ❐ $50,001–75,000
- ❐ $75,001–100,000
- ❐ More than $100,000

In the third category, "$50,001" is necessary to avoid overlap with the figure "$50,000" in the second category. Without this distinction, the categories would not be mutually exclusive.

Even experienced researchers find it difficult to spot ambiguities or other problems in their own questionnaires. Before sending the survey to a large population, run a pilot test with a small sample of respondents or, at a minimum, ask a colleague to edit your instrument with a critical eye. Then, you can make revisions before distributing the final version.

9-3d Writing a Survey Email

After you develop your survey, you need to convince respondents to complete it. Programs like SurveyMonkey will create a link that you can copy into an email. Fidelity uses several persuasive strategies, discussed in Chapter 7, in the example shown in Figure 9.

Figure 9 | Email to Introduce a Survey

Secure Login

Your Opinion Makes a Difference.

You were recently invited to join ***My Fidelity Connection***, an exclusive online Customer Forum, to gather YOUR feedback on the services, materials and tools Fidelity currently provides to you through your employer. If you have already joined, thank you! If you haven't, we'd still like to include your voice.

Customer feedback helps us design, prioritize and deliver the most effective workplace benefits and experiences; as a Forum member, you will be invited to share your personal needs and experiences with your Retirement plan (e.g., 401(k), 403(b), 457) and, in some cases, your other workplace benefits (e.g., healthcare choices, student debt support, financial wellness programs).

You'll also have the opportunity to weigh in on new ideas Fidelity is considering.

To join the Forum, please click **here** to begin.

If you decide to join, we will ask you a few questions about yourself. This process will take 5-10 minutes to complete. As a member of this Forum, you will be invited to give feedback through online interviews, activities, and short surveys, no more than twice a month. There is no required length of membership, and you can cancel at any time.

Fidelity is working with Ipsos®, an independent market research firm, to conduct surveys and administer the Forum. Please be assured that your information will not be used for individual marketing purposes.

We look forward to your invaluable insights!

Margin annotations:

- Uses "you" and "my" throughout; presents the opportunity as "exclusive" (scarcity principle).
- Explains the purpose of the survey and how results will be used to benefit the reader (starts with "why").
- Indicates how much time it will take and encourages a longer-term commitment (commitment and consistency principle).
- Addresses a potential security concern to demonstrate transparency and integrity (credibility).
- Refers to the reader's "valuable insights" (emotional appeal).

Source: FMR LLC (Fidelity Management and Research Company)

9-4 Visualizing Data

LO4 Choose a data visualization for a given business situation.

At some point, you'll have enough data from your secondary and primary sources to help you make a decision. (Of course, when analyzing the data, writing a report, or preparing a presentation, you may realize that you need to collect more information.)

Next, your job is to convert your raw data (from journal articles, completed surveys, company reports, and so on) into information. This information—meaningful facts, statistics, and conclusions—will help your audience make a decision. In addition to interpreting your findings in narrative form, you will likely prepare visuals—tables, charts, or other graphics—to improve comprehension and add interest to your report or presentation.

9-4a Creating Tables

A table is an orderly arrangement of data into columns and rows. As the most basic form of statistical analysis, a table is useful for showing a large amount of numerical data in a small space and in a more efficient and interesting way than with narrative text. Figure 10 shows results from the Maror survey in a table that might appear in a report.

Simple Data Table | **Figure 10**

Table 4. Responses to the Question, "To what extent do you agree with the following statements?"	Strongly Agree		Agree		Neither Agree nor Disagree		Disagree		Strongly Disagree	
	N	%	N	%	N	%	N	%	N	%
Q1. The Maror app is easy to use.	2	**3.5**	5	**8.8**	11	**19.3**	23	**38.6**	17	**29.8**
Q2. The Maror app is worth the subscription fee.	23	**40.4**	12	**21.1**	12	**21.1**	5	**8.8**	5	**8.8**

A table provides more information than a chart does, although with less visual impact. In one study, respondents chose more accurate answers about data displayed in tables than data in charts.[21] However, trends are more obvious when presented in graphs. To increase visual impact and improve readability in tables, choose alternating colors for rows and use font enhancements, for example, bold for data you want to highlight, as you see in Figure 10.

Your reader must be able to understand each table on its own, without having to read the surrounding text. At a minimum, each table should contain a table number, a descriptive but concise title, column headings, and the body (the items under each column heading). If you need footnotes to explain individual items within the table, put them immediately below the body of the table, not at the bottom of the page. Similarly, if the table is based on secondary data, add a source note below the body giving the appropriate citation.

Depending on the situation, you might include additional columns, described as follows:[22]

- ***Minimum:*** *the lowest value collected*
- ***Maximum:*** *the highest value collected*
- ***Mean:*** *the average of all values collected*
- ***Median:*** *the midpoint of your dataset (the middle of all values collected when they are organized from smallest to largest)*
- ***Standard Deviation:*** *the amount of variation or dispersion of values collected*
- ***Variance:*** *the spread between numbers in your dataset*
- ***Responses:*** *the total number of responses collected that contribute to the dataset*

Each percentage is rounded to its nearest whole. These practices are important to illustrate attention to detail:

- Any number with a decimal less than 0.50 gets rounded *down* to the next nearest whole number; any number with a decimal greater than 0.50 gets rounded *up*.
- To avoid bias, odd numbers with a decimal of exactly 0.50 get rounded *up*; even numbers with a decimal of exactly .50 get rounded *down*.
- If your table shows the total percentages and your rounding efforts result in totals that do not equal 100% (such as 99% or 101%), you have the option of either (1) showing the actual resulting totals or (2) readjusting one of the rounded numbers (the one that will cause the least distortion to the number) to "force" a 100% total.

9-4b Designing Simple, Clear Charts

Well-designed charts and graphs can improve reader comprehension, emphasize certain data, create interest, and save time and space. Charts help readers understand main points from large amounts of statistical data.

Because of their visual impact, charts receive more emphasis than tables or narrative text. Use charts when the overall picture is more important than the individual numbers. Also, charts are ideal when using visual support for an oral presentation; tables with a lot of data are difficult to read during online meetings and when shown on a screen. However, avoid using too many charts. In a written report, because charts have strong visual appeal, the more charts you include, the less impact each chart will have.

When creating a chart for a report or to support an oral presentation, first determine the main point you wish to convey. For a persuasive report, use your audience analysis skills to design a chart that emphasizes the most important information.

Cramming too much information into one chart will confuse the reader and lessen the impact of the graphic. Avoid chartjunk—visual elements that call attention to themselves instead of the information on a chart. Compare the charts in Figure 11. The revision is much easier to read with better color contrast, reduced percentage decimals, fewer lines and data points, consistent fonts, and no shadows. Months and vertical lines are added to clarify data points, so labels can be used only for major inflection points.

Figure 11 | Removing Chartjunk

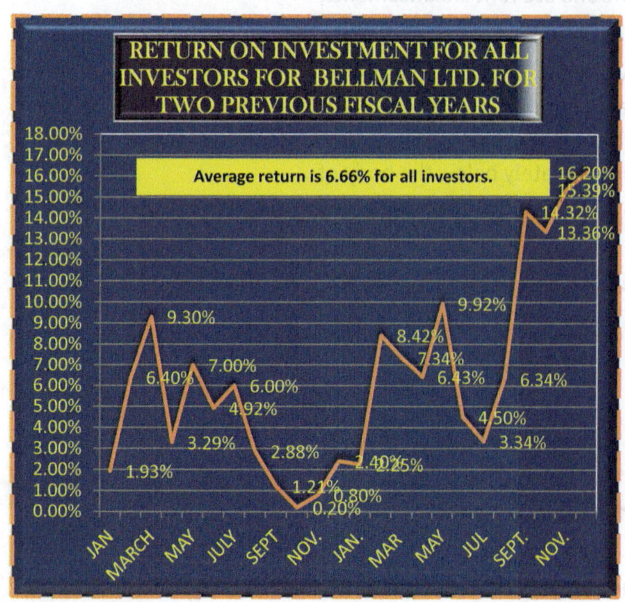

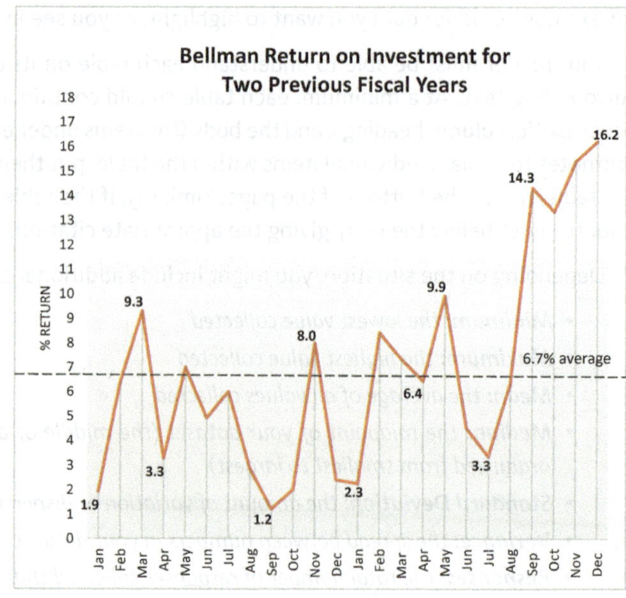

9-4c Choosing an Appropriate Chart Type

Choose a chart type or other graphic to meet your communication objectives. Bar and line charts are most common,[23] with many creative variations and additional options available. Let's explore charts that an investment company might provide to its customers.

Comparisons

Data without context has little meaning. If you discovered that a stock gained 9%, would you be impressed? It's a good percentage, but what if that was over a 9-year period? Or what if a competitor's stock gained 14%?

Several chart types show comparisons. *Bar charts* are most typical to show how items compare in size, either at a point in time or over time. In Excel, you'll see horizontal rectangles in a bar chart and vertical rectangles in a column chart, but both are commonly referred to as bar charts.

In the bar chart shown in Figure 12, Vanguard investment management firm compares market and individual returns over a ten-year period. The purpose is to discourage investors from trying to "time" the market—adjusting their portfolio by buying and selling instead of holding stocks for longer periods of time.[24] As in this example, bars may be grouped and arranged in some logical order with values labeled for quicker comprehension.

Bar Charts Show Comparison | **Figure 12**

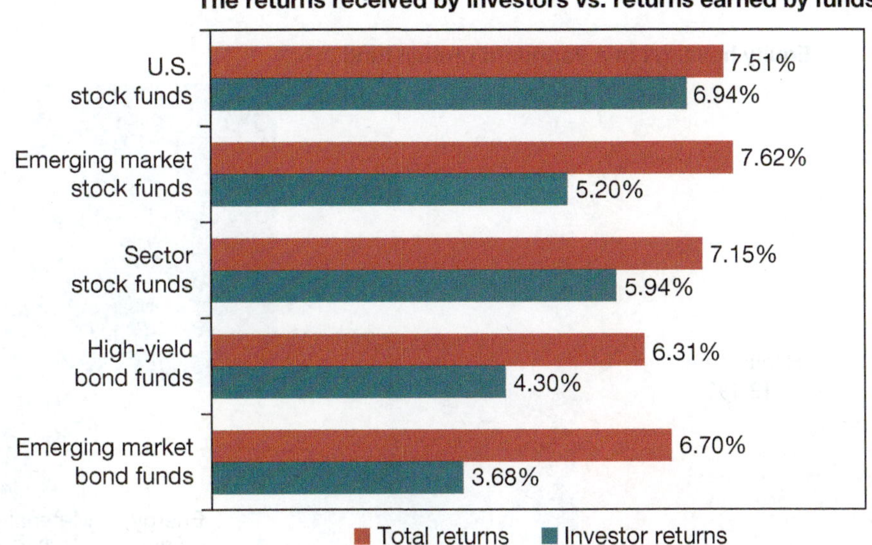

Consider your audience and the complexity of a chart to decide whether to include axis labels. More traditional charts will have X (horizontal) and Y (vertical) labeled axes, as you saw in Figure 11. But more modern-looking charts omit one axis and place values within the chart, as you see in Figure 12. In its most recent annual report, JPMorgan Chase has multiple charts, and not one includes vertical axis labels.[25]

Parts of a Whole

Charts are useful for showing composition—how parts relate to a whole. *Pie charts* are most typical, but *donuts* and *treemaps* (also called *Marimekkos* or, simply, *mekkos*), shown in Figure 13,[26] look more modern. Note that these charts, like the stacked bar from Vanguard in Figure 13,[27] also show comparisons.

Keep these charts simple and easy to read. For pie and donut charts, limit the number of components and begin "slicing" the pie at the 12 o'clock position, moving clockwise in some logical

Figure 13 | Donut, Treemap, and Stacked Bar Show Parts of a Whole

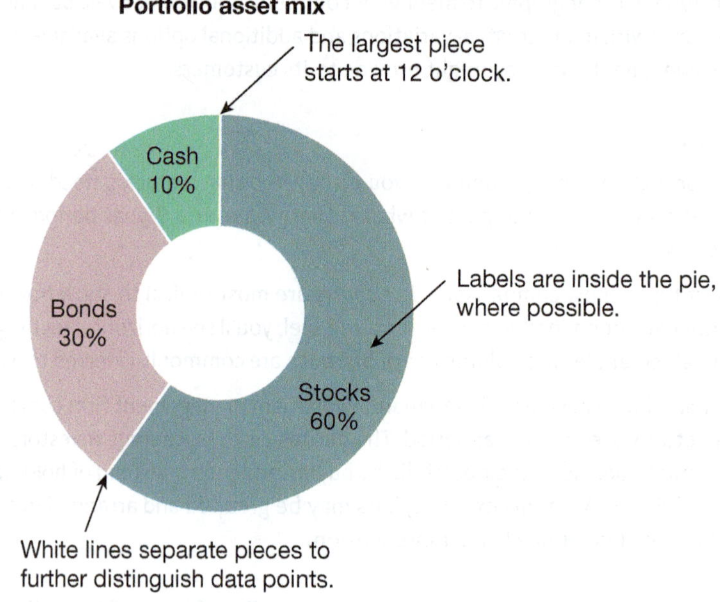

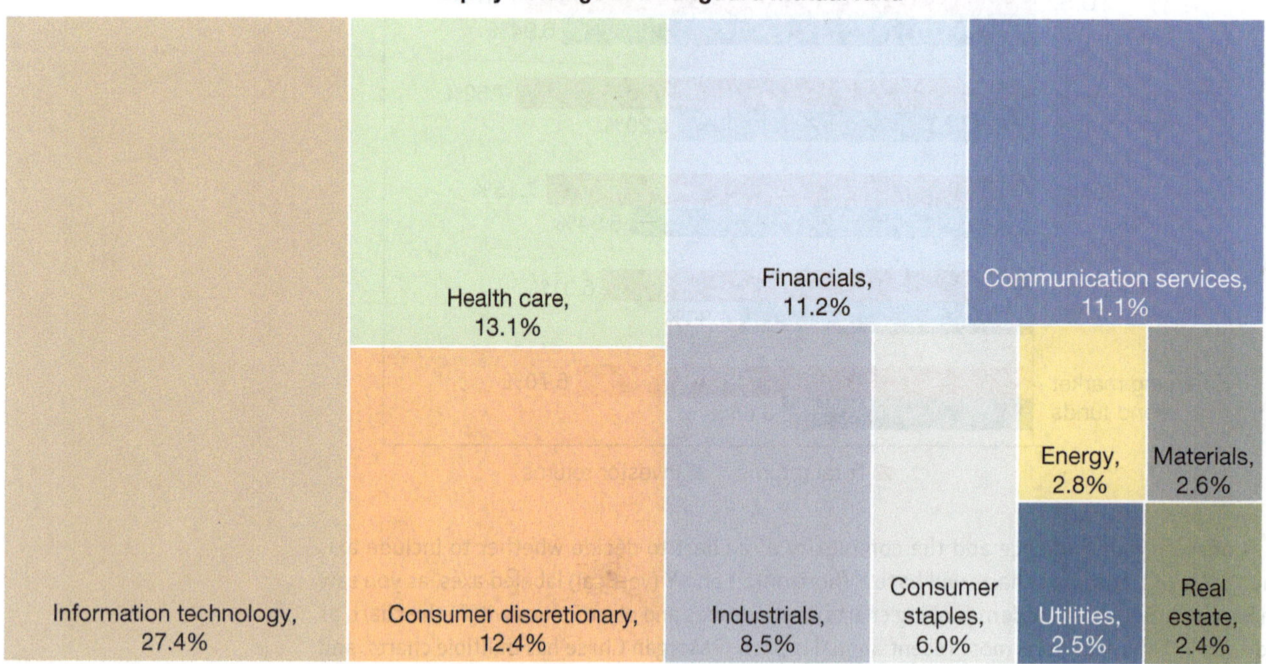

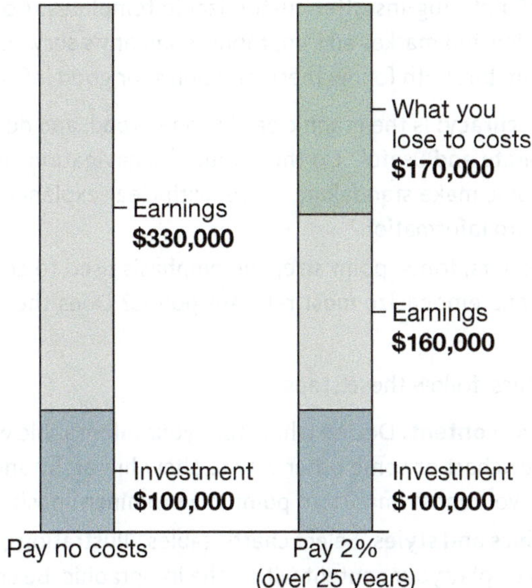

order (often in order of descending size). Place labels either inside each wedge or directly opposite the wedge outside the pie. Avoid a separate legend, which would appear as a box, typically below or beside the chart; labels within the chart are easier to understand. To distinguish each wedge, use shading, cross-hatched lines, different colors, or some other visual device.

Changes Over Time

Although bar charts can show changes over time, *line charts* are the most common and easiest to read for trends. The Bellmore example in Figure 11 illustrates a typical line chart: the vertical dimension represents values, and the horizontal dimension represents time. If you choose to label axes, mark them clearly and place them at equal intervals.

Stories and Compilations

You'll find more chart types in programs like Excel and Tableau. Bubble, waterfall, scatter, funnel, radar, and other graphics may fit your purpose well and add more visual appeal to a report or presentation.

For complex data and multiple main points, you might choose a combination of graphics. But be careful about overwhelming your audience. Instead, programs like Tableau provide tools for you to turn your data into a story. An interactive series of sheets—called *story points*—allows readers to sift through a large amount of data that supports your main points.[28]

9-4d Creating Infographics

Infographics are another option for presenting complex data. These graphics pack a lot of information into a small space and help an audience understand your story. More comprehensive and graphical than a table or chart alone, infographics show information simply and clearly.

Useful infographics may go viral. With relevant information, a catchy design, search engine optimization, and social marketing, your infographic may be viewed by many. You'll also find plenty of bad infographics that favor kitschy graphics over actionable information.

You don't have to be an expert designer to create an infographic. Programs like Canva, Infogram, and PowerPoint plug-ins offer customizable templates. Compare the examples in Figure 14, which describe and market an infographic company's services. Which do you prefer? They are quite different, but both follow these principles for good infographic design:[29]

- **Clarity and accuracy:** Is the graphic easily understood, and does it tell a clear story? Is the data accurate and useful? Do the layout and navigation support the main points? Does the graphic make standalone sense, with clear explanatory text where required to turn data into information?
- **Design:** Are colors, fonts, point size, and emphasis used to create hierarchy, organize information, and emphasize most relevant points? Does the design complement the message?

To create infographics, follow these steps:

- **Storyboard the content.** Decide what story your infographic will tell. You may choose to create a flowchart or some other way to show hierarchy and relationships of information. Place your most important point in a prominent position.
- **Choose graphics and styles.** Select charts, tables, illustrations, maps, and other graphics to visually display your content within the infographic. Be creative, but find ways to give meaning to your data rather than distract from it. Choose eye-catching visuals and attractive colors—pastels and bright hues—but not too many of them.
- **Explain the data:** Write clear, simple text to help the audience find meaning. Craft a compelling title to summarize your main point.

Figure 14 | Infographics to Market a Company's Services

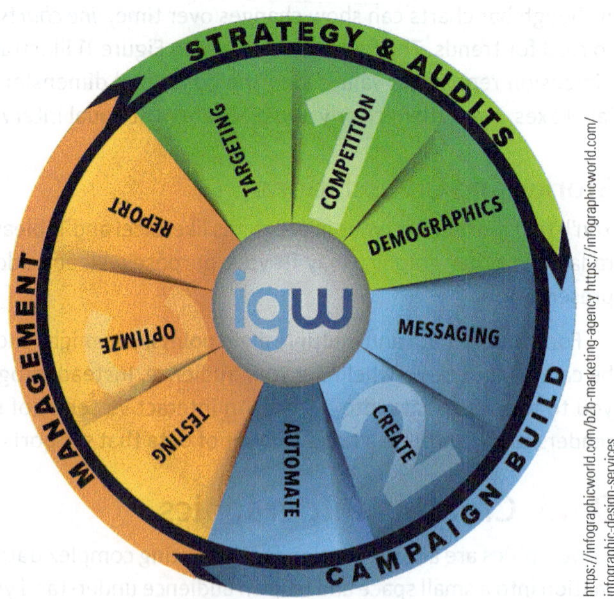

https://infographicworld.com/b2b-marketing-agency https://infographicworld.com/infographic-design-services

LO5 Describe three ways to avoid presenting misleading information.

9-5 Analyzing and Presenting Data

As the name visual *aids* implies, charts act as a *help*—not a substitute—for narrative interpretation and presentation. Data is meaningless without your analysis.

Data analysis takes time and skill. The more familiar you become with the data and the more insight you can provide the reader about the *meaning* of the data, the more helpful your information will be. Data analysts are in high demand today to describe and understand trends, predict the future, and recommend actions.

Your analysis reflects on your character. A credible leader presents information clearly and accurately, without misleading the audience. If you're using data to persuade rather than merely to inform, you'll want to present the best possible picture—but not at the expense of ethics.

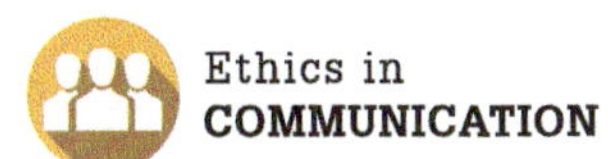

9-5a Making Sense of the Data

From your research, you'll have several sources of data to compare and analyze. Use the process in Figure 15 to interpret your data in three steps: isolation, context, and synthesis. The approach is to zoom in closely, and then zoom out to see the bigger picture and implications.

Three Steps in Interpreting Data | **Figure 15**

Scenario: Imagine that you're trying to determine the exercise habits of college students. Perhaps you're considering opening a fitness center or offering yoga classes.

For this example, let's also assume that you gathered only three pieces of information: a paraphrase from a newspaper article, a chart you developed from a recent study published in a journal article, and primary data from a survey you distributed on campus.

Step 1: Isolation	Look at each piece of data in isolation. If the newspaper article were the only piece of data you collected, what would that mean for your business idea? For example, if the article discussed students throughout the United States, what, if any, conclusions could you draw about your local campus? Follow the same process for the study and your survey, examining each in isolation, without considering any other data.
Step 2: Context	Look at each piece of data in combination with the other bits. For example, the newspaper article may lead you to believe that few students exercise regularly, but 67% of students who responded to your survey reported belonging to a gym. What could this combination of data mean (e.g., perhaps students belong to a gym but rarely go)? If your data sources reinforce each other, you can use stronger, more conclusive language in your analysis. If not, you may want to use less certain language or perhaps not draw any conclusions at all.
Step 3: Synthesis	Synthesize all the information you've collected. When you consider all the facts and their relationships together, what do they mean for your business idea? Do you have enough data to conclude whether the business has a good chance of success? If so, you're ready to begin the detailed analysis and presentation that will help the reader—perhaps a business investor—understand your findings. If not, you must backtrack and start the research process again.

When you present data in a report or presentation, you don't have to discuss *all* the data in the tables and charts; that would be boring and insulting to the reader's intelligence. Instead, discuss the implications of data most relevant to the business question.

Once you've discussed the overall finding, describe other relevant points. Look for trends, unexpected findings, data that reinforces or contradicts other data, extreme values, and data that raises questions. If possible, discuss the *reasons* for these differences. You might include descriptive statistics (e.g., the mean, median, mode, range, and standard deviation) or inference (significance) testing to determine whether the qualities found in your sample data are also likely to exist in the general population.

Present specific numbers—within reason. Depending on the situation, writing or saying "12.5 million" may be accurate enough and less awkward than 12,516,023.11. In most cases when discussing dollar figures, you can omit cents.

For large numbers that are difficult to imagine, consider providing context. Comparing data to concrete objects helps people understand the magnitude. Choose relevant, meaningful comparisons. Also scale long time periods down to minutes or days, and scale large dollar amounts down to a household budget.[30]

☒ NOT 1.3 billion tons of food produced for human consumption is lost or wasted globally each year[31]—that's the weight of 216,666,666 elephants!

☑ BUT With the amount of food wasted each year globally, we could feed every American every day for four years.[32]

After all your data collection and analysis, you'll likely know more about the topic than your audience does. Help the reader by pointing out the important implications, findings, and relationships of your data. With your guidance and well-chosen graphics, the audience will draw the same conclusions you have.

Have you made bad data look good for personal gain? What was the effect?

9-5b Avoiding Misleading Data Presentations

An ethical manager ensures that data presentations don't mislead the audience. Cherry-picking, apple-polishing, and comparing apples to oranges are three common problems in how we select and present data.[33] These tactics make bad data look good and may cause audiences to question our integrity.

Cherry-Picking

Cherry-picking means selecting data that supports your argument, while downplaying or omitting data that opposes it. Of course, instead of including all results, you might choose data when you create a chart, and you might not show all data in a table. But when you intentionally exclude data to sway your audience, you are acting unethically.

For example, imagine that you're reporting sales for the year. Sales dipped in June because you lost a valuable employee to a competitor. To hide this loss and show a continuous upward trend on a line chart, you present average sales for every other month: January, March, May, July, and so on.

When pharmaceutical companies were rushing to develop vaccines against COVID-19, AstraZeneca made several missteps. The company reported a 79% effectiveness rate against the virus, but later results were between 69 and 75%. An independent group of experts called the data "already outdated and potentially misleading"—cherry picked. In a letter, the group highlighted the negative impact:

> [The data] they chose to release was the most favorable for the study as opposed to the most recent and most complete. Decisions like this are what erode public trust in the scientific process.[34]

When you review others' charts, ask what is missing. What data points do not appear, and what could they mean?

Apple-Polishing

Apple-polishing means manipulating data to look better than it is. Notice how the chart on the right side in Figure 16 exaggerates the difference between the columns. This happens when the vertical axis is truncated—it doesn't start at 0. If you must start an axis at a point other than zero to show differences in large numbers, use a symbol to acknowledge the break, such as those in Figure 17.

A Truncated Axis Skews Data | **Figure 16**

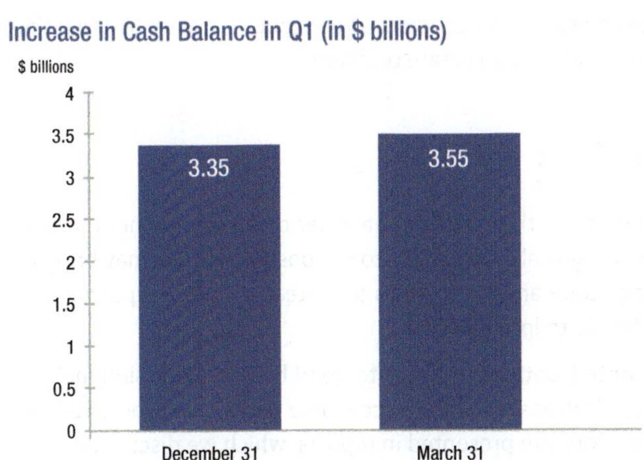

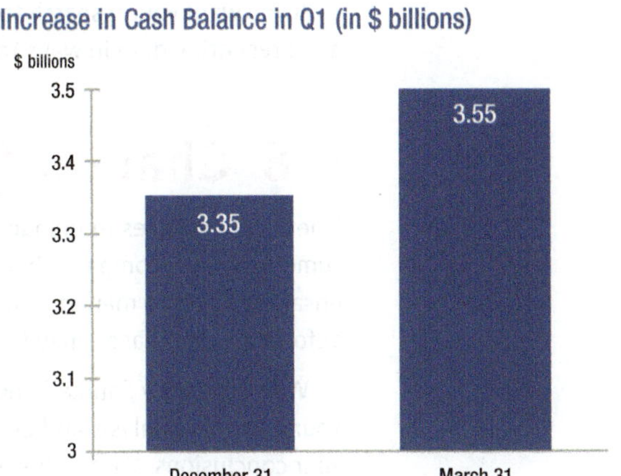

Three-dimensional graphs contribute to chartjunk and can look misleading. Compare the pie charts in Figure 18. Because the left pie is slanted away from the viewer, the slices farthest away appear smaller than they are. *A* may not look twice the size of *C*, which you see clearly on the right side. Shape and text effects should never be used just for visual appeal, particularly when they mislead the audience.

Symbols to Show an Axis Break | **Figure 17**

Comparing Apples to Oranges

Comparing apples to oranges refers to finding similarities between two items that are not similar and, as a result, drawing a faulty conclusion. For example, imagine that you lead a company's North American sales division. You compare your group's revenue to that of the European division, which is significantly lower, and conclude that your account managers are better trained. The European division leader might refute your argument, pointing out regional differences in customer preferences or product availability.

Data needs context to be meaningful and accurately compared. Imagine comparing a small company's turnover to that of a large company. If only the *numbers* of employees who quit each

Three-Dimensional Pie Charts Skew Data | **Figure 18**

Misleading pie chart

A
B
C
D

Regular pie chart

11%
42%
5%
42%

year were reported, you might conclude that the smaller company has less turnover. In most cases, a percentage rather than a raw number will be the more useful, fairer comparison.

If you want your research to guide decision making, demonstrate good character by collecting and presenting data in ways that solve rather than create problems.

9-6 Chapter Closing

Unethical practices in managing and presenting data can have serious consequences. A consumer products company that bribes drug trial participants to get positive results may bring an unsafe product to market. A mortgage company that reveals only "teaser" interest payments—before rates increase—may force a family to lose its home.

When properly sourced and presented, data contributes to good business decision making. Your accurate analysis and clear visualizations make data accessible and allow people to trust your conclusions. Often, these conclusions are presented in reports, which we discuss next.

Provide Feedback on the Softbank Chart

Consider the chapter introduction, which described Softbank's charts. Imagine that you work as Softbank's head of investor relations. Before he delivers his presentation to the press, CEO Masayoshi Son asks for your feedback on his charts. Using the CAM model, what questions might you consider before providing your feedback?

>>> CHARACTER CHECK

1. **What is my feedback about the charts?**
   I'm concerned about reporters' reactions. I want to suggest that the CEO present more data about WeWork. The loss is obvious, so he might as well be honest about the situation. Realistically, more losses may follow.
2. **What might hold me back from telling him my full reaction?**
   The CEO's purpose is to inspire investors, and he does that well. He is running an incredibly successful company, despite these losses. He's also my boss, and I want to keep my job. Still, I feel a responsibility to say something now that he is asking for my feedback.

>>> AUDIENCE ANALYSIS

1. **How might the CEO react?**
   He'll probably be annoyed at me. The slides illustrate the message he wants to convey: an optimistic view of WeWork. He wants to reassure investors.
2. **What can I suggest in response?**
   I'm going to find data that might be useful to show; it's not all bad news. I'll also suggest eliminating some slides, particularly those without any data support. Maybe he can describe his enthusiasm with fewer charts.

>>> MESSAGE AND MEDIUM

1. **What are the main points of my message?**
   His optimism is inspiring. His message will be taken more seriously with more accurate charts.
2. **In what medium will I communicate the message?**
   I'll talk with him about this. An email can't convey my respect for him, while balancing my concerns.

› IN PRACTICE

Prepare a Chart for the Softbank CEO to Present

Imagine that you are the head of investor relations and are preparing a chart for the Softbank CEO to present. The primary audience is the press, who will write stories about the investment. Find recent data about WeWork to include.

››› CHARACTER CHECK

1. What is my personal motivation for creating the chart?
2. How will I be sure to present data ethically and not mislead the audience?

››› AUDIENCE ANALYSIS

1. What is CEO Masayoshi Son looking for in my chart?
2. The primary audience of the chart is the press. What are their interests? Why might they be skeptical?

››› MESSAGE AND MEDIUM

1. What are the main points I want to convey in the chart?
2. Create the chart using PowerPoint or another visual program.

REFLECTING ON YOUR COMMUNICATION AND CHARACTER DEVELOPMENT

1. **Consider your approach to research.**

   When you want to find an answer to a question, how do you start? Do you use different sources for different types of information, or do you rely on Google or another web browser for your answers?

   Why do you use this approach? What other approach could offer better results, even if it takes more time initially?

2. **Reflect on cognitive bias.**

   Think of a time when you struggled with too much information, not enough meaning, the need to act fast, or limited memory. What was the result? To which of the biases in Figure 3 are you most prone? How can you avoid this problem in the future?

3. **Assess your news sources.**

   Where do you get your news? How might those sources—and your social media sites—give you biased information? What could you do to get additional points of view?

4. **Reflect on a time when you spread misinformation.**

   Think about a time when you liked, forwarded, or reposted something online that turned out to be untrue or misleading. Or have you told a friend or family member something you read that wasn't verified? What was the result? Which of the steps in Figure 4 did you miss? In retrospect, what could you have done differently to check the information first?

5. **Consider your participation in research.**

   Have you participated in primary research, for example, by taking a survey online? What was the purpose, and who or what organization asked for your responses? What inspired you to participate? How thoughtful were your responses? In what ways do you believe your participation helped the researcher?

DEVELOPING YOUR BUSINESS COMMUNICATION SKILLS

IDENTIFYING TYPES OF SOURCES AND DATA

LO1 Identify types of data.

1. **Find public information about a company.**

   Choose a public company to research. If you're not sure whether a U.S. company is public, search the Securities and Exchange Commission database at https://www.sec.gov/edgar/searchedgar/companysearch.html. Next, find the following information:

   - Number of employees
   - Headquarters location
   - Board of directors and senior leadership team members
   - Stock price for the past five years
   - Revenue for the past fiscal year by major product or service group

   You might try the company's investor relations web pages to start. What other sources do you find?

   Now try to find other information that may be harder to source online:

   - Employee demographics
   - Employee turnover rate
   - Corporate sustainability goals
   - Anything else that interests you

How easy is it to find this information? Compare results with students who researched different companies. Was it easier to find information about some companies than others? Why do you think this was the case?

2. **Find relevant sources for business information.**
   Choose one of the following small business situations—or another situation that interests you:
   - You own a clothing store and want to know whether to offer hats.
   - You own a jewelry store and want to know which precious gems are most popular.
   - You're developing an app for booking youth hostels and want to know the potential customer base.
   - You own a sporting goods store and want to know the most popular bicycle brands by age group.
   - You own an event planning company and want to know how strong the wedding business will be next year in your region.
   - You own a computer repair business and want to know what services customers want.

   Conduct research and provide a list of the most relevant sources you found.

3. **Compare search results on Google, Google Scholar, and a library database.**
   Enter a few keywords into Google, Google Scholar, and a library database. You may use a scenario from Exercise 2 or choose a different situation. Try to get the most relevant, reliable results from each search by narrowing results a few times.

4. **Find data to decide whether to start a business.**
   If you could start any business, what would it be? Maybe you have already been working on a business or have done so in the past. Write a list of questions you need answered before deciding whether the business is viable. Then, find information for each of your questions. Provide citations for all sources and be sure to include conflicting information or data that does not support your idea. You don't want to start a business that you know will fail from the start.

5. **Compare and modify social media feeds.**
   With a friend, compare social media feeds. What type of information do you see on each feed? Does the content reinforce what you think you already know? Now try to change what appears in your feed. Do your favorite platforms allow you to see the latest or most recent information instead of what is curated for you by an algorithm? If so, keep the new settings for a couple of days to see how the information varies.

LO2 Explain criteria for evaluating information.

EVALUATING SOURCES OF INFORMATION

6. **Assess media bias.**
   Find a media bias chart, which shows political leanings of news organizations. In small groups, discuss what might surprise you or confirm what you previously thought. Also consider the limitations of this type of information.[35]

7. **Prepare a presentation about evaluating internet sources.**
   Imagine that you're giving a presentation to middle school children to help them distinguish between credible and false information online. Using the steps in Figure 4 and your own thinking, make the process relevant to kids. Provide a couple of examples to illustrate your points. Create a few slides in Google Slides or another program for your presentation.

8. **Evaluate the quality of internet resources.**

   Select two internet resources and evaluate them based on the criteria in Figure 4. You might search for news about a company that interests you. Submit a one-page summary of your analysis to your instructor.

9. **Distinguish between high- and low-quality internet sources.**

   Imagine that a person you admire is coming to speak on campus. You have been selected to introduce the speaker to your entire graduating class. Of course, you want to ensure you have accurate information about this person. Search the internet for information about the person and identify at least five resources. Use the principles in Figure 4 to guide your research. Write a list of information and include your sources.

10. **Explain a study retraction.**

    Find an article about a study that was retracted from an academic journal. You might search for "retractions in academic journals" or something similar. Choose one that interests you. Read two or three articles and write a summary about the situation. Include background about the research issues and reasons for the retraction but focus most of your writing on the implications—why does the retraction matter?

11. **Evaluate studies for a report.**

    Imagine that you're the corporate communications vice president for Harley-Davidson Motor Company. To promote motorcycle use in the United States, you're planning a communication campaign focused on safety. Your objective is to overcome the public's perception that motorcycles are dangerous.

    You decide to include some scholarly research to support your point of view. But, of course, you want to present an ethical argument, so you'll evaluate each study carefully. Use the following questions from Figure 5, Evaluating Research Studies, to ensure the studies meet your quality standards:

    - What was the purpose of the study?
    - How was the data collected?
    - How was the data analyzed?
    - How consistent is the data with that from other studies?
    - How old is the data?

    Write a few paragraphs that you plan to put on the Harley-Davidson website. Remember your objective: you want people to believe that motorcycles are safe (or, at least, aren't as dangerous as people perceive them to be). Include references to the articles you decide to use so that your instructor can evaluate your choices.

COLLECTING DATA THROUGH SURVEYS

LO3 Write an effective survey question for a given research question.

12. **Analyze a survey.**

    Find a survey you were asked to complete recently. You might see one in your email, or you might see one appear when you're on a web page. As you complete the survey, answer the following questions:

    a. How persuasive is the message asking you to complete the survey? What is the stated purpose and value of participation to you? How could the message be more persuasive?

    b. How easy is the survey to complete? How long does it take? Do you find it a burden or interesting to answer the questions?

    c. What types of questions are used? Do you see a variety of open- and closed-ended questions? Are they chosen well?

d. How are questions worded? Are they clear and easy to understand? Are they written to avoid bias? Are the answer choices mutually exclusive, with no overlap?

e. What demographic information is collected? How comfortable do you feel answering those questions? If you skipped a question, why did you? Could it have been worded differently to make it easier to answer?

13. Create a survey for a new business.

Return to Exercise 4, which asked you to collect information on a new business idea. Now create a survey to collect primary data by following these steps:

a. Identify your audience. Who is the ideal respondent to answer your questions?

b. Identify information that you want answered. What information would you like to know that isn't available online?

c. Write a few questions. Choose a good variety of question types, for example, rating and ranking.

d. Order the questions in a logical sequence.

e. Write a cover message.

Exchange drafts with two other students for feedback. Which questions work best, and which will you revise?

14. Create an online survey for your classmates.

(For this exercise, you may use your questions from the previous exercise if the target audience is students.) Working in small groups, imagine that you're planning a business targeted to students. First, decide on your business concept. This can be anything: a service (e.g., laundry or grocery shopping) or a product (e.g., custom T-shirts or imported hats).

Next, write about ten questions to determine whether your idea will be popular. When you're satisfied that your questions meet the criteria for a well-designed survey, create the survey using SurveyMonkey or another program. Then distribute the survey to your classmates. (See the next exercise for a related activity.)

Finally, with your group, analyze the responses and make a preliminary judgment about whether your business would be successful.

15. Evaluate your classmates' online surveys.

For Exercise 14, you worked in a group to create a survey for other students in your class. Pair up with another group to evaluate each other's survey. In class, meet with your partner group and provide each other with feedback on your surveys. Which questions were most effective, and why? Which questions were least effective, and why? Next, revise your questions.

LO4 Choose a data visualization for a given business situation.

VISUALIZING DATA

16. Eliminate chartjunk.

Find a messy chart online. Look for garish colors, too many lines or variables, shadows or shading, and other distractions from the main point. Create a new chart without these design features. Compare revisions with a classmate and suggest additional improvements.

17. Analyze a chart.

The text and chart in Figure 19 are from the U.S. Federal Reserve.[36] In small groups, identify a list of questions you have about the data collection and presentation. In other words, what else do you want to know before drawing conclusions based on the data?

18. Redesign a chart.

Review the chart in Figure 19. How could the data be presented in a better way to improve comprehension? Also include a more descriptive title to summarize the main point. Redraw the chart and compare your approach with that of other students.

Text and Chart About Income and Risk-Taking | **Figure 19**

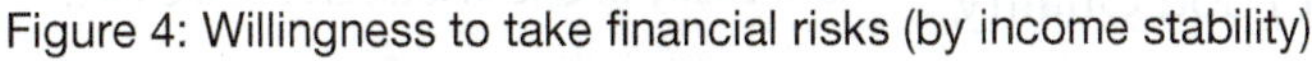

Figure 4: Willingness to take financial risks (by income stability)

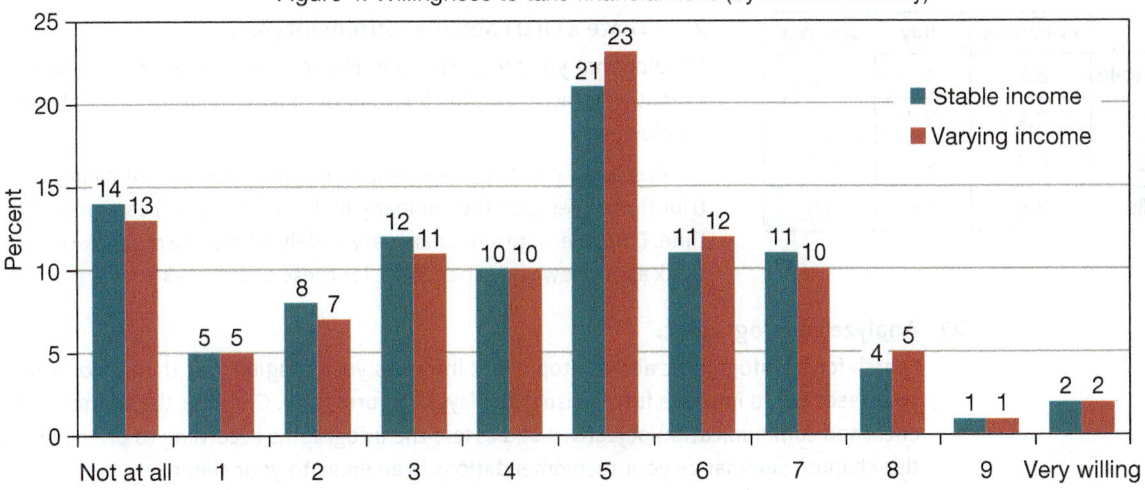

"More risk-tolerant individuals may be willing to accept income that is more volatile. On a scale of zero to ten, with 'zero' being unwilling to take risks and 'ten' being very willing to take risks, more risk-tolerant individuals are somewhat more likely to have varying income than those who are less risk tolerant (figure 4). However, the difference in income volatility by risk tolerance is modest. This suggests that factors other than individual risk preferences likely drive income volatility."[37]

19. Determine which type of visual is best.

For the following situations, select the most appropriate visual aid for presenting the data and explain why it is the best option. First, identify the primary purpose: comparison, parts of a whole, trends over time, stories and compilations, or something else. Then, decide what type of chart—bar, line, donut, and so on—would work best and why.

a. To show the daily sales for your small computer business for the past six months
b. To show the proportion of your budget spent on each of the four fixed costs for your company during the year
c. To show the results of six survey questions asking people's opinion regarding the economy
d. To show the first quarter's net sales for departments A, B, and C
e. To show the locations of your international offices
f. To show the history of native advertising in web pages
g. To show total sales by region and the percentage of increase or decrease from the previous year
h. To show the average annual rainfall in selected cities in the nation

20. Construct a chart from data presented in a table.

Imagine that you're the F&B director for a hotel group with four properties in the New York area. The owner has asked you for data about food quality at each location.

You collected the guest feedback shown in Figure 20. Ratings are based on responses to the question, "How would you rate the quality of food at this restaurant?" and the scale is 1 = very poor, 2 = poor, 3 = acceptable, 4 = good, 5 = very good. You distributed surveys at three points in time at each location.

Figure 20 Data from Guests About Restaurant Food Quality

	February	July	October
New Rochelle	3.9	4.1	4.2
Park Slope	2.4	2.7	2.3
Glen Cove	4.8	4.9	4.7
Forest Hills	3.6	3.6	3.5

To show off your data presentation skills and help the owner see the data easily in one visual, create a chart.

21. Create a chart about a retirement plan.

Imagine that you are the head of HR and received approval from the executive director and the board to offer a 401(k) retirement plan for employees.

Prepare a chart to show employees how much their salary contribution of 6% plus the company match of 3% (50%) can grow over time. Employee age and salary vary widely within the organization, so think about how you can account for these differences in your graphic.

22. Analyze an infographic.

Search for an infographic about a topic that interests you. Imagine that the author wants your feedback to improve future visual displays of information. Consider the source, audience, and communication objectives and assess the infographic according to principles in this chapter. Summarize your recommendations in an email to your client.

23. Create an infographic.

With two or three other students, choose one of these topics or find data about a subject that interests you:

- Major banks: Which are the biggest banks according to market share, assets, employees, or other measures?
- News websites: Which are the most popular news websites in the world?
- Students at your school: What majors and career paths do students choose?
- Baseball: How do two teams compare for the past five years?
- Reality television: Who watches which shows?

As a group, agree on at least three sets of data that will become sections of an infographic. Then, working independently, create an infographic to display the data. Consider which data should get the most and least attention and which requires explanatory text.

When you're finished, compare infographics with the other students. What decisions did you make in choosing text and graphics? Which work best and why?

LO5 Describe three ways to avoid presenting misleading information.

ANALYZING AND PRESENTING DATA

24. Discover what data analysts do.

Find three or four job postings for data analysts. Compare the descriptions, including required qualifications. With another student in class, discuss your interest in these positions. Would you like to apply for these jobs? Why or why not?

25. Make sense of performance review data.

Imagine that you are a team leader at Anders Consulting and manage a group of junior consultants. Your manager asks you to consider whether Kyle, one of your direct reports, is ready for promotion to team leader. You have the data collected from 15 of Kyle's peers (Figure 21). Write an email to your manager with your assessment. Be sure to provide a clear picture of Kyle's strengths and areas for development. Support your opinion with specific examples of Kyle's behavior, which you may invent.

26. Interpret data you collected.

Revisit the survey you created for Exercise 14 and revised for Exercise 15. Distribute the survey to students and gather at least 50 responses.

Ratings Based on 15 Team Evaluations | **Figure 21**

Major Assessment Categories	Specific Behaviors	Kyle Houston
Ratings Key 3 = The member has performed very well in this area; 2 = The member has performed OK in this area; 1 = The member has not performed very well in this area; 0 = The member has performed poorly in this area.		
Overall Rating		***Mean*** **(2.42)** ***Mode*** **(2)**
Contributing	Offers ideas, suggestions, etc. Attends all meetings. Meets all deadlines.	Mean (2.83) Range (2 to 3)
Listening	Lets other members talk. Limits discussion to main point of meeting. Summarizes or clarifies other members' ideas. Resists telling other members what to think.	Mean (1.96) Range (0 to 3)
Facilitating Group Problem Solving	Asks questions to organize discussion. Defines questions in order to stay on topic. Selects criteria for evaluating suggested ideas. Encourages suggestions of alternative solutions. Discards all but the best solution.	Mean (2.18) Range (0 to 3)

Next, interpretate your data in three steps: isolation, context, and synthesis. Write a summary of your results. How, if at all, do your conclusions differ from your preliminary judgment?

27. Provide a concrete comparison for data.

Compare the number of people who are food insecure to something concrete. First, find raw data about people who are food insecure either within a country or worldwide—your choice. In addition to presenting the raw number, provide a way for people to understand the magnitude of this population.

28. Find misleading charts.

Try to find three charts that illustrate each of the problems discussed in this chapter that mislead the audience: cherry-picking, apple-polishing, and comparing apples to oranges. Describe the issue and potential impact—how each presentation is problematic and how it could affect decision making. Also redraw the charts or explain what data is needed for a more accurate representation of the information.

CHAPTER SUMMARY

LO1 Identify types of data.

Search for data that will achieve your purpose, for example, to solve a problem or make a decision. By factoring the problem, you'll determine what primary and secondary data are needed to answer important questions. Where available, choose library databases over broad internet searches to get the best sources. Avoid bias by using a variety of sources, including those that contradict your way of thinking.

LO2 Explain criteria for evaluating information.

The quality of information publicly available varies widely. When evaluating online content, assess the website, check the author, read carefully, follow links, check dates, consider the joke, check your biases, and ask experts. When using research studies as secondary sources, consider the purpose of the study, how the data was collected and analyzed, how consistent the data is with other studies, and how old the data is.

LO3 Write an effective survey question for a given research question.

Surveys are the most common method for collecting primary data. Survey tools provide templates with several types of open- and closed-ended questions. Ensure that all survey questions are necessary, clearly worded, complete, and unbiased. Organize the questions logically and include a persuasive message for respondents to understand the purpose and value of completing the survey.

LO4 Choose a data visualization for a given business situation.

Data is converted into information and explained in tables and other graphics. Create tables to show large amounts of numerical data in a small space. Create clear charts to show data more visually and to increase comprehension. Choose a chart type based on your purpose: a comparison, parts of a whole, or changes over time. For more complex stories and information, consider combination charts and infographics.

LO5 Describe three ways to avoid presenting misleading information.

Interpret important points from your data, pointing out the major findings, trends, and contradictions. Avoid misleading your audience by cherry-picking data, apple-polishing data, and comparing apples to oranges, which might reflect poorly on your character.

Endnotes

1. Polina Marinova, "SoftBank Created the Earnings Deck to End All Earnings Decks," *Fortune*, November 7, 2019, https://fortune.com/2019/11/07/softbank-wework-earnings-deck/, accessed April 25, 2021.
2. Vijay Govindarajan and Anup Srivastava, "No, WeWork Isn't a Tech Company. Here's Why That Matters," *Harvard Business Review*, August 21, 2019, https://hbr.org/2019/08/no-wework-isnt-a-tech-company-heres-why-that-matters, accessed April 24, 2021.
3. SoftBank slides shown in Shona Ghosh, "Check out SoftBank CEO Masayoshi Son's Wildly Optimistic Slides About Turning WeWork Profitable," Business Insider, November 7, 2019, www.businessinsider.com/softbank-ceo-masayoshi-son-turnaround-presentation-slides-wework-2019-11, accessed April 24, 2021.
4. "FTC Charges Volkswagen Deceived Consumers with Its 'Clean Diesel' Campaign," Federal Trade Commission, March 29, 2016, www.ftc.gov/news-events/press-releases/2016/03/ftc-charges-volkswagen-deceived-consumers-its-clean-diesel, accessed April 24, 2021.
5. Versions of this quote date back to the 1970s and refer to the era of TV. "You're Not the Customer; You're the Product," QuoteInvestigator.com, https://quoteinvestigator.com/2017/07/16/product, accessed April 2, 2021.
6. "The Social Dilemma (2020)—Transcript," Posted by Scraps from the Loft, https://scrapsfromtheloft.com/2020/10/03/the-social-dilemma-movie-transcript/, accessed April 2, 2021.
7. For a strong case for the singular form, see Daniel Oberhaus, "It's Time to End the 'Data Is' vs 'Data Are' Debate," Vice, August 20, 2018, www.vice.com/en/article/594aj8/its-time-to-end-the-data-is-vs-data-are-debate, accessed April 18, 2021.
8. Dariusz Jemielniak, "Wikipedia: Why Is the Common Knowledge Resource Still Neglected by Academics?" *GigaScience* 8 (2019), https://doi.org/10.1093/gigascience/giz139.
9. Joanna Stern, "Social-Media Algorithms Rule How We See the World. Good Luck Trying to Stop Them," *The Wall Street Journal*, January 17, 2021, www.wsj.com/articles/social-media-algorithms-rule-how-we-see-the-world-good-luck-trying-to-stop-them-11610884800, accessed April 2, 2021.
10. Buster Benson, "Cognitive Bias Cheat Sheet," September 1, 2016, BetterHumans, https://betterhumans.pub/cognitive-bias-cheat-sheet-55a472476b18, accessed April 2, 2021.
11. Cited by Adam Grant, *Think Again* (New York: Viking, 2021). See David J. Lick, Adam L. Alter, and Jonathan B. Freeman, "Superior Pattern Detectors Efficiently Learn, Activate, Apply, and Update Social Stereotypes," *Journal of Experimental Psychology: General* 147 (2017): 209–227. https://doi.org/10.1037/xge0000349. Also see Danim Kahan et. al, "Motivated Numeracy and Enlightened Self-Government," *Behavioural Public Policy* 1 (2017): 54-86, https://scholarsbank.uoregon.edu/xmlui/bitstream/handle/1794/22105/833.pdf, accessed April 11, 2021.
12. Sam Wineburg et al., "Evaluating Information: The Cornerstone of Civic Online Reasoning. Stanford Digital Repository," Stanford University Digital Repository, http://purl.stanford.edu/fv751yt5934, accessed April 4, 2021.
13. For ways to identify a deepfake, see Elyse Samuels, Sarah Cahlan, Emily Sabens, "How to Spot a Fake Video," *The Washington Post*, March 19, 2021, www.washingtonpost.com/politics/2021/03/19/how-spot-fake-video/, accessed April 4, 2021.
14. Eli Rosenberg, "Alex Jones Apologizes for Promoting 'Pizzagate' Hoax," *The New York Times*, March 25, 2017, www.nytimes.com/2017/03/25/business/alex-jones-pizzagate-apology-comet-ping-pong.html, accessed April 4, 2021.
15. Cecilia Kang and Sheera Frenkel, "'PizzaGate' Conspiracy Theory Thrives Anew in the TikTok Era," *The New York Times*, July 14, 2020, www.nytimes.com/2020/06/27/technology/pizzagate-justin-bieber-qanon-tiktok.html, accessed April 4, 2021.
16. "How to Spot Fake News," International Federation of Library Associations and Institutions (IFLA), www.ifla.org/publications/node/11174, accessed April 3, 2021.
17. Frank DeStefano and Tom T. Shimabukuro, "The MMR Vaccine and Autism," *Annual Review of Virology* 6 (2019), https://doi.org/10.1146/annurev-virology-092818-015515.
18. "Chipotle Feedback Customer Satisfaction Survey Sweepstakes Official Rules," Chipotle.com, www.chipotle.com/about-us/feedback-rules, accessed April 5, 2021.
19. "Voice of the Guest," Chipotle.com, www.chipotlefeedback.com/Index.aspx, accessed April 5, 2021.
20. "Types of Survey Questions," SurveyMonkey.com, www.surveymonkey.com/mp/survey-question-types, accessed April 5, 2021.
21. Matthias Schonlau and Ellen Peters, "Graph Comprehension," Working Paper, Rand Labor and Population, September 2008, www.rand.org/pubs/workingpapers/2008/RANDWR618.pdf, accessed April 7, 2021.
22. Adapted from "Statistics Table Visualization," Qualtrics.com, www.qualtrics.com/support/survey-platform/reports-module/reports-section/reports-visualizations/table-visualizations/statistics-table-visualization/#CustomizationOptions, accessed April 6, 2021.
23. "Guidance for Data Visuals," Connecting Cognitive Science and Climate Science, http://guidance.climatesciencecognition.com, accessed April 7, 2021.
24. "Keeping Performance in Perspective," Vanguard.com, https://investor.vanguard.com/investing/portfolio-management/performance-overview, accessed April 7, 2021.
25. JPMorgan Chase, "Annual Report 2020," JPMorgan Chase Website, https://reports.jpmorganchase.com/investor-relations/2020/ar-ceo-letters.htm, accessed April 8, 2021.

26. Data from "Vanguard 500 Index Fund Admiral Shares (VFIAX)," Vanguard.com, https://investor.vanguard.com/mutual-funds/profile/VFIAX, accessed April 7, 2021.
27. "Don't Let High Costs Eat Away your Returns," Vanguard.com, https://investor.vanguard.com/investing/how-to-invest/impact-of-costs, accessed April 7, 2021.
28. "What Is Tableau?" Tableau, www.tableau.com/why-tableau/what-is-tableau, accessed August 16, 2021.
29. For more advice on creating infographics, see "Ultimate Infographic Design Guide," Worcester Polytechnic Institute Academic Technology, https://canvas.wpi.edu/courses/14090/pages/ultimate-infographic-design-guide, accessed April 8, 2021.
30. Aiyana Green and Steven Strogatz, "Who's Afraid of Big Numbers?" *The New York Times*, June 17, 2021, www.nytimes.com/2021/06/17/science/math-numbers-federal-budget-tao.html, accessed August 23, 2021.
31. "Food Loss and Food Waste," Food and Agriculture Organization of the United Nations, www.fao.org/food-loss-and-food-waste/flw-data), accessed April 9, 2021
32. Based on the U.S. population of about 328,000,000 and estimates that Americans eat about 1 ton of food each year. 328 million * 4 = 1.312 billion. Allison Aubrey, "The Average American Ate (Literally) a Ton This Year," NPR, www.npr.org/sections/thesalt/2011/12/31/144478009/the-average-american-ate-literally-a-ton-this-year, accessed April 9, 2021.
33. Charles Seife, *Proofiness* (Penguin Books, 2011), Chapter 1.
34. Carolyn Y. Johnson et al., "AstraZeneca Used 'Outdated and Potentially Misleading Data' That Overstated the Effectiveness of Its Vaccine, Independent Panel Says," *The Washington Post*, March 23, 2021, www.washingtonpost.com/world/astrazeneca-oxford-vaccine-concerns/2021/03/23/2f931d34-8bc3-11eb-a33e-da28941cb9ac_story.html, accessed August 16, 2021.
35. Jake Sheridan, "Should You Trust Media Bias Charts?" Poynter, March 24, 2021, www.poynter.org/fact-checking/media-literacy/2021/should-you-trust-media-bias-charts/, accessed April 11, 2021.
36. "Report on the Economic Well-Being of U.S. Households in 2018–May 2019," Board of Governors of the Federal Reserve System, www.federalreserve.gov/publications/2019-economic-well-being-of-us-households-in-2018-income.htm, accessed April 11, 2021.
37. "Report on the Economic Well-Being of U.S. Households."

CHAPTER

10 Writing Reports

Learning Objectives

After you have finished this chapter, you should be able to

LO1 Determine an appropriate report format and organization in a business situation.

LO2 Describe typical components of a business report.

LO3 Explain how the writing style for a report may differ from other types of writing.

LO4 Format a footnote to cite a given source.

LO5 Distinguish design and formatting guidelines for slide decks from other types of reports.

> "*McKinsey continued to design and develop ways that Purdue could increase sales of OxyContin well after the opioid epidemic peaked.*"[1]
>
> —Keith Ellison, State of Minnesota Attorney General

Chapter Introduction

McKinsey Report Helped Purdue Increase Sales of OxyContin

In the midst of the opioid epidemic in the United States, McKinsey management consultants proposed ways that Purdue Pharma could increase sales of OxyContin. The drug is a brand name for oxycodone, at one point the leading cause of drug overdose deaths.[2]

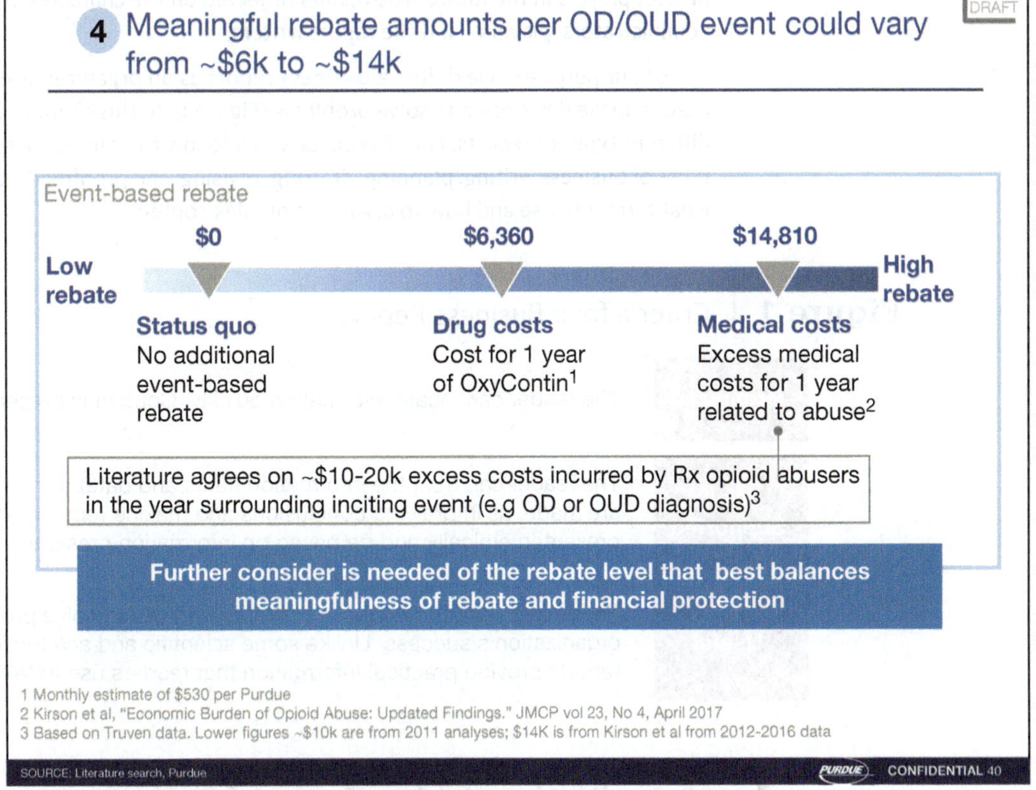

DRAFT
4 Meaningful rebate amounts per OD/OUD event could vary from ~$6k to ~$14k
Event-based rebate
Low rebate
$0
$6,360
$14,810
High rebate
Status quo
No additional event-based rebate
Drug costs
Cost for 1 year of OxyContin[1]
Medical costs
Excess medical costs for 1 year related to abuse[2]
Literature agrees on ~$10-20k excess costs incurred by Rx opioid abusers in the year surrounding inciting event (e.g OD or OUD diagnosis)[3]
Further consider is needed of the rebate level that best balances meaningfulness of rebate and financial protection
1 Monthly estimate of $530 per Purdue
2 Kirson et al, "Economic Burden of Opioid Abuse: Updated Findings." JMCP vol 23, No 4, April 2017
3 Based on Truven data. Lower figures ~$10k are from 2011 analyses; $14K is from Kirson et al from 2012-2016 data
SOURCE: Literature search, Purdue
PURDUE
CONFIDENTIAL 40

McKinsey's deck recommends ways to continue opioid prescriptions.

McKinsey & Company, "High impact interventions to rapidly address market access challenges," December 2017 [Exhibit R, filed November 18, 2020], https://assets.documentcloud.org/documents/20421781/mckinsey-docs.pdf, accessed April 12, 2021.

Throughout its 15-year consulting relationship with Purdue, McKinsey recommended marketing strategies to boost sales. Consultants suggested targeting new patients, veterans, and the most prolific prescribers.[3]

A McKinsey slide deck became public after several lawsuits about its role in the opioid crisis.[4] On the page shown here, the company recommends a rebate program. To make OxyContin more attractive, the company suggested offering pharmacies up to $14,810 for each person who overdosed.[5]

McKinsey settled several lawsuits and published an apology, excerpts of which you read in Chapter 5. The report was well designed (despite the typo) and persuasive but became an embarrassment and a liability to the company.

The type in the blue box, "Further consider," should be "Further consideration."

LO1 Determine an appropriate report format and organization in a business situation.

10-1 Planning the Report

Reports are a tough sell to today's business audience. Leaders may prefer shorter documents, but decisions that affect people's lives, the environment, or company profits deserve careful consideration. Complex situations require deep analysis, which could mean multiple data presentations and detailed, nuanced explanations.

For example, an independent commission that investigated the University of Maryland football culture produced a 198-page report.[6] The situation was serious: Jordan McNair, who played offensive tackle, died of heat stroke after a strenuous football practice. From interviews, complaint records, communications, and other sources of data, the report provided enough detail to support sound recommendations for the university to improve the football program and protect players in the future. The results reflected on the character of those involved: coaches, administrators, players—and the report writers.

For our purposes, we define a **business report** as an organized presentation of information used to make decisions and solve problems (Figure 1). In this chapter, you learn how to develop different types of reports. For all reports, you'll follow the same process we discussed for other types of business writing: planning, drafting, revising, and proofreading. You also need to decide what format to use and how to organize complex content.

Figure 1 | Criteria for a Business Report

Organized	The reader can locate information quickly. Content is presented in a logical order.
Well Supported	The reader can trust the information (facts and data). Where subjective judgments are made, as in drawing conclusions and making recommendations, they must be presented ethically and be based on information presented in the report.
Useful	The reader uses the report to make decisions and solve problems that affect the organization's success. Unlike some scientific and academic reports, business reports provide practical information that readers use to take action.

10-1a Distinguishing Types of Reports

At work, you're likely to see many reports for a variety of audiences. In any organization, unique problems and opportunities require **situational reports**, which are produced only once. These reports are often more challenging than ongoing reports, such as a weekly time log or monthly sales analysis, because they require the writer to start from scratch. For each report, writers need to determine what and how much information to include and how best to organize and present the findings. These one-of-a-kind projects are the focus of this chapter.

Reports may be written in response to a company or government request. A **request for information (RFI)** is a preliminary document asking for general background from potential suppliers. Purdue Pharma might have asked several consulting firms about their experience working with drug manufacturers and how they might approach the issue of declining sales. A **request for proposal (RFP)** is a more formal, detailed document looking for bids. After gathering a short list of potential consulting firms, Purdue Pharma might have asked for formal proposals addressing research plans, timelines, costs, and other questions. In response to an RFP, firms submit reports that meet the client's requirements, sometimes in a highly specific format.

When writers initiate a report, they have more flexibility and may choose a less formal approach. Next, we discuss several options.

Which report type do you prefer—one that's mostly text or mostly graphics? Should your own preference factor into your decision about which to choose for an audience?

10-1b Selecting a Report Format

When initiating your own report, which format you choose depends on the context—the audience, purpose, content, and organizational norms. In Figure 2, you see examples along a continuum. Numerical reports and short reports sent in email are least graphical. Reports that combine text and graphics may be created in Microsoft Word, Google Docs, Google Slides, PowerPoint, or other programs. When developed using presentation software in landscape rather than portrait layout, they are often referred to as "decks."

For an audience accustomed to more traditional reports, a document that is primarily text may be best; however, for a more progressive audience who is pressed for time, a deck may be a better choice. If your company typically produces text-based reports, then that format may be preferable. If you are illustrating your points with extensive charts and images, then a deck may be a better choice.

For short, text-based, less formal reports, you may include the report within an email message. This approach is appropriate if your manager asked you to research a question, as you see in the example shown in Figure 3. Within the email, you can include links to more information, which avoids awkward citations in an email.

For longer, more formal reports, consider how much text and how many graphics you need to explain and support your points. A primarily text-based report is written in narrative (paragraph) form, with headings and subheadings separating each section. In a deck, very little, if any, paragraph text is used. Instead, text is written in bulleted form, often incorporated into graphical elements, such as tables or shapes. Each slide is a separate page of the report: the pages function as section divisions, and the slide titles function as headings.

Comparing the reports in Figure 2, you can see why decks have become so popular. In many ways, these reports are easier to create and easier to read than text-based reports. With more graphics and less dense text, the format has much more visual appeal and is far more skimmable than a paragraph-based report. But don't confuse these reports with PowerPoint or Google Slides you would show on a screen or monitor during an oral presentation; the deck example in Figure 2 is far too dense for an audience to read as slides during an oral presentation, which we discuss in the next chapter.

10-1c Organizing the Report

A well-organized report leads the reader through your findings, conclusions, and recommendations. With logical sequencing, your reader will find your report clear and easy to navigate.

Findings, Conclusions, and Recommendations

The differences among findings, conclusions, and recommendations are illustrated in Figure 4. Findings include your evidence, for example, results from a survey, expert opinion from articles, quotations from an interview, or data from internal records. Conclusions are drawn from your findings; in a recommendation report, these are also considered your claims. Recommendations are solutions to address your conclusions.

As discussed earlier in the book, most business reports for American audiences use the direct organization plan, with the conclusions and recommendations up front. This is the preferable structure for your manager, for audiences who will be receptive to your conclusions and recommendations, and for readers to have context before reading the details of your report. However, the indirect style may be appropriate in some situations. Consider the indirect style when your

Figure 2 | Report Formats

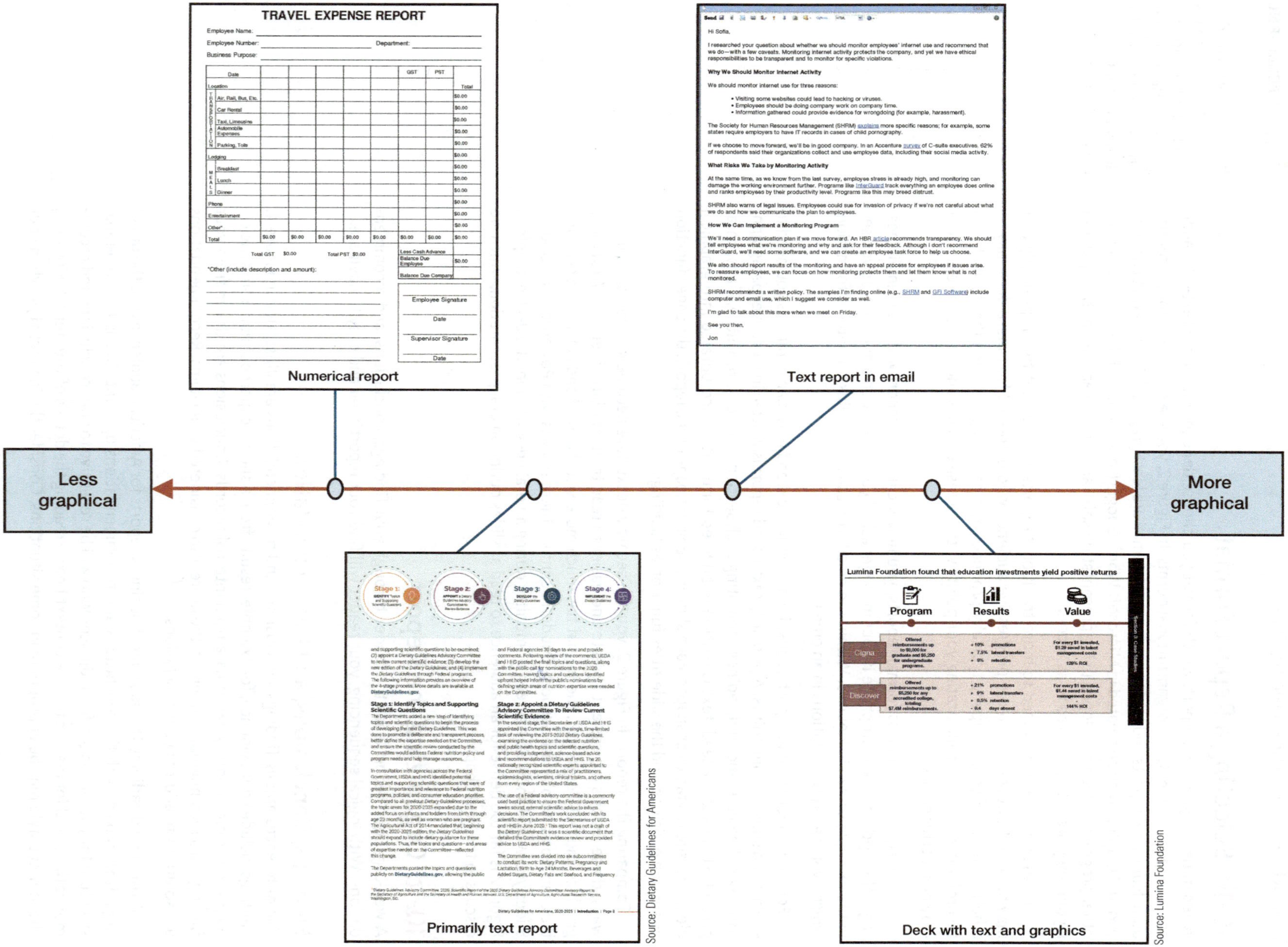

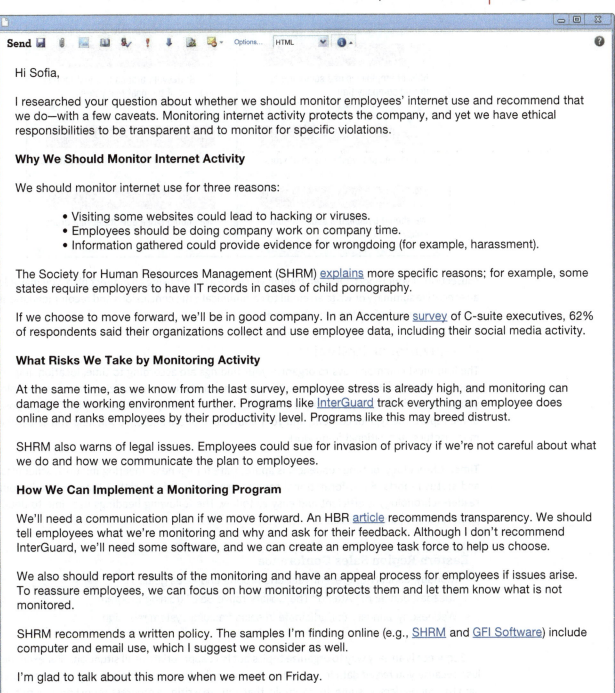

Send Options... HTML

Hi Sofia,

I researched your question about whether we should monitor employees' internet use and recommend that we do—with a few caveats. Monitoring internet activity protects the company, and yet we have ethical responsibilities to be transparent and to monitor for specific violations.

Why We Should Monitor Internet Activity

We should monitor internet use for three reasons:

- Visiting some websites could lead to hacking or viruses.
- Employees should be doing company work on company time.
- Information gathered could provide evidence for wrongdoing (for example, harassment).

The Society for Human Resources Management (SHRM) explains more specific reasons; for example, some states require employers to have IT records in cases of child pornography.

If we choose to move forward, we'll be in good company. In an Accenture survey of C-suite executives, 62% of respondents said their organizations collect and use employee data, including their social media activity.

What Risks We Take by Monitoring Activity

At the same time, as we know from the last survey, employee stress is already high, and monitoring can damage the working environment further. Programs like InterGuard track everything an employee does online and ranks employees by their productivity level. Programs like this may breed distrust.

SHRM also warns of legal issues. Employees could sue for invasion of privacy if we're not careful about what we do and how we communicate the plan to employees.

How We Can Implement a Monitoring Program

We'll need a communication plan if we move forward. An HBR article recommends transparency. We should tell employees what we're monitoring and why and ask for their feedback. Although I don't recommend InterGuard, we'll need some software, and we can create an employee task force to help us choose.

We also should report results of the monitoring and have an appeal process for employees if issues arise. To reassure employees, we can focus on how monitoring protects them and let them know what is not monitored.

SHRM recommends a written policy. The samples I'm finding online (e.g., SHRM and GFI Software) include computer and email use, which I suggest we consider as well.

I'm glad to talk about this more when we meet on Friday.

See you then,

Jon

audience prefers this approach (e.g., some international audiences), when your audience may be resistant to your conclusions and recommendations, or when the topic is so complex that the reader needs detailed explanations to understand your conclusions.

You can use a hybrid approach. For example, instead of putting all the conclusions and recommendations either first or last, you might split them up, discussing each in the appropriate

Figure 4 | Examples of Findings, Conclusions, and Recommendations

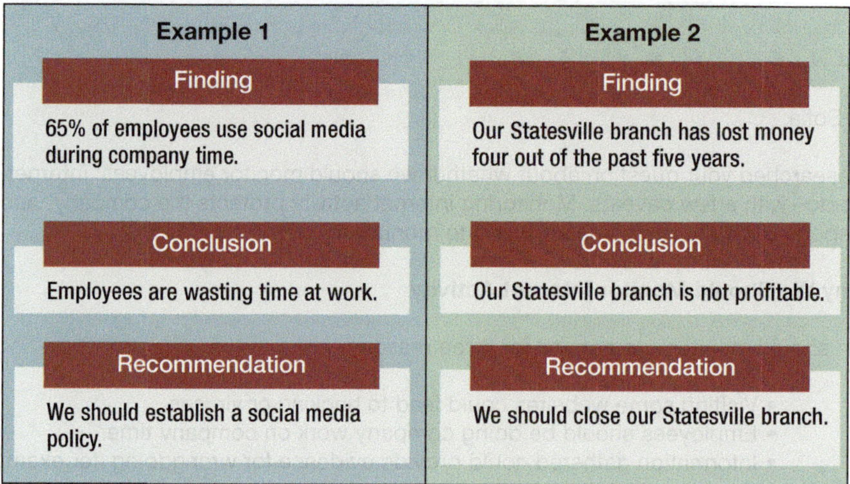

subsection of your report. Or, even though you write a report using an indirect plan, you may add an executive summary or write an email to communicate the conclusions and recommendations to your audience before the report is read.

Example 1
Finding
65% of employees use social media during company time.
Conclusion
Employees are wasting time at work.
Recommendation
We should establish a social media policy.
Example 2
Finding
Our Statesville branch has lost money four out of the past five years.
Conclusion
Our Statesville branch is not profitable.
Recommendation
We should close our Statesville branch.

Organizational Strategies

The four most common ways to organize your findings are according to time, location, importance, and criteria. Of course, you may choose other patterns for organizing data; for example, you can move from the known to the unknown or from the simple to the complex. The purpose of the report, the type of content, and your knowledge of the audience will help you select the most useful organizational framework.

Time. Chronology, or time sequence, is appropriate for agendas, meeting minutes, schedules, and status reports. For informational reports—to simply inform rather than persuade your reader—chronology is efficient and easy to follow. The following headings use time to detail plans for a companywide event.

Eastern Region Sales Conference

- Monday, January 6: Present year-end reports and sales goals.
- Tuesday, January 7: Attend "The Collaborative Sale" training program.
- Wednesday, January 8: Participate in sales tracking system redesign.

Sequence is an easy way to organize topics but isn't appropriate in all situations. For example, just because you *record* data in sequence, it may not be the most efficient way to *present* that data to your readers. Assume, for example, that you are writing a progress report on a recruiting trip you made to four college campuses. The first passage, given in time sequence, is hard to follow and not relevant to the reader.

☒ NOT On Monday morning, I interviewed one candidate for the budget analyst position and two candidates for the junior accountant position. Then, in the afternoon, I interviewed two candidates for the asset manager position and another for the budget analyst position. Finally, on Tuesday, I interviewed another candidate for budget analyst and two for junior accountant.

☑ BUT On Monday and Tuesday, I interviewed three candidates for the budget analyst position, four for the junior accountant position, and two for the asset manager position.

Location. Like time sequence, location as the basis for organizing a report is often appropriate for simple informational reports. Discussing topics according to their geographical or physical location (e.g., describing an office layout) may be the most efficient way to present the data.

The following example uses location to organize the topics; however, the writer is probably using a second variable—for example, time (when the projects will be started or completed) or importance (how much each project will cost). In most cases, you'll use more than one variable for organizing among and within sections.

Renovation Plans for the SAS Dallas Office

- Converting the Cafeteria to Office Space
- Replacing the Roof
- Redecorating the Executive Suite
- Upgrading the Bathroom Facilities

Importance. For the busy reader, the most efficient organizational plan may be to have the most important topic discussed first, followed in order by topics of decreasing importance. The reader then gets the major idea up front and can skim the less important information as desired or needed.

The following example uses level of importance to organize information for a progress report about a renovation.

Progress on SAS Renovation Project

- Renovation Is on Budget
- Time Schedule Has Slipped One Month
- Houston Office Was Added to Project

Criteria. For most analytical and recommendation reports, for which the purpose is to analyze the data, draw conclusions, and recommend a solution, the most logical arrangement is by criteria. For these reports, you may develop a hypothesis and break down recommendations or causes of a problem. The following example uses criteria against which the writer evaluates consultants.

Selecting a Consultant for the Communication Audit

- Although the Most Expensive, Bain Offers the Most Depth
- Deloitte Has Experience with the Northeast Region
- Boston Consulting Group Is the Least Expensive Option

By focusing attention on the criteria—in this case, cost and experience—you lead the reader to the same conclusion you reached. This strategy is another good option if your reader might be resistant to your recommendations.

LO2 Describe typical components of a business report.

10-2 Drafting the Report

Even if you spent months collecting data, your final report is the only way your audience knows how much time and effort you dedicated to the project. Your skillful data analysis will be lost unless your written report explains the significance of your data and helps the reader reach a decision or solve a problem.

Everything you learned about the writing process applies directly to report writing: choosing a productive work environment, scheduling a reasonable block of time, letting ideas flow quickly during the drafting stage, and leaving time for revising. However, report writing requires several additional considerations when creating report sections and drafting the body and supplementary sections.

10-2a Creating Report Sections

At some point, you'll decide on the major and minor sections of your report. As for any business writing, you might find an outline or mind map useful to help you plan which points are to be covered, in what order they will be covered, and how the topics relate to the rest of the report.

Create a working draft of headings and subheadings that will help orient your reader and give your report unity and coherence. Use any combination of multilevel numbers, letters, or bullets. As you write the report, you'll refine the wording and decide how many you'll need. Next, you learn ways to choose descriptive, logical headings.

Generic Headings and Message Titles

Imagine reading proposals from four energy auditors about your company's property. Each wants to sell you energy-saving solutions, such as a new heating system or new windows. "Benefits," "Costs," and "Implementation" explain major sections of the reports, but they're hardly descriptive—and they do nothing to distinguish one report from the others. These are generic headings, which identify only the topic of a section without giving the conclusion.

Message titles (or talking headings), unlike generic headings, identify the main points of a report section or deck page. Also used in newspapers and magazines, descriptive headings allow the reader to skim an article for the most important ideas.

You might use generic headings if you didn't want to reveal your main points, as in these examples about the energy audit:

- Decreasing Heat Loss
- Upgrading Exterior Features
- Improving Efficiency

Now compare the previous headings to these message titles, which convey the main points but might scare the client because of perceived costs:

- Insulating the Walls and Attic Will Decrease Heat Loss
- Replacing the Windows and Doors Will Reduce Air Leaks and Improve Appearance
- Installing an Efficient Furnace Will Reduce Fuel Costs

Read the entire Valex tuition report—and slides for an oral presentation for comparison—in the Reference Manual.

When you read message titles across a report, including slide titles in decks, you understand the entire argument. The headings in Figure 5 are for a report recommending a college tuition assistance program. When you write page titles in decks, check that each page conveys one well-supported point and that the title (like a topic sentence for a paragraph) covers the entire idea on the page but doesn't mention points that aren't supported.

Parallelism

Although full sentences are the most descriptive message titles, you may phrase your headings in a variety of ways. Consider using phrases (e.g., Saving Heating Costs by Replacing Windows) or questions (e.g., How Much Will Replacing Windows Save?).

Figure 5 Message Titles Convey an Argument

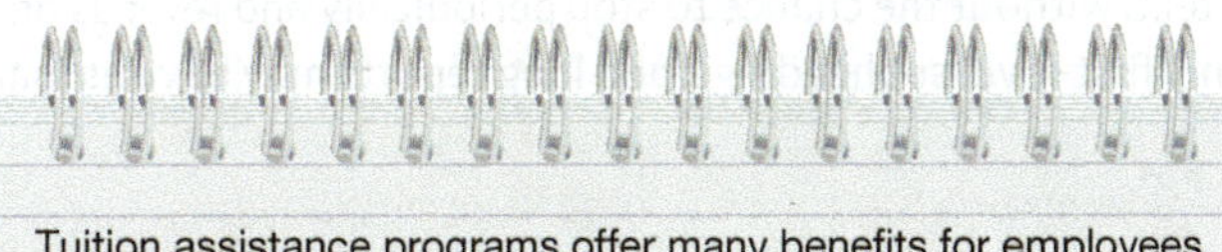

- Tuition assistance programs offer many benefits for employees
- Tuition assistance programs offer many benefits for employers
- Turnover is costly, but tuition assistance programs are not
- Most Valex employees are educated, but we can increase numbers
- Lumina Foundation found positive returns at Cigna and Discover
- Our competitors already offer tuition reimbursement programs
- The proposal includes reimbursement for approved degree programs
- Valex will partner with colleges to create tailored programs

Whichever form of heading you select, be consistent within each level of heading. If the first major heading (a first-level heading) is a full sentence, all first-level headings should be full sentences. As you move from level to level, you may switch to another form of heading if this works better, but all headings within the same level and section should be parallel for more logical, easier reading. See Figure 6 for an example from a report about Snapchat.

Figure 6 Parallel Headings in a Report

Improving Snapchat's Reputation: Table of Contents

Introduction 1
Snapchat Responding to Public Backlash Regarding Privacy 1
- Third-Party Applications Hack and Deceive Snapchat's Servers 1
  - Nude Photograph Leak 1
  - User Information Leak 2
- FTC Reviews Snapchat's Privacy Policy 3

Snapchat Improving Its Reputation 4
- Publicly Apologize for Hacks 4
- Inform Users of Updated Privacy Policy 6
- Market Snapchat Appropriately 7
- Prevent Screenshots and Third-Party Hacks 8
  - Research Different Methods 8
  - Invest in Testing Different Methods 8

Length and Number of Headings

For either a text report or a slide deck, full-sentence message titles may be quite long. As a title for a deck page, a sentence can span two lines. Four to eight words is about the right length for most headings but focus more on conveying meaning than on word count.

Similarly, choose an appropriate number of headings. Including too many headings weakens the unity of a report—they chop the report up too much, making it look more like an outline than a reasoned analysis. Having too few headings, however, overwhelms the reader with an entire page of solid text, without the chance to stop periodically and refocus on the topic. Short reports may have only first-level subheadings, and long reports may have as many as four levels of headings.

Balance

Maintain a sense of balance within and among sections. Other than introductions and conclusions, it would be unusual to give one section of a report five subsections and give the following section none. Similarly, it would be unusual to have one section five pages long and another section only half a page long. Also, ensure that the most important ideas appear in the highest levels of headings. For example, if you are discussing four criteria for a topic, all four should be in the same level of heading—most logically in first-level headings.

When you divide a section into subsections, it must have at least two subsections. You cannot logically have just one second-level heading within a section because when you divide something, it divides into more than one part.

10-2b Drafting the Body

The report body consists of the introduction, findings, and summary or conclusion. As stated earlier, the conclusions may be presented first—and for recommendation reports, they are presented up front in an executive summary.

Introduction

The introduction sets the stage for understanding the findings that follow. In the University of Maryland football report, the introduction includes university history, the role of football in university life, and National Collegiate Athletic Association (NCAA) principles.

The topics and amount of detail in an introduction vary according to the type and complexity of the report and the audience's needs. Decks omit the introduction entirely, merging this information into the executive summary or the first page of the deck.

Findings

Discuss and interpret relevant primary and secondary data you gathered—your evidence. Using objective language, present the information clearly, concisely, and accurately. The Maryland report provides detail about several incidents, which are itemized in the table of contents, for example, "Player Removed from Meeting for Smiling" and "Player Compelled to Eat Candy Bars."[7] These are jarring to read but set the tone for objective reporting from interviews.

Within the body, most reports include data visualizations. The information in these displays should be self-explanatory; that is, readers should understand them without having to refer to the text. At the same time, you should refer to and explain all tables and figures so that the text, too, is self-explanatory.

Label all your charts in a report as *figures*, and assign them consecutive numbers, as you see throughout this book. In a formal report, table numbers are labeled separately (not in sequence with figures) and are captioned at the top, while charts may be captioned at the top or bottom.

Give enough interpretation to help the reader comprehend the table or figure, but don't repeat all the information it contains. Discuss data most relevant to your main points, describing important items, implications, trends, contradictions, unexpected findings, and similarities and differences. The text in Figure 7, from a report on dietary guidelines,[8] explains the data by comparing consumption levels to recommended intake.

Explaining a Graphic | **Figure 7**

stevemart/Shutterstock.com

Figure 4-4

Average Intakes of Subgroups Compared to Recommended Intake Ranges: Ages 31 Through 59

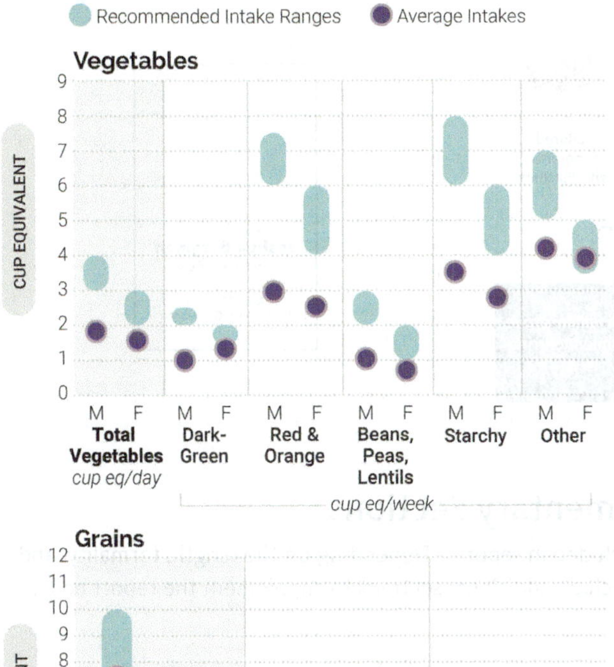

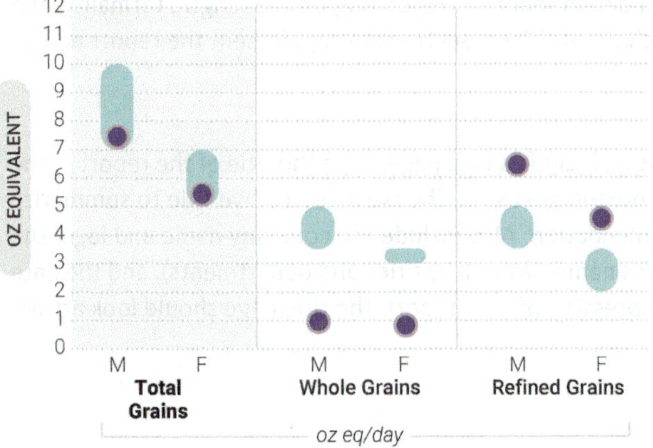

Average intakes of fruits, vegetables, and dairy fall below the range of recommended intakes for all adults. Although average total grains intakes meets recommendations, **Figures 4-2** and **4-4** show that intake of whole grains is well below recommendations, and intakes of refined grains exceeds the upper end of the recommended intake range for adults in both age groups. Intakes of protein foods generally meets or exceeds recommended intake levels. Current patterns generally include meats, poultry, eggs, and nuts, seeds, and soy, while average intake of seafood falls well below recommendations. Beans, peas, and lentils—a subgroup of both the vegetable and protein foods groups—also are underconsumed by most adults.

Figures 4-1 and **4-3** show that adults are exceeding recommendations for added sugars, saturated fat, and sodium. About 60 percent of men and 65 percent of women exceed the limit for intakes of added sugars. This is an average daily intake of about 330 calories from added sugars for men and around 250 calories for women.

Source: Dietary Guidelines for Americans

Avoid presenting so many facts and figures that the reader is overwhelmed with data. How much is too much? Be sure to make the transition from your extensive work on the project to how much information the reader needs to draw conclusions and make a decision.

Summary and Conclusions

The length of your summary depends on the length and complexity of the report. A two-page report may need only a one-paragraph summary. Longer or more complex reports, however, should include a more extensive summary. You may briefly review the issues and provide an overview of the major findings.

If your report only analyzes the information presented and does not make recommendations, you might label the final section of the report "Summary" or "Summary and Conclusions." If your report includes both conclusions and recommendations, ensure that the conclusions stem directly from your findings and that the recommendations stem directly from the conclusions. Either way, end your report with a clear concluding statement. Don't leave your reader wondering if more pages will follow.

For recommendation reports, such as proposals, the summary briefly repeats conclusions or recommendations presented in the executive summary at the beginning. The Valex tuition assistance deck ends with a summary of why the program is worthwhile (Figure 8).

Figure 8 | Summary Page for the Tuition Assistance Deck

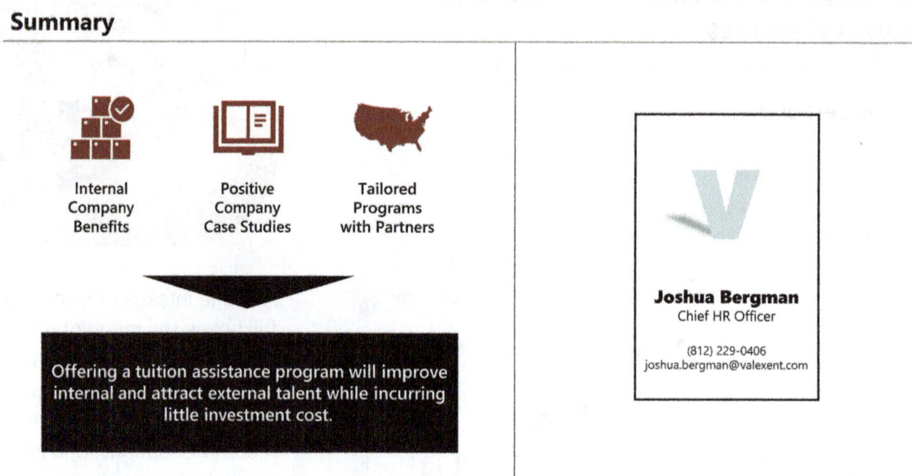

10-2c Drafting Supplementary Sections

What additional components are included in reports? Depending on the length, formality, and complexity of the report, you may include additional sections to supplement the report body.

Title Page

For reports longer than about two pages, include a title page. Type the title of the report in the largest font size and a subtitle in the next-largest size. Choose a descriptive title to summarize the main point, conclusion, or recommendation. Also include the company name and logo, the writer's name (and perhaps the reader's name—as well as titles and departments), and the date the report was written. As the first impression of your report, the title page should look attractive and inviting to read.

Cover Note

Include a cover note with longer reports. Most typically, this will be an email with the report attached. Consider saving your report as a PDF before attaching it to an email to preserve your formatting and reduce the chance of changes.

In your cover note, provide a summary of the report. State up front that the report is attached, and provide background information, for example, that the report responds to a request. Perhaps give an overview of the conclusions and recommendations of the report (unless you want the reader to read your evidence first); this is a short, more conversational, personal version of your executive summary. Briefly discuss any other information that will help the reader understand and make use of the report (e.g., "The report covers data through March; when we receive financials for April, we'll send an update"). Include a goodwill ending, for example, "Thank you for the opportunity to present this proposal. We enjoyed the process and hope we can continue to work together" or "If you want to discuss the report in detail, let's schedule time next week."

Executive Summary

An executive summary, similar to an abstract in an academic report, is a condensed version of the body of the report (including introduction, findings, and any conclusions or recommendations). Although some readers may scan the entire report, most will read the executive summary carefully—and some will read *only* the executive summary. Some companies that conduct original research make an executive summary of a report publicly available, while charging a hefty fee (e.g., $2,500) for the detailed findings.

The executive summary is an optional part of the report, most commonly used for long reports. Because it saves the reader time, this part should be short—no more than 10% of the entire report. Think of the executive summary as a standalone document: assume that the reader will not read the whole report, so include as much useful information as possible.

Figure 9 shows the executive summary for the tuition assistance report. For comparison, the executive summary of the University of Maryland report is 15 pages, which seems long but is less than 10% of the 192-page total.

Executive Summary of the Tuition Assistance Deck | **Figure 9**

Executive Summary

Proposal: Offer a tuition assistance program consisting of tuition reimbursement and tailored college programs.

Creating positive employee sentiment and return on investment

Because employees understand that companies invest in them, they reciprocate with increased satisfaction and loyalty. Employees participating in tuition assistance programs benefit from increased wage gains and knowledge and skills to better execute their jobs. Valex benefits from reduced turnover and increased employee retention, saving potential losses in labor value. Additionally, Valex may write off up to a **$5,250 tax deduction per year per employee** for tuition reimbursement. With minimal investment costs, Valex can decrease talent management costs and increase employee value.

Examining programs and results from other companies

Companies have seen a positive return on investment when offering these programs. They have seen higher rates of retention, promotion, and lateral transfers while avoiding talent management costs. Studies by the Lumina Foundation found **return on investments of 129% and 144%** for Cigna and Discover, respectively. Tuition assistance programs are already offered by most companies across the country, and even more offer professional development programs. Many of Valex's competitors, including AT&T, Apple, Comcast, and Disney, already offer tuition assistance and/or company-tailored college programs. Implementing a program with low cost will improve internal talent development and external competitiveness.

Implementing a tuition reimbursement and college program plan

With the many benefits of a tuition assistance program, Valex should offer a program consisting of tuition reimbursement and college partnerships. All employees will be offered up to $5,250 in tuition reimbursement. Valex will **partner with four colleges** (Santa Clara University, UCLA, NYU, and American University) to create specific, tailored programs built for our employees. Employees may earn bachelor's and master's degrees in business administration, computer science, digital media, and engineering, among others. Developing partnerships with reputable universities will entice employees looking to offset education costs while gaining fundamental knowledge to improve their work—and their career prospects.

Section 1: Executive Summary

1

Table of Contents

Long reports with many headings and subheadings benefit from a table of contents. Use the same wording in the table of contents that you use in the body of the report. Typically, only two or three levels of headings are included in the table of contents—even if more levels are used in the body of the report. Include a list of tables and figures for formal reports but not in slide decks.

Page numbers in the table of contents, as you saw in Figure 6, identify where each section begins. You may find it useful to automate the pagination in a program such as Microsoft Word. This way, the page numbers in the table of contents automatically update as you edit the report.

Appendix

You may include supplementary information or documents in an appendix at the end of a report. For example, you might include a questionnaire used to collect data, detailed calculations, or additional tables helpful to the reader but not important enough to include in the body of the report. Label each appendix separately, by letter—for example, "Appendix A: Questionnaire" and "Appendix B: Calculations." In the body of the report, refer by letter to any items placed in an appendix.

References

The reference list contains all secondary sources cited in the report. The reference list for the tuition assistance report is shown in Figure 10. For a printed report, you may remove the hyperlinks to web addresses and keep the plain text.

Figure 10 | Reference Page for the Tuition Assistance Deck

References

"Amazon Career Choice," Amazon, www.amazoncareerchoice.com/home, accessed November 19, 2021.

Peter Cappelli, "Why Do Employers Pay for College?" *Journal of Econometrics* 121 (2004): 213–241, http://dx.doi.org/10.1016/j.jeconom.2003.10.014.

Courtney Connley, "10 Companies That Will Help Pay Your Tuition," *CNBC*, November 14, 2017, www.cnbc.com/2017/11/14/10-companies-that-will-help-pay-your-tuition.html, accessed November 15, 2021.

"Disney Invests in Employees' Futures with Unprecedented Education Program," The Walt Disney Company, February 5, 2019, thewaltdisneycompany.com/disney-invests-in-employees-futures-with-unprecedented-education-program, December 15, 2021.

Lindsay Northon, "2016 Human Capital Benchmarking Report," Society for Human Resource Management, November 2016, https://www.shrm.org/hr-today/trends-and-forecasting/research-and-surveys/Documents/2016-Human-Capital-Report.pdf, accessed December 2, 2021.

Bridget Perry, "New Study Shows the Lasting Impact of Tuition Assistance," *Business Wire*, January 8, 2018, www.businesswire.com/news/home/20180108006550/en/New-Study-Shows-the-Lasting-Impact-of-Tuition-Assistance, accessed November 15, 2021.

"Talent Investments Pay Off: Cigna's ROI from Tuition Benefits," Lumina Foundation, April 2, 2016, www.luminafoundation.org/resource/talent-investments-pay-off/, accessed November 15, 2021.

"Talent Investments Pay Off (Discover Financial Services)," Lumina Foundation, November 30, 2016, www.luminafoundation.org/resource/talent-investments-pay-off-discover-financial-services/, accessed December 14, 2021.

Tim Stobierski, "Average Salary by Education Level: Value of a College Degree," Northeastern University, June 2, 2020, www.northeastern.edu/bachelors-completion/news/average-salary-by-education-level/, accessed December 15, 2021.

"Weighing the Pros and Cons of Offering Tuition Assistance for Your Employees," Brandman University, August 27, 2019, www.brandman.edu/news-and-events/blog/weighing-the-pros-and-cons-of-offering-tuition-assistance-for-your-employees, accessed November 11, 2021.

3

A good indication of a report writer's scholarship is the accuracy of the reference list—in terms of both content and format—so proofread this part of your report carefully.

10-3 Developing an Effective Writing Style

LO3 Explain how the writing style for a report may differ from other types of writing.

An effective writing style will improve how well your report is received. Writing principles from Chapters 4 and 5 apply, and a few more guidelines will ensure that your report is professional and easily read.

10-3a Tone

Depending on the context, you still may use your professional, natural writing style. For example, the report about the University of Maryland football program is serious, but the stilted language is unnecessary:

☒ NOT This report is the result of an investigation of the University of Maryland football program conducted by an eight-person commission reporting to the school's board of regents.[9]

☑ BUT An eight-person commission investigated the University of Maryland football program and submitted this report to the school's board of regents.

In the original version, the hidden noun *investigation* hides the perfectly good verb *investigate* and causes wordiness. Active voice also improves the sentence.

At the same time, the writing style for a report is typically more objective than in an email. Avoid colloquial expressions, attempts at humor, subjectivity, bias, and exaggeration.

☒ NOT The company *hit the jackpot* with its new MRP program.

☑ BUT The new MRP program saved the company $125,000 in the first year.

☒ NOT He *claimed* that half his projects involved name-brand advertising.

☑ BUT He stated that half his projects involved name-brand advertising.

10-3b Pronouns

Reports tend to focus on the information rather than on the writer. Where you can, use third-person pronouns and avoid using *I*, *we*, and *you*. However, if your perspective is emphasized, or if using *you* improves the readability of the report, you may use these pronouns, particularly for less formal reports.

You can avoid the awkward substitute "the writer" by revising the sentence. Most often, the reader knows that the writer is the person doing the action.

Informal: I recommend that the project be canceled.

Awkward: The writer recommends that the project be canceled.

Formal: The project should be canceled.

Using the passive voice is a common device for avoiding the use of *I* in formal reports but doing so weakens the impact. Instead, revise some sentences to avoid overusing the passive voice.

Informal: I interviewed Jan Smith.

Passive: Jan Smith was interviewed.

Formal: In a personal interview, Jan Smith stated . . .

10-3c Verb Tense

Use the verb tense (past, present, or future) that is appropriate at the time the reader *reads* the report—not necessarily when you *wrote* the report. Use past tense to describe procedures and to describe the findings of other studies already completed but use present tense for conclusions from those studies.

When possible, use the stronger present tense to explain the data from your study. You can assume that your findings continue to be true—if your findings are no longer true, then you probably should not use them in the report.

☒ NOT These findings *were based* on interviews with 62 football fans.

☑ BUT These findings *are based* on interviews with 62 football fans.

☒ NOT All managers *believed* the annual meeting *was* effective.

☑ BUT All managers *believe* the annual meeting *is* effective.

Procedure: Nearly 500 people *responded* to this survey.

Findings: Only 11% of the managers *received* any specific training on the new procedure.

Conclusion: Most managers *do not receive* any specific training on the new procedures.

10-3d Emphasis and Subordination

Wouldn't it be nice if all your data pointed to one conclusion? That rarely happens—and if it does, you might question the accuracy of your data. More likely, you'll have a mix of data and will have to evaluate the relative merits of each point for your reader. To help your reader understand how important you view each point, use emphasis and subordination techniques when discussing your findings. Consider an excerpt from a research report and how the authors show the relative importance of their findings (Figure 11).[10]

Figure 11 | How Authors Use Emphasis and Subordination

A sixth of cell phone owners have bumped into someone or something while using their handhelds.

Of the 82% of American adults who own cell phones, fully 17% say they have bumped into another person or an object because they were distracted by talking or texting on their mobile phones. That amounts to 14% of all American adults who have been so engrossed in talking, texting, or otherwise using their cell phones that they bumped into something or someone.

Devote an appropriate amount of space to a topic.

This section (with two more paragraphs) takes up only one-third of a page. Data about cell phone distractions while driving fill the remaining 3.5 pages of the findings section of the report.

Position your major ideas first for the direct plan.

This section appears last in the report, after the more dangerous cell phone behaviors.

Use language that directly tells what is more and less important.

Words such as "fully" express the authors' view of the data. Without this emphasis, the reader might interpret 17% to be a smaller number.

Use emphasis and subordination to let the reader know what you consider most and least important—but not to inappropriately sway the reader. If the data honestly leads to a strong, definite conclusion, then make your conclusion strong and definite. But if the data permits only a tentative conclusion, then say so.

Also avoid overstating conclusions by using weak descriptions. Words such as *plethora*, *constantly*, and *countless* are inaccurate and could make your reader question your results—or worse, distrust you personally.

10-3e Coherence

One of the difficulties of writing any long document—especially when the document is drafted in sections and then put together—is making the finished product read smoothly and coherently, like a unified presentation rather than a cut-and-paste job. The problem is even greater for team-written reports.

One way to achieve coherence in a report is to use previews, summaries, and transitions. At the beginning of each major section, preview what is discussed in that section. At the conclusion of each major section, summarize what was presented and provide a smooth transition to the next topic. For long sections, the preview, summary, and transition might each be a separate paragraph; for short sections, a sentence might suffice.

Note how preview, summary, and transition are used in the following example of a report section opening and closing.

> **Training System Users**
>
> The training program can be evaluated in two ways: user opinion and training cost as a percentage of total system costs. . . . *(After this topic preview, several paragraphs follow that discuss the users' opinions and the cost of the training program.)*
>
> Even though a slight majority of users now feel competent in using the system, the training falls far short of the 20% of total system cost recommended by experts. This low level of training may have caused the high rate of system errors. *(The first sentence summarizes this section, and the second provides a transition to the next.)*

Don't depend on your heading structure for coherence. Your report should read smoothly and coherently without the headings. For variety and to reflect a sophisticated writing style, avoid repeating the exact words of the heading in the subsequent narrative.

☒ NOT **The finance and accounting departments should be merged.** The reason is that there is a duplication of services.

☑ BUT **The finance and accounting departments should be merged.** Merging the two departments will eliminate the duplication of services.

Always introduce a topic before dividing it into subtopics. You should never have one heading following another without some intervening text; these are called stacked headings. (The exception to this guideline is that the heading "Introduction" may be used immediately after the report title or subtitle.) Instead, use a section overview to preview for the reader how the topic will be divided before you actually make the division. Section overviews also highlight main points to follow. Compare the stacked headings and section overview in Figure 12.

Avoiding Stacked Headings with a Section Overview | **Figure 12**

Stacked headings lack introductory text for a section.

> **Selecting a Consultant for the Communication Audit**
>
> ***Although the Most Expensive, McKinsey Offers the Most Depth***
> text text text text text text text text text text text text text text text text
>
> ***Deloitte Has Experience with the Northeast Region***
> text text text text text text text text text text text text text text text text
>
> ***BCG Is the Least Expensive Option***
> text text text text text text text text text text text text text text text text

Section overviews highlight main points covered under subheadings.

> **Selecting a Consultant for the Communication Audit**
>
> McKinsey is the best choice for the communication audit. Competitors Deloitte and BCG offer advantages, but McKinsey has the most depth in this area.
>
> ***Although the Most Expensive, McKinsey Offers the Most Depth***
> text text text text text text text text text text text text text text text text
>
> ***Deloitte Has Experience with the Northeast Region***
> text text text text text text text text text text text text text text text text
>
> ***BCG Is the Least Expensive Option***
> text text text text text text text text text text text text text text text text

LO4 Format a footnote to cite a given source.

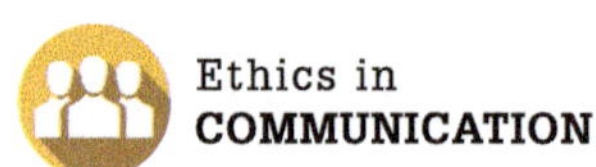

CHARACTER

10-4 Documenting Your Sources

When you write a report, you'll include information from other sources that must be documented. Unless you identify a source, your audience will assume all ideas are your own. Citing original work is a sign of good character—and good work. Documenting your sources will save you from embarrassment and potentially worse consequences: at school, you may violate a code of academic integrity, and at work, you may lose credibility and, in some situations, your job.

10-4a Why We Document Sources

At the Republican National Convention where her husband was nominated for president of the United States, Melania Trump gave a speech that was plagiarized. Within a one-minute segment, about 50% of the content was the same as First Lady Michelle Obama's speech when her husband was nominated for president.[11] A speechwriter took responsibility for the mistake.[12]

When writing for business audiences, we document sources for several reasons:

- To avoid accusations of plagiarism
- To give credit to the originator of information
- To demonstrate the validity of our work with credible sources
- To instruct readers where to find additional information.

Ethics in COMMUNICATION

International COMMUNICATION

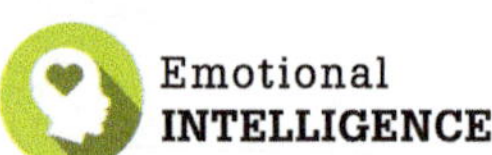

Emotional INTELLIGENCE

What's your view of documenting sources? Do you find it important, an inconvenience, or something else?

Plagiarism means using another person's words or ideas without giving proper credit. Although every country has different laws regarding the use of others' written work, in the United States, copyright and other laws provide clear guidance of how we treat writers' words—as legal property. Using words without permission or acknowledgment is considered theft. With search engines and programs like Turnitin, plagiarism is easily caught.

Documentation means identifying sources by giving credit to others, either in the text or in a reference list, for using their words or ideas. For many business reports, secondary information may be the *only* data you use. This is entirely acceptable, but you must provide appropriate documentation whenever you quote, paraphrase, or summarize someone else's work.

10-4b What Must Be Documented

All content from secondary sources (information or ideas that aren't your own) must be documented: articles, books, website content, blogs, quotations, graphics, interviews, and so on. However, you do not need to cite information considered common knowledge, for example, "Customer satisfaction is important in the retail industry," or information that is easily verifiable, for example, "Allen Zhang led the development of WeChat." If in doubt, it's always safer to provide a reference.

Most of your references to secondary data should be in the form of paraphrases. A **paraphrase** is a summary or restatement of a passage in your own words. A **direct quotation**, on the other hand, contains the exact words of someone else. Use direct quotations (always enclosed in quotation marks) for definitions or for text written in a unique way that is not easily paraphrased.

Paraphrasing involves more than just rearranging words or leaving out a word or two. Instead, try to understand the writer's idea and then restate it in your own language. When you paraphrase, change the sentence structure, and do not use any three consecutive words from the original source, unless the words represent, for example, a company name that cannot be changed.

Avoid online tools that paraphrase for you. Figure 13 shows original text about a woman who falsified her qualifications to get a job.[13] The middle column shows a revision, but the writing is terrible—clunky and still too similar to the original, including four identical words at the end. The last column omits the timing because the human decides that this isn't relevant to the story; instead, the emphasis is on her mental health issues. The human keeps "mental health" because "psychological well-being" is not a suitable substitute. Both human examples change the sentence subject and structure.

Poorly Paraphrased Text from an Online Tool | **Figure 13**

Original text	Her case became suspicious to the department after her mental health deteriorated shortly after she started working in the position.
Paraphrased text by an online tool	Her case got dubious to the office after her psychological well-being disintegrated not long after she began working in the position.
Paraphrased text by a human	When department managers noticed mental health issues, they questioned her job qualifications. OR After the employee suffered increasing mental health issues, her initial application came into question.

Although all secondary sources must be documented, unpublished sources (e.g., not in a journal or on a website) do not need a formal citation. Instead, provide enough text to explain the source, as in these examples.

> According to the company's "Phone Use Policy," the company "has the right to monitor calls not made within normal business hours."
>
> The contractor's letter stated, "We agree to modify Blueprint 3884 by widening the southeast entrance from 10 to 12 feet for an additional charge."

Occasionally, you can provide enough information in the narrative so that a formal citation is unnecessary even for published sources. This format is most appropriate when only one or two sources are used in a report.

> In her seminal book *The Death and Life of Great American Cities*, Jane Jacobs opposed urban planning approaches that disregarded neighborhood residents.

After you cite a source once, you may mention it again on the same or even on the next page without another citation, as long as the reference is clear.

10-4c How to Document Sources

The three major forms for documenting sources in a business report are footnotes, endnotes, and author-date references. The method you select depends on organizational norms, the formality of the report, the audience—and, for school reports, your instructor's guidelines.

Footnotes and Endnotes

Footnotes and endnotes are the business standard for documenting sources. For writers, footnotes and endnotes are easy to create in programs like Microsoft Word; for readers, footnotes are easy to view because they appear on the same page as the referenced text. Endnotes follow the same format as footnotes but simply shift the reference to the end of the paper. This is useful when you have so many footnotes on one page that your text is dwarfed by the citations. In this case, endnotes are preferable for better design and easier reading. When you use footnotes, you do not need a separate bibliography or reference page.

Although footnotes are ideal for text-based reports, they tend to clutter slide design in PowerPoint decks. For these graphical reports, you may include a separate reference page. To connect your slide content to a source, use descriptive text, for example, "According to PKF's lodging report . . ."

Footnotes appear as superscript text at the end of each sentence—or part of a sentence—that requires a citation. If one source is used for an entire paragraph, you do not need to add a footnote after each sentence; instead, you may use only one footnote at the end of the paragraph. Footnotes appear after all punctuation, as shown below.

> SeaWorld and Southwest ended their promotional partnership, which began in 1988. The joint press release describes the reason as "shifting priorities,"[11] but news articles blame backlash from the movie *Blackfish*.[12]

To appropriately describe a source, use the guidelines in Figure 14. These guidelines are recommended by Harvard Business School and are a simpler variation of those recommended by *The Chicago Manual of Style*. This is an easy way to identify the author, title of the work,

Figure 14 | How to Format Sources in Footnotes

TYPE OF REFERENCE MATERIAL	HOW TO FORMAT THE FOOTNOTE	NOTES/ALTERNATIVES
Article from a periodical	Alex M. Susskind and Peggy R. Odom-Reed, "Team Members' Centrality, Cohesion, Conflict, and Performance in Multi-University Geographically Distributed Project Teams," *Communication Research* 46 (2019): 151–178.	Although some academic citation formats suggest including the database you used to find articles (e.g., Factiva or ProQuest), this is not necessary for footnoting in business writing.
Article from a newspaper accessed online	Shivani Vora, "An Enduring Paris Hotel in a New Light," *The New York Times*, June 1, 2018, www.nytimes.com/2018/06/01/travel/lutetia-hotel-paris-reopening.html, accessed March 2, 2022.	If you retrieved this article from the print newspaper, include the section and page number instead of the website and accessed date.
Article from a website	Vaughan Rouesnel, "Don't We All Just Want to Use SQL on the Frontend?" Medium, April 16, 2021, https://vjpr.medium.com/dont-we-all-just-want-to-use-sql-on-the-frontend-6b9d38c08146, accessed April 17, 2022.	To save space, you may shorten URLs to include only the main site reference (including ".com" in this case), as long as the reader can find the original source easily. If an article doesn't identify an author, simply start with the title.
Book	Richard H. Penner, Lawrence Adams, and Stephani Robson, *Hotel Design, Planning, and Development*, 2nd edition (New York: Routledge, 2013).	For books and articles with more than three authors, include only the first author's name, followed by "et al.," to mean "and others."
Class discussion notes	Katherine Morley, "Services as Experiences," ACCT 209 class discussion, April 19, 2022, Drury University, Springfield, MO.	To cite PPT slides or handouts, simply replace "class discussion" with the name of the source material.
Personal conversations or interviews	Khalil Bey, Drury, MO, August 2, 2022.	Another variation may be, "Khalil Bey, phone interview by author, August 2, 2022."
Tweet	Missouri State (@MissouriState), "Featuring this incredible man as Pacha. #GoMaroon," Twitter, April 13, 2021, https://twitter.com/MissouriState/status/1382057311368224770, accessed August 2, 2021.	If you include the entire tweet within your text, you can omit the quoted tweet in your footnote. Click on the tweet to find the URL.
Website content	Marriott International, Inc., "Who We Support," Marriott company website, www.marriott.com, accessed April 22, 2022.	Providing the date accessed is particularly important for content that exists only online because pages may be moved or removed. You also may include the time if the site changes frequently.

publication, date, and other information to tell your reader that your source is credible and retrievable. If your source material isn't included in this chart, use a format that mirrors these, or you can find additional guidelines in the most recent *Harvard Business School Citation Guide*.[14]

Author-Date Format

For the author-date format, the writer inserts the last name of the author and the year of publication in parentheses, for example, (Yuan, 2020). Complete bibliographic information is then included in the References section at the end of the report. More typically used for American Psychological Association (APA) and Modern Language Association (MLA) formats, these in-text citations tend to interrupt the flow of a paragraph.

10-4d How to Avoid Distortion by Omission

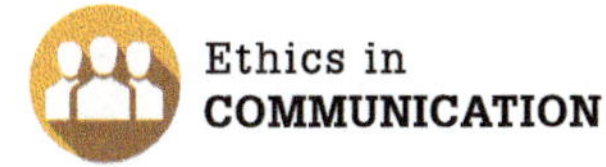

It would be unethical to leave an inaccurate impression, even when what you do report is true. Distortion by omission occurs when using quotations out of context, omitting relevant background information, or including only interesting or favorable data (cherry-picking). For example, it would be inappropriate to include one employee's comment from a company review site and imply that this view represents how all employees feel.

Be especially careful to quote and paraphrase accurately from interview sources. Provide enough information to ensure that the passage reflects the interviewee's *intention*. Examples of possible distortions are in Figure 15.

Distortions of an Interview Statement | **Figure 15**

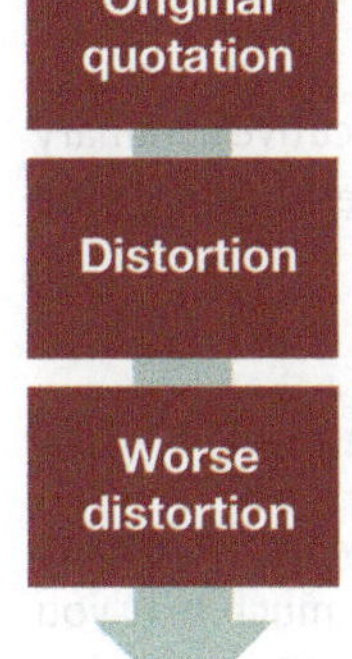

"I think the Boxster is an excellent car for anyone who does not need to worry about fuel economy."

Johnson stated that the Boxster "is an excellent car."

Johnson stated that the Boxster "is an excellent car for anyone."

10-5 Designing, Formatting, and Refining the Report

LO5 Distinguish design and formatting guidelines for slide decks from other types of reports.

A well-designed and formatted report improves how easily the reader understands your information. The last step is refining it: revising the text and proofreading. We discuss principles for text-based reports and slide decks.

10-5a Designing and Formatting Text-Based Reports

When creating a report that is primarily text, for example, in Microsoft Word, you'll incorporate graphics to complement text and increase visual appeal; choose spacing and fonts for easier reading; and use headers, footers, and page numbers for clear organization.

Graphics

Typically place a table or figure immediately *below* the first paragraph that describes the graphic. This provides readers with your interpretation before they see the illustration. Refer to the number (e.g., Figure 3 or Table 4), and be careful with phrases such as "as shown below" because the table or figure might actually appear at the top of the following page.

Avoid splitting a table or figure between two pages. If not enough space is available on the page for the display, continue with the narrative to the bottom of the page and then place the display at the top of the following page.

Spacing and Fonts

Spacing and fonts make your report easier to read. Use a two-inch top margin for the first page of each special part (e.g., the table of contents, the executive summary, the first page of the body of the report, and the first page of the reference list). Leave a one-inch top margin for all other pages and at least a one-inch bottom and side margin on all pages.

Business reports are typically single-spaced. Although you may indent at the beginning of paragraphs, this is not necessary. Instead, left-justify all paragraphs with one line space between paragraphs.

Use a standard business font and size, for example, Times New Roman 12, Arial 10, or Calibri 11. With different fonts, colors, or enhancements (e.g., bold or italic), make sure that the reader can easily distinguish between major and minor headings.

Headers, Footers, and Page Numbers

Typically, business reports have the report title (and perhaps the subtitle) and page number in either the header or footer of body pages. Some reports may include the date, the name of the writer or organization, or a copyright notice. Whether these appear in the header or footer depends on organizational standards and your preference.

Preliminary pages may take lowercase Roman numerals; for example, the executive summary might be page ii and the table of contents might be page iii. Then, Arabic numbers begin on the first page of the report body.

10-5b Designing and Formatting Slide Decks

See the Valex tuition report in the Reference Manual.

For graphical report decks, the executive summary, table of contents, summary, and reference slides may be mostly text, but all main pages balance text and graphics. How much text you include in a deck depends on the purpose and audience, as you see along the Figure 16 continuum. For audiences who will read the deck on their own, the report should make "standalone sense"—without any presentation or instruction. Readers can take more time on each slide and move along at any pace. Decks for this audience are most dense with detailed charts and descriptive text.

For an audience who will discuss your report, perhaps in small groups, you can provide less text because you'll walk them through the deck, and they'll provide feedback and ask questions throughout. They also can request that you go faster or slower on certain slides.

The last row shows a slide for a more formal presentation. In these situations, you may present to a large group of people and have slides as visual support, but what you say is more important than what is on the slides. The audience has no control over the pace, so they won't be able to read much while a slide is displayed. We discuss these types of slides in the next chapter.

Deck Density for Different Purposes and Audiences | **Figure 16**

Most — Slide density — Least

Least — Presentation formality — Most

Individual reading (one person at an individual pace)

</>

Tuition Assistance Programs offer many benefits for employees

Employers value a college education, according to the Association of American Colleges and Universities.

Most business executives (82%) said that completing a college education is either "very" or "absolutely" important.

Eighty-eight percent of executives believe that getting a college degree is worth the time and money.

Employers note that learned/developed college skills including oral communication, critical thinking, and working effectively in teams are very valuable.

Executives agree that no matter the study, the college degree and experience allows positive interaction with people of high-level positions.

Median salary jumps 40% from associate to bachelor's and 20% from bachelor's to master's, according to the U.S. Census.

$30,784 $38,792 $43,316 $46,124 $64,896 $77,844 $97,916

+40.7% +20.0%

Some High School Ed. | High School Diploma | Some College | Associate Degree | Bachelor's Degree | Master's Degree | Doctorate Degree

Section 2: Benefits

3

Discussion or sales pitch (small group at a varied pace)

Tuition Assistance Program offers many benefits for employees

Employers value a college education (AACU survey)

- Important to the company
- Worth the time and money
- Effective for skill development
- Valuable for positive interactions with senior management

Median salaries increase with additional degrees (U.S. Census)

$30,784 $38,792 $43,316 $46,124 $64,896 $77,844 $97,916

+40.7% +20.0%

Some High School Ed. | High School Diploma | Some College | Associate Degree | Bachelor's Degree | Master's Degree | Doctorate Degree

Benefits

3

Presentation or briefing (larger group at a set pace)

Median salary increases by degree obtained

$30,784 $38,792 $43,316 $46,124 $64,896 $77,844 $97,916

+40.7% +20.0%

Some High School Ed. | High School Diploma | Some College | Associate Degree | Bachelor's Degree | Master's Degree | Doctorate Degree

3

Designing decks can be challenging. Follow the guidelines below and summarized in Figure 17.

Graphics

Although the page shown in Figure 17 is mostly text, the author uses boxes, colors, and bullets to connect points and add visual interest. Try to visualize your information. Use parallel text boxes, diagrams, arrows, and other tools, such as SmartArt embedded in Microsoft products.

Figure 17 | Guidelines for Creating a PowerPoint Report Page

A white background improves readability; check contrast by printing in both color and black and white.

Message titles describe the main point in full sentences using sentence case. When read in sequence across the report, titles convey a cohesive argument.

Detailed, explanatory text allows the report to stand alone; check that you have enough evidence to prove your message title.

Business fonts, sizes 11–16, are used.

Bullets are preferred over paragraph text; check for parallel phrasing within lists, and check for proper alignment under bullets.

Main points are reinforced on each page.

Mars has already started down a socially responsible path by choosing sustainable cocoa but has the opportunity to expand.

Mars takes initiative to be a leader in sustainable practices.

A commitment to sustainability builds off an ethical commitment to the individual and the larger community. This commitment is demonstrated by these practices:

- Engagement in cocoa production research to find new and more environmentally friendly production techniques.
- Involvement in organizations such as the World Cocoa Foundation that brings education about sustainable practices to farmers.
- Development research labs to eliminate or reduce the fungal diseases that kill off many cocoa plants.
- Innovation in waste management. The technique of mixing the cocoa waste with piglet food helps pigs transition from mother's milk to solid food. Prior to this, piglets would lose significant weight during this transition.

TransFair shares this commitment to sustainability.

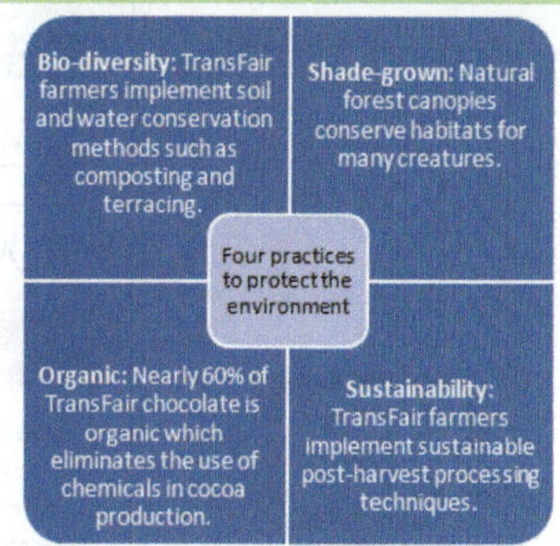

Bio-diversity: TransFair farmers implement soil and water conservation methods such as composting and terracing.
Shade-grown: Natural forest canopies conserve habitats for many creatures.
Four practices to protect the environment
Organic: Nearly 60% of TransFair chocolate is organic which eliminates the use of chemicals in cocoa production.
Sustainability: TransFair farmers implement sustainable post-harvest processing techniques.

Each page uses a mix of text and graphics. Only relevant graphics are included (no photos just for visual appeal).

Sustainability limits the focus on helping the earth. Fair trade focuses both on this earth-friendly impact through sustainability and a positive impact for others who share this earth.

9

All pages except the title page are numbered.

Courtesy of Mars

Unlike a report that is primarily text, you don't have to label graphics in a deck, but you do need to explain them. Place explanatory text near graphics or use text boxes and arrows. All visuals should be relevant to the main point. Skip the clip art and photos that you might use in a PowerPoint slide for an oral presentation just for visual interest.

Follow these guidelines when choosing colors for your deck:[15]

- Avoid dark-colored backgrounds; white is a safe choice. But dark-colored text boxes may be used for message titles and other headings.
- Avoid using too many colors. Choose a professional-looking color scheme and create a visual template for your deck.
- Use colors in a meaningful way: they may signal connections, progression, contrasting ideas (with contrasting colors), and so on. This color symbolism will intensify your point, but your reader still needs enough explanation.
- Avoid color combinations that may be problematic for some readers (e.g., people who are colorblind have trouble distinguishing shades of red and green next to each other).[16]
- Print a test page to make sure the deck will look as you planned.

Fonts, Spacing, and Page Numbers

Follow these guidelines when choosing fonts and formatting the deck:

- Use consistent fonts and font sizes for titles, subheadings, and body text on each page.
- Use the same size for all message titles (usually between 20 and 28 points).
- Use the same size for all subheadings (e.g., headings over text boxes), and make these smaller than the message titles.
- Use the same size for similar body text (usually between 11 and 16 points).

- Choose business or more creative fonts depending on the context, but don't use more than two to avoid busyness.
- Use sentence case. Set message titles flush left rather than centered.
- For bulleted or numbered lists, fix the alignment to avoid a hanging indentation. Check that multilevel bullets vary by level.
- Insert page numbers but omit numbers on the first two pages—your title page and table of contents.

10-5c Refining Your Report

Once you have produced a first draft of your report, put it away for a few days. This will give you a fresh perspective and will help you find new ways of communicating your ideas.

Revising

As you revise your draft, don't try to correct all problems in one review. Instead, look at this process as having three steps, as discussed for all business writing—revising for content, style, and correctness (Figure 18).

Steps for Revising | **Figure 18**

1. Revise for content.	• Have you included sufficient information to support each point? • Have you excluded extraneous information (regardless of how interesting it might be or how hard you worked to gather the information)? • Is all information accurate? • Is the information presented in an efficient and logical sequence?
2. Revise for style.	• Are words clear, simple, and concise? • Are you using a variety of sentence types? • Do your paragraphs have unity and coherence, and are they of reasonable length? • Have you maintained an overall tone of confidence, sincerity, and objectivity? • Have you used appropriate emphasis and subordination?
3. Revise for correctness.	• Do you find any errors in grammar, spelling, punctuation, and word usage? • Does a colleague catch any errors you may have overlooked?

Proofreading

How would you react if you saw a typo or data error in a report? Some managers and prospective clients will let this go, but others will judge the writer negatively.

After making all your revisions and formatting the pages, give each page one final proofread. Check closely for errors and appearance. Do you have blank lines, extra page breaks, inconsistent use of fonts and colors, misused words, or inconsistent punctuation?

Let your pride of authorship show through in every facet of your report. Appearances and details count. Review your entire document to ensure that you can answer "yes" to every question in the Checklist for Reviewing Your Report Draft.

Checklist for Reviewing Your Report Draft

INTRODUCTION AND SUPPLEMENTARY PAGES

☑ Is the report title accurate and descriptive?
☑ Does the introduction convey the main points?
☑ Does the executive summary provide a comprehensive overview of the report?
☑ Is the table of contents accurate, with correct page numbers and wording that matches the report headings?
☑ Is appendix material labeled and referred to in the body of the report?

FINDINGS AND ORGANIZATION

☑ Is the data analyzed completely, accurately, and appropriately?
☑ Is the analysis free of bias and misrepresentation?
☑ Is the data interpreted (its importance and implications discussed) rather than just presented?
☑ Are the sections logically divided and sequenced?
☑ Does each major section contain a preview, summary, and transition?
☑ Are the headings descriptive, parallel, and appropriate in number?
☑ Are headings and subheadings clearly distinguished?

WRITING STYLE AND TONE

☑ Is the report appropriately tailored to the audience?
☑ Are emphasis and subordination used effectively?
☑ Has proper verb tense been used throughout?
☑ Has an appropriate level of formality been used?

SUMMARY, CONCLUSIONS, AND RECOMMENDATIONS

☑ Is the wording used in the summary consistent with that used initially to present the data?
☑ Are the conclusions drawn supported by ample, credible evidence?
☑ Do the conclusions answer the questions or issues raised in the introduction?
☑ Are the recommendations reasonable in light of the conclusions?
☑ Does the report end with a sense of completion and convey an impression that the project is important?

DESIGN AND FORMAT

☑ Have the principles of document design been followed?
☑ Does the report include appropriate graphics, and are the graphics explained sufficiently in the text?
☑ Are graphics correct, clear, appropriately sized and positioned, and correctly labeled?
☑ Is the report free from spelling, grammar, and punctuation errors?
☑ Are all sources properly documented and consistently formatted?
☑ Does the report make a positive impression overall?

10-6 Chapter Closing

Richard Sackler, former Purdue Pharma president and board member, gave eight hours of testimony denying his company's role in the opioid crisis. When asked how many people died from OxyContin, he said, "To the best of my knowledge, recollection, that data is not available."[17]

Of course, those numbers were available at the time. Today, they are increasingly available in many reports, such as one from the Wisconsin Department of Health Services. That report described "initiatives to be funded through the McKinsey & Company settlement"—a hopeful look toward the future.[18]

When well written and supported, reports provide information for problem solving and decision making. In the case of the opioid crisis, reports help officials decide how to support people struggling with addiction and how to prevent future deaths.

A *New York Times* writer described Sackler as "evasive and defiant" during his video testimony.[19] Next, we discuss developing and delivering presentations and visuals. As always, we keep our purpose and the audience in mind.

Decline Work to Market Opioids

Consider the chapter introduction, which described McKinsey's role in the opioid crisis. Imagine that you're a senior consultant who is asked to help Purdue Pharma increase marketing of OxyContin.

You decline the work. Using the CAM model, what questions might you consider before responding to the request?

>>> CHARACTER CHECK

1. **What is my motivation for declining the work?**
   McKinsey is a reputable firm and cannot be associated with the opioid crisis. We have an ethical obligation to uphold high standards.
2. **How do I personally feel about the work?**
   Mixed. The revenue would be significant, and the work is interesting. However, I could not sleep well if I were involved in increasing the already high numbers of addiction and deaths attributed to this drug.

>>> AUDIENCE ANALYSIS

1. **How will Purdue likely react?**
   The company will be surprised and disappointed. We have had a long relationship. The management team also might be offended.
2. **How could I handle the decision and their potential reaction?**
   I could lie and say that we're too busy to handle the work, but I will be truthful and explain my reasons. I want to be respectful and, at the same time, I will be critical of the company's plans.

>>> MESSAGE AND MEDIUM

1. **What are the main points of my message?**
   I'll provide evidence of the opioid crisis, which the management team might already know but is important for context. I'll also explain McKinsey's principles and the risks of our involvement.
2. **In what medium will I communicate the message?**
   A short report within an email will be sufficient.

CAM

› IN PRACTICE

Create a Deck About the Opioid Crisis

Imagine that you sent the email described in the previous section. In response, the Purdue management team rethinks their strategy and asks you to submit a report about the opioid crisis and the company's role. (Let's just imagine.)

››› CHARACTER CHECK

1. How do I feel about the idea of writing this report?
2. How might my feelings or experience with the opioid crisis affect my approach to writing the report?

››› AUDIENCE ANALYSIS

1. Considering that I'm writing this report at their request, how might the management team respond?
2. What tone and level of detail might work best?

››› MESSAGE AND MEDIUM

1. What will be my main points? What other information will I include?
2. What report format is best for the purpose and audience?

REFLECTING ON YOUR COMMUNICATION AND CHARACTER DEVELOPMENT

1. **Reflect on your views about reading reports.**
   How do you feel about reading reports? When faced with a long, dense report, what is your approach? Do you relish every word or delay reading and then skim as much as possible? Why do you think you react this way, and what's the effect?

2. **Reflect on your views about writing reports.**
   How do you feel about writing reports? In what ways might your feelings about reading reports affect your feelings about writing them—or vice versa? What have you learned about business writing so far in this book and in your class that might help you approach a big task like writing a report differently?

3. **Consider your preferred report format.**
   Do you prefer more graphical reports or reports that have more explanatory text? How might your preference influence your choice to write one type of report or another? Could this preference interfere with the best choice for your purpose and audience?

4. **Reflect on your experience with plagiarism.**
   Have you ever taken someone else's work and presented it as your own? What was the situation, and why did you take this action? How do you feel about it in retrospect? Would you do it again in a similar situation?

5. **Consider different perspectives on citations.**
   Norms for citing sources—and even copyright laws—differ depending on country, region, and often by company or department. What are your own views about citing sources? Do the guidelines described in this chapter align with your thinking, or do you think they are too strict or too lax? How will you approach citing sources in your work outside this class?

DEVELOPING YOUR BUSINESS COMMUNICATION SKILLS

PLANNING THE REPORT

LO1 Determine an appropriate report format and organization in a business situation.

1. **Determine which report format is best.**
   For each of the following scenarios, which report format would you choose and why? Would you create a primarily text report or create a more graphical deck? How much text and how many graphics do you anticipate using? (Note: You will find more than one "correct" answer, but whichever you choose, be prepared to justify your response.)
   a. You work for a traditional university as the head of the residence halls. You write a report to the dean of students to provide unsolicited information about the number of false fire alarms in the 16 campus dorms. Your purpose is to request an upgraded fire alarm system for all dorms.
   b. You work as a consultant, and you're trying to win new business from a prospective client, a software developer. You propose a training program to improve customer service skills for call center representatives. The estimated costs are $15,000.
   c. You work for an independent clothing store and have been asked to compare the number of items made in China, South America, and the United States. The report will be sent to the store manager, who works on-site, and the owner, who works in another state.

d. You work for a regional bank and have been asked to research new ATMs. Your report will be sent to the chief technology officer and the head of the consumer banking division.

2. **Explain the different report formats.**
   Imagine that a colleague asks for your help in deciding what format to use for a report for a prospective client. Write an email describing the differences between a primarily text-based report and a deck. Without knowing more about the situation, you probably can't advise which is best, but be sure to include criteria for choosing the most appropriate format. In other words, what considerations should your colleague use when making the decision?

3. **Write an executive summary.**
   Find a report that you wrote in the past for school or work that doesn't have an executive summary. Write one that is about 10% of the total report.

4. **Convert an executive summary from a deck.**
   Imagine that you wrote the executive summary in Figure 9 about tuition assistance in PowerPoint. When you showed your draft to a couple of coworkers, they suggested that you rewrite it for a more conservative audience in Microsoft Word. After revising the text and design, compare your drafts in small groups. What changes did each of you make? Which work best and why?

5. **Write an outline about a potential investment.**
   Imagine that you're a business consultant who has been hired to explore an idea for a start-up and write a report. Choose any prospective business that interests you—maybe an idea you are already pursuing. Working in small groups, brainstorm what information would be valuable in helping your client make the decision. Next, create a preliminary outline of major topics, with at least two minor topics under each.

6. **Convert generic headings to message titles.**
   From a preliminary outline for a report, you have the following major and minor generic headings. Convert these to message titles that you'll include in your final report. You may add information to make each heading more descriptive. Either research each topic or, if your instructor allows, invent information just for the purpose of the exercise.

   Internet Access in North America

   - Country Comparisons
     — United States
     — Canada
   - Regional Comparisons
     — Rural
     — Urban
     — Suburban
   - Available Technologies
     — Broadband
     — Wireless
     — Dial-Up
   - Implications
     — Educational
     — Social
     — Political

DRAFTING THE REPORT

LO2 Describe typical components of a business report.

7. Write an introduction for a report.

Imagine that you're writing a report to convince your school's dean of students to provide additional funding for your student club. What will the report include? What are your main points? After you consider the report as a whole, write a short introduction.

8. Analyze parts of a report.

Find three reports longer than 15 pages on any topic that interests you. What components are included in the body? What supplementary sections do you see? What conclusions can you draw about the reports based on the writers, audience, purpose, and other factors? Which report do you find most effective and why?

9. Write a short report within an email.

The Federal Trade Commission, a government agency that protects consumers, has hired you to summarize the issue of rising U.S. consumer debt. Your task is to write a short report within the body of an email that the agency will send to other government constituencies. The agency wants to highlight the importance of its work by showing the seriousness of the problem.

Working in groups of three or four, complete the following:

a. Independently research current data about consumer debt. Be sure to use credible sources, primarily government and academic research.

b. As a group, discuss your research and select the most relevant data for your purpose. In your short report, you won't be able to cover all data, so be selective and focus on three or four points.

c. Create an outline for your email report.

d. Draft the first paragraph, which will include the purpose and main points (your conclusions).

e. Draft the email and share your group's version with the rest of the class.

f. Vote on which group's email works best. What makes this email most effective?

DEVELOPING AN EFFECTIVE WRITING STYLE

LO3 Explain how the writing style for a report may differ from other types of writing.

10. Adjust the tone of a report section.

You are a consultant working in the education division of a major firm. One of your group's clients is a federal government agency trying to increase how much time people spend reading. As part of the argument—and the final report—your client asks you how much time people spend on social networking sites.

You find this interesting story online. It's a good starting point, but to present this in a credible way for your client, you'll need to find updated data and, of course, present the data using a more objective tone. Write one or two paragraphs with the most recent data you can find.

> Astonishingly, the average person will spend nearly two hours (approximately 116 minutes) on social media every day, which translates to a total of 5 years and 4 months spent over a lifetime. Even more, time spent on social is only expected to increase as platforms develop and is expected to eat further into traditional media—most notably TV. Right now, the average person will spend 7 years and 8 months watching TV in a lifetime. However, as digital media consumption continues to grow at unprecedented rates, this number is expected to shrink in counter to that expansion.[20]

11. **Manage your tone in a report.**

Choose a topic you're passionate about. What about the world breaks your heart or makes you angry? Imagine that you're writing a report to a group of people who can make a difference. Write a brief introduction to your report. Include preliminary research, but the purpose of this exercise is to manage your tone. You don't need to squelch your passion but try to maintain an objective tone so that people who may not agree with you can trust your conclusions.

12. **Analyze emphasis and subordination.**

Text in a JPMorgan Chase Letter to Shareholders describes a table of data (Figure 19) showing how banks have grown in the past 20 years.[21] In small groups, discuss the purpose of this section. In other words, what claims is the company making? What data is chosen as evidence to support those claims? How does CEO Jamie Dimon use emphasis and subordination to explain the data (shown following the chart)?

Figure 19 | Data and Text from a JPMorgan Chase Annual Report

SIZE OF THE FINANCIAL SECTOR / INDUSTRY				
($ IN TRILLIONS)		**2000**	**2010**	**2020**
Size of banks	U.S. banks market capitalization[1]	1.2	1.3	2.2
	U.S. GSIB market capitalization	0.9	0.8	1.2
	European banks market capitalization[1]	1.1	1.5	1.1
	U.S. bank loans[2]	3.7	6.6	10.5
	Total U.S. broker dealer inventories	2.0	3.5	3.7
	U.S. bank common equity[3]	0.4	1.0	1.5
	U.S. bank liquid assets[2,4]	1.1	2.8	7.0
Market size	Total U.S. debt and equity market	33.6	57.2	118.4
	Total U.S. GDP[5]	13.3	15.8	18.8
Shadow banks	Total private direct credit	7.6	13.8	18.4
	Total U.S. passives and ETFs[6]	6.9	13.6	30.5
	Total U.S. money market funds	1.8	2.8	4.3
	Hedge fund and private equity AUM[7]	0.6	3.0	8.0
Size of evolving competitors	Google, Amazon, Facebook, Apple[8]	NM	0.5	5.6
	Payments[9]	NA	0.1	1.2
	Private and public fintech companies[9]	NA	NA	0.8

GSIB = Global Systemically Important Banks
NA = Not applicable
NM = Not material
Sources: FactSet. S&P Global Market Intelligence, Federal Reserve Z.I, Federal Reserve H.8, Preqin and Federal Reserve Economic Data (FRED).

Whether you look at the chart above over 10 or 20 years, U.S. banks have become much smaller relative to U.S. financial markets and to the size of most of the shadow banks. You can also see the rapid growth of payment and fintech companies and the extraordinary size of Big Tech companies. . . .

Some regulators will look at the chart above and point out that risk has been moved out of the banking system, which they wanted and which clearly makes banks safer. That may be true, but there is a flip side—banks are reliable, less-costly, and consistent credit providers throughout good times and in bad times, whereas many of the credit providers listed in the chart above are not. More important, transactions made by well-controlled, well-supervised, and well-capitalized banks may be less risky to the system than those transactions that are pushed into the shadows.

13. Write a section overview.

Assume that you're writing a report with the following headings within one section. Write a brief section overview after the major heading to preview topics within the section and summarize the main points. Avoid using the same wording; instead, rephrase the subheadings to form a meaningful section overview.

The Alliam Hotel Can Conserve Water by Making a Few Minor Changes

- Install Dual-Flush Toilets
- Install Oxygen-Assisted Shower Heads
- Capture Rainwater for Landscaping

DOCUMENTING YOUR SOURCES

LO4 Format a footnote to cite a given source.

14. Determine whether information must be documented.

Imagine that you're writing a case study about the bookseller Barnes & Noble. Which of the following information needs to be documented in a report?

a. Barnes & Noble's corporate headquarters is located at 122 Fifth Avenue, New York City, New York.

b. The company's online division uses the website www.bn.com.

c. The company's online division generates 10% of the company's revenue.

d. Michael Huseby is the CEO of Barnes & Noble.

e. Barnes & Noble closed its Lincoln Center store in New York City.

f. Most stores are between 10,000 and 60,000 square feet.

15. Choose quotations from a report.

Write up your analysis from Exercise 12. In a couple of paragraphs, explain how Jamie Dimon described the data. Include original quotations to illustrate your points, but make sure that most of the text is your own writing.

16. Improve paraphrasing.

Find a paraphrasing tool online (e.g., https://paraphrasing-tool.com). Write your own or copy and paste a sentence into the tool. What are the results? What issues do you find with the computer paraphrasing? Rewrite the sentence as a better example. Show both versions to a classmate for comparison.

17. Use footnotes to document sources.

Assume you are writing a report and have used the following secondary sources.[22]

a. An article written by Marie Callen on pages 45–48 of the June 6, 2022, edition of *Bloomberg Businessweek* titled "Little Bits of Bitcoin."

b. A quotation by Tre Simpson in an article titled "Best Online Python Courses" on Medium.com on August 22, 2022.

c. Statistics from page 233 in a book titled *Service in Your Backyard* written by Jonathan Della Santi in 2021 and published by Harper Publishing in New York.

d. A quote from an interview conducted on September 30, 2022, with T. Warren Towes, a professor of economics at the University of Wisconsin.

Using these sources and the guidelines in the chapter, prepare footnotes for your report. Assume that you accessed online content today.

18. Use secondary sources to write a report about women leaders in business.

Imagine that you're writing a report to a group of CEOs dedicated to increase the number of women who are CEOs. Identify three women who are CEOs of publicly traded companies. Find secondary sources for information on their backgrounds. Did they make it to the top by rising through the ranks or by following some other path?

Analyze the effectiveness of these three individuals. How profitable are the companies they head in relation to others in the industry? Are their companies more or less profitable now than when they assumed the top job? Finally, try to uncover information regarding their management styles—how they see their role, how they relate to their employees, how they have handled challenges, and so on.

From your study of these three individuals, can you draw any valid conclusions? Write a report objectively presenting and analyzing the information you've gathered. Then, write a cover note about the sources you found. Which are most and least credible and why?

19. Research secondary data and create a deck.

Your client is a community foundation, which provides funding to small, local, nonprofit organizations. With an endowment of $1 million, the foundation is looking for sound investments to grow funds available to support the community. Choose any publicly traded company that interests you, and research whether this company would be a worthy investment for some of the foundation's endowment funds. Your purpose is to identify *whether* the company is a good choice—you do not need to give a positive recommendation.[23]

To formulate your argument, you might research some of the following about your company of choice:

- Background Information: What does your client need to know about the company?
- Mission and Vision: Does the company align with the foundation's mission?
- Stock Trend and Analysts' Recommendations: Is this a sound investment likely to give positive returns?
- Growth Trends: What do you know about the company's revenue and profits? What plans (e.g., for new products and new locations) might be relevant to the foundation?
- Management: Does the company have a strong, stable management team capable of running the company well in the future?
- Ethics: How well does the company uphold ethical standards in its relationships with people and the environment? Have issues with misconduct been reported?
- Current News: What news items about the company might be relevant to the decision?

Prepare a deck to the foundation's board of directors. Include a title page, executive summary, table of contents, several pages of findings, and a summary.

20. **Use primary and secondary sources to write a report about your future career.**

Explore a job that interests you. Determine the job outlook, present level of employment, salary trends, typical responsibilities, educational or experience requirements, and so on. If possible, interview someone holding this position to gain firsthand impressions. Then write up your findings in a report to your instructor. Include at least five secondary sources and at least three tables or graphs in your report.

DESIGNING, FORMATTING, AND REFINING THE REPORT

LO5 Distinguish design and formatting guidelines for slide decks from other types of reports.

21. **Analyze a report design.**

Find any report online. You might look at government reports or at an annual report of a company you admire. What principles from this chapter does the report follow, and in what ways could the report be improved? Do you find the format appropriate for the purpose and audience? Are text and graphics balanced well? Are explanations clear, and is the report easy to follow?

22. **Improve a deck page.**

Imagine that you work for the U.S. government, focusing on dietary guidelines. One of your direct reports created the deck page shown in Figure 20.[24] The purpose is to provide nutritional advice to American citizens. Write an email to compliment the strengths and suggest ways to improve the design. You may use bullet points for your comments.

23. **Write a complex report.**

To practice researching information and writing complex reports, you may use the following prompts. Follow your instructor's directions in terms of report length, format, degree of formality, and supplements.

Figure 20 Sample Deck Page

Try the MyPlate Plan

A healthy eating routine is important at every stage of life and can have positive effects that add up over time. It's important to eat a variety of fruits, vegetables, grains, dairy or fortified soy alternatives, and protein foods. When deciding what to eat or drink, choose options that are full of nutrients. Make every bite count.

Think about how the following recommendations can come together over the course of your day or week to help you create a healthy eating routine:

Fruits
Grains
Dairy
Vegetables
Protein
MyPlate.gov

To learn what the right amounts are for you, try the personalized **MyPlate Plan**.[2]

Based on decades of solid science, MyPlate advice can help you day to day and over time.

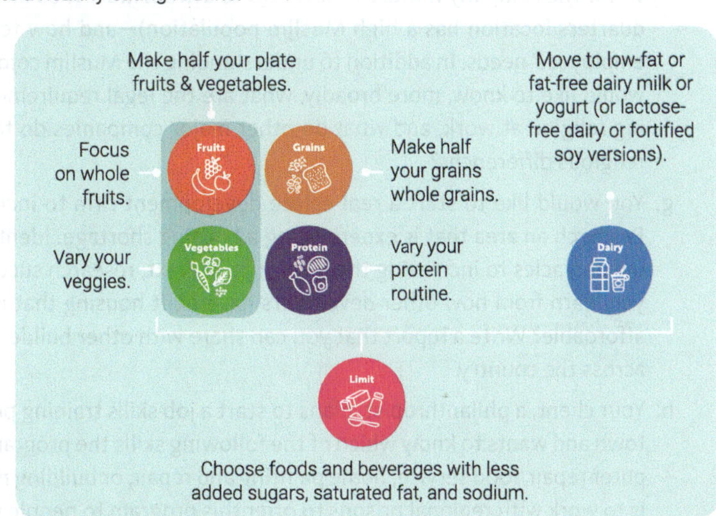

Make half your plate fruits & vegetables.
Move to low-fat or fat-free dairy milk or yogurt (or lactose-free dairy or fortified soy versions).
Focus on whole fruits.
Fruits
Grains
Make half your grains whole grains.
Vary your veggies.
Vegetables
Protein
Vary your protein routine.
Dairy
Limit
Choose foods and beverages with less added sugars, saturated fat, and sodium.

The benefits of healthy eating add up over time, bite by bite. Small changes matter. **Start Simple with MyPlate.**

DGA
Dietary Guidelines for Americans

Start simple with MyPlate

a. Imagine that your client is in the airline, retail, or hotel industry and wants advice for using social media to connect with customers. Identify five companies within the industry and compare their use of social media. Look at each company's presence on social media sites. How are they engaging and responding to customers? Also research news stories and other reports about these companies' social media use: which are seen as models within the industry? Use this research to provide recommendations for your client company.

b. Choose a company that handled a crisis situation recently. Imagine that you're a consultant for a similar business. How would you advise the management team to avoid such a crisis in the future? According to crisis communication research, what are the best practices for handling a crisis, and how should your client adapt these practices for the company?

c. Where should graduating students start their career? Your client is the career management office at your school, wanting to know which companies to pursue for on-campus recruiting. Recommend five companies to work for within one industry that interests you and base your recommendation on published "best company" lists, financial performance, management, growth potential, organizational culture, career opportunities, and so on. Include at least 15 different sources.

d. How have women in business fared over the past decade? Your client is the Women's Opportunity Center, a regional organization that wants to encourage women, yet give them a realistic view of their chances of success. Looking at women in various companies and industries in the past ten years, what would you conclude about their progress, particularly their ability to reach the highest levels in organizations? The Center also wants to tell women how they can improve their chances of reaching senior-level positions. Research experts' opinions and studies to provide a list of advice. Try to avoid obvious, surface advice, such as "dress for success"; rather, what should women do in terms of education, performance, communication, relationships, and so on?

e. What are the retail trends among 18- to 25-year-olds? This is a highly coveted market for retailers, and your client, a major clothing manufacturer, wants to understand what this group is buying and how they buy. Research the data and provide your client with recommendations for types of products, quality, service, and marketing strategies to reach this target group.

f. How do companies today support religious differences? A major consumer products company is finding that an increasing number of Muslims need prayer time during work. The company wants to know how to attract more Muslim employees (the headquarters location has a high Muslim population)—and how to accommodate these employees' needs. In addition to understanding the Muslim community, management would like to know, more broadly, what are the legal requirements for accommodating religion at work, and what do other major companies do to support employees' religious differences?

g. You would like to start a real estate development firm to increase housing supply. Research an area that is experiencing a housing shortage. Identify the issues, including obstacles to increasing the local supply. Next, research success stories. What can you learn from how other developers have built housing that is both accessible and affordable? Write a report that you can share with other builders to inspire initiatives across the country.

h. Your client, a philanthropist, plans to start a job skills training program in your hometown and wants to know which of the following skills the program should target: computer repair, food service, home painting and repair, or building maintenance. Her plan is to work with regional prisons to offer this program to people who are incarcerated.

The objective is to reduce recidivism by giving people in prison marketable skills they can use when they are released. To support your recommendation, you'll need to (1) research the success of similar reentry job training programs that focus on each skill area and (2) find data about job availability in your area.

i. Under what situations can an employer fire someone for posting negative information online? Your client, a mid-sized technology company, wants to know the prevailing thinking. To provide a balanced perspective, research recent cases and provide several examples of situations where employees were terminated, whether the company was sued, and what the outcome was in each case. Also research information from the National Labor Relations Board to understand the concept of "protected concerted activity." Finally, look at companies' social media policies and guidelines and recommend an approach for your client—to prevent this situation in the first place.

j. Your client wants to protect its office and employees from environmental disasters. Choose a location that interests you and research vulnerabilities. Include what the company leaders can do now to avert major damage.

CHAPTER SUMMARY

LO1 Determine an appropriate report format and organization in a business situation.

Reports may be formatted as primarily text documents or as a combination of text and graphics, as in a deck created in PowerPoint or other presentation software. The most common ways to organize the findings of a report are by time, location, importance, and criteria. Conclusions typically are presented at the beginning of the report.

LO2 Describe typical components of a business report.

Major and minor sections clarify your organization and help readers navigate the report. Message titles are descriptive headings that convey main points. The body of the report consists of the introduction; findings; and, as needed, the summary, conclusions, and recommendations. Long, formal reports might also require supplementary components: title page, cover note, executive summary, table of contents, appendix, and reference list.

LO3 Explain how the writing style for a report may differ from other types of writing.

Use an objective writing style, appropriate pronouns, and accurate verb tenses that reflect the reader's time frame (rather than yours, as the writer). Use emphasis and subordination techniques to help alert the reader to what you consider important; and use preview, summary, and transitional devices to help maintain coherence.

LO4 Format a footnote to cite a given source.

Use direct quotations sparingly; most references to secondary data should be paraphrases. Provide appropriate documentation whenever you quote, paraphrase, or summarize someone else's work by using footnotes, endnotes, or the author-date method of citation. Do not omit important, relevant information from the report.

LO5 Distinguish design and formatting guidelines for slide decks from other types of reports.

For primarily text reports, incorporate graphics to complement the text. For visual appeal and easier reading, choose appropriate spacing and fonts. Use page numbers and other features to clarify the organization. For slide decks, balance text and graphics and follow other report guidelines for fonts, spacing, and page numbers. Choose density—how much to include on each page—depending on the purpose and audience.

Endnotes

1. State of Minnesota, County of Ramsey, "Complaint," February 4, 2021, www.ag.state.mn.us/Office/Communications/2021/docs/McKinsey_Complaint.pdf, p. 6, accessed April 12, 2021.
2. "Deaths: United States, 2011–2016," Center for Disease Control, *National Vital Statistics Reports* 67 (2018), www.cdc.gov/nchs/data/nvsr/nvsr67/nvsr67_09-508.pdf, accessed April 12, 2021.
3. Commonwealth of Massachusetts, "First Amended Complaint and Jury Demand," Superior Court C.A. No. 1884-cv-01808, January 31, 2019, www.documentcloud.org/documents/5715954-Massachusetts-AGO-Amended-Complaint-2019-01-31.html, accessed April 12, 2021, and State of Minnesota, County of Ramsey, "Complaint," February 4, 2021.
4. McKinsey & Company, "High Impact Interventions to Rapidly Address Market Access Challenges," December 2017 (Exhibit R, filed November 18, 2020), https://assets.documentcloud.org/documents/20421781/mckinsey-docs.pdf, accessed April 12, 2021.
5. Walt Bogdanich and Michael Forsythe, "McKinsey Proposed Paying Pharmacy Companies Rebates for OxyContin Overdoses," *The New York Times*, November 27, 2020, www.nytimes.com/2020/11/27/business/mckinsey-purdue-oxycontin-opioids.html, accessed April 12, 2021.
6. Frederick M. Azar et al., "Report to the University System of Maryland of an Independent Investigation of the University of Maryland Football Program," October 23, 2018, www.documentcloud.org/documents/5020884-Maryland-football-program-culture-report, April 12, 2021.
7. Descriptive text in DocumentCloud.
8. "Dietary Guidelines for Americans, 2020–2025," USDA, December 2020, www.dietaryguidelines.gov/sites/default/files/2020-12/Dietary_Guidelines_for_Americans_2020-2025.pdf, p. 100, accessed April 15, 2021.
9. Frederick M. Azar, et al., p. 1.
10. Mary Madden and Lee Rainie, "Adults and Cell Phone Distractions," Pew Internet, June 18, 2010, www.pewresearch.org/internet/2010/06/18/adults-and-cell-phone-distractions-2/, accessed April 19, 2021.
11. Amita Kelly, "Section of Melania Trump's Monday Speech Mirrors Michelle Obama's in 2008," *NPR*, July 19, 2016, www.npr.org/2016/07/19/486560186/section-of-melania-trumps-monday-speech-closely-imitates-michelle-obama-in-2008, accessed April 17, 2021.
12. Brett Neely, "Trump Speechwriter Accepts Responsibility for Using Michelle Obama's Words," *NPR*, July 20, 2016, www.npr.org/2016/07/20/486758596/trump-speechwriter-accepts-responsibility-for-using-michelle-obamas-words, accessed April 17, 2021.
13. Eric Cheung, "A Woman Lied on Her Resume to Land a $185,000-a-Year Job. Now She's Going to Jail," CNN, December 4, 2019, www.cnn.com/2019/12/04/australia/australia-woman-jailed-fake-resume-intl-hnk-scli/index.html, accessed April 17, 2021.
14. Harvard Business School, Baker Library, Bloomberg Center, *HBS Citation Guide*, www.library.hbs.edu/citations/hbs-citation-guide, April 17, 2021.
15. Adapted from Maria Wolfe, "Guidelines for PowerPoint Reports," Cornell University.
16. Jennifer Birch, "Red Tape, White Lies," *The Guardian*, www.theguardian.com/notesandqueries/query/0,,-1327,00.html, accessed June 9, 2021.
17. "Watch 8-hour Deposition of Richard Sackler as He Denies Family's Role in the Opioid Crisis," Posted by ProPublica, YouTube, August 4, 2021, www.youtube.com/watch?v=zUNrhPUV6Ew, accessed August 23, 2021.
18. "Opioid Overdose Incidents and the COVID-19 Pandemic in Wisconsin," Wisconsin Department of Health Services, August 10, 2021, www.dhs.wisconsin.gov/news/releases/081021.htm, accessed August 23, 2021.
19. Jan Hoffman, "Richard Sackler Says Family and Purdue Bear No Responsibility for Opioid Crisis," *The New York Times*, August 8, 2021, www.nytimes.com/2021/08/18/health/richard-sackler-purdue-testimony.html, accessed August 23, 2021.
20. Evan Asano, "How Much Time Do People Spend on Social Media?" SocialMediaToday, January 4, 2017, www.socialmediatoday.com/marketing/how-much-time-do-people-spend-social-media-infographic, accessed April 19, 2021.
21. Jamie Dimon, "Letter to Shareholders," JPMorgan Chase, April 7, 2021, www.jpmorganchase.com/content/dam/jpmc/jpmorgan-chase-and-co/investor-relations/documents/ceo-letter-to-shareholders-2020.pdf, p. 27, accessed April 19, 2021.
22. Examples are fictionalized.
23. Adapted from an assignment by Daphne Jameson, Cornell University.
24. "Dietary Guidelines for Americans, 2020–2025," p. 13.

Part 5

Developing and Delivering Presentations and Visuals

CHAPTER

11

Developing Presentations and Visuals

Learning Objectives

After you have finished this chapter, you should be able to

LO1 Describe ways to adapt your presentation for an audience in a given business situation.

LO2 Identify steps for developing a presentation as a story.

LO3 Redesign a given slide to improve visual appeal.

LO4 Identify ways to reinforce a main point in a presentation.

LO5 Explain the value of using video and handouts in a presentation.

"I realized that we had to go on offense, or we were going to go down a very dark road."[1]

—Sonia Syngal, CEO, Gap Inc.

Chapter Introduction

Gap CEO Opens Investor Meeting With Visuals

At an annual investor meeting, Gap Inc. CEO Sonia Syngal set the stage. On the job less than a year and starting right when the COVID-19 pandemic hit the United States in full force, Syngal needed to inspire enthusiasm for the company's brands.

After a short introduction, Syngal started her presentation with a dynamic video set to the song "I'm Crazy for Love" by Craig Reever.[2] We see people happy, active, and in love. The video reinforces company brands and generates excitement.

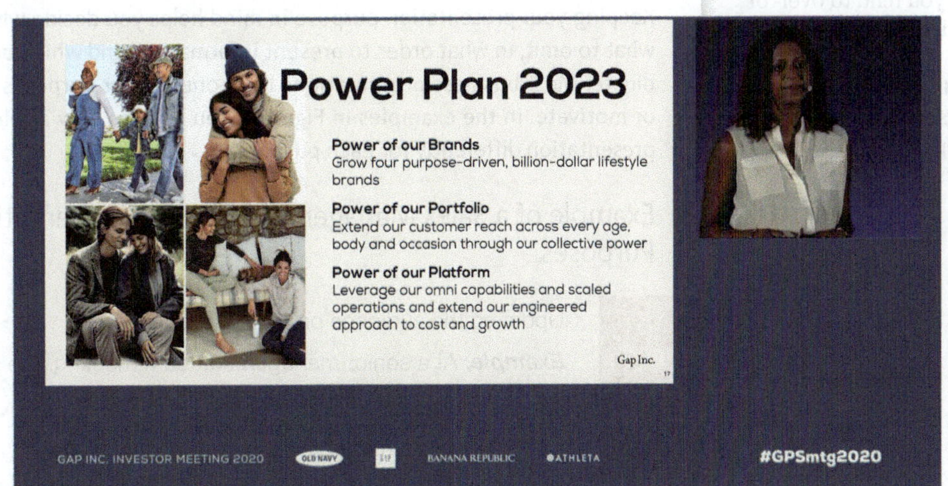

With visuals, Gap Inc. CEO Sonia Syngal reinforces the company's "power."

Source: YouTube, LLC, https://www.youtube.com/watch?v=mjN5kQqDfPw (approx. 13:40)

Next, Syngal showed a few visuals to complement her presentation. The slides are minimal—some data points but mostly photos of people wearing Gap, Old Navy, Banana Republic, and Athleta clothes.

"Power" is an obvious theme. The company strategy is "Power Plan 2023," and the word is repeated on several slides. Throughout the presentation, Syngal focuses on growth, convincing her audience that Gap Inc. is a worthy investment.

LO1 Describe ways to adapt your presentation for an audience in a given business situation.

How do you usually prepare for a presentation? Do you tend to over- or under-prepare, and what is the result? How might your feelings about delivering presentations affect your preparation?

11-1 Adapting a Presentation

Whether you're a CEO addressing thousands of investors or a new employee speaking with your coworkers, your presentation can inspire and motivate or bore and disappoint. We discuss delivering presentations in the next chapter. For now, let's focus on your preparation.

You and your character are on full display during a presentation—not only in your delivery but in how you plan and organize your presentation and in what visuals you choose to show. Your ability to adapt to different situations and audiences is critical to how the message will be received.

One sure way to fail at developing presentations is to try to "wing it." Planning a presentation involves determining the purpose of the presentation and analyzing the audience. Then, you can feel relaxed when you deliver it.

11-1a Purpose

Keeping your presentation purpose in mind helps you decide what information to include and what to omit, in what order to present information, and which points to emphasize and subordinate. Most business presentations have one of four purposes: to report, explain, persuade, or motivate. In the examples in Figure 1, you can see how a sales manager might approach a presentation differently for each purpose.

Figure 1 Example of a Sales Manager Making Four Presentations with Different Purposes

To Report	Updating the audience on a project or event ***Example:*** At a senior management team meeting, the sales manager provides a monthly report of actual sales against targets.
To Explain	Detailing how to carry out a process or procedure ***Example:*** The sales manager shows sales associates how to accurately complete expense reports.
To Persuade	Convincing the audience to purchase something or to accept an idea ***Example:*** The sales manager encourages a new client to use the company's services.
To Motivate	Inspiring the audience to take some action ***Example:*** At a monthly sales team meeting, the sales manager gets the associates excited about a new incentive plan.

When the presentation is over, the sales manager determines whether the presentation fulfilled its purpose. Does the senior management team understand the sales report? Do associates complete expense reports properly? Does the client sign a contract? Do associates increase sales to earn incentives? No matter how well or how poorly you spoke, and no matter how impressive or ineffective your visual support, the most important question is whether you accomplished your purpose.

11-1b Audience Analysis

To analyze the audience of a presentation, use the same principles you use for writing messages and reports. What you discover gives you clues about what content to present, how to organize your presentation, and what questions you might receive.

Sample agenda slides for two presentations are shown in Figure 2. Even with the same content—a monthly sales report—you can see how the audience and purpose of the presentation determine the chosen approach.

Agenda Slide Tailored to Different Audiences | **Figure 2**

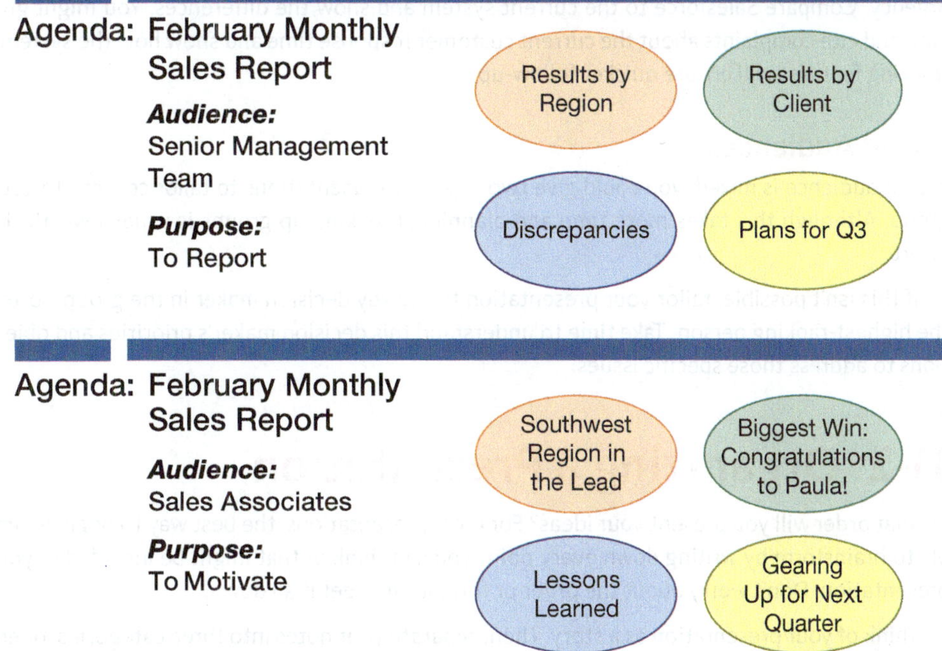

In addition to obvious factors, for example, organizational level and job function, the audience's attitude affects your presentation. Try not to go into a presentation cold. Meeting with decision makers before your presentation can help predispose the audience in your favor, or at least tell you what resistance you might encounter. For example, if you know that a prospective client is unhappy with the service provided by the current vendor, you can spend more time talking about your company's high level of personalized service.

Strategies discussed earlier for persuasive messages and bad-news messages will help you prepare for most business audiences. In addition, consider a few particularly challenging situations for group presentations: hostile, skeptical, laid-back, and mixed audiences. Let's use the example of encouraging company leaders to use Salesforce, a platform for managing customer data.

Hostile Audiences

If you think your listeners will be hostile—either to you personally or to your message—try to build common ground.[3] Focus on shared goals. For example, if you're proposing Salesforce, you might focus on the company's goals to grow the business or improve customer service. You might start with a neutral argument or an assertion that will get the least resistance, for example, how the system connects remote workers. Also, demonstrate humility by acknowledging opposing arguments and costs.

Skeptical Audiences

Like hostile audiences, skeptics resist your ideas and need more convincing. In addition to establishing your own credibility, you may need extensive research to bolster your case. Instead of giving one or two examples, give several. Show how Salesforce works for your competitors.

Address resistance directly. Consider mentioning a big point of contention up front, so you can argue against it throughout your presentation. You might acknowledge the costs of using Salesforce, and then show how the benefits will outweigh those costs.

Don't hesitate to admit your own uncertainty. This also demonstrates humility—that you don't know everything and are willing to learn, just as you're asking your audience to be open to learning.[4]

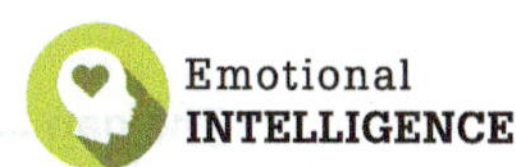

How well can you "read" audiences? Accurately gauging people's reactions to you increases the chance that you'll respond appropriately.

Laid-Back Audiences

When audiences are laid-back, or attached to the status quo, you'll need to create a sense of urgency. Compare Salesforce to the current system and show the differences. You might give data and cite complaints about the current customer response time and show how the system's tracking features will ensure quicker follow-up.

Mixed Audiences

If your audience is mixed, you could give two separate presentations to tailor content to each group. Although this takes more time and planning, breaking up groups is usually worth the effort.

If this isn't possible, tailor your presentation to the key decision maker in the group—often the highest-ranking person. Take time to understand this decision maker's priorities and objections to address those specific issues.

LO2 Identify steps for developing a presentation as a story.

11-2 Organizing a Presentation

In what order will you present your ideas? For most presentations, the best way to begin is simply to brainstorm by writing down every point you can think of that might be included in your presentation. Don't worry about the order or format—just get it all down.

Think of your presentation as a story. Then, separate your notes into three categories: opening, body, and ending.

11-2a The Story

We watch movies and read books because we love stories. Most TED Talks are organized around stories. As discussed for persuasive messages, the best stories create and build tension.

You might think of your entire presentation as a story, or you might develop a story as part of your presentation. Figure 3 illustrates the rhythm of a story, bringing the audience on a journey from how things are today to how they could be in the future.[5] For a presentation about Salesforce, you might start with an example of a customer who needs your company's product. Then, describe a series of problems with the current sales (what is) and provide evidence of how the system works for other companies (what could be). The visual is a roller-coaster ride, building excitement until your call to action—to adopt the system and reap the rewards.

Figure 3 | A Presentation Organized as a Story

Beginning
Paint a picture of the current situation.
Middle
Present contrasting content, alternating between *what is* and *what could be.*
End
Summarize the positive results.
What could be
What could be
What could be
Reward: New bliss
The gap
What is
What is
What is
What is
Turning point 1
Turning point 2
Call to adventure
Create tension between *what is* and *what could be.*
Call to action
Invite your audience to follow your recommendation.

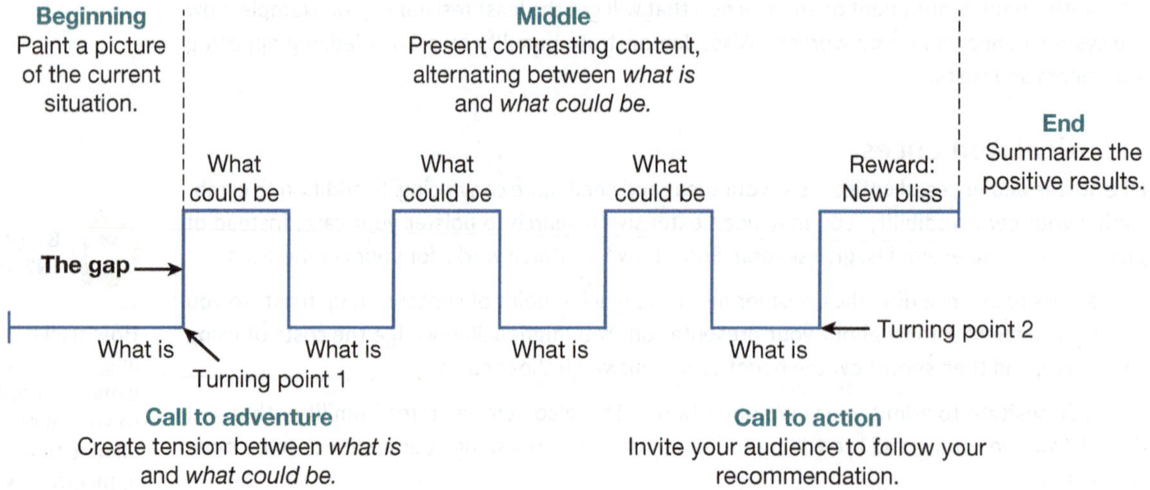

Each cycle in the story uses the ABT structure described for persuasive messages, as in this example:

> On average, our customer service team receives 141.4 emails per day. (What is)
>
> **AND,** 21.6 of these turn into sales.
>
> **BUT,** the rest are lost opportunities. We have no way of tracking these customer inquiries.
>
> **THEREFORE,** we need a way to retain these email contacts and a system for following up. Salesforce turns these leads into sales. (What could be)

Before you begin to design your slides, consider creating a storyboard. A storyboard is a visual representation of your presentation—how your presentation will unfold and what will be on each slide. The example in Figure 4 shows a mix of text and graphics for part of the Salesforce pitch. You can use special software, modify the storyboard template in PowerPoint, or just draw a series of boxes by hand on a large piece of paper or on movable sticky notes.

Storyboard to Plan a Presentation | **Figure 4**

Salesforce Presentation to Executive Committee, July 14

Slide 4

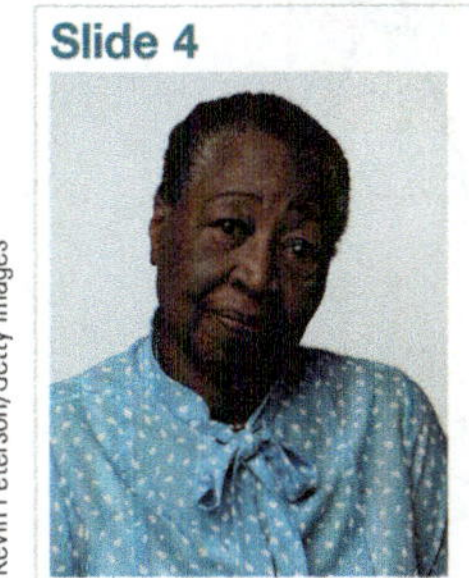

Kevin Peterson/Getty Images

Description

Picture of customer persona with demographic descriptions

Text

Include frustrations and reasons for calling customer service.

Notes

Pull example from customer log.

Slide 5

	5-Jul	6-Jul	7-Jul	8-Jul	9-Jul	Weekly average
Calls Logged	144	178	122	99	164	141.4
Sales	16	22	10	35	25	21.6
Leads	128	156	112	64	139	119.8

Description

Data from the previous week showing sales from customer service calls.

Text

Brief description, but let numbers speak for themselves.

Notes

Focus on lost leads.

Slide 6

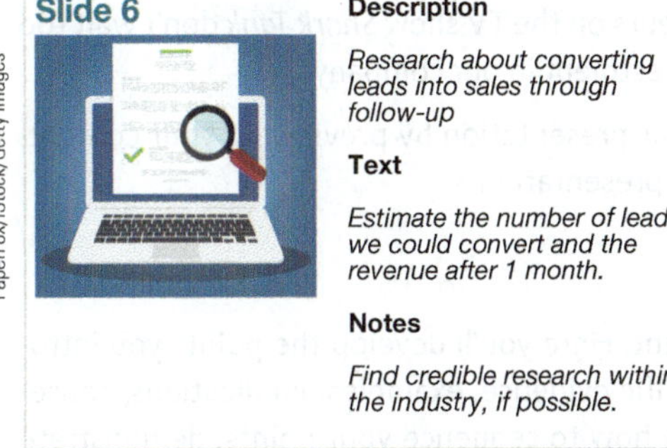

Paperfox/iStock/Getty Images

Description

Research about converting leads into sales through follow-up

Text

Estimate the number of leads we could convert and the revenue after 1 month.

Notes

Find credible research within the industry, if possible.

Slide 7

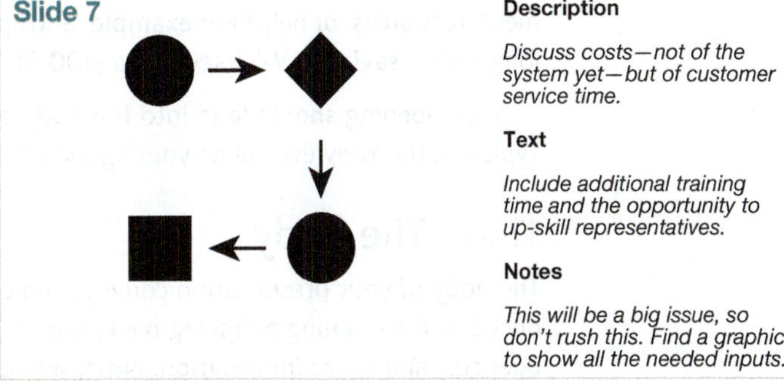

Description

Discuss costs—not of the system yet—but of customer service time.

Text

Include additional training time and the opportunity to up-skill representatives.

Notes

This will be a big issue, so don't rush this. Find a graphic to show all the needed inputs.

With your overall organization drafted, you can begin work on your presentation opening.

11-2b The Opening

The best opening depends on your topic, how well you know the audience, and how well they know you. If, for example, you're giving a weekly status report on a project, you can immediately announce your main points (e.g., that the project is on schedule). If, however, you're presenting a new proposal to a resistant audience, you may first have to introduce the topic and provide background information.

Consider capturing attention with a creative opening. You could start with an interesting fact, a question to the audience, or a story. But use your judgment. You might make a strong first impression—or you might immediately lose the audience. Pay careful attention to the organizational culture and know your audience well before taking a big risk. Avoid starting with a joke, which could fall flat, or a quote, which could minimize your credibility. Quotations are overused, and you want your listeners to hear *your* words—not someone else's.

Strong visuals in your presentation can serve as an alternative, engaging opening. When a presenter wanted to convince Dunkin' Donuts to offer soymilk, she captured attention with a bold opening slide (Figure 5). Shown after the title slide but before the agenda, this slide uses builds (or animations) to display an "X" over each container—a visual way to explain the lack of options for soymilk drinkers.

Figure 5 | Engaging Opening Presentation Slide

For most business presentations, let the audience know up front what you expect of them. Are you simply presenting information for them to absorb, or are you asking for their endorsement, resources, or help? For example, entrepreneurs on the TV show *Shark Tank* don't wait too long before saying, "We're seeking a $100,000 investment in our company."

Your opening should lead into the body of your presentation by previewing your content. Typically, this preview will be your agenda for the presentation.

11-2c The Body

The body of your presentation conveys the content. Here you'll develop the points you introduced in the opening by giving background, specific evidence, examples, implications, consequences, and other information. Next, we review how to sequence your points, demonstrate your credibility, and manage negative information.

Choose a Logical Sequence

Just as you do when writing a letter, email, or report, choose an organizational plan that suits your purpose and your audience's needs. Common organizational plans and examples related to the Salesforce presentation are described in Figure 6. The left column is the primary organizational strategy, and you'll notice that some are used in conjunction with others.

Demonstrate Your Credibility

CHARACTER

Convince the audience that you've done a thorough job of collecting and analyzing the data and that your points are reasonable. Support your arguments with credible evidence—statistics, experiences, examples, and support from experts. Use objective language; let the data—not

Sample Organizational Patterns for a Presentation | **Figure 6**

ORGANIZATIONAL STRATEGY	DESCRIPTION	EXAMPLE FOR SALESFORCE
Benefits	Describe benefits the company will achieve. Best for proposals or recommendations to ensure that you address given criteria.	Present major positive results the company will see from using the software (e.g., a streamlined billing process).
Issues or Goals	Address concerns or shared goals and provide evidence for each. Useful as a less direct strategy when you have a hostile or resistant audience.	Identify major problems (e.g., long customer wait times) or goals (e.g., retaining more customers).
Order of Importance	Sequence points according to their importance. You may use this in combination with other strategies.	Typically, start with your strongest argument—the biggest benefit (e.g., increasing sales revenue) or issue (e.g., cancelled subscriptions).
Chronology	Describe a process or implementation plan by presenting points in time sequence.	Create a timeline to show necessary steps to purchase, customize, implement, and evaluate the software.
Problem Solving	Identify causes, effects, and possible solutions. Useful for complex problems and collaborative presentations.	Engage the sales associates in identifying problems with the current process and how Salesforces might mitigate each.
Elimination of Alternatives	Present possible options and evaluate each. Useful when many solutions may be viable.	List Salesforce and competitive products and show how each measures up against your criteria.

exaggeration or emotion—persuade the audience. Be guided by the same principles you use when writing a persuasive letter or report.

At the same time, avoid saturating your presentation with so many facts and figures that your audience won't be able to absorb them. Regardless of their relevance, statistics will not strengthen your presentation if the audience can't digest all the data. Instead, you might prepare handouts or distribute copies of additional slides with detailed statistics.

Manage Negative Information

What should you do about negative information, which, if presented, might weaken your argument? During an earnings call with analysts, Gap Inc. Executive VP and Chief Financial Officer Katrina O'Connell addressed obvious problems facing the company:

> Recognizing the COVID-related challenges faced during 2020, I am very proud of our team and how we remain focused on driving these strategic initiatives to drive long-term shareholder value. As we look to 2021, despite the significant uncertainty that remains related to the COVID pandemic, we are pleased to provide a 2021 outlook today.[6]

In your own presentations, if you ignore possible downsides of or contradictions to your ideas, a savvy audience may question your credibility—and your character.

When faced with negative information, think about your data analysis. Despite criticism, you still believe in your idea. The best approach is to present all the important information—pro and con—and to show through your own analysis that your recommendations are valid. Use emphasis and subordination techniques to let your listeners know which points you consider major and which you consider minor.

Although you should discuss the important negative points, you may reasonably omit discussing minor ones. But be prepared to discuss all issues that the audience may raise during and after the presentation.

11-2d The Ending

The ending of your presentation is your last opportunity to achieve your objective. Don't waste it. A presentation without a strong ending is like a joke without a punch line. Your closing should summarize the main points of your presentation, especially if it was long. Leave the audience with a clear and simple message, including next steps—what you expect or request after the meeting.

After you've developed some experience in giving presentations, you'll be able to judge fairly accurately how long to spend on each point so that you can finish on time. Until then, practice your presentation with a stopwatch. If necessary, insert reminders at critical points in your notes, indicating where you should be at what point. Avoid having to drop important sections or rush through the conclusion of your presentation because you misjudged your timing.

LO3 Redesign a given slide to improve visual appeal.

11-3 Designing Presentation Slides

As you organize your presentation, you'll probably sketch a few visuals, particularly as part of your storyboard. Most business presentations include some visual support. Visuals complement your message, increase comprehension, and make your presentation easier to follow—for you as well as your audience.

When planning a presentation, you'll decide what, if any, visual support you'll use. If you choose slides, use an attractive design, minimal text, and meaningful graphics.

11-3a Choosing Visual Support

When you are asked to give a presentation for a business audience, the default is to create slides to be projected onto a screen or shown on a large monitor. Although PowerPoint, as a Microsoft product, is the business standard for presentation slides, other tools are available. You might choose Google Slides for collaboration, Canva for a free app, Ludus for creative designs, Beautiful.ai for intuitive designs, Powtoon for video, Prezi for nonlinear designs, Genially for interactivity, or others.[7]

Slides aren't right for every presentation. Guests at an award or ribbon-cutting ceremony might receive only a printed program. Team members at a daily check-in meeting might receive only an agenda in advance.

Here, we focus on creating presentation slides that you deliver to groups. In Chapter 10, you learned that different levels of slide density are appropriate for different situations (shown again in Figure 7). During formal presentations, briefings, discussions, and proposals, you are the main visual. The audience cannot read slides and listen to you at the same time. In these situations, you'll create slides that complement your message rather than detract from it.

11-3b Creating an Attractive, Appropriate Design

Design is never as important as content, but visual appeal can affect the audience's comprehension. Unless your company has a standard design that you must use, you can adapt one of the many templates available for presentation slides.

A template is a good starting point for your slide design, but the few offered with PowerPoint get old fast. Adjust templates, at a minimum, by changing the colors, fonts, and background.

Deck Density for Different Purposes and Audiences | **Figure 7**

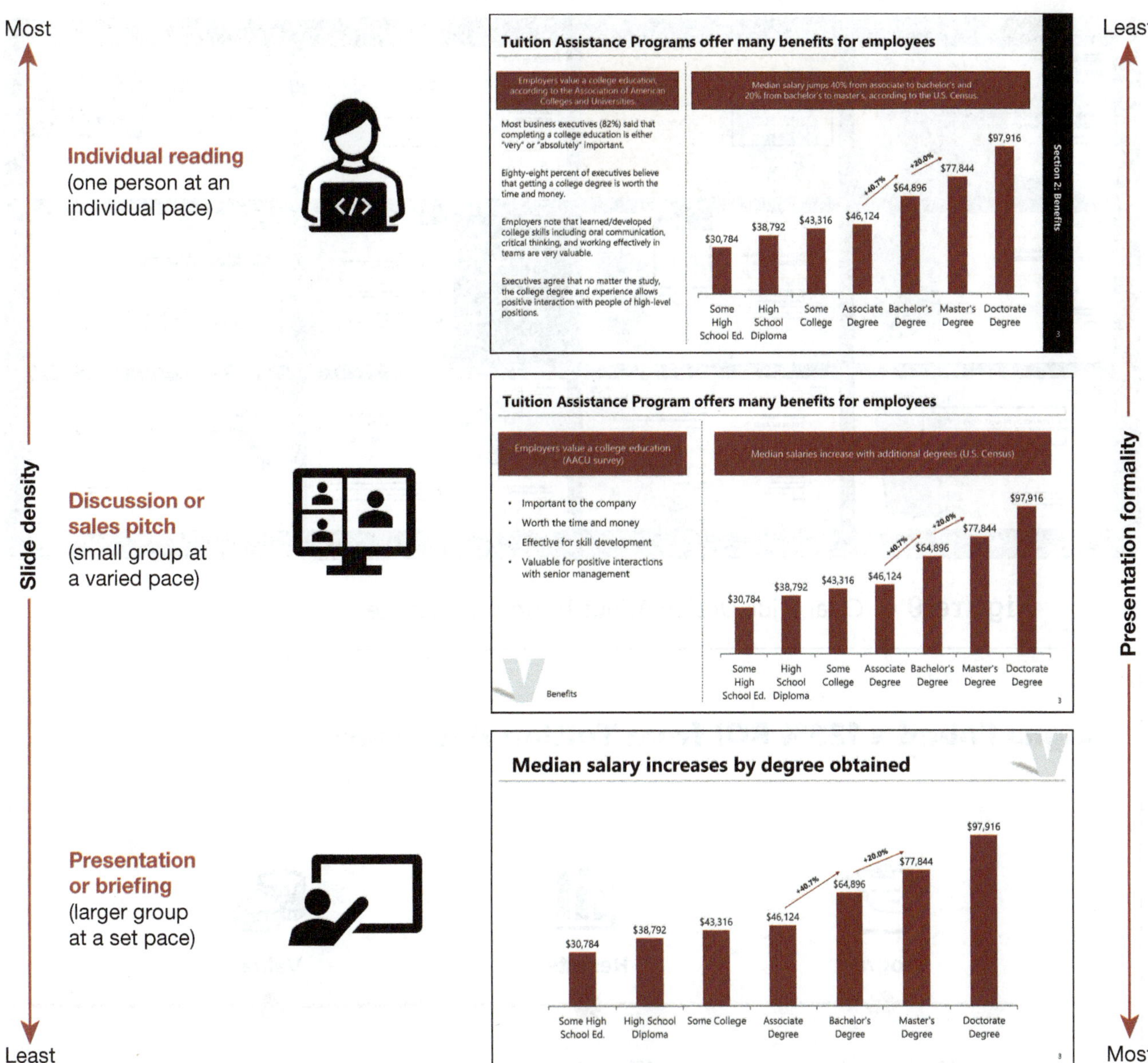

Figure 8 shows a custom design with a simple color palette. You may use more colors but avoid too many that conflict with each other. You might also consider a color scheme that reflects your company's colors.

Design principles discussed in Chapter 4 for written documents and web pages apply to presentation slides as well. Applying C.R.A.P. principles—contrast, repetition, alignment, and proximity—on each slide allows your audience to grasp information quickly. Also remember that our eyes typically follow a "Z-Pattern," so most slides start with a title, aligned left. The slide about tuition assistance shown in Figure 9 is clear and easy to follow.

You'll notice lots of white space in Figure 9. Again, the amount of text and graphics depends on your setting and audience. Projected in a large room, this slide has about as much text as you would want. For this situation, white space draws the reader's eye to a few important words and graphics.

Instead of adding clutter, consider balance. Think of each slide divided into halves, thirds, or quarters. The template in Figure 8 offers segmented places for text and photos or other graphics.

Figure 8 | Custom Design with a Simple Color Palette

GraphicPapa/Shutterstock.com

Figure 9 | Clear Slide Design About Tuition Assistance

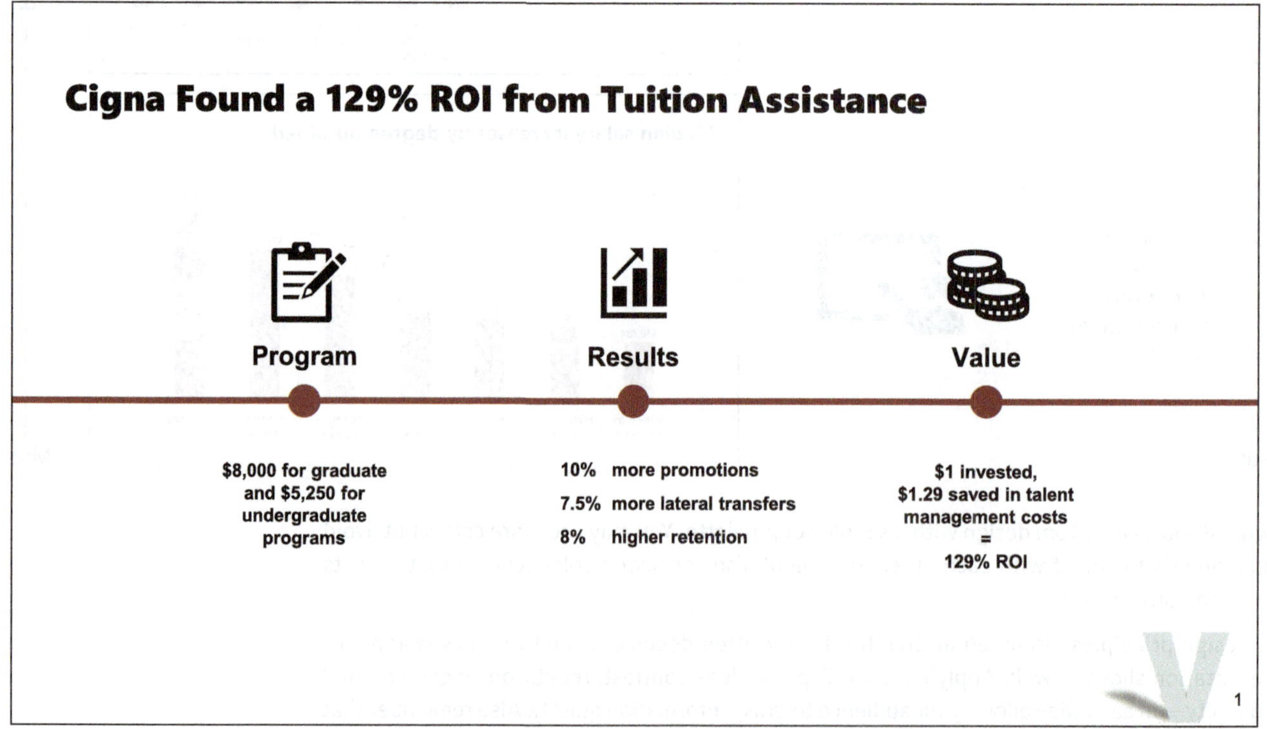

Simple backgrounds are best for slides. Choose a solid color, a light image that travels along just the edges of the slide, or a bold image with a few words of light text for an occasional, dramatic slide.

If possible, look at your slides projected in the room where you'll deliver your presentation. You may use either a dark background with light text or a light background with dark text, depending on the room. All projectors show colors slightly differently, which could affect, for example, your company's logo. Also, only with the appropriate room lighting can you determine whether your color contrast is sufficient.

Choose no more than two fonts for your slides. One font for a slide title and another for the body works well, but more may look busy. Unless you're presenting to a creative audience, choose standard business fonts. Serif fonts, which have small lines connecting to the letters, such as Cambria, have a more classic look. But you might avoid Times New Roman, which is most typical for written documents. Fonts without serifs, such as Arial and Calibri, convey a more modern look. Sometimes these fonts are easier to read on a projected screen, so check the fonts when you do your presentation run-through in the room as well.

11-3c Replacing Text with Meaningful Graphics

For large groups, slides with few or no words are best. For highly creative presentations, the speaker's delivery skills are most prominent. The slides might be simply a series of photographs. The Gap Inc. investor presentation has minimal text throughout. The slide shown in Figure 10, like most of the 91 slides, focuses on the company's clothes. Notice that the text is listed—without bullets. Bullets would not add value to this slide, only visual clutter.

Minimal Text on a Slide | **Figure 10**

Source: Gap Inc.

Even for more traditional presentations, for example, in the banking industry, avoid slide after slide of bulleted text. Some text on slides is useful for audiences—and will serve as a guide for you as the presenter. But too much text tempts you to read off the slides rather than rely on your own preparation. Text-only slides are mind-numbing for your audience and inspire jokes about "death by PowerPoint."

Instead, use your creativity to convert text into graphics. Graphics make your slides more visually appealing and, more important, show your audience how concepts relate to each other, as the Gap slide illustrates in Figure 11. The text and graphics show how all digital touchpoints connect to the customer.

Look at programs for ideas. PowerPoint's shapes, icons, and SmartArt are simple ways to turn text into graphics. Also consider using photos to replace text. But beware of arrows pointing nowhere, overused funnels, irrelevant images, and goofy clip art, which detract from your main points. You'll find more creative options on other applications.

Equally mind-numbing as text-heavy slides are large tables of data projected for your audience. A table of dense numbers is fine for a printed report deck but not for a slide. Columns and rows of numbers are hard to see and do nothing to help your audience make sense of the data. Instead, convert tables into charts.

Finally, you can use graphics and animations (builds) to highlight data and help the audience follow along. Change colors and text enhancements, such as boldface, to draw attention to key points as you review a slide. Use animations to control when the audience sees certain text and graphics.

Figure 11 | Graphics Show How Points Relate

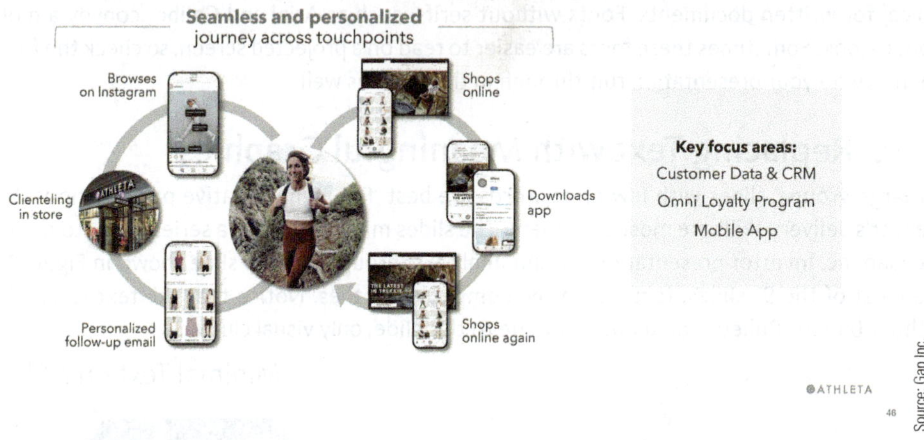

Source: Gap Inc.

But keep animations simple and avoid overusing them. Nobody needs to see a line of text travel around the slide, accompanied by a Gwen Stefani song, before it finally lands next to a bullet. Similarly, you don't need to control every word for your audience. Presenters who bring in one line of an agenda slide at a time are keeping their audience in suspense for no reason—and missing the chance for audience members to read at their own pace and see the overall plan for the presentation.

LO4 Identify ways to reinforce a main point in a presentation.

11-4 Reinforcing Main Points on Slides

For most business presentations, you'll present your main points up front and reinforce them throughout your slides. Gap Inc. slides mention "power" 44 times to drive home the message. In this section, you learn ways to focus on your message by surfacing main points in your slides, making your presentation easy to follow, and writing simply and clearly.

11-4a Surfacing Your Main Points

Begin with explicit main points on your title, main point, and agenda slides, as shown in Figure 12. A main point slide, presented before the agenda, conveys your most important message. This slide is optional but makes your communication objective clear and ensures that you don't rush through your introduction.

Next, customize your agenda with a few words to reinforce your main points. Choose phrases that differentiate you and your idea from other presentations.

Also surface your main points with message titles at the top of each slide. We discussed using descriptive headings for reports; the same applies to slide titles. But shorter titles—either full sentences or phrases—are better for easier reading during a presentation. Check that your slide titles meet the following criteria:

- **Logically sequenced.** Do they tell the story of your presentation?
- **Descriptive.** Do they convey your main point?
- **Parallel.** Are they all full sentences or similar phrases?
- **Proven.** Does the slide provide evidence to prove the main point?

To test the last criterion—whether the title is proven—think of each slide on its own. The title is a promise of what you will cover. Does it accurately summarize all points? Are any points included in the slide that the title doesn't include? Or does the title encompass points that are missing from the slide? Clear, cohesive titles are one step toward making your presentation easy to follow, which we discuss next.

Clear Main Points Up Front in a Presentation | **Figure 12**

GoodStudio/Shutterstock.com

Proposal

Offer a tax-deducible tuition assistance program to improve employee recruitment, retention, and skills.

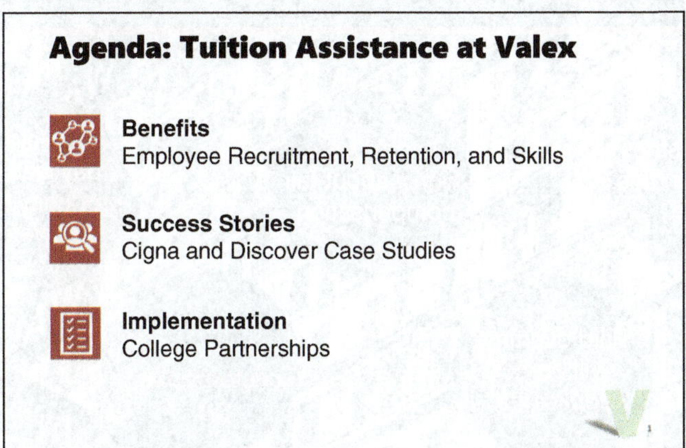

11-4b Making Your Presentation Easy to Follow

Developing a well-organized presentation is only half the battle; you also need to reflect that clear organization through your visuals to keep you and your audience focused. In your slide deck, you can include divider slides or a slide tracker. Divider slides show the topic for the next part of your presentation in either a new slide or a copy of the agenda slide highlighting it. Divider slides are particularly useful for team presentations as you transition to different presenters.

For the investor presentation, Gap Inc. used the divider slide shown in Figure 13. When a presenter showed this slide, the third part of Gap's strategy, Omni-Experience, was enlarged, new text appeared, and the background image receded with a gray filter.

An alternative to divider slides is a slide tracker to show where you are within the presentation. A slide tracker lists the major divisions of your presentation and is repeated on all slides after the agenda. With each section of the presentation highlighted as you get to it, a tracker is the audience's guide (see "Conclusion" in Figure 14). Although trackers typically appear at the bottom of a slide, they may appear at the top instead.

Figure 13 | Divider Slide for Clear Organization

As a verb, *has* should be capitalized in the slide title.

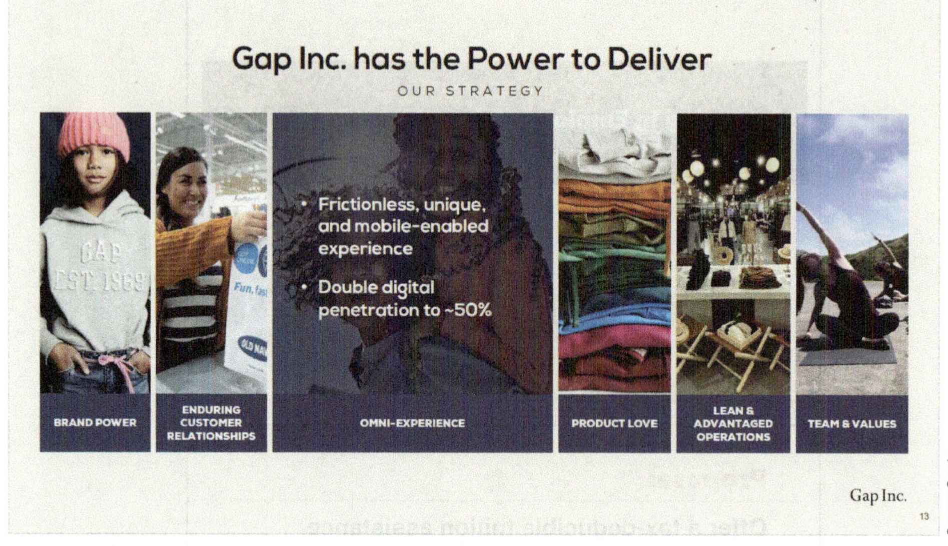

Source: Gap Inc.

Figure 14 | Slide Tracker for Clear Organization

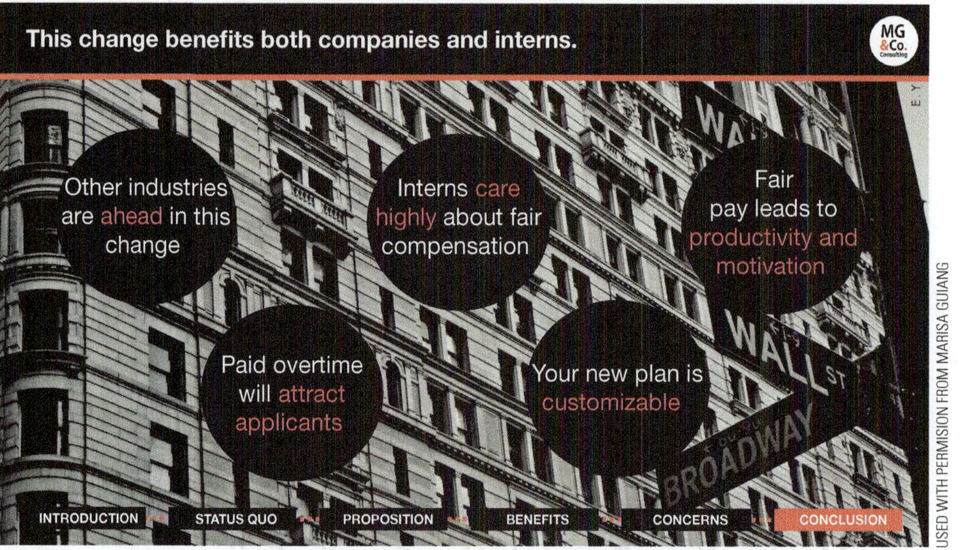

USED WITH PERMISION FROM MARISA GUIANG

11-4c Writing Simply and Clearly

When you do use text, keep it simple and clear. Edit relentlessly to keep just the most important points. The example in Figure 15 shows how you can convert paragraph text to bulleted text, and then to minimal text on a slide. The middle version might be appropriate for an online meeting, while the last would be more appropriate for a briefing in a larger, more formal setting.

Use all your proficient revising and editing skills to perfect the words you include on your slides. Notice how parallel phrasing is used in Figure 15 for each level of bullets. Once you have the text narrowed down, you can decide how to present it visually.

Converting a Paragraph to Bullets and Minimal Slide Text | **Figure 15**

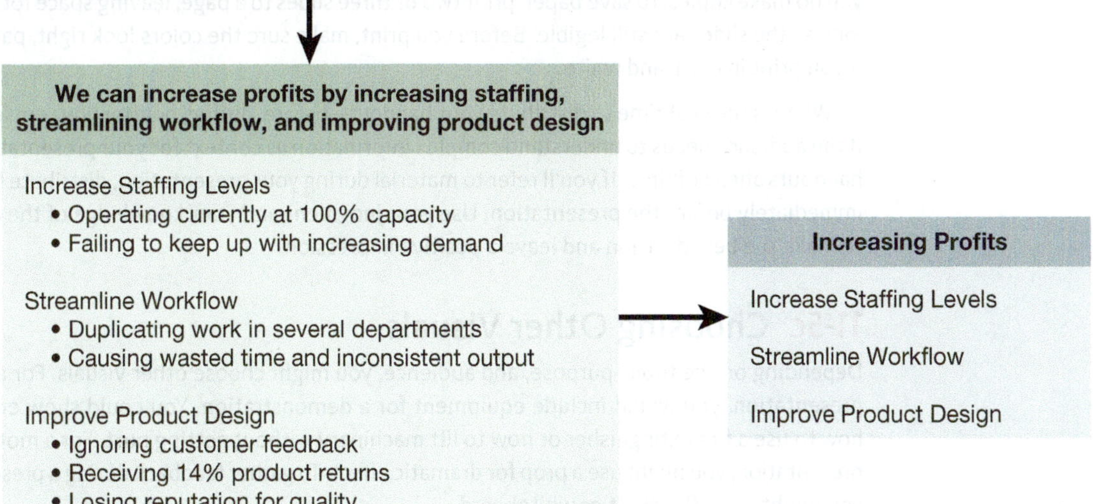

Three major initiatives will ensure that profits increase over the next 12 months. First, we must increase our staffing levels. We are currently operating at 100% capacity, yet we cannot keep up with demand, which has increased over 20% in the past six months alone. Second, we need to improve our workflow. We have people duplicating work in several departments, and this is leading to wasted time and inconsistent output. Finally, we need better product design. Customer feedback tells us that our design should be simpler and easier to use. With a product return rate of 14%, we're losing our reputation for quality.
We can increase profits by increasing staffing, streamlining workflow, and improving product design
Increase Staffing Levels
• Operating currently at 100% capacity
• Failing to keep up with increasing demand
Streamline Workflow
• Duplicating work in several departments
• Causing wasted time and inconsistent output
Improve Product Design
• Ignoring customer feedback
• Receiving 14% product returns
• Losing reputation for quality
Increasing Profits
Increase Staffing Levels
Streamline Workflow
Improve Product Design

11-5 Developing Additional Visuals

LO5 Explain the value of using video and handouts in a presentation.

Slides aren't the only visuals you can use in a presentation. At times, videos, handouts, or other visual aids will help the audience understand and remember your message.

11-5a Using Video

Including video in a presentation is a good way to engage the audience, illustrate a point, and make an emotional appeal. If you want in-store customer service associates to improve their sales skills, you could show a video of interactions with customers. If you want to convince restaurant workers to improve cleanliness, you might show how dirt accumulates on tables.

But don't use video just to break up your presentation. Your video should have a clear purpose—otherwise, it may detract from your message. Irrelevant or, worse, silly videos may make your audience question why your content isn't strong enough to stand alone. Use just enough to make your point, editing content to keep only the relevant parts.

Also integrate your video into the presentation. Tell your audience what to expect—why you're showing it, generally what it's about, and how long it will be. At the end, summarize the relevance and transition to your next point.

Practice so that you can show the video smoothly and seamlessly. Embed videos into your presentation slides rather than switching programs or linking to YouTube. Embedded videos will look more professional and will eliminate embarrassing downtime during your presentation. Check the sound in the presentation room and set the volume level in advance to make sure your audience won't miss the first few seconds of your video.

11-5b Creating Handouts

International COMMUNICATION

Handouts—copies of slides, notes, tables, or illustrations—help the audience follow a presentation and provide a "takeaway" for additional information. For audiences whose primary language differs from that of the speaker, a handout provides more time for comprehension after the presentation. For an online presentation, send a link or an attachment for people to download.

For an in-person presentation, decide what, if anything, you need to print. Audiences might object to wasted paper, so you might send slides digitally even for in-person presentations. If you do make copies, to save paper, print two or three slides to a page, leaving space for notes, as long as the slides are still legible. Before you print, make sure the colors look right, particularly if you print in black and white.

When is the best time to distribute your handout—before, during, or after your presentation? If the audience needs to understand complex information as context for your presentation, send handouts ahead of time. If you'll refer to material during your presentation, distribute handouts immediately before the presentation. Use your judgment and your knowledge of the audience to make the best decision and leave a positive impression.

11-5c Choosing Other Visuals

Depending on the topic, purpose, and audience, you might choose other visuals. For a training presentation, you would include equipment for a demonstration. You could show employees how to use a fire extinguisher or how to lift machinery without getting hurt. For a motivational presentation, you might use a prop for dramatic effect. To gather feedback during a presentation, you might use a flip chart or whiteboard.

For topics that can't be described in words alone, you could be more creative. To improve interpersonal relationships, you might bring in actors to role-play a situation. Or you might invite a customer to describe a service experience.

In business, we default to PowerPoint for presentations just as we default to email for written communication. Finding original ways to deliver information might engage your audience more and make it more likely that you'll get the result you want.

11-6 Chapter Closing

As of this writing, the consensus among investment analysts is a "hold" rating for Gap Inc. stock. Company performance is better for some brands (e.g., Athleta) than others (e.g., Banana Republic). In a recent presentation, one slide is titled "Rationalizing Our Store Fleet," a positive way of saying that 350 Gap and Banana Republic stores are closing.[8]

In business, we use presentations to tell our story—for better or for worse. With a clear message and a good understanding of our audience, we develop a presentation with visuals that meets our communication objectives. Next, we prepare to deliver the presentation to our audience.

Prepare an In-Person Presentation for a Monthly Report About Athleta

Consider the chapter introduction, which described Gap Inc.'s investor presentation. Imagine that you're Mary Beth Laughton, the president and CEO of the Athleta brand, and you're preparing your monthly presentation to the board of directors. Using the CAM model, what questions might you consider before preparing the presentation?

>>> CHARACTER CHECK

1. **What's my view of the company and Athleta brand performance?**
   Gap is a classic brand and a great company, but not all brands are equal. Athleta's performance is doing well and much better than some of the others, like Banana Republic. I had better watch my humility about this because I am proud of our brand.
2. **How might my view affect my presentation?**
   I need to stay focused on our strengths but also include challenges, and we do have a lot of competition in the activewear space. I won't make comparisons between Athleta and the other Gap Inc. brands.

>>> AUDIENCE ANALYSIS

1. **Who is my audience and what is their purpose for asking me to present?**
   The CEO and board of directors want good news. The company is relying on my brand (and others) to contribute to the bottom line and tell a good story to investors.
2. **What do I know about them that will help me prepare the presentation?**
   They want just the facts—our numbers since last month and expectations for next. They also want to know about any challenges so they're not blindsided if the situation changes. I want to be accurate, but with this group, it's better if I exceed expectations than come up short.

>>> MESSAGE AND MEDIUM

1. **What are the main points of my message?**
   I'll present our financials and report on progress against our initiatives for the year. We have gotten good press for being a certified B Corp (business as a force for good) and for our inclusive design and marketing. I want to emphasize that because some board members were skeptical about our initial approach.

2. **In what medium will I communicate the message?**
   The monthly presentations are fairly standard. I'll create a PowerPoint presentation using the brand template.

Prepare an Online Presentation to Athleta Store Managers

IN PRACTICE

Imagine that you're the sales director for Athleta. You helped Mary Beth Laughton, the president and CEO of the Athleta brand, prepare her presentation described on the previous page to the board of directors. Now you would like to present similar—but tailored—information to your sales department. Some employees work remotely, so you will present via Microsoft Teams online.

>>> CHARACTER CHECK

1. What drives me to present to my staff? Of course, I want to increase sales. What else?
2. What is at stake for me personally?

>>> AUDIENCE ANALYSIS

1. Who is my audience, and what do they need to hear?
2. What resistance might I encounter?

>>> MESSAGE AND MEDIUM

1. What will be my main points? How will they differ for this audience?
2. What visuals will I use? How will they differ for the online format?

REFLECTING ON YOUR COMMUNICATION AND CHARACTER DEVELOPMENT

1. **Consider your own views about developing presentations.**
   Before you consider delivering a presentation, think about preparing one. How do you feel about the work? If you feel anxious, try to reframe the prospect. Focus on your knowledge of the subject and the chance to convey it to others. Or imagine achieving your objective and how that will make you feel.

2. **Transfer your skills.**
   Do you feel more competent preparing content or delivering a presentation? How can you use your skills from one to improve your competence at the other?

   For example, are you good at organizing a presentation? If so, how can you apply your sense of timing and transitions to reinforce your message during delivery? Or, if you enjoy interacting with people during delivery, how can you develop a presentation that engages the audience and invites their participation?

3. **Reflect on visuals you have seen.**
   How do you perceive others' visuals during presentations? Have you been harsh in criticizing PowerPoints and other visuals? What can you learn for your own development process?

4. **Consider a demonstration.**
   How comfortable would you be using a demonstration as part of a presentation? Imagine that you want to reduce sexual harassment in an organization. Could you include a role play by actors or employees to illustrate a situation and then have the audience discuss what could be done differently? Consider the potential benefits and drawbacks of this approach. Include your own feelings about facilitating the activity.

DEVELOPING YOUR BUSINESS COMMUNICATION SKILLS

LO1 Describe ways to adapt your presentation for an audience in a given business situation.

ADAPTING A PRESENTATION

1. **Prepare a presentation about your business idea for different audiences.**
   Imagine that you have a great idea for a new business—and maybe you already have one. Plan to present your idea to two different audiences: potential investors and prospective employees. In small groups, describe your communication objectives for each audience. What do you hope each group will think, do, and feel after hearing your presentation? What does each group want to know? Prepare an agenda for each audience.

2. **Prepare a presentation for different campus audiences.**
   Imagine that you work for a university as the head of transportation. You want to encourage people to take the bus rather than park on campus because spots are limited. Prepare agenda slides for two different audiences: faculty who live off campus and students who live on campus.

   Your presentation may include the challenges of parking on campus, the bus schedule, a cost comparison between driving and taking the bus, and any other information you believe may be relevant to persuade each of your audiences.

3. **Plan a presentation for a job interview.**
   Imagine that you made it through first-round interviews with a company you admire. For the second round, they ask you to prepare a three-minute presentation on any topic. You'll

deliver this to the hiring manager, three people who would be your coworkers, and two representatives from HR. To prepare for your presentation, answer the following questions:

a. What is the purpose of your presentation?
b. What do you know about your audience that will help you prepare?
c. What topic will you choose for your presentation and why?
d. What points will you include in your presentation?
e. What visual support will you use?

4. Describe audience types

To prepare for a presentation, imagine different audiences. In small groups, describe how you would identify audiences that are hostile, skeptical, or laid-back. Try to be specific about their body language, questions they might ask, and other behaviors.

5. Identify audience types in person or online.

Watch a presentation or meeting in person or online. Identify audience reactions by observing each person carefully. Would you describe anyone as hostile, skeptical, or laid-back? What about their behavior leads to your conclusion?

Do you get the sense that the presenter planned well for these reactions, or was the presenter taken by surprise? What about the presentation content, organization, and visuals leads to your conclusion?

6. Prepare for different employee audiences.

Imagine that you're preparing to talk with your team of employees about a new inventory management system at a retail store. You have noticed items missing and want a better tracking system. The system also will help you predict sales more accurately, so you'll know when to restock items. You expect that employees will respond differently to the idea. How would you adapt the presentation for a hostile, skeptical, and laid-back audience? Consider what content you would focus on and how you would organize the presentation differently for each.

ORGANIZING A PRESENTATION

LO2 Identify steps for developing a presentation as a story.

7. Identify a story in presentations.

Watch two TED Talks. Identify stories—either parts of a presentation or the entire presentation as a story. How does each story follow the format shown in Figure 3? In what ways does it differ? How does the speaker create and build tension or suspense?

8. Describe suspense in a series.

Think about a show you watch that has multiple episodes. How is suspense used to keep you engaged? What happens at the end of each episode that makes you want to watch the next one? Give a few examples of the story plot to illustrate highs and lows.

9. Create a storyboard.

To prepare for an upcoming presentation, create a storyboard. Use software, a PowerPoint template, or paper and sticky notes. Draw pictures and write a few words to capture what you would create on each slide.

If you do this activity in groups, walk through your storyboard with another team for their feedback. How might you reorder sections and change content to improve the organization? Also give each other feedback on the storyboard itself. Is it clear? Do you have enough content to develop the slides? What else would be helpful to include at this point in the planning process?

10. **Prepare an opening for a presentation.**

For an upcoming presentation, prepare an engaging opening. Try something original and creative but consider the audience carefully so you don't lose credibility by trying to capture attention in a way that will be a turnoff. When you think you have a good start, discuss your approach with another student for feedback.

11. **Discuss how to organize a presentation.**

In small groups, discuss the following and identify which organizational pattern might work best in each situation. Review Figure 6 for a description and example of each pattern: benefits, issues or goals, order of importance, chronology, problem solving, and elimination of alternatives. You also may consider other patterns or a combination of these patterns.

a. You're explaining a new procedure for hosts to upload their podcasts.

b. You're pitching a proposal to a prospective client who has had the same supplier for more than five years.

c. You're proposing a new way for your student organization to run meetings.

d. You're concerned about your team's increased expenses in the past year and decide to talk with them.

e. You're proposing a particular company to clean the office; you already have approval to have it professionally cleaned.

f. You're communicating to your team that they can no longer work from home every day.

LO3 Redesign a given slide to improve visual appeal.

DESIGNING PRESENTATION SLIDES

12. **Find slide templates that appeal to you.**

Go to Canva or another design website. Look at the available slide templates and choose two that appeal to you. Why are you drawn to these examples? What about the colors or format do you like? What aspects of the template don't appeal to you? Remember these choices so that you can incorporate some design elements and avoid others in your own slides.

13. **Create a customized slide template.**

You are the owner of a mid-sized insurance company. You have 25 agents who travel throughout the country, making presentations to small groups of 10–20 people.

You want to create a template that all agents can use for their presentations. Your agents have been making their own slides or using no visuals at all, but you want consistency across all regions.

Invent a company name and logo, and then create a template that all agents can use. You may start with a standard template but customize it for the team. Choose a design, colors, and a few standard graphics. Include five or six slides in your sample deck—title slide, agenda slide, two or three examples of graphical slides, and a closing slide.

14. **Evaluate visuals used for a presentation.**

Attend a business meeting, city council meeting, student organization meeting, conference, or some other event where presentations will take place. Imagine that you were hired as a consultant to help the group improve their presentation visuals.

Write a one-page email to summarize your feedback. What, if any, visuals are used? Does the presenter have handouts? When are handouts distributed? How effective are the visuals, and what changes could improve them?

15. **Convert a report to slides for two presentations.**
If you created a report deck for individual reading (discussed in Chapter 10), this is your chance to use it to create new decks for two presentations. First, imagine a presentation for a small group. Reduce the heavy text and convert tables to charts. Next, imagine a briefing type of presentation for a large audience. Reduce the text further so that you are speaking more and the audience is reading less. Edit all text until it's concise and readable.

16. **Reduce text on a slide.**
If a colleague showed you the slide in Figure 16, how would you change it? Working in trios, reduce the text on this slide to make it easier to read, more logically organized, and more graphical. Compare your revision to another group's. What are the best features of each?

Reduce Text on a Slide | **Figure 16**

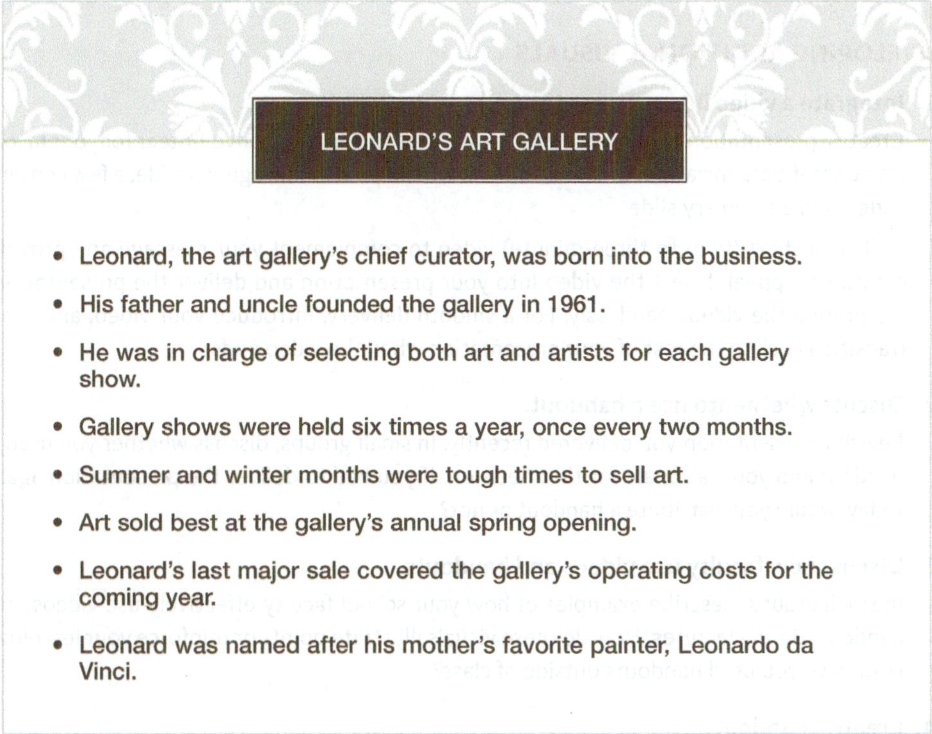

LEONARD'S ART GALLERY

- Leonard, the art gallery's chief curator, was born into the business.
- His father and uncle founded the gallery in 1961.
- He was in charge of selecting both art and artists for each gallery show.
- Gallery shows were held six times a year, once every two months.
- Summer and winter months were tough times to sell art.
- Art sold best at the gallery's annual spring opening.
- Leonard's last major sale covered the gallery's operating costs for the coming year.
- Leonard was named after his mother's favorite painter, Leonardo da Vinci.

REINFORCING MAIN POINTS ON SLIDES

LO4 Identify ways to reinforce a main point in a presentation.

17. **Revise opening slides in a presentation.**
Find a slide presentation you created. Revise the title and agenda slides to include your main points if you didn't in the original version. You might have to add descriptive text or remove generic points in the agenda. Did you use a main point slide? If not, create one. Try to capture the presentation in a few words or a sentence.

18. **Revise titles in a presentation.**
For the same presentation you revised in Exercise 17 or another one, revise the slide titles. Read them all first. Are they logically sequenced, descriptive, and parallel? If not, revise them to meet these criteria. Then read them in sequence. Do they tell the story of your

presentation? Finally, read each slide individually. Does the slide title convey all points on that slide? Do you find missing information or overlap between slides? Revise the slides as you need to, and then read the titles again in sequence to double-check for logic and cohesiveness.

19. Add dividers and a tracker.

For the same slides used in the previous exercise, add divider slides. You might repeat the agenda slide and highlight each part, or you might use images and other text as dividers.

Also add a tracker. Create one that matches your slide color and style yet doesn't overpower the rest of the slides.

20. Convert paragraph text to graphics.

Imagine that you want to present the ideas for using video in presentations from this chapter to a group of people. Convert the "Using Video" section of this chapter (11-5a) to one slide. Use only a few words to focus on your main points, and then arrange them graphically.

LO5 Explain the value of using video and handouts in a presentation.

DEVELOPING ADDITIONAL VISUALS

21. Integrate a video into a presentation.

Create a presentation to convince your classmates to donate to or volunteer for your favorite nonprofit organization. Create a title slide, main point slide, agenda slide, a few content slides, and a summary slide.

Find a short (two- to three-minute) video to complement your message and provide emotional appeal. Insert the video into your presentation and deliver the presentation, integrating the video seamlessly. For a smooth delivery, introduce your video, and then transition back to the rest of your presentation when the video ends.

22. Discuss whether to use a handout.

Revisit a presentation you delivered recently. In small groups, discuss whether you used a handout and your rationale for that decision. If you had to deliver the presentation again today, would you distribute a handout or not?

23. Discuss how faculty use videos and handouts.

In small groups, describe examples of how your school faculty effectively use videos and handouts during lectures. How do these visuals illustrate points or reinforce your learning? How have you used handouts outside of class?

24. Create a handout.

For your second-round job interview, a prospective employer has asked you to deliver a presentation on any topic (Exercise 3). To make the best impression—and to leave something for the audience to remember you—create a handout. Include a summary of your main points and your contact information.

CHAPTER SUMMARY

LO1 Describe ways to adapt your presentation for an audience in a given business situation.

Avoiding "winging" a presentation. Instead, spend time preparing by determining the purpose of the presentation and analyzing the audience. The same content should be delivered differently based on the context. Also prepare for particularly challenging groups, for example, hostile, skeptical, laid-back, and mixed audiences.

LO2 Identify steps for developing a presentation as a story.

Think of your presentation as a story and consider telling a story within a presentation. Create a storyboard to identify the presentation sequence and to introduce and build tension. Begin with an opening to engage the audience, and then organize your topics logically around benefits, issues, chronology, or another pattern. End strongly by summarizing your main points or discussing next steps.

LO3 Redesign a given slide to improve visual appeal.

Choose a slide design and format based on the presentation context. Use more text for discussions with small groups and less text for briefings to large groups. Replace text with meaningful graphics where possible. Customize a slide template to create an original-looking design with complementary colors and graphics.

LO4 Identify ways to reinforce a main point in a presentation.

Reinforce your main points throughout your slides with title, main point, and agenda slides. Include message titles to summarize main points on each slide and consider divider slides or a tracker to help the audience follow along with your presentation.

LO5 Explain the value of using video and handouts in a presentation.

Consider using visuals other than slides for a presentation. Videos engage the audience, illustrate a point, and make an emotional appeal. Handouts give the audience a way to remember the presentation and find more information. Demonstrations are useful for training and for challenging presentation topics.

Endnotes

1. "Can Gap Escape the Whirlwind?: New CEO Confronts Years of Decline," *The Wall Street Journal*, October 26, 2020, www.wsj.com/articles/gap-stores-ceo-sonia-syngal-retail-economy-11603424943, accessed June 7, 2021.
2. Sonia Syngal, "Gap Inc. Investor Meeting 2020," October 20, 2020, YouTube, posted October 28, 2020, www.youtube.com/watch?v=mjN5kQqDfPw, accessed April 20, 2021.
3. Read more from Adam Grant, *Think Again* (New York: Viking, 2021), Chapter 5.
4. Grant, p. 171.
5. Adapted from Nancy Duarte, "Structure Your Presentation Like a Story," *Harvard Business Review*, October 31, 2012, https://hbr.org/2012/10/structure-your-presentation-li, accessed June 7, 2021, and Orana Velarde, "7 Ways to Structure Your Presentation to Keep Your Audience Wanting More," Visme, https://visme.co/blog/presentation-structure, accessed June 7, 2021.
6. "Q4 2020 Gap Inc Earnings Call, San Francisco," March 5, 2021, edited transcript, Yahoo, www.yahoo.com/now/edited-transcript-gps-n-earnings-220000892.html, accessed June 7, 2021.
7. Kiera Abbamonte, "The Best Presentation Software in 2021," Zapier, April 29, 2021, https://zapier.com/blog/best-powerpoint-alternatives/, accessed June 9, 2021.
8. "Gap Inc. Fiscal 2021, First Quarter Earnings Results," PowerPoint Presentation, Gap Inc., https://gapinc-prod.azureedge.net/gapmedia/gapcorporatesite/media/images/investors/realestate/1q21-slides-final_1.pdf, accessed June 12, 2021.

CHAPTER

12 Delivering Presentations

Learning Objectives

After you have finished this chapter, you should be able to

LO1 Identify five strategies to feel more confident for a presentation.

LO2 Describe how to use body movement and voice during a large-group presentation.

LO3 List ways to prepare for an online presentation.

LO4 Describe how to adapt your delivery to a specific, challenging audience.

LO5 Identify a list of challenging questions for a given presentation and practice responding.

“*I want to hang out with you. . . . Best pitch ever.*”[1]

—Mark Cuban, on *Shark Tank* about Wen Muenyi

Chapter Introduction

Entrepreneur Impresses *Shark Tank* Investors

Investors on the TV show *Shark Tank* provide financing for businesses they believe will be successful—and for entrepreneurs they can trust with their money. Wen Muenyi received accolades from the Sharks after presenting Jax Sheets, a copper-infused, silk and cotton bedsheet marketed to men.

Michael Desmond/Disney General Entertainment Content/Getty Images

Shark Tank investors appreciate honesty from entrepreneurs who present on the show.

Muenyi presented himself authentically, showing a picture of the messy garage where he sits in a lawn chair and works. The Sharks could relate. Daymond John said, "I've been there."

After a commercial break, the show announcer said, "The Sharks are charmed by Wen's honesty." Kevin O'Leary said, "I don't care about the underwear and T-shirt business. Returns are horrific." Muenyi responded, "I agree. You're right." At another point, Mark Cuban said, "That was a great answer. You're an honest guy, man." Muenyi responded, "I don't lie."

In the end, Muenyi did not get an investment. The Sharks felt that he didn't need a partner at the time, but they invited him back when he has more sales and more data.

They'll remember him. Robert Herjavec said, "When someone comes out that's pure and honest and full of joy, that's why we get so excited."[2]

LO1 Identify five strategies to feel more confident for a presentation.

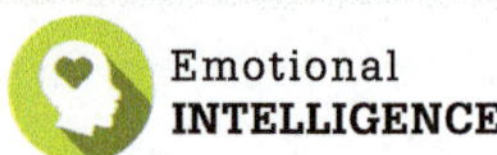
Emotional INTELLIGENCE

How do you feel about giving presentations? For what types of presentations, settings, and audiences do you feel most and least comfortable?

CHARACTER

12-1 Preparing Yourself to Present

You may have heard that one of Americans' top fears is public speaking—perhaps it's one of yours. Presentations are inescapable in business for winning sales, rallying support for an idea, communicating change, and many other situations. Just about everyone in business will give at least one major presentation and many smaller ones each year to employees, clients, managers, and colleagues. Your presentation skills also are useful for your personal life—in social situations and at community meetings.

The good news is that you can be yourself and develop your own style. A presentation is an opportunity to present your authentic self, project confidence, and show who you are as a person—your character. You do this in presentations that feel more like conversations than formal speeches.

12-1a Projecting Confidence and Demonstrating Presence

You might agree with the famous quote "There are two types of speakers—those who are nervous and those who are liars."[3] For many people, giving a presentation makes them feel faint or nauseated ("butterflies in the stomach"); makes their hands or legs shake and their palms sweat; gives them a rapid, loud heartbeat; makes their face or neck look red and blotchy; or makes them speak too fast and in a high-pitched voice. If you have experienced these symptoms, you're not alone.

The Oscar-winning movie *The King's Speech* portrayed England's King George VI, who suffered with a stammer. The film raised awareness of how many people—even kings—suffer from speech anxiety and other hurdles to speaking in public.

Some level of nervousness is useful for presentations. Anxiety indicates that we have an important task ahead of us and challenges us to prepare well. But too much anxiety can control us and damage our performance.

Fortunately, people can use their anxiety to become more confident speakers. For many people, nervousness itself is the only issue. Simply changing how we think about ourselves and our delivery skills can reduce speech anxiety.

Anxiety affects people differently. How we experience nervousness—how it manifests in our bodies—and how we can combat counterproductive thoughts and feelings vary. What works for one person will not necessarily work for another.

Find the speech tool at speaking.amynewman.com.

A web-based tool, "How to Feel Confident for a Presentation and Manage Speech Anxiety," describes 24 possible strategies (Figure 1). Cognitive approaches involve changing what you believe or how you think about your fears, your audience, your presentations, or yourself. Behavioral (or physical) strategies focus on how you prepare, understand, and use your body. Affective strategies relate to emotions. Working through how you feel helps you focus on your success.

With tactics to try before, the day of, and after a presentation, this tool generates a custom plan. Following are a few examples:

- **Before the Presentation:** How you prepare for and think about a presentation can help reduce anxiety. Writing coping statements and practicing in front of others are among the strategies that can reduce nervousness.
- **The Day of the Presentation:** On the day of the presentation, presenters can improve their delivery by, for example, breathing deeply, visualizing success, and distracting themselves from negative thoughts—focusing on something other than the presentation.
- **After the Presentation:** Research shows that watching a video of yourself with an open mind, letting yourself relax, and writing down what went well can improve how you feel about your presentation.

Some nervousness is good, so don't fret it too much. Anxiety during a presentation gets the adrenaline flowing and gives your speech an edge. If you do make a mistake, don't apologize for it. Dropped the remote? Just pick it up. Lost your place? Refer briefly to your notes. If you

Online Tool: "How to Feel Confident for a Presentation and Manage Speech Anxiety" | **Figure 1**

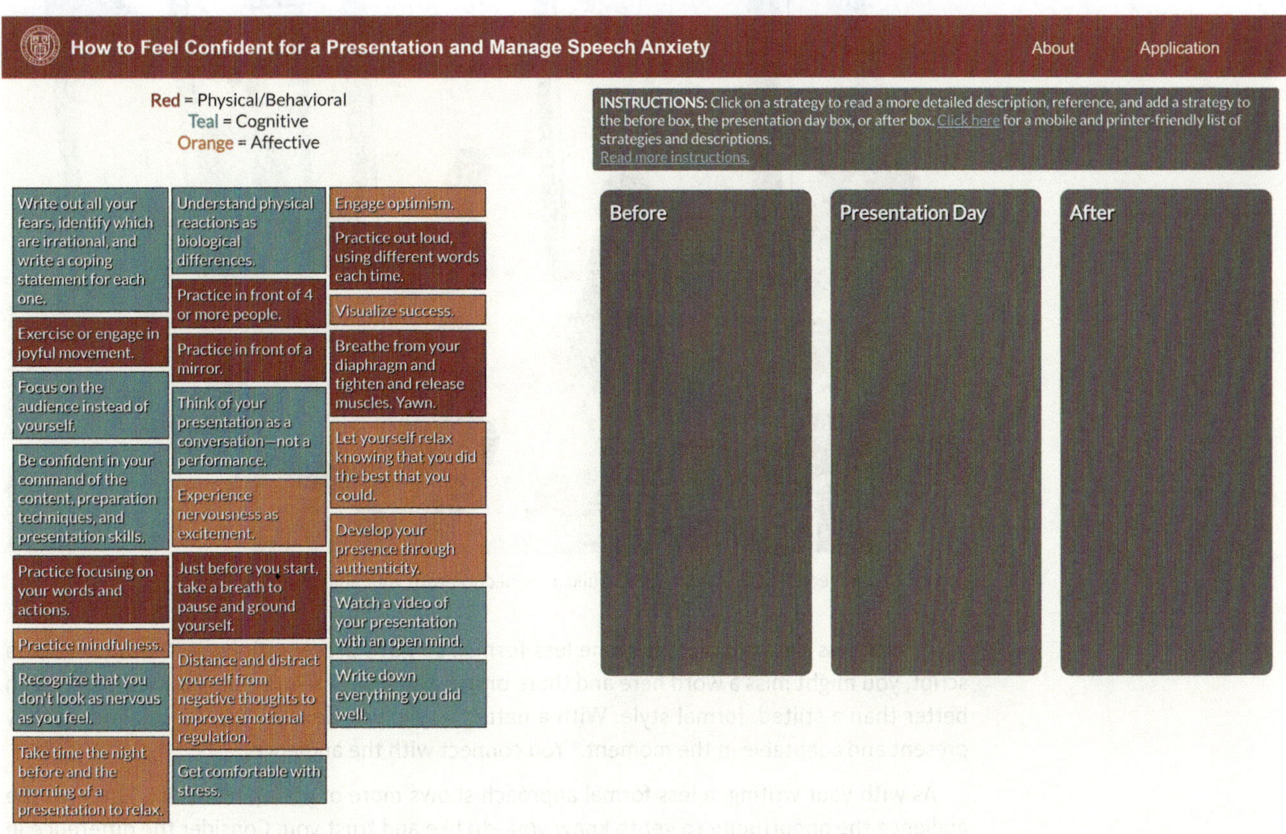

handle mishaps smoothly and with grace, your audience will remember your recovery more than the mistake.

12-1b Choosing a Delivery Style

As you become more comfortable as a presenter, you can adapt your speaking style to any situation and audience. Plotted along a continuum in Figure 2, delivery styles span informal and formal formats.

Delivery Styles | **Figure 2**

Informal

Formal

Impromptu

Scripted

Extemporaneous

Memorized

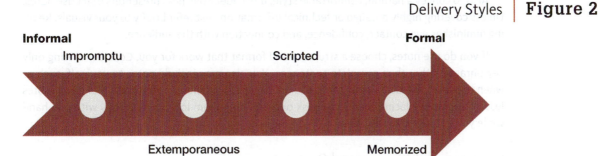

Impromptu and Extemporaneous Presentations

Most business presentations are impromptu or extemporaneous. You can't prepare much for an impromptu presentation; for example, during a meeting, someone might ask you for your opinion on a new product. If you did your homework, you would be able to answer the question well. But you wouldn't have any visuals, and you would speak in a conversational, unrehearsed style. Like an impromptu presentation, an extemporaneous presentation is unrehearsed and conversational. But it is prepared, so the presenter sounds organized and fluid.

Monkey Business Images/Shutterstock.com

An extemporaneous speaking style helps build a connection with your audience.

As business environments become less formal, so have presentations. Without notes or a script, you might miss a word here and there or use a couple of fillers, but this method is much better than a stilted, formal style. With a natural style, you develop "presence"—being fully present and adaptable in the moment.[4] You connect with the audience.

As with your writing, a less formal approach shows more of your personality. You give the audience the opportunity to get to know you—to like and trust you. Consider the difference in tone in these sentences:

☒ NOT Today, I will be reviewing the project timeline and the extent to which the deliverables have met previously set targets.

☑ BUT Let's take a look at where we are in the project plan.

The second version uses natural, conversational language, such as contractions, and is much shorter.

Also to convey a natural, comfortable style, most adept business presenters don't use notes. Unless covering highly detailed or technical information, just refer briefly to your visuals. Reading diminishes eye contact, confidence, and connection with the audience.

If you do use notes, choose a structure and format that work for you. Consider writing only key phrases rather than complete sentences. You also may include notes to yourself, such as when to pause. Instead of index cards, use full pages to look more professional. Make your notes less obtrusive by placing them on a desk or by holding them low on your body with one hand while you gesture with the other.

Emotional **INTELLIGENCE**

Have you memorized a speech to avoid the extemporaneous delivery style? What worked well about this approach, and in what ways did it fall short?

Scripted and Memorized Presentations

In a few business situations, a scripted or memorized style may be appropriate. For a scripted presentation, the presenter reads directly from notes, as you see business leaders and politicians do at news conferences. For crisis situations, for example, this is a good approach to make sure you don't say anything on camera that you'll later regret. You also may read notes for ceremonial speeches—for example, at a retirement dinner.

Very few situations call for a memorized speech. When you memorize, you prepare to present for *any* audience—not the audience to whom you're presenting, so you'll be less able to

Mark Wilson/Getty Images News/Getty Images

GM CEO Mary Barra testifies in Washington, D.C., about ignition switch recalls.

adapt to their reactions. Trying to build a client relationship or motivate a team with a memorized speech would be off-putting. You're likely to sound mechanical rather than authentic and confident. Finally, memorizing takes time, which isn't always possible when preparing a presentation.

If you do deliver a memorized speech, you must be completely comfortable with it. TED Talks are presented in ways that appear natural but are scripted and memorized.[5] Speakers so thoroughly rehearse that they can focus on the audience instead of on themselves.

General Motors delayed car recalls and, by some accounts, caused 124 deaths.[6] After reaching a settlement agreement, CEO Mary Barra held a town hall meeting with employees and spoke plainly: "Before I talk about the settlement agreement, let's pause for a moment and remember that people were hurt, and people died in our cars. That's why we're here."[7] She made an emotional connection with her audience, which was critical to help them accept responsibility and learn from their mistakes.

As the CEO of a Fortune 500 company, Barra has delivered many different types of presentations. In addition to internal audiences, she speaks at academic and leadership conferences and on TV business news programs. She adapts to different settings and audiences just as you will throughout your career. Next, we discuss delivering in-person presentations.

12-2 Delivering In-Person Presentations

LO2 Describe ways to use body movement and voice during a large-group presentation.

When presenting in person, you are on full display and have every tool available for engaging with your audience. In this section, you learn how to start and end strongly, use your body and voice, interact with visuals, and practice.

As you read these suggestions, you'll discover ways to deliver different types of presentations. The purpose, audience, and setting are always important to consider as you prepare.

Emotional **INTELLIGENCE**

How have you adapted to different types of presentations in the past? How adept were you in making adjustments to different audiences?

12-2a Setting the Stage and Ending Strongly

The first 90 seconds of your presentation are crucial to capture the audience's attention. Whether your presentation is formal or informal, the audience will be observing and making judgments about your dress, posture, facial expressions, voice qualities, visuals, and of course, what you say.

Plan what you'll wear, erring on more conservative clothes. As the presenter, dress just slightly better than the audience, but don't go overboard. If the office is casual, you can dress casually too.

Before you begin your presentation, build a relationship with your audience—not just for the duration of your presentation, but for the long term. Focus on your presence. Are you fully engaged and connecting with everyone? Consider introducing yourself and making small talk with people as they walk into the space. Use your strategies from the tool, "How to Feel Confident for a Presentation," to convey a sense of calm, confidence, and focus.

Because the opening of your presentation is so crucial to establish rapport, consider writing out the first one or two sentences and practicing them more carefully. Pause just a beat before beginning to command control of the room, and then speak clearly and confidently.

Don't start your presentation with an apology or excuse. If you say, "I'm not really much of a speaker," the audience may agree with you! Also avoid apologizing for a cold or scratchy voice. Most people wouldn't notice otherwise. Why start off by telling your audience to question your credibility or delivery skills?

As you prepare your opening, also prepare your closing. What will you say at the end of the presentation, so people leave with a positive impression? You might change your plan depending on the audience reaction but have a sentence or two in mind to end strongly and connect back to your beginning. Your audience may most remember your last words—choose them carefully and deliver them confidently.

12-2b Moving Your Body

In addition to the type of presentation, the size of your audience and the room determine how you'll move within the space. For large groups and in big spaces, your movement might be more deliberate, your gestures more exaggerated, and your eye contact more intentional.

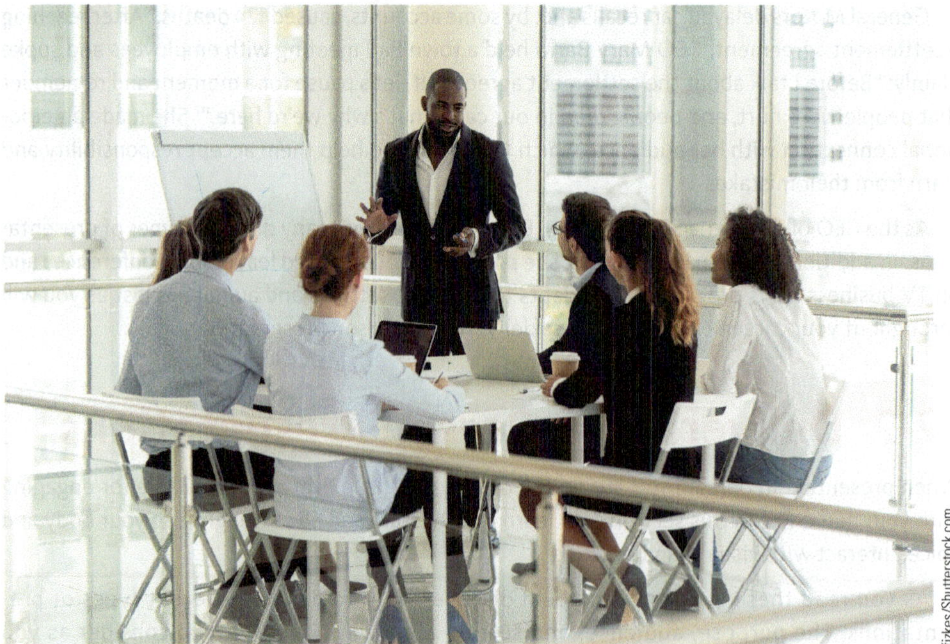

fizkes/Shutterstock.com

Consider dressing slightly more formally than your audience.

Also get a sense of the energy in the room. Who seems most engaged? Where do you feel most present? Where are you most drawn? Zooming out will help you see how to engage the audience and what relationships might evolve. Then, you can decide how to move your body, use hand and arm gestures, and make eye contact.

Body Movement

Aim for natural body movement. As you present, take a few steps and avoid swaying or pacing. Take purposeful walks, which can release nervous energy. You might walk toward someone who asks a question and then take a step back while answering. Or you might take a couple of steps to the side when transitioning from one part of your presentation to another.

For more formal presentations, some body movement may be choreographed, but try to use your body in a way that complements your message rather than detracts from it. Knowing your audience will ensure you're moving appropriately for the setting. For example, leaning against a table might convey that you're relaxed, or disinterested.

Hand and Arm Gestures

Some presenters struggle with what to do with their hands. Try to use natural hand gestures as you would in any conversation. Practice by observing yourself as you speak with friends you meet in a hallway. How do you "talk with your hands" during these informal interactions?

Use your arms and hands to complement your message. Avoid crossing your arms, clasping your hands in front of you, or placing your hands on your hips. Instead, keep your arms at your sides and lift them to gesture. Use one hand and vary your gestures by extending your full arm at times, for example, to refer to a visual or to signal someone to ask a question. Use broader gestures for larger group settings.

Gestures convey openness and confidence. Using your hands and arms helps you avoid nervous distractions, such as jingling coins or keys in your pocket or playing with your hair or jewelry. But avoid using too many hand gestures. They become distracting when they are in front of a presenter's face or when they're repetitive.

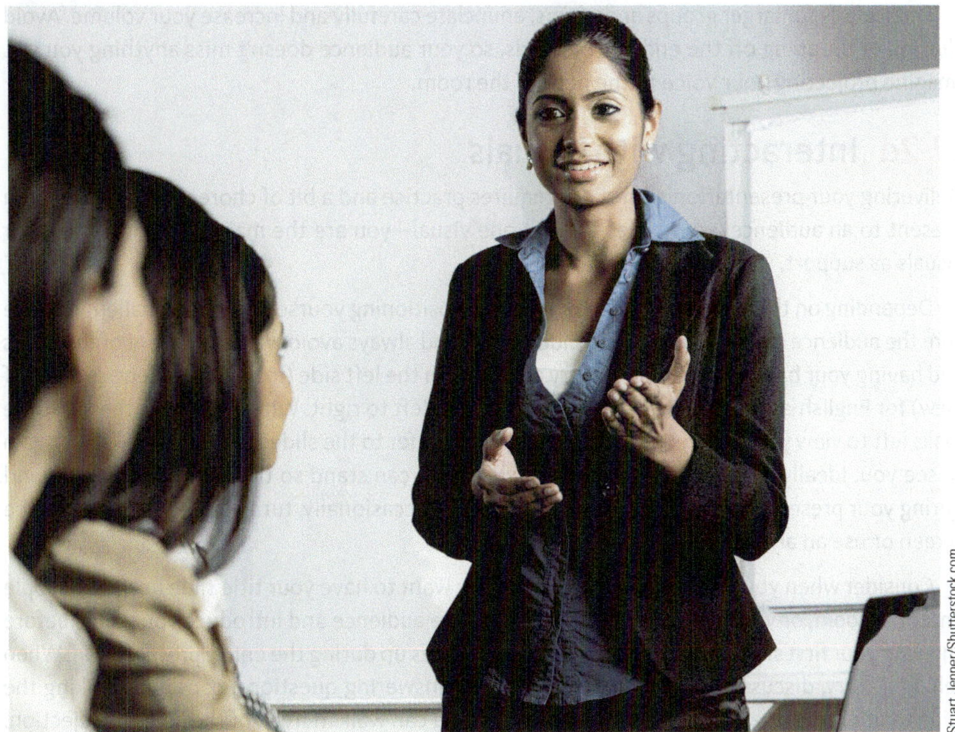

Stuart Jenner/Shutterstock.com

Use natural hand and arm gestures to add interest and emphasize points in your presentation.

Eye Contact

Try to make eye contact with everyone. Hold eye contact for just a couple of seconds and imagine having mini-conversations with each member of the audience. Don't miss people all the way in the back or on the sides of the room. You might find a friendly face in the group and focus on that person for a little while, particularly at the beginning if you feel nervous.

12-2c Finding Your Natural Speaking Voice

For even the most formal presentations, try to use your natural speaking voice. You may have a range of styles for different contexts, but for each, your tone should be engaging and conversational. Your goal is to sound authentic, confident, and trustworthy.

Practice by recording your voice as you imagine different settings. Stand up and either say a few lines from a prepared presentation or read from an article or book. You might have a friend play different roles as you deliver these short presentations. Although it will be awkward at first, get comfortable hearing how you sound.

As you practice for each setting, vary your pitch—with high and low notes—to convey energy and interest. A monotone voice is boring. To train your voice, first practice by using the same note; say your few lines using only that pitch. Then, say your lines in your natural voice. How do they compare?

Do the same to practice varying your pace. Say a few lines as if every syllable is part of the same steady beat. Then, again, say your lines in your natural voice. Notice the conversational rhythm that conveys interest and meaning. You can slow down when presenting important or complex information and speed up when summarizing or making side-bar comments that aren't central to your point.

Also pause between important phrases and sentences. For emphasis, say words more loudly and add a little space around them. Avoid peppering your speech with fillers, for example, *um*, *uh*, *like*, or *you know*. Get comfortable with a bit of silence. At the same time, don't worry about a filler here and there. With a more conversational style, an occasional "um" makes you sound natural and comfortable.

Particularly for larger groups and rooms, enunciate carefully and increase your volume. Avoid slurring or dropping off the endings of words, so your audience doesn't miss anything you say. Imagine projecting your voice to the back of the room.

12-2d Interacting with Visuals

Delivering your presentation with slides requires practice and a bit of choreography. When you present to an audience, your slides are just one visual—you are the main attraction. Use your visuals as support, with the main focus on you.

Depending on the room and screen or monitor, positioning yourself may be a challenge. Make sure the audience can see you and the slides easily, and always avoid walking in front of the slides and having your back to the audience. Try standing on the left side (from the audience's point of view) for English-speaking audiences, who read from left to right. With this setup, the audience looks left to view you, glances slightly to the right to refer to the slides, and then looks left again to see you. Ideally, find at least two places where you can stand so that you can move around during your presentation. To draw attention to slides occasionally, turn your body to look at the screen or use an arm gesture or a laser pointer.

Consider when you'll show your slides. You may want to have your title slide up when people enter the room, or you may want to connect with the audience and introduce your topic before showing your first slide. Also, you don't need your slides up during the entire presentation. When telling a story, discussing a controversial topic, or answering questions, consider blanking the slide temporarily to engage the audience so that you can walk in front of the screen projection. During a PowerPoint slideshow, you can press the B key to show a black blank slide, and then

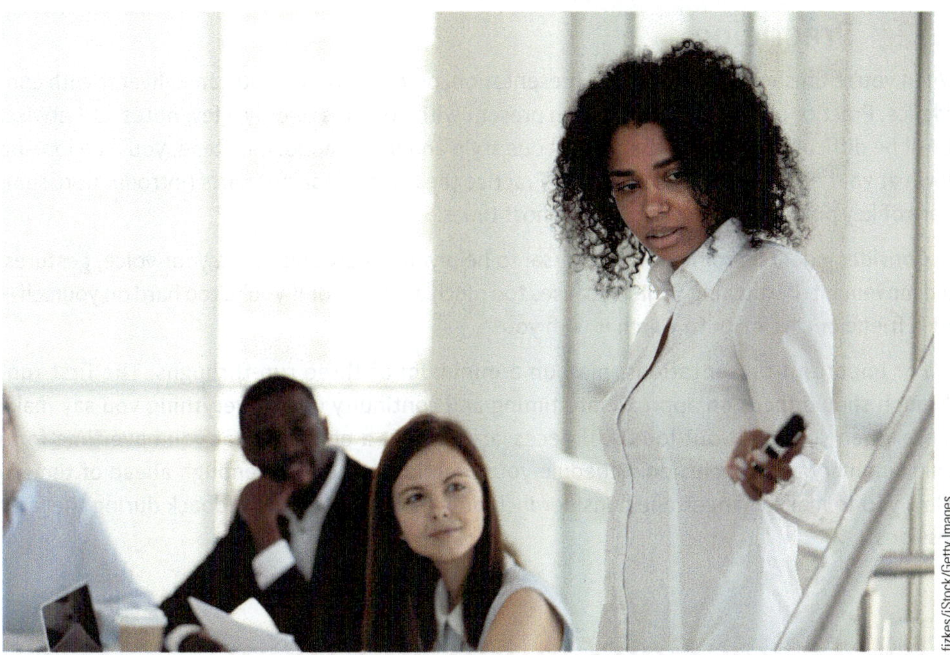
fizkes/iStock/Getty Images

Stand to the side of your visuals and show your audience where to look.

hit this key again when you're ready to continue. Or you can use the slide remote to "blank" or "mute" the light for the same effect.

Use a remote so you can walk around. To advance slides, you don't need to point your remote to the screen or the projector. Just continue with your natural hand and arm gestures and push the button when you're ready to go to the next slide. Give yourself time to practice using the remote to prevent stumbles.

For more interactive presentations, you might develop visuals during the presentation. If you're creating a scrum board for project management or using a whiteboard or flip chart for problem solving, make sure your audience can see the writing easily. Also plan for enough wall space as your visual grows.

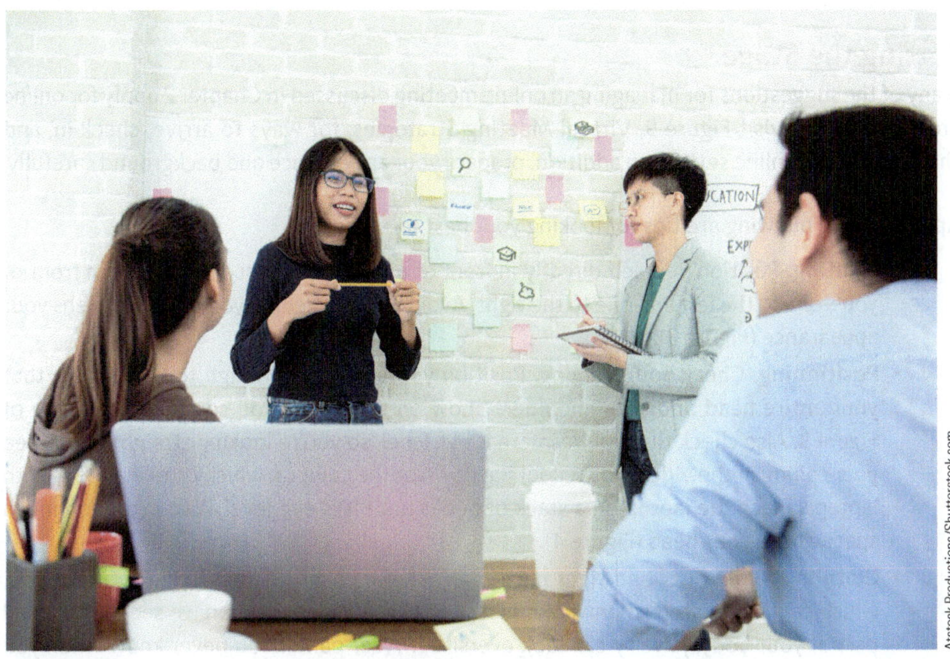
Atstock Productions/Shutterstock.com

Plan for easy viewing and enough space when creating visuals during a presentation.

12-2e Practicing

When you're finished preparing your presentation, practice so that you can deliver it with confidence. Practice enough so that you can present with no notes or only a few notes. Otherwise, it will be difficult to use an extemporaneous style and build rapport. Instead, you'll be looking down at your notes or at a slide for help. Practice the most important parts (introduction, summary of key points, and conclusion) the most times.

Consider videorecording your rehearsal to help you review and refine your voice, gestures, and movement. If watching yourself causes too much anxiety—or if you're too hard on yourself—ask a friend or classmate to watch it with you.

For important presentations, plan on a minimum of three run-throughs. The first run-through should focus on approximate timing and continuity (does everything you say make sense when you say it out loud?). If necessary, cut out a point so that you have time for a solid summary and conclusion. Schedule your practice sessions far enough ahead of time to allow you to make changes and consider including more people for feedback during the later sessions.

LO3 List ways to prepare for an online presentation.

12-3 Delivering Online and Team Presentations

When you present online or in teams, you adapt to the technology or to other members of your group. You set the stage, move your body, use your natural voice, interact with visuals, and practice differently than for an in-person presentation.

12-3a Delivering Online Presentations

Online presentations may be via Zoom, Microsoft Teams, or other programs, and they may be presented to one person or to many. Webinar formats are designed for many people and include little audience interaction, with only the presenters on-screen. Technology staff often orchestrate these events. Here we focus on more typical formats in which you see and interact with the audience.

Setting the Stage

Many of the suggestions for managing an online meeting discussed in Chapter 2 apply for online presentations. Revisit Figure 9, Virtual Meeting Strategies, for ways to arrive, check in, and check out of the online setting. In addition, prepare your appearance and background carefully.

Appearance Following are tips for looking your best on video:

- **Lighting.** Position yourself directly in front of a window or place two lamps in front of you—one to the left and one to the right. Avoid lighting behind you, which darkens your appearance (Figure 3).
- **Positioning.** Check your framing. Position yourself close enough to the camera that your entire head and your shoulders show on-screen, as you see in the left side of Figure 3. Also check that your camera is eye level, so you're looking straight. If you see your ceiling in the video, you're looking down at the camera, which often happens with laptops. Place the laptop on a stack of books until it is eye level. Also avoid too much space above your head (Figure 4).
- **Clothing.** Avoid busy and tight patterns, including some stripes, checks, and plaids, which can look distorted on video. Also avoid large jewelry. When we see only a small part of your body, jewelry can look oversized. Wear pants! You never know when you might need to stand up, and you might forget that everyone can see you.

Good and Bad Lighting for Video | **Figure 3**

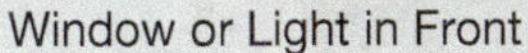

Background Choose a professional-looking background. A bookcase with a few items is ideal if that's possible in your home or office space. A wall with simple art also works. Otherwise, you might choose a filter to blur a messy background—or upload a picture. Zoom backgrounds are fun but overused, and they can distort your image.

Bad Framing on Video | **Figure 4**

If you're working from home or in a shared space, try your best to schedule uninterrupted time during your presentation. This may be challenging with pets and family members, and most people will be sympathetic if a video is interrupted or if they hear noise in the background. When this happens, smile and apologize briefly, but don't make a big deal of it, which only causes more embarrassment.

Moving Your Body

Once your framing is set within the video, your audience will see little of you, so be thoughtful about how you move and where you look. Relax your head and shoulders so that you move naturally. Small movements show that you're engaged and feel confident and comfortable.

As discussed in Chapter 2, typically look just below the camera for the best eye contact. Move video images to avoid looking to one side of the screen. In Zoom, you may have an advanced video setting to allow up to 49 people on one screen, which is useful to feel as though you're speaking to everyone.

Using Your Natural Voice

Speak naturally and conversationally—even more so on video than in person. You might be tempted, but reading is more obvious than you might think. The audience can see your eyes moving back and forth, and you will probably sound scripted. Presenting by video challenges you to build rapport with an audience; don't make it worse by being too formal or sounding too rehearsed. Be your authentic self, particularly when presenting from home.

insta_photos/Shutterstock.com

Use small hand gestures when presenting online.

Interacting with Visuals

Join the video meeting early and decide whether to have your slides visible when people arrive. You might wait until you welcome the group and do introductions, or you might share your screen immediately if you and the audience are ready to start quickly. If you use slides, put them in slide show, or presentation, mode before you share your screen so the transition is seamless.

When you share your screen, be mindful about what else people can see. If you share your desktop instead of your slides, close open websites, hide bookmarked sites, and pause notifications and other pop-ups.

Plan how you'll close the presentation. Will you keep your slides up until the end, or will you stop sharing your screen when the audience asks questions or provides comments at the end? Also consider how to end on time. Typically, thank everyone as you would during an in-person presentation, wave or smile briefly, and then end the meeting. You also might say that you'll stay if people have more questions or comments. This mirrors what happens in an in-person presentation: a couple of people might linger to speak with you individually.

Practicing

A lot can go wrong when you present online. Take steps to give yourself the best chance for success. Most important, check your internet connection. A hardwired Ethernet connection is more secure and may be faster than a Wi-Fi connection.

Practice the entire presentation online. As the presenter, you will be perceived as the person in control. Navigate into and out of slide sharing, open and close polls, and rearrange chat and video windows. Select "New Share" in Zoom to avoid exiting out of one share to start another. If you're showing a video, make sure your sound settings are correct.

Get so comfortable that you can manage the entire presentation without people noticing. Avoid narrating, for example, "Let's see . . . I'm going to open my chat window now." Let the audience focus on the content of your presentation rather than on the technology behind it.

Check settings ahead of time to ensure that you look your best, can hear, and aren't muted. If you're relying on natural lighting, make sure it still looks good at the time of day when you're scheduled to present—rain or shine. Go to zoom.us/test or another program to check your speakers and microphone.

Always have a backup plan for the worst-case scenario. If you lose your connection, how can you continue the presentation? Consider preparing a backup presenter or dialing into the meeting if you must. As for in-person presentations, how you recover from a mishap is often more memorable than the incident itself.

12-3b Delivering Team Presentations

Team presentations are common for communicating about complex projects. For example, describing a large company's marketing strategy or updating a five-year plan demands time and expertise from several people.

Like team writing projects, team presentations require extensive planning and quite a bit of patience. You will need to coordinate how you set the stage, move, and interact with visuals. A full rehearsal will ensure that you present as a cohesive team.

Setting the Stage and Ending Strongly

When facing an audience, your team will want to present as a well-coordinated unit. Unity takes precedence over whatever challenges or conflicts you worked through during the creation process.

Because people have different styles, appearing cohesive is a challenge for team presentations. In advance, decide with your team on the presentation purpose and format, audience expectations, organization, and visuals. Use a slide template to maintain one "look and feel." Have one editor review all slides for consistency throughout the presentation. Also agree on what to wear, how to handle questions, and how to transition from one speaker to another.

You will all speak differently but try to get close to each other's style and aim for balance. A loud presenter will overshadow someone with a soft voice. You don't need equal time in front of the audience, but it's odd to have one person speak for 20 minutes and another for only two.

When you begin the presentation, have one speaker introduce the team, or have team members introduce themselves. Try to have everyone speak within the first few minutes, so the audience views you as giving a team rather than an individual presentation.

Moving Your Body

If the presentation is delivered in person, decide where each of you will stand or sit. When others are speaking, consider sitting down rather than creating a "line-up" in which presenters nervously look at their notes and mouth the words to their upcoming section.

Consider yourself on stage during the entire team presentation—no matter who is presenting. If two of you are delivering at the same time, take a step forward when you're speaking and back when you're not. If you're waiting for your turn, pay attention to the presenter (even though you may have heard the content a dozen times), and nod or smile as appropriate. Model what you want the audience to do. Also try to read the audience for nonverbal signs of confusion, boredom, or disagreement.

When you transition, make eye contact with the next person. Act as if you like each other and enjoy working together. These small interactions among the team convey credibility—that you have consensus on your ideas. Otherwise, the audience might not trust your recommendations or conclusions.

Interacting with Visuals

Plan carefully how you'll manage visuals. Relying on one person to advance the slides in person or online can lead to someone repeating, "Next slide" and "Go to the next one." This gets tiresome for your audience and indicates a lack of coordination. Instead, consider passing the remote or screensharing to each other. Include this in your choreography—a way of connecting with and transitioning to the next person.

Datacraft Co Ltd/Photolibrary/Getty Images

This team is being photographed, but during a presentation, people who aren't presenting should sit down to wait their turn.

Practicing

A full-scale rehearsal with visuals—in the room where the presentation will take place—is crucial for in-person team presentations. If possible, videorecord the practice presentation so you can review it later. Schedule your final practice session early enough to have time for changes. A thorough rehearsal reveals any inconsistencies or repetition in content.

Emotional **INTELLIGENCE**

What feedback have you received from team members about your delivery skills? How well did you respond to the feedback?

Practice your transitions until they are smooth. To avoid overlap, decide what both the exiting and entering speaker will say. Practice sitting down, standing up, and walking so you aren't in each other's way.

Critiquing the performance of a colleague requires tact and empathy, and accepting feedback requires grace and maturity. Revisit the guidelines for "Commenting on Team Writing" in Chapter 2—similar techniques apply to oral presentations.

LO4 Describe how to adapt your delivery to a specific, challenging audience.

12-4 Connecting with Specific Audiences

When planning your presentation, you analyzed your audience to determine the best approach. When you deliver your presentation, you will see the audience's reactions in full force. Responding well requires you to accurately diagnose their emotions and skillfully manage your own—to use your emotional intelligence abilities. Let's revisit the challenging groups discussed earlier, and then consider how you might use humor to connect with your audience.

12-4a Presenting to Challenging Audiences

Most presentations go well. People want you to succeed and will support you by smiling, nodding, and demonstrating genuine curiosity by asking questions. Unfortunately, not every audience will react positively. How you respond to audiences through your delivery style increases your chance of success with even the most challenging audiences.

Mark Wilson/Getty Images News/Getty Images

GM CEO Mary Barra presented in front of an anguished audience.

Hostile Audiences

Earlier, you read about GM CEO Mary Barra's heartfelt delivery to employees. But when she was called to testify about recalls during a Congressional hearing,[8] she seemed stiff. Although she apologized—"I am deeply sorry"—the setting was tragic. Families held photos of mangled cars and people who died, and they didn't get the response they wanted. One father said, "She's not doing anything except stonewalling."[9] Barra may have felt constrained by the legal proceedings, stereotypes about women who express emotion, her own feelings about the deaths—or her inexperience. She was in the CEO job for only three months at this point. Regardless, families found her inauthentic.

When delivering to a hostile audience, maintain a sense of calm and confidence. Cultivate flexibility to sound measured and balanced—clear about your own position, yet empathic about the audience's concerns.

Expect challenging questions and comments, which we discuss in the next section. Try to adopt a mindset that welcomes them. You want to hear what others think and feel so that you can address their concerns and put people at ease as much as possible. This requires the full strength of your character, particularly humility—your ability to learn from your mistakes and from your audience's issues with your plans, your argument, or you.

Skeptical Audiences

During the COVID-19 pandemic, officials around the world struggled with decisions about restrictions, such as stay-at-home orders. New Zealand Prime Minister Jacinda Ardern created a video from her home to "check in with everyone, really." With a conversational, natural style, PM Ardern asked people to "stay at home, break the chain, and you'll save lives." She addressed skepticism directly, explaining the potential 10-day lag between social isolation and a reduction in illnesses and deaths, warning, "Don't be disheartened. Our numbers are going to go up. . . . We may see several thousand cases."[10] PM Ardern developed credibility with her audience.

When facing skeptics, you might be tempted to appear overly confident. But this could be perceived as arrogance and might entrench your audience further into their own beliefs. Instead, present yourself as confident but not a know-it-all; you certainly don't know everything and may be surprised by what you learn from your audience.

Consider dressing just a bit more professionally than you would for other presentations. Business audiences might judge you on your appearance, particularly when they don't trust or agree with you at the start.

When presenting, how well do you focus on the audience instead of your content? Try to accurately assess reactions.

Laid-Back Audiences

To inspire a disinterested audience that is stuck in the status quo, present with an energetic, enthusiastic style. Don't go overboard: you're not a cheerleader. But you do want to convince the audience that your ideas are worth their attention and action.

Delivering to a sleepy or bored audience can be demoralizing. Try moving around the space more or breaking up your presentation with more interaction. Ask a few questions to encourage participation and interest.

For laid-back groups and all situations, be attentive. An indifferent audience can suddenly turn hostile or the other way around. Stay present and observe changes in attitudes. You don't want to miss important feedback as you mindlessly go through your slides.

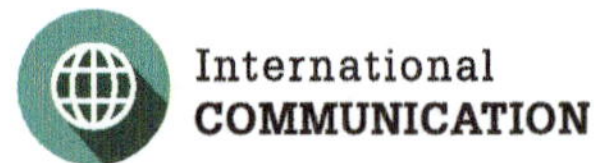

International Audiences

When you present to international audiences, you'll use all the intercultural communication skills you learned in Chapter 3. Revisit suggestions in that chapter for verbal behavior, visuals and nonverbals, pace, comprehension, and support. Presenting—and listening—to people whose primary language differs from yours takes skill and patience.

12-4b Using Humor in Business Presentations

Humor creates a connection between the speaker and the audience. Saying something funny helps build rapport and, when appropriate, could lighten the mood of a presentation. In addition, humor helps audiences remember information.[11]

What makes something funny? Typically, we laugh when something is unexpected or said in an atypical way.[12] At the beginning of PM Ardern's video presentation, she said, "It can be messy business putting toddlers to bed, so I'm not in my work clothes."[13] This was a surprising comment from a world leader, and audiences most likely smiled at the thought.

If you plan to tell a funny story, it must be in good taste and appropriate to the situation. Never tell an off-color or sexist joke; use offensive language; single out an ethnic, racial, or religious group; or imitate an accent when telling a story. Also avoid humor if your presentation topic is serious or has negative consequences for the audience.

In presentations, the best humor is spontaneous. As you develop your presence, you'll attune to what is happening in the moment and might make a witty, relevant comment.[14]

Personal, unexpected stories also might get a good laugh. Self-deprecating humor shows that you're human and can laugh at yourself. But be careful not to damage your credibility. Joking about your lack of PowerPoint skills won't reflect well on your presentation. Instead, surprise the audience by telling a story about yourself that becomes funny.

Relate your story to the next part of your presentation. If the audience laughs, this transition will be smooth. You might also get just a smile, which is enough; you don't need people doubled over with laughter. If the audience doesn't react at all—it happens—just continue on with confidence.

Don't warn the audience that a joke is coming, which could disappoint them. Also avoid saying, "Just joking." If the humor isn't obvious, then it's not funny.

Even if you're an expert joke teller, use humor sparingly. You want your audience to respect your ideas and remember you as a person of good character—not a comedian.

Mark Mitchell/Pool/Getty Images News/Getty Images

PM Ardern declared the tooth fairy and Easter bunny as essential workers during the pandemic.

12-5 Responding to Questions and Feedback

LO5 Identify a list of challenging questions for a given presentation and practice responding.

Preparing for questions and comments in advance will help you respond with ease. But of course you can't prepare for every audience reaction. You will need to be nimble and think quickly. In this section, you learn the best ways to plan and address questions and feedback, whether in person, with a team, or online.

12-5a Preparing for Questions

As you prepare your presentation, anticipate questions you might get from the audience. Consider costs of your proposal, competition for your business idea, holes in your argument, alternative explanations, curious data points, and so on. If your list of questions is very long, consider revising your presentation to incorporate some of the answers into your main content.

Prepare answers. Just as you rehearse your presentation, practice answering questions out loud. When the time comes, you may not get the exact question, but you'll likely hear something similar and can address it well. You also may incorporate your prepared answer into a different question to show your thorough preparation—that you considered the audience's point of view.

When presenting as a team, plan how you'll handle questions. Given your list of possible questions, who will respond? Typically, the person who covered a particular content area responds to a question about that topic. But all members of the team should know the content well and be ready to answer any question.

12-5b Deciding Whether to Take Questions Throughout a Presentation

Will you take questions throughout your presentation or only at the end? For large, formal presentations, holding questions until the end helps you avoid being interrupted and losing your train of thought, or running out of time and not being able to complete your prepared content. Also, a question may be answered later in your presentation.

However, for senior-level audiences, prospective clients or investors, complex topics, and informal settings, you should take questions throughout your presentation. In these situations, you'll be able to adapt your presentation based on questions and help audiences understand the content without getting too lost. You also demonstrate humility by allowing people to interrupt you and by reflecting on their questions, comments, and suggestions.

If you take questions throughout the presentation, you must manage them well. For a hostile audience, at the beginning of the presentation, consider showing a detailed agenda and acknowledging potential concerns up front. This tells your audience that you will address their concerns, which could prevent or reduce early interruptions.

To handle questions during the presentation, you have three options, shown in Figure 5 with examples from a business pitch. In most cases, when you ask permission to defer a question, the person will nod and let you continue.

Figure 5 | Three Strategies for Managing Questions During a Presentation

Strategy	Rationale	Example
Defer the question until later.	The question is complex, is far off topic, and/or will be addressed soon in the presentation.	"Yes, I considered market saturation. If you don't mind waiting a bit, I'll address that in the next section."
Answer briefly.	The answer is quick, so deferring it might appear controlling.	"I'd like to pilot the system by November, and I'll show a full implementation plan later."
Answer the question fully.	Although a question may be off topic, if it's emotional or critical, and you believe others might feel similarly, deferring a question could derail your presentation more than addressing it when raised. Sometimes, these types of questions indicate poor organization.	"I planned to show the costs later, but let me jump ahead so you can see what the investment looks like before I get into more detail."

If questions get unmanageable, say something like, "I know you have more questions. I want to end on time, and I think these next slides will address many of them. May I go through these quickly? I can also stay late to answer more questions." Asking permission to continue may put the audience at ease and help you maintain control of the presentation. If the audience insists, you will have to be flexible and go with the flow; you can't force people to listen and accept your ideas.

12-5c Responding to Questions

Always listen carefully to the question. Repeat a question, if necessary, for the benefit of the entire audience, and look at everyone as you answer—not just the questioner. You might say, "That's a good question," if you mean it, but don't start every response that way; every question is unlikely a good question.

Hostile and skeptical audiences will ask particularly difficult questions. Treat each questioner with unfailing courtesy even if the question is antagonistic. After a presentation, people may or may not remember a snarky audience member, but they will remember how you responded.

Don't make a bad situation worse. Instead, stay calm, take a breath, and show your unwavering professionalism and good character. Use the strategies in Figure 6 to address challenging questions or statements.

Figure 6 Strategies to Address Challenging Questions or Statements

Demonstrate understanding by first validating or empathizing.

Q: We can't implement the system this year when we just started the recovery.

A: We know this will be another challenging year. Our concern is that if we delay implementation further, we'll miss the chance to…

Provide more evidence to support your points.

Q: This was just one bad year.

A: Actually, this was a *particularly* bad year. If you look at the data [show another prepared slide], you see the negative trend for the past six years.

Avoid yes-or-no or leading questions; transition to your main point.

Q: Shouldn't we just wait for government regulations?

A: What's most important is that the public sees how we're addressing privacy issues now. We want to be perceived as leaders among our peers.

Avoid repeating negative language; paraphrase.

Q: This will increase expenses by 10%!

A: This will be a large initial investment for the company, but we risk more cancelled accounts and serious damage to our reputation if we don't take action soon.

You don't have to know all the answers or dispute every question or statement. If someone raises a question you hadn't thought of, you may say so. If someone presents a contradictory point of view that you agree with, admit it. As discussed earlier, research shows that, when you have credibility on a topic, admitting uncertainty makes you *more* persuasive, not less.[15]

Generally, avoid "I think" and "I believe" when you are certain. But you may use these qualifiers to emphasize your well-reasoned opinion. Consider responses to the question, "When do you think we'll see a return on our investment?"

☒ NOT We'll see a return within three years. (*gives an unrealistic guarantee*)

☒ NOT I think we'll see a return within three years. (*sounds wishy-washy*)

☑ BUT Based on our revenue model, I believe we'll see a return within three years. (*justifies your opinion and sounds credible*)

☑ BUT Based on our revenue model, we'll see a return within three years. (*focuses more on the model than on your opinion, which might not be credible with the audience*)

Answer questions concisely. Stick to the main point and refer back to your argument so the response is clear and cohesive. For complex concerns raised or complex answers, consider checking back with the questioner to confirm that you addressed all issues.

If no one asks a question, you did a great job of explaining your topic, the audience is disinterested, or people are reluctant. To break the ice, you might start the questions yourself by saying something like, "One question I'm frequently asked is…" or "You might be wondering…" Or you may ask someone ahead of time to raise the first question if no one else does.

For team presentations, give each other space to answer. If a question comes up during your section that a team member will address later, you might say, "Dylan will cover that point in a few minutes." Or you might make eye contact with Dylan and ask if he wants to address the question.

When a team member answers a question, refrain from adding on unless what you contribute is truly an important point not covered in the original answer. A second response—and particularly, a third—may confuse the audience or appear that you are unprepared or distrustful of each other.

12-5d Asking Questions

As an engaged audience member, ask good questions when you participate in a presentation. Just as you brainstorm questions you might receive as a presenter, consider preparing questions you might ask and practice saying them out loud if the situation will be uncomfortable for you.

You might ask questions that delve deeper into the topic, draw connections between points, or test assumptions. Consider asking for examples, paraphrasing what you heard and asking for confirmation, checking whether the presenter's idea might work in a different context, or wondering about consequences of a plan. Be curious and courageous when asking questions but avoid being hostile. You don't want to be the audience that every presenter, including you, dreads.

12-5e Addressing Comments Online

During presentations online, questions will come in several forms. At the beginning of your presentation, you might encourage the audience to type questions in chat or raise their virtual hand in programs such as Zoom and Microsoft Teams.

If possible, ask for help in managing questions and feedback. Someone who knows you and your content well—or another team member—could interrupt you to ask questions where appropriate. This person can monitor the chat and combine similar questions or comments for you to respond.

Otherwise, you will need to monitor feedback yourself. Reading the chat and presenting at the same time is challenging. You might move the chat box to the center of your screen to avoid looking left or right. This box might cover your slides, as you see in Figure 7, but you should know your presentation well enough without seeing all the content. Also keep a close watch for hands raised.

Figure 7 | Zoom with Videos and Chat Box Arranged

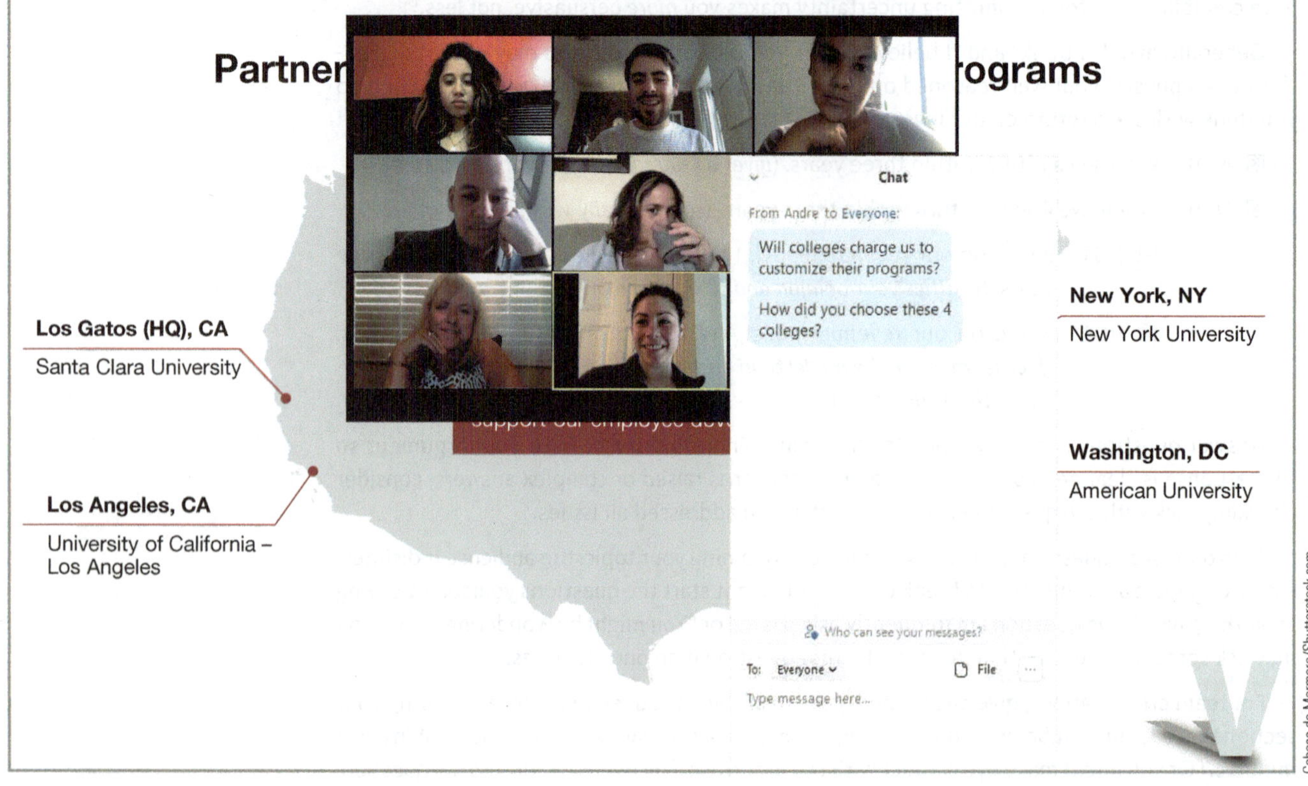

Cabeca de Marmore/Shutterstock.com

If this is too much to manage, then take a break from your content periodically and check for questions and feedback. People understand the difficulty with monitoring chat and presenting at the same time.

During in-person and online presentations, audiences also might participate by using the "backchannel." For larger presentations, seeing people post on Twitter and other sites may feel daunting—having your ideas shared or criticized so immediately and so publicly. But you might decide to encourage, rather than limit, the backchannel. Setting up a Twitter hashtag lets presenters and participants continue discussions. During presentations at conferences, a speaker may project tweets during breaks. This is risky—you never know what people will write—but is a good way to include the audience in the presentation, keep people engaged, and demonstrate your confidence.

12-6 Chapter Closing

New Zealand Prime Minister Jacinda Ardern won reelection in a landslide vote in what was described as a "historic shift" for her party.[16] Her success is attributed to her response to COVID-19.[17] An *Atlantic* article was titled "New Zealand's Prime Minister May Be the Most Effective Leader on the Planet."[18] Not everyone agreed with her strict lockdown policy, but she was authentic and likable.

The more you present, the more comfortable you will be. When you evaluate your presentations—not with an overly critical eye—you will always find ways to improve. Over time, you'll sound and feel more confident, read group reactions more accurately, and respond to questions with grace and ease.

No presentation is perfect. Setting a standard too high may lead to disappointment and unnecessary anxiety. Strive to do your best, to be perceived as a knowledgeable professional who can command an audience—and learn from one as well.

Provide Feedback to Wen Muenyi

Consider the chapter introduction, which described an entrepreneur on *Shark Tank*. Imagine that you are an employee of Wen Muenyi, the founder of Jax Sheets.

Muenyi has asked for your feedback on his presentation before he delivers it on the show. Using the CAM model, what questions might you consider as you prepare to give feedback?

>>> CHARACTER CHECK

1. **Why am I giving feedback, and what are the risks to me?**
   Wen Muenyi asked for my feedback, and I report to him, so I have to be careful. He wants me to be honest, which I will be, but I also have to be tactful. I don't want him to be angry at me for giving him negative feedback.
2. **What personal motivation do I have in Wen Muenyi's success?**
   I want Jax Sheets to get an investment so we can continue to grow the business, and so I'll continue to have a job at the company. I also want him to be realistic; we don't want to get funding and then fail to deliver on an investor's expectations.

>>> AUDIENCE ANALYSIS

1. **How is Wen Muenyi likely to react?**
   Wen Muenyi wants to be successful, so he wants the truth. He also is a positive person and is open to negative feedback.
2. **To what feedback might Wen Muenyi react negatively?**
   I think it's too soon for Jax Sheets to get an investment, but if I say this, Wen Muenyi will be disappointed and may not accept the feedback. At this point, he is already scheduled for the show! The best I can offer now is suggestions on how to present the pitch.

>>> MESSAGE AND MEDIUM

1. **What are the main points of my message?**
   I'll give feedback on the presentation organization, content, and delivery. Overall, Wen makes a good connection with the audience, but his organization could be improved.
2. **In what medium will I communicate the message?**
   This will take place in person, and I'll make a few notes to myself (Figure 8) to remember my feedback.

Presentation Feedback | **Figure 8**

	Not at all	Somewhat	Yes	Definitely
1. The organization works well for the topic and is easy to follow.	1	2	(3)	4
Comments: The structure is logical and easy to follow. However, Wen should move the sales figures earlier; that's the most compelling part of the pitch.				
2. The content is clear and is well supported with details and examples.	1	2	(3)	4
Comments: The content is clearly focused on Jax Sheets and the market need. Wen should choose the amount he's asking for to something more rational. The number $212 sounds odd and may raise questions.				
3. The delivery style is engaging and appropriate for the audience.	1	2	3	(4)
Comments: Wen sounds authentic and natural. He is also energetic and exudes enthusiasm about the business.				

› IN PRACTICE

Provide Feedback to Another *Shark Tank* Presenter

Imagine that you're asked to give feedback to a scheduled *Shark Tank* entrepreneur. Take the role of a current investor in the business. In other words, imagine that you already have a stake in the company's success and want the entrepreneur to get more funding.

Find any episode online, and use the questions about organization, content, and delivery from Figure 8 to comment as if the presentation were a rehearsal.

››› CHARACTER CHECK

1. How does the outcome of the *Shark Tank* presentation affect me personally?
2. How do I feel about giving feedback to the entrepreneur?

››› AUDIENCE ANALYSIS

1. How is the entrepreneur likely to react? (Take a guess based on how the person responded to questions during the show.)
2. With what feedback might the entrepreneur react negatively?

››› MESSAGE AND MEDIUM

1. What are the main points of my message?
2. I'll complete the questions in Figure 8.

REFLECTING ON YOUR COMMUNICATION AND CHARACTER DEVELOPMENT

1. **How do you feel about delivering presentations?**
   To what extent are you anxious or excited about giving presentations? In what situations are you more comfortable, and in what situations are you more nervous?

   How do you think your reaction compares to other people's? Try to put your feelings—both positive and negative—into perspective by understanding that everyone feels what you feel to some extent.

2. **Reflect on your previous success giving a presentation.**
   Think about presentations you have given in the past. Identify one that makes you feel proud. Write a list of what you did that contributed to your success. Try to be specific. What and how did you prepare ahead of time? How did you practice? How did you move, use your voice, interact with visuals, connect with the audience, respond to questions, and so on? What can you learn from that experience for your future presentations?

3. **Watch a video of a previous presentation you delivered.**
   If available, watch a video of a presentation you delivered in the past. On a scale of 1 to 5, how nervous did you feel? How nervous do you look? Ask a friend to watch the video as well. How does your friend rate how nervous you look? You probably don't look as nervous as you felt. Also ask your friend to give you feedback on your organization, content, and delivery. What suggestions can you use for future presentations?

4. **Find ways to feel more confident about delivering presentations.**
   Use the tool at speaking.amynewman.com to identify strategies to try before, during, and after a presentation. Which have you used successfully in the past? Which five or six would be most useful for you to incorporate in the future?

5. **Identify coping strategies for your fears about delivering presentations.**
   One of the ideas in the speaking tool is to write out your fears and identify coping strategies for each, particularly those that aren't rational. Complete this activity. For example, if you write, "I have a lot to cover, and I'll forget something." Identify ways to manage that situation; for example, you might add more points on a particular slide, you might include an appendix, or you might tell yourself, "If I forget something, it's not a disaster. Not everything is critically important, and if I do miss an important point, the audience will ask about it, and then I can address it."

6. **Reflect on your reactions to others' presentations.**
   How quickly do you judge others' presentations? Think about the opening of a presentation you saw recently. How did it start? Did the speaker capture your attention? For a similar presentation, would you use a similar approach? How could you adapt what you observed to your own style?

DEVELOPING YOUR BUSINESS COMMUNICATION SKILLS

PREPARING YOURSELF TO PRESENT

LO1 Identify five strategies to feel more confident for a presentation.

1. **Share your strategies for feeling more confident for a presentation.**
   After completing the speaking tool (speaking.amynewman.com), share your results with another student in class. Identify five or six strategies you will try before, during, or after a presentation. Also discuss what you have done in the past to feel more confident for a presentation.

2. **Prepare a presentation about speech anxiety.**

   Prepare a three-minute presentation, using an outline, about one strategy for managing speech anxiety. You may include sources in the speaking tool or from your own research.

   Before delivering the presentation, write a list of the questions you anticipate being asked and possible answers to those questions. Then, in groups of four or five, take turns delivering your presentation. After each presentation, the audience should ask the presenter questions about the chosen topic.

   Submit an email to your instructor. The email should include your outline, a list of the questions you anticipated, your answers to those questions, the actual questions asked (if different from the ones you anticipated), and your answers to those questions. Also give your instructor a short post-presentation evaluation of what you did well and what changes you would make to improve your presentation.

3. **Identify styles of delivery.**

   Over the next few days, consider how presenters use different methods of delivery in different situations. You might see professors teaching classes, a student addressing members in an organization, a coach speaking to a team, etc. In each of these situations, identify the delivery style: impromptu, extemporaneous, scripted, or memorized. How do you distinguish each? In other words, what does the presenter do that causes you to categorize the talk as you do? Finally, do you believe the style was appropriate for each situation and audience? Why or why not?

4. **Analyze delivery styles.**

   Find any video of an executive giving a talk about a company or find an entrepreneur pitching an idea on *Shark Tank*. How would you describe the style of presentation? In what ways do you find it effective? Also observe how the style changes when the person answers questions. Often, you'll notice a switch between a scripted or planned style and a more conversational style, during which you'll see more of the presenter's personality.

5. **Practice different delivery styles.**

   In small groups, deliver two versions of the same presentation. Choose a topic that interests you: a hobby, service work, business idea, or something else. Prepare to deliver two or three sentences of a presentation about the topic.

   First, write out a script and deliver it. Next, put the script away and speak extemporaneously. What differences do you and other students observe? Which was clearer? With which did more of your personality show through? What can you learn from this experience for future presentations?

LO2 Describe how to use body movement and voice during a large-group presentation.

DELIVERING IN-PERSON PRESENTATIONS

6. **Analyze two presentations.**

   Watch any two presentations. Search for a company executive, a commencement speaker, a politician, or someone else. Try to find two different types of presentations—one formal and one more extemporaneous. Use the template in Figure 8 for your feedback on each.

7. **Analyze movement, gestures, and eye contact.**

   Watch the videos from Exercise 6 again. This time, observe the delivery skills more closely. What do you find effective and ineffective in each presenter's movement, gestures, and eye contact? Stop the video and rewatch parts so you can identify specific behavioral examples.

8. **Prepare a presentation opening.**

   For an upcoming presentation, prepare your first couple of sentences. Say them out loud to a small group of students for feedback.

Ask for feedback. Is your main point clearly up front? Did you make a strong connection with the audience? Did you seem confident? Is the audience engaged and interested in hearing more? Identify adjustments that you can make for your final presentation.

9. **Use your natural delivery skills.**

In small groups, take turns delivering short presentations to each other. Speak for between one and three minutes at a time. Talk about any topic that interests you: your favorite TV show, movie, sports team, performer, place to travel, or anything else. Don't think about it too much; present as though you're talking to a friend about something you like to watch or do.

When you're finished, ask the group for feedback about your movement, gestures, and eye contact. Did they seem natural and appropriate? How do you move and use your hands naturally?

Deliver the presentation again and incorporate the feedback. Stay natural, but you might, for example, use a few more gestures or vary them. Ask for feedback the second time to see how you have improved—and whether you still came across naturally.

10. **Practice a presentation and track your progress.**

Practice an upcoming presentation three times—at least once in the room where you will deliver it. Each time you practice, write notes about your observations and plans for improvements. Use the format in Figure 9 for your notes.

Presentation Practice Notes | **Figure 9**

	Location	Timing	Major Strengths	Areas to Improve
Practice Round 1				
Practice Round 2				
Practice Round 3				

DELIVERING ONLINE AND TEAM PRESENTATIONS

LO3 List ways to prepare for an online presentation.

11. **Prepare for an online presentation with remote offices.**

Imagine that you work as a data analyst for a technology company and have prepared a presentation about data security. You'll deliver your presentation to employees in three countries in addition to your own. Choose the three locations, and then list the steps you will take to prepare for the presentation. Include everything you would do, up to the point of starting the presentation. Remember to consider time differences. Compare notes with another student to see what steps you might have missed.

12. **Practice delivering and participating in an online presentation.**

Working in groups of three or four, have one person deliver a short presentation online to the rest of the team. Choose Zoom, Google Meet, or any other program.

Select a presenter, who will be in a separate room or location from the rest of the team. The presenter can choose any topic relevant to the rest of the team, and this can be an informal presentation.

During the presentation, the rest of the team takes notes using the criteria in Figure 10. After the presentation, the audience gives feedback to the presenter.

Figure 10 | Online Presentation Feedback Form

	Not at all	Somewhat	Yes	Definitely
1. Engaged the audience throughout.	1	2	3	4
Comments:				
2. Demonstrated proficiency with the technology.	1	2	3	4
Comments:				
3. Used a backup plan effectively.	1	2	3	4
Comments:				

13. Prepare for an online presentation to fail.

As you did for the previous exercise, plan for one person in another room to present to two or three team members online. This time, something goes wrong. The audience can invent whatever mishap they choose. For example, you might use the wrong microphone or camera option, have your computer sound off, or lose your internet connection in the middle.

Don't tell the presenter what the technology issue is and see how the presenter handles the situation. After the presentation, discuss lessons you learned for the future.

14. Divide speaking responsibilities for a team presentation.

In teams of three or four, plan how to divide parts of a presentation. Choose a topic that interests your team: a business idea, a current news item, an upcoming campus event, and so on. Follow these steps to plan your team presentation:

a. Identify your audience. What group would be interested in your topic?

b. Brainstorm a list of topics for your presentation. Consider what would be valuable to your audience.

c. Create an outline of topics for your presentation. Plan a logical sequence.

d. Identify how much time you would dedicate to each topic.

e. Divide topics among the team members and select someone to open and close the presentation.

After you have finished your plan, discuss your team process. Is everyone happy with how responsibilities were shared and how the team worked together? Why or why not?

15. Prepare and deliver a team presentation.

Divide into teams of four or five students. Your instructor will assign you to either the pro or the con side of one of the following topics:

a. Drug testing should be mandatory for all warehouse employees.

b. All forms of smoking should be banned from campus.

c. Remote employees should work in the office at least once per month.

d. Employers should provide flextime (flexible working hours) for all office employees.

e. Employers should provide on-site childcare facilities for the preschool children of their employees.

f. Employees who work with the public should be required to wear a company uniform.

Assume that your employee group has been asked to present its views to a management committee that will make the final decision regarding your topic. Gather whatever data you think will be helpful to your case, organize it, divide up the speaking roles, and prepare speaker notes. (Hint: Gather information on both the pro and the con sides of the issue to prepare for the rebuttal.) The presentations will be given as follows:

a. Each side (beginning with the pro side) will have eight minutes to present its views.

b. Each side will then have three minutes to confer.

c. Each side (beginning with the con side) will deliver a two-minute rebuttal—to refute the arguments and address the issues raised by the other side.

d. Each side (beginning with the pro side) will give a one-minute summary.

e. The management committee (the rest of the class) will then vote by secret ballot on which side (pro or con) presented its case more effectively.

CONNECTING WITH SPECIFIC AUDIENCES

LO4 Describe how to adapt your delivery to a specific, challenging audience.

16. Adapt to different audiences.

Working in small groups, plan a presentation to different audiences. Imagine that you're the management team of a moving company and are announcing the acquisition of a storage company. The storage units will provide another service for customers who are moving and need short-term storage. You also plan to offer long-term storage, which you have identified as a business in high demand.

Discuss how you would deliver your presentation for each of the following audiences:

- Corporate staff, who will be skeptical about the idea and worried that the core moving business will suffer
- Customer service staff, who will be hostile because this complicates their work
- Truckers, who are laid-back and indifferent about the change
- Investors, who will be happy about the expanding business and a new revenue stream

17. Deliver a presentation to different audiences.

Revisit Exercise 6 in Chapter 11, when you prepared a presentation about a new inventory management system at a retail store. Working in small groups, plan the first few minutes of the presentation.

Then have one person deliver the beginning of the presentation and have others play the role of a hostile or skeptical audience who interrupts with challenging questions. Provide feedback on how well the presenter managed the group.

Repeat the process for a laid-back audience. Have a different member of the group present the beginning of the presentation to an audience who doesn't say anything! They sit with their arms crossed and don't respond at all. In some ways, this can be more difficult to manage than an openly hostile audience. How does the presenter handle this situation, and what could improve the response?

18. **Discuss humor in presentations.**

In this chapter, you read about using humor in presentations. In small groups, discuss your experience and views on the topic. When have you used humor successfully in a presentation? Describe the context, what you said, and how the audience reacted. Have you tried to be funny and failed? From your own experience, how do you feel about using humor? What works and doesn't work for each of you?

LO5 Identify a list of challenging questions for a given presentation and practice responding.

RESPONDING TO QUESTIONS AND FEEDBACK

19. **Analyze how an executive responds to questions.**

Find an interview with a company leader on a business news program. Identify the types of questions the reporter asks: easy, hostile, leading, negative, or something else. What strategies does the leader use to answer the questions? How would you describe the leader's communication objective for the interview? In other words, what key message does the leader want to convey? Overall, how would you assess the leader's preparation and response?

20. **Prepare for questions as a team.**

For an upcoming team presentation, brainstorm a list of questions you might receive. Then, practice your presentation and interrupt each other with the most challenging questions. After each, pause and give feedback on how well the presenter handled each. With this intense practice, you'll be well prepared for tough interruptions.

21. **Analyze questions asked.**

Attend a presentation or meeting that includes time for questions. You might attend a campus event, a company presentation at a job fair, or a local community meeting. What types of questions do people ask? Are they useful to others? Are they relevant to the topic? Are they hostile or curious? What can you learn from these audience members for your own participation in presentations?

22. **Practice using the backchannel.**

In class, have one student deliver a three-minute presentation on any topic. Before the presentation, five students in the audience sign on to Twitter. During the presentation, using the same hashtag (e.g., #BusComm402), students tweet one encouraging comment and one question. After the presentation, show the Twitter feed, and discuss the benefits and challenges of using the backchannel in this way.

Then, have the speaker continue the presentation by debriefing comments and answering questions from the Twitter feed. Try to do this within three minutes (you won't be able to address everything) to summarize the presentation.

CHAPTER SUMMARY

LO1 Identify five strategies to feel more confident for a presentation.

Almost everyone feels nervous before a presentation. Prepare yourself by learning which strategies work for you before, during, and after a presentation. Choose a delivery method appropriate to the situation—usually a natural style that allows you to be your authentic self.

LO2 Describe how to use body movement and voice during a large-group presentation.

How you move and use your voice depend on the situation and audience. Movement and voice projection will be greater when you deliver to more people in a larger room. Walk and use gestures naturally in ways that complement your presentation. Find your natural speaking voice that is varied, fluid, and engaging. Practice interacting with visuals until transitions are seamless, so audiences can focus on you and your message.

LO3 List ways to prepare for an online presentation.

Online presentations require agility with the technology so that nothing detracts from your presentation. Look your best with lighting in front of you and by framing your head and shoulders. Practice sharing your screen and identify backup plans in case the technology fails. Your team should look and sound cohesive during a presentation. Check for repetition and contradictions, and practice how you'll move, transition, and manage visuals.

LO4 Describe how to adapt your delivery to a specific, challenging audience.

Prepare to deliver your presentation to particularly challenging groups, for example, hostile, skeptical, and laid-back audiences. Maintain your calm and confidence but be human. Demonstrate humility as you listen openly to your audience's concerns. Humor in presentations builds rapport and increases what people remember. Unexpected stories and spontaneous comments might get a laugh or a smile.

LO5 Identify a list of challenging questions for a given presentation and practice responding.

Prepare for questions by identifying a list of possibilities and answering each out loud. Most typically, you'll take questions throughout a presentation. On the spot, depending on the question and context, you'll decide whether to defer the question, answer briefly, or answer fully. Respond to challenging questions by demonstrating confidence and humility, by providing additional evidence, and by avoiding traps of leading and negative questions.

Endnotes

1. Mark Cuban, "Jax Sheets," *Shark Tank*, Season 12, Episode 13, YouTube, February 12, 2021, https://youtu.be/1mlFdXpcf9c, accessed June 14, 2021.
2. "Jax Sheets."
3. This quote has been attributed to Mark Twain, but the original author is unknown. See "There Are Two Types of Speakers: Those Who Are Nervous and Those Who Are Liars," Quote Investigator, https://quoteinvestigator.com/2020/03/05/nervous, accessed September 2, 2021.
4. For more about presence, see Amy Cuddy, *Presence: Bringing Your Boldest Self to Your Biggest Challenges* (New York: Little, Brown, 2018).
5. "Prepare Your Speaker," TED website, www.ted.com/participate/organize-a-local-tedx-event/tedx-organizer-guide/speakers-program/prepare-your-speaker, accessed September 2, 2021.
6. David Shepardson, "GM Compensation Fund Completes Review with 124 deaths," *The Detroit News*, August 24, 2015, www.detroitnews.com/story/business/autos/general-motors/2015/08/24/gm-ignition-fund-completes-review/32287697/, accessed June 14, 2021.
7. Mary Barra, "GM CEO Addresses Employees in Town Hall Meeting," General Motors Company, www.gm.com, September 17, 2015, http://media.gm.com/media/us/en/gm/news.detail.html/content/Pages/news/us/en/2015/sep/0917-barra.html, accessed June 2021.
8. "The GM Ignition Switch Recall: Why Did It Take So Long?" The Energy and Commerce Committee, April 1, 2014, https://energycommerce.house.gov/hearings-and-votes/hearings/gm-ignition-switch-recall-why-did-it-take-so-long, accessed May 8, 2017.
9. Matthew L. Wald, "Highlights from Senate Hearing on G.M. Defects," *The New York Times*, The Lede Blogging the News with Robert Mackey, April 2, 2014, https://thelede.blogs.nytimes.com/2014/04/02/live-video-from-senate-hearing-on-g-m-defects, accessed May 8, 2017.
10. Prime Minister Jacinda Ardern, "COVID-19, Jacinda Ardern Hosts Coronavirus QA from Home After Putting Child to Bed," *The Guardian*, YouTube, May 27, 2020, www.youtube.com/watch?v=xMA6Gz82iiQ&t=61s, accessed June 23, 2021.
11. Jason C. Coronel et al., "Political Humor, Sharing, and Remembering: Insights from Neuroimaging," *Journal of Communication* 71 (February 2021): 129–161, https://doi.org/10.1093/joc/jqaa041.
12. Michael Cundall, "Using Humor in Business Communication," in Stephanie Kelly (ed.), *Computer-Mediated Communication in Business: Theory and Practice* (Newcastle upon Tyne, UK: Cambridge Scholars, 2019), p. 67.
13. Prime Minister Jacinda Ardern.
14. For more advice, see Jennifer Aaker and Naomi Bagdonas, *Humor, Seriously: Why Humor Is a Secret Weapon in Business and Life* (New York: Currency, 2021).
15. Adam Grant, *Think Again* (New York: Viking, 2021), p. 171.
16. Praveen Menon, "New Zealand's Ardern Wins 'Historic' Re-election for Crushing COVID-19," Reuters, October 16, 2020, www.reuters.com/article/uk-newzealand-election/new-zealands-ardern-wins-historic-re-election-for-crushing-covid-19-idUSKBN2712ZI, accessed June 27, 2021.
17. Matthew Schwartz, "New Zealand PM Ardern Wins Re-Election in Best Showing for Labour Party in Decades," NPR, October 17, 2020, www.npr.org/2020/10/17/924934728/new-zealand-pm-ardern-wins-re-election-in-best-showing-for-labour-party-in-decad, accessed June 27, 2021.
18. Uri Friedman, "New Zealand's Prime Minister May Be the Most Effective Leader on the Planet," *The Atlantic*, April 19, 2020, www.theatlantic.com/politics/archive/2020/04/jacinda-ardern-new-zealand-leadership-coronavirus/610237, accessed September 6, 2021.

Part 6 Presenting Yourself for Employment

CHAPTER 13

Writing for the Job Search

Learning Objectives

After you have finished this chapter, you should be able to

LO1 Describe your strengths for a position that interests you.

LO2 Identify questions to guide decisions about resume content.

LO3 Assess whether a LinkedIn profile meets given criteria.

LO4 Tailor a cover letter for a given position.

"I was inspired by Emily Vu's creative resume for Spotify, and coincidentally, I found Pinterest is looking for UX apprentices!"[1]

—Crystal Chan, UX/UI designer

Chapter Introduction

Creative Resumes Attract Attention

Creative approaches to the job search can pay off. Emily Vu, a student at the University of California, Irvine, created a Spotify-themed resume.[2] A Spotify manager saw Vu's tweet and encouraged her to apply for a product manager internship.

Vu inspired Crystal Chan, who created a themed resume for Pinterest, shown here. Chan highlighted her skills and experience relevant to the company and her desired position. This approach might not work for every industry, but a creative technology company would likely appreciate an applicant's design skills.

For Vu, her risk paid off: she got the Spotify job. In a crowded field of applicants for a popular company, Vu's qualifications stood out.

Crystal Chan

UX/UI Designer × Show all

skylight.cloud@gmail.com | +1 999-999-9999 | linkedin.com/in/cryschan/

Experience

- Graphic Designer and Marketing Lead for Breaking Barriers, Codeswitch (present)
- Social Media Content Creator and Co-Manager for SoNE1 (2 years), EKHO (10 months)
- Hackathons participated = 6

Education

University of California, Davis

B.A in Design, Communication
Sept 2017 – Dec 2020

Skills

- Figma
- Adobe Illustrator
- Adobe Photoshop
- Adobe InDesign
- Adobe AfterEffects
- Adobe XD
- Canva
- Google Suite
- Social Media (Instagram, Youtube)
- Traditional Art
- Wireframing
- User Research
- Active Listening
- Perceptive to Details
- Rapid Iterations for Feedback
- Empathetic
- Up to Date with Trends
- Co-Creating

Projects

Ensured — Apr 9-11, 2021
Healthcare Application
A community funded program for small gig economy workers, such as Uber, Lyft, and Doordash, to earn afforadable and portable health benefits. Riders can customize their healthcare plan. Built during a 3 day protothon organized by Product Buds.
1st Place Winner — figma.com/prototype

From U — Feb 26-28, 2021
Self Care Application
Aimed to users who feel like they are lacking connection and motivation, users are sent a daily challenge to complete based on their emotions for the day. User will also enter chatrooms to talk with others who have completed the same self care challenge. Built during a 3 day protothon organized by TechTogether Atlanta.
Best Social Good Hack — devpost.com

VCON — Feb 13, 2021
Entertainment and Media Application
Implementing Agora's 3D spatial features, AR features, and online broadcasting features to create an immersive virtual music concert experience for music lovers to connect with music artists. Built during a 24 hour UX hackathon organized by DubsTech.
canva.com

https://www.linkedin.com/posts/cryschan_crystal-chan-pinterest-apprenticeship-resume-activity-6796226837577134081-aW9w/.

Creative resumes may differentiate candidates.

LO1 Describe your strengths for a position that interests you.

13-1 Presenting Your Best Self

Applying for a job puts all your communication skills to the test. This is your chance to impress an employer and land a great job. Because companies often receive resumes from many qualified candidates, how you represent yourself during the employment process may determine whether you are the selected candidate.

Like Warren Buffett, described in Chapter 1, Ray Dalio describes character as the primary qualification of job candidates for the hedge fund Bridgewater Associates:

> What I look for is really character—character is number one. . . . And then, it applies to the particular job that they have. So when I'm referring to values, I'm referring to, is this a person of good character?[3]

***Resume* is used throughout the book to follow the business convention instead of the academic convention of *résumé*.**

Of course, skills are important to a job too. But Dalio believes that the company can train employees to learn skills. Character is developed over time and is more difficult to teach.

In this chapter, we explore ways to present your best self—your skills, character, and other qualifications—for a job. First, you'll learn how to identify your strengths.

13-1a Being Yourself

Throughout the book, we discuss authenticity as an important character dimension. Presenting your genuine self throughout the selection process increases the chance that employers get to know and feel comfortable with you—and they may be more likely to hire you. Once hired, people who are "themselves" at work tend to be happier and more productive.[4]

When communicating during a job search, being authentic means using your natural writing and speaking style—professional but not overly formal. Being authentic also means presenting yourself as you are, which raises a few decisions for you to make. Will you include on your resume the religious or political organization where you have volunteered for the past four years? Will you explain your employment gap? Will you highlight or downplay your race, ethnicity, or international status?

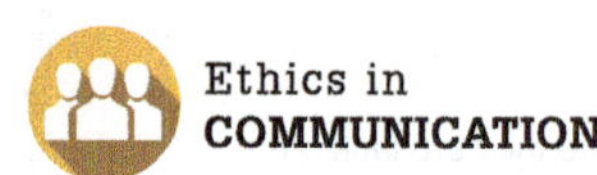

In Chapter 3, you read that some employers use "blind hiring" strategies to omit such characteristics as name, address, dates, hobbies, interests, volunteer work, and/or college.[5] They do this to reduce inherent bias in the selection process, including discrimination based on race and ethnicity. Sadly, research shows that applicants who "whiten" their resumes—that is, omit references to their race—are more likely to be called for interviews than those who reveal their race.[6] The results were the same for companies that post notices on job descriptions such as "equal opportunity employer" or "minorities are strongly encouraged to apply."[7]

Applicants have a difficult choice in deciding whether to downplay their race and other affiliations. Some students choose to do so to avoid bias—to increase their chances of getting hired when they are at a disadvantage in the selection process. Others downplay their identities for a different reason: if an employer does want to increase diversity, they don't want to be hired to "fill that quota."[8]

How will you present your identities during the job search? Are you more inclined to highlight or downplay them?

Yet other students choose not to downplay—or choose to highlight—their identities. As one student said, "I wouldn't consider whitening my resume because if they don't accept my racial identity, I don't see how I would fit in that job."[9] Some students feel that their identities are what they "bring to the table." As a university student services director explains, your value to an organization is "who you are."[10] Other students won't hide their identities because of moral beliefs about the issue.

How you present yourself is your choice. You might exclude information that you do not consider part of your workplace identity, and, over time, you may change your mind. You also might decide to keep your involvement in a religious, political, or other group because it exemplifies your strengths for a position, which we explore next.

13-1b Identifying Your Strengths

Before you begin writing details on your resume, you might spend time thinking about your qualifications more broadly. What character dimensions, strengths, and gifts would you bring to an organization? What distinguishes you from other candidates? What experience and competencies (knowledge, skills, or abilities) qualify you for the type of work you want to do? What opportunities have made your experience unique and valuable?

In other words, what is your personal brand? Just as companies have brands, think about your reputation. Consulting firm PwC provides an extensive workbook for developing your brand, which the company calls, "what you're known for and how people experience you."[11]

What are you most proud of about yourself and your experience? How will you make this clear on your resume?

In addition to what you bring, consider where your talents are most needed. What is your vocation—a strong inclination toward a career or service work? In other words, where might your abilities be most useful to the world?

Answer the questions in Figure 1 as you begin to shape the story of who you are and what you will contribute. Your responses will influence how you communicate throughout the selection process, which we discuss next.

Figure 1 Questions to Prepare Yourself for the Job Search

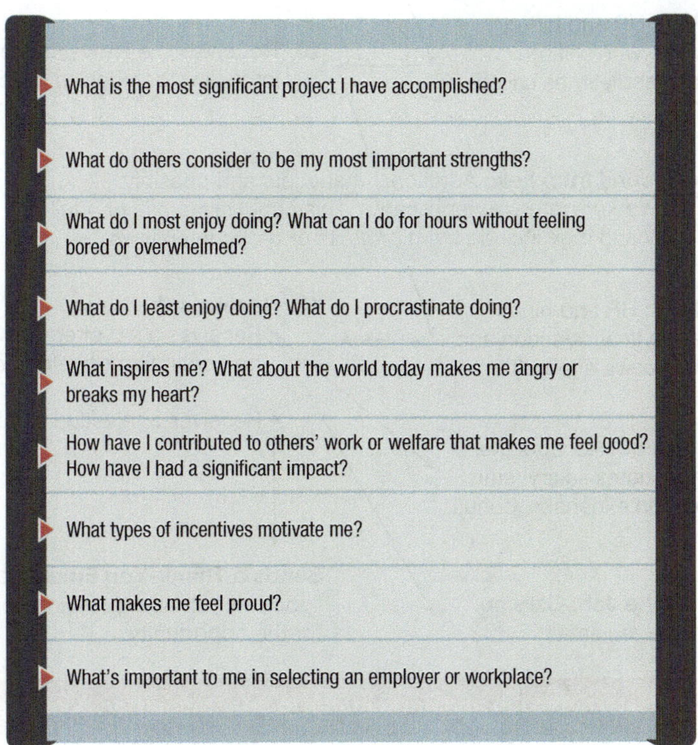

What is the most significant project I have accomplished?
What do others consider to be my most important strengths?
What do I most enjoy doing? What can I do for hours without feeling bored or overwhelmed?
What do I least enjoy doing? What do I procrastinate doing?
What inspires me? What about the world today makes me angry or breaks my heart?
How have I contributed to others' work or welfare that makes me feel good? How have I had a significant impact?
What types of incentives motivate me?
What makes me feel proud?
What's important to me in selecting an employer or workplace?

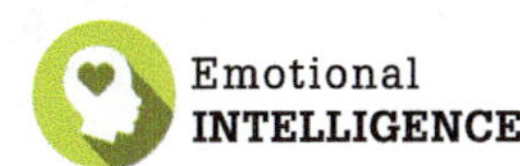

Emotional
INTELLIGENCE

Most people think about their future career in terms of jobs. Try something different: when you think of yourself as a 60-year-old person, what relationships and experiences would you like to have had?

13-1c Following the Selection Process

Typically, a company will follow a selection process like the one shown in Figure 2. This process varies by company and position, but these are the usual steps from when a company identifies a hiring need to when a new employee starts the job.

Throughout this process, you are putting your best self forward and—if the process goes well—regularly communicating with your future employer. Next, we discuss your first step in finding a job: preparing your resume.

Figure 2 | Typical Selection Process

Company	Applicant
1. Posts the Job: HR and hiring manager determine hiring needs and job requirements.	**2. Applies for the Job:** Submits an application and/or email or letter and resume.
3. Screens Resume: HR manager, recruiter, or hiring manager (or applicant tracking system) reviews resume and selects a few candidates for the first interview.	**4. Receives the News:** Receives a request for an interview or receives a rejection email or letter.
5. Screening Interview: HR typically conducts the first interview in person, by phone, or online.	
6. Narrows the Pool: HR determines who will be called back for a full interview.	**7. Receives the News:** Invited for an interview or receives rejection email.
8. First Interview: HR and hiring manager typically will conduct one-hour interviews with applicants in person or online.	
9. Narrows the Pool: HR and hiring manager determine who will be interviewed again (sometimes called "second round").	**10. Receives the News:** Invited for more interviews or receives rejection email.
11. Second Interview: Additional managers and possibly coworkers interview applicants. This could last a half or a full day and may include team projects or group interviews.	
12. Narrows the Pool: HR and hiring manager make the final selection and decide who will receive a job offer.	**13. Receives the News:** • Receives a job offer. The offer may be contingent on reference checks. • Receives a rejection email.
14. Accepts the Job: Accepts the terms or negotiates salary, start date, relocation expenses, bonus, etc.	
Turns Down the Job: Calls or sends a thank-you email.	**Sends a Thank-You Email:** Sends a "goodwill" email expressing appreciation for the opportunity.

New employee starts the job and participates in orientation ("on boarding").

LO2 Identify questions to guide decisions about resume content.

13-2 Preparing Your Resume

Throughout your career, you'll update your resume, continually revising it to reflect who you are and what you have achieved. Typically packed into one page, your resume gives employers a snapshot of how you can contribute to their organization. The best resume is tailored to highlight your qualifications for a specific job.

Most people have a generic version of their resume that they revise for different positions. This compilation represents all your qualifications for any job—a complete picture of you. Then, when you apply for a position, you choose which parts will be most relevant.

The purpose of the resume is to get an interview, and the purpose of the interview is to get a job. You will not likely be hired based on the resume alone, but your resume and cover letter will set you apart from potentially thousands of applicants.

In addition to representing yourself authentically, as we discussed, you have other strategic decisions to make when writing your resume. You'll decide the length, format, and content, and then prepare it for screening software.

13-2a Strategic Decisions About Your Resume

Resumes for college students are fairly standard, but you have many decisions about how to present yourself. Consider the questions in Figure 3 to guide your choices.[12] When responding to these questions, also consider the attributes employers look for on students' resumes (Figure 4).[13]

Let's take an example. You are the leader of a conservative political organization on campus, and you're applying for a marketing position at Ben & Jerry's, the ice cream company, which you believe is politically liberal. Your knowledge may be based on company contributions to political parties, news stories, products and services, or other factors.

Questions to Guide Resume Decisions | **Figure 3**

Example: The leader of a conservative political organization applying for a marketing position at Ben & Jerry's.

Q Is the item relevant to the position and valuable to the employer?
Yes, I organized and hosted several campus events that had good turnouts. I created graphics, marketed events on social media, and partnered with other campus organizations.

Q Is the item either recent or your only example using the competency (knowledge, skill, or ability)?
Sort-of both. I don't have a lot of marketing experience other than selling candy bars for a church fundraiser when I was 13.

Q Could the item cause an employer to disqualify you?
It's possible. I love Ben & Jerry's ice cream. Obviously, it's not just for liberals, but I'm not sure whether they would hire someone like me. On the other hand, maybe I wouldn't want to work there. It might be a difficult place to be myself.

Q Is the item important to your identity or to demonstrate your authenticity?
Pretty much. I'm proud of my membership in the organization, and my political views are an important part of who I am.

Q Is the item accurate and does it reflect well on your integrity?
Yes, the leadership position carried a lot of responsibilities, and I was involved in a few senior-level meetings with campus administrators. It feels dishonest to remove it.

DECISION: I'll leave it on my resume. Without it, I'm not really qualified for the position. I'll take the risk and, if they call me for an interview, I'll see how I feel about the environment and whether it's the right fit for me.

Another approach to deciding what to include on your resume is to use the CAM (character, audience, message and medium) model. You'll see an example of how to work through this process at the end of the chapter.

Figure 4 What Employers Look for on Students' Resumes

ATTRIBUTE	% OF RESPONDENTS
Problem-solving skills	91.2
Ability to work in a team	86.3
Strong work ethic	80.4
Analytical/quantitative skills	79.4
Communication skills (written)	77.5
Leadership	72.5
Communication skills (verbal)	69.6
Initiative	69.6
Detail-oriented	67.6
Technical skills	65.7
Flexibility/adaptability	62.7
Interpersonal skills (relates well to others)	62.7
Computer skills	54.9
Organizational ability	47.1
Strategic planning skills	45.1
Friendly/outgoing personality	29.4
Entrepreneurial skills/risk-taker	24.5
Tactfulness	24.5
Creativity	23.5

The last question in Figure 3 about integrity is important. Here are a few lies that people have told on their resumes:

- Included Microsoft as an employer but didn't know who Bill Gates was.
- Invented a school that didn't exist.
- Claimed to have worked for the hiring manager but didn't.
- Wrote that he worked for the CIA during a time when he would have been in elementary school.[14,15]

How comfortable are you stretching the truth on your resume? If you had to choose between underselling or overselling yourself, what would you do?

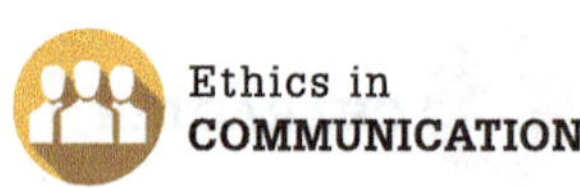

Although these examples are outrageous, one survey found that 78% of applicants exaggerate their qualifications, including skills, dates, and schools.[16] Some employers may overlook these claims, but many will not.

Of course, you want to present yourself well, and you'll highlight your strengths and minimize your weaknesses. However, falsifying information could disqualify you from a search and damage your reputation. A simple review of your LinkedIn profile or phone call can verify any statement on your resume. During an interview, the employer will push for details about your past responsibilities. If you didn't do what you claim on your resume, this may be embarrassing for you—and you could find yourself in a job that you can't perform successfully.

13-2b Resume Length

How long should your resume be? One consideration is how much time HR professionals and hiring managers spend reviewing a resume. According to one study, most employers spend less than two minutes,[17] while an eye-tracking study cites a mere 7.4 seconds for the initial screen.[18] This probably seems absurd, considering how much time and energy you devote to perfecting your resume, but this is enough time for an experienced employer to decide whether you meet the minimum qualifications for the job.

One page is usually enough space for students and new graduates. However, in one study, 83% of employers accepted a two-page resume[19] and, in another study, two-page resumes were viewed more favorably—even for entry-level positions.[20] If you have more experience, use a second page if you need to. Preferences also vary by industry and by recruiter. Follow your college career counselor's advice: they know local employers and those who recruit on campus.

Writing a one-page resume doesn't mean cramming two pages of information into one page by using tiny text and narrow margins. Your resume must be attractive and easy to read, as is the sample in Figure 5.

Sample Resume 1 (Chronological) | **Figure 5**

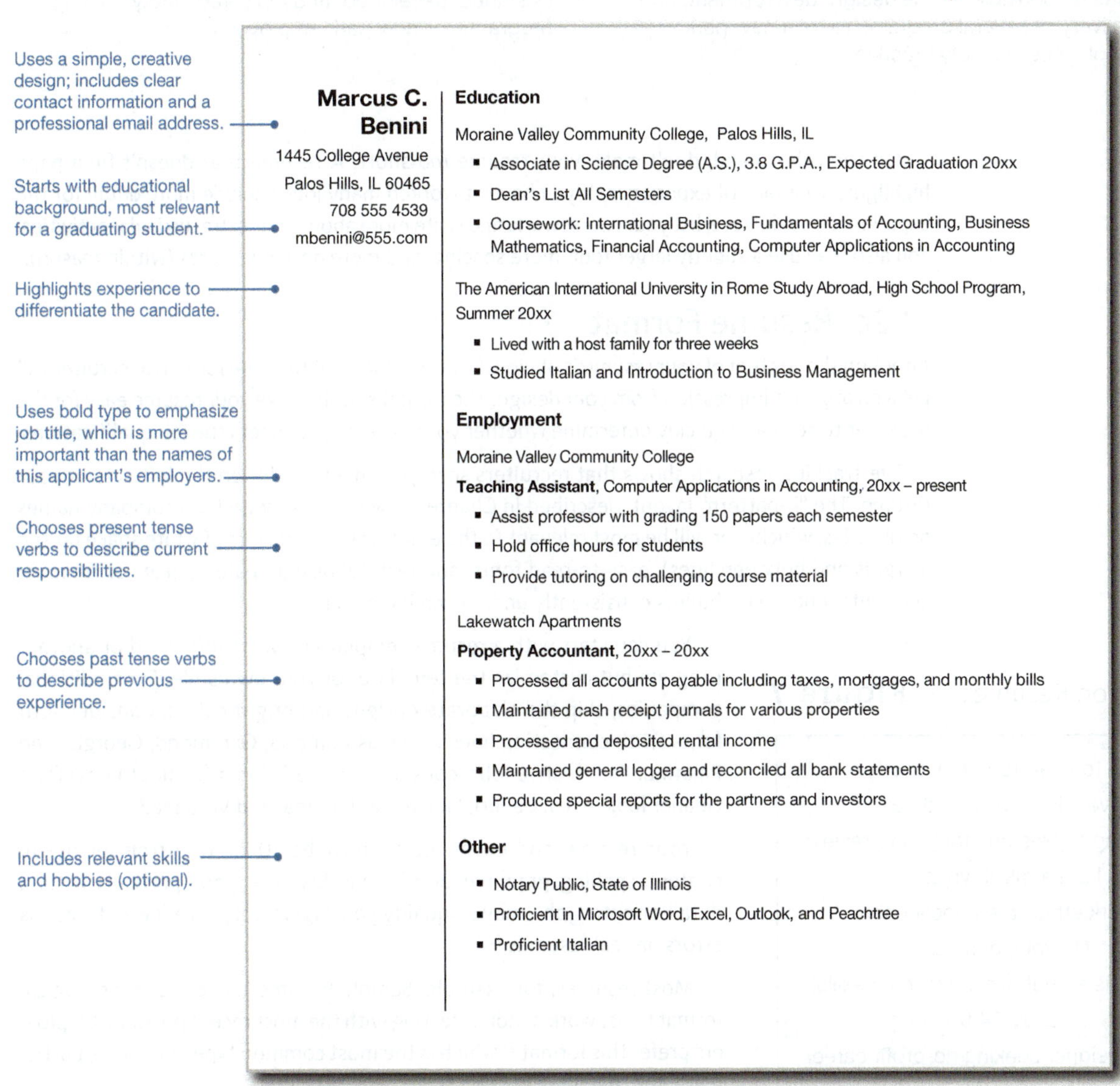

Uses a simple, creative design; includes clear contact information and a professional email address.
Starts with educational background, most relevant for a graduating student.
Highlights experience to differentiate the candidate.
Uses bold type to emphasize job title, which is more important than the names of this applicant's employers.
Chooses present tense verbs to describe current responsibilities.
Chooses past tense verbs to describe previous experience.
Includes relevant skills and hobbies (optional).

Marcus C. Benini
1445 College Avenue
Palos Hills, IL 60465
708 555 4539
mbenini@555.com

Education

Moraine Valley Community College, Palos Hills, IL

- Associate in Science Degree (A.S.), 3.8 G.P.A., Expected Graduation 20xx
- Dean's List All Semesters
- Coursework: International Business, Fundamentals of Accounting, Business Mathematics, Financial Accounting, Computer Applications in Accounting

The American International University in Rome Study Abroad, High School Program, Summer 20xx

- Lived with a host family for three weeks
- Studied Italian and Introduction to Business Management

Employment

Moraine Valley Community College
Teaching Assistant, Computer Applications in Accounting, 20xx – present

- Assist professor with grading 150 papers each semester
- Hold office hours for students
- Provide tutoring on challenging course material

Lakewatch Apartments
Property Accountant, 20xx – 20xx

- Processed all accounts payable including taxes, mortgages, and monthly bills
- Maintained cash receipt journals for various properties
- Processed and deposited rental income
- Maintained general ledger and reconciled all bank statements
- Produced special reports for the partners and investors

Other

- Notary Public, State of Illinois
- Proficient in Microsoft Word, Excel, Outlook, and Peachtree
- Proficient Italian

Shorten your resume by including only what is most relevant to the particular job and by using concise language. Use the questions in Figure 3 to help you decide what to omit; for example, do you really need to include your high school choir experience? This may have been important to you, but perhaps you have more relevant and more recent experience. The before-and-after examples in Figure 6 show how to describe your experience concisely. In both examples, revise the text using the principles from Chapter 5 to save valuable resume space.

Figure 6 | Using Concise Language

Before	After
Was put in charge of managing one of the company's retail stores, which had the most revenue, including overseeing three sales associates.	Managed the company's largest revenue-producing store with three sales associates.

Before	After
Was responsible for the design, development, and delivery of several programs to train new park employees in safety practices.	Designed, developed, and delivered safety training programs for new park employees.

On the other hand, don't make your resume *too* short. A resume that doesn't fill a page highlights your lack of experience. If you haven't worked many jobs, include more detail for the experience you do have, list your coursework, and write more about your extracurricular activities. You also may use a slightly larger font, more spacing, and more design features (within reason).

13-2c Resume Format

Although the content of your resume is obviously more important than the format, a recruiter will get a strong first impression from your design. The format should make your resume easy for the recruiter to scan and quickly determine whether your background meets the job qualifications.

Eye-tracking research shows that recruiters scan your name and then the left side of your resume. The "F-pattern" layout, described in Chapter 4, works best, with bold company names or job titles, whichever will be most relevant to the employer. Include lots of white space (at the margins and between lines), easy-to-read fonts, and tasteful design features (e.g., columns or horizontal lines). Use bullets consistently under each job or activity.

You can start with a resume template in Microsoft Word or another program but customize the template for your own style. For traditional companies, skip the elaborate designs and bright colors. Consider serif fonts (with connecting lines), such as Cambria, Garamond, Georgia, and Palatino. For creative jobs, consider sans serif fonts (without lines) for a cleaner look: Arial, Calibri, Helvetica, Tahoma, and Verdana.[21]

Your resume and cover letter must be 100% free from error—in content, spelling, grammar, and format. Just one typo—particularly for a detail-oriented job—may disqualify you. Figure 7 shows a few outrageous errors on real resumes.[22]

Real Errors on Resumes | **Figure 7**

Real Errors on Resumes
Hope to hear from you, shorty.
Have a keen eye for derail
I'm attacking my resume for you to review.
I am a rabid typist.
My work ethics are impeachable.
Nervous of steel
Following is a grief overview of my skills.
GPA: 34.0
Graphic designer seeking no-profit career

Most resumes, for example, Sample Resume 1, use the chronological format to list work history, starting with the most recent position. Employers prefer this format,[23] which is the most common type of resume, particularly for college students.

However, in some situations, a functional resume—organized around skills or job functions—is a better choice. Functional resumes are most appropriate when you're changing industries, moving into an entirely different line of work, or reentering the workforce after a long period of unemployment. In these situations, functional resumes emphasize your skills rather than your employment history.

Sample Resume 2 (Figure 8) is an example of a functional resume. For Dina Fowler, a functional resume is a good choice because she has changed careers—and now wants to make another switch (from a nonprofit organization to a for-profit company). With a chronological format, Dina's resume would highlight her previous jobs, which do not match her job objective. Instead, Dina needs to emphasize the *skills* that qualify her for a future position. This format is a clever disguise for an imperfect history but makes the screening process more difficult for recruiters.

13-2d Resume Content

Every resume is different, but recruiters expect to see some standard parts included. Figure 9 shows content typically included in a college student's resume.

Contact Information

How will you represent yourself in the contact section of your resume? If you decide to use your given name and you use a nickname, you can include both, for example, Matsuko (Mike) Takahashi. Include a middle initial if you use one on social media accounts and as part of your signature. Include either your school or home mailing address; employers probably won't send a letter, but they might like to know if you're applying for a job in your hometown.

Consider the employer before adding identifying information. For U.S.-based jobs, avoid a photo or personal information (e.g., age, ethnicity, marital status). In the United States, it's illegal to hire or not hire someone based on these characteristics. Applications for international jobs often require a curriculum vitae (CV), a longer version of a resume. Although personal information, such as height, weight, marital status, and children, is more common on CVs than on resumes, this information is not required and is best omitted.

Job Objective and Summary of Qualifications

Job objectives on resumes have fallen out of favor.[24] Some recruiters believe an objective is obvious—you want the position. Also, you can explain your career objective in your cover letter.

However, you could use an objective to clarify your career goals if, for example, your experience doesn't match the job for which you're applying. If you do include an objective, write one that is clear and specific—but not so specific that you exclude yourself from positions that may interest you.

☒ NOT A position that offers an opportunity for growth.

☒ NOT A challenging position in a progressive organization.

☒ NOT A responsible position that lets me use my education and experience and provides opportunities for increased responsibilities.

☑ BUT A paid, one-semester internship in marketing or advertising in the Atlanta area.

☑ BUT A sales position in a medium-sized manufacturing firm.

☑ BUT A public relations position requiring well-developed communication, administrative, and computer skills.

Instead of an objective, some career professionals suggest a summary of qualifications (shown in Sample Resume 2 in Figure 8), which identifies your key skills and experience. This is more typical for applicants who have significant full-time work experience.

Figure 8 | Sample Resume 2 (Functional)

Dina Fowler **dinafowler555@gmail.com**

612 Madeline Road, Apt. 3B, Newark, NJ 07102 **(973) 555-9648**

Qualifications Summary

Highly organized manager with experience in the corporate, nonprofit, and government sectors. Proven ability to successfully manage projects and develop diversified fundraising strategies. Exceptional presentation skills; adept at communicating at all organizational levels and with community partners.

Selected Accomplishments

Nonprofit Leadership and Fundraising

- Provided leadership, management and vision for Bailey Community Center; coordinated fundraising drives, program development, volunteer services, and daily operations; worked with community coalitions and served as the primary spokesperson.
- Created and implemented comprehensive fundraising plan to diversify revenue sources, evaluate results, and engage board members in soliciting donations.
- Instituted new major donor solicitations and direct-mail fundraising campaigns resulting in 20% increase in annual fundraising revenues.
- Researched and secured new foundation and government grants through meticulous proposal writing. Managed and improved profit margin of large-scale fundraising events.
- Implemented structured volunteer services including recruitment, communications, and appreciation events for almost 100 regular volunteers at Bailey.

Project Management

- Administered all aspects of scholarship program for low-income students attending college. Managed collaboration between Newark County and private scholarship foundation, applicant recruitment, selection process, and annual press event.
- Organized and expanded annual conference on housing issues; increased attendance 25% to almost 450 participants over three years; managed logistics and tasks for volunteer committee.

- Recommended and advocated for public policy changes. Tracked developments in policy on the local, state, and national levels to advise executive director on appropriate positions.
- Coordinated coalition of more than 50 nonprofit and advocacy agencies to work for passage of community housing legislation.
- Worked on corporate-wide, human resources computer system conversion for Black & Decker. Analyzed and redesigned all business processes for most effective use of new technology and alignment with corporate standards.

Training and Education

- Created and managed new computer training department for 2,800 employees at the University of Maryland; responsible for computer and furniture procurement, internal marketing, scheduling, enrollment, training delivery, and management reporting.
- Designed and delivered hands-on computer training in PeopleSoft HRMS; Microsoft Word, Excel, PowerPoint, and Access.
- Developed, marketed, and presented training programs on hunger and homelessness issues for hundreds of people in law enforcement, social service agencies, schools, corporations, and religious organizations.

Work History

20xx – present	Assistant Executive Director, Newark Coalition for the Food Insecurity and Housing, Newark, NJ
20xx – 20xx	Executive Director, Bailey Community Services Center, Newark, NJ
20xx – 20xx	Computer Instructor, University of Maryland, College Park, MD
20xx – 20xx	Programmer/Analyst, Black & Decker Corporation, Baltimore, MD

Education and Skills

Rutgers University, Rutgers Business School, B.S. in Management, 20xx

Intermediate Spanish Language Skills

Figure 9 | Typical Resume Content

Contact Information	Education	Work Experience	Other Skills and Experience
• Name • Address • Email Address • Phone Number • LinkedIn Profile URL	• College Name • Major • Degree • Date of Graduation • Relevant Coursework	• Companies • Job Titles • Responsibilities/Achievements • Dates of Employment	• Extracurricular Activities • Languages • Computer Skills • Special Skills

Education

Figure 10 addresses typical questions from students about the education section of a resume.

Figure 10 | Q&A About Education

Which should come first—my education or experience?	Unless you have extensive work experience, your education is probably your strongest job qualification and therefore comes first on the resume. After your first full-time job, you might start with your experience and move the education section to the bottom of your resume.
What if I didn't graduate yet?	Include language such as "Expected date of graduation." (See Sample Resume 1 for an example.)
Should I include my grade-point average?	Include your grade-point average (GPA) if it will set you apart from others (generally, at least a 3.3 or 3.5 on a 4.0 scale). If you made the dean's list, write which semesters you achieved this distinction.
Should I include the name of my high school and grade-point average or rank?	After your first year in college, you can probably omit your high school information unless it might attract attention from a recruiter (e.g., if you attended a highly selective or unique school or if you were valedictorian). By your junior or senior year, you may find that you have more worthy information (work and leadership experience) to fill your one-page resume.
Should I include a list of classes?	Most employers want to see coursework, particularly classes relevant to the job.[25] Choose courses that distinguish you from other applicants.

Work Experience

The work experience section of your resume shows how your previous jobs have prepared you for a future job. Your employment history demonstrates what you've learned that will benefit the organization. From your research about the job you're seeking, highlight your skills and experience that will transfer to the new position. For example, if a position description emphasizes teamwork, be sure to describe examples of your work with others.

☒ NOT Updated employee profiles on the intranet.

☑ BUT Worked with department heads and HR managers to update employee profiles on the intranet.

Complete sentences are not necessary. Instead, start your descriptions with action verbs, using present tense for current responsibilities and past tense for previous job responsibilities or accomplishments. Use concrete words to explain your work experience. Choose from the action verbs in Figure 11 or find your own. The bold words are among those that employers want to see on resumes, according to one survey.[26]

Action Verbs to Start Bulleted Descriptions | **Figure 11**

accomplished	conducted	guided	**mentored**	researched
achieved	constructed	hired	modified	**resolved**
administered	coordinated	implemented	**negotiated**	revised
analyzed	**created**	**improved**	operated	screened
applied	delegated	increased	organized	secured
approved	designed	**influenced**	oversaw	simplified
arranged	determined	instituted	planned	sold
budgeted	developed	interviewed	prepared	supervised
built	diagnosed	introduced	presented	**trained**
changed	directed	investigated	produced	transformed
communicated	edited	**launched**	purchased	updated
completed	established	led	recommended	**volunteered**
conceived	evaluated	maintained	renovated	**won**
concluded	generated	**managed**	reported	wrote

Avoid weak verbs such as *attempted*, *hoped*, and *tried*. When possible, list specific accomplishments, giving numbers or dollar amounts. Highlight accomplishments directly relevant to the job.

☒ NOT I was responsible for a large sales territory.

☑ BUT Managed a six-county sales territory; increased sales by 13% during first full year.

☒ NOT Streamlined data entry.

☑ BUT Automated data entry by creating an Excel spreadsheet; saved an estimated four hours per week for each of eight accountants.

☒ NOT Worked as a bouncer at a local bar.

☑ BUT Maintained order at Nick's Side-Door; resolved several disputes and reduced police interventions by 60% from the previous year.

☒ NOT Sold tickets for Art Reach.

☑ BUT Sold more than $1,000 in tickets to the annual benefit dance; introduced "Each One, Reach One" membership drive that increased membership every year during my three-year term as membership chair.

In the experience section, you may include unpaid internships and volunteer work. Employers are divided on whether you should always include volunteer activities or only when they are relevant to the job.[27] Use the questions in Figure 3 to help you decide. Consider whether you demonstrated transferrable skills used in many professional positions, for example, managing time, working with groups, handling money, organizing tasks, and managing people.

Definitely include volunteer work if you have limited paid work experience. Employers will not likely care whether you were paid for jobs; they are more interested in the skills you developed. However, employers may consider it a stretch to include volunteer work under "Work Experience." Instead, consider adding a section called "Other Relevant Experience" or broadening the "Work Experience" title to "Relevant Experience."

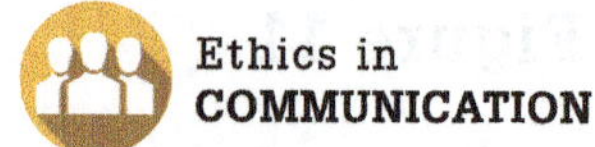

If you started your own business, include it in the work experience section. Emphasize your entrepreneurial skills but be careful about exaggerating your achievements or inflating your title (e.g., referring to yourself as "CEO, President, and COO"). Here's one description of a start-up business.

Cathy Lin Bracelets, New York, NY
Founder and Owner

- Managed business to earn $15,500 in revenue last fiscal year
- Designed and sold custom bracelets for more than 250 customers since inception
- Marketed through email, word-of-mouth, and social media
- Maintained all records in Microsoft Excel
- Managed large inventory of handmade beads

Other Relevant Information

Figure 12 addresses questions students typically have about other information to include on a resume.[28]

Because your resume is about you, it's probably the most personal business document you'll ever write. Use everything you know about effective communication to tell your story in the best way possible.

Figure 12 | Q&A About Other Relevant Information

What should I call the last section on my resume where I have additional skills?	Here are a few options: "Leadership and Other Experience," "Other Relevant Experience," "Extracurricular Activities," or "Other Skills and Qualifications." Choose a heading that summarizes your additional qualifications for the job.
What type of information should I include?	Include anything relevant to the job or interesting to an employer: professional, athletic, or social clubs and organizations; volunteer experience; language skills; honors and awards; and computer skills, particularly programs important for an industry. If you held a leadership position in a club or organization, include the title and your responsibilities.
Should I include personality or other attributes?	Avoid subjective qualities, such as "detail oriented" or "team player." Instead, prove these attributes in your experience descriptions.
How do I represent my language skills?	Consider these categories to describe your language skills: basic, conversational, intermediate, proficient, fluent. If you're unsure, ask your language instructor for an assessment. Also, imagine yourself in front of an interviewer who is fluent in this language. How would you do?
Where do I include my study abroad experience?	You may include your study abroad experience in the last section or within the education section at the beginning of your resume. Consider including the university name, location, dates, and possibly your coursework.
Should I include names of references or "References on Request"?	You should omit both. Although some recruiters might prefer to see references, they take up valuable space and can be presented later in the selection process. Just prepare a list of people who can vouch for you so you're ready when an employer asks.

13-2e Resume Screening Software

About 75% of resumes are never seen by a real person.[29] Almost all Fortune 500 companies—and many smaller ones—use an applicant tracking system, which scans and sorts resumes.[30] When you submit your resume online, the system will search for terms that match the job description. Unfortunately, 90% of employers surveyed believe that their automated systems weed out otherwise highly skilled candidates,[31] but they still use them to manage the large number of resumes they receive.

Follow these tips to increase the chance of your resume ending up in the "yes" pile:[32]

- **Keywords.** Include terms that you see in the job description and provide them in context. To see which words appear most often, copy and paste the description into Wordle or another word cloud program. Typically, keywords are nouns, and you may find terms spelled out or abbreviated, so include both in your resume. Mention each two or three times, once in your descriptive bullets, taking time to integrate the word. This avoids keyword "stuffing," which is a turnoff for most employers. Instead, prove that you have experience with the term.[33]
- **Fonts and formatting.** Choose standard computer fonts and round bullets. Fancy fonts, bullets, and other graphics may get garbled by older systems. Test your resume by saving it as a plain text document (.txt) to see how well it converts.
- **File type and organization.** Be sure to upload an acceptable type of file and choose Microsoft Word over PDF because it's more easily read by some systems. Avoid placing contact and other information in the header or footer, which can be missed. Also stick to common section titles suggested earlier rather than, for example, "How I Contribute," which might not be recognized as a heading.[34]

Figures 13 and 14 show keywords on a job posting and how you might incorporate them into bulleted descriptions on a resume. Keywords aren't just for your resume. Without overdoing it,

Keywords in an Ad | **Figure 13**

HUMAN RESOURCES RECRUITER

Core Job Responsibilities:

- Write job descriptions and identify job requirements
- Screen resumes
- Conduct screening interviews in person and online
- Conduct in-person behavioral interviews
- Organize candidates' interview schedules with managers
- Make selection decisions working with managers
- Manage high school and college intern programs
- Work with an assistant for administrative support

Qualifications and Skills:

- Bachelor's degree required
- Ability to work with all levels of management
- Proficient use of Microsoft Office software
- Strong writing and editing skills
- Experience working with a recruitment management system a plus
- Meticulous organization and follow-up skills
- Professional in Human Resources (PHR) certification preferred

Figure 14 | Keywords on a Resume

KEYWORDS: job descriptions, selection decisions

- Worked with managers to write job descriptions and make final selection decisions.

KEYWORDS: resumes, intern

- Screened resumes of interns and full-time applicants to determine qualifications.

KEYWORDS: behavioral interviews, online, intern

- Conducted behavioral interviews in person, by phone, and online for full-time and intern hires.

KEYWORDS: Microsoft Office, recruitment management system

- Used Microsoft Office products (Word, Excel, and PowerPoint) and Yello Recruitment Management System (RMS).

KEYWORDS: writing, organization

- Wrote and edited guidelines for on-campus recruitment.
- Organized recruitment events at 15 campuses for more than 300 students.

weaving the same terms into your cover letter, LinkedIn profile, interview, and thank-you note may increase your chances of being selected and will ensure a cohesive approach to your application.

LO3 Assess whether a LinkedIn profile meets given criteria.

13-3 Developing a Professional Online Presence

When recruiters search for you online, what do they find? In this section, we discuss how to manage your online reputation, create a LinkedIn profile, and connect with people to increase your chance of getting hired via social networking.

13-3a Managing Your Online Reputation

How you present yourself online can make or break a hiring decision. Does your online presence reflect how you want to be perceived? Do you come across as a person of good character? Would others want to work with you? Your professional image will be judged partly by your **online reputation**—how you are represented on the web.

Most employers search for candidates online, with estimates between 70[35] and 90%.[36] Employers want to know whether you'll fit within the organization; your online presence gives them a better sense of your personality, communication, and relationships. Employers report using search engines and checking social networks for the following reasons:

- To verify a candidate's qualifications for the job (58%).
- To see whether the candidate has a professional online persona (50%).
- To read what other people post about the candidate (34%).[37]

Imagine your first-choice employer googling you and finding a LinkedIn article you wrote about the industry or an Instagram photo caption you wrote about your school club. Or maybe a recruiter finds your blog about food, fashion, sports, or whatever interests you. Later, we discuss how you can reinforce your interests, knowledge, and personal brand—how you would like to be known.

In addition to the reasons above, 22% of employers search online to look for "a reason *not* to hire the candidate"—and they find them.[38] "Red flags" that caused employers to eliminate a candidate from the selection pool include those in Figure 15.[39]

Figure 15 Reasons Employers Didn't Hire Candidates

40%	Posted provocative or inappropriate photographs, videos, or information
36%	Shared information about drinking or using drugs
31%	Wrote discriminatory comments related to race, gender, religion, etc.
30%	Had a link to criminal behavior
27%	Lied about qualifications
27%	Demonstrated poor communication skills
25%	Bad-mouthed a previous company or coworker
22%	Chose an unprofessional screen name
20%	Shared confidential information from previous employer
16%	Lied about an absence
12%	Posted too frequently

In another study, hiring managers judged "self-absorption" and "opinionatedness" negatively. Managers saw two different captions on images. For example, they saw a young person sitting with an older person holding a gift. One caption was about his grandmother's birthday, and the other was about his "birthday week" and how he looked in the photo. When photo captions were overly focused on the candidate or expressed strong opinions about political issues or social issues, the candidate was evaluated more negatively.[40]

In yet another study, hiring managers identified spelling and grammar errors as the biggest turnoff in social posts. This group also reacted negatively to "pictures of bodies showing skin."[41]

You can protect yourself by managing your online content:

- **Search for yourself.** Type your name in Google and Bing and review the images and videos in addition to the default page results. Scroll down to at least page 10. Next, search for your name with your hometown, school, former employer, and other terms.
- **Take an external view.** How do you appear to someone who doesn't know you? Does your online presence represent your best self? Do you see any "red flags" for employers?
- **Differentiate yourself.** If you find negative information about someone else with your name, find a "clean version" of your name (e.g., with your middle name) and use it consistently on your resume, cover letter, and social profiles.[42]
- **Cull content.** Remove content and un-tag photos and videos that don't represent you well. If you can't remove negative content, be prepared to discuss it honestly during an interview.
- **Manage privacy settings.** Consider being more selective about who sees your online posts.
- **Think twice before posting.** Imagine your favorite company seeing everything you post about your opinions, beliefs, family, friends, coworkers, and customers.
- **Create positive content.** Often, the best way to overcome negative content is to post new content that will appear in search engines and feeds. Write well and portray yourself as a person of high character. This starts with your social profile, which we discuss next.

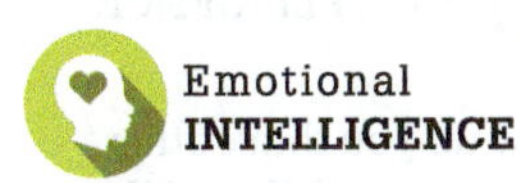

Do any online posts by or about you cause you concern? How can you remove the information, drown it out, or make peace with it?

Once you're hired, continue to be diligent about what you post online. Follow your company's social media policy, described in Chapter 1. Companies have been criticized and, in some cases, sued for their response to online posts, but why spoil your professional image and put your job in jeopardy?

13-3b Creating a Social Profile

Part of developing a professional online presence is creating a social profile, particularly on LinkedIn. Employers report getting the highest quality candidates from the network. Although less often than in previous years, employers use LinkedIn for recruiting more than any other social media site.[43]

Employers use LinkedIn to post jobs and to search for, screen, contact, and keep track of candidates. Follow these tips to create a professional, compelling profile.[44]

General Introduction

Include the following in your profile introduction:

- **Name:** Write your name as you do on your resume, cover letter, and other social platforms. Include pronouns if you'd like to, and on the mobile app, you can record and add your name pronunciation.
- **Profile photo:** Use a professional-looking headshot that takes up about 60% of the space. Wear what you would to work. Smile.
- **Background photo:** Add a photo to show what's important to you and to make your profile stand out.
- **Headline:** Write your current job title—or something else. Try to summarize your career interest or personal brand.

Summary

The summary tells recruiters the story of who you are—beyond the details of your resume. Within about 100 words, show how what you do matters. In your natural writing style, demonstrate your personality and good character. Skip the buzzwords but include keywords in your area of interest. See Figure 16 for an example of a LinkedIn introduction and summary.

How do you think others perceive you? Would they say you are generally more positive or negative? What do you think contributes to this assessment?

If you have trouble writing the summary, revisit the questions in Figure 1 at the beginning of the chapter. Here are a few variations to ask yourself:

- A turning point in my life was . . .
- The world would be a better place if . . .
- I'm known for . . .
- I'm happiest doing . . .
- Work feels like play when . . .
- What motivates me to get up every morning is . . .

Experience

List your previous jobs as they appear on your resume. Recruiters use LinkedIn to verify the details on your employment application. Include paid work, internships, volunteer work, military experience, and so on.

Education

Write your official school names and dates you attended, including your expected year of graduation.

Skills and Endorsements

Choose a few skills you feel confident using. LinkedIn offers skills assessments for popular technologies and tools. Initial LinkedIn research shows that applicants with verified skills are 30%

Sample LinkedIn Introduction and Summary | **Figure 16**

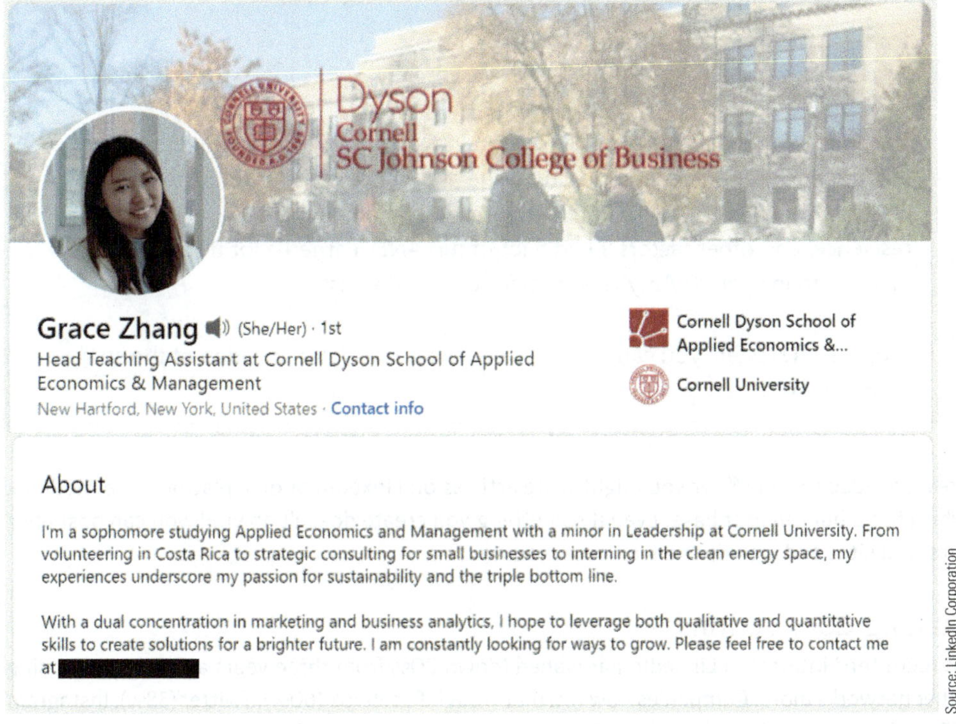

Source: LinkedIn Corporation

more likely to be hired.[45] For consistency, align your top three skills with the keywords you include in all your employment communications.

Allow endorsements and actively endorse others' skills, which will encourage them to endorse yours. You also may request recommendations from people who know you well and whose opinion will be valued. Ask them to endorse specific skills that represent work they observed you doing.

Additional Content

Take the time to round out your profile. Include relevant licenses and certifications, interests, courses, honors and awards, languages, organizations, and projects. Also include examples of your work. Within the experience section, you can add links to examples of slide decks, reports, a video, a blog, and so on. Consider creating new content and making connections on LinkedIn—and on other social sites, which we discuss next.

12-3c Strengthening Your Online Presence

Bolster your qualifications by presenting yourself as an engaged professional. By developing original content to demonstrate your interests and expertise and by making connections, you'll build your network, which could lead to job opportunities.

Developing Content

Consider creating original content that you can share online. You can start small by posting regular updates on LinkedIn, Twitter, or other sites. To keep your profile in front of people, let your network know what you are up to, as Grace Zhang did, shown in Figure 17. If you want more likes and shares, post content that's relevant and interesting.

If your goal is to attract attention, try innovative approaches like the examples you read about in the chapter introduction. You can create an infographic resume in Canva or other sites or

Figure 17 | Sample Status Update on LinkedIn

Grace Zhang (She/Her) • 1st
Head Teaching Assistant at Cornell Dyson School of Applied Economics & Manag...
2mo • Edited •

This past week, I had the pleasure of working with Sherri Kimes to design a reading deck/report based on a study she and her colleague conducted on how hotels responded to COVID in terms of revenue management, price wars, human resilience, and other factors. I had a lot of fun AND learned a lot through the process; thank you to Amy Newman for connecting us!

If you're interested, you can find my deck and a presentation video of the study on her website.

Source: LinkedIn Corporation

create a video resume.[46] Or you might write articles on LinkedIn or on a platform like Medium, which has a built-in user base. Even if something you create doesn't go viral, you can post links on social sites and include them on your resume.

Making Connections

As recruiters' interest in LinkedIn has waned (down 20% from three years ago), they are using other networks more. Companies now recruit through Facebook (60%), Twitter (38%), Instagram (37%), Glassdoor (36%), YouTube (27%), Snapchat (13%), and TikTok (7%).[47] They post content about their company and look for candidates.

Build your network by sending requests to friends, classmates, former employers, and others you know. On LinkedIn, you can sync your email address book with your profile to get recommendations for connections. If you want to connect with people you don't know, write personal invitations about your interest in them or their work. Similarly, you might consider accepting invitations from people you don't know.

On all social networks, join groups and follow people who interest you. After spending some time observing how others post, begin to participate in discussions. Comment on posts thoughtfully, making sure that everything you write reflects well on you. Grace Zhang likes and comments on others' posts regularly—including responses to her own, as you see in Figure 18. Proofread carefully and avoid posting anything you may regret.

Figure 18 | Example of Responding to a LinkedIn Comment

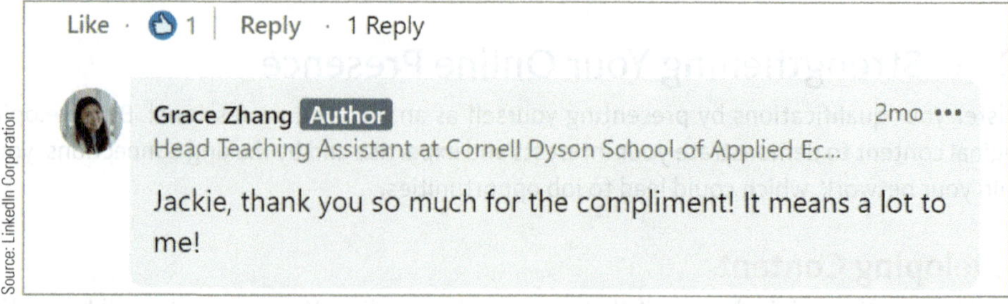

Source: LinkedIn Corporation

Building your network is best done when you're not actively looking for a job. People often find jobs through people they know,[48] but the relationship is key. When you think about what, how, and when to post, consider how content might be received. What will people find useful for their own careers? How can you be of service to others who are seeking jobs? If you find ways to develop genuine connections, your network will serve you in the long run.

13-4 Writing Cover Letters and Networking Messages

LO4 Tailor a cover letter for a given position.

In addition to your resume and social profile, cover letters and networking messages provide prospective employers with information about your interests and qualifications. You might send a cover letter as an email with a resume attached, or you may be asked by on-campus recruiters to submit a cover letter with your resume. To expand your job search, you may contact people who don't have advertised jobs. All these communications require your natural, professional writing style.

13-4a Cover Letters

A cover letter tells a prospective employer that you are interested in and qualified for a position within the organization. An effective cover letter will achieve the following:

- Express your interest in the company and the position
- Highlight how your background specifically matches the job qualifications
- Reveal some of your personality and character
- Demonstrate your business writing skills

Your cover letter is a sales letter—you're selling your qualifications to the prospective employer. This is your chance to differentiate yourself and pique the employer's interest in you as a candidate. Ideally, a recruiter reads your cover letter and thinks, "I'd like to meet this person." Aim to sound confident and professional, without being too boastful or presumptuous.

Read a cover letter you wrote in the past. How do you come across? Do you sound confident but not boastful?

Typically, cover letters for entry-level jobs are one page long, as in the sample shown in Figure 19. This should be enough space to achieve your goals.

Although it's often still referred to as a "letter," a cover letter is typically sent as an attachment or email. Follow each company's instructions, for example, to attach the letter in a particular file format or to include it within the body of the email. If a cover letter isn't requested, shorten your traditional cover letter and place the body text (without the letter formatting) within the email (Figure 20). This avoids the receiver having to open two attachments.

Address and Salutation

Your letter should be addressed to an individual rather than to an organization or department. You might write to an HR manager listed as the contact on a job posting or to the department manager you'll report to if you get the job. Make sure you have the right name, spelling, and position title. As discussed in Chapter 3, use the person's full first and last name to avoid assumptions about gender and marital status: "Dear Katrina Williams." If you don't have someone's name, use a generic title: "Dear Human Resources Manager" or "Dear Hiring Manager."

Opening

The opening paragraph of a solicited cover letter is fairly straightforward. Because the organization has advertised the position, recruiters want to receive applications, so use a direct organization with the main points up front: state (or imply) the reason for your letter, identify the position for which you're applying, and indicate how you learned about the opening.

Tailor your opening to the job and to the specific organization. For traditional companies (e.g., financial services firms), use a restrained opening. For more creative work (e.g., sales, advertising, and public relations), you might start out on a more imaginative note.

Finally, for unsolicited cover letters, which you initiate without a specific job posting, first get the reader's attention. Try mentioning the company—a recent project or a new product launch—and then show how you can contribute to the corporate effort, without stretching too much.

Figure 19 | Sample Cover Letter

Uses traditional letter formatting.

45 East 4th Street
Hempstead, NY 11549

December 14, 20xx

Marley Catona
VP, Recruiting
Vanguard
100 Vanguard Blvd.
Malvern, PA 19355

Dear Marley Catona:

Attracts attention

Mentions the position.

I was excited to see the Investment Trainee Internship at Vanguard, posted by my high school classmate Caroline Madison. Caroline told me about her great experience last summer working in the Private Wealth division. My finance skills and experience, ESG interest, and leadership make me a great fit for the role.

Begins with the strongest qualification.

Shows a connection to the company.

I'm the founder and president of Duke's first student investment club, and we focus on ESG stocks. Just an idea during my sophomore year, the club has grown to more than 75 student members and has served as a model for three other universities. We have a small portfolio that tracks Vanguard's FTSE Social Index Fund, and we research additional ESG stocks. Last year, we worked with club advisors, including two managers at Blackstone, to research new evaluation tools.

Uses topic sentences for readers who skim.

Provides a specific example.

Includes external evidence to verify skills.

My internship at Morgan Stanley prepared me well for the investment club. Working in Wealth Management, I learned a lot about evaluating cash flows, balance sheets, and financial statements. One highlight of my summer was presenting an investment opportunity to the team, which they adopted and earned a 14.4% return on within two months. I received good feedback on the presentation, and my manager said she would use my PPT deck as an example for future interns.

Demonstrates enthusiasm and impact on others.

My three favorite classes at Duke are Financial Markets, Python, and Excel Modeling. I serve as a teaching assistant for the Excel course, holding office hours for students and grading homework assignments. Although students see it as a challenging course, it's great seeing how much they learn from their first homework assignment to the mid-term exam after they come to office hours.

Shows personality and community interest.

In addition to these experiences, I volunteer for Habitat for Humanity at home and in Durham. My trip to rebuild homes in Florida last summer taught me a lot about how the environment affects people's lives and how much people rely on their local communities in difficult times. Since I started school, I worked on four new homes in Durham. I enjoy the physical work with a team, but meeting the families is the best part.

Closes confidently.

I look forward to hearing from you to discuss more of my qualifications, which you'll find in the attached resume. You may reach me at (516) 555-6229 or sebastianfavela@555.com.

Sincerely,

Sebastian Favela

Sebastian Favela

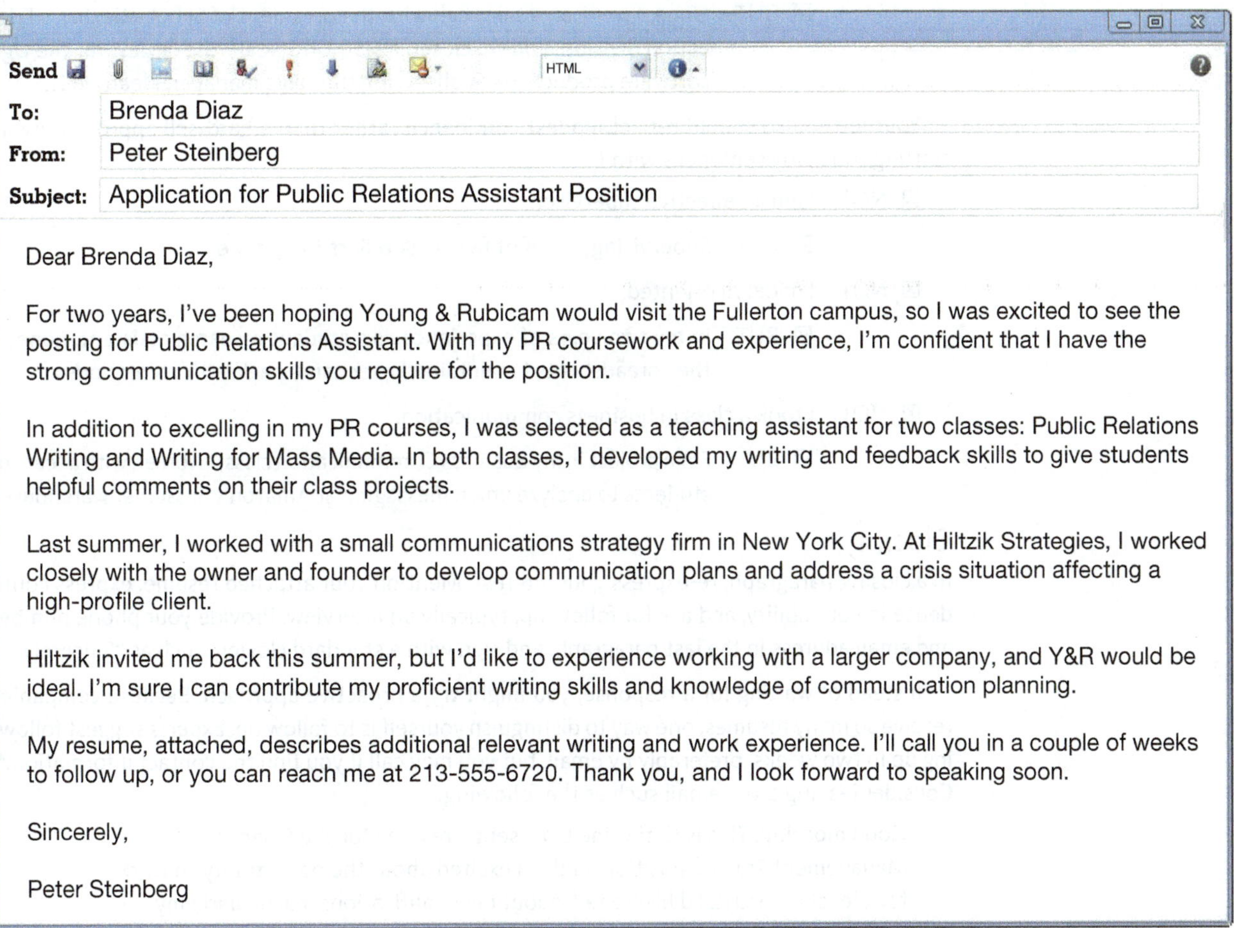
Send HTML
To: Brenda Diaz
From: Peter Steinberg
Subject: Application for Public Relations Assistant Position

Dear Brenda Diaz,

For two years, I've been hoping Young & Rubicam would visit the Fullerton campus, so I was excited to see the posting for Public Relations Assistant. With my PR coursework and experience, I'm confident that I have the strong communication skills you require for the position.

In addition to excelling in my PR courses, I was selected as a teaching assistant for two classes: Public Relations Writing and Writing for Mass Media. In both classes, I developed my writing and feedback skills to give students helpful comments on their class projects.

Last summer, I worked with a small communications strategy firm in New York City. At Hiltzik Strategies, I worked closely with the owner and founder to develop communication plans and address a crisis situation affecting a high-profile client.

Hiltzik invited me back this summer, but I'd like to experience working with a larger company, and Y&R would be ideal. I'm sure I can contribute my proficient writing skills and knowledge of communication planning.

My resume, attached, describes additional relevant writing and work experience. I'll call you in a couple of weeks to follow up, or you can reach me at 213-555-6720. Thank you, and I look forward to speaking soon.

Sincerely,

Peter Steinberg

☒ NOT As a native Brazilian, I'm sure I can help Chobani's expansion plans in South America.

☑ BUT As a native Brazilian, I have great interest in Chobani's expansion plans in Rio de Janeiro, where four generations of my family have lived.

☑ BUT With my experience as a marketing intern at Sabra, I would look forward to finding innovative ways to improve Chobani's social media presence.

Your opening should be short, interesting, and reader oriented. Avoid tired, formal openings that sound robotic. Yet avoid being too cute, which may sound unprofessional and detract from your qualifications.

☒ NOT Please consider this letter of application for . . .

☒ NOT Lucky me for finding this job posting!

☑ BUT The social media intern position describes my experience perfectly, and I'm confident that I can transfer my learning about SEO to Chobani.

Body

In a paragraph or two, highlight your strongest qualifications and show how they can benefit the employer. Provide specific, credible evidence to support your statements, using different wording from that used in the resume. Give an example to make the bullets on your resume come alive and help the recruiter visualize your experience.

☒ NOT As stated on my resume, I sometimes went on sales calls.

☑ BUT Once, I went on a sales call with the president of Scholastic, Inc.'s Education division, and we closed a $150,000 deal—the largest for the Ugo software product. From observing the sales manager, I learned ...

Your letter also should reflect modest confidence rather than a hard-sell approach. Avoid starting too many sentences with *I*.

☒ NOT I am an effective supervisor.

☑ BUT Supervising a staff of five bank tellers taught me ...

☒ NOT I'm detail oriented.

☑ BUT In my two years of experience as a student research assistant, none of the spreadsheets I maintained ever came back with corrections.

☒ NOT I took a class in business communication.

☑ BUT For a project in my Business Communication class, I worked with a team of students to analyze union messaging at Amazon's Bessemer warehouse.

Closing

In a closing paragraph, re-express your interest. Mention your attached resume, express confidence in your ability, and ask for follow-up, typically an interview. Provide your phone number and email address in the last paragraph, and sign with a standard closing, such as "Sincerely."

Instead of waiting for a response, you might try a proactive approach. Because companies receive so many resumes, one way to distinguish yourself is to follow up. Experts suggest following up in two weeks, preferably by email, but you may call if you find the contact information.[49] Consider leaving a voicemail such as the following:

> Good morning. This is Catherine Lin. I sent a resume for the Finance Management Trainee position, and I'm excited about the opportunity to work for Cleveland Trust. I'd like to talk about my qualifications, particularly my experience at Ernst & Young, and possibly set up an interview. You can reach me at 555-555-1212. Thank you, and I look forward to hearing from you.

You may not hear back, but the receiver will likely remember your name while reading through the stack of resumes—and perhaps yours will get a second look.

13-4b Networking Messages

When you don't know of a specific job opening but want to express interest in a company, you can send an email—sometimes called a **networking email** or a request for an informational interview. Typically, this inquiry email is shorter than a cover letter. The example in Figure 21 might be sent to someone who owns a financial planning practice in your hometown.

Networking is a good way to find job openings that may not be advertised or to learn more about a company and professionals in your area of interest. Find contacts through your school's alumni database, friends and family, the company's website, articles about the company, and LinkedIn. The example in Figure 22 illustrates changes from the email in Figure 21. On LinkedIn, you may need to get connected to the person before sending a message without a premium (paid) account.

The message in Figure 22 is low stakes. It doesn't require much of Amar, who is probably happy to talk about his career with a college student from the town where he runs a business. One day, Marie might become a client—or maybe Amar will simply be generous with his time. You'll probably get better results with this type of message than one that refers to an internship, but be careful: you don't want to be disingenuous about your reason for reaching out. If you meet and suddenly ask about an internship, Amar may feel duped. Either keep the conversation general and focused on him or see whether he raises the topic of work experience during the meeting.

You won't hear back from everyone who receives your inquiry email, but it's worth a shot. Making these connections is a good way to practice your networking skills.

Sample Networking Email | **Figure 21**

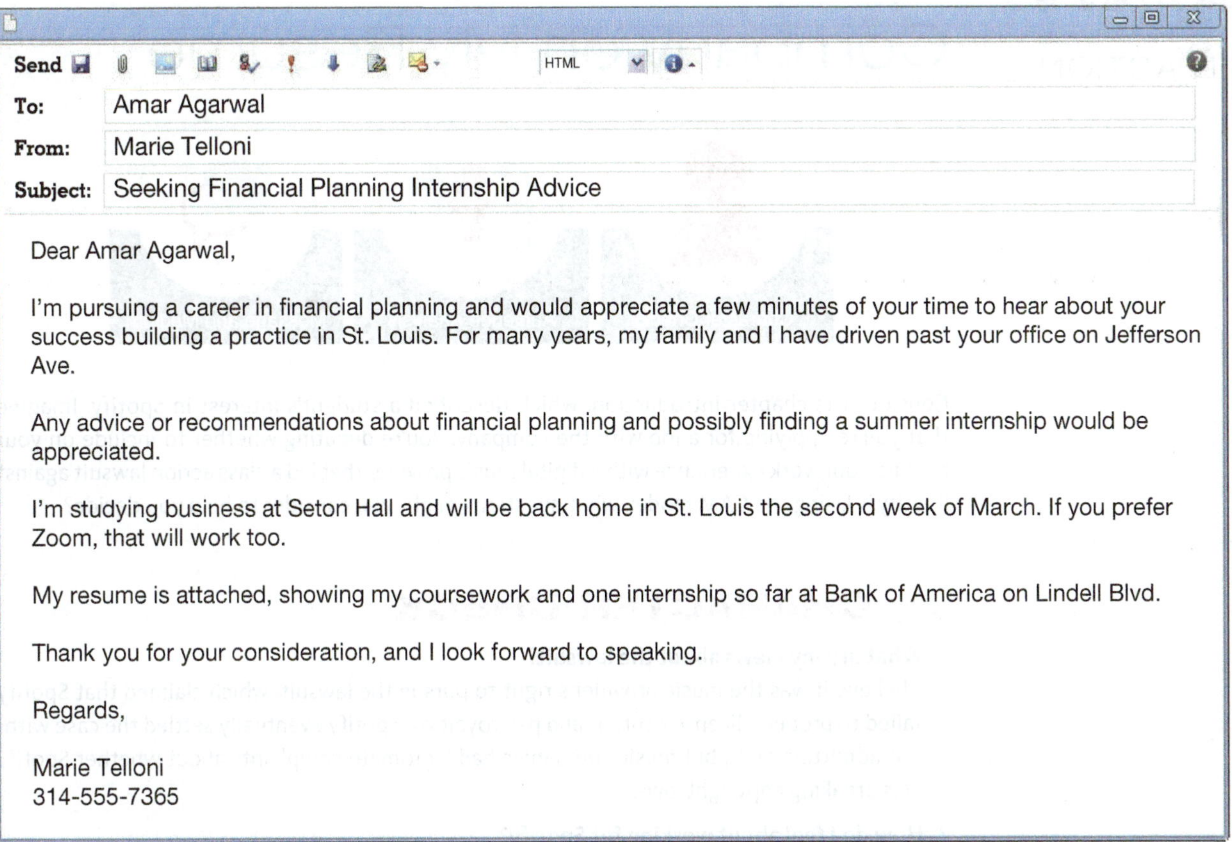

Dear Amar Agarwal,

I'm pursuing a career in financial planning and would appreciate a few minutes of your time to hear about your success building a practice in St. Louis. For many years, my family and I have driven past your office on Jefferson Ave.

Any advice or recommendations about financial planning and possibly finding a summer internship would be appreciated.

I'm studying business at Seton Hall and will be back home in St. Louis the second week of March. If you prefer Zoom, that will work too.

My resume is attached, showing my coursework and one internship so far at Bank of America on Lindell Blvd.

Thank you for your consideration, and I look forward to speaking.

Regards,

Marie Telloni
314-555-7365

Sample LinkedIn Networking Message | **Figure 22**

Hello Amar,

I'm a sophomore studying business at Seton Hall. I see that you own a financial planning company in St. Louis, my hometown.

Would you have a few minutes to chat about your career? I'm trying to decide whether financial planning is right for me and would appreciate hearing your experience.

You can reach me here or by email: _______

Thanks so much,

Marie

13-5 Chapter Closing

Throughout your life, you might spend more time on your resume than on any other document. Resume and cover letter formats have changed surprisingly little over the years, and yet you have many options for adding your own style and creativity as you read in the chapter introduction.

Finding a job is more than simply writing out your accomplishments. As a college student, you can start developing your online presence by making connections and helping others.

Someday, you will be in a leadership position and can change how people are hired for jobs. You might find ways to reduce bias in the selection process to make sure the best person is hired for an open position. Next, we explore more steps in the selection process: interviewing and, finally, landing a job.

Decide Whether to Include a Company on My Resume

Consider the chapter introduction, which described a student's interest in Spotify. Imagine that you're applying for a job with the company. You're debating whether to include on your resume your work experience with a digital music provider that led a class action lawsuit against Spotify.[50] Using the CAM model, what questions might you consider to help you decide?

>>> CHARACTER CHECK

1. **What are my views about the lawsuit?**
   I believe it was the music provider's right to pursue the lawsuit, which claimed that Spotify failed to properly license content and pay royalties. Spotify eventually settled the case without admitting guilt, but music companies had legitimate complaints about whether Spotify was breaking copyright laws.
2. **How do I feel about working for Spotify?**
   The case was resolved, and I think Spotify is a great company. I feel no conflict having worked for the music provider. I was in the marketing group and not part of the legal action.

>>> AUDIENCE ANALYSIS

1. **How might a Spotify recruiter react to my application?**
   Well, maybe not positively, although my marketing role is clear. Besides, I would guess that many people who worked for music companies later join Spotify, and others may have been involved in the lawsuit. That was a few years ago.
2. **How might the recruiter view my qualifications without the experience on my resume?**
   The marketing position is very relevant to the Spotify job. Without it, my resume shows a gap, which isn't great either. I think I need to include it. It feels dishonest to omit it.
3. **Would the recruiter pass on my application if someone else is equally qualified?**
   Maybe, if our experience is about the same. I'll have to distinguish myself in other ways, demonstrating my commitment to the company.

>>> MESSAGE AND MEDIUM

1. **What are the main points of my message?**
   I need to show how much I like the company, which I do! I've been a premium subscriber for several years.
2. **In what medium will I communicate the message?**
   I'll mention my history with Spotify in my cover letter. I'll also find the recruiter on LinkedIn or try to find an email address. Then, I can send a personal message.

Write a Cover Letter

‹ IN PRACTICE

For this activity, you can use the situation described on the previous page, or you can use your own situation. Imagine that you're writing a cover letter for a job, and you are concerned that an experience might disqualify you. This can be anything potentially controversial or negative about your background that you have already decided to keep on your resume. Using the CAM model, how will you describe the experience?

››› CHARACTER CHECK

1. What motivated me to participate in the experience that is now in question?
2. How do I feel about the experience and my role in it?
3. If I had to do it over, would I? Why or why not?
4. How central to my identity is the experience? In other words, is it a matter of authenticity and/or integrity that persuaded me to include it?

››› AUDIENCE ANALYSIS

1. How might the employer react to my experience?
2. What could be the employer's concerns about hiring me, given my background? In other words, what risks could the employer be concerned about in deciding to hire me?

››› MESSAGE AND MEDIUM

1. What will be my main points about my experience? How can I convince the employer that my experience is relevant and valuable—and that the hire risk is minimal?
2. I'll write a cover letter that describes the experience.

REFLECTING ON YOUR COMMUNICATION AND CHARACTER DEVELOPMENT

1. **Assess your strengths.**
   First, answer the questions in Figure 1. Next, think about five times in your life when you felt that you were your "best self"—or at your best. Jot down notes about each situation, particularly your actions and the impact on or reactions from others.

   From these exercises, what three or four top strengths surface? Write them down with a short description of each.

   Now discuss your notes with two or three family members or friends who know you well. What are their views of your assessment? Do they agree with the strengths you identified? Do they see others that you didn't identify? How, if at all, do their opinions of you influence how you feel about your strengths?

   How does this exercise help you think about your future career?

2. **Consider your career choices.**
   Given the previous exercise and your own thinking about your career, how would you describe the best job situation for you? Next, consider two more options in case your idea doesn't work out. What else could you do that would use your skills, experience, and talents? How else could you contribute to society? It's OK if you are unsure because these ideas are still evolving for you.

3. **Develop confidence about your resume.**
   How do you feel about your resume—your present one and the prospect of updating it? When you read it, what makes you feel proud? What makes you feel sad, worried, or inadequate?

   Try to reframe your feelings of inadequacy. For example, you might consider that everyone has room to grow and that not everyone has had the same opportunities that others have had. Think about what you can do in the future so that your resume represents you in a way that makes you feel good about yourself and your qualifications.

4. **Reassess a former application.**
   Have you ever stretched the truth on an application? What were the consequences—positive and negative? How do you feel about your decision now? Would you make the same decision again if you had another chance? Why or why not?

5. **Manage your online content.**
   Follow the steps described in the chapter to manage your online reputation. What did you find in a thorough search that included different search engines, name and term combinations, and videos and images? What changes can you make to ensure that your online presence represents your good character?

6. **Assess online connections.**
   How do you interact with people in public online spaces? Consider social networks where employers might see and judge your relationships. Are you professional, helpful to others, and engaged? Are your experience, interests, and knowledge evident? How can you improve your online interactions to expand your network and reflect well on your character and professionalism?

DEVELOPING YOUR BUSINESS COMMUNICATION SKILLS

PRESENTING YOUR BEST SELF

LO1 Describe your strengths for a position that interests you.

1. **Discuss your strengths.**
   Review your answers to the first question in the previous section, Reflecting on Your Communication and Character Development. With a classmate, share as much as you're comfortable revealing. Find as many commonalties between you as you can.

   Also discuss the process of identifying your strengths. What else can you do to clarify your strengths and how you can most contribute to an organization?

2. **Identify work and personal values.**
   Complete the Work and Personal Values form at https://career.berkeley.edu/Plan/Values. Identifying what is most important to you provides direction as you consider potential careers and places to work. What you value will change over time, so repeating this exercise periodically will be helpful as you make decisions throughout your career.

3. **Evaluate a company's career pages.**
   Choose a company that interests you. Go to the website and find the careers section. In small groups, answer the following questions:
   - How easy is it to find information about careers or jobs at the company?
   - How are the pages within that section organized?
   - What is emphasized? In other words, what seems to be most important to the company? What do they value in new hires?
   - How, if at all, does the company describe its commitment to diversity, equity, and inclusion?
   - What jobs are posted? What categories of positions do you find?
   - What is written about the selection process? Do you know what to expect after submitting your application or resume?
   - Overall, does your evaluation of the website increase or diminish your interest in the company?

PREPARING YOUR RESUME

LO2 Identify questions to guide decisions about resume content.

4. **Give and receive feedback to improve generic resumes.**
   Exchange generic resumes (not for a particular job) with two classmates. Using the principles in this chapter, analyze each other's resume. Imagine that you're a human resources manager who reviews hundreds of resumes every day. Use the criteria in Figure 23 to provide feedback to each other.

5. **Customize your resume for a job.**
   After you incorporate feedback on your generic resume, revise your resume for a particular job. Find a job posting that interests you and tailor your experience and other information to fit that description.

   Use guidelines throughout this chapter to include what is most relevant and valuable to the employer. Integrate keywords from the job posting where relevant. Also use the questions in Figure 3 to guide you.

6. **Give and receive feedback to improve tailored resumes.**
   Share the job posting you used for the previous exercise with two classmates. Use the questions in Figure 24 to provide feedback to each other.

Figure 23 | Feedback About a Generic Resume

CRITERIA	STRENGTHS	SUGGESTIONS
Formatting is attractive and easy to read.		
Contact information is clear.		
Education section is accurate and emphasizes key points.		
Work experience section is well organized.		
Work experience section includes companies, job titles, and dates.		
Bulleted job responsibilities start with action verbs and are phrased clearly.		
Job responsibility descriptions highlight accomplishments.		
Other activities are relevant and clearly explained.		
Resume is 100% accurate.		

Discuss your feedback in trios. When you do, explain choices you made on your resume and be open to hearing other students' choices. You don't have to accept all the feedback you receive.

Like your classmates' feedback, employers' decisions based on resumes are subjective. What will cause one employer to eliminate a candidate may be a selling point for another. You might have good reasons (e.g., your identity or integrity) for including some information—and that is your choice.

LO3 Assess whether a LinkedIn profile meets given criteria.

DEVELOPING A PROFESSIONAL ONLINE PRESENCE

7. Ask two people to search for you online.

Before you do this exercise, complete Exercise in the previous section, Reflecting on Your Communication and Character Development. After you're satisfied with your review, ask two friends, family members, or classmates to search for you online. Ask them to spend

Feedback About a Tailored Resume | **Figure 24**

QUESTIONS	NOTES
Is the education section, including coursework, appropriate for the position?	
How is the work experience section tailored to the position? Compare the generic and custom resume. Does the revised resume emphasize what is most relevant to the job and valuable to the employer?	
How are keywords incorporated into the resume? Are they used in context and throughout the resume—and not overused?	
Are other activities relevant to the job? What, if anything, from the generic version was changed in the later sections? Are these changes appropriate for the position?	
Is this version of the resume 100% accurate?	

at least 15 minutes to do a thorough review. Do they find anything additional that you would like to change?

8. **Give and receive feedback to improve LinkedIn profiles.**

   Connect with two classmates to share LinkedIn profiles. Use the criteria in Figure 25 to provide feedback to each other.

9. **Participate in LinkedIn groups.**

   Join a LinkedIn professional group that interests you. Spend a couple of weeks observing the online discussions, and then post a question and see what, if any, responses you get. Share your posts and the responses with a classmate for feedback about what you did well and how you can improve your connections.

10. **Consider developing new content.**

    Imagine that you have some extra time and want to develop new content online. What most interests you that could also attract attention? Brainstorm a few ideas.

    Next, find a couple of people who are writing in your area of interest. Analyze their approach, content, writing style, followers, and so on. Could you see yourself doing something similar? Describe the benefits and obstacles of developing content.

11. **Expand your network.**

    Find ways to expand your LinkedIn network. If you haven't already, consider syncing your email address book to get recommendations for connections. Spend time thinking about everyone in your life: friends, family, family friends, faculty, classmates in college and high school, and so on. Send requests through LinkedIn; keep them short but personalize them as appropriate.

Figure 25 Feedback About a LinkedIn Profile

CRITERIA	STRENGTHS	SUGGESTIONS
Name is consistent with cover letter and resume. Audio pronunciation, if included, is clear.		
Profile photo looks professional, takes up about 60% of the space, and shows the student smiling.		
Background photo distinguishes the student's profile from others and highlights something relevant to a prospective employer.		
Headline reflects well on the student—either a job title or a short description.		
Summary sounds natural, reflects well on the writer, and describes what's important to the student.		
Experience and education sections match jobs listed on the resume.		
Skills and endorsements sections are completed and ready for comments.		
Overall, profile is professional and error free.		

WRITING COVER LETTERS AND NETWORKING MESSAGES

LO4 Tailor a cover letter for a given position.

12. **Customize a cover letter.**

    Revisit the job posting for which you customized your resume in Exercise 5. Now write a cover letter for that position. How will you express interest in this specific company? Which experiences will you highlight? Exchange letters with a classmate for feedback.

13. **Change your cover letter to an email message.**

    Revise a cover letter you wrote previously (or the one you wrote for Exercise 12) to a version you'll send as an email. Imagine that the company didn't request a cover letter—just a resume. Think of your email as a brief introduction to your attached resume. What changes will you make in the salutation and formatting? How can you reduce the length of the letter? What else will you change to make it more appropriate for an email message?

14. **Revise a networking email.**

    Imagine that your friend Ron asks you to review a draft networking email before he sends it (Figure 26). His goal is to get a summer internship in the marketing department of the company. What advice would you give to your friend? If you were Ron, how would you revise the email?

Networking Email for Feedback | **Figure 26**

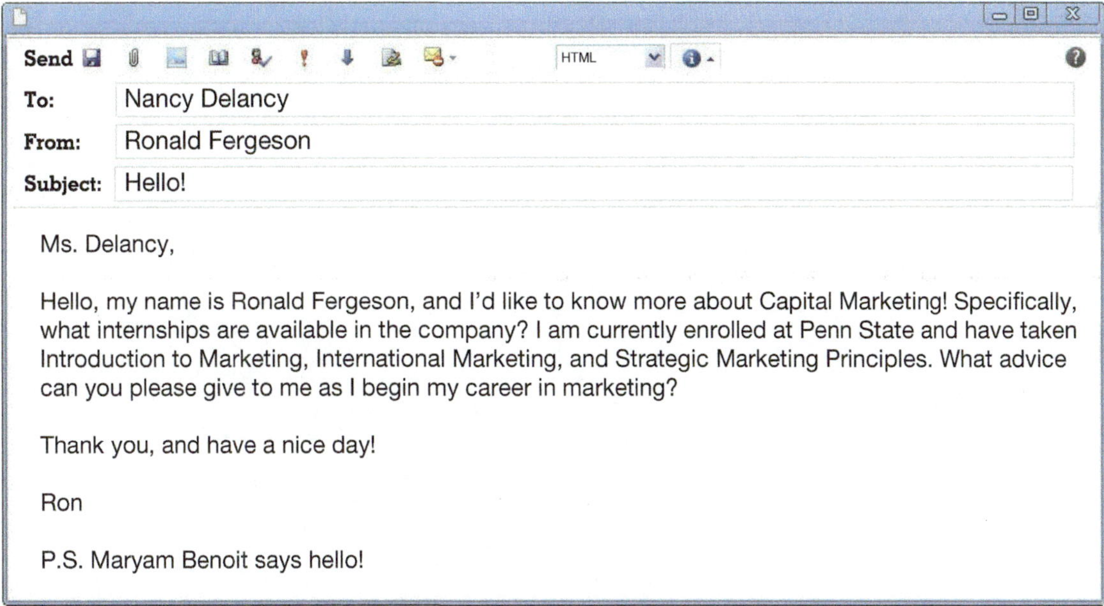

To: Nancy Delancy

From: Ronald Fergeson

Subject: Hello!

Ms. Delancy,

Hello, my name is Ronald Fergeson, and I'd like to know more about Capital Marketing! Specifically, what internships are available in the company? I am currently enrolled at Penn State and have taken Introduction to Marketing, International Marketing, and Strategic Marketing Principles. What advice can you please give to me as I begin my career in marketing?

Thank you, and have a nice day!

Ron

P.S. Maryam Benoit says hello!

15. **Expand your network by meeting new people.**

    To expand your job search, push yourself to join groups that may be uncomfortable for you. Most of us have some social anxiety when meeting people for the first time, but the more you meet new people, the easier it may be. Look for professional associations near you and register to attend a meeting. At the meeting, look for one or two friendly looking people and introduce yourself. Spend some time observing how people behave and interact with each other and decide whether this is a place where you could feel comfortable returning. If you do, try to make one or two new connections each time.

16. **Send LinkedIn networking messages.**

    Find a few businesspeople with whom you would like to network. For this exercise, you can decide—based on your own career goals—what you would like to get out of the experience.

This could be a chance to meet with someone to see what it's like to work for a company you admire, to gather more information about a field that interests you, or to find a summer internship. Just be realistic and avoid placing a burden on someone you don't know.

To find people to contact, you might search your college's alumni database, ask friends or family for recommendations, look at companies' websites, or search online for people's names and titles. Also look at your network's connections on LinkedIn. The more people you include, the more likely you will get responses.

Prepare a draft message. Then, tailor the message to each person on your list. Think about ways to connect with each person to encourage a positive response.

Send at least ten messages. After two weeks, share the results with the class. How many people responded? If some of your classmates had better responses than others, analyze their approach, message content, writing style, or field of interest to understand why. Try to incorporate what you learn into your next ten messages to see whether your results improve.

CHAPTER SUMMARY

LO1 Describe your strengths for a position that interests you.

Before you begin looking for a job, consider how you'll present yourself. Research shows advantages for people who are authentic at work, and yet, sometimes, being your genuine self carries risk. Identifying your strengths and vocation will help guide you through the selection process, improving the chance that you'll get a position that you enjoy with a company where you feel you belong and can fully contribute.

LO2 Identify questions to guide decisions about resume content.

The purpose of your resume is to get you a job interview. Take a strategic approach to decisions about what to include by focusing, for example, on what is most relevant, valuable, recent, and accurate—and on content that reflects your integrity. Strive for a concise, one-page document with a simple, readable format. Describe your education, work experience, and other qualifications to demonstrate how your past prepares you for the particular job for which you're applying. Pay attention to keywords that will increase the likelihood that an applicant tracking system selects your resume.

LO3 Assess whether a LinkedIn profile meets given criteria.

Develop a professional online presence by representing yourself and your character well. When recruiters google you, they shouldn't find any "red flags" or questionable behavior that might eliminate you from the selection pool. Instead, they should find a professional, fully completed LinkedIn profile and, perhaps, original content that you developed. Enhance your online image by connecting with others and demonstrating your interests, knowledge, and relational skills. Build your network and find ways to be helpful to others in their job search.

LO4 Tailor a cover letter for a given position.

Compose a cover letter that highlights your strongest qualifications for a particular position. Use your professional, natural writing style so the reader sees your personality. Write networking messages to people whose careers interest you. Focus on building relationships rather than getting a job, although that may come as a result.

Endnotes

1. Crystal Chan (@cryschan), LinkedIn, May 2020, www.linkedin.com/posts/cryschan_crystal-chan-pinterest-apprenticecship-resume-activity-6796226837577134081-aW9w/, accessed July 14, 2021.
2. Emily Vu (@emvutweets), "f*ck it, Spotify-themed resume for my dream PM job at @Spotify," Twitter, March 3, 2021, 4:14 PM, https://twitter.com/emvutweets/status/1367221816985407488, accessed July 14, 2021.
3. Ray Dalio, "What Ray Dalio Looks for in an Employee," Bloomberg Markets and Finance, YouTube, https://youtu.be/xiwTpBKw01Q, October 30, 2019, accessed July 14, 2021.
4. For example, see Ralph Van den Bosch and Toon W. Taris, "Authenticity at Work: Development and Validation of an Individual Authenticity Measure at Work," *Journal of Happiness Studies* 15 (2014): 1–18.
5. Daniel Bortz, "Can Blind Hiring Improve Workplace Diversity?" The Society for Human Resources Management, March 20, 2018, www.shrm.org/hr-today/news/hr-magazine/0418/pages/can-blind-hiring-improve-workplace-diversity.aspx, accessed January 22, 2021.
6. Sonia K. Kang et al., "Whitened Resumes: Race and Self-Presentation in the Labor Market," *Administrative Science Quarterly* 61 (2016): 469–502. https://doi.org/10.1177%2F0001839216639577.
7. Kang, p. 29.
8. Kang, p. 18.
9. Kang, p. 19.
10. Victor Younger, "Ownership in the Family: Representation, Identity, and Diversity," eCornell Panel Discussion, February 25, 2021, https://ecornell.cornell.edu/keynotes/overview/K022521, accessed July 19, 2021.
11. PwC, "Personal Brand Workbook," www.pwc.com/c1/en/assets/downloads/personal_brand_workbook.pdf, accessed July 19, 2021.
12. Questions adapted from Chalice Randazzo, "A Framework for Resume Decisions: Comparing Applicants' and Employers' Reasons," *Business and Professional Communication Quarterly* 83 (2020): 409–433.
13. NACE Staff, "Key Attributes Employers Want to See on Students' Resumes," National Association for Colleges and Employers, January 13, 2021, www.naceweb.org/talent-acquisition/candidate-selection/key-attributes-employers-want-to-see-on-students-resumes/, accessed July 20, 2021.
14. Nicole Lyn Pesce, "These Are the Most Outrageous Lies People Have Put on Their Resumes," MarketWatch, August 19, 2019, www.marketwatch.com/story/these-are-the-most-hilarious-lies-people-have-put-on-their-resumes-2018-08-24, accessed July 20, 2021.
15. "Nearly Half of Employers Have Caught a Lie on a Resume, CareerBuilder Survey Shows," Career Builder, July 30, 2008, www.careerbuilder.com, accessed July 20, 2021.
16. Dawn Papandrea, "The Biggest Resume Lies to Avoid," Monster, Checkster 2020 Survey, www.monster.com/career-advice/article/the-truth-about-resume-lies-hot-jobs, accessed July 20, 2021.
17. "Hiring Managers Rank Best and Worst Words to Use in a Resume in New CareerBuilder Survey," CareerBuilder, March 13, 2014, http://press.careerbuilder.com/2014-03-13-Hiring-Managers-Rank-Best-and-Worst-Words-to-Use-in-a-Resume-in-New-CareerBuilder-Survey, accessed July 20, 2021.
18. "Eye-Tracking Study," Ladders, 2018, www.theladders.com/static/images/basicSite/pdfs/TheLadders-EyeTracking-StudyC2.pdf, accessed July 20, 2021.
19. Chalice Randazzo, "A Framework for Resume Decisions: Comparing Applicants' and Employers' Reasons," *Business and Professional Communication Quarterly* 83 (2020): 409–433.
20. Peter Yang, "Settling the Debate: One- or Two-Page Resumes," ResumeGo, 2018, www.resumego.net/research/one-or-two-page-resumes, accessed July 20, 2021.
21. Carrie Morris, "Strategies to Beat the Applicant Tracking System and Land the Interview," Indeed, March 29, 2021, www.indeed.com/career-advice/finding-a-job/expert-advice-applicant-tracking-system, accessed July 21, 2021.
22. "Have a Keen Eye for Derail," Accountemps, News Release, http://accountemps.com, accessed December 30, 2014.
23. Randazzo.
24. Randazzo.
25. See Randazzo, particularly for questions about coursework.
26. "Hiring Managers Rank Best and Worst Words to Use in a Resume in New CareerBuilder Survey," CareerBuilder, March 13, 2014, http://press.careerbuilder.com/2014-03-13-Hiring-Managers-Rank-Best-and-Worst-Words-to-Use-in-a-Resume-in-New-CareerBuilder-Survey, accessed July 20, 2021.
27. Randazzo.
28. See Randazzo, particularly for questions about subjective qualities.
29. Terena Bell, "Applicant Tracking System: The Secret to Beating a Resume-filtering ATS," *CIO*, April 17, 2018, www.cio.com/article/2398753/applicant-tracking-system.html, accessed July 21, 2021.
30. Joseph B. Fuller et al., "Hidden Workers: Untapped Talent," Accenture and Harvard Business School, August 2021, www.hbs.edu/managing-the-future-of-work/Documents

/research/hiddenworkers09032021.pdf, accessed September 8, 2021.

31. Fuller et al.

32. Kerri Anne Renzulli, "75% of Resumes Are Never Read by a Human–Here's How to Make Sure Your Resume Beats the Bots," CNBC, February 28, 2019, www.cnbc.com/2019/02/28/resume-how-yours-can-beat-the-applicant-tracking-system.html, accessed July 21, 2021.

33. "Eye-Tracking Study," Ladders, 2018, www.theladders.com/static/images/basicSite/pdfs/TheLadders-EyeTracking-StudyC2.pdf, p. 4, accessed July 20, 2021.

34. Wendy Enelow, "Leveraging Keywords to Advance Your Career," SHRM, www.shrm.org/resourcesandtools/hr-topics/organizational-and-employee-development/pages/leveraging-keywords-to-advance-your-career.aspx, accessed July 21, 2021.

35. "More Than Half of Employers Have Found Content on Social Media That Caused Them NOT to Hire a Candidate, According to Recent CareerBuilder Survey," Harris Poll sponsored by CareerBuilder, August 9, 2018, http://press.careerbuilder.com/2018-08-09-More-Than-Half-of-Employers-Have-Found-Content-on-Social-Media-That-Caused-Them-NOT-to-Hire-a-Candidate-According-to-Recent-CareerBuilder-Survey, accessed July 21, 2021.

36. Kelsey McKeon, "5 Personal Branding Tips for Your Job Search," The Manifest, April 28, 2020, https://themanifest.com/digital-marketing/5-personal-branding-tips-job-search, accessed July 21, 2021.

37. CareerBuilder/Harris Poll.

38. CareerBuilder/Harris Poll.

39. CareerBuilder/Harris Poll

40. Michael Tews, Kathyrn Stafford, and Ethan Kudler, "The Effects of Negative Content in Social Networking Profiles on Perceptions of Employment Suitability," *International Journal of Selection and Assessment* 28 (2019): 17–30, doi: 10.1111/ijsa.12277.

41. "2020 Recruiter Nation Survey," Jobvite, www.jobvite.com/lp/2020-recruiter-nation-survey, accessed July 22, 2021.

42. Susan P. Joyce, "Smart Job Search Strategy: Defensive Googling," Huffington Post, February 18, 2014, www.huffingtonpost.com/susan-p-joyce/smart-job-search-strategy_b_4777881.html, accessed July 22, 2021.

43. "2020 Recruiter National Survey."

44. Advice adapted from Jane Fleming, "20 Steps to a Better LinkedIn Profile in 2020," LinkedIn, February 20, 2020, https://business.linkedin.com/en-uk/marketing-solutions/blog/posts/content-marketing/2017/17-steps-to-a-better-LinkedIn-profile-in-2017, accessed July 22, 2021; and Grace Zhang, "LinkedIn: Purposes and Uses of the Platform. Writing and Editing Strategies," PowerPoint for AEM 3000, Management Communication, Cornell Dyson School of Applied Economics and Management, Fall 2020.

45. John Jersin, "Announcing Skill Assessments to Help You Showcase Your Skills," LinkedIn, September 17, 2019, https://blog.linkedin.com/2019/september/17/announcing-skill-assessments-to-help-you-showcase-your-skills, accessed July 22, 2021.

46. For tips, read Alison Doyle, "Tips for Creating a Video Resume (and When You Need One)," The Balance Careers, January 25, 2020, www.thebalancecareers.com/tips-for-creating-a-video-resume-2064219, accessed July 22, 2021.

47. "2020 Recruiter National Survey."

48. Julia Freeland Fisher, "How to Get a Job Often Comes Down to One Elite Personal Asset, and Many People Still Don't Realize It," CNBC, December 27, 2019, www.cnbc.com/2019/12/27/how-to-get-a-job-often-comes-down-to-one-elite-personal-asset.html, accessed July 22, 2021.

49. Indeed Editorial Team, "How to Follow Up on a Job Application," Indeed, June 23, 2021, www.indeed.com/career-advice/finding-a-job/follow-up-on-job-application, accessed July 24, 2021.

50. Anandashankar Mazumdar, "Spotify to Pay $113M to Settle Copyright Class Action," Bloomberg Law, May 24, 2018, https://news.bloomberglaw.com/business-and-practice/spotify-to-pay-113m-to-settle-copyright-class-action, accessed September 10, 2021.

CHAPTER

14 Interviewing and Landing the Job

Learning Objectives

After you have finished this chapter, you should be able to

LO1 Provide a response to a behavioral interview question in the "STAR" format.

LO2 Describe ways to make a good first impression during a job interview.

LO3 Write a thank-you email for a given job offer.

LO4 Write an email to decline a job offer.

LO5 List behaviors that describe professionalism.

"*I don't get how some of the people there are considered Googley as this guy hadn't had a bit of Googleyness in him.*"[1]

—Anonymous interview candidate, Glassdoor

Chapter Introduction

Prepare for an Interview with Company Research

If Google invites you for an interview, you'll find good information online. The company's career page shows an overview of the entire hiring process.[2]

For more detail, Glassdoor can be a wealth of information. One applicant posted questions asked during an interview for a product manager position, including, "Design a search engine for a cat gif library" and "How do you see the future of ridesharing evolving? If you had to create a 10-year strategy for Uber, what would that look like?"[3]

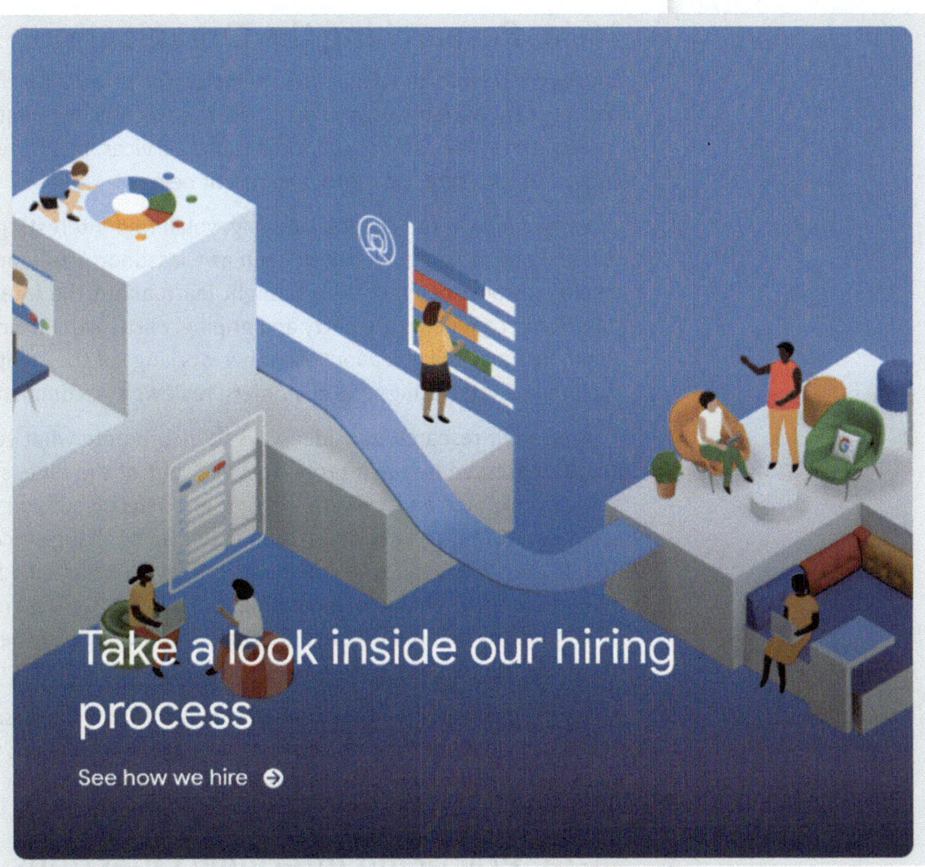

Google illustrates its selection process.

Candor, a company that helps employees manage pay equity, describes more details about selection at Google. For example, according to insiders, "A typical onsite interview consists of 4–5 interviews at 45 minutes each. Some are 1:1; others are a panel."[4]

Interviews vary depending on the industry, company, position, location—and individual interviewer. Still, online research could give you an advantage when competition is fierce, and working for Google certainly is competitive: the acceptance rate is about 0.2%.[5]

LO1 Provide a response to a behavioral interview question in the "STAR" format.

14-1 Preparing for a Job Interview

Any reputable employer will require at least one employment interview before extending a job offer, even for summer internships. Employers use interviews to verify information on the resume, learn more about your experience, and get to know you personally.

As you read throughout this book, employers will assess your character. Your skills and experience are important, but a hiring manager also wants to know what it will be like to manage you and how you will interact with others.

In this section, you learn how to prepare for a job interview by researching the organization, practicing interview questions, and preparing your own questions.

14-1a Researching the Organization

Employers want to know that you are motivated to work for the company. Learn everything you possibly can about the organization. Use the research techniques you developed from Chapter 9 to learn about the company's products and services, history, vision and values, financial health, corporate structure, locations, and recent news.

As you read in the chapter opening, you'll find interesting information about the company online. Look at career websites, such as Glassdoor, Vault, and Indeed, where candidates and employees post comments. You might learn about the interview process and company culture. Some comments are petty and griping, particularly from former employees, but repeated comments may tell you about the inner workings of the company and management style. Also explore analysts' ratings and customers' reviews and comments.

After your research, consider ways to incorporate what you learned into the interview. No one is impressed by the interviewee who, out of the blue, spouts, "I see your stock went up $5 last week," and an interviewer might get defensive if you raise a former employee's snarky comments. But if an interviewer admits to a lot of change recently, you can say something like, "Yes, I saw some employee comments online about layoffs. I read that the new structure will allow more focus on digital marketing" or "It looks like the entire industry took a hit this year." By connecting comments to your broader knowledge of the industry, you can discuss issues affecting the company more intelligently.

Bring up information that flows naturally into the conversation. If you don't get a chance to talk about what you learned, at least you'll know a lot about the company, which will help you make an informed decision about whether to accept a job.

14-1b Practicing Interview Questions

Employers take different approaches to interviewing candidates. Many use a structured interview, which typically means they ask set questions and have a set way of scoring responses. During these interviews, recruiters or hiring managers have less discretion in what they ask and how they interpret the answers.[6] But during even the most structured interview, you can tell your story—what makes you the best candidate for the position.[7]

Next, we review how to prepare for different types of interviews: standard, behavioral, case, and stress interviews, which, thankfully, are increasingly rare. You may experience a combination of these during the selection process or within one interview.

Standard Interviews

Some interviews are fairly straightforward. The interviewer may review your resume with you, asking questions about your interests (e.g., "Why did you apply for this job?") and experience (e.g., "What did you like about working for Walgreens?"). With standard and all interview questions, the employer is interested not only in the content of your responses but also in how you react to the questions themselves and how you communicate your thoughts and ideas. Before an interview, practice answering each of the questions in Figure 1.

Standard Interview Questions | **Figure 1**

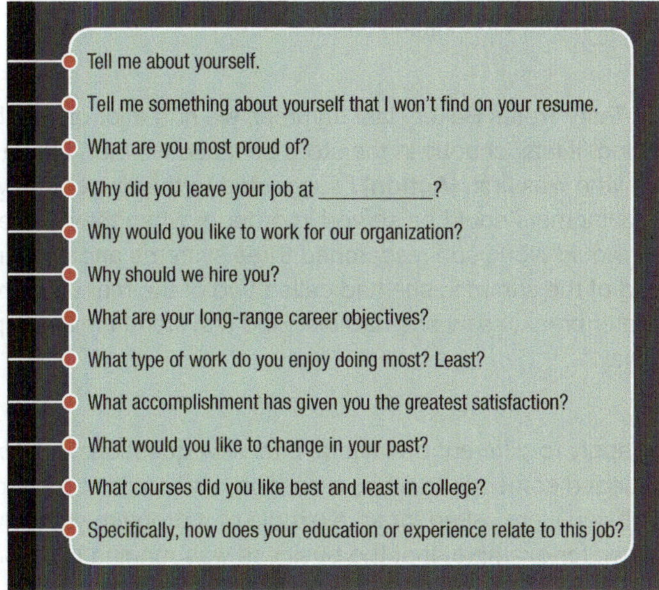
Tell me about yourself.
Tell me something about yourself that I won't find on your resume.
What are you most proud of?
Why did you leave your job at __________?
Why would you like to work for our organization?
Why should we hire you?
What are your long-range career objectives?
What type of work do you enjoy doing most? Least?
What accomplishment has given you the greatest satisfaction?
What would you like to change in your past?
What courses did you like best and least in college?
Specifically, how does your education or experience relate to this job?

Behavioral Interviews

Behavioral interviews are based on the theory that past behavior predicts future performance. Common for entry-level hires, these interviews include structured questions related to competencies identified for a job.[8] When interviewers ask these questions, they are looking for a specific example that demonstrates your ability to fulfill key job requirements—they want to hear a story. The best response follows the "STAR" format:

- **S**ituation or **T**ask: What brief context is important for the interviewer to understand?
- **A**ction: How did you handle the situation? What did you do?
- **R**esult: How did the situation turn out? How can you prove that your action was appropriate in the situation?

Two typical job competencies, behavioral interview questions, and sample responses are shown in Figure 2. Additional questions and associated competencies are shown in Figure 3.

You can prepare for a behavioral interview by doing the following:

- **Determine possible competencies for the job.** Look at the job description for a list of requirements. Some of the keywords you identified earlier also will be competencies.
- **Identify possible questions.** See Figure 3 for sample questions and write your own that would elicit information about each competency.
- **Plan between 10 and 15 examples.** Think about your work, academic, and extracurricular experience. What specific examples could you provide that might fit behavioral interview questions?
- **Write out your answers.** For each story, write the "STAR," typically with most emphasis on the "A" or action—what you did. Each story should be between 1 and 3 minutes.
- **Practice your responses.** Rehearse your examples and record yourself to see how you come across. Try not to memorize every word; your natural, conversational style will be best for making a connection.

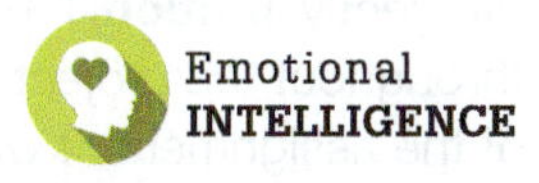

How do you know when you're overtalking during an interview? What signs might an interviewer give you?

Figure 2 | Sample Behavioral Interview Questions and Responses

COMPETENCY AREA: INITIATIVE

Sample Behavioral Interview Question:

"Tell me about a time when you saw a problem and took initiative to solve it."

Sample Response:

"**[Situation]** Sure, when I was working for Tasty Treats Bakery last summer, we had a lot of very busy times when 15 to 20 customers were waiting. It was chaotic in the store because we didn't have enough space for a line, and people argued about who was first. [**Action**] I suggested to the owner that we implement a 'Take-a-Number' system so customers could be served in order of when they arrive. She was concerned about the cost and how it would work, so I researched three systems and explained the process in more detail. [**Result**] By the end of the summer, she had called two of the manufacturers in for quotes. When I visited the bakery over winter break, I saw she had installed a system! I felt very proud that I could contribute to the business in this way."

Notes:

With some variations, this situation could apply to different behavioral interview questions. For example, if you were asked for a time when you persuaded someone to make a change, you could focus more on the steps you took to convince the owner. Or if you were asked for an example of a problem you solved, you could focus more on the result for the owner, for example, that the business was running more smoothly and fewer customers left without ordering.

COMPETENCY AREA: TEAMWORK

Sample Behavioral Interview Question:

"Tell me about a time you worked as part of a team that didn't function too well. What did you do about it?" (Note that behavioral questions may ask for negative examples. In these situations, you should be honest and focus on what you learned from the experience.)

Sample Response:

"[**Situation**] For my marketing class in school, I worked with three other students to create a marketing plan. We started off well by assigning responsibilities and deadlines, but one student didn't submit her work on time. This was a problem for all of us because she was supposed to do the initial research, and this held up the rest of our work. [**Action**] I jumped in and did her work because I was worried about the project and wanted to move it along. [**Result**] We finished the marketing plan on time and got a B+, but looking back, I'm not sure this was the best solution—everyone should participate equally, and this student got the same grade as the rest of us but didn't pull her weight. We didn't think this was fair."

Notes:

At this point during the interview, you may present another example to demonstrate what you learned from the experience and how you improved your teamwork skills. You may ask the interviewer for permission to give another example, and then describe the situation:

"[**Situation**] I had a similar situation for a finance project just last semester, but this time I did two things differently. [**Action**] First, I set up a Slack channel for the team so we could track everyone's progress throughout the project. This made accountability easier because when someone didn't complete a part of the assignment, it was public, and this put more pressure on each team member. Second, when one person didn't do his part on time, instead of jumping in, I took the initiative to talk to the student to see what was going on. He was having trouble finding data we needed, so I helped him but didn't complete the work for him. [**Result**] He was a couple of days late, but I'm glad he contributed his assigned part to the project. The team received an A, and I think it's partly because everyone contributed fairly equally."

Sample Competencies and Behavioral Interview Questions | **Figure 3**

Business Communication: Tell me about a time when you delivered a presentation. | Describe a report you wrote for a business audience. | Can you tell me about a time when you worked with people who are different from you? What communication challenges did you face, and how did you resolve them?

Relationship Building: Describe the best working relationship you've had. What did you do to make it successful? | Tell me about a time when you had to work with someone you didn't like. | Describe a time when it was particularly difficult for you to gain credibility with someone. What did you do?

Problem Solving: Tell me about a time when you were assigned work that you didn't know how to do or had difficulty completing on your own. How did you handle it? | Please give me an example of when you had to solve a particularly challenging problem.

Teamwork: Tell me about a time when you had to step in to help a group or team complete a task/project/assignment. What did you do? | Give an example of a conflict with a coworker. How did you handle it? | Think of a time when you had a major role in developing a team that became very successful. Tell me one or two things you did that contributed to the team's success.

Time Management or Planning and Organizing: Tell me about a time when you faced a strict deadline and how you handled it. | We all miss deadlines sometimes. Can you think of when this happened to you? How did it happen, and what was the result? | Tell me about a time when you had too many things to do, and you had to prioritize your tasks.

Work Ethic: Tell me about a time when you had to cut corners in order to finish a project or meet a manager's expectations. | Describe a task you truly disliked and how you handled it. | Tell me about a time when you had to go above and beyond in order to get a job done.

Ethics: Please give me an example of when you felt that your personal ethics didn't align with a company's. | Tell me about a time when your manager or client asked you to do something that you didn't think was appropriate. How did you respond? | Can you think of a time when your ethics and those of a coworker or teammate caused a conflict between you? What happened?

Decision Making: Give me an example of a time when you had to make a split-second decision. | Tell me about a policy you didn't agree with but had to comply with anyway. What did you do? | Tell me about a difficult decision you've made in the last year.

Persuasion or Influence: Tell me about a time when you convinced someone to see your point of view. | Can you give me an example of how you successfully persuaded another person even when that person didn't personally like you (or vice versa)? | Please describe how you persuaded someone to implement an idea you proposed.

Customer Service: Tell me about a recent situation in which you had to deal with a very upset customer or coworker. | I'd like to hear an example of when you exceeded a customer's expectations. | Tell me about a time when you had to bend a policy to accommodate a customer. What happened?

Case Interviews

Some companies—particularly management consulting firms—use case interviews that present you with a problem to be solved. These companies are testing your analytical skills, creativity, problem-solving skills, ability to think on your feet, logic and reasoning, quantitative skills, and of course, communication skills. For these types of interviews, your approach to solving the problem is as important as the solution you offer.

Case questions may be quite complex and typically last between 20 and 40 minutes. Questions may be short, such as, "How many pieces of luggage go through JFK airport on an average day?" or long, such as, "One of our clients, a retailer in the jewelry and luxury watch market, has experienced declining profits in the past 12 months. How would you go about assessing this problem?"

The major consulting firms have tips and sample cases on their websites. Bain's site includes a mock interview, so you can experience the process.[9] McKinsey posts sample "problem-solving cases" with "helpful hints" throughout. The example shown in Figure 4 is for an Eastern European client wanting to improve its educational system.[10]

Figure 4 | "Helpful Hints" on a McKinsey Practice Case

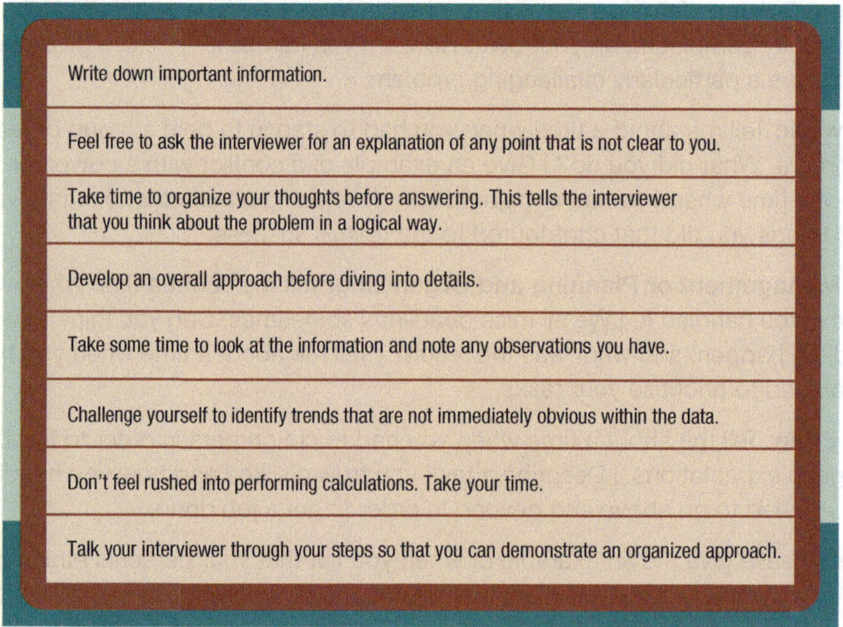

Write down important information.
Feel free to ask the interviewer for an explanation of any point that is not clear to you.
Take time to organize your thoughts before answering. This tells the interviewer that you think about the problem in a logical way.
Develop an overall approach before diving into details.
Take some time to look at the information and note any observations you have.
Challenge yourself to identify trends that are not immediately obvious within the data.
Don't feel rushed into performing calculations. Take your time.
Talk your interviewer through your steps so that you can demonstrate an organized approach.

The theme of McKinsey's hints is clear: take your time. A well-reasoned, thoughtful approach demonstrates your depth and analytical skills. Practice as many cases as you can so you feel comfortable with this type of interview.

Stress Interviews

Some companies simulate a stressful environment to see how well you work under pressure. In these situations, your interviewer may ask you pointed or inappropriate questions, interrupt you, or be sarcastic and just generally rude.

Try to maintain your composure if this happens. Keep telling yourself that you're qualified for the job and can handle the interview. You're under no obligation to answer inappropriate questions, and you have every right to defend your performance and experience. If an interviewer says, "You really don't have the background to work here," be clear and confident: "Yes, I do. I have strong analytical skills from my experience at . . ."

Of course, you may decide that a company that chooses to use stress interviews isn't the place for you. If you are offered the job, you don't have to take it.

14-1c Preparing Your Own Questions

During an interview, you're evaluating the organization as much as the interviewer is evaluating you. Is this the right place for *you*? You'll learn about the company from the questions interviewers ask, how they react to you and your responses, and how they answer your questions.

Asking questions such as those in Figure 5 shows the recruiter that you're engaged in the interview and interested in the job and company.

Possible Questions to Ask During an Interview | **Figure 5**

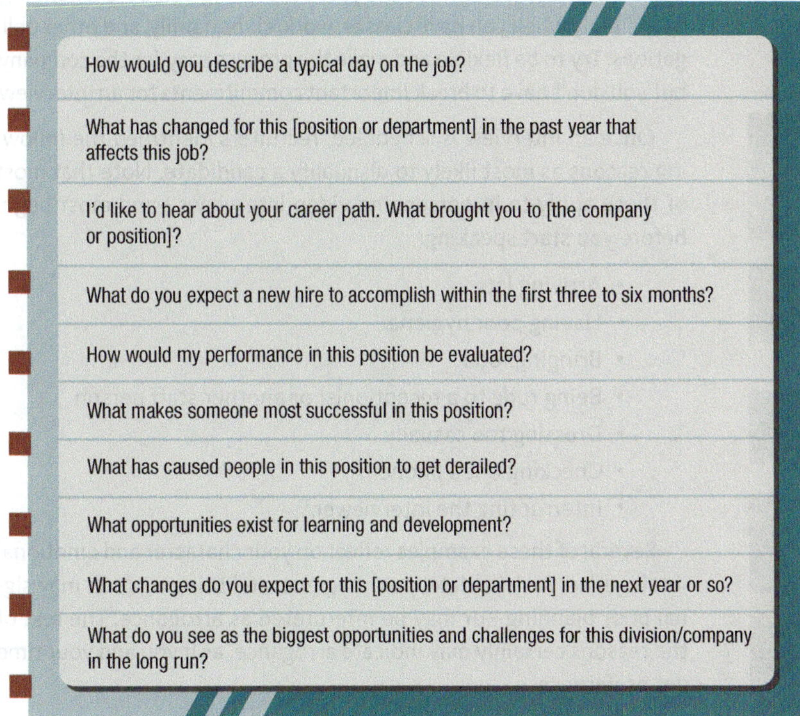
How would you describe a typical day on the job?

What has changed for this [position or department] in the past year that affects this job?

I'd like to hear about your career path. What brought you to [the company or position]?

What do you expect a new hire to accomplish within the first three to six months?

How would my performance in this position be evaluated?

What makes someone most successful in this position?

What has caused people in this position to get derailed?

What opportunities exist for learning and development?

What changes do you expect for this [position or department] in the next year or so?

What do you see as the biggest opportunities and challenges for this division/company in the long run?

In addition to these questions, you can ask about what's important to you. In a recent survey, recruiters said, compared to the previous year, more candidates asked about mental-health benefits, accommodations for working parents, and diversity and inclusion initiatives.[11] Instead of asking about diversity initiatives, which could yield a pat response, consider more personal questions. Ask about your interviewer's and prospective coworkers' own experience, for example, "In what ways do you, as a person, feel valued by the organization?" You could ask a follow-up question for a specific example, and you might ask for a time when they didn't feel valued. For these types of questions, consider waiting until the second interview, when you evaluate the company more seriously.

Some of the best interviews are more like conversations. In these situations, you may ask questions throughout. If this happens, just relax and focus on talking with the interviewer as someone you respect and from whom you want to learn.

Finally, know when the interview is over. If the interviewer seems to be wrapping up, you may have to end your questions. You may ask about next steps in the selection process, including the time frame for decisions.

14-2 Presenting Yourself During an Interview

LO2 Describe ways to make a good first impression during an interview.

Making a good first impression during an interview is critical. Research shows that people form judgments about charisma, status, leadership potential, and trustworthiness within seconds.[12]

The interview is your time to persuade the employer that you're the best person for the job and will be a good employee and coworker. In this section, we discuss ways to make a good impression, demonstrate confidence in your qualifications, manage phone or video interviews, and respond to multiple interviewers.

14-2a Making a Good Impression

Long before an interview, you're making a first impression. When setting up interviews, respond quickly and be sure to express your appreciation and enthusiasm for the job. Scheduling can be challenging, particularly when you have classes, work, clubs, family, and other obligations. Try to be flexible and make the process easy for the company, but you don't have to break important commitments for an interview.

Djomas/Shutterstock.com

How would you sequence these photos from most to least casual? For what industries might each be appropriate?

Once an interview is scheduled, recruiters identified the following reasons as most likely to disqualify a candidate. Note that most of these apply to in-person and video interviews—and most begin before you start speaking:

- Arriving late
- Having poor hygiene
- Bringing food
- Being rude to a receptionist or another staff person
- Dressing too casually
- Checking one's phone
- Interrupting the interviewer.[13]

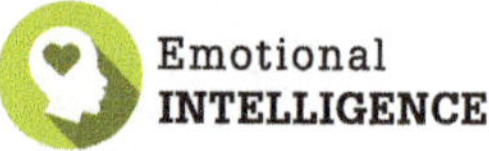

When have you come across as arrogant, without intending to? What was the situation and your role in the judgment?

Do you have some social anxiety, or do you get nervous when meeting new people? Try to approach an interview as a meeting with someone interesting. Your goals are simply to let the person know you and for you to know that person and the company a little better.

Several of these examples reflect on your character and emotional intelligence. Arriving late, poor hygiene, and bringing food may signal poor planning—or may be interpreted as arrogance. The rest of the reasons certainly may indicate arrogance, as if you and your time get preference.

During an interview, try to be your natural, likeable self. Imagine that you're talking with a trusted friend of the family and use your conversational speaking style. One recruiter put it well when she said, "After a day of back-to-back interviews, I may not remember what everyone said, but I'll remember how I felt about each of them."[14] People want to work with people they like.

If you have social anxiety, revisit the tool "How to Feel Confident for a Presentation and Manage Speech Anxiety" (*http://speaking.amynewman.com*). The strategies for an interview are similar to those for a presentation. You might find that reframing your anxiety as excitement, focusing on the interviewer instead of on yourself, distracting yourself before an interview, and other strategies help you feel more confident.

For video or in-person interviews, dress appropriately. Deciding what to wear can be tricky: every industry and company is different. Dress more formally than what people typically wear at work. Choose clean lines and neutral colors. Business attire typically means suits (matching jackets and pants or a skirt) and ties for men. In general, when recruiters ask you to wear "business casual," you can skip the full suit. On the more formal end of business casual, consider a blazer (tie optional), button-down shirt, and dress pants, or a jacket and skirt with a button-down or jewel-neck shell shirt. Less formal business casual can mean a button-down shirt with chinos or khakis, or a sweater or blouse with dress pants or a skirt.

For in-person interviews, greet the interviewer by name with direct eye contact and a smile. Extend a firm handshake if the interviewer extends a hand first. If you're not asked to sit immediately, wait until the interviewer is seated and then take your seat. Lean forward a bit in your seat and maintain comfortable eye contact with the interviewer. Avoid taking notes, except perhaps for a specific name or date.

Throughout the interview, try to attune to the interviewer to build rapport. At the same time, recognize that some interviewers aren't great at making an emotional connection. In fact, some people believe that they shouldn't express any emotion—even if they think you would be a good candidate—so they don't give a false impression of a callback or job offer before the final decision is made. This attitude can leave you feeling as though the interview didn't go well, and you may be surprised to hear back from the company. Sometimes it's simply hard to judge, so just do your best regardless and try not to get discouraged during the interview time.

djile/Shutterstock.com

Follow your interviewer's lead about whether to shake hands.

14-2b Demonstrating Confidence in Your Qualifications

To get hired for any position, you must demonstrate that you meet the job qualifications. If you're invited for an interview, the employer believes you have the minimal qualifications, which you explained on your resume. During the interview, you provide more detail and evidence to support your claims.

Study the job description to remind yourself what the company needs. With enough practice—during mock interviews on campus or with a friend—you should be well prepared for even the toughest questions.

Listen carefully to each question rather than focusing on what you'll say next. What is the interviewer seeking? Work backward from your behavioral interview practice to connect each question with a probable job competency or qualification. As you see in Figure 6, you can tell your stories, whether it's a behavioral question or not, to prove that you have what it takes to do the job.

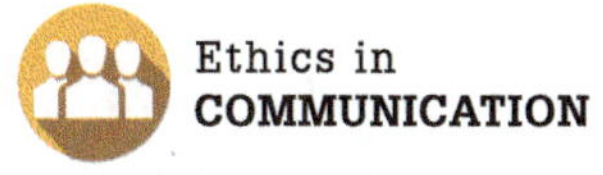

Presenting yourself as confident but not overconfident is a delicate balance. Avoid an attitude that suggests, "You're lucky to have me here." The interviewer might not agree. Don't try to oversell yourself, or you may end up in a job for which you're unprepared.

On the other hand, you don't have to fawn or grovel either. You're *applying*—not begging—for a job. Show how you're qualified with clear stories and evidence. If the interviewer doesn't address one of your skills, try to work it into the discussion. At the end of an interview, many recruiters will ask you, "Is there anything else we didn't cover that you'd like to tell me?" That's your chance to talk about the business fraternity you joined or the speaker series you started.

14-2c Managing Video and Phone Interviews

Video and phone interviews are increasingly common. Although 77% of recruiters in one survey said that in-person interviews are most effective, 40% said that video calls will be the default in the future.[15]

In a recent survey, recruiters cited connectivity issues, inappropriate dress, and weak eye contact as the "biggest video interview mistakes" candidates made.[16] Be sure that you have a reliable internet connection; consider hardwiring your computer to an ethernet cable so you don't have WiFi issues. Dress as you would for an in-person interview and look at eye level directly at the camera—not at the screen. This strategy is particularly useful when you have multiple interviewers because you will appear to be looking at everyone individually.[17]

All other suggestions you learned earlier for video meetings and presentations apply. Follow the tips in Figure 7 for a successful video interview.

Figure 6 | Mapping Your Qualifications to Interview Questions and Comments

QUESTION/ COMMENT	QUALIFICATION	EXAMPLE	HIGHLIGHTS OF MY STORY
"Tell me about a time when you had a conflict with someone."	Probably trying to assess strong interpersonal skills, which is listed first on the job description	My coworker at Zappos	I'll be specific about her behavior (raising her voice, ending Zoom abruptly) but will focus more on my action—what I did to resolve the situation (asked to speak with her separately about our working relationship, described how her behavior affected me, and avoided saying that the rest of the team had complained about her). Finally, I'll explain how her behavior changed and how she thanked me at the end of the summer.
"I see you left Carmichael's after only two weeks . . ."	Probably worried about my commitment and whether I'll stay the whole summer	When my mother called me	I'll be honest and describe my family situation. My father was ill, and I wanted to be home in Minneapolis. The internship was in New York, which was too far to drive if I needed to be there quickly. My mother didn't ask, but she clearly needed help managing my little brother and two sisters. I made the very difficult decision to leave the internship and discussed the situation with my manager. He was really understanding. I thought about doing some work remotely, but with my father in the hospital and my mother working full time, I had my hands full with the kids. I'll say that this was the only time I didn't fulfill a commitment and felt really bad about it. I'll also point out that my manager asked me to come back the next summer, but I decided to stay closer to home.
"What is your favorite type of work?"	Probably looking for logical thinking or detail orientation because this is a data analytics job	I don't have any direct work experience, so I'll focus on the experience I do have: the project I did for my Data Science class.	I learned so much in my Data Science class last semester. I thought I would like it, but I had no idea how much. During the semester, I worked on a project to predict employee attrition at a client company. It was fascinating! What I liked most was looking at a ton of data that the HR department had for 10 years and figuring out a way for it to be useful. I developed a few algorithms to help the company so they could do a better job of talent planning, and I got great feedback from my professor and from the head of HR.

Tips for a Successful Video Interview | **Figure 7**

Before the Interview

- Get comfortable with the technology: practice with someone ahead of time.
- Arrange for a quiet, uninterrupted place.
- Practice responding to interview questions if you receive them in advance.
- Check the time zone difference.
- Check your lighting and framing so your image looks clear and balanced.
- Make sure that your background looks professional—not like a messy room.
- Dress as you would for an in-person interview, but avoid loud plaid or striped clothing, which can look distorted on video.
- Close other programs on your computer to avoid alerts and other sounds.

During the Interview

- Log on a couple of minutes before the call starts.
- Check your posture and positioning—not too far or too close.
- Maintain eye contact and avoid looking left and right.
- Speak and act naturally, even for virtual interviews.
- Keep the window of your image open during the interview so you can check yourself occasionally.

One-way, or virtual, video interviews are becoming more popular. You log onto a system, such as HireVue, and answer automated questions. Be sure to use a compatible device and to answer the practice questions so you're prepared for the experience. As for any video interview, dress as you would for an in-person interview and check your eye contact by taking screen shots ahead of time. You might have an option to re-record an answer, which will help you perfect the final product.[18]

Instead of a video interview, companies may request a phone interview, particularly for initial screening. Typically, these interviews are shorter than in-person interviews and include general or behavioral questions. Avoid distractions and background noise just as you would for a video interview. You might find it helpful to stand during the interview, which may improve your voice quality and help you feel more confident. But don't walk around or move papers too much because the interviewer may hear the noise. Also use a good-quality headset or just keep the phone at your ear rather than use a speaker phone.

The real challenge of phone interviews is not having nonverbal cues from your interviewer, such as nodding and smiling—or trying to jump in. You might keep your answers shorter to allow the interviewer to interrupt; otherwise, you could be way off track and not know it.

14-2d Responding to Multiple Interviewers

If you're called back for a second (or third) round after a screening or initial interview, you will meet multiple people—either one after the other or at the same time. These interviews tend to be longer and more intense than a screening interview.

If you have separate interviews with different people, be sure to give consistent answers because the interviewers will talk to each other about you. They might even, intentionally, ask you the same or a similar question to check for consistent responses. If they ask a similar behavioral question, give a different story to demonstrate more experience with the competency.

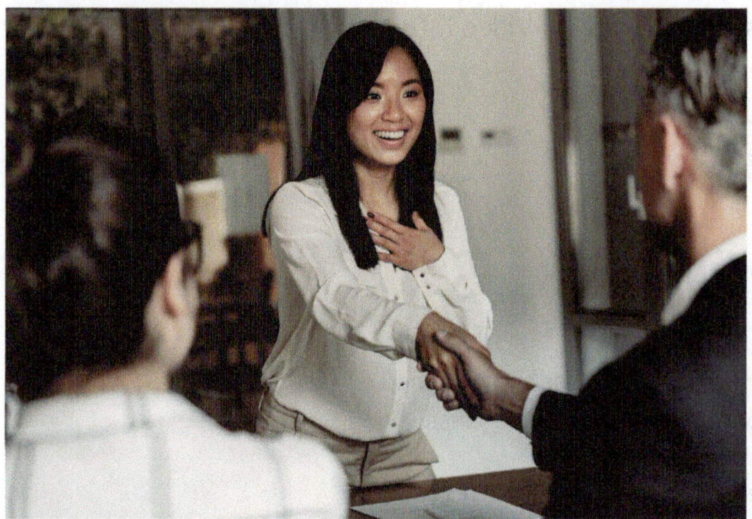

Dean Drobot/Shutterstock.com

Although panel interviews can be stressful, try to be natural and show your personality and enthusiasm.

You also might participate in a panel interview, with several people asking you questions at the same time. If possible, find out about this practice ahead of time so you can prepare yourself mentally. Address your responses to everyone, not just to the person who asked the question or to the most senior person present.

Some companies, particularly investment banks, will have "superdays," when they invite several candidates back at one time. At this point in the process, everyone has the baseline technical skills to do the job, so recruiters and hiring managers will assess your personality, character, and communication. Network as much as possible before and during the day to get to know people and to have them know you. If you're asked to deliver a presentation or participate in a team problem-solving activity, demonstrate your strong delivery and interpersonal communication skills. You'll need to distinguish yourself as a leader yet show your humility—your willingness to learn and to bring others along.

CHARACTER

Day-long interviews can be draining. You might feel as though you're "on" the entire time, and this may be the case, with multiple people watching you to decide whether you're the best candidate and whether they want to work with you. Try to get a good night's sleep, eat well, and exercise beforehand, so you can relax, be yourself, and enjoy the process as much as possible. You will learn a lot about the company—and possibly about yourself.

After your interviews, follow up with everyone you met—not just your main contact. Next, we discuss thank-you notes and other actions you can take while waiting for an offer.

LO3 Write a thank-you email for a given job offer.

14-3 Following Up After the Interview

Every interview is a learning experience—some will go well and some won't. You'll get some job offers but not others, and you'll want to work for some companies but not others. Regardless, spend time after an interview to evaluate the experience and send thank-you notes. In this section, we also discuss ways to handle disappointing responses.

14-3a Assessing Yourself and the Company

Emotional INTELLIGENCE

How do you regulate your emotions after an interview? The process can be stressful; allowing yourself time to reflect and recognize what's within your control—whether you receive an offer or not—can help you relax.

After an interview, assess your experience so you can improve for future interviews and gauge your interest in the company. Asking the questions in Figure 8—about yourself and the company—puts you back in control and helps you develop your interview skills.

Reflecting on your experience, you may decide that the position isn't right for you. Either way, you'll want to send a thank-you note.

14-3b Sending a Thank-You Note

A thank-you note after an interview can distinguish you—and it's the right thing to do to express your gratitude for the interviewer's time. In one survey of HR managers, 80% reported finding thank-you notes helpful to the hiring decision, yet only 24% received them.[19]

Questions to Ask Yourself After an Interview | **Figure 8**

ASSESS YOURSELF	ASSESS THE COMPANY
How well did you present yourself? Did you dress appropriately? If this was a video or phone interview, did you manage the technology well?	How do you feel about the company? Did you feel respected and valued during the selection process? Is this a place you could see yourself working?
What qualifications did the interviewer emphasize for this job? How can you change your cover letter, resume, and social profiles to address qualifications more directly in the future?	How was your relationship with the interviewer and people on the team? Did you connect with them? Did you feel comfortable and able to be yourself?
Which interview questions did you answer most easily? Which descriptions or stories were best?	What are the job responsibilities? Could you see yourself doing this job for the next two to three years?
Which questions did you have trouble answering? How can you address these differently in the future?	How does this company compare to others you're considering? What are the advantages and disadvantages?
What questions were you asked about your resume? What should you clarify or delete as a result?	Do you think you'll get a job offer? Do you feel excited, indifferent, anxious, or something else at the prospect?

After each interview, send a thank-you email within 24 hours. Wait at least a few hours, or your email might look canned—too quick and not thoughtful. If you made a personal connection with the interviewer, you may send a handwritten note—86% of HR managers find this method appropriate[20]—but this shouldn't replace your email. Decisions may be made quickly, and you want the chance to influence them.

Send a customized thank-you email for each interview. Express genuine appreciation for the interview, reiterate your interest in the job, and reinforce your qualifications. Consider a short, catchy subject line:

- Thank you, (interviewer's name)
- Thank you from (your name)
- Thank you for meeting with me
- Thank you for the interview
- Great to meet you today

The sample email shown in Figure 9 mentions the response time the recruiter promised. You may include this, subtly, to encourage a response, which we discuss next.

14-3c Handling Disappointing Responses

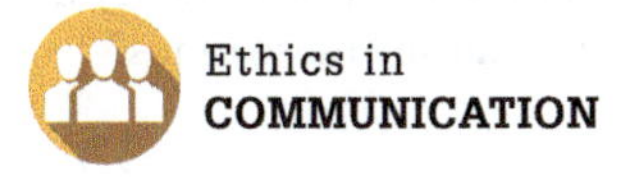

You may have had this experience: you had a great interview, the company and job seem perfect—and then nothing. You don't hear back within the two weeks the recruiter promised.

This "ghosting" is quite common. Try not to take the lack of response personally; in one survey, 77% of candidates reported having experienced ghosting. People are busy and, sadly, some

Figure 9 | Sample Thank-You Email

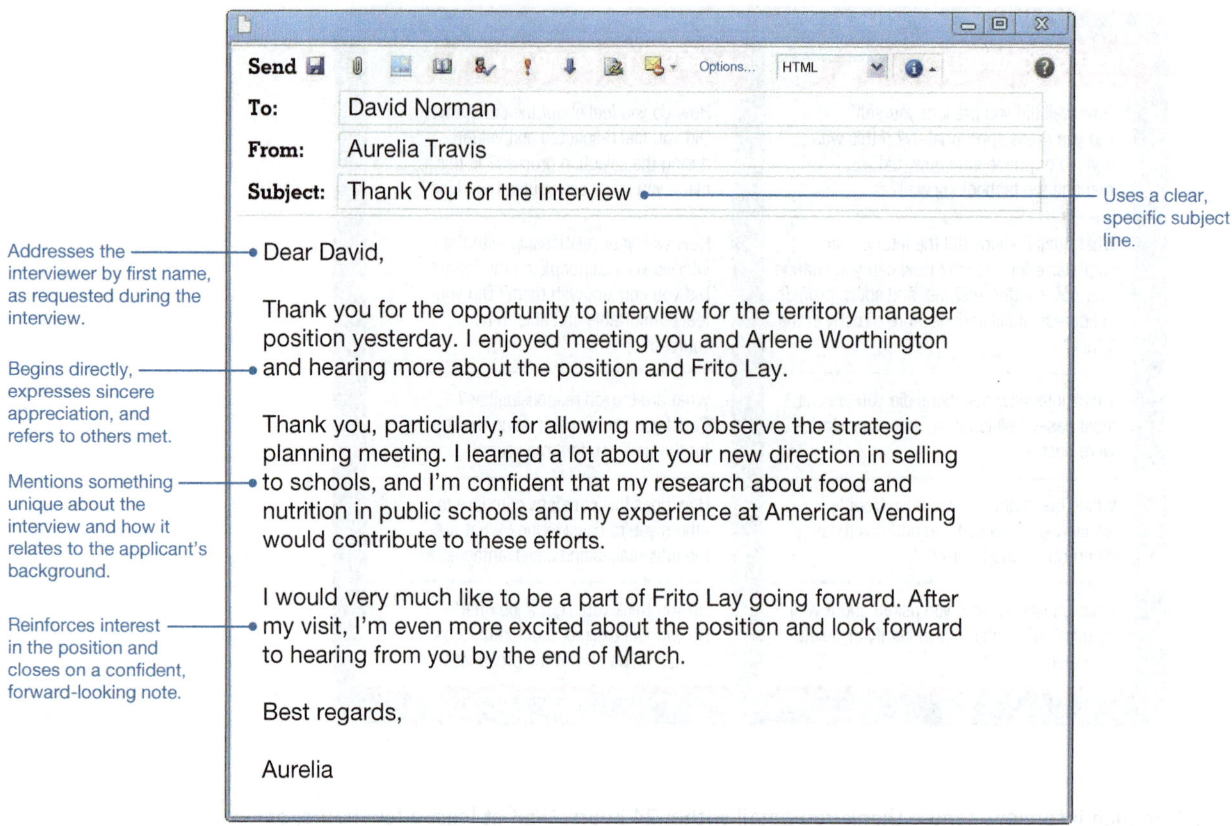

Send
Options...
HTML
To: David Norman
From: Aurelia Travis
Subject: Thank You for the Interview
Uses a clear, specific subject line.
Addresses the interviewer by first name, as requested during the interview.
Dear David,
Begins directly, expresses sincere appreciation, and refers to others met.
Thank you for the opportunity to interview for the territory manager position yesterday. I enjoyed meeting you and Arlene Worthington and hearing more about the position and Frito Lay.
Mentions something unique about the interview and how it relates to the applicant's background.
Thank you, particularly, for allowing me to observe the strategic planning meeting. I learned a lot about your new direction in selling to schools, and I'm confident that my research about food and nutrition in public schools and my experience at American Vending would contribute to these efforts.
Reinforces interest in the position and closes on a confident, forward-looking note.
I would very much like to be a part of Frito Lay going forward. After my visit, I'm even more excited about the position and look forward to hearing from you by the end of March.
Best regards,
Aurelia

CHARACTER

don't see the importance of following up. On the other hand, many HR managers report being ghosted by job candidates—56% of them after the candidate had accepted a job offer![21] From both parties, this behavior is unprofessional and lacks integrity, a failure to follow through on a commitment.

If you don't hear back from a company within the promised time, wait about another week before following up. Then, follow up with either a phone call or an email, such as the example shown in Figure 10. If no decision has been made, your inquiry will keep your name and interest in the interviewer's mind.

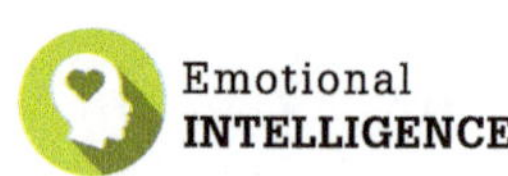

How do you feel when you're waiting for an employer's response? What stress-management strategies have worked for you during these times?

If you don't hear back after your email, try one more time. Wait another week, and then email or call again. When emailing, forward your previous message and, if you have another offer, mention it, as shown in Figure 11. You can send a similar email before the response deadline if you are pressed to decide about another offer. You also can ask for more time from your second-choice employer. All these communications require tactful navigation, and your college's career management office may be able to help.

If you *still* don't receive a response to your second follow-up message, it's time to move on. At this point, typically, you can assume that the company will not pursue you as a candidate.

Everyone gets rejected from companies, even when they believe it's their "ideal" place to work. You might revisit the assessment questions in Figure 8. Did you miss something that would indicate a poor fit between you and the company? Maybe so—or maybe not. Searching for high-demand jobs, particularly in a strong economy, is always challenging. Many times, someone is simply more qualified or a better choice than you at the time. When candidates move on to pursue other opportunities, they often find that, in the long run, a different company or position works out for the best, anyway.

Follow-Up Email | **Figure 10**

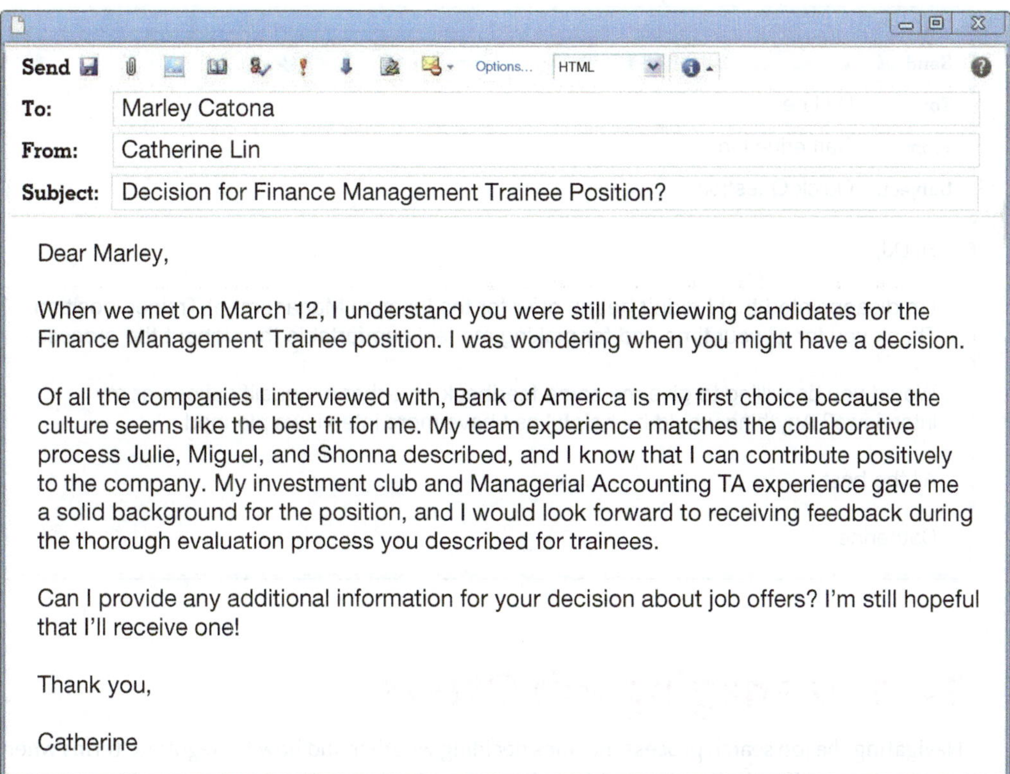
Send | Options... | HTML

To: Marley Catona

From: Catherine Lin

Subject: Decision for Finance Management Trainee Position?

Dear Marley,

When we met on March 12, I understand you were still interviewing candidates for the Finance Management Trainee position. I was wondering when you might have a decision.

Of all the companies I interviewed with, Bank of America is my first choice because the culture seems like the best fit for me. My team experience matches the collaborative process Julie, Miguel, and Shonna described, and I know that I can contribute positively to the company. My investment club and Managerial Accounting TA experience gave me a solid background for the position, and I would look forward to receiving feedback during the thorough evaluation process you described for trainees.

Can I provide any additional information for your decision about job offers? I'm still hopeful that I'll receive one!

Thank you,

Catherine

Second Follow-Up Email | **Figure 11**

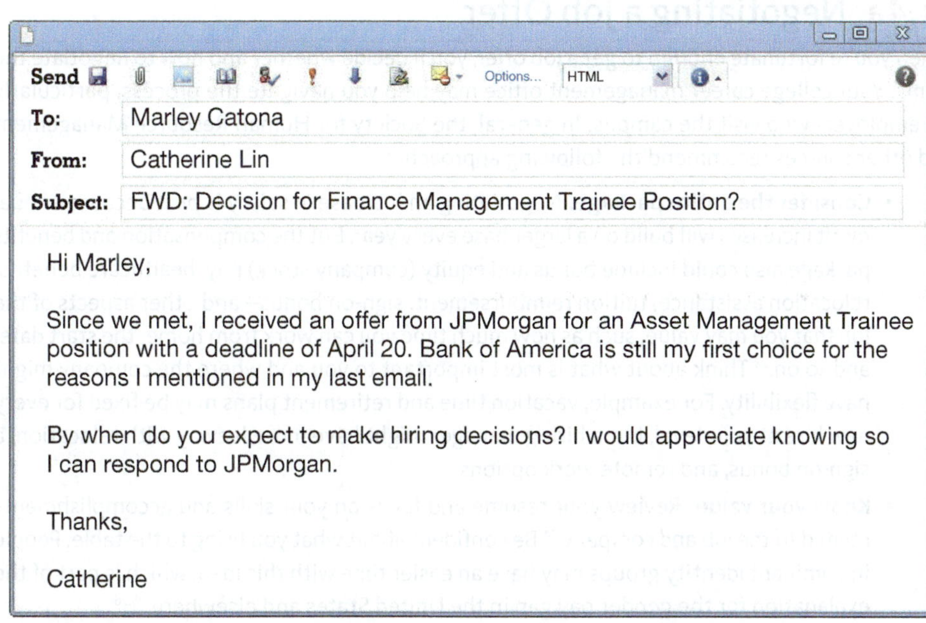
Send | Options... | HTML

To: Marley Catona

From: Catherine Lin

Subject: FWD: Decision for Finance Management Trainee Position?

Hi Marley,

Since we met, I received an offer from JPMorgan for an Asset Management Trainee position with a deadline of April 20. Bank of America is still my first choice for the reasons I mentioned in my last email.

By when do you expect to make hiring decisions? I would appreciate knowing so I can respond to JPMorgan.

Thanks,

Catherine

When you receive a rejection, consider writing a brief reply to thank the interviewer for the time and opportunity. Although you may not get a response, you could ask for feedback, as the email to an HR manager shows in Figure 12. If you take this approach, keep it short and make it easy for the interviewer to reply.

Figure 12 | Response to a Rejection

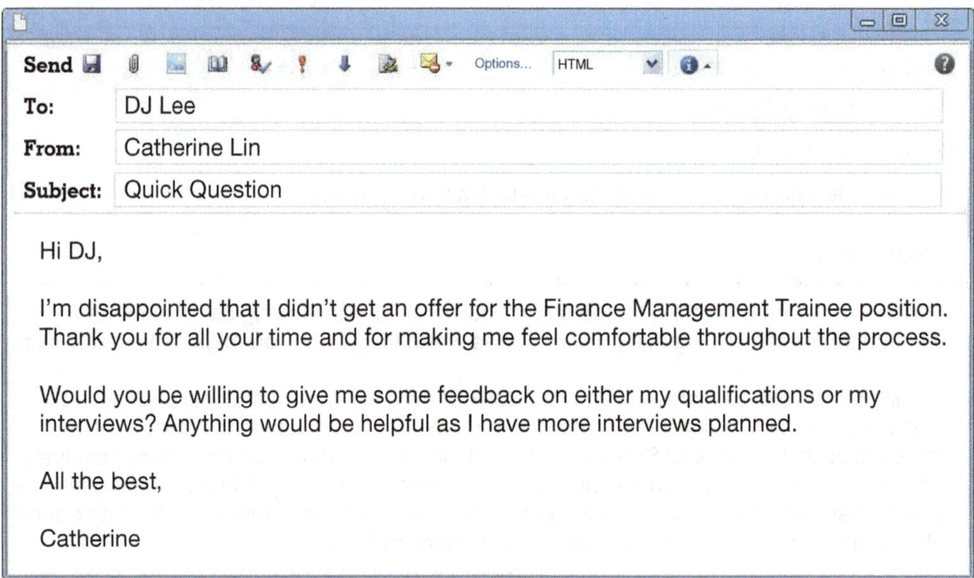
To: DJ Lee
From: Catherine Lin
Subject: Quick Question

Hi DJ,

I'm disappointed that I didn't get an offer for the Finance Management Trainee position. Thank you for all your time and for making me feel comfortable throughout the process.

Would you be willing to give me some feedback on either my qualifications or my interviews? Anything would be helpful as I have more interviews planned.

All the best,

Catherine

LO4 Write an email to decline a job offer.

14-4 Managing Job Offers

Navigating the job search process includes deciding whether and how to negotiate terms when you receive an offer, declining a position when you either have a better option or choose to wait for one, and turning down a candidate if you're in a management position. None of these messages are easy and all require a degree of confidence, savvy relational skills, and strong character.

14-4a Negotiating a Job Offer

When you're fortunate enough to get a job offer, you'll decide whether and how to negotiate the terms. Your college career management office may help you navigate the process, particularly for employers who visit the campus. In general, the Society for Human Resource Management and other sources recommend the following approach:[22]

- **Consider the entire package.** Negotiating an increase in salary is best because annual merit increases will build on a larger base every year. But the compensation and benefits package also could include bonus and equity (company stock) pay, healthcare benefits, relocation assistance, tuition reimbursement, sign-on bonus—and other aspects of the job that you may value, such as how much time you can work from home, the start date, and so on.[23] Think about what is most important to you and where the company might have flexibility. For example, vacation time and retirement plans may be fixed for every new hire at your level, but a hiring manager might have more leeway with relocation, a sign-on bonus, and remote work options.
- **Know your value.** Review your resume and focus on your skills and accomplishments related to the job and company.[24] Be confident about what you bring to the table. People in dominant identity groups may have an easier time with this idea, which is part of the explanation for the gender pay gap in the United States and elsewhere.[25,26]
- **Research starting salaries.** Explore your college's career management office, Glassdoor, PayScale, Salary.com, and other sites to determine the likely range for the position and location. You might share your offer with other students; people are surprisingly willing to talk about their finances today,[27] and transparency helps reduce the pay gap.[28] Keep your expectations realistic. You can ask a recruiter about a salary range—but not too early in the process. Negotiations typically don't start until after you have a job offer. If

asked about your requirements, try to get a salary range from the employer first, so you don't "low-ball" yourself. Research local laws that govern questions employers cannot ask and information they must provide.

- **Highlight your assets.** When you begin to negotiate, give concrete examples, for example, similar work and accomplishments at other companies. Think about why the employer should pay you more. Often, they are looking for your motivation level.[29] In other words, how can you prove—with evidence—that you'll work harder than other employees and, therefore, be worth the extra compensation? Avoid talking about your needs, for example, student loans; other than relocation, an employer will pay more for what you can contribute—not for your expenses.[30]
- **Decide on your approach.** Include all your requests up front so the employer doesn't get frustrated and feel manipulated when you negotiate each term separately. If you don't get the salary or other terms you request, what will you do? Be clear about what you're willing to compromise and at what point you will decline the offer.
- **Practice.** Practice what you'll say with friends and others to address counterarguments and hold your ground. You don't need to apologize ("Sorry to bother you with this. I know you're busy"). Instead, adopt a confident, persuasive, yet friendly tone ("I'm very excited about the position and joining the team, and I know I'll bring a lot of value to the table, particularly because of my experience at __________ [or something relevant you accomplished]. I'm wondering if we can explore a slightly higher starting salary of $ __________").[31] Your goal is to convince the employer, without sounding too demanding, that you're worth the higher salary.[32]

Can you imagine yourself negotiating a job offer? What concerns you, for example, the hiring manager's reaction? How can you overcome your concerns?

Negotiating your offer may be the first indication of how you'll communicate with your hiring manager in the future. This is an opportunity to gain respect at the start. Asking for more is risky; an employer might rescind an offer. You'll have to read the hiring manager to check reactions throughout the conversation. But asking for reasonable increases in compensation and benefits—and making a request rather than a demand—may improve your total starting package.

14-4b Declining a Job Offer

After an interview, if you decide that the position isn't right for you, let your main contact know so the company can move on to other candidates. Send an email explaining that you would like to withdraw from the selection process. In these situations—and after you receive an offer—communicating your decision gracefully conveys your professionalism and good character. Consider these questions as you plan your messages:

- What relationships did you build during the selection process? Did you make a special connection with someone who took extra steps to make you feel comfortable? Express your appreciation in a way that respects the time people invested and how well they accommodated you throughout the process.
- Did you meet with multiple people? Did they reimburse your travel expenses? In these situations, you'll want to take extra care in how you tell your main contact that you won't be accepting the job. You also may want to reach out (typically, through email) to others who interviewed you.
- What is your reason for declining the job? Try to be tactful in how you explain your decision. Saying that another company offered you more money may be off-putting. Is the other job in a city where you prefer to work? Are the job responsibilities closer to what you hoped to be doing? You may choose not to give a reason at all ("I've decided to pursue other opportunities").

In most cases, email is the most appropriate way to decline an offer. The emails in Figure 13 are from a candidate who is in a delicate situation: a good family friend recommended her for the position. Both emails maintain good relationships—and you can tell that the candidate has been in continuous communication with everyone involved.

Figure 13 | Declining a Job Offer

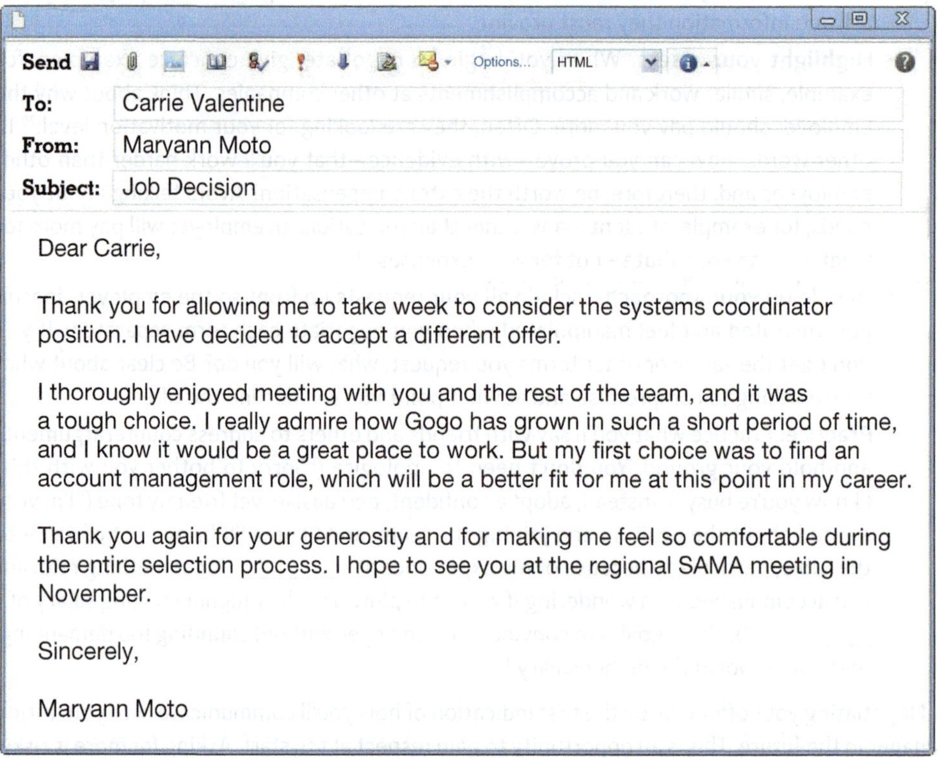

Send | Options... | HTML

To: Carrie Valentine

From: Maryann Moto

Subject: Job Decision

Dear Carrie,

Thank you for allowing me to take week to consider the systems coordinator position. I have decided to accept a different offer.

I thoroughly enjoyed meeting with you and the rest of the team, and it was a tough choice. I really admire how Gogo has grown in such a short period of time, and I know it would be a great place to work. But my first choice was to find an account management role, which will be a better fit for me at this point in my career.

Thank you again for your generosity and for making me feel so comfortable during the entire selection process. I hope to see you at the regional SAMA meeting in November.

Sincerely,

Maryann Moto

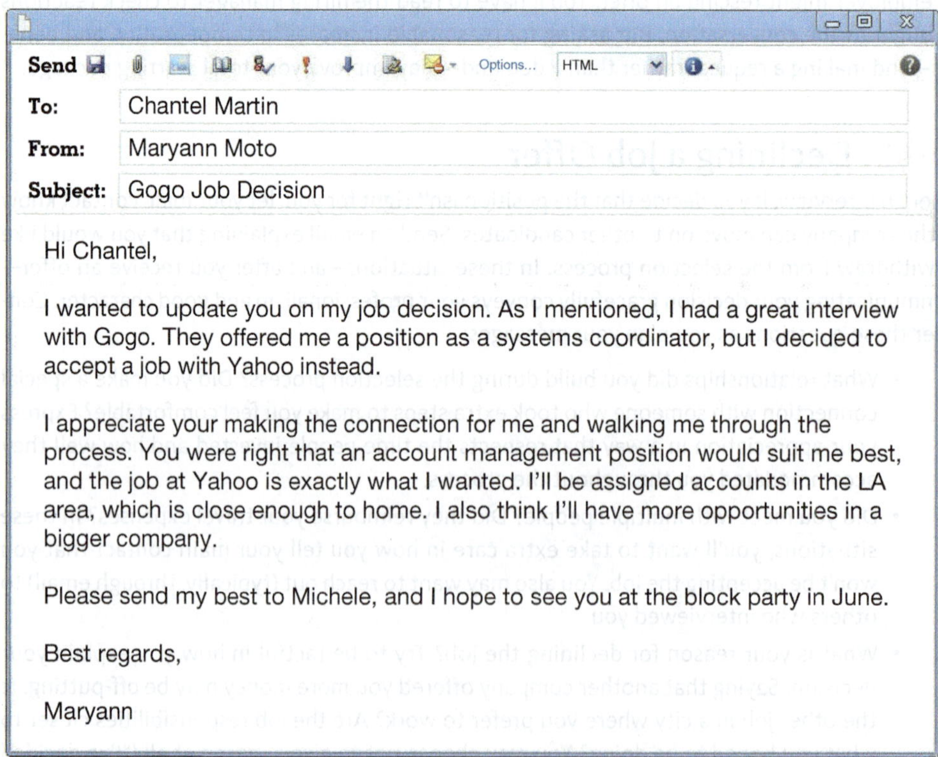

Send | Options... | HTML

To: Chantel Martin

From: Maryann Moto

Subject: Gogo Job Decision

Hi Chantel,

I wanted to update you on my job decision. As I mentioned, I had a great interview with Gogo. They offered me a position as a systems coordinator, but I decided to accept a job with Yahoo instead.

I appreciate your making the connection for me and walking me through the process. You were right that an account management position would suit me best, and the job at Yahoo is exactly what I wanted. I'll be assigned accounts in the LA area, which is close enough to home. I also think I'll have more opportunities in a bigger company.

Please send my best to Michele, and I hope to see you at the block party in June.

Best regards,

Maryann

14-4c Turning Down a Job Candidate

Almost everyone will apply for a job but not get an offer, and this can be a painful process. If you're a hiring manager, you will want to handle these situations with sensitivity.

Employers seldom give job candidates feedback. They fear discrimination lawsuits and having to further explain the decision.[33] Figure 14 is a template job rejection email recommended by the Society for Human Resource Management.[34] As a manager, you may customize this to sound more personal. The last line, particularly, sounds cliché.

Figure 14 Form Rejection Email

Dear [Insert Name],

It was a pleasure meeting with you to discuss your background and interest in the [job title] position within our organization. We appreciate your time, attentiveness, and patience throughout the interview process. We did have several highly qualified candidates for the position, and it has been a difficult decision, but we have chosen to pursue another candidate for this position who we feel is best qualified.

We do thank you for your interest in [Company Name], and we wish you good luck in your future endeavors.

Sincerely,

[Name]
[Title]
[Company Name]

With your employer's consent, you may choose to give feedback to candidates despite the risks. For an internal candidate, feedback will be expected and is important to the person's development. For students—as discussed earlier—it's nice to get feedback to improve their chances for other jobs. If you made a personal connection with someone and want to give more specific reasons, have a phone conversation rather than send email. Also focus on specific job qualifications (e.g., "We had other candidates with more management experience" or "who had previous accounting internships") rather than vague, personal issues (e.g., "You didn't seem to be very motivated" or "We hired someone who seemed more confident"). Can you see how these last two statements could leave a candidate feeling that the decision was subjective?

As a manager, be sure to communicate decisions as soon as someone accepts an offer. Let candidates know that the job has been filled so they can move on to other opportunities. As with all bad news, delaying it only makes the situation worse for the receiver.

14-5 Demonstrating Professionalism at Work

LO5 List behaviors that describe professionalism.

Once hired, your professionalism will determine how you're perceived and how your work is evaluated. As a result, you may get better projects and opportunities—and be promoted to take on more responsibility. A taskforce of college and business recruiting staff (National Association of Colleges and Employers [NACE]) defined professionalism as a competency: "understand and demonstrate effective work habits and act in the interest of the larger community and workplace."[35]

In this definition, you notice the foundations of emotional intelligence and character discussed throughout the book. Emotional intelligence is required to be aware of yourself and others, the "larger community and workplace." Character is required to consider our impact on others—acting in others' interest. Often, professionalism is perceived in small ways, and we discuss a few in this section: scanning the environment; meeting and greeting, sharing meals, and exchanging gifts; and socializing outside of work and connecting on social media.

14-5a Scanning the Environment

The NACE taskforce identified the behaviors listed in Figure 15 to describe professionalism.[36] Reading these behaviors, you have an idea of what employers most value in new graduates: honesty, positivity, timeliness, accountability, work output, detail orientation, and dedication.

Figure 15 | Behaviors to Describe Professionalism

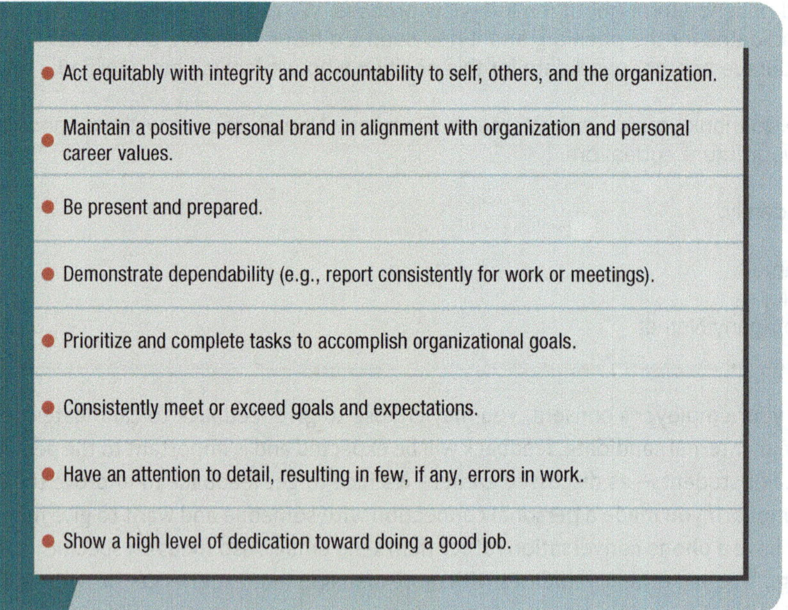

Act equitably with integrity and accountability to self, others, and the organization.
Maintain a positive personal brand in alignment with organization and personal career values.
Be present and prepared.
Demonstrate dependability (e.g., report consistently for work or meetings).
Prioritize and complete tasks to accomplish organizational goals.
Consistently meet or exceed goals and expectations.
Have an attention to detail, resulting in few, if any, errors in work.
Show a high level of dedication toward doing a good job.

International
COMMUNICATION

Also notable is the introduction to the NACE definition: "work environments differ greatly."[37] Each organization has its own rules about what is considered appropriate in terms of dress, interactions with senior-level managers, punctuality, and other subtle forms of communication in the workplace. In addition, every country and culture has its own rules that guide workplace behavior. Furthermore, expectations vary even within an organization. What's considered acceptable in the IT department (e.g., casual dress and abbreviations in instant messages) may be perceived negatively in the sales department. Generally, these rules are not written down but are learned informally or through observation.

Closely observe how others behave; pay attention to social cues. What do people wear? How do they greet each other and talk about projects? How do they respect one another's privacy in

an open office with cubicles? What's common practice when people come into work and when they leave for the day?

How do people interact when they work remotely? When employees join online meetings, are they on time with their video on or off? How do they use chat during meetings? How do they end calls?

Research shows a bias against people who work from home. Without in-person contact with company leaders, remote workers may miss out on mentoring opportunities and promotions.[38] Consider keeping your video camera on even if you're in the minority, so people see and remember you. Also consider how you'll document your work. Ask your manager if a weekly (or daily) list of activities or accomplishments would be helpful.

How astute are you at reading social cues at work? Attune to subtleties to understand what's considered professional behavior.

14-5b Meeting and Greeting, Sharing Meals, and Exchanging Gifts

Interactions at work can be awkward. Here, we discuss a few that often challenge new employees: meeting and greeting, dining, and giving and receiving gifts.

Everett Collection

Tight quarters—and some strange personalities—cause people to annoy their coworkers in the classic movie *Office Space*.

Meeting and Greeting

When you meet people for the first time, take the initiative to introduce yourself. This shows confidence and will help you meet more people at your company or in your industry. Follow others' lead about whether to shake hands, and to remember names, repeat them. When you have more experience with the company, introduce others to help them network.

Engage in small talk as you see others doing. Who stops to chat? For how long do they talk and about what? How do they end conversations? Be attuned to when people want to move on, so you don't take too much of their time.

Sharing Lunch and Formal Meals

As you scan the environment, also pay attention to when and how people eat lunch. Do people eat quickly at their desks or go out in pairs or groups? Who is included and who is excluded? Your coworkers might invite you along, so be prepared. Follow their lead on conversation topics, which may be social or work related.

In the book *Hillbilly Elegy*, autobiographer J.D. Vance describes a formal dinner when he was interviewing with a law firm. He was daunted by "an absurd number of instruments," unsure which to use for what food.[39] Whether at an upscale restaurant or a casual café, these etiquette guidelines will help you enjoy a business meal:

- **Before the meal.** Arrive at the restaurant a couple of minutes before the reservation time and take your host's lead for where to sit at the table. Order something easy to eat and in the middle price range of the menu.

  If the host orders wine and you drink alcohol, have a glass. If someone offers a toast, "clink" glasses with a couple of people to your right and left. If it's a big group, you can lift your glass to others without reaching across the table. If you don't drink, decline the wine politely. During a toast, just pick up your water glass instead.

- **During the meal.** When the food arrives, don't begin eating until others do. If your dish is the only one missing, invite others to begin rather than wait—they may or may not.

At a formal place setting, the glass or cup on the right side and the bread plate on the left side are yours.

At your place setting, the bread plate at left and glassware at right are yours. When using silverware, start from the outside in (the smaller fork is for your salad). If you *must* use salt (only after tasting the food), ask someone to please pass it to you, rather than reach across the table for it.

A business meal is about the conversation—not the food. Stay engaged throughout the meal and follow your mother's advice: keep your elbows off the table and don't talk with your mouth full. Take small bites so you can participate in the conversation and pace your eating so you finish about when others do. Take your host's lead for topics. Sometimes, like lunch with your coworkers, business meals are more social, and discussing too much business is considered inappropriate.

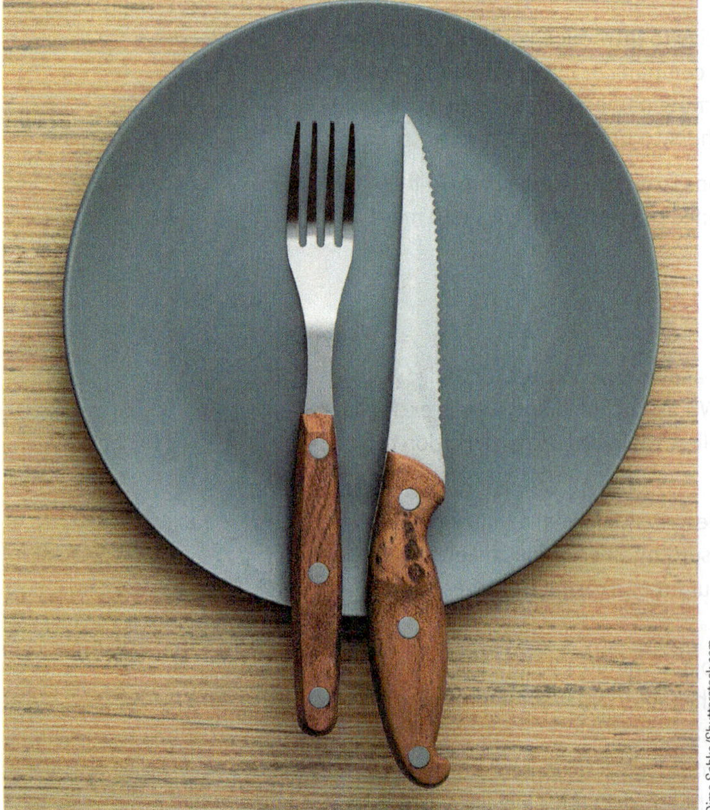

To signal to the server that you are finished, place the knife and fork together on your plate.

If you leave the table during the meal, leave your napkin on your chair. At the end of the meal, place the napkin, unfolded, on the table. Place the knife across the top edge of the plate, with the cutting edge toward you when it is not being used; don't keep silverware leveraged on the table and plate like oars. If you drop a utensil—it happens—don't pick it up; the server will take care of it and give you a new one, or you can subtly ask for a replacement. To signal to the server that you're finished, place your knife and fork together on the plate.

- **After the meal.** For business meals, it's typically inappropriate to take leftovers home. If the server asks, politely decline.

The person who extended the invitation is expected to pay the bill. If someone else paid, be sure to say thank you before you get up from the table.

If you're the host, when the server comes with the check, indicate that you will accept it. If it's placed on the table, just pick it up. Tip at least 20% of the bill before tax.[40] If it's unclear who will pay, you should always offer. If your host declines your offer, say a polite, thank you.

For formal occasions, send a thank-you note immediately after the meal. Be sure to write more than a token note, mentioning something special about the décor, food, service, and/or meal companions.

Exchanging Gifts

Giving gifts to suppliers, customers, or workers is typical at many companies, especially at the end of the year. Although gifts are often appreciated, check your company's policy. Many companies restrict both giving and receiving gifts to avoid improprieties.

Check to ensure that a gift you give or receive is appropriate. Gifts should not be too expensive and should be impersonal, for example, something connected to the office or work. Gifts are also for the past—not to create obligations for the future, which might be interpreted as a bribe. Finally, avoid singling out one person for a gift, which could look like favoritism and might be embarrassing.

A manager is more likely to give an employee a gift than the other way around. For special occasions, coworkers may contribute to a gift for the boss and present it from the entire group.

14-5c Socializing Outside of Work and Connecting on Social Media

Naturally, you may meet friends and have romantic interests at work. Particularly if you're joining a company right out of school with a cohort of students, you'll likely go out together and connect on social media.

Socializing to build relationships will help your career. In addition to learning more about the company, you'll develop a network of people you can rely on for advice and support. Having people you know well and trust within the company increases your sense of belonging and may improve your chance of success.

On the other hand, relationships can get awkward. If your work friends are your *only* friends, you might lose perspective and become dependent on them. Without other advice, you might find it difficult to leave a bad employment situation. In addition, too much socializing or flirting during work time could affect your productivity and job performance.

Embarrassing situations after work—or during company events—also may cause problems. Heavy drinking or other behaviors get memorialized on social media for your employer to see. Avoid doing anything that will reflect poorly on you so you don't regret it later.

Most people connect with coworkers on social media. But if your boss or others send a request, you don't have to accept. Instead, you could send a LinkedIn invitation. Or you might make your profile on other apps private or restrict access. Of course, another approach is to be public—and share everywhere judiciously. Before you send invitations to coworkers, consider waiting until you've developed a relationship with them. After you develop trust, you can both connect online more comfortably.

14-6 Chapter Closing

Finding a job can be a rewarding but also a grueling and demoralizing process. While you present yourself, the company is presenting itself to you—letting you know, throughout a selection process, what it will be like to work there. Pay attention to the signs to determine where you—with all your experience, talents, and motivations—can best contribute and be happy.

Your first job is an important milestone in your life, but it's only one step. You'll have a long career with many twists and turns, setbacks and successes. As you progress through your journey, you'll continuously develop your business communication skills and your character to become the best person you can be.

Decide Whether to Write a Negative Review on Glassdoor

Consider the chapter introduction, which described reviews about companies on Glassdoor. Imagine that you are interning at a company and are not having a good experience. Using the CAM model, what questions might you consider before writing a review on Glassdoor?

>>> CHARACTER CHECK

1. **What is my motivation for writing a Glassdoor review?**
   The internship was supposed to be a rotational program. The plan was for me to spend one week in at least five different departments. So far, I've spent three weeks in accounting, the area I find least interesting.
2. **How do I feel about the situation?**
   I turned down another internship offer because I thought I would get exposure to different areas of the company and meet a lot of people. I'm bored and angry.

>>> AUDIENCE ANALYSIS

1. **Who are the primary and secondary audiences of a Glassdoor review?**
   Primarily, students who consider an internship with this company will read the review and may take other, better offers. Company HR managers probably monitor the site too.
2. **How might HR managers who read the review react?**
   Not well. To be fair, they have been apologetic about the situation. Apparently, managers in other departments didn't plan well, so they don't have work for me to do.
3. **How helpful would this review be to potential future interns?**
   Very! On the other hand, I don't need to write the review now because the company won't start recruiting again until the fall. Maybe I'll wait until after I leave.

>>> MESSAGE AND MEDIUM

1. **What are the main points of my message?**
   I feel duped into this internship, and I would suggest that students not accept the job if they think they will spend time in different departments.
2. **In what medium will I communicate the message?**
   Well, I should probably talk to my recruiter about my frustration. I've been gracious about the situation, but I am really disappointed. If things don't change, I'll write a review after I leave—when I don't feel so angry.

Raise a Sensitive Topic During an Interview

IN PRACTICE

Imagine that you just accepted an interview invitation from a company, described on the previous page. The recruiter said you will spend one week in each of at least five departments, but two Glassdoor reviews said this didn't happen for interns last summer. The rotation is important to you if you accept the position. Use the CAM model to plan how to address this issue.

>>> CHARACTER CHECK

1. What motivates me to address the rotation issue? Why is this important to me?
2. I have conflicting information from the recruiter and former interns. Which do I trust? How can I reconcile the information?

>>> AUDIENCE ANALYSIS

1. How would the recruiter react to my expressing concern based on what I read on Glassdoor?
2. How might my raising the issue affect my candidacy for the position?

>>> MESSAGE AND MEDIUM

1. How can I raise the concern in a way that is respectful?
2. What questions can I ask about the rotations that would give me more confidence? How can I get more detail about the summer plan?
3. What is the best medium for my questions? We have been communicating by email, and we have an interview scheduled for one week from today.

REFLECTING ON YOUR COMMUNICATION AND CHARACTER DEVELOPMENT

1. **Reflect on your interview history.**

   How have your interviews for jobs, clubs, or other organizations gone in the past? How would you describe your comfort level? What were your strengths, and in what ways did you fall short?

   Describe what you can do to improve your interview success—even if you did well in the past. Consider ways to research the organization, practice and prepare questions, build rapport with the interviewer, demonstrate confidence, and so on.

2. **Imagine an interview "do-over."**

   Think about an interview during which you didn't do as well as you had hoped. Don't spend too much time fretting about what went wrong. Instead, visualize a "do-over": imagine watching a movie of yourself doing better. Try to recreate the original details, but this time, you do everything well. If you flubbed a question, practice responding now, out loud.

3. **Assess your confidence level.**

   Read a job description that interests you. Compare your qualifications for the position. Imagine that you're someone else reviewing your resume and matching up skills and experience. What are your application strengths? What might be a weakness in your application?

   Practice answering a direct interview question about a weakness, for example, "I see you don't have any experience working with customers." Practice responding in a way that demonstrates your qualifications, for example, by describing how you worked with children's demanding parents when you were a lifeguard or how you created customer profiles in your Consumer Behavior class.

4. **Reflect on ghosting and being ghosted.**

   In this chapter, you read that ghosting happens on both sides of the selection process. What is your experience—in your personal or your professional life—with being ghosted? How did you feel at the time? How do you feel now, reflecting on the experience?

   What is your experience ghosting others? What prevented you from responding? What were the possible consequences for the other person then, and what might be lingering for that person still? Can you commit to doing better during the job search process by communicating and following up more consistently?

5. **Clarify feelings about negotiating.**

   How did you feel reading the chapter section about negotiating offers? How comfortable have you been in the past asking for a higher salary? What might hold you back in the future? How might your identity, culture, upbringing, and other factors affect your comfort level? What information or practice would give you more clarity and confidence?

DEVELOPING YOUR BUSINESS COMMUNICATION SKILLS

LO1 Provide a response to a behavioral interview question in the "STAR" format.

PREPARING FOR A JOB INTERVIEW

1. **Research a potential employer.**

   Assume that your favorite company has invited you to an interview. To prepare for the interview, research the company by reviewing its website, reading news stories, and exploring websites like Glassdoor. Concentrate on information most likely to help you during the interview.

Now assume that another student, who is also interested in the company, asks you what you have learned. Write an email to this student summarizing your research.

2. **Identify job competencies and possible interview questions.**
Find a job description that interests you. Based on the tasks and qualifications, list the job competencies and specialized skills the company seeks, for example, detail orientation, customer service, innovation, data analysis, financial modeling, and so on.

   Now write at least one behavioral interview question that would elicit information about each competency. Figure 3 will give you some ideas, and you can invent your own.

3. **Prepare your stories.**
Based on the competencies you identified for Exercise 2—and for other competencies you may need for jobs that interest you—identify between 10 and 15 examples of stories from your experience, as described in this chapter. Write each out in the STAR (situation/task, action, result) format. Practice saying them out loud, and then revise each to take between one and three minutes.

4. **Practice answering behavioral interview questions.**
Working in groups of three, practice answering a behavioral interview question from Figure 3 and others you wrote for Exercise 2. Take turns, with one of you asking the question, another responding, and the third person observing and taking notes, using the feedback form in Figure 16 to evaluate the candidate's response.

Figure 16 Behavioral Interview Question Feedback Form

Content and Organization	❑ Did you get a complete story (STAR)? ❑ Did it demonstrate the competency you were looking for? ❑ Was it well organized? ❑ Did you get the right amount of detail (enough, not too much)? ❑ COMMENTS:
Delivery	❑ Easy to understand ❑ Good eye contact ❑ Appropriate pace ❑ Good volume ❑ Effective hand gestures ❑ Few fillers (*uh, um*) ❑ Appropriate pauses ❑ COMMENTS:

5. **Prepare a list of questions for a potential employer.**
For an upcoming interview (or from your research completed in Exercise 1), prepare a list of questions you might ask. You may not have the time to ask everything but prepare at least ten questions, just in case.

6. **Prepare a career preparation portfolio.**
To prepare for your job search, conduct research and meet with people who can help you. First, target specific people within companies where you might like to work. You will need

to send a few networking emails to ask for assistance. Your goal is to complete the following activities within one or more companies:

- Job shadow someone who holds a position that interests you.
- Observe a meeting or formal presentation.
- Attend a training program.
- Meet with people in your field (informational interviews).

In addition, to understand your field of interest, pursue professional development activities, such as the following:

- Find two professional associations for your field of interest. You may search online for these organizations. Study their websites to understand the purpose, membership, and mission of each organization.
- Attend a local meeting of one of the professional organizations that interests you.
- Connect on LinkedIn with three organizations that interest you. Follow conversations for two weeks.
- Find two professional journals within your field of interest, and study one article from each.
- Search for news stories or credible blogs about your field. Study what these sources say about important trends or developments within your field.

Prepare a portfolio of your work and submit it to your instructor. You might be instructed to include the following:

- A cover memo summarizing what you learned from these activities
- Observations from your job-shadowing experience
- Copies of handouts or presentation decks you received during meetings or training programs
- Notes from your informational interviews
- Notes from LinkedIn and other social media posts
- Observations about professional associations in your field
- Notes from the professional association meeting you attended
- Summaries of journal articles you read
- An analysis of trends and developments that might affect your career choice in the future.

Organize your portfolio in a way that makes sense to you—not necessarily in the order presented here. Include a table of contents for your materials and a title page.

LO2 Describe ways to make a good first impression during a job interview.

PRESENTING YOURSELF DURING AN INTERVIEW

7. Assess a mock interview.

Find a sample interview by searching for "mock interview" on YouTube or another video site. Watch at least two questions and answers with a classmate. How did the candidate do? What improvements would you suggest about the candidate's presentation and interaction? Would you like to have the candidate as a coworker? Why or why not?

8. Practice interviewing.

Ask someone to do a complete practice interview with you. Your school's career management office might offer mock interviews, or you can reach out to a business professional you know or an alumnus of your school. You may do this in person or on video, whichever is the more likely way you'll have your next interview. If you have the opportunity, do one of each.

Rehearse everything. Ask the interviewer to schedule time with you, and show up in appropriate dress. Greet each other, answer an entire set of questions, ask questions at the end, and close the interview.

Ask for feedback about every aspect of the process. Overall, what impression did you make? What came across as your strengths? How can you improve your interview skills?

9. **Identify and address challenging questions.**
Thinking about jobs that interest you, what could a hiring manager ask that would be difficult for you to answer? Consider questions about your experience, coursework, grades, and so on. Write a few possible questions and prepare to answer them. Find ways to convince the interviewer that you're qualified for the job despite these weaker areas. Try to balance over- and underselling yourself.

10. **Prepare for a one-way video interview.**
Imagine that you are asked to interview through HireVue. Visit the website and review guidelines to ensure that your device is compatible. Next, answer a few of the practice questions. Say your answers a couple of times until you're comfortable. As always, avoid memorizing your responses; you'll want to appear confident and sound natural and conversational.

FOLLOWING UP AFTER THE INTERVIEW

LO3 Write a thank-you email for a given job offer.

11. **Assess yourself and a company.**
After an interview, answer the questions in Figure 8. Write your responses and submit them to your instructor. At the end, summarize your conclusions by answering one more question: under what, if any, conditions would you take the job if offered?

12. **Give and receive feedback on a thank-you email.**
Find an email you sent in the past to thank someone for an interview. Exchange messages with a classmate and give each other feedback. Assess the tone, writing style, tailored content, and so on.

13. **Write a thank-you email.**
Imagine that you had a great interview for a job. Write a thank-you email to your interviewer to summarize your qualifications and reinforce your interest in the position. Invent whatever details you would like. Send the email to your instructor for feedback.

14. **Follow up after an interview.**
Have you had an interview in the past, and the interviewer never got back to you? Or have you sent a resume and not received a response? Think about one of these situations and write an email to follow up. Exchange drafts with a classmate to make sure your request is clear and your tone is appropriate.

15. **Request feedback.**
Have you been declined a job offer? Write an email to request feedback. It might be too late to send it, but this is good practice for next time. Exchange drafts with a classmate to make sure your request is easy to answer and your tone is appropriate.

MANAGING JOB OFFERS

LO4 Write an email to decline a job offer.

16. **Research salaries.**
Find two other students who have career interests similar to yours. Think about a job you would all like when you graduate. Then, separately, search online at Glassdoor, PayScale, Salary.com, and other sites to find a typical salary range for the position in a particular location. Compare results. You might check your ranges with your college career office.

17. **Determine compensation and benefits priorities.**
When you think about compensation and benefits for a future job, what is most important to you? Consider the salary, healthcare benefits, retirement plan, bonus, equity, location,

relocation assistance, remote work option, tuition reimbursement, flexible time, vacation days, training opportunities, and so on. How would you prioritize these and other aspects that are important to you? Try to put them in rank order, which, of course, will vary depending on the job—and your perspective when the time comes to negotiate.

18. **Practice negotiating.**

Revisit the guidelines in this chapter for negotiating a job offer. Then, with the two classmates you worked with for Exercise 16, practice negotiating. Divide roles: the hiring manager, candidate, and observer. The hiring manager and observer should meet privately first to decide on an offer. At a minimum, include the salary, bonus, vacation time, remote work schedule, and relocation assistance.

The hiring manager then presents the offer, and the candidate responds. After some back-and-forth conversation, discuss the results. The observer should give feedback to both negotiators, and they can weigh in as well.

19. **Decline a job offer.**

Imagine that you received an offer that you don't accept. Instead, you accepted an offer for a higher starting salary in your hometown. Write an email declining the offer. Your goal is to express appreciation and keep the door open for future opportunities. In a short cover note to your instructor, explain your communication choices more fully than what you wrote to the hiring manager.

20. **Decline another job offer.**

Just for fun, imagine that you received a great job offer from your favorite company, but alas, you have been cast as your favorite actor's love interest in an upcoming movie. You cannot pass up the opportunity. Write an email to the company hiring manager to turn down the job. Invent whatever details you would like.

21. **Write a job rejection email—to yourself.**

Think about a recent job for which you applied but weren't offered a position. If you received a generic or template rejection, write something more specific and personal. Even if you weren't the best candidate for the job, what would you have liked to have received from the employer?

LO5 List behaviors that describe professionalism.

DEMONSTRATING PROFESSIONALISM AT WORK

22. **Describe professionalism.**

With two classmates, discuss the culture of an organization where you have worked or that you know well. How would you define professionalism at that location? Specifically, what type of behavior was valued and what was discouraged? What, if anything, surprised you about how people acted at work?

23. **Assess your professionalism.**

Consider your own professional behavior. Looking at the list of behaviors in Figure 15, which do you consider assets? Of which do you feel most proud? How can you emphasize these qualities throughout the job search?

Which behaviors don't describe you? What prevents you from demonstrating professionalism in these ways, and how could you improve?

24. **Discuss your view of socializing outside of work.**

In small groups, discuss your personal relationships at past jobs. How were friendships and romantic relationships perceived at the office? In what ways did you benefit from your relationships at work, and in what ways did they cause problems on the job? Consider any ramifications from social media. What, if anything, would you do differently in a future job?

CHAPTER SUMMARY

LO1 Provide a response to a behavioral interview question in the "STAR" format.

For a successful interview, prepare by researching the company so you can ask good questions. Also practice responding to questions asked in different types of interviews: standard, behavioral, case, and stress. For behavioral interviews, which are most common, give specific examples from your experience in the STAR (situation/task, action, result) format.

LO2 Describe ways to make a good first impression during a job interview.

An interview is your chance to demonstrate your character and personality. Avoid giving the company reason to disqualify you. Instead, demonstrate confidence in your qualifications for the job. Prepare well when you are scheduled for a video interview or to meet with multiple interviewers.

LO3 Write a thank-you email for a given job offer.

After an interview, evaluate your performance and your view of the company so you can do better the next time. Write a personalized thank-you note and consider following up if you do not hear from the employer within the time frame promised. Try to handle disappointment gracefully, knowing that everyone gets rejected from some jobs.

LO4 Write an email to decline a job offer.

Consider negotiating a job offer to address aspects of the compensation and benefits that are important to you and where the employer might have flexibility. If you're fortunate enough to have multiple opportunities, decline other offers when you decide a position isn't right for you. As a hiring manager, turn down candidates gently, just as you would like to be treated.

LO5 List behaviors that describe professionalism.

Demonstrating professionalism depends on the company and working environment. Be an active observer of how others behave and follow etiquette guidelines for meeting people, sharing meals, and exchanging gifts. It's natural to develop personal relationships at work. However, be careful about how those relationships might affect you negatively back at the office.

Endnotes

1. Anonymous Interview Candidate in Dublin, "Account Manager Interview," Glassdoor, July 21, 2021, www.glassdoor.com/Interview/Google-Account-Manager-Interview-Questions-EI_IE90,79.0,6_KO7,22.htm, accessed July 27, 2021.
2. "Our Hiring Process," Google website, https://careers.google.com/how-we-hire/, accessed July 27, 2021.
3. Anonymous Interview Candidate, "Product Manager Interview," Glassdoor, July 18, 2021, www.glassdoor.com/Interview/Google-Product-Manager-Interview-Questions-EI_IE9079.0,6_KO7,22.htm, accessed July 27, 2021.
4. Kindra Cooper, "Google Interview Process + Interview Questions," Candor, July 19, 2020, https://candor.co/articles/interview-prep/google-interview-process-interview-questions, accessed July 27, 2021.
5. Tom Popomaronis, "Here's How Many Google Interviews It Takes to Hire a Googler," CNBC, April 17, 2019, www.cnbc.com/2019/04/17/heres-how-many-google-job-interviews-it-takes-to-hire-a-googler.html, accessed July 27, 2021.
6. Julia Levashina et al., "The Structured Employment Interview: Narrative and Quantitative Review of the Research Literature," *Personnel Psychology* 67 (2014): 241–293, https://doi.org/10.1111/peps.12052.
7. Karl L. Smart and Jerry DiMaria, "Using Storytelling as a Job-Search Strategy," *Business and Professional Communication Quarterly* 81 (2018): 185–198.
8. "A Guide to Conducting Behavioral Interviews with Early Career Job Candidates," Society for Human Resources Management, www.shrm.org/LearningAndCareer/learning/Documents/Behavioral%20Interviewing%20Guide%20for%20Early%20Career%20Candidates.pdf, accessed July 28, 2021.
9. "Video: Consultant Mock Interview," Bain & Company Website, www.bain.com/careers/interview-prep/case-interview/cons-video/, accessed July 28, 2021.
10. "Transforming a National Education System," McKinsey & Company, Practice Case, www.mckinsey.com/careers/interviewing/national-education, accessed September 15, 2021.
11. "2020 Recruiter Nation Survey," Jobvite, www.jobvite.com/lp/2020-recruiter-nation-survey, accessed July 22, 2021.
12. Rachel Premack and Shana Lebowitz, "Science Says People Decide These 12 Things Within Seconds of Meeting You," Business Insider, April 24, 2019, www.businessinsider.com/science-of-first-impressions-2015-2, accessed July 29, 2021.
13. "2020 Recruiter Nation Survey," p. 18.
14. Paraphrased from a Cornell University recruiter, Ithaca, NY, in-person conversation circa 2017. A similar quote is often attributed to Maya Angelou; however, the original author appears to be Richard Evans. See "They May Forget What You Said, But They Will Never Forget How You Made Them Feel," Quote Investigator, https://quoteinvestigator.com/2014/04/06/they-feel, accessed September 28, 2021.
15. "2020 Recruiter Nation Survey," p. 11.
16. "2020 Recruiter Nation Survey," p. 11.
17. Kenneth T. Rocker, Christopher Bell, and Stephanie Kelly, "Online Interviews," in Stephanie Kelly (ed.), *Computer-Mediated Communication for Business: Theory and Practice* (Newcastle upon Tyne: Cambridge Scholars Publishing, 2019), p. 112.
18. "Tips for Facing Your Virtual Interview," HireVue, www.hirevue.com/candidates/interview-tips, accessed September 16, 2021.
19. "A Little Thanks Goes a Long Way," Robert Half Talent Solutions, November 17, 2017, www.roberthalf.com/blog/job-interview-tips/a-little-thanks-goes-a-long-way, accessed July 31, 2021.
20. "A Little Thanks Goes a Long Way."
21. Jenny Taitz, "Honest Communication in the Age of Ghosting," *The Wall Street Journal*, August 21, 2021, www.wsj.com/articles/honest-communication-in-the-age-of-ghosting-11630070801, accessed September 17, 2021.
22. Andrew Deichler, "How to Negotiate Salary as a Recent Graduate," SHRM, www.shrm.org/membership/student-resources/pages/recent-graduate-salary-negotiation.aspx, accessed August 1, 2021.
23. "How to Negotiate Salary: Tips for Recent College Graduates," Robert Half Talent Solutions, June 13, 2018, www.roberthalf.com/blog/salaries-and-skills/salary-negotiation-tips-for-recent-college-graduates, accessed August 1, 2021.
24. NACE Staff, "Teach Students to Understand Their Value, Negotiate Salaries to Overcome the Gender Pay Gap," NACE, August 3, 2016, www.naceweb.org/job-market/compensation/teach-students-to-understand-their-value-negotiate-salaries-to-overcome-the-gender-pay-gap/, accessed August 1, 2021.
25. NACE.
26. "Gender Pay-Gap: Women Undervalue Their Own Contributions, Study Finds," BV.World, July 12, 2018, https://bv.world/corporate-finance/2018/07/gender-pay-gap-women-undervalue-their-own-contributions-study-finds/, accessed August 1, 2021.
27. Svati Kirsten Narula, "How Much Money Do Millennials Make? It's No Longer a Taboo Question," *The Wall Street Journal*, May 3, 2021, www.wsj.com/articles/how-money-much-do-millennials-make-theyre-more-than-happy-to-tell-you-11620061103, accessed August 1, 2021.
28. Kristin Wong, "Want to Close the Pay Gap? Pay Transparency Will Help," *The New York Times*, January 20, 2019, www.nytimes.com/2019/01/20/smarter-living/pay-wage-gap-salary-secrecy-transparency.html, accessed August 1, 2021.
29. "What Should an Employer Tell a Candidate Who Is Not Selected for the Position?" SHRM, www.shrm.org/ResourcesAndTools/tools-and-samples/hr-qa/Pages/whatshouldanemployertellarejectedcandidate.aspx, accessed March 21, 2021.

30. "What Should an Employer Tell a Candidate Who is Not Selected for the Position?"

31. Adapted from Robin Madell, "What to Say When Negotiating Salary in a Job Offer," U.S. News, Money, February 12, 2021, https://money.usnews.com/money/blogs/outside-voices-careers/articles/the-exact-words-to-use-when-negotiating-salary-in-a-job-offer, accessed September 17, 2021.

32. "How to Negotiate Salary: Tips for Recent College Graduates."

33. "What Should an Employer Tell a Candidate Who is Not Selected for the Position?"

34. "Candidate Rejection Letter—Position Filled," www.shrm.org/resourcesandtools/tools-and-samples/hr-forms/pages/interview_rejectionletter-positionfilled.aspx, accessed March 21, 2021.

35. "What Is Career Readiness?" National Association of Colleges and Employers, Revised 2020, www.naceweb.org/career-readiness/competencies/career-readiness-defined/, accessed August 2, 2021.

36. "What Is Career Readiness?"

37. "What Is Career Readiness?"

38. Sarah Kessler, "Will Remote Workers Get Left Behind in the Hybrid Office?" *The New York Times*, August 5, 2021, www.nytimes.com/2021/08/05/business/dealbook/remote-work-bias.html, accessed September 17, 2021.

39. J.D. Vance, *Hillbilly Elegy* (New York: HarperCollins, 2016), p. 212.

40. Libby Wells, "Tipping Do's and Don'ts: When and How Much to Tip in Every Situation," Bankrate, December 7, 2020, www.bankrate.com/personal-finance/smart-money/a-cheat-sheet-on-tipping-dos-and-donts, accessed September 17, 2021.

Reference Manual

Section A

Section B

Section C

Section D

A Language Arts Basics

Lab 1: Parts of Speech

We use words, of course, to communicate. Of the hundreds of thousands of words in an unabridged dictionary, each can be classified as one of just eight parts of speech: noun, pronoun, verb, adjective, adverb, preposition, conjunction, or interjection. These eight parts of speech are illustrated in the sentence below:

Interjection Pronoun Adverb Verb Preposition Adjective Noun Conjunction Noun

Oh, I eagerly waited for new computers and printers.

Many words can act as different parts of speech, depending on how they are used in a sentence. (A *sentence* is a group of words that contains a subject and predicate and that expresses a complete thought.)

Consider, for example, the different parts of speech played by the word *following*:

We agree to do the *following. (noun)*

I was only *following* orders. *(verb)*

We met the *following* day. *(adjective)*

Following his remarks, he sat down. *(preposition)*

Not all words serve more than one function, but many do. Following is a brief introduction to the eight parts of speech.

1.1 Nouns A *noun* is a word that names something—for example, a person, place, thing, or idea:

Person:	employee, Mr. Watkins
Place:	office, Chicago
Thing:	animal, computer
Idea:	concentration, impatience, week, typing

The words in italics in the following sentences are all nouns.

Olaf promoted his *idea* to the *vice president* on *Wednesday*.

Problem solving is just one of the *skills* you'll need as an *intern*.

How much does one *quart* of *water* weigh on our bathroom *scale*?

The animal *doctor* treated my *animal* well in *Houston*.

If you were asked to give an example of a noun, you would probably think of a *concrete noun*—that is, a *physical* object that you can see, hear, feel, taste, or smell. An *abstract noun,* on the other hand, names a quality or concept and not something physical.

Concrete Noun	Abstract Noun
book	success
stapler	patience
computer	skills
dictionary	character

A *common noun*, as its name suggests, is the name of a *general* person, place, thing, or idea. If you want to give the name of a *specific* person, place, thing, or idea, you would use a *proper noun*. Proper nouns are always capitalized.

Common Noun	Proper Noun
man	Rodolfo Escobar
city	Los Angeles
car	Corvette
religion	Judaism

A *singular noun* names one person, place, thing, or idea. A *plural noun* names more than one.

Singular Noun	Plural Noun
Smith	Smiths
watch	watches
computer	computers
victory	victories

1.2 Pronouns A *pronoun* is a word used in place of a noun. Consider the following sentence:

> *Anna* went to *Anna's* kitchen and made *Anna's* favorite dessert because *Anna* was going to a party with *Anna's* friends.

The noun *Anna* is used five times in this awkward sentence. A smoother, less monotonous version of the sentence substitutes pronouns for all but the first *Anna*:

> Anna went to *her* kitchen and made *her* favorite dessert because *she* was going to a party with *her* friends.

The words in italics in the following sentences are pronouns. The nouns to which they refer are underlined:

> <u>Angélica</u> thought *she* might get the promotion.
>
> *None* of the <u>speakers</u> were interesting.
>
> <u>Juan</u> forgot to bring *his* slides.

1.3 Verbs A *verb* is a word (or group of words) that expresses either action or a state of being. The first kind of verb is called an *action verb*; the second kind is known as a *linking verb*. Without a verb, you have no sentence because the verb makes a statement about the subject.

Most verbs express action of some sort—either physical or mental—as indicated by the words in italics in the following sentences:

Iram *planted* his garden while Lian *pulled* weeds.

I *solved* my problems as I *baked* bread.

Jeremy *decided* he should *call* a meeting.

A small (but important) group of verbs do not express action. Instead, they simply link the subject with words that describe it. The most common linking verbs are forms of the verb *to be*, such as *is*, *am*, *are*, *was*, *were*, and *will*. Other forms of linking verbs involve the senses, such as *feels*, *looks*, *smells*, *sounds*, and *tastes*. The following words in italics are verbs (note that verbs can comprise one or more words):

Rosemary *was* angry because Shantel *looked* impatient.

If Franz *is having* a party, I *should have been* invited.

Jason *had* already *seen* the report.

1.4 Adjectives You can make sentences consisting of only nouns or pronouns and verbs (such as "Dogs bark."), but most of the time you'll need to add other parts of speech to make the meaning of the sentence clearer or more complete. An *adjective* is a word that modifies a noun or pronoun. Adjectives answer questions about the nouns or pronouns they describe, such as *how many?*, *what kind?*, and *which one?* (*Articles* are a special group of adjectives that include the words *a*, *an*, and *the*.)

As shown by the words in italics in the following sentences, adjectives may come before or after the nouns or pronouns they modify:

Seventeen applicants took the *typing* test.

The interview was *short*, but *comprehensive*.

She took the *last* plane and landed at a *small Mexican* airport.

1.5 Adverbs An *adverb* is a word that modifies a verb (usually), an adjective, or another adverb. Adverbs often answer the questions *when?*, *where?*, *how?*, or *to what extent?* The words in italics in the following sentences are adverbs:

Please perform the procedure *now. (When?)*

Put the papers *here. (Where?)*

Alice performed *brilliantly. (How?)*

I am *almost* finished. *(To what extent?)*

The *exceedingly* expensive car was *very carefully* protected.

In the last sentence, the adverb *exceedingly* modifies the adjective *expensive* (how expensive?) and the adverb *very* modifies the adverb *carefully* (how carefully?).

Many (but by no means all) adverbs end in *-ly*, such as *loudly*, *quickly*, *really*, and *carefully*. However, not all words that end in *-ly* are adverbs; for example, *friendly*, *stately*, and *ugly* are all adjectives.

1.6 Prepositions A *preposition* is a word (such as *to*, *for*, *from*, *of*, and *with*) that shows the relationship between a noun or pronoun and some other word in the sentence. The noun or pronoun following the preposition is called the *object* of the preposition, and the entire group of words is called a *prepositional phrase*. In the following sentences, the preposition is shown in italics; the entire prepositional phrase is underlined:

The ceremony occurred *on* the covered bridge.

The ceremony occurred *under* the covered bridge.

Lucia talked *with* Mr. Hines.

Lucia talked *about* Mr. Hines.

1.7 Conjunctions A *conjunction* is a word (such as *and*, *or*, and *but*) that joins words or groups of words. For example, in the sentence "Ari and Alice are brokers," the conjunction *and* connects the two nouns *Ari* and *Alice*. In the following sentences, the conjunction is shown in italics; the words it joins are underlined:

Francesca *or* Teresa will attend the conference. *(joins two nouns)*

Chang spoke quietly *and* deliberately. *(joins two adverbs)*

Tamika tripped *but* caught her balance. *(joins two verbs)*

1.8 Interjections An *interjection* is a word that expresses strong emotions. Interjections are used more often in oral communication than in written communication. If an interjection stands alone, it is followed by a period (for a mild emotion) or an exclamation point (to express a stronger emotion). If an interjection is a part of the sentence, it is followed by a comma. Some words can serve as interjections in some sentences and as other parts of speech in other sentences. In the following sentences, the interjection is shown in italics:

Good! I'm glad to learn that the new employee does good work.

Oh. I didn't realize this is your first job.

Um, I wouldn't do that.

Yikes, that was an exhausting exercise. *Whew!*

Application

Directions Label each part of speech in Sentences 1–8 with the abbreviation shown below.

adjective	*adj.*
adverb	*adv.*
conjunction	*conj.*
interjection	*interj.*
noun	*n.*
preposition	*prep.*
pronoun	*pron.*
verb	*v.*

1. Oh, don't tell me I missed my flight.
2. My, your new chair is comfortable.
3. When I received your package, I was relieved. Whew!
4. Gosh! I could not believe the depth of the raging water in the river.

5. When the quail and her chicks came into the yard, the hen carefully checked the area for predators.
6. Alas! By the time he received her report, the decision had been made.
7. I was disappointed we missed your input to the decision-making process.
8. Valerie Renoir, the major conference speaker, was delayed at O'Hare and did not arrive at the hall until 2:00 p.m.

Lab 2: Punctuation—Commas

Punctuation serves as a roadmap to help guide the reader through the twists and turns of your message—pointing out what is important (italics or underlines), subordinate (commas), copied from another source (quotation marks), explained further (colon), considered as a unit (hyphens), and so on. Sometimes correct punctuation is absolutely essential for comprehension. Consider, for example, the different meanings of the following sentences, depending on the punctuation:

What's the latest, dope?
What's the latest dope?

The social secretary called the guests names as they arrived.
The social secretary called the guests' names as they arrived.

Our new model comes in red, green and brown, and white.
Our new model comes in red, green, and brown and white.

The play ended, happily.
The play ended happily.

A clever dog knows it's master.
A clever dog knows its master.

We must still play Michigan, which tied Ohio State, and Minnesota.
We must still play Michigan, which tied Ohio State and Minnesota.

"Medics Help Dog Bite Victim"
"Medics Help Dog-Bite Victim"

The comma rules presented in Lab 2 and the other punctuation rules presented in Lab 3 do not cover every possible situation. These 11 comma rules cover the most frequent uses of punctuation in business writing.

Commas are used to connect ideas and to set off elements within a sentence. Many writers use commas inappropriately. No matter how long the sentence, make sure you have a legitimate reason before inserting a comma.

Commas Used *Between* Expressions

Three types of expressions (an expression is words or groups of words) typically require commas between them: independent clauses, adjacent adjectives, and items in a series.

, ind **2.1 Independent Clauses** Use a comma between two independent clauses joined by a coordinate conjunction (unless both clauses are short and closely related).

Calvin discussed last month's performance, and Aditi presented the sales projections.

The meeting was running late, but Emma was in no hurry to leave.

But: The firm hadn't paid and Valentina was angry.

The major coordinate conjunctions are *and*, *but*, *or*, and *nor*. An independent clause is a subject–predicate combination that can stand alone as a complete sentence.

Don't confuse two independent clauses joined by a coordinate conjunction and a comma with a compound predicate, whose verbs are not separated by a comma. *Hint:* Cover up the conjunction with your thumb. If what's on both sides of your thumb could stand alone as complete sentences, a comma is needed.

No comma:	Qiang had read the report_but had not discussed it with his team. *("Had not discussed it with his team" is not an independent clause; it lacks a subject.)*
Comma:	Qiang had read the report, but he had not discussed it with his team.

2.2 Adjacent Adjectives Use a comma between two adjacent adjectives that modify the same noun. *, adj*

He was an aggressive, unpleasant manager.

But: He was an aggressive_and unpleasant manager. *(The two adjectives are not adjacent; they are separated by the conjunction "and.")*

Don't use a comma if the first adjective modifies the combined idea of the second adjective plus the noun. *Hint:* Mentally insert the word *and* between the two consecutive adjectives. If it doesn't make sense, don't use a comma.

Please order a new bulletin board for the executive_conference room.

Don't use a comma between the last adjective and the noun.

Wednesday was a long, hot, humid_day.

2.3 Items in a Series Use a comma between each item in a series of three or more. Don't use a comma after the last item in the series. *, ser*

The committee may meet on Wednesday, Thursday, or Friday_of next week.

Carl wrote the questionnaire, Anna distributed the forms, and Jacinto tabulated the results_for our survey on employee satisfaction.

Some style manuals indicate that the last comma before the conjunction is optional. However, to avoid ambiguity in business writing, you should insert this comma.

Not: We were served salads, macaroni and cheese and crackers.

But: We were served salads, macaroni and cheese, and crackers.

Or: We were served salads, macaroni, and cheese and crackers.

Commas Used *After* Expressions

Two types of expressions typically require commas after them: introductory expressions and complimentary closings in letters.

2.4 Introductory Expressions Use a comma after an introductory expression. An *introductory expression* is a word, phrase, or clause that comes before the subject and verb of the independent clause. When the same expression occurs at the end of the sentence, no comma is used. *, intro*

No, the status report is not ready. *(introductory word)*

Of course, you are not required to sign the petition. *(introductory phrase)*

When the status report is ready, I will call you. *(introductory clause)*

But: I will call you when the status report is ready.

Don't use a comma between the subject and verb—no matter how long or complex the subject is.

To finish that boring and time-consuming task in time for the monthly sales meeting_was a major challenge.

The effort to bring all our products into compliance with ISO standards and to be eligible to sell in Europe_required a full year of detailed planning.

, clos **2.5 Complimentary Closing** Use a comma after the complimentary closing in a letter or email.

Sincerely,	All the best,
Yours truly,	With warm regards,

Commas Used *Before* and *After* Expressions

Many types of expressions typically require commas before *and* after them. Of course, if the expression comes at the beginning of a sentence, use a comma only after the expression; if it comes at the end of a sentence, use a comma only before it.

, nonr **2.6 Nonrestrictive Expressions** Use commas before and after a nonrestrictive expression. A *restrictive expression* is one that limits (restricts) the meaning of the noun or pronoun that it follows and is, therefore, essential to complete the basic meaning of the sentence. A *nonrestrictive expression*, on the other hand, may be omitted without changing the basic meaning of the sentence.

Restrictive:	Anyone *with some experience* should apply for the position. ("With some experience" restricts which "anyone" should apply.)
Nonrestrictive:	Anne Suárez, *a clerk with extensive experience*, should apply for the position. (Because Anne Suárez can be only one person, the phrase "a clerk with extensive experience" does not serve to further restrict the noun and is, therefore, not essential to the meaning of the sentence.)
Restrictive:	Only the papers *left on the conference table* are missing. (identifies which papers are missing)
Nonrestrictive:	Lever Brothers, *one of our best customers*, is expanding in Europe. ("One of our best customers" could be omitted without changing the basic meaning of the sentence.)
Restrictive:	The manager *using a great deal of tact* was Ellis.
Nonrestrictive:	Ellis, *using a great deal of tact*, disagreed with her.

An *appositive* is a noun or noun phrase that identifies another noun or pronoun that comes immediately before it. If the appositive is nonrestrictive, insert commas before and after the appositive.

Restrictive:	The word *plagiarism* strikes fear into the heart of many. ("Plagiarism" is an appositive that identifies which word.)
Nonrestrictive:	Mr. Bayrami, *president of the corporation*, is planning to resign. ("President of the corporation" is an appositive that provides additional, but nonessential, information about Mr. Bayrami.)

2.7 Interrupting Expressions Use commas before and after an interrupting expression. An *interrupting expression* breaks the normal flow of a sentence. Common examples are *in addition*, *as a result*, *therefore*, *in summary*, *on the other hand*, *however*, *unfortunately*, and *as a matter of fact*—when these expressions come in the middle of the sentence. *, inter*

You may, of course, cancel your subscription at any time.

One suggestion, for example, was to consider a leveraged buyout.

Ebay offers more services, however, charges higher fees.

You could, I think, ask for an extension.

Aida's present salary, you must admit, is not in line with those of other network managers.

But: You must admit_Aida's present salary is not in line with those of other network managers.

If the expression does not interrupt the normal flow of the sentence, don't use a comma.

There is no doubt that you are qualified for the position.

But: There is, no doubt, a good explanation for his actions.

2.8 Dates Use commas before and after the year when it follows the month and day. Don't use a comma after a partial date or when the date is formatted in day-month-year order. If the name of the day precedes the date, also use a comma *after* the name of the day. *, date*

The note is due on May 31, 2027, at 5:00 p.m.

But: The note is due on May 31 at 5:00 p.m.

But: The note is due in May 2027.

But: The note is due on 31 May 2027 at 5:00 p.m.

Let's plan to meet on Wednesday, December 15, 2027, for our year-end review.

2.9 Places Use commas before and after a state or country that follows a city and between elements of an address in narrative writing. *, place*

The sales conference will be held in Phoenix, Arizona, in May.

Our business agent is located in Brussels, Belgium, in the P.O.M. Building.

You may contact her at 500 Beaufort Drive, LaCrosse, VA 23950. *(Note that there is no comma between the state abbreviation and the zip code.)*

, dir ad **2.10 Direct Address** Use commas before and after a name used in direct address. A name is used in *direct address* when the writer speaks directly to (i.e., directly addresses) another person.

Thank you, Dr. Zhao, for bringing the matter to our attention.

Ladies and gentlemen, we appreciate your attending our session today.

, quote **2.11 Direct Quotation** Use commas before and after a direct quotation in a sentence.

The president said, "You have nothing to fear," and then changed the subject.

"I assure you," the human resources director said, "that no positions will be terminated."

If the quotation is a question, use a question mark instead of a comma.

"How many have applied?" she asked.

Application

Directions Insert any needed commas in the following sentences. Above each comma, indicate the reason for the comma. If the sentence needs no commas, leave it blank.

Example: As a matter of fact, *(intro)* you may tell her yourself.

1. A comma comes between two adjacent adjectives that modify the same noun but don't use a comma if the first adjective modifies the combined idea of the second adjective and the noun.
2. Steven generated questions and I supplied responses.
3. At the request of your accountant we are summarizing all charitable deductions in a new format.
4. By asking the right questions we gained all the pertinent information we needed.
5. Everyone please use the door in the rear of the hall.
6. His bid for the congressional seat was successful this time.
7. I disagree with Ariana but do feel some change in policy is needed.
8. I feel as a matter of fact that the proposed legislation will fall short of the required votes.
9. Ethan will prepare the presentation graphics and let you know when they are ready.
10. Determining purpose analyzing the audience and making content and organization decisions are critical planning steps.
11. It is appropriate I believe to make a preliminary announcement about the new position.
12. A goodwill message is prompt direct sincere specific and brief.
13. Look this decision affects me as much as it does you.
14. The teacher using one of her favorite techniques prompted the student into action.
15. Subordinate bad news by using the direct plan by avoiding negative terms and by presenting the news after the reasons are given.
16. My favorite destination is Atlanta Georgia.
17. The team presented a well-planned logical scenario to explain the company's status.
18. Evan plans to conclude his investigation and explain the results by Friday but would not promise a written report until Tuesday.
19. We appreciate your business.

    Sincerely
    Medea Haddad

20. Those instructors who were from southern schools were anxious to see the results of the study completed in Birmingham.
21. A group of teachers from Michigan attended the conference this year.
22. Our next training session will be located in Madison Wisconsin sometime in the spring.
23. The next meeting of our professional organization will be held in the winter not in the spring.
24. The brochure states "Satisfaction is guaranteed or your money will be freely refunded."
25. The department meeting you will note will be held every other Monday.
26. This assignment is due on April 20 which is one week before the end of the semester.
27. I need the cabinets installed by the week before my family arrives.
28. To qualify for promotion will require recommendations and long hours of preparation.
29. To qualify for promotion you will need recommendations from previous managers.
30. To earn an award for outstanding sales is an achievable goal for Mary.
31. To earn an award for outstanding sales Mary must set intermittent goals that are attainable.
32. Dave was promoted in his job by working hard.
33. Shayna's sister was born on June 6 2014, in Munster Indiana.
34. Ted could paint the house himself or he could hire a professional to do the job.
35. I am telling you Tyrell that your report has been misplaced.

Lab 3: Punctuation—Other Marks

Hyphens

Hyphens are used to form some compound adjectives, to link some prefixes to root words (such as *quasi-public*), and to divide words at the ends of lines. When typing, don't leave a space before or after a regular hyphen. Likewise, don't use a hyphen with a space before and after to substitute for a dash. Make a dash by typing two hyphens with no space before, between, or after. Most software programs automatically reformat two hyphens into a dash.

3.1 Compound Adjective Hyphenate a compound adjective that comes *before* a noun (unless the adjective is a proper noun or unless the first word is an adverb ending in *-ly*). *-adj*

We hired a first-class management team.

But: Our new management team is first_class.

The long-term outlook for our investments is excellent.

But: We intend to hold our investments for the long_term.

But: The General_Motors warranty received high ratings.

But: Huang presented a poorly_conceived proposal.

Note: Don't confuse compound adjectives (which are generally temporary combinations) with compound nouns (which are generally well-established concepts). Compound nouns (such as *Social Security*, *life insurance*, *washing machine*, and *high school*) are not hyphenated when used as adjectives that come before a noun; thus, use *income_tax form*, *real_estate agent*, *public_relations firm*, and *data_processing center*.

-num **3.2 Numbers** Hyphenate fractions and compound numbers 21 through 99 when they are spelled out.

Nearly three-fourths of our new applicants were unqualified.

Seventy-two orders were processed incorrectly last week.

Semicolons

Semicolons are used to show where elements in a sentence are separated. The separation is stronger than a comma but not as strong as a period. When typing, leave one space after a semicolon and begin the following word with a lowercase letter.

; comma **3.3 Independent Clauses with Commas** If a misreading might otherwise occur, use a semicolon (instead of a comma) to separate independent clauses that contain internal commas. Make sure that the semicolon is inserted *between* the independent clauses, not *within* one of the clauses.

Confusing: I ordered juice, toast, and bacon, and eggs, toast, and sausage were sent instead.

Clear: I ordered juice, toast, and bacon; eggs, toast, and sausage were sent instead.

But: Although high-quality paper was used, the copier still jammed, and neither of us knew how to repair it. *(no misreading likely to occur)*

; no conj **3.4 Independent Clauses Without a Conjunction** Use a semicolon between independent clauses that are not connected by a coordinate conjunction (such as *and*, *but*, *or*, and *nor*). You have already learned to use a comma before coordinate conjunctions when they connect independent clauses. This rule applies to independent clauses *not* connected by a conjunction.

The president was eager to proceed with the plans; the board still had some reservations.

But: The president was eager to proceed with the plans, but the board still had some reservations. *(Use a comma instead of a semicolon if the clauses are joined by a coordinate conjunction.)*

Bannon Corporation exceeded its sales goal this quarter; furthermore, it rang up its highest net profit ever.

But: Bannon Corporation exceeded its sales goal this quarter, and furthermore, it rang up its highest net profit ever. *(Use a comma instead of a semicolon if the clauses are joined by a coordinate conjunction.)*

; ser **3.5 Series with Internal Commas** Use a semicolon after each item in a series if any of the items already contain a comma. Normally, we separate items in a series with commas. However, if any of those items already contain a comma, we need a stronger mark (semicolon) between the items.

The human resources department will hold interviews in Dallas, Texas; Stillwater, Oklahoma; and Little Rock, Arkansas, for the new position.

Among the guests were Henry Halston, our attorney; Phaedra Hart Wilder; and Isabella Grimes, our new controller.

Colons

A colon is used after an independent clause that introduces explanatory material and after the salutation of a business letter that uses the standard punctuation style. When typing, leave one space after a colon; don't begin the following word with a capital letter unless it begins a quoted sentence.

3.6 Explanatory Material Use a colon to introduce explanatory material that is preceded by an independent clause. *:exp*

His directions were as follows: turn right and proceed to the third house on the left.

I now have openings on the following dates: January 18, 19, and 20.

Just remember this: you may need a reference from her in the future.

The fall trade show offers the following advantages: inexpensive show space, abundant traffic, and free press publicity.

Expressions commonly used to introduce explanatory material are *the following*, *as follows*, *this*, and *these*. Make sure the clause preceding the explanatory material can stand alone as a complete sentence. Don't place a colon after a verb or a preposition that introduces a list.

☒ NOT My responsibilities were: opening the mail, sorting it, and delivering it to each department.

☑ BUT My responsibilities were opening the mail, sorting it, and delivering it to each department.

3.7 Salutations Use a colon after the salutation of a business letter. *:salut*

Dear Hwan Jeong: Dear Human Resources Manager: Dear Ruben:

In an email, a comma follows the salutation.

Apostrophes

Apostrophes are used to show that letters have been omitted (as in contractions) and to show possession. When typing, do not space before or after an apostrophe (unless a space after is needed before another word).

Remember this helpful hint: whenever a noun ending in *s* is followed by another noun, the first noun is probably a possessive, requiring an apostrophe. However, if the first noun *describes* rather than establishes ownership, no apostrophe is used.

Bernie's department *(shows ownership; therefore, an apostrophe)*

the sales department *(describes; therefore, no apostrophe)*

3.8 Singular Nouns To form the possessive of a singular noun, add an apostrophe plus *s*. *'sing*

my accountant's fee	a child's toy
the company's stock	Eva's choice
Alzheimer's disease	Akira's home
a year's time	the boss's contract
Morris's office	Liz's promotion
Gil Hodges's record	Carl Bissett Jr.'s birthday

'plur + s **3.9 Plural Nouns Ending in *s*** To form the possessive of a plural noun that ends in *s* (i.e., most plural nouns), add an apostrophe only.

our accountants' fees — both companies' stock

the Dyes' home — two years' time

'plur – s **3.10 Plural Nouns Not Ending in *s*** To form the possessive of a plural noun that does not end in *s*, add an apostrophe plus *s* (just as you would for singular nouns).

the children's hour — the men's room

the alumni's contribution

Hint: To avoid confusion in forming the possessive of plural nouns, first form the plural then apply the appropriate rule.

Singular	**Plural**	**Plural Possessive**
employee	employees	employees' bonuses
hero	heroes	heroes' welcome
Mr. and Mrs. Lake	the Lakes	the Lakes' home
woman	women	women's clothing

'pro **3.11 Pronouns** To form the possessive of an indefinite pronoun, add an apostrophe plus *s*. Don't use an apostrophe to form the possessive of personal pronouns.

It is *someone's* responsibility.

But: The responsibility is *theirs*.

I will review *everybody's* figures.

But: The bank will review *its* figures.

Note: Examples of indefinite possessive pronouns are *anybody's*, *everyone's*, *no one's*, *nobody's*, *one's*, and *somebody's*. Examples of personal possessive pronouns are *hers*, *his*, *its*, *ours*, *theirs*, and *yours*. Don't confuse the possessive pronouns *its*, *theirs*, and *whose* with the contractions *it's*, *there's*, and *who's*.

It's time to put litter in *its* place.

There's no reason to take *theirs*.

Who's determining *whose* jobs will be eliminated?

'ger **3.12 Gerunds** Use the possessive form for a noun or pronoun that comes before a gerund. (A gerund is the *-ing* form of a verb used as a noun.)

Garth questioned *Karen's* leaving so soon.

Stockholders' raising so many questions delayed the adjournment.

Mr. Matsumoto knew Karl and objected to *his* going to the meeting.

Periods

Periods are used at the ends of declarative sentences and in abbreviations. When typing, leave one space after a period (or any other punctuation mark).

Quotation Marks

Quotation marks are used around direct quotations, article and episode titles, and special terms. Type the closing quotation mark after a period or comma but before a colon or semicolon. Type the closing quotation mark after a question mark or exclamation point if the quoted material itself is a question or an exclamation; otherwise, type it before the question mark or exclamation. Capitalize the first word of a quotation that begins a sentence.

3.13 Direct Quotation Use quotation marks around a direct quotation—that is, around the exact words someone said. "quote

"When we return on Thursday," Luis said, "we need to meet with you."

But: Luis said that when we return on Thursday, we need to meet with you. *(no quotation marks needed in an indirect quotation)*

Did Helen say, "He will represent us"?

Helen asked, "Will he represent us?"

3.14 Term Use quotation marks around a term to clarify its meaning or to show that it is being used in a special way. "term

Net income after taxes is known as "the bottom line"; that's what's important around here.

The job title changed from "chairman" to "chief executive officer."

The president misused the word "effect" in last night's press conference.

3.15 Title Use quotation marks around the title of a newspaper or magazine article, program episode, chapter in a book, report, conference, and similar items. "title

Read the article titled "Wall Street Recovery."

Chapter 4, "Market Segmentation," of *Industrial Marketing* is of special interest.

Did you watch the "The One After the Superbowl," the most-watched *Friends* episode?

The report "Common Carriers" shows the extent of the transportation problems.

Note: The titles of *complete* published works are shown in italics (see below). The titles of *parts* of published works and most other titles are enclosed in quotation marks.

Italics

Use italics to emphasize words and for certain titles.

3.16 Titles Italicize the title of a book, magazine, newspaper, and other *complete* published works. Title

Liang's newest book, *All That Glitters*, was reviewed in *The New York Times* and in *The Los Angeles Times*.

The cover story in last week's *Time* magazine was "Is the Economic Expansion Over?"

Ellipses

An ellipsis signals an omission. Three periods, with one space before and after each, are used to show that something has been left out of a quotation. Four periods (the sentence period plus the three ellipsis periods) indicate the omission of the last part of a quoted sentence, the first part of the next sentence, or a whole sentence or paragraph.

3.17 Omission Use ellipsis periods to indicate that one or more words have been omitted from quoted material.

> According to *Bloomberg Businessweek*, "Protests, which have been ongoing since January, could affect the company's IPO planned for March. CEO Melissa Mandel has not addressed the controversy publicly. Company social media accounts make no mention of customer complaints." (*original quote*)

> According to *Bloomberg Businessweek*, "Protests . . . could affect the company's IPO planned for March. CEO Melissa Mandel has not addressed the controversy publicly."

> According to *Bloomberg Businessweek*, "Protests, which have been ongoing since January, could affect the company's IPO planned for March. . . . Company social media accounts make no mention of customer complaints."

Note: The typing sequence for the first ellipsis is *space period space period space period space*. The sequence for the second ellipsis is *period space period space period space period space*.

Application

Directions Insert any needed punctuation (including commas) in the following sentences. Underline any expression that should be italicized. Above each mark of punctuation, indicate the reason for the punctuation. If the sentence needs no punctuation, leave it blank.

Example: We received our money's worth. (*Sing* written above the apostrophe)

1. Bernice tried to use the new software but she had trouble with the computer.
2. Juanita Johnsons raising the expectations for promotion was hotly debated.
3. The short term goal of the department was improvement in software utilization.
4. It was a poorly designed office.
5. Approximately one half of the orders came from Spokane Washington.
6. Bertram preferred soda hamburgers and fries but iced tea, hot dogs and onion rings were served instead.
7. The classes started on time the school was entirely on schedule.
8. Did you meet Sally Henley our manager Paul Krause and Ana Chávez our attorney?
9. Remember this the best recommendation is a job well done.
10. Dear Shondra Kimes
11. Did you get the total from the sales department?
12. Jasons boss will distribute the new guidelines for his department.
13. Within two years time the neighborhood will double in size.
14. Locking the door to the department was someones responsibility.
15. Fabians guiding the discussion was a departure from the usual procedure.
16. Would you please sort these responses for me
17. The teacher said The samples you submitted were excellent.
18. Would you believe he misspelled the word their in his report?
19. The articles titled Technology for Fitness should be required reading
20. Time magazine features a person of the year each December.
21. I want her to know she is a highly respected employee.
22. The meetings date was rescheduled.

23. If the tickets sell we will tell Jon she will take it from there.
24. The hotels guests thought the conference rooms temperatures were too cold.
25. They were watching the demonstration nevertheless they didn't understand.
26. Can we keep this off the record?
27. You will receive the materials tomorrow but stop by today to see Alberto our corporate trainer for a quick preview.
28. I can do this for you either on December 5 2022 or January 13 2023.
29. This is a once in a lifetime opportunity for our employees families.
30. Mr. Henry will see you after the meeting Mr. Perez will not be available.

Lab 4: Grammar

Grammar refers to the rules for combining words into sentences. The most frequent grammar problems faced by business writers are discussed below.

Complete Sentences

4.1 Fragment Avoid sentence fragments.

☒ NOT He had always wanted to be a marketing representative. Because he liked to interact with people.

☑ BUT He had always wanted to be a marketing representative because he liked to interact with people.

Note: A fragment is a part of a sentence that is incorrectly punctuated as a complete sentence. Each sentence must contain a complete thought.

4.2 Run-on Sentences Avoid run-on sentences.

☒ NOT Fidélia Padilla is a hard worker she even frequently works through lunch.

☒ NOT Fidélia Padilla is a hard worker, she even frequently works through lunch.

☑ BUT Fidélia Padilla is a hard worker; she even frequently works through lunch.

☑ BUT Fidélia Padilla is a hard worker. She even frequently works through lunch.

Note: A run-on sentence is two independent clauses run together without any punctuation between them or with only a comma between them (the latter error is called a *comma splice*).

Modifiers (Adjectives and Adverbs)

An adjective modifies a noun or pronoun; an adverb modifies a verb, an adjective, or another adverb.

4.3 Modifiers Use a comparative adjective or adverb (*-er*, *more*, or *less*) to refer to two persons, places, or things and a superlative adjective or adverb (*-est*, *most*, or *least*) to refer to more than two.

The Datascan is the fast**er** of the two machines.

The XR 75 is the slow**est** of all the machines.

Rose Marie is the **less** qualified of the two applicants.

Rose Marie is the **least** qualified of the three applicants.

Note: Don't use double comparisons, such as "more faster."

Agreement (Subject/Verb/Pronoun)

Agreement refers to correspondence in number between related subjects, verbs, and pronouns. All must be singular if they refer to one, plural if they refer to more than one.

4.4 Agreement Use a singular verb or pronoun with a singular subject and a plural verb or pronoun with a plural subject.

The four **workers have** copies of **their** assignments.

Roger's **sister was** quite late for **her** appointment.

Liam and Olivia plan to forgo **their** bonuses.

Included in this envelope **are a contract and an affidavit.**

Note: This is the general rule; variations are discussed below. In the first sentence, the plural subject (*workers*) requires a plural verb (*have*) and a plural pronoun (*their*). In the second sentence, the singular subject (*sister*) requires a singular verb (*was*) and a singular pronoun (*her*). In the third sentence, the plural subject (*Liam and Olivia*) requires a plural verb (*plan*) and a plural pronoun (*their*). In the last sentence, the subject is *a contract and an affidavit*—not *envelope.*

4.5 Company Names Treat company names as singular.

Facebook is declining to comment on the story.

Etsy is in a good position to expand its user base.

4.6 Expletives In sentences that begin with an expletive, the true subject follows the verb. Use *is* or *are*, as appropriate.

There **is** no **reason** for his behavior.

There **are** many **reasons** for his behavior.

Note: An expletive is an expression such as *there is*, *there are*, *here is*, and *here are* that comes at the beginning of a clause or sentence. Try to avoid expletives and use stronger subjects and verbs instead.

4.7 Intervening Words Disregard any words that come between the subject and verb when establishing agreement. See, however, Rule 4.8 regarding special treatment of certain pronouns.

The **appearance** of the workers, not their competence, **was** being questioned.

The **administrative assistant**, as well as the clerks, **was** late filing **her** form. (not *their forms*)

Note: First, determine the subject; then make the verb agree. Other intervening words that don't affect the number of the verb are *together with*, *rather than*, *accompanied by*, *in addition to*, and *except*.

4.8 Pronouns Some pronouns (*anybody, each, either, everybody, everyone, much, neither, no one, nobody*, and *one*) are always singular. Other pronouns (*all, any, more, most, none,* and *some*) may be singular or plural, depending on the noun to which they refer. *They* is increasingly acceptable as a singular pronoun, but you can often avoid it.

☒ NOT **Everybody** is required to take **his or her** turn at the booth. (not *their turn*)

☑ BUT **Everybody** is required to take **a** turn at the booth.

☒ NOT **Each** of the employees **has** a different view of **his or her** job.

☑ BUT Each employee has a different view of the job.

Neither of the models **is** doing **her** job well.

All the **pie has** been eaten.

All the **cookies have** been eaten.

None of the **work is** finished.

None of the **workers are** finished.

4.9 Subject Nearer to Verb If two subjects are joined by correlative conjunctions (*or*, *either/or*, *nor*, *neither/nor*, or *not only/but also*), the verb and any pronoun should agree with the subject that is nearer to the verb.

Either Pablo or **Harold is** at **his** desk.

Neither the receptionist nor the **operators were** able to finish **their** tasks.

Not only the actor but also the **dancer has** to practice **his** routine.

The tellers or the **clerks have** to balance **their** cash drawers before leaving.

Note: The first noun in this type of construction may be disregarded when determining whether the verb should be singular or plural. Note that subjects joined by *and* or *both/and* are always plural: *Both* **the actor and the dancer have** to practice **their** routines.

4.10 Subjunctive Mood Verbs in the subjunctive mood require the plural form, even when the subject is singular.

I wish the situation **were** reversed.

If I **were** you, I would not mention the matter.

Note: Verbs in the subjunctive mood refer to conditions that are impossible or improbable.

Case

Case refers to the form of a pronoun and indicates its use in a sentence. The three cases are nominative, objective, and possessive. (Possessive case pronouns are covered under "Apostrophes" in the section on punctuation in Lab 3.) Reflexive pronouns, which end in *self* or *selves*, refer to nouns or other pronouns.

4.11 Nominative Case Use nominative pronouns (*I*, *he*, *she*, *we*, *they*, *who*, *whoever*) as subjects of a sentence or clause and with the verb *to be*.

The customer representative and **he** are furnishing the figures. (***he** is furnishing*)

Dr. Quigley asked if Oscar and **I** were ready to begin. (***I** was ready to begin*)

We old-timers can provide some background. (***we** can provide*)

It was **she** who agreed to the proposal. (***she** agreed*)

Who is chairing the meeting? (***he** is chairing*)

Elijah wanted to know **who** was responsible. (***she** was responsible*)

Mia is the type of person **who** can be depended on. (***she** can be depended on*)

Note: If you have trouble determining which pronoun to use, ignore the plural subject or substitute another pronoun. See the reworded clauses in parentheses.

4.12 Objective Case Use objective pronouns (*me, him, her, us, them, whom, whomever*) as objects in a sentence, clause, or phrase.

Thomas emailed Noah and **me**. (emailed ***me***)

This policy applies to Eric and **her**. (*applies to* ***her***)

Habib asked **us** old timers to provide some background. (*Habib asked* ***us*** *to provide*)

The work was assigned to **her** and **me.** (*the work was assigned to* ***me***)

To **whom** shall we mail the specifications? (*mail them to* ***him***)

Guadalupe is the type of person **whom** we can depend on. (*we can depend on* ***her***)

Note: For *who/whom* constructions, if *he* or *she* can be substituted, *who* is the correct choice; if *him* or *her* can be substituted, *whom* is the correct choice. Remember: *who he, whom him*. The difference is apparent in the final examples shown here and under "Nominative Case," Rule 4.11: ***who*** *can be depended on* versus ***whom*** *we can depend on*.

4.13 Reflexive Pronouns Use reflexive pronouns (*myself, yourself, himself, herself, itself, ourselves, yourselves*, or *themselves*) to refer to or emphasize a noun or pronoun *that has already been named*. Don't use reflexive pronouns to *substitute for* nominative or objective pronouns.

I **myself** have some doubts about the proposal.

You should see the exhibit **yourself.**

☒ NOT Virginia and **myself** will take care of the details.

☑ BUT Virginia and **I** will take care of the details.

☒ NOT Maya Louise administered the test to Thomas and **myself**.

☑ BUT Maya Louise administered the test to Thomas and **me.**

Application

Directions Select the correct word or words in parentheses.

1. (Who/Whom) is your favorite new chef? Laura Buraston, who along with Frederico Fox, (are/is) a new chef in Tucson. Some of my friends (has/have) eaten at their restaurants. Laura, they say, is the (better/best) of the two.
2. Merchant Associates is presenting (its/it's/their/there) seminar in Kansas City. The associates will work with seven or eight participants in developing (their/there) portfolios. Not only Dr. Merchant but also his associates (is/are) willing to mentor faculty members. Dr. Merchant asked all participants to acknowledge the invitation with written responses to (he/him).
3. If I (was/were) you, I would be (more/most) helpful with organizing the conference. You can work directly with Sandra and (me/myself). After all, Sandra knows that it was (I/me) (who/whom) made key contacts. This opportunity is open to the type of person (who/whom) we can depend on.
4. The report on sales volume (is/are) finally on my desk. (Us/We) managers may be somewhat apprehensive about these reports, but sales results tend to predict (who/whom) can be depended on.

5. Not only the lawyer but also the manager (was/were) able to attend the conference on ethics. Everybody in the firm (is/are) trying to participate as a way to improve (their/his or her) performance. Each of the employees (is/are) eager to attend the next session.
6. There (was/were) several students in the class (who/whom) challenged whether each of the assignments (was/were) comparable in complexity. The professor asked (us/we) group leaders to evaluate the students' concerns.
7. Neither the professors nor the dean (was/were) able to meet Dr. Phyllis Hart, the conference speaker, at the airport. In fact, neither of the professors (was/were) able to pick her up at the hotel either. However, Dean Dye, as well as two other professors, (is/are) escorting her to the banquet.
8. Martin's and Ricardo's groups are the (more quicker/most quicker/quicker/quickest) in the class. Ricardo's group is the (more slow/most slow/slower/slowest) of these two groups. In any case, all of the jobs (has/have) been submitted for both groups.
9. (Who/Whom) will you ask to participate in the evaluation process? If I (was/were) you, I'd consider Hillary. While Jane is the (more/most) competent software expert we have available, Hillary is the type of team player (who/whom) can provide the leadership we need.
10. I wish it (was/ were) possible for Machiko and (I/me/myself) to see both Marty and Alex in (his/their) last performance this season. Machiko and (I/me/myself) have always had a gathering in our home after they finished. Watching their reactions to the reviewers' comments as they were given (is/are) exciting, but as we are leaving too, it remains to be seen (who/whom) will assume that function next year.

Directions Revise the following paragraph to eliminate any fragments and run on sentences.

FunTimes by Travel Log is a prepaid vacation program designed with families in mind. Club owners have permanent usage rights in a continually growing system of outstanding resorts. Unlike the traditional time-share plans. Members may select any of the club resorts as a destination with optional access to other resorts through exchange programs, the owners may select additional vacation sites, both in the United States and internationally. The membership fee entitles an owner to a fixed number of points each year, up to three years' worth can be accumulated so a selected vacation can be upgraded or lengthened. Future points can be "borrowed" to use on a current vacation. Reservations may be made up to 13 months in advance these features make this plan an economical and flexible way to create family vacation memories.

Lab 5: Mechanics

Writing mechanics refer to those elements in communication that are evident only in written form: abbreviations, capitalization, number expression, spelling, and word division. (Punctuation, also a form of writing mechanics, was covered in Labs 2 and 3.) While creating a first draft, you need not be too concerned about the mechanics of your writing. However, you should be especially alert during the editing and proofreading stages to follow these common rules.

Abbreviations

Use abbreviations according to organizational norms for business writing. Be sure that your audience will understand your abbreviation, or follow the rule "When in doubt, write it out." When typing, do not space within abbreviations except to separate each initial of a person's name. Leave one space after an abbreviation unless another mark of punctuation follows immediately.

5.1 Not Abbreviated In most business writing, don't abbreviate common nouns (such as *acct.*, *assoc.*, *bldg.*, *co.*, *dept.*, *misc.*, and *pkg.*).

5.2 With Periods Use periods to indicate many abbreviations.

8:00 a.m.	4 ft.
P.O. Box 45	e.g.

5.3 Without Periods Write some abbreviations in all capitals, with no periods—including all two-letter state abbreviations used in addresses with zip codes.

CPA	IRS	CT
AI	MBA	OK

Capitalization

The function of capitalization is to emphasize words or to show their importance. For example, the first word of a sentence is capitalized to emphasize that a new sentence has begun.

5.4 Compass Point Capitalize a compass point that designates a definite region or that is part of an official name. (Don't capitalize compass points used as directions.)

Margot lives in the **S**outh.

Our display window faces **w**est.

Is **E**ast Orange in **W**est Virginia?

5.5 Letter Part Capitalize the first word and any proper nouns in the salutation and complimentary closing of a business letter.

Dear **D**r. **F**edorov:	**S**incerely **y**ours,
Dear **M**r. and **M**rs. **A**mes:	**Y**ours **t**ruly,

5.6 Noun Plus Number Capitalize a noun followed by a number or letter (except for page and size numbers).

Table 3	**p**age 79
Flight 1062	**s**ize 8D

5.7 Position Title Capitalize an official position title that comes before a personal name, unless the personal name is an appositive set off by commas. Don't capitalize a position title used alone except, by convention, in employment communications.

Vice **P**resident Alfredo Tenegco	Shirley Wilhite, **d**ean,
our **p**resident, Joanne Rathburn,	The **c**hief **e**xecutive **o**fficer retired.

5.8 Proper Noun Capitalize proper nouns and adjectives derived from proper nouns. Don't capitalize articles, conjunctions, and prepositions typically of four or fewer letters (e.g., *a*, *an*, *the*, *and*, *of*, and *from*). The names of the seasons and the names of generic school courses are not proper nouns and are not capitalized.

Xerox copier	**A**mherst **C**ollege (*but:* the **c**ollege)
New **Y**ork **C**ity (*but:* the **c**ity)	the **M**exican border
the **F**ourth of **J**uly	**F**riday, **M**arch 3,
Chrysler **B**uilding	**B**ank of **A**merica

First **C**lass **S**torage **C**ompany | **M**argaret **A**dams **W**hite

business **c**ommunication | the **w**inter holidays

5.9 Quotation Capitalize the first word of a quoted sentence. (Don't capitalize the first word of an indirect quotation.)

According to Hall, "**T**he goal of quality control is specified uniform quality."

Hall thinks we should work toward "**s**pecified uniform quality."

Hall said that **u**niform quality is the goal.

5.10 Title In a published title, capitalize the first and last words, the first word after a colon or dash, and all other words except articles, conjunctions, and prepositions of four or fewer letters.

"**A** **W**ord to the **W**ise"

*Pricing **S**trategies: **T**he **L**ink with **R**eality*

Numbers

Authorities don't agree on a single style for expressing numbers—whether to spell out a number in words or to write it in figures. The following guidelines apply to typical business writing. When typing numbers in figures, separate thousands, millions, and billions with commas and leave a space between a whole number figure and its fraction unless the fraction is a character on the keyboard or is created automatically by your word processing software.

5.11 General Spell out numbers for zero through ten and use figures for 11 and higher.

the first three pages | ten complaints

18 photocopies | 5,376 stockholders

Note: Follow this rule only when none of the following special rules apply.

5.12 Figures Use figures for the following:

- Dates (Use the endings *-st*, *-d*, *-rd*, or *-th* only when the day precedes the month.)
- All numbers if two or more *related* numbers both above and below ten are used in the same sentence
- Measurements—such as time, money, distance, weight, and percentage; be consistent in using either the word *percent* or the symbol %

May 9 (or the 9th of May) | 10 miles

4 men and 18 women | *But:* The **18** women had **four** cars.

$6 | 5:00 p.m. (or 5 o'clock)

5 percent (or 5%) | 6½

5.13 Words Spell out the following:

- A number used as the first word of a sentence
- The smaller number when two numbers come together
- Fractions
- The words *million* and *billion* in even numbers

Thirty-two people attended.	nearly two-thirds of them
three 41-cent stamps	150 two-page brochures
37 million	$4.8 billion

Note: When fractions and the numbers 21 through 99 are spelled out, they should be hyphenated.

Spelling

Correct spelling is essential to effective communication. A misspelled word can distract the reader, cause misunderstanding, and send a negative message about the writer's competence. Because of the many variations in the spelling of English words, no spelling guidelines or spellcheckers are foolproof. The five rules that follow, however, may be safely applied to most business writing situations.

5.14 Doubling a Final Consonant If the last syllable of a root word is stressed, double the final consonant when adding a suffix.

Last Syllable Stressed		**Last Syllable Not Stressed**	
prefer	preferring	happen	happening
control	controlling	total	totaling
occur	occurrence	differ	differed

5.15 One-Syllable Words If a one-syllable word ends in a consonant preceded by a single vowel, double the final consonant before a suffix starting with a vowel.

Suffix Starting with Vowel		**Suffix Starting with Consonant**	
ship	shipper	ship	shipment
drop	dropped	glad	gladness
bag	baggage	bad	badly

5.16 Final *e* If a final *e* is preceded by a consonant, drop the *e* before a suffix starting with a vowel.

Suffix Starting with Vowel		**Suffix Starting with Consonant**	
come	coming	hope	hopeful
use	usable	manage	management
sincere	sincerity	sincere	sincerely

Note: Words ending in *ce* or *ge* usually retain the *e* before a suffix starting with a vowel: *noticeable, advantageous*.

5.17 Final *y* If a final *y* is preceded by a consonant, change *y* to *i* before any suffix except one starting with *i*.

Most Suffixes		**Suffix Starting with i**	
company	companies	try	trying
ordinary	ordinarily	forty	fortyish
hurry	hurried		

5.18 *ei* and *ie* Words Remember the rhyme:

Use *i* before *e*	bel**ie**ve	y**ie**ld
Except after *c*	rec**ei**ve	dec**ei**t
Or when sounded like *a*	fr**ei**ght	th**ei**r
As in *neighbor* and *weigh*.		

Word and Paragraph Division

When possible, avoid dividing words at the end of a line because word divisions tend to slow down or even confuse a reader (e.g., *rear range* for *rearrange* or *read just* for *readjust*). However, when necessary to avoid grossly uneven right margins, use the following rules. Most word processing software programs have a hyphenation feature that automatically divides words to make a more even right margin; you can change these word divisions manually, if necessary. When you are typing, do not space before a hyphen.

5.19 Compound Word Divide a compound word either after the hyphen or where the two words join to make a solid compound.

self- service free- way battle- field

5.20 Division Point Leave at least two letters on the upper line and carry at least three letters to the next line.

ex- treme typ- ing

5.21 Not Divided Don't divide a one syllable word, contraction, or abbreviation.

straight shouldn't

UNESCO approx.

5.22 Syllables Divide words only between syllables.

re- sources knowl- edge

Note: When in doubt about where a syllable ends, consult a dictionary.

5.23 Web Addresses Avoid breaking a URL (web address) or email address to a second line. If you must, break it before a period. Never add a hyphen, which the reader may misunderstand to be part of the address.

5.24 Paragraphs If it is necessary to divide a paragraph between two pages, leave at least two lines of the paragraph at the bottom of the first page and carry forward at least two lines to the top of the next page.

Application

Directions Rewrite the following paragraphs so that all words and numbers are expressed correctly. Do not change the wording in any sentences.

1. 100 of our elementary students will receive passes to Holly's Heartland Amusement Park today. Mrs. freda t. albertson, principal, indicated students from every grade were randomly selected to receive the free passes. The students represent about a 1/5 of the school's population.
2. As of Sept. 1st, nearly ¾ of our parents have attended at least one learning style orientation seminar. The School Psychologist, John Sibilsky, summarized the response of the participants and reported a favorable evaluation by ninety-six parents.

3. The Athletes for Freedom participants sponsored 12 2-hour presentations in a 3-week period. The last stop was east St. Louis, before the long ride home.
4. As reported on Page 2 of today's newspaper, the price of a barrel of oil has continued to climb. According to president Victoria payton, the price is 1 ½ times higher than last year.
5. This month's issue of Time magazine reports an interview with justin lake who said, "Service to our country is measured by many things, but a gift of time is one of the more significant." Our employees gave a total of two-hundred-ninety-five hours.

Directions Correct the one misspelling in each line.

1. preferring	controlling	occurence
2. shipper	droped	baggage
3. totalling	badly	shipment
4. differred	happening	gladness
5. sincerity	sincerly	noticeable
6. trying	fortyish	ordinarly
7. deceit	yeild	believe
8. advantagous	hopeful	companies
9. changeable	boundary	arguement
10. catagory	apparent	criticize
11. recommend	accomodate	weird
12. plausable	indispensable	allotted
13. camouflage	innocence	seperately
14. nickle	miniature	embarrassing
15. liaison	exhilarated	inadvertent

Directions Write the following words, inserting a hyphen or blank space at the first correct division point. If a word cannot be divided, write it without a hyphen.

Examples: mis-spelled
thought

1. freeway	chairperson	lien
2. express	exploitation	right
3. MADD	soared	solitary
4. wouldn't	mayor-elect	reliance
5. agree	recourse	Ohio

6. www.homemadesimple.com

7. Saddlebrooke_tripticket@yahoo.com

Lab 6: Word Usage

The following words and phrases are often used incorrectly in everyday speech and in business writing. Learn to use them correctly to help achieve your communication goals.

In some cases in the following list, one word is often confused with another similar word; in other cases, the structure of our language requires that certain words be used only in certain ways. Because of space, only brief and incomplete definitions are given here. Consult a dictionary for more complete or additional meanings.

6.1 Accept/Except *Accept* means "to agree to"; *except* means "with the exclusion of."

I will **accept** all the recommendations **except** the last one.

6.2 Advice/Advise *Advice* is a noun meaning "counsel"; *advise* is a verb meaning "to recommend."

If I ask for her **advice**, she may **advise** me to quit.

6.3 Affect/Effect *Affect* is most often used as a verb meaning "to influence" or "to change"; *effect* is most often used as a noun meaning "result" or "impression."

The legislation may **affect** sales but should have no **effect** on gross margin.

6.4 All Right/Alright Use *all right*. (*Alright* is considered substandard.)

The arrangement is **all right** (not *alright*) with me.

6.5 A Lot/Alot Use *a lot*. (*Alot* is considered substandard.)

We used **a lot** (not *alot*) of overtime on the project.

6.6 Among/Between Use *among* when referring to three or more; use *between* when referring to two.

Among the three candidates was one manager who divided his time **between** London and New York.

6.7 Amount/Number Use *amount* to refer to money or to things that cannot be counted; use *number* to refer to things that can be counted.

The **amount** of consumer interest was measured by the **number** of coupons returned.

6.8 Anxious/Eager Use *anxious* only if great concern or worry is involved.

Andrés was **eager** to get the new car, although he was **anxious** about making such high payments.

6.9 Any One/Anyone Spell as two words when followed by *of;* spell as one word when the accent is on *any*.

Anyone is allowed to attend **any one** of the sessions.

Between See *Among/Between*.

6.10 Can/May *Can* indicates ability; *may* indicates permission.

I **can** finish the project on time if I **may** hire an additional secretary.

6.11 Cite/Sight/Site *Cite* means "to quote" or "to mention"; *sight* is either a verb meaning "to look at" or a noun meaning "something seen"; *site* is most often a noun meaning "location."

The **sight** of the high-rise building on the **site** of the old battlefield reminded Monica to **cite** several other examples to the commission members.

6.12 Complement/Compliment *Complement* means "to complete" or "something that completes"; *compliment* means "to praise" or "words of praise."

I must **compliment** you on the new model, which will **complement** our line.

6.13 Could of/Could've Use *could've* (or *could have*). (*Could of* is incorrect.)

We **could've** (not *could of*) prevented that loss had we been more alert.

6.14 Different from/Different than Use *different from.* (*Different than* is considered substandard.)

Your computer is **different from** (not *different than*) mine.

6.15 Each Other/One Another Use *each other* when referring to two; use *one another* when referring to three or more.

The two workers helped **each other**, but their three visitors would not even look at **one another**.

Eager See *Anxious/Eager*.

Effect See *Affect/Effect*.

6.16 e.g./i.e. The abbreviation *e.g.* means "for example"; *i.e.* means "that is." Use *i.e.* to introduce a restatement or explanation of a preceding expression. Both abbreviations, like the expressions for which they stand, are followed by commas. (Many writers prefer the full English terms to the abbreviations because they are clearer.)

The proposal has merit; **e.g.**, it is economical, forward looking, and timely.

Or: The proposal has merit; for example, it is economical, forward looking, and timely.
Unfortunately, it is also a hot potato; **i.e.**, it will generate unfavorable publicity.

Or: Unfortunately, it is also a hot potato; that is, it will generate unfavorable publicity.

6.17 Eminent/Imminent *Eminent* means "well known"; *imminent* means "about to happen."

The arrival of the **eminent** scientist from Russia is **imminent**.

6.18 Enthused/Enthusiastic Use *enthusiastic*. (*Enthused* is considered substandard.)

I have become quite **enthusiastic** (not *enthused*) about the possibilities.

Except See *Accept/Except*.

6.19 Farther/Further *Farther* refers to distance; *further* refers to extent or degree.

We drove 10 miles **farther** while we discussed the matter **further**.

6.20 Fewer/Less Use *fewer* to refer to things that can be counted; use *less* to refer to money or to things that cannot be counted.

Alvin worked **fewer** hours at the exhibit and therefore generated **less** interest.

Further See *Farther/Further*.

6.21 Good/Well *Good* is an adjective; *well* is an adverb or (with reference to health) an adjective.

Joe does a **good** job and performs **well** on tests, even when he does not feel **well**.

i.e. See *e.g./i.e.*

Imminent See *Eminent/Imminent*.

6.22 Imply/Infer Imply means "to hint" or "to suggest"; *infer* means "to draw a conclusion." Speakers and writers *imply*; readers and listeners *infer*.

The president **implied** that changes will be forthcoming; I **inferred** from his tone of voice that these changes will not be pleasant.

6.23 Irregardless/Regardless Use *regardless*. (*Irregardless* is considered substandard.)

He wants to proceed, **regardless** (not *irregardless*) of the costs.

6.24 Its/It's *Its* is a possessive pronoun; *it's* is a contraction for "it is."

It's time to let the department increase **its** budget.

6.25 Lay/Lie *Lay* (principal forms: *lay*, *laid*, *laid*, *laying*) means "to put" and requires an object to complete its meaning; *lie* (principal forms: *lie*, *lay*, *lain*, *lying*) means "to rest."

Please **lay** the supplies on the shelf.

I **laid** the folders in the drawer.

She had **laid** the notes on her desk.

I **lie** on the couch after lunch each day.

The report **lay** on his desk yesterday.

The job has **lain** untouched for a week.

Less See *Fewer/Less*.

Lie See *Lay/Lie*.

6.26 Loose/Lose *Loose* means "not fastened"; *lose* means "to be unable to find."

Do not **lose** the **loose** change in your pocket.

May See *Can/May*.

Number See *Amount/Number*.

One Another See *Each Other/One Another*.

6.27 Passed/Past Passed is a verb (the past tense or past participle of *pass*, meaning "to move on or by"); *past* is an adjective, adverb, or preposition meaning "earlier."

The committee **passed** the no-confidence motion at a **past** meeting.

6.28 Percent/Percentage With figures, use *percent*; without figures, use *percentage*.

We took a commission of 6 **percent** (or 6%), which was a lower **percentage** than last year.

6.29 Personal/Personnel *Personal* means "private" or "belonging to one individual"; *personnel* means "employees."

I used my **personal** time to draft a memo to all **personnel**.

6.30 Principal/Principle *Principal* means "primary" (adjective) or "sum of money" (noun); *principle* means "rule" or "law."

The guiding **principle** is fair play, and the **principal** means of achieving it is a code of ethics.

6.31 Real/Really *Real* is an adjective; *really* is an adverb. Do not use *real* to modify another adjective.

She was **really** (not *real*) proud that her necklace contained **real** pearls.

6.32 Reason Is Because/Reason Is That Use *reason is that*. (*Reason is because* is considered substandard.)

The **reason** for such low attendance **is that** (not *is because*) the weather was stormy.

Regardless See *Irregardless/Regardless*.

6.33 Same Do not use *same* to refer to a previously mentioned item. Use *it* or some other wording instead.

We have received your order and will ship **it** (not *same*) in three days.

6.34 Set/Sit *Set* (principal forms: *set*, *set*, *set*, *setting*) means "to place"; *sit* (principal forms: *sit*, *sat*, *sat*, *sitting*) means "to be seated."

Please **set** your papers on the table.

She **set** the computer on the desk.

I have **set** the computer there before.

Please **sit** in the chair.

She **sat** in the first-class section.

I had not **sat** there before.

6.35 Should of/Should've Use *should've* (or *should have*). (*Should of* is incorrect.)

We **should've** (not *should of*) been more careful.

Sight See *Cite/Sight/Site*.

Sit See *Set/Sit*.

Site See *Cite/Sight/Site*.

6.36 Stationary/Stationery *Stationary* means "remaining in one place"; *stationery* is writing paper.

I used my personal **stationery** to write a letter about the **stationary** bike.

6.37 Sure/Surely *Sure* is an adjective; *surely* is an adverb. Do not use *sure* to modify another adjective.

I'm **surely** (not *sure*) glad that she is running and feel **sure** that she will be nominated.

6.38 Sure and/Sure to Use *sure to*. (*Sure and* is considered substandard.)

Be **sure to** (not *sure and*) attend the meeting.

6.39 Their/There/They're *Their* means "belonging to them"; *there* means "in that place"; and *they're* is a contraction for "they are."

They're too busy with **their** reports to be **there** for the hearing.

6.40 Theirs/There's *Theirs* is a possessive pronoun; *there's* is a contraction for "there is."

We finished our meal, but **there's** no time for them to finish **theirs**.

They're See *Their/There/They're*.

6.41 Try and/Try to Use *try to*. (*Try and* is considered substandard.)

Please **try to** (not *try and*) attend the meeting.

Well See *Good/Well*.

6.42 Whose/Who's *Whose* is a possessive pronoun; *who's* is a contraction for "who is."

Who's going to let us know **whose** turn it is to make coffee?

6.43 Your/You're *Your* means "belonging to you"; *you're* is a contraction for "you are."

You're going to present **your** report first.

Application

Directions Select the correct words in parentheses.

1. I will (accept/except) your (advice/advise), but the (affect/effect) of doing so may bring (alot/a lot) of change.
2. The seminar was (all right/alright), but (among/between) Ludwig and me, most participants were (anxious/eager) to complete the training.
3. The (amount/number) of political activity generated (fewer/less) interest than anticipated.
4. (Any one/Anyone) of the students (may/can) apply that (principal/principle) if (theirs/there's) time.
5. The first (sight/cite/site) for the new office (could of/could've) (complimented/complemented) the surrounding community, mainly because it is (different from/different than) the typical building.
6. The program will succeed; (e.g./i.e.), it is positive, forward looking, and cost effective.
7. The group members supported (each other/one another) and were (enthused/enthusiastic) about their presentation.
8. The CEO (implied/inferred) that arrangements with an (eminent/imminent) scientist have been finalized, and (irregardless/regardless) of the number who are invited, we will be included.
9. How much (farther/further) can we pursue this if (its/it's) not (passed/past) on through regular channels?
10. Please (lay/lie) your (loose/lose) change on the dresser, and I'll be (real/really) pleased.
11. You (should of/should've) taken advantage of the opportunity to refinance your home under the lower (percent/percentage) rates.
12. The new investment program is open to all (personal/personnel) and will (sure/surely) build security for (their/there) future.
13. The reason for the increase in deli foods in grocery stores is (that/because) more people are buying food prepared outside the home.

14. I use my personal (stationery/stationary), and please (try to/try and) use yours.
15. Tell Henri to be (sure and/sure to) lock up before he leaves and (sit/set) the late afternoon mail on my desk.
16. We have the document and will forward (it/same) to the actuary so that (you're/your) department is included in the transaction.
17. (Who's/Whose) turn is it to clean the refrigerator because it (sure/surely) needs it?
18. I'll follow the guidelines you (advise/advice), (except/accept) the one involving the (eminent/imminent) staff change in sales.
19. There was wide disparity (between/among) the five candidates, but they supported (each other/one another).
20. Dr. Zhoa was excited about the new job but (eager/anxious) about the research required.
21. Be sure the (cites/sights/sites) are interesting because we want to do a (good/well) job.
22. What did you (imply/infer) from her (compliment/complement)?
23. The (principle/principal) reason for (their/there/they're) success is the lawyer, (whose/who's) a specialist in international law.
24. A (stationery/stationary) pump for the well was (complemented/complimented) by a mobile emergency backup.
25. They wanted us to work (less/fewer) hours so the (number/amount) of savings could be increased.

B Formatting Business Documents

Formatting Letters and Memos

The most common features of business letters and memos are discussed in the following sections and illustrated in Figure 1.

Letter and Punctuation Styles

The *block style* is the simplest letter style to type because all lines begin at the left margin. In the *modified block style*, the date and closing lines begin at the center point. Offsetting these parts from the left margin enables the reader to locate them quickly. The *standard punctuation style*—the most common format—uses a colon after the salutation and a comma after the complimentary closing.

Paper and Margins

When letters and memos are printed, typically use standard-sized paper, 8½ × 11 inches. Include a logo and/or address on the first page only.

Side, top, and bottom margins should be 1 to 1¼ inches (the default in programs such as Microsoft Word). Vertically center one-page letters and memos. Set a tab at the center point if you're formatting a modified block style letter.

Required Letter Parts

The required letter parts are as follows:

Date Line Type the current month (spelled out), day, and year on the first line. Begin either at the center point for modified block style or at the left margin for the block style.

Inside Address The inside address gives the name and location of the person to whom you're writing. Skip between one and four lines below the date, depending on the size of the letter, and type at the left margin. If you use the addressee's job title, type it either on the same line as the name (separated from the name by a comma) or on the following line by itself. In the address, use the two-letter U.S. Postal Service abbreviation, typed in all capitals with no period, and leave one space between the state and the zip code. For international letters, type the name of the country in all-capital letters on the last line by itself.

Salutation Use the same name in both the inside address and the salutation. If the letter is addressed to a job position rather than to a person, use a generic greeting, such as "Dear Human Resources Manager." If you typically address the reader in person by first name, use the first name in the salutation (e.g., "Dear Cara"); otherwise, use the full name to avoid assumptions about gender and marital status (e.g., "Dear Cara Currigan"). Leave one blank line before and after the salutation.

Figure 1 | Letter and Memo Formats

May 18, 20xx

Calvin Finch
5223 Monroe Street, Apt. 6A
Pittsburgh, PA 15216

Dear Calvin:

Please accept my deepest gratitude for your generous in-kind gift of food. Your gift will help feed our Southern Tier neighbors in need. The Food Bank's network of hunger-relief agencies is currently serving more households than in previous years. Within the last year, existing clients needed assistance more frequently than before, and our network experienced an increase in first-time users, many of them employed but unable to make ends meet, as well as seniors who struggle to live on fixed incomes.

Without people like you, we would not be able to keep up with the increasing demand for emergency food assistance. I am very thankful that we have such wonderful, caring donors who want to alleviate the stress that some families face.

Thank you for your generosity and support for the Food Bank's hunger-relief efforts.

Sincerely,

Natasha R. Thompson
President & CEO

NRT/lce

Block style letter

May 18, 20xx

Calvin Finch
5223 Monroe Street, Apt. 6A
Pittsburgh, PA 15216

Dear Calvin:

Please accept my deepest gratitude for your generous in-kind gift of food. Your gift will help feed our Southern Tier neighbors in need. The Food Bank's network of hunger-relief agencies is currently serving more households than in previous years. Within the last year, existing clients needed assistance more frequently than before, and our network experienced an increase in first-time users, many of them employed but unable to make ends meet, as well as seniors who struggle to live on fixed incomes.

Without people like you, we would not be able to keep up with the increasing demand for emergency food assistance. I am very thankful that we have such wonderful, caring donors who want to alleviate the stress that some families face.

Thank you for your generosity and support for the Food Bank's hunger-relief efforts.

Sincerely,

Natasha R. Thompson
President & CEO

NRT/lce

Modified block style letter

Calaway Movers

To: All Calaway Staff
From: Bill Calaway, CEO
Subject: Reorganizing Our Sales Teams
Date: September 9, 20xx

As we discussed last week, we are reorganizing the corporate office to focus more closely on customer needs. Instead of sales functions serving regional customers, we will organize around types of customers: consumer, small business, and corporate. This will allow Calaway to tailor our products and services to specific customer groups and leverage services within customer segments. The former regional model worked well for a long time, but we have outgrown this structure and must adapt, particularly to our growing base of corporate clients, who demand more customized services from Calaway.

Our goal is to make this transition as smooth as possible. Over the next 90 days, we will implement the transition plan:

- **Transfer sales representatives to new divisions (by October 15)**

  Each sales representative will be moved from our current regional teams to a new team: consumer, small business, or corporate. Managers will work closely with representatives to determine strengths, experiences, and preferences.

- **Identify account type (by October 31)**

  All sales representatives will categorize current accounts for the new divisions: consumer, small business, and corporate.

- **Transition accounts to new teams (by November 30)**

  Where accounts are changing sales representatives, we will follow this process:

  - For small business accounts, the former and new sales representative will send an email to the account contact, followed by a phone call and visit (if possible) by the new sales representative.
  - For corporate accounts, the former sales representative will send an email and schedule a conference call or visit by the account contact and new sales representative.

Seamless communication with our clients during this transition is essential. Each segment is working on email templates to ensure that our communication is clear and consistent across all divisions.

Interoffice memo (page 1)

Sales Reorganization Page 2 September 9, 20xx

I am pleased to announce the following leaders in the newly formed sales organization:

- **Melissa Chowdhury, Vice President, Sales**

  Formerly the vice president of the Northeast region, Melissa will oversee all sales functions. Melissa will report directly to me, and the following sales directors will report to Melissa.

- **Bruce Gorman, Director, Consumer Accounts**

  Bruce will move from the Midwest region to oversee the new Consumer Accounts division.

- **Ryan Korman, Director, Small Business Accounts**

  Ryan will move from the Southern region to oversee the Small Business Accounts division.

- **Manny Fernandez, Director, Corporate Accounts**

  Formerly director, customer service, Manny will oversee the Corporate Accounts division.

Please join me in congratulating these folks in their new roles.

I am very excited about the future of Calaway. With our new organizational structure, we will continue to grow—and move people safely to new homes and offices across the country. I look forward to taking this journey with all of you.

Interoffice memo (page 2)

Body Single-space the lines of each paragraph and leave one blank line between paragraphs.

Page 2 Insert the page number in the header or footer, centered or on the right side. Omit the page number on page 1. Carry forward to a second page at least two lines of text; if you have only one line, adjust margins or edit text to fit on one page.

Complimentary Closing Begin the complimentary closing at the same margin point as the date line. Capitalize the first word only and leave one blank line before and approximately three blank lines after, to allow room for your signature before your full typed name.

Signature Sign your name legibly in blue or black ink or insert an image of your signature if you send the document digitally.

Writer's Identification The writer's identification (name or job title or both) begins approximately on the fourth line immediately below the complimentary closing. The job title may go either on the same line as the typed name, separated by a comma, or on the following line by itself.

Reference Initials When used, reference initials (the initials of the typist) are typed at the left margin in lowercase letters without periods, with one blank line before. In Figure 1, we see the CEO's initials followed by the typist's. Do not include reference initials if you type your own letter.

Envelopes Business envelopes have a printed return address. You may type your name above this address if you wish. Use plain envelopes for personal business letters; type the return address (your home address) at the upper left corner or use an address label. On large (No. 10) envelopes, type the mailing address 2 inches from the top edge and 4 inches from the left edge. On small (No. 6¾) envelopes, type the mailing address 2 inches from the top edge and 2½ inches from the left edge. Fold 8½ × 11 letters in thirds and small notepaper in half to fit the envelope.

Optional Letter Parts

Optional letter parts are as follows:

Subject Line You may include a subject line in letters (identified by the words *Subject* or *Re* followed by a colon) to identify the topic of the letter. Type it below the salutation, with one blank line before and one after.

Numbered or Bulleted Lists in the Body You may include a numbered list (if the sequence of the items is important) or a bulleted list (when the sequence is not important). Single-space each item and double-space or use 6-point spacing between items. Leave one blank line before and after the list.

Enclosure Notation You may use an enclosure notation if items are included in the envelope and are not obvious. Type "Enclosure" (or "Attachment" if the items are physically attached) on the line immediately below the reference initials, and as an option, add the description of what is enclosed.

Copy Notation If someone other than the addressee will receive a copy of the letter, type a copy notation ("c:") immediately below the enclosure notation or reference initials, whichever comes last. Then follow the copy notation with the names of the people who will receive copies.

Postscript If you add a postscript to a letter, type it as the last item, preceded by one blank line and starting with "P.S." Postscripts are used most often in sales letters.

Memo Header Format

Internal memos may be printed, attached to email messages, or uploaded onto company intranet sites. Double-space the memo header and include the following:

To: Type the first and last name of the receiver or a group name, for example, "All Employees." You may include a job title after a receiver's name and a comma, for example, "Jason Matthews, CFO."

From: Type your first and last name. If you wrote a title after the receiver's name, include yours here. For printed memos, sign your initials after your name if this is standard in your organization.

Date: Type the full date: month, day, and year.

Subject: Include a descriptive subject line as you would for an email message.

Formatting Reports

In Chapter 10, you read suggestions for designing and formatting text-based reports and report decks. The executive summary of the report, *Dietary Guidelines for Americans*, with traditional text formatting, is shown in Figure 2. Note that the report uses several graphical elements to break up the text (e.g., images, column formatting, boxes, and lines).

Decks created in presentation software are intended as standalone documents without a presenter to explain the detail. Therefore, compared to slides used to complement an oral presentation, a report will be far denser with text and graphics and may use standard business font sizes. Compare the full Valex report on tuition assistance (Figure 3) with the oral presentation slides (Figure 4). Both were created in PowerPoint, but the content and formatting are quite different.

Monkey Business Images/Shutterstock.com

Executive Summary

The foods and beverages that people consume have a profound impact on their health. The scientific connection between food and health has been well documented for many decades, with substantial and increasingly robust evidence showing that a healthy lifestyle—including following a healthy dietary pattern—can help people achieve and maintain good health and reduce the risk of chronic diseases throughout all stages of the lifespan: infancy and toddlerhood, childhood and adolescence, adulthood, pregnancy and lactation, and older adulthood. The core elements of a healthy dietary pattern are remarkably consistent across the lifespan and across health outcomes.

Since the first edition was published in 1980, the *Dietary Guidelines for Americans* have provided science-based advice on what to eat and drink to promote health, reduce risk of chronic disease, and meet nutrient needs. Publication of the *Dietary Guidelines* is required under the 1990 National Nutrition Monitoring and Related Research Act, which states that at least every 5 years, the U.S. Departments of Agriculture (USDA) and of Health and Human Services (HHS) must jointly publish a report containing nutritional and dietary information and guidelines for the general public. The statute (Public Law 101-445, 7 United States Code 5341 et seq.) requires that the *Dietary Guidelines* be based on the preponderance of current scientific and medical knowledge. The 2020-2025 edition of the *Dietary Guidelines* builds from the 2015 edition, with revisions grounded in the *Scientific Report of the 2020 Dietary Guidelines Advisory Committee* and consideration of Federal agency and public comments.

The *Dietary Guidelines* is designed for policymakers and nutrition and health professionals to help all individuals and their families consume a healthy, nutritionally adequate diet. The information in the *Dietary Guidelines* is used to develop, implement, and evaluate Federal food, nutrition, and health policies

Page vii | Dietary Guidelines for Americans, 2020-2025 | **Executive Summary**

Figure 2 | *(continued)*

and programs. It also is the basis for Federal nutrition education materials designed for the public and for the nutrition education components of USDA and HHS nutrition programs. State and local governments, schools, the food industry, other businesses, community groups, and media also use *Dietary Guidelines* information to develop programs, policies, and communication for the general public.

The aim of the *Dietary Guidelines* is to promote health and prevent disease. Because of this public health orientation, the *Dietary Guidelines* is not intended to contain clinical guidelines for treating chronic diseases. Chronic diseases result from a complex mix of genetic, biological, behavioral, socioeconomic, and environmental factors, and people with these conditions have unique health care requirements that require careful oversight by a health professional. The body of scientific evidence on diet and health reviewed to inform the *Dietary Guidelines* is representative of the U.S. population—it includes people who are healthy, people at risk for diet-related chronic conditions and diseases, such as cardiovascular disease, type 2 diabetes, and obesity, and some people who are living with one or more of these diet-related chronic illnesses. At the same time, it is essential that Federal agencies, medical organizations, and health professionals adapt the *Dietary Guidelines* to meet the specific needs of their patients as part of an individual, multifaceted treatment plan for the specific chronic disease.

Consistent and Evolving

Although many recommendations have remained relatively consistent over time, the *Dietary Guidelines* also has built upon previous editions and evolved as scientific knowledge has grown. The *Dietary Guidelines for Americans, 2020-2025* reflects this in three important ways:

The first is its recognition that diet-related chronic diseases, such as cardiovascular disease, type 2 diabetes, obesity, and some types of cancer, are very prevalent among Americans and pose a major public health problem. Today, more than half of adults have one or more diet-related chronic diseases. As a result, recent editions of the *Dietary Guidelines* have focused on healthy individuals, as well as those with overweight or obesity and those who are at risk of chronic disease. A fundamental premise of the *2020-2025 Dietary Guidelines* is that just about everyone, no matter their health status, can benefit from shifting food and beverage choices to better support healthy dietary patterns.

The second is its focus on dietary patterns. Researchers and public health experts, including registered dietitians, understand that nutrients and foods are not consumed in isolation. Rather, people consume them in various combinations over time—a dietary pattern—and these foods and beverages act synergistically to affect health. The *Dietary Guidelines for Americans, 2015-2020* puts this understanding into action by focusing its recommendations on consuming a healthy dietary pattern. The *2020-2025 Dietary Guidelines* carries forward this emphasis on the importance of a healthy dietary pattern as a whole—rather than on individual nutrients, foods, or food groups in isolation.

The third is its focus on a lifespan approach. This edition of the *Dietary Guidelines* highlights the importance of encouraging healthy dietary patterns at every life stage from infancy through older adulthood. It provides recommendations for healthy dietary patterns by life stage, identifying needs specific to each life stage and considering healthy dietary pattern characteristics that should be carried forward into the next stage of life. For the first time since the 1985 edition, the *2020-2025 Dietary Guidelines* includes recommendations for healthy dietary patterns for infants and toddlers.

The Guidelines

The *2020-2025 Dietary Guidelines* provides four overarching Guidelines that encourage healthy eating patterns at each stage of life and recognize that individuals will need to make shifts in their food and beverage choices to achieve a healthy pattern. The Guidelines also explicitly emphasize that a healthy dietary pattern is not a rigid prescription. Rather, the Guidelines are a customizable framework of core elements within which individuals make tailored and affordable choices that meet their personal, cultural, and traditional preferences. Several examples of healthy dietary patterns that translate and integrate the recommendations in overall healthy ways to eat are provided. The Guidelines are supported by Key Recommendations that provide further guidance on healthy eating across the lifespan.

Dietary Guidelines for Americans, 2020-2025 | **Executive Summary** | Page viii

The Guidelines

Make every bite count with the *Dietary Guidelines for Americans*. Here's how:

1 **Follow a healthy dietary pattern at every life stage.**

At every life stage—infancy, toddlerhood, childhood, adolescence, adulthood, pregnancy, lactation, and older adulthood—it is never too early or too late to eat healthfully.

- **For about the first 6 months of life,** exclusively feed infants human milk. Continue to feed infants human milk through at least the first year of life, and longer if desired. Feed infants iron-fortified infant formula during the first year of life when human milk is unavailable. Provide infants with supplemental vitamin D beginning soon after birth.
- **At about 6 months,** introduce infants to nutrient-dense complementary foods. Introduce infants to potentially allergenic foods along with other complementary foods. Encourage infants and toddlers to consume a variety of foods from all food groups. Include foods rich in iron and zinc, particularly for infants fed human milk.
- **From 12 months through older adulthood,** follow a healthy dietary pattern across the lifespan to meet nutrient needs, help achieve a healthy body weight, and reduce the risk of chronic disease.

2 **Customize and enjoy nutrient-dense food and beverage choices to reflect personal preferences, cultural traditions, and budgetary considerations.**

A healthy dietary pattern can benefit all individuals regardless of age, race, or ethnicity, or current health status. The *Dietary Guidelines* provides a framework intended to be customized to individual needs and preferences, as well as the foodways of the diverse cultures in the United States.

3 **Focus on meeting food group needs with nutrient-dense foods and beverages, and stay within calorie limits.**

An underlying premise of the *Dietary Guidelines* is that nutritional needs should be met primarily from foods and beverages—specifically, nutrient-dense foods and beverages. Nutrient-dense foods provide vitamins, minerals, and other health-promoting components and have no or little added sugars, saturated fat, and sodium. A healthy dietary pattern consists of nutrient-dense forms of foods and beverages across all food groups, in recommended amounts, and within calorie limits.

The core elements that make up a healthy dietary pattern include:

- **Vegetables of all types**—dark green; red and orange; beans, peas, and lentils; starchy; and other vegetables
- **Fruits,** especially whole fruit
- **Grains,** at least half of which are whole grain
- **Dairy,** including fat-free or low-fat milk, yogurt, and cheese, and/or lactose-free versions and fortified soy beverages and yogurt as alternatives
- **Protein foods,** including lean meats, poultry, and eggs; seafood; beans, peas, and lentils; and nuts, seeds, and soy products
- **Oils,** including vegetable oils and oils in food, such as seafood and nuts

Page ix | Dietary Guidelines for Americans, 2020-2025 | **Executive Summary**

Figure 2 | (*continued*)

4 **Limit foods and beverages higher in added sugars, saturated fat, and sodium, and limit alcoholic beverages.**

At every life stage, meeting food group recommendations—even with nutrient-dense choices—requires most of a person's daily calorie needs and sodium limits. A healthy dietary pattern doesn't have much room for extra added sugars, saturated fat, or sodium—or for alcoholic beverages. A small amount of added sugars, saturated fat, or sodium can be added to nutrient-dense foods and beverages to help meet food group recommendations, but foods and beverages high in these components should be limited. Limits are:

- **Added sugars**—Less than 10 percent of calories per day starting at age 2. Avoid foods and beverages with added sugars for those younger than age 2.
- **Saturated fat**—Less than 10 percent of calories per day starting at age 2.
- **Sodium**—Less than 2,300 milligrams per day—and even less for children younger than age 14.
- **Alcoholic beverages**—Adults of legal drinking age can choose not to drink, or to drink in moderation by limiting intake to 2 drinks or less in a day for men and 1 drink or less in a day for women, when alcohol is consumed. Drinking less is better for health than drinking more. There are some adults who should not drink alcohol, such as women who are pregnant.

Terms to Know

Several terms are used throughout the *Dietary Guidelines* and are essential to understanding the Guidelines and putting them into action. These terms are defined here:

- **Dietary pattern:** It is the combination of foods and beverages that constitutes an individual's complete dietary intake over time. This may be a description of a customary way of eating or a description of a combination of foods recommended for consumption.
- **Nutrient dense:** Nutrient-dense foods and beverages provide vitamins, minerals, and other health-promoting components and have little added sugars, saturated fat, and sodium. Vegetables, fruits, whole grains, seafood, eggs, beans, peas, and lentils, unsalted nuts and seeds, fat-free and low-fat dairy products, and lean meats and poultry—when prepared with no or little added sugars, saturated fat, and sodium—are nutrient-dense foods.

For most individuals, no matter their age or health status, achieving a healthy dietary pattern will require changes in food and beverage choices. Some of these changes can be accomplished by making simple substitutions, while others will require greater effort to accomplish. This edition of the *Dietary Guidelines* presents overall guidance on choosing nutrient-dense foods and beverages in place of less healthy choices and also discusses special nutrition considerations for individuals at each life stage—infants and toddlers, children and adolescents, adults, women who are pregnant or lactating, and older adults.

Although individuals ultimately decide what and how much to consume, their personal relationships; the settings in which they live, learn, work, play, and gather; and other contextual factors—including their ability to consistently access healthy and affordable food—strongly influence their choices. Health professionals, communities, businesses and industries, organizations, government, and other segments of society all have a role to play in supporting individuals and families in making choices that align with the *Dietary Guidelines* and ensuring that all people have access to a healthy and affordable food supply. Resources, including Federal programs that support households, regardless of size and make-up, in choosing a healthy diet and improving access to healthy food, are highlighted throughout this edition of the *Dietary Guidelines for Americans.*

Dietary Guidelines for Americans, 2020-2025 | **Executive Summary** | Page x

Valex Tuition Assistance Report | Figure 3

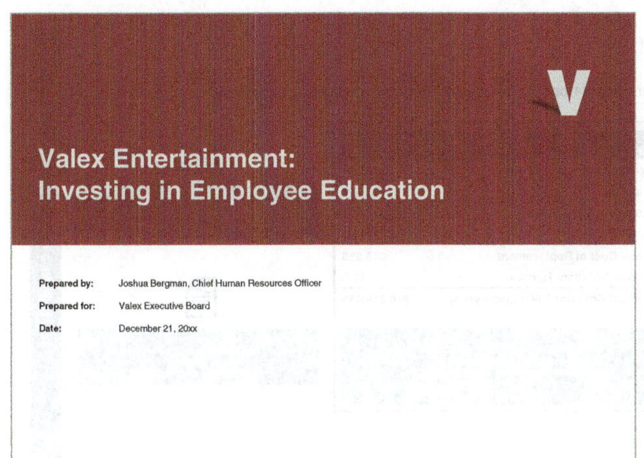

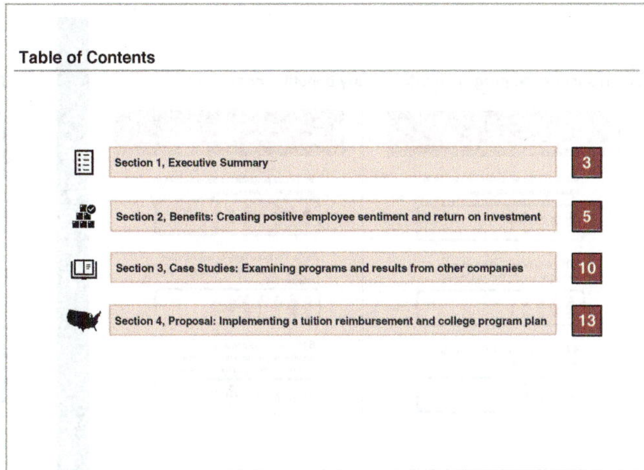

Table of Contents
Section 1, Executive Summary 3
Section 2, Benefits: Creating positive employee sentiment and return on investment 5
Section 3, Case Studies: Examining programs and results from other companies 10
Section 4, Proposal: Implementing a tuition reimbursement and college program plan 13

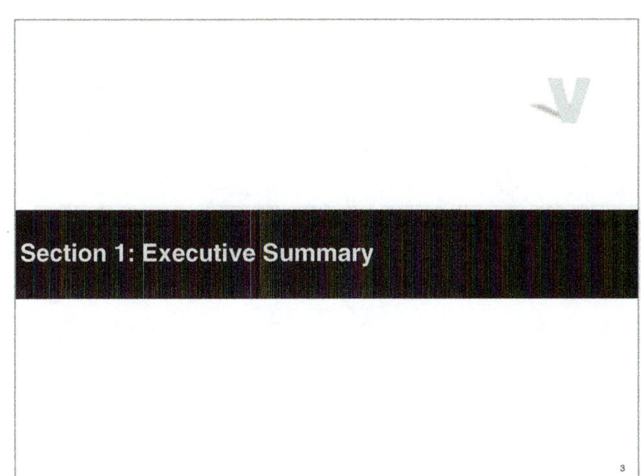

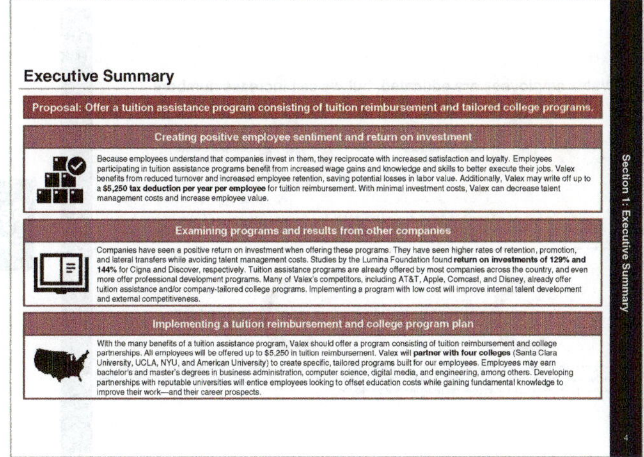

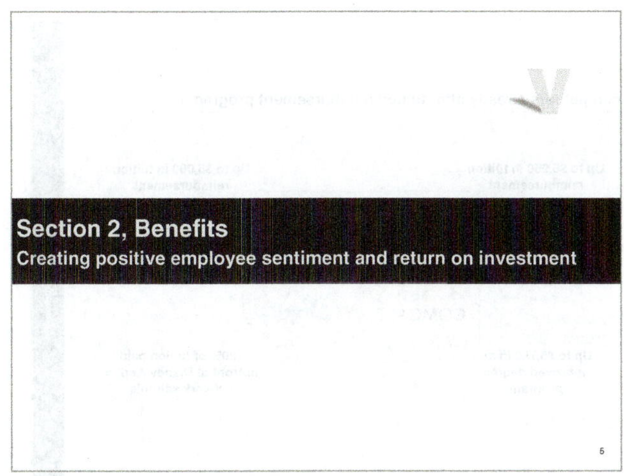

Tuition assistance programs offer many benefits for employees

Employers value a college education, according to the Association of American Colleges and Universities.

Most business executives (82%) said that completing a college education is either "very" or "absolutely" important.

Eighty-eight percent of executives believe that getting a college degree is worth the time and money.

Employers note that learned/developed college skills including oral communication, critical thinking, and working effectively in teams are very valuable.

Executives agree that no matter the study, the college degree and experience allows positive interaction with people of high-level positions.

Median salary jumps 40% from associate to bachelor's and 20% from bachelor's to master's, according to the U.S. Census.

$30,784
$38,792
$43,316
$46,124
$64,896
$77,844
$97,916
+40.7%
+20.0%
Some High School Ed.
High School Diploma
Some College
Associate Degree
Bachelor's Degree
Master's Degree
Doctorate Degree

Section 2: Benefits

6

SOURCE: REPORT TO SHAREHOLDERS YILIN ZHANG

Figure 3 | *(continued)*

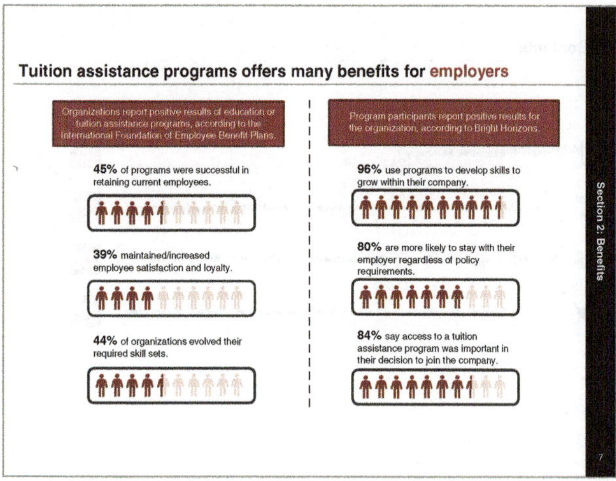

Tuition assistance programs offers many benefits for employers
Organizations report positive results of education or tuition assistance programs, according to the International Foundation of Employee Benefit Plans.
45% of programs were successful in retaining current employees.
39% maintained/increased employee satisfaction and loyalty.
44% of organizations evolved their required skill sets.
Program participants report positive results for the organization, according to Bright Horizons.
96% use programs to develop skills to grow within their company.
80% are more likely to stay with their employer regardless of policy requirements.
84% say access to a tuition assistance program was important in their decision to join the company.
Section 2: Benefits
7

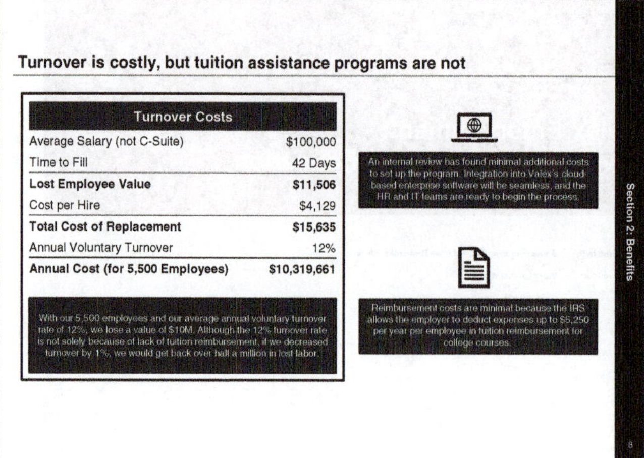

Turnover is costly, but tuition assistance programs are not
Turnover Costs
Average Salary (not C-Suite) $100,000
Time to Fill 42 Days
Lost Employee Value $11,506
Cost per Hire $4,129
Total Cost of Replacement $15,635
Annual Voluntary Turnover 12%
Annual Cost (for 5,500 Employees) $10,319,661
With our 5,500 employees and our average annual voluntary turnover rate of 12%, we lose a value of $10M. Although the 12% turnover rate is not solely because of lack of tuition reimbursement, if we decreased turnover by 1%, we would get back over half a million in lost labor.
An internal review has found minimal additional costs to set up the program. Integration into Valex's cloud-based enterprise software will be seamless, and the HR and IT teams are ready to begin the process.
Reimbursement costs are minimal because the IRS allows the employer to deduct expenses up to $5,250 per year per employee in tuition reimbursement for college courses.
Section 2: Benefits

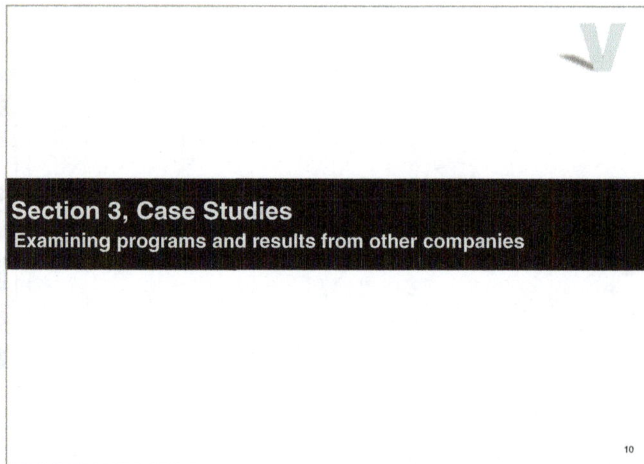

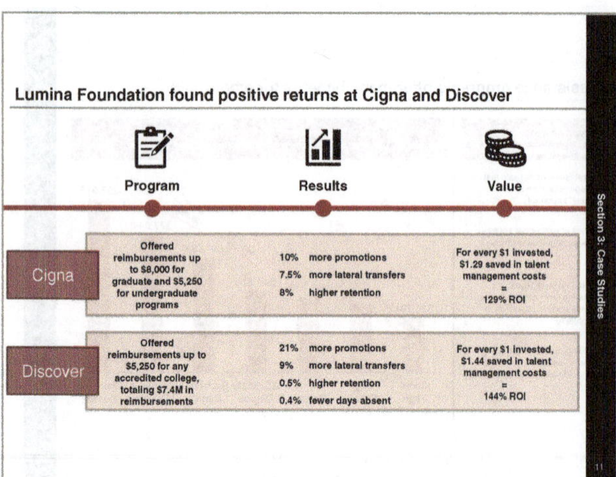

Lumina Foundation found positive returns at Cigna and Discover
Program
Results
Value
Cigna
Offered reimbursements up to $8,000 for graduate and $5,250 for undergraduate programs
10% more promotions
7.5% more lateral transfers
8% higher retention
For every $1 invested, $1.29 saved in talent management costs = 129% ROI
Discover
Offered reimbursements up to $5,250 for any accredited college, totaling $7.4M in reimbursements
21% more promotions
9% more lateral transfers
0.5% higher retention
0.4% fewer days absent
For every $1 invested, $1.44 saved in talent management costs = 144% ROI
Section 3: Case Studies
11

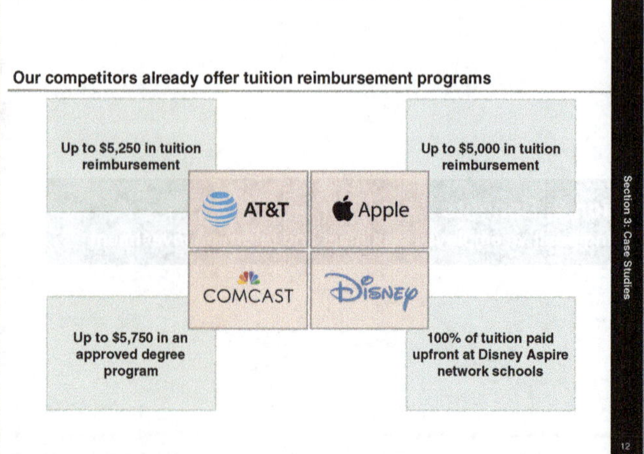

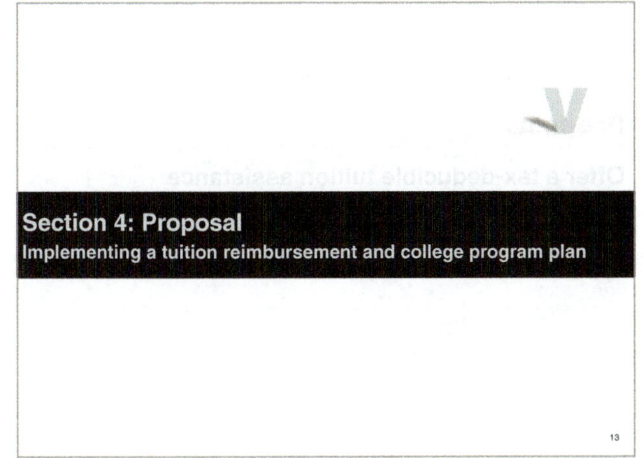

Section 4: Proposal
Implementing a tuition reimbursement and college program plan
13

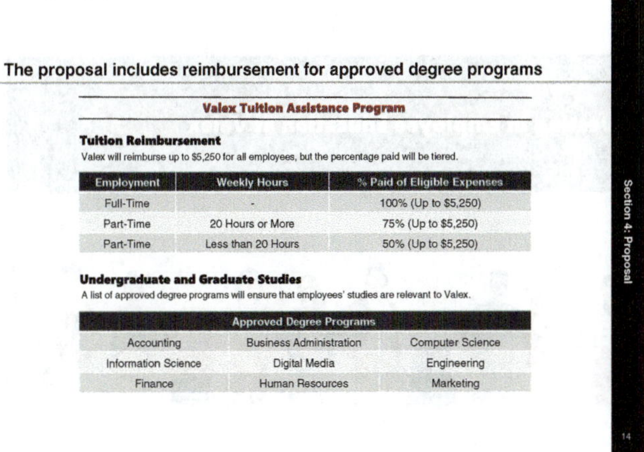

The proposal includes reimbursement for approved degree programs
Valex Tuition Assistance Program
Tuition Reimbursement
Valex will reimburse up to $5,250 for all employees, but the percentage paid will be tiered.
Employment | Weekly Hours | % Paid of Eligible Expenses
Full-Time | - | 100% (Up to $5,250)
Part-Time | 20 Hours or More | 75% (Up to $5,250)
Part-Time | Less than 20 Hours | 50% (Up to $5,250)
Undergraduate and Graduate Studies
A list of approved degree programs will ensure that employees' studies are relevant to Valex.
Approved Degree Programs
Accounting | Business Administration | Computer Science
Information Science | Digital Media | Engineering
Finance | Human Resources | Marketing
Section 4: Proposal
14

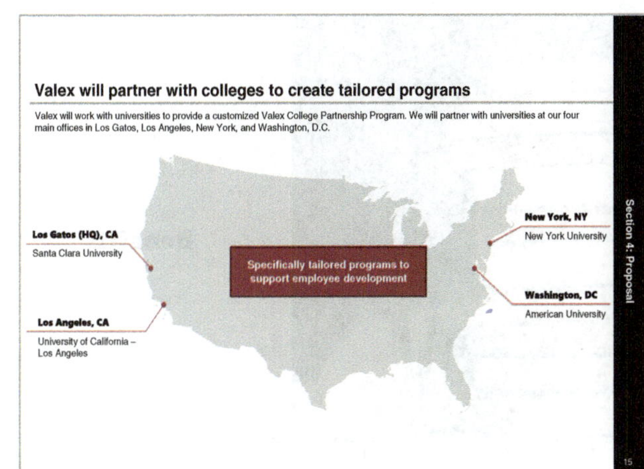

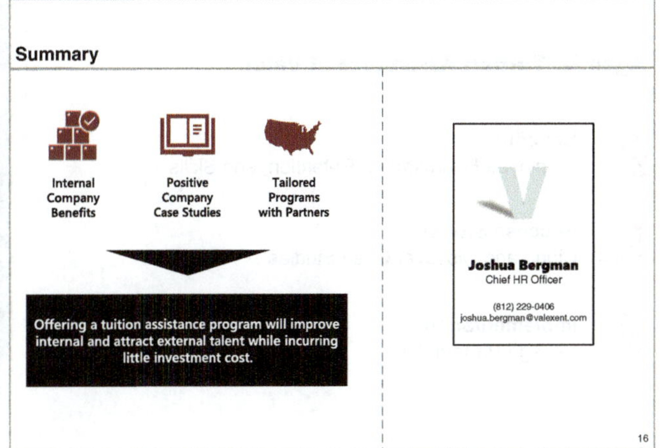

References

"Amazon Career Choice," Amazon, www.amazoncareerchoice.com/home, accessed November 19, 2021.

Peter Cappelli, "Why Do Employers Pay for College?" *Journal of Econometrics* 121 (2004): 213–241, http://dx.doi.org/10.1016/j.jeconom.2003.10.014.

Courtney Connley, "10 Companies That Will Help Pay Your Tuition," *CNBC*, November 14, 2017, www.cnbc.com/2017/11/14/10-companies-that-will-help-pay-your-tuition.html, accessed November 15, 2021.

"Disney Invests in Employees' Futures with Unprecedented Education Program," The Walt Disney Company, February 5, 2019, thewaltdisneycompany.com/disney-invests-in-employees-futures-with-unprecedented-education-program, December 15, 2021.

Lindsay Northon, "2016 Human Capital Benchmarking Report," Society for Human Resource Management, November 2016, https://www.shrm.org/hr-today/trends-and-forecasting/research-and-surveys/Documents/2016-Human-Capital-Report.pdf, accessed December 2, 2021.

Bridget Perry, "New Study Shows the Lasting Impact of Tuition Assistance," Business Wire, January 8, 2018, www.businesswire.com/news/home/20180108006550/en/New-Study-Shows-the-Lasting-Impact-of-Tuition-Assistance, accessed November 15, 2021.

"Talent Investments Pay Off: Cigna's ROI from Tuition Benefits," Lumina Foundation, April 2, 2016, www.luminafoundation.org/resource/talent-investments-pay-off/, accessed November 15, 2021.

"Talent Investments Pay Off (Discover Financial Services)," Lumina Foundation, November 30, 2016, www.luminafoundation.org/resource/talent-investments-pay-off-discover-financial-services, accessed December 14, 2021.

Tim Stobierski, "Average Salary by Education Level: Value of a College Degree," Northeastern University, June 2, 2020, www.northeastern.edu/bachelors-completion/news/average-salary-by-education-level, accessed December 15, 2021.

"Weighing the Pros and Cons of Offering Tuition Assistance for Your Employees," Brandman University, August 27, 2019, www.brandman.edu/news-and-events/blog/weighing-the-pros-and-cons-of-offering-tuition-assistance-for-your-employees, accessed November 11, 2021.

17

Figure 4 | Valex Tuition Assistance Presentation Slides

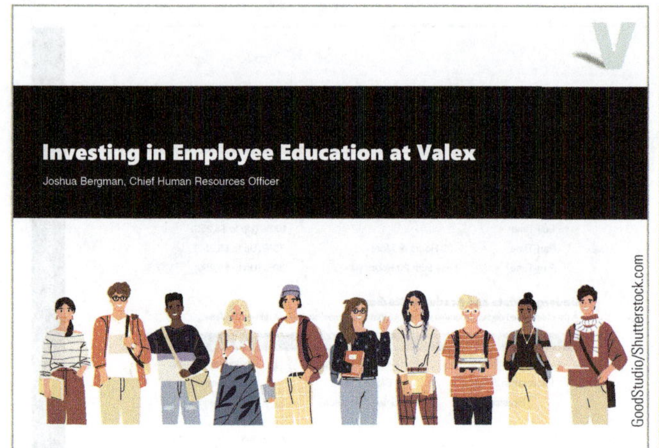

Investing in Employee Education at Valex
Joshua Bergman, Chief Human Resources Officer
GoodStudio/Shutterstock.com

Proposal

Offer a tax-deducible tuition assistance program to improve employee recruitment, retention, and skills.

2

Agenda: Tuition Assistance at Valex

 **Benefits**
Employee Recruitment, Retention, and Skills

 **Success Stories**
Cigna and Discover Case Studies

 **Implementation**
College Partnerships

3

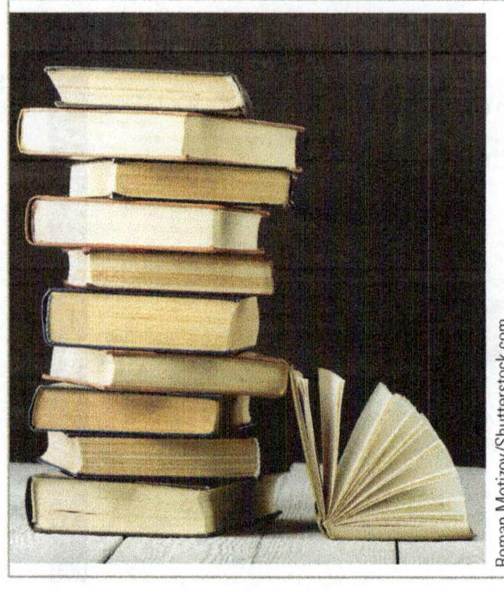
Roman Motizov/Shutterstock.com

Benefits

4

Tuition Assistance Will Improve Recruitment

84% of employees who participate say access to a tuition assistance program was important in their decision to join the company.

5

Most Employers Offer Tuition Programs

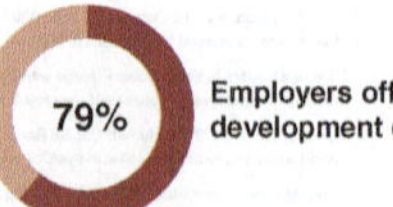

Employers offer professional development opportunities.

Employers offer tuition reimbursement.

6

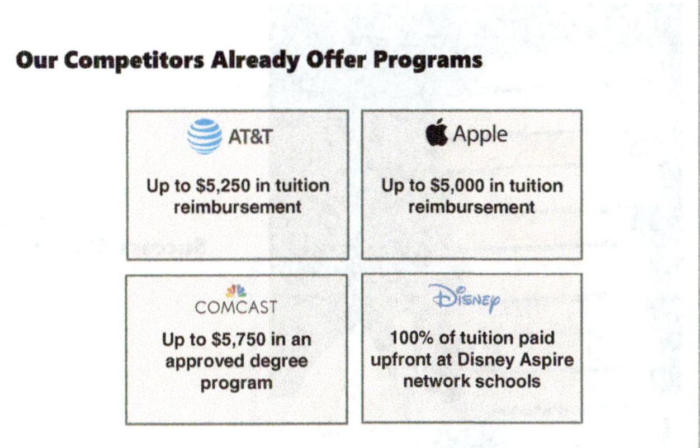

Our Competitors Already Offer Programs
AT&T
Up to $5,250 in tuition reimbursement
Apple
Up to $5,000 in tuition reimbursement
COMCAST
Up to $5,750 in an approved degree program
Disney
100% of tuition paid upfront at Disney Aspire network schools
7

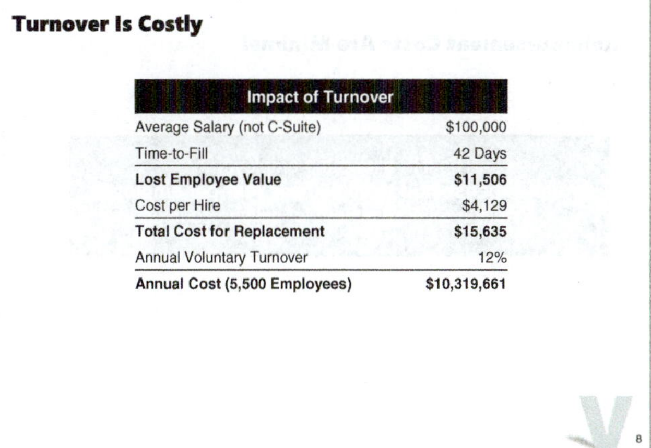

Impact of Turnover	
Average Salary (not C-Suite)	$100,000
Time-to-Fill	42 Days
Lost Employee Value	**$11,506**
Cost per Hire	$4,129
Total Cost for Replacement	**$15,635**
Annual Voluntary Turnover	12%
Annual Cost (5,500 Employees)	**$10,319,661**

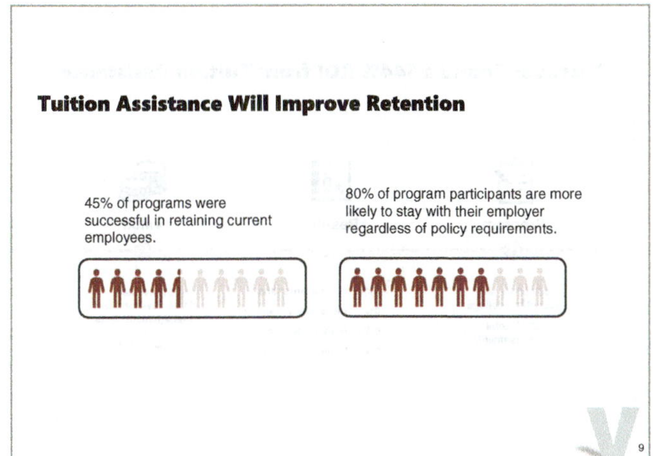

Tuition Assistance Will Improve Retention
45% of programs were successful in retaining current employees.
80% of program participants are more likely to stay with their employer regardless of policy requirements.
9

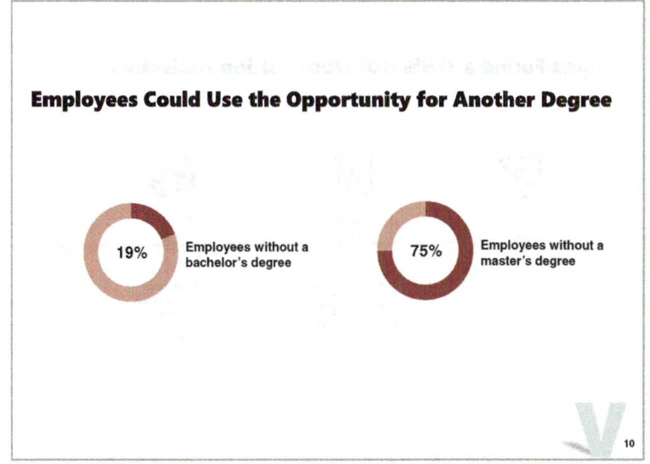

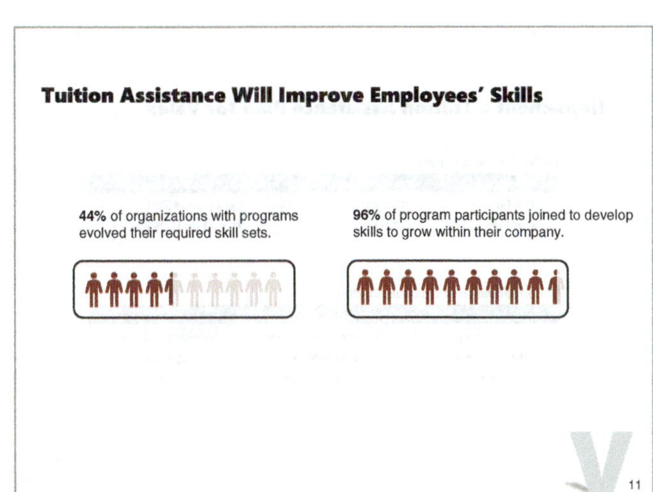

Tuition Assistance Will Improve Employees' Skills
44% of organizations with programs evolved their required skill sets.
96% of program participants joined to develop skills to grow within their company.
11

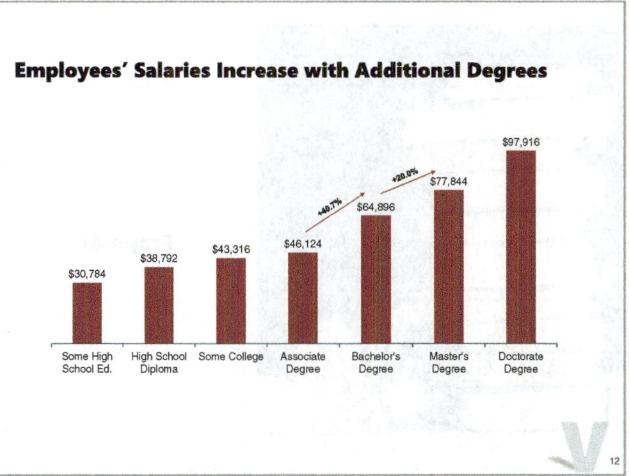

Figure 4 | *(continued)*

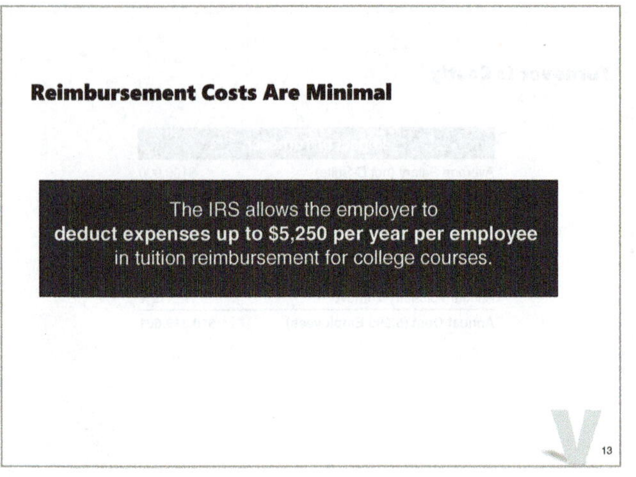

Reimbursement Costs Are Minimal
The IRS allows the employer to
deduct expenses up to $5,250 per year per employee
in tuition reimbursement for college courses.
13

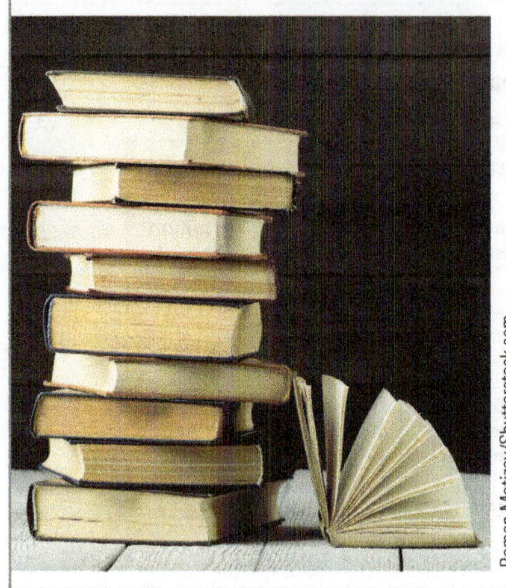

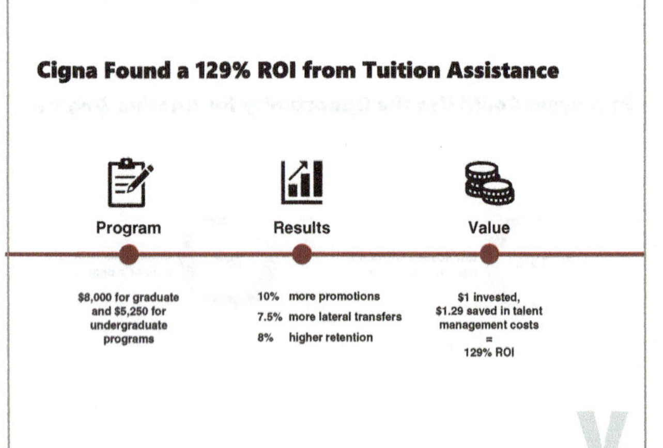

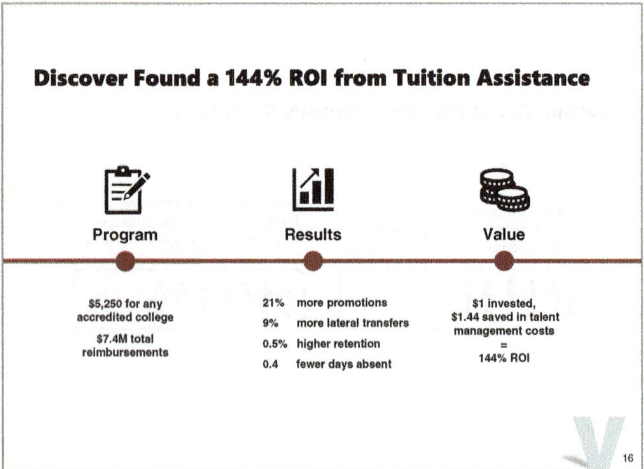

Discover Found a 144% ROI from Tuition Assistance
Program
Results
Value
$5,250 for any accredited college
$7.4M total reimbursements
21% more promotions
9% more lateral transfers
0.5% higher retention
0.4 fewer days absent
$1 invested, $1.44 saved in talent management costs = 144% ROI
16

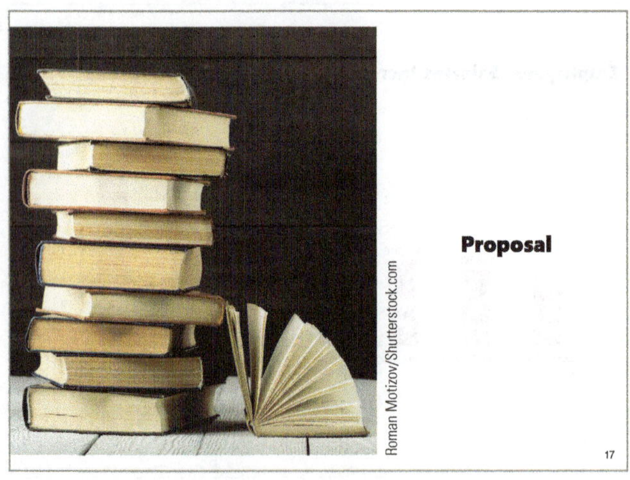

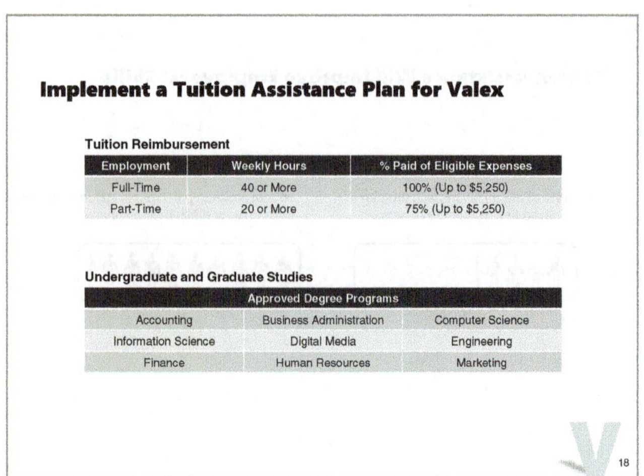

Implement a Tuition Assistance Plan for Valex
Tuition Reimbursement
Employment | Weekly Hours | % Paid of Eligible Expenses
Full-Time | 40 or More | 100% (Up to $5,250)
Part-Time | 20 or More | 75% (Up to $5,250)
Undergraduate and Graduate Studies
Approved Degree Programs
Accounting | Business Administration | Computer Science
Information Science | Digital Media | Engineering
Finance | Human Resources | Marketing
18

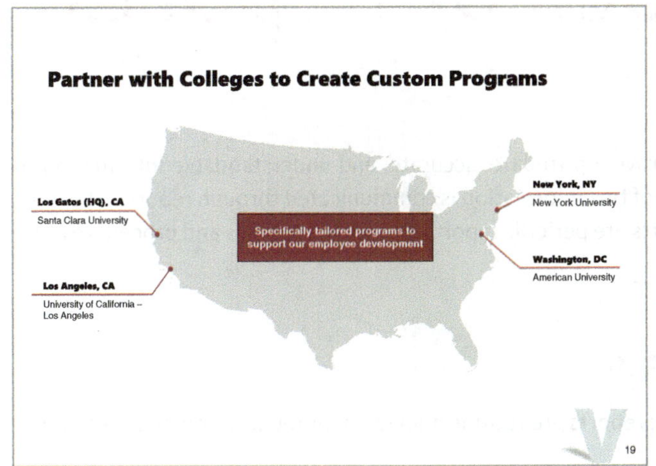

References

"Amazon Career Choice," Amazon, www.amazoncareerchoice.com/home, accessed November 19, 2021.

Peter Cappelli, "Why Do Employers Pay for College?" *Journal of Econometrics* 121 (2004): 213–241, http://dx.doi.org/10.1016/j.jeconom.2003.10.014.

Courtney Connley, "10 Companies That Will Help Pay Your Tuition," *CNBC*, November 14, 2017, www.cnbc.com/2017/11/14/10-companies-that-will-help-pay-your-tuition.html, accessed November 15, 2021.

"Disney Invests in Employees' Futures with Unprecedented Education Program," The Walt Disney Company, February 5, 2019, thewaltdisneycompany.com/disney-invests-in-employees-futures-with-unprecedented-education-program, December 15, 2021.

Lindsay Northon, "2016 Human Capital Benchmarking Report," Society for Human Resource Management, November 2016, https://www.shrm.org/hr-today/trends-and-forecasting/research-and-surveys/Documents/2016-Human-Capital-Report.pdf, accessed December 2, 2021.

Bridget Perry, "New Study Shows the Lasting Impact of Tuition Assistance," Business Wire, January 8, 2018, www.businesswire.com/news/home/20180108006550/en/New-Study-Shows-the-Lasting-Impact-of-Tuition-Assistance, accessed November 15, 2021.

"Talent Investments Pay Off: Cigna's ROI from Tuition Benefits," Lumina Foundation, April 2, 2016, www.luminafoundation.org/resource/talent-investments-pay-off/, accessed November 15, 2021.

"Talent Investments Pay Off (Discover Financial Services)," Lumina Foundation, November 30, 2016, www.luminafoundation.org/resource/talent-investments-pay-off-discover-financial-services, accessed December 14, 2021.

Tim Stobierski, "Average Salary by Education Level: Value of a College Degree," Northeastern University, June 2, 2020, www.northeastern.edu/bachelors-completion/news/average-salary-by-education-level, accessed December 15, 2021.

"Weighing the Pros and Cons of Offering Tuition Assistance for Your Employees," Brandman University, August 27, 2019, www.brandman.edu/news-and-events/blog/weighing-the-pros-and-cons-of-offering-tuition-assistance-for-your-employees, accessed November 11, 2021.

21

C Common Types of Reports

Management needs comprehensive, up-to-date, accurate, and understandable information to meet business objectives. Much of this information is communicated through reports. The most common types of business reports are periodic reports, proposals, policies and procedures, and situational reports.

Periodic Reports

Three common types of periodic reports are routine management reports, compliance reports, and progress reports.

Routine Management Reports

Every organization has its own recurring reports to provide information for making decisions and solving problems. Some of these routine management reports are statistical and may be just a spreadsheet; others are primarily narrative. Examples of routine management reports are quarterly earnings, annual headcount, and monthly revenue.

Compliance Reports

Many state and federal government agencies require companies to file reports showing that they are complying with labor relations, safety, financial, and environmental regulations. Completing these compliance reports is often mostly a matter of gathering the data and reporting the information honestly and completely. Typically, very little analysis of the data is required.

Progress Reports

Interim progress reports are often used to communicate the status of long-term projects. They are submitted periodically to management for internal projects, to customers for external projects, and to investors for an accounting of venture capital expenses or stock performance. Typically, these reports (1) tell what has been accomplished since the last progress report, (2) document how well the project is adhering to the schedule and budget, (3) describe any problems encountered and how they were solved, and (4) outline future plans. Often these reports will be produced using project management software and will include at-a-glance or "dashboard" charts.

Proposals

A proposal is a report written to persuade the reader to accept a suggested plan of action. Two types of business proposals are project proposals and, less common, research proposals.

Project Proposals

A manager may write a project proposal, for example, to persuade a potential customer to purchase products or services, to persuade the federal government to locate a new research facility in a particular city, or to persuade a foundation to fund a project. Proposals may be solicited or unsolicited.

Government agencies and many large companies routinely solicit proposals from potential suppliers. For example, the government might publish a request for proposal (RFP) stating its intention to purchase 5,000 computers, giving detailed specifications about the features it needs and inviting prospective suppliers to bid on the project. Similarly, the computer manufacturer that submits the successful bid might itself publish an RFP to invite parts manufacturers to bid on supplying some component the manufacturer needs for the computers.

Unlike solicited proposals, unsolicited proposals typically require more background information and more persuasion. Because the reader may not be familiar with the project, the writer must present more evidence to convince the reader of the proposal's merits.

When writing a proposal, keep in mind that it may become legally binding. In spelling out exactly what the writer's organization will provide, when, under what circumstances, and at what price, the proposal report writer creates the *offer* part of a contract that, if accepted, may become binding on the organization.

As discussed in Chapter 10, proposals vary in length, organization, complexity, and format. Longer, more formal proposals include the following sections:

1. *Background:* Introduce the problem you're addressing and discuss why it merits the reader's consideration.
2. *Objectives:* Provide specific information about what the outcomes of the project will be.
3. *Process or Plan:* Discuss in detail how you will achieve these objectives. Include a step-by-step discussion of what will be done, when, and exactly how much each component or phase will cost. (Alternatively, you may include costs in an appendix.)
4. *Qualifications:* Show how you, your organization, and any others who would be involved are qualified.
5. *Request for approval:* Directly ask for approval of your proposal. Depending on the reader's needs, this request could come either at the beginning or at the end of the proposal.
6. *Supporting data:* Include additional information that might bolster your arguments.

Research Proposals

Because research is a cost to the organization in terms of labor and expenses, senior management may want to know what they will gain in return for expending these resources. A research proposal identifies the problem you want to solve or issue you seek to understand, how you will conduct the research, what costs are involved, and how the research will provide useful, actionable information for the organization.

Policies and Procedures

Policies are broad operating guidelines that govern the general direction and activities of an organization; procedures are the recommended methods or sequential steps to follow when performing a specific activity. An organization's attitude toward promoting from within a company would constitute a policy, and the steps for applying for promotion would constitute a procedure. Policy statements are typically written by top management, while procedures may be written by the managers and supervisors who are involved in the day-to-day operation of the organization.

Policies

Begin a policy statement by setting the stage—that is, justify the need for a policy. Your justification should be general enough that the policy covers a broad range of situations but not so general that it has no real "teeth." Ensure that the reader knows exactly who is covered by the policy, what is required, and any other needed information. Finally, show how the reader, the organization, or *someone* benefits from this policy. You will find sample policies online or through professional associations. These are good starting points, but always have legal counsel review a policy before publishing it to employees or clients.

Procedures

Write procedures using the active voice and a natural tone. Imagine that you are explaining the procedure to someone. Go step by step through the process, explaining, when necessary, what should *not* be done as well as what should be done. Use visuals and supplemental videos as much as possible.

Try to put yourself in the role of the reader. How much background information is needed; how much jargon can safely be used; what reading level is appropriate? Anticipate questions and problems but recognize that it's impossible to answer every conceivable question; therefore, concentrate on the high-risk components—those tasks that are difficult to perform or that have serious safety or financial implications if performed incorrectly.

Minimize the amount of conceptual information included, concentrating instead on the practical information. (Someone can learn to drive a car safely without needing to learn how the engine propels the car forward.) Usually, numbered steps are appropriate, but use a narrative approach if it seems more effective.

After you have written a draft, have several employees follow the steps to see if they work. The Society for Human Resource Management suggests the steps in Figure 5 for handling a harassment, discrimination, or retaliation complaint within the company.[1] This procedure provides guidance and consistency, but these situations are enormously varied and complex. You see the complexity acknowledged in how the procedure allows HR directors, with "other management staff as appropriate," to determine specific outcomes.

Figure 5 | Sample Complaint Procedure

[Insert the company's name] has established the following procedure for lodging a complaint of harassment, discrimination, or retaliation. The company will treat all aspects of the procedure confidentially to the extent reasonably possible.

Complaints should be submitted as soon as possible after an incident has occurred, preferably in writing. The HR director may assist the complainant in completing a written statement or, in the event an employee refuses to provide information in writing, the HR director will dictate the verbal complaint.

Upon receiving a complaint or being advised by a supervisor or manager that violation of this policy may be occurring, the HR director will notify senior management and review the complaint with the company's legal counsel.

---

[1] "Anti-harassment Policy and Complaint Procedure (includes Dating/Consensual Relationship Policy Provision)," Society for Human Resource Management, https://www.shrm.org/resourcesandtools/tools-and-samples/policies/pages/cms_000534.aspx, accessed October 1, 2021.

The HR director will initiate an investigation to determine whether there is a reasonable basis for believing that the alleged violation of this policy occurred.

If necessary, the complainant and the respondent will be separated during the investigation, either through internal transfer or administrative leave.

During the investigation, the HR director, together with legal counsel or other management employees, will interview the complainant, the respondent, and any witnesses to determine whether the alleged conduct occurred.

Upon conclusion, the HR director or other person conducting the investigation will submit a written report of findings to the company. If it is determined that a violation of this policy has occurred, the HR director will recommend appropriate disciplinary action. The appropriate action will depend on the following factors:

a) the severity, frequency, and pervasiveness of the conduct
b) prior complaints made by the complainant
c) prior complaints made against the respondent
d) the quality of the evidence (e.g., firsthand knowledge, credible corroboration)

If the investigation is inconclusive or if it is determined that there has been no violation of policy but potentially problematic conduct may have occurred, the HR director may recommend appropriate preventive action.

Senior management will review the investigative report and any statements submitted by the complainant or respondent, discuss results of the investigation with the HR director and other management staff as appropriate, and decide what action, if any, will be taken.

Once a final decision is made by senior management, the HR director will meet with the complainant and the respondent separately and notify them of the findings of the investigation. If disciplinary action is to be taken, the respondent will be informed of the nature of the discipline and how it will be executed.

Situational Reports

Unique problems and opportunities often require reports that will be written only once. These *situational reports* are perhaps the most challenging for the report writer. Because they involve a unique issue or question, the writer has no previous reports to use as a guide and must decide what types of information to include, how much research is needed, and how best to organize and present the findings. A sample situational report is shown in Figure 3 in Chapter 10.

D Glossary

A

Abstract word A word that identifies an idea or feeling instead of a concrete object. (5)

ABT The *and, but, therefore* story format used to create and build tension. (7)

Accountability Taking responsibility. (1)

Active voice The sentence form in which the subject performs the action expressed by the verb. (5)

Agenda A list of topics to be covered at a meeting, often including the name of the person responsible for covering each topic and the timing for each topic. (2)

AIDA plan The process of gaining the reader's attention, creating interest in and desire for the benefits of your product, and motivating action. (7)

Alignment Matching up text and graphics to convey order. (4)

Apple-polishing Manipulating data so it looks better than it is. (9)

Applicant tracking system A system companies use to scan and screen job applicants and resumes. (13)

Audience The receiver of a message. (1)

Audience analysis A critical step in communication for the writer to understand what the audience needs and how they may react to a message. (4)

Audience The receiver of a message. (1)

Authenticity Living as your genuine self. (1)

B

Behavioral interviews Interviews based on the theory that past behavior predicts future performance. (14)

Belonging A feeling of being valued and part of a community. (3)

Benefits Advantages a reader or potential customer receives from accepting a proposal or buying a product or service. (7)

Blind hiring Redacting applicants' name, address, dates, hobbies and interests, volunteer work, and/or college to reduce bias in the selection process. (3)

Brainstorming Jotting down ideas, facts, and anything else—without evaluating the output—that might be helpful in constructing a message. (4)

Buffer A neutral opening statement in a bad-news message. (8)

Business report An organized presentation of information used to make decisions and solve problems. (10)

Buzzwords Important-sounding expressions used mainly to impress other people. (5)

C

Cascading communication Conveying information from the top of the organization down to each level in sequence. (1)

Character The sum of who you are as a person; your ideas, what you value, and how you engage with those around you. (1)

Chartjunk Visual elements that call attention to themselves instead of information on a chart. (9)

Cherry-picking Selecting data that supports your argument, while downplaying or omitting data that opposes your argument. (9)

Cliché An expression that has become monotonous through overuse. (5)

Closed-ended question A question that includes a list of predefined answers. (9)

Coercion Force or intimidation used to get someone to comply. (7)

Coherence When each sentence of a paragraph links smoothly to the sentences before and after it. (5)

Communication The process of sending and receiving messages. (1)

Communication barriers Verbal and nonverbal impediments to an audience receiving a message as we intend. (1)

Communication need The reason for communicating in organizations—what starts the process. (1)

Comparing apples to oranges Finding similarities between two items that are not similar and therefore drawing a faulty conclusion. (9)

Compassion Caring for others and for yourself; noticing and acting to relieve someone's suffering. (1, 2)

Competencies The knowledge, skills, and abilities required for a specific job. (13)

Complex sentence A sentence that has one independent clause and at least one dependent clause. (5)

Compound sentence A sentence that has two or more independent clauses. (5)

Computer-mediated communication (CMC) Communication that takes place using two or more digital devices. (1)

Concrete word A word that identifies something the senses can perceive. (5)

Confirmation bias The tendency to interpret new evidence as confirmation of one's existing beliefs or theories. (9)

Connotation The subjective or emotional feeling associated with a word. (1)

Consensus Reaching a decision that best reflects the thinking of all team members. (2)

Consumer-generated media (CGM) Any media (e.g., videos, images, blogs) about a company posted by consumers for public viewing (also called *user-generated content*). (1)

Contrast The way elements stand out and are easily distinguished. (4)

Courage Standing up for principles despite the risks. (1)

Crisis communication Attempts to protect and defend the company's reputation. (7)

Crisis situation A significant threat to the organization. (7)

Cross-functional communication Lateral, or horizonal, communication to another division or department. (1)

Cultural agility Being adept in various cross-cultural situations; navigating with grace and ease. (3)

Cultural competence Understanding and engaging effectively with people from different cultures. (3)

Cultural humility Believing that our culture is neither inferior nor superior to others' cultures; reflecting and recognizing that learning about cultural difference is a continuous process. (3)

Culture The customary traits, attitudes, and behaviors of a group of people. (3)

Curiosity Being genuinely open to learning about others' values and beliefs; asking others about themselves and their perspectives. (3)

Curriculum vitae (CV) A longer version of a resume that is more typical for international (and academic) jobs. (13)

Cyberbullying Intimidating, offending, or humiliating people online. (3)

Dangling expression Any part of a sentence that does not logically connect to the rest of the sentence. (5)

Data Facts and statistics. (9)

Data integrity The accuracy and consistency of facts and statistics over time. (9)

Denotation The literal, dictionary meaning of a word. (1)

Direct organizational plan A plan in which the major purpose of the message is communicated first, followed by the explanation and the details. (4)

Direct quotation The exact words of another person. (10)

Distracting noise Competing demands on attention, such as too much schoolwork or a messy workspace. (1)

Diversity Demographic differences among people. (3)

Document design The visual appearance of fonts, spacing, graphics, and other elements in a document. (4)

Documentation Identifying sources by giving credit to others' words or ideas. (10)

Downward communication The flow of information from managers to their employees. (1)

Drafting Composing a preliminary version of a message. (4)

E

Editing The stage of revision that ensures that writing conforms to standard English. (4)

Emotional intelligence Recognizing and managing feelings. (1)

Empathy Understanding and sharing someone else's feelings. (2)

Employee engagement A culture in which employees feel passionate about their company and are enthusiastic about their jobs. (6)

Environmental noise Competing demands on attention, such as construction, an uncomfortable chair, or a family member during a Zoom call. (1)

Ethics Moral principles that go beyond legal rules to guide how to act. (1)

Ethnocentrism The belief that one's own cultural group is superior. (3)

Ethos A persuasive appeal based on credibility. (7)

Euphemism An expression used in place of words that may be offensive or inappropriate. (5)

Executive summary A condensed version of the report body (also called an *abstract* or *synopsis*). (10)

Expletive An expression such as *there is* or *it has been* that begins a clause and for which the pronoun has no antecedent. (5)

Extemporaneous presentation A presentation delivered using an unrehearsed, enhanced, and conversational style. (12)

Extranet A private computer network for a select group of people outside of the company (e.g., for customers or franchisees). (1)

F

Fact Indisputably verifiable information. (7)

Factoring Breaking a problem down to determine what data needs to be collected. (9)

Feature An aspect of how a product or service works. (7)

Filter Perception based on one's knowledge, experience, and viewpoints. (1)

Formal communication network The transmission of information through downward, upward, and lateral paths within an organization. (1)

Framing Using language to present an idea to be most relevant to an audience. (7)

Gender A social construct that reflects how people feel and behave. (3)

Gender identity An individual's concept of the self as male, female, a blend of both, or neither; how individuals perceive themselves and what they call themselves. (3)

Generic heading Text that identifies only the topic of a section, without giving the conclusion. (10)

Goodwill message A message sent out of a sense of kindness and to maintain or build relationships with no true business objective (6)

Grapevine The flow of information through nonofficial channels within the organization (also called *informal communication network*). (1)

Groupthink A hindrance to team performance that happens when individuals think too similarly. (2)

Horizontal communication The flow of information among peers within an organization (also called *lateral communication*). (1)

Humility Seeing and handling our own and others' limitations; being willing to learn. (1, 3)

Implicit bias A preference for (or aversion to) a person or group of people about which we are unaware or mistaken (also called *unconscious bias*). (3)

Impromptu presentation A presentation delivered without preparation. (12)

Inclusion Creating an environment where all people are valued and can contribute to their fullest potential. (3)

Indirect organizational plan A plan in which the reasons or rationale are presented first, followed by the major idea. (4)

Individual ethics Ethics defined by a person, which are based on family values, heritage, personal experience, and other factors. (1)

Inference Information that can probably be verified. (7)

Infographics An engaging way of showing data visually. (9)

Informal communication network The flow of information through nonofficial channels within the organization (also called the *grapevine*). (1)

Information Meaningful facts, statistics, and conclusions. (9)

Integrity Acting consistently with your own and with societal values. (1)

Intercultural communication When a message is created by someone from one culture to be understood by someone from another culture (also called *cross-cultural communication*). (3)

Intranet A private computer network within an organization for employee access. (1)

J

Jargon Technical terminology used within specialized groups. (5)

L

Lateral communication The flow of information among peers within an organization (also called *horizontal communication*). (1)

Lawn-mower pattern Reading with eyes beginning in the top left corner, traveling to the right, and then dropping down to the next line. (4)

Lean media Communication methods that are static, or one-way, and provide few or no social cues. (1)

Letter A message written to people outside the organization and typically reserved for formal communication. (4)

Logos A persuasive appeal based on logic. (7)

M

Main points The major conclusions of a message. (4)

Mechanics Elements in communication that show up only in writing (e.g., spelling, punctuation, abbreviations, capitalization, number expression, word division). (5)

Medium How a message is transmitted (e.g., email, video call). (1)

Memo A message written to someone within (or internal to) an organization; sometimes used generically to mean an important message, whether sent as an email or posted on a company intranet. (4)

Mentions Social media posts that include a company's name, products, or services. (6)

Message The information (either verbal or nonverbal) that is communicated. (1)

Message title Unlike a generic heading, text that identifies your main points on each page or section of a report (also called a *talking heading*). (10)

Mind mapping Generating ideas for a message by connecting them in a graphical way. (4)

Minutes An official record of a meeting that summarizes what was discussed, what decisions were made, and what actions participants will take. (2)

Multicommunicating Overlapping conversations using various forms of communication. (1)

Multiculturalism Appreciating diversity among people, typically beyond differences in countries of origin. (3)

N

Networking email An email sent to a person at a company or in a field of interest for the purpose of obtaining career information or job leads. (13)

Nonverbal message What is communicated without words (e.g., body language). (1)

O

Online reputation The way a company or an individual is represented on the web. (13)

Open-ended question A question that allows respondents to create their own answers. (9)

Opinion Information that is possibly verifiable. (7)

Organizational savvy The ability to navigate and adapt to individual personalities and styles as well as organizational culture, history, and structure (also called *political savvy*). (1)

P

Parallelism Using a similar grammatical structure to express similar ideas. (5)

Paraphrase A summary or restatement of a passage in one's own words. (2, 10)

Passive voice The sentence form in which the subject receives the action expressed by the verb. (5)

Pathos A persuasive appeal based on emotion. (7)

Personal brand The way you're known and how people experience you. (13)

Perspective taking Adopting another point of view; seeking to understand others' thoughts, feelings, and motivations. (3)

Persuasion Using communication to change another person's beliefs, feelings, or behaviors. (7)

Plagiarism Using another person's words or ideas without giving proper credit. (10)

Platitude A trite, obvious statement. (5)

Preview An overview of what the audience can expect in a message. (4)

Primary audience The most important receiver of a message (e.g., the decision maker). (4)

Primary data Data collected by a researcher to solve a specific problem. (9)

Professional ethics Ethics defined by an organization. (1)

Professionalism Work habits that consider the working environment and interests of other employees. (14)

Prosocial messaging Persuasive messages that promote the welfare of others instead of self-interest. (7)

Proximity Grouping or placing elements together to convey relationships. (4)

Purpose The reason for which a message is created. (4)

Q

Qualitative data Descriptive data that cannot be measured. (9)

Quantitative data Numerical data. (9)

Questionnaire A written document containing questions to obtain information from recipients; commonly referred to as a survey. (9)

R

Receiver benefit How an audience benefits from message content. (5)

Redundancy The unnecessary repetition of an idea that has already been expressed or intimated. (5)

Reflecting Listening in a way to convey that you hear, understand, and care about the underlying message. (2)

Relationship conflict Disagreements caused by differing personalities or styles. (3)

Repetition The use of consistent sizes and colors of text and graphical elements that allow readers to scan and find information easily. (4)

Request for information (RFI) A preliminary document seeking general information from potential suppliers. (10)

Request for proposal (RFP) A formal, detailed document seeking bids from potential suppliers. (10)

Revising Modifying the content and style of a draft to increase its effectiveness. (4)

Rhetorical devices A stylistic way to persuade and evoke emotion. (7)

Rich media Communication methods that allow for real-time interactivity and cues, such as body language. (1)

S

Scripted presentation A presentation delivered by reading from notes. (12)

Search engine optimization Ranking highly in search engine results to drive traffic to a website. (4)

Secondary audience Receivers of a message who are not the primary audience but who will also read or view and be affected by a message. (4)

Secondary data Data (published or unpublished) collected by someone else for another purpose. (9)

Section overview Text that previews for the reader how a report section is divided and what main points follow. (10)

Self-awareness Accurately identifying our strengths and development needs; knowing ourselves and knowing how others perceive us. (1)

Self-righteousness A steadfast belief that your way is the right way. (3)

Service recovery Responding to a service failure in a way that turns an upset customer into a satisfied customer. (7)

Sex A trait that determines reproductive function; refers to an individual's biology. (3)

Simple sentence A sentence that has one independent clause. (5)

Situational ethics Ethics that are based on particular circumstances. (1)

Situational report A report that is produced only once to address unique problems and opportunities. (10)

Slang An expression, often short-lived, that is identified with a specific group of people. (5)

Slide tracker Text or an image that repeats on every slide after the agenda to show the major divisions of a presentation, highlighting each topic as it is presented. (11)

Social ethics Ethics defined by society. (1)

Social listening Monitoring online conversations related to a company's brand. (6)

Social network An app on which communities of people share common interests or activities that can form relationships (a subset of social media). (1)

Social presence The extent to which we perceive someone close and real through technology. (2)

Stacked headings Two consecutive headings without intervening text. (10)

Stereotype Attributing to an individual an assumption we have about the group to which that person belongs, which may or may not be true. (1, 3)

Stereotype threat The risk of confirming negative stereotypes about an individual's racial, ethnic, gender, or other group. (3)

Storyboard A visual representation of your presentation; the way your presentation will unfold and what will be on each slide. (11)

Structured interview The process of job recruiters asking set questions and having an established way of scoring responses. (14)

Style How an idea is expressed (rather than the substance of the idea). (5)

Survey A data-collection method that gathers information through questionnaires, telephone inquiries, or interviews; commonly refers to a questionnaire. (9)

Sympathy Understanding and providing comfort to another person. (2)

Synchronous communication Messages that happen in real time—at the same time; the opposite is asynchronous. (1)

T

Table An orderly arrangement of data into columns and rows. (9)

Tailored messages Messages that are adapted to individuals. (7)

Talking heading A report heading or slide title that identifies the major conclusion of a section or slide (also called a *message title*). (10)

Targeted messages Messages that are adapted to different audience segments. (7)

Task conflict Disagreements about work (e.g., assignments, resource allocation, expectations, opinions about policies and procedures). (3)

Team A group of individuals who depend on one another to accomplish a common objective. (2)

Tone How the writer's attitude toward the reader and the subject of the message is reflected. (5)

Topic sentence The main idea of a paragraph, usually introduced at the beginning of a passage. (5)

Transgender Relating to someone whose gender identity and/or gender expression is different from cultural expectations based on their birth sex. (3)

Transparency Sharing timely, accurate information. (1)

U

Unity When all parts of a paragraph work together to convey a single idea consistently and logically. (5)

Upward communication The flow of information from lower-level employees to upper-level employees or managers. (1)

User-generated content (UGC) Any media (e.g., videos, images, blogs) about a company posted by consumers for public viewing (also called *consumer-generated media*). (1)

V

Values conflict Disagreements caused by differences in politics, religion, morals, identities, and other factors. (3)

Verbal message The part of a communication that uses words to convey meaning. (1)

Vocation A strong inclination toward a career or service work; a calling. (13)

Vulnerability Being willing to accept emotional exposure. (1)

W

White space The unused parts of a page. (4)

Workplace bullying Intimidating, offending, or humiliating people at work. (3)

Workplace civility Showing respect and concern for others—a baseline way of interacting at work. (3)

Writer's block The inability to focus one's attention on the writing process and to draft a message. (4)

Y

"You" attitude Emphasizing what the reader wants to know and how the reader will be affected by the message. (5)

Z

Zoom fatigue Exhaustion from online meetings caused by excessive focus and cognitive processing. (2)

Index

Note: Page numbers followed by "f" indicate figures.

A

B

C

D

E

F

G

H

I

J

K

L

M

N

O

P

Q

R

S

T

U

V

W

Y

Z